W9-AOP-987

PERSONNEL

THE HUMAN PROBLEMS
OF MANAGEMENT

GEORGE STRAUSS Professor of Business Administration
and Associate Dean, Schools of
Business Administration,
University of California, Berkeley

LEONARD R. SAYLES Professor of Business Administration
Graduate School of Business,
Columbia University

PRENTICE-HALL, INC. / ENGLEWOOD CLIFFS, N.J.

PERSONNEL
THE HUMAN PROBLEMS
OF MANAGEMENT

Third Edition

PERSONNEL: The Human Problems of Management

Third Edition

George Strauss and Leonard R. Sayles

ISBN: 0-13-657783-0

10 9 8 7 6 5 4 3 2

PRENTICE-HALL INTERNATIONAL, INC., *London*
PRENTICE-HALL OF AUSTRALIA, PTY. LTD., *Sydney*
PRENTICE-HALL OF CANADA, LTD., *Toronto*
PRENTICE-HALL OF INDIA PRIVATE LTD., *New Delhi*
PRENTICE-HALL OF JAPAN, INC., *Tokyo*

TO OUR FATHERS: FRANK STRAUSS
AND IN MEMORY OF ROBERT SAYLES

CONTENTS

PART TWO: MOTIVATION AND LEADERSHIP

PART THREE: MANAGERIAL SKILLS

PREFACE

This is our third edition. In a field already well-endowed with a number of fine books, what was our justification for writing a new book in the first place? And now that we have a third edition, how does this edition differ from the second? Let us answer these questions in order.

From the beginning, our purpose has been to place personnel administration in the context of the social sciences. Traditionally, the teaching in this field emphasized description ("This is the way companies handle problems") or prescription ("This is the way companies should handle problems"). We felt that this "cook-book" (and often excessively dogmatic) approach tended to make an intrinsically exciting subject dull; further, it ill-prepared the student for the realities of organizational life. After all, the manager needs analytic techniques that go beyond the transitory practices of specific companies at the time that the material was written. Otherwise, the student or manager is limited to the rote application of old techniques that may become wholly irrelevant to new problems.

On the other hand, we wanted to provide a broader perspective than was provided by specialized works dealing with personnel problems from the one-sided viewpoint of specific disciplines, such as industrial psychology, sociology, labor relations, or industrial engineering. Each of these fields provides important insights, but our purpose here has been to integrate their various contributions and apply them to personnel problems. Thus we make considerable use of theories, not as abstract propositions, but as tools for analyzing and solving real-life problems.

To put it in other words, our major purpose has been not just to build a bridge between managerial practice and the behavioral sciences, but to lay firm foundations in both areas as well.

We had a number of other objectives. When we were writing our first edition, most texts in the field dealt with personnel problems from the viewpoint of the personnel department rather than management generally; they concentrated on unionized blue-collar employees and gave little attention to managers, professionals, and nonmanufacturing employees; and they were concerned almost exclusively with business organizations, ignoring the important lessons to be learned from hospitals, educational institutions, government organizations, and the like.

We have tried to rectify these limitations. We have sought to place personnel problems in the context of management problems generally and have dealt extensively with questions of motivation, leadership, communications, and control—questions that every manager must face, whether he is staff or line, a foreman on the production floor or a vice-president on executive row. In so doing, we have tried to show that personnel problems can best be dealt with by consistent integrated policies, not as a series of isolated crises.

Reflecting changes in our labor force, each successive edition has given greater emphasis to white-collar employees, especially managers and professionals, for personnel policies must recognize that the special interests of these groups often differ considerably from those of blue-collar employees. Furthermore, we have compared business problems with those involving other institutions, in hopes that this comparative approach would provide insights for students from both business and nonbusiness fields.

Finally, perhaps our most important objective was to portray the drama and excitement of real-life organizations, doing so with illustrations based on our own research and that of others. In addition, case problems at the end of most of our chapters are designed to test the students' analytical ability and to provide a springboard for class discussion. We have tried to give a feel for the complexities and ambiguities that managers constantly face, and in this way place abstract behavioral science findings in context. Of necessity, this produces a systems approach, because in the real world there are no neat compartments separating the study of work groups, for example, from wage and salary administration or separating leadership from incentives.

Few of the questions we raise have simple answers. We have tried to indicate the main areas of disagreement and the main arguments on each side. Our field is far from cut and dried. The student must make up his mind on a wide variety of issues, but he should do so on the basis of sound analysis, not untutored "common sense."

So much for the general theme of all three editions. In writing this third edition, we naturally wanted to preserve the best of the old and to make room for new developments. Unless our book was to grow enormously, some drastic and painful cutting was required. (In fact, the third edition is shorter than the second.) To help us in this difficult task, we obtained some very useful suggestions from a panel of distinguished colleagues whose names are listed on the opposite page. We are very grateful for their helpful recommendations, which are reflected in additions, deletions, and changes throughout the book.

Professor Hrach Bedrosian
Department of Management and
Industrial Relations
College of Business and Public
Administration
New York University

Dr. Stephen J. Carroll, Jr.
Behavioral Sciences Division
College of Business and Public
Administration
University of Maryland

Professor Hal P. Eastman, Jr.
Graduate School of Business
Administration
Rutgers University

Professor Alice M. Harrison
School of Business
East Carolina University

Associate Professor Allan Nash
University of Maryland

Professor Gerald Silver
Chairman, Department of
Management and Computer Sciences
(Graduate and Undergraduate)
College of Business Administration
Fairleigh Dickinson University

Miss Carol Stewart
Marketing Retailing Department
Nassau Community College

Assistant Professor Shirley L. Teeter
Management Department
School of Business and Economics
San Fernando Valley State College

Professor Keith E. Voelker
Department of Economics
Wisconsin State University/Oshkosh

Eventually, cuts were made in almost every chapter, the chapters dealing with organization being pruned especially heavily. Two chapters (Conference Leadership and Safety) were eliminated altogether. The chapter on work measurement techniques was integrated with our previous chapter on individual incentive systems. A completely new chapter on manpower planning was written to take into account much recent interest in this area, and it includes suitably updated material from our old chapter on promotions, transfers, and seniority. Another completely new chapter deals with minority employment problems, perhaps the area of greatest urgency today. This chapter deals with discrimination on the basis of sex as well as race. It outlines the nature and causes of the problem as well as the major remedial measures available to management. It also summarizes legal developments to the time of writing.

Considerable change was made in other chapters. Among the most significant are the following: The work of McClelland on the achievement motive has been brought into Chapter 1 (The Meaning of Work). Chapter 3 (Technology and Job Satisfaction in the Office and Laboratory) now deals more extensively and systematically with professionals and managers. On the basis of requests from many instructors, our discussion of union-management relations in Chapter 5 (Unions and Labor Relations) has been considerably expanded, with special emphasis being given white-collar and governmental unions and the structure of collective bargaining.

Chapter 6 (Motivating People to Work) has been expanded to take account of current research findings, especially the paths-goals analysis of Porter and Lawler. A new section on resistance to management science computerized techniques has been added to Chapter 12 (Introducing Change). Chapter 17 (The Role of Personnel Administration) has been largely recast with greater emphasis given to personnel's audit and stabilization roles.

The testing field has changed greatly in the last ten years as a result of new research and civil rights pressures. These changes are reflected in our new Chapter 19 (Recruitment and Selection), which has been substantially rewritten to incorporate recently developed approaches, such as synthetic validation. Among other changes, we added some new material on managerial career patterns to Chapter 22 (Management Development). Chapter 23 (Performance Appraisal) now deals more heavily (and critically) with Management by Objectives, again based on recent research and company experiences. Chapter 24 (Management Training and Organization Development) has been renamed to indicate its current emphasis. We have attempted to provide a critical evaluation of sensitivity training and other forms of Organization Development.

Our section on management compensation in Chapter 25 (Wage and Salary Administration) has been updated and expanded. Chapter 26 (Benefit Programs: Rewards for Loyalty) has been totally revised. It deals with a host of new topics, among others the four-day week. A new section on white-collar incentives has been added to Chapter 27 (Incentives and Performance Standards), which formerly dealt primarily with blue-collar incentives—thus permitting comparison. A short discussion of worker participation in management outside the U.S. has been incorporated into Chapter 28 (Organization-Wide Incentives), along with added emphasis on profit sharing, in line with current interests.

Over the years, many teachers and colleagues have contributed to this book. When we were graduate students at MIT in the late 1940's, our interests were greatly influenced by the late Douglas McGregor and by Professor Charles A. Myers, Douglas V. Brown, and Paul Pigors; at Cornell, William F. Whyte was a colleague, teacher, and friend. In the preparation of this third edition, Peter Feuille provided invaluable research and editorial assistance. Raymond Miles and Sidney Ingerman read and criticized several chapters. Above all we owe a debt of gratitude to three long-suffering people, our patient secretaries, Mrs. Barbara Porter and Fanny Williams, and to our indomitable editor, Mrs. Maurine Lewis.

Individuals,
Jobs, and
Groups

Studying the human problems of organizations can be exciting but frustrating too. As with so many problems in behavioral science, one often feels the need to know everything before one can know something. Human organizations are organic in the sense that the various parts are interdependent. For example, you can't understand why an engineer complains about the work he receives from the model shop without knowing something about his needs (and those of his counterpart in the other department), the structure and policies of the larger organization, small group norms, how various supervisors behave, and many other things.

But one has to begin some place to build knowledge and understanding. We think that it is easier to start with some of the building blocks of the organization—individuals, jobs, and groups—and then look at the complex interrelationships involved in administration.

Individuals place a variety of demands on their work; in fact, the workplace is one of the most important institutions for providing human satisfactions. What motivates people? Do individuals differ in the relative importance they place on various needs and how stable are these demands? These are some of the questions which Chapter 1 ("The Meaning of Work") endeavors to answer by mustering relevant behavioral research findings.

But individual demands or needs are just one side of the equation. Different kinds of jobs provide more or less of various human satisfactions. In other words, management can predict the impact of technological decisions on employee reactions to work. Chapter 2 ("Technology and Job Satisfaction: Manual Work") contrasts worker responses to three typical blue-collar types of jobs: craft, machine tending and assembly line, and continuous processing automation.

The world of offices and laboratories is explored in Chapter 3 ("Technology and Job Satisfaction: Office and Laboratory"). Particular emphasis is placed on managers, professionals, and service occupations: employees whose jobs require a great deal of human interaction and intellectual activity.

Motivation and on-the-job behavior are influenced profoundly by still another factor: group identifications. In a sense, every organization gets fractionated over time into a number of smaller groups because people need the close, more personal associations these groups provide in contrast to the effects of impersonal, larger institutions. In turn, these informal groups come to modify both individual needs and objectives, the character of the job and the organization. The dynamics of small group elaborations are analyzed in Chapter 4 ("Work Groups and Informal Organization").

Another type of group which has an impact on the larger organization is the labor union, which is, of course, a much more formal, complex entity than the work group. Not every firm has union relations, but because of their crucial importance to the human problems of management and their pervasive influence, it would be unrealistic to endeavor to understand the functioning of organizations without some knowledge of union structure and behavior. Chapter 5 ("Unions and Labor Relations") provides some historical perspective on union growth, their structure and impact on management decision-making.

THE MEANING OF WORK 1

It's hard to imagine the changes in human life that have come about in western civilization over the past century and a half. For thousands of years the material conditions of our existence (the way food, clothing, and shelter were produced) remained relatively unchanged. And then, since 1800, at an ever faster pace, we have had steam engines, locomotives, the telegraph, automobiles, airplanes, radio, atomic energy, and space exploration. Our way of life has changed unbelievably—but perhaps in no area has the change been greater than in the way men earn their living.

Let us look for a moment at the "industrial relations" of yesteryear—for only by examining the past can we bring into focus the problems of today. Back in 1800, 90 per cent of the American people lived on farms, and the percentage was not much lower in Europe. Although there were large plantations in some sections of the country, most men owned and worked their own farms, receiving aid at harvest time when neighbor helped neighbor. The family was the basic economic unit. Father worked in the fields. Mother processed the food (in a way housewives rarely do in this age of supermarkets), cooked the meals, spun the wool, made the clothes, and did the household chores. Brother and sister were assigned simple tasks almost as soon as they could walk. Labor relations and family relations were the same.

Economically, the farm was almost self-sufficient. A man was his own boss. No one could tell him when to plant or harvest, or could give him a written warning if he started work three minutes late. True, nature and the weather might prove more tyrannical than any foreman, but what a man produced was his own. His motivation was clear: If he was lazy, his own family suffered.

Furthermore (in contrast to what prevails in many jobs today) his efforts brought tangible fruit. Looking at his growing fields, he could say with real satisfaction, "Look what *I* have created." He, his family, his life, and his job were all tied together in a rich oneness that many look back on with nostalgia. (Few farmers today, however, would give up the benefits of tractors or electricity, nor would their wives long enjoy dipping candles and spinning wool. The earlier farmer's hours were long and his frustrations many. The continuing exodus from farm to city over the last century indicates that, for all its disadvantages, many prefer our urban civilization to the simple country life.)

Even in earlier days, in the city perhaps the farmer had a younger brother, a journeyman wagon-maker. He was a wage-earner, not his own boss. And yet, how different the meaning of his job was to him than to his great-great-grandson who tightens bolts on the final line of Chevy No. 3! He knew he would not be a journeyman for long. If he saved his money, he might expect to set himself up in business within a few years. Relations between himself and his boss were simple and easy—at times almost like the relations between father and son. The older man taught the younger what he knew and together they performed the same job. The work was creative and satisfying. Building a wagon required skill, and when the job was finished the worker could see what he had done. He could be proud of his craftsmanship and sure of his place in the world.

Such was the way some men earned their living not so many years ago— even though our picture is admittedly somewhat idyllic. After all, a slave on a plantation or a peasant in Europe was often just a working beast, and few wage-earners had the sense of skill enjoyed by our journeyman wagon-maker. In fact, it may well be "that in modern society there is a far greater scope for skill and craftsmanship than in any previous society, and that far more people are in a position to use such skills." [1]

THE IMPACT OF THE INDUSTRIAL REVOLUTION

The last century and a half has brought a dramatic revolution, not only in what we make, but in how we make it. The industrial revolution has been a revolution not only in technology but also in human relations. As technology grew more and more complex, people became more dependent on one another and the problems of working together became more troublesome. Today the typical American is no longer his own boss; he is not a farmer, but a city dweller. Furthermore, the industrial revolution has brought major changes in what it means to be an employee.

Specialization

The journeyman wagon-maker did a whole job from beginning to end. But one of the distinguishing marks of the industrial revolution is specialization. Here

[1] J. A. C. Brown, *The Social Psychology of Industry* (Baltimore: Pelican, 1954), p. 207. See also Robert Blauner, "Work Satisfaction and Industrial Trends in Modern Society," Walter Galenson and S. M. Lipset, eds., *Labor and Trade Unionism* (New York: Wiley, 1960).

4

is Adam Smith's famous description of the changes that were taking place in pinmaking almost two centuries ago, in England:

A workman not educated to this business ... could scarce, perhaps, with utmost industry, make one pin a day, and certainly not make twenty. But in the way in which this business is now carried on ... one man draws out the wire, another straightens it, a third cuts it, a fourth points it, a fifth grinds it at the top for receiving the head; to make the head requires two or three distinct operations; to put it on is a peculiar business. ... I have seen a small manufactory of this sort where ten men only were employed and where some of them consequently performed two or three distinct operations. But though they were very poor, and therefore but indifferently accommodated with the necessary machinery, they could, when they exerted themselves, make upwards of forty-eight thousand pins in a day. [2]

Economically, specialization has brought great advantages. But it has brought many disadvantages as well: boredom and the loss of a sense of individual importance, of accomplishment, of pride in work. How much satisfaction can a man obtain from spending his entire day pointing pins?

Further, workers feel that they are shackled to work processes they have had no hand in developing. The Industrial Engineering Department frequently determines every detail of the job, depriving the individual of any chance to show initiative or originality. Specialization has sharpened the dividing line between workers and management.

Specialization has also developed within management. Instead of a single owner-manager with complete control over the plant, or a foreman with complete control over his department, we have staff departments such as engineering, production scheduling, purchasing, and personnel. No man performs more than a small part of the whole job; no man has significant control over what he does. A dozen staff agencies may be involved in making a simple decision, and the worker is at the very bottom: "Everybody gets consulted but me. I just carry out their orders."

Opportunity To Get Ahead

To make the industrial revolution possible, elaborate machinery was necessary—and machinery requires money. The journeyman craftsman needed little more than his own tools to set himself up in business, but the man on the automobile assembly line cannot hope to compete with General Motors. Unless he wants to operate a small store or a gas station, the modern worker has far less chance to own his own business than did his great-grandfather.

Even after the average man's chance to become an *independent* industrialist had vanished, the avenue of promotion within a company remained wide open for many years. Fifty years ago an able and ambitious man might conceivably work himself up from sweeper to president. Today, as our technology and business life become more and more complicated, opportunities for the noncollege man become increasingly limited. Sociologists call this phenomenon *blocked mobility*. A man can still get ahead through hard work, but unless he is a college graduate it is a much more arduous task than it used to be.

2 *The Wealth of Nations* (New York: Modern Library, 1937), p. 4.

Organizational Growth

The industrial revolution has made business organizations larger and the boss more remote. The journeyman wagon-maker had no trouble talking to his boss; communication was easy. Today, however, a man may spend his lifetime in a steel mill and never talk to the plant manager, let alone the president.

The owner of a wagon shop could easily supervise all phases of manufacture. In a business like AT&T, supervision and coordination require the services of thousands of executives. All this leads to the process of bureaucratization, the making of rules that restrict individual discretion even to the point where top executives find themselves tied down.

Constant Change

In the simple society of the early 1800's, changes were rare. Behavior was governed by tradition: There was no need to tell a man what to do—all he had to do was follow the patterns laid down by his ancestors.

Modern industry is subject to constant change. The very fact of change creates two types of problem: (1) Less can be left to routine; careful planning, deliberate orders, and elaborate communications are essential. Since personal experience and tradition are less valued, there is a correspondingly greater need for rules and regulations. (2) People often resist change, particularly when it is imposed upon them. Consequently the problems of motivating people to work together have grown more complex.

In short, the industrial revolution has done wonders to make life easier for all of us, but at a serious cost in terms of the rewards and enjoyments that individuals derive from their jobs.

The rest of this chapter will be concerned with three questions: What sorts of needs are satisfied through work? How can these needs be ranked in relative importance? And how important as a source of satisfaction is one's *job* compared with other means of satisfaction available in life?[3]

NEEDS SATISFIED BY WORKING

Although the authors recognize that all attempts to categorize needs are somewhat artificial, we shall speak of three forms of need satisfaction.

1. *Physical and security needs.* These relate to the satisfaction of bodily functions, such as hunger, thirst, shelter, and the like, as well as the need to be secure in the enjoyment of these.

2. *Social needs.* Since human beings are dependent on each other, there are some needs which can be satisfied only when the individual is helped or recognized by other people.

---

[3] We are indebted to our teacher, the late Douglas McGregor, for many of the concepts discussed in this chapter.

3. *Egoistic needs.* These relate to man's desire to be independent, to do things on his own and to sense accomplishment.

Another way of categorizing needs is in terms of the means by which they are satisfied. Some forms of satisfaction are enjoyed *off the job*—for example, a man spends his pay check after work and away from the job. Other needs are satisfied through having a happy, satisfying work environment *around the job*. A third form of satisfaction can be obtained only through the process of working and so can be called intrinsic or *through-the-job* satisfaction. As we shall see in later chapters (Chapter 6 in particular), this three-way distinction is critical for the motivation of employees. When management emphasizes off-the-job satisfactions, it assumes, in effect, that work is a punishment which employees endure in exchange for rewards to be enjoyed after work. Managers who stress around-the-job satisfactions seek to make the work environment a pleasant one, but do not provide direct, positive motivation for men to work harder. To the extent that through-the-job satisfactions are provided, employees work hard; the harder they work the greater their satisfaction.

As will be seen, both sets of categories—types of needs and ways in which needs are satisfied—overlap a bit and many needs can be placed in more than one category. Nor is there any hard-and-fast relationship between the sets of categories. To a considerable extent, however, physical needs are satisfied off the job, social needs are satisfied through personal contacts around the job, whereas egoistic needs are chiefly satisfied through the job. There are, of course, many exceptions to this "rule." For example, safe working conditions satisfy an important physical need, yet they are enjoyed on the job; status is a social need, yet the status derived from holding an important position is enjoyed away from work as much as on the job; praise is another social need, yet praise from one's boss is often best obtained through doing one's job well; a salesman may satisfy his social needs through his work—the more sales he makes, the greater his opportunity to meet people.

With the above warnings in mind, let us now look at the various forms of need satisfaction obtained from work, starting with physical and security needs.

PRIMARILY PHYSICAL AND SECURITY NEEDS

Money

Ask a man why he works and chances are he will tell you, "to make money." Certainly the need to earn a living is the most powerful single reason why people work, though, as we shall see, nonmonetary incentives are also important.

Money satisfies all types of needs. Its principal use may be to provide the physical necessities of life as well as security; however, social status in our society depends largely on the size of one's earnings; and earning a good income provides many people with an egoistic sense of accomplishment.

The first demand most people make of a job, then, is that it provide them with enough to enjoy a "proper" standard of living. But what we accept as "proper" tends to rise over time. Today we consider a house substandard if it lacks running water or central heating; this was not so a hundred years ago. To many people today, an automobile and a TV set are among the essentials of life. Moreover, our concept of the proper standard of living depends a good bit on what our neighbors have. If the man next door buys a shiny new Buick, our five-year-old Chevy becomes less adequate.

This tremendous interest in material goods is not a natural characteristic of man but a special trait of our own culture. Many other societies ascribe far less importance to material goods than to holiness or physical or military power. The individual's place in society may be determined purely by who his ancestors were; displays of wealth may be regarded as poor taste. Among certain tribes competitiveness is socially tabu; when the missionaries taught these people how to run races, they insisted that every race must end in a dead heat.

Even in our own culture, money is ordinarily more important to the salesman than to the teacher or the minister. Some men refuse a promotion with a higher salary simply because it involves "too much responsibility." And today there is an entire "hippie" culture, which has "dropped out of the rat race" and rejected money as a standard of value or achievement.

Although in the larger community income may be only a rough measure of status, within an organization it measures very precisely the importance of a job. Even the difference of a cent in hourly rates may assume great significance. If one job pays $3.62 an hour and another $3.63, employees feel that (a) the $3.63 job is more important or (b) the $3.62 job should be higher paid.

Who is more important, the plumber or the electrician? If the plumber gets a 50 cent raise, the electrician wants the same—otherwise he feels he is suffering a cut. The National War Labor Board perhaps only slightly exaggerated when it said: "There is no single factor in the entire field of labor relations which does more to break down morale, create individual dissatisfaction, encourage absenteeism, increase labor turnover, and hamper production than obviously unjust inequalities in the wage rates paid to the same individuals in the same labor group within the same plant."

Security

Job security is a fundamental human need; for many people it is more important than either pay or advancement. The forces driving toward unionism, the most serious problems of superior-subordinate relations, the fears surrounding changing technology—all revolve around the need for security.

It is not enough for a man to have his physical needs satisfied from day to day; he wants to make sure they will continue to be satisfied in the future. In some cases, seniority offers the unskilled worker a sense of security akin to that of the farmer who owns his property or the craftsman who possesses special skills. In recent years, however, automation and other economic changes have brought unemployment to many who once thought their jobs secure. Older men, members of minority groups, and those with limited education or outmoded skills find it extremely hard to find steady work. As a consequence, losing a job can be a catastrophe, both physically and psychologically. No wonder workers' desires to hold on to their "property rights" to their jobs have led to labor-management disputes over working rules and featherbedding, particularly in industries with declining employment.

Illness and old age provide similar threats to security. Understandably, many companies and unions now seek to provide employees with "total" or "employment-to-grave" security against all forms of income interruption.

Advancement

The urge to advance, "to get ahead," is particularly strong in America. In many other societies a man is born to a rigidly defined class and follows his father's occupation without question; bootblack or king, he fulfills as best he can "the station to which God has called him."

Deep in the heart of every "true" American lies the Horatio Alger dream of unlimited occupational mobility, the belief that every man, no matter how humble his birth, can rise to the highest positions in the land. Indeed, our fondest stories concern men like Abe Lincoln who through honesty and hard work make their way from log cabin to White House.

Children are taught that any virtuous man can work his way to the top. "Your future is strictly up to you,"[4] said a National Association of Manufacturers pamphlet in 1951. "Your opportunities will be limited only by your vision of what your future may become, your abilities and how you use them, your character and your determination." At one time it was believed that poverty was largely due to moral weakness, that failure was the fault, not of the system, but of personal character.

Historians and sociologists are finding increasing evidence that the "sweeper-to-president" phenomenon has always been something of a myth.[5] Even a century ago opportunities to get ahead were considerably limited. Yet for a long time this myth of unlimited opportunities for "upward mobility" was generally believed and provided hopes for millions. Today this dream may be fading.[6] True, a child born in the 1970's has as good a chance to advance in social status as did his grandfather. But once a man reaches the age of 25 without having gone to college, his chances for advancement in the old-fashioned sense are limited. Such men may still want to get ahead, but they must redefine what they mean by getting ahead in terms that are realistically related to their actual opportunities.

A generalization of this sort, however, is much too broad, and needs careful qualification. In fact, as we shall discuss in future chapters, the very meaning of

[4] As quoted in Ely Chinoy, *The American Automobile Worker and the American Dream* (New York: Doubleday, 1955), pp. 9-10.

[5] Seymour Martin Lipset and Reinhard Bendix, *Social Mobility and Industrial Society* (Berkeley: University of California Press, 1960).

[6] Chinoy, *op. cit.*; Bennett M. Berger, *Working Class Suburb* (Berkeley: University of California Press, 1960), p. 88.

advancement differs substantially from one segment of the population to another: whether more security, more responsible jobs, higher incomes, greater status, or recognition from one's colleagues. The measure chosen depends in part on the kind of work one does.

PRIMARILY SOCIAL NEEDS

Man is a social animal. He craves *friendship,* is unhappy when left alone for too long, and often associates with his fellows just because he is hungry for companionship. Particularly for employees who have an unsatisfactory home life, the job provides a large part of their social-need satisfaction.

It is social banter that makes many jobs bearable. If there is nothing more constructive to talk about, small issues can be magnified and boredom can be relieved through circulating rumors. In the informal social life of the plant, too, many a worker has a chance to demonstrate skill and initiative. And even the work itself may be socially rewarding for some employees, such as telephone operators and salesclerks who gain satisfaction from talking to customers.

The job frequently satisfies other social needs besides the need for friendship. Belonging to a clique provides employees with a sense of *identification* and belonging, and they insist on forming "informal groups" even in the face of management opposition. When they are unable to achieve such identification, the job becomes less desirable. Indeed, there is evidence that workers who belong to small, integrated work groups have higher morale than those who work either alone or among large masses of employees with whom they have few social ties. One study explains why steelworkers are more satisfied with their job than automobile assembly-line workers partly on the grounds that steelworkers typically work in small teams; in contrast, on an assembly line a worker can talk only to the men flanking him, thus making cohesive social groups difficult to form.

Merely working together, *teamwork,* helps to build morale. Most people like *helping others.* Also, when we need it, we like to be *helped* by others.

Another set of social needs develops out of the subordinate's relationship to his supervisor. Naturally the subordinate wants *to be treated fairly:* He wants a fair hearing when he thinks his supervisor has made a wrong decision, and he wants the right to appeal over the supervisor's head. Most people like recognition when they do something well (though sometimes praise from a fellow worker is more meaningful than praise from management). The average worker also expects acceptance from his supervisor—that is, understanding and consideration when he makes a mistake. Finally, he wants to *know where he stands.*

Regardless of whether he is doing badly or well, the typical worker wants some *attention* from both his boss and his fellow workers. Individuals differ in the amount of attention they desire, however, for some want to be left strictly alone and others constantly run to the boss for reassurance. The supervisor must adjust his supervisory practices accordingly (and yet avoid charges of favoritism). But we shall have more to say about this later on.

Achievement

"The trouble with this work is that I don't have any feeling of achievement. I'm just nobody, doing nothing, getting nowhere. I'm just a cog, so small I'd never be missed." So one worker explained his dislike for his job, even though it was one of the highest-paying jobs in the plant.

One of man's strongest needs is the need for a sense of achievement, for the feeling that he is getting something done, that his work is of importance. The word *achievement* is rather nebulous, however, for it means many things to different people. Let us examine some of the dimensions of this term.

Importance of the work. Work that seems pointless is bound to lead to frustration. One of the most unpleasant forms of punishment used by the military is to have men dig holes and then fill them in again. Compare this with the rich reward that people who perform even menial tasks in a hospital get from "helping people."

Two English researchers, in a study of a candy factory, once found that the greatest dissatisfaction centered in a small work group whose job consisted of unwrapping defective chocolates as part of a salvage operation.[7] The workers felt that their job was less useful than that of the other operators. Telephone supervisors report that production and morale are usually higher during an emergency. As one said, "It's amazing. An operator may be a low producer, and often tardy and absent, but come a blizzard when the highways are closed, she will walk long distances to come to work."

The satisfied worker takes pride in the product he makes: "I get a big kick every time I see it in the store," he may say, or "Our widgets are made to the finest tolerance in the industry." The various forms that this sense of achievement may take are suggested by the following quotations:[8]

Responsibility for the welfare of others: "I am very proud of my job because I examine the mine to make sure it is safe. I save a lot of lives by taking chances for them."—*Miner.*

Service to others: "There is a lot of satisfaction out of putting something on a man you know looks well on him, and that he is going to get a lot of compliments and he's going to be pleased and all that."—*Salesclerk.*

Satisfaction in product: "When you are selling sterling silver, you've got something to talk about and you talk about it truthfully. It's something that turns into a heirloom—never wears out."—*Salesclerk.*

The elevator operator, the janitor, and the groundskeeper—all *want* to feel that their job is important, and good supervision can do much to enhance their

---

[7] S. Wyatt and J. N. Langdon, *Fatigue and Boredom in Repetitive Work,* Industrial Health Research Council, Report No. 77 (London: H. M. Stationery Office, 1938).

[8] Eugene A. Friedmann and Robert J. Havighurst, *The Meaning of Work and Retirement* (Chicago: University of Chicago Press, 1954), pp. 77, 110, 119.

sense of achievement and their feeling of self-respect, as we shall see in later chapters.

Studies suggest that there is a close correlation between an occupation's prestige and the satisfaction people get from working at it. "Jobs that have high prestige will tend to be valued for their status rewards even when 'objective' aspects of the work are undesirable; similarly, low-status jobs will tend to be undervalued and disliked." [9] Low-status work is considered unimportant. "The best way to improve the job may often be, in fact, to change what the outside public thinks about it and its doers." [10]

A final point: having considerable freedom in determining how the job is to be done may well increase the importance of the job to the individual, since it is a test of his ability to plan his own work.

How the work fits into the whole. During World War II, the morale in a small plant was very low and turnover was high. Most of the employees were women who spent their days producing a small metal part that had no obvious importance. The women had no idea what it was used for, nor would management tell them. Then one day they were taken by bus to a nearby aircraft plant where they were shown that the part was an important component of the tail assembly of the B-29. For a while at least, production and morale soared.

In modern industry it is often extremely difficult for the worker "to see his place in the scheme of things, to appreciate his contributions to the total process. Too often the individual job is like the isolated pieces of a jigsaw puzzle. And because there are so many 'pieces,' those at the work level generally have only the haziest notion of the total pattern. ... In a real sense, therefore, the job loses its meaning for the worker—the meaning that is in all terms except the pay envelope." [11]

Skill. All of us enjoy the sense of creativity that springs from doing something well, from being "on top" of our job. The housewife is proud of her cleanliness or her shortbread, the safecracker of his sensitive fingers, the professor of his brilliant lecture or his searching questions.

We also like to imagine that our job requires unusual skill, and as a consequence we tend to exaggerate its importance. When describing his job, a worker often stresses its difficulty, complexity, and the length of time required to learn it. Every machine seems to have special quirks in the eyes of its operator. Every trade has its tricks which require skill, ingenuity, and expertise. Even the janitor feels he has developed a number of special techniques (knowing that Executive A likes his desk dusted, but that Executive B never wants his desk touched) that raise him above the level of unskilled labor. "The bricklayer as a rule is more than a workman. He is a craftsman," says the

[9] Robert Blauner, *Alienation and Freedom* (Chicago: University of Chicago Press, 1964), p. 63.

[10] Whiting Williams, *The Mainsprings of Man* (New York: Scribner's, 1925), p. 63.

[11] James C. Worthy, *Some Observations on Frederick W. Taylor and the Scientific Management Movement,* paper delivered before the Society for Applied Anthropology, Columbia University, New York City, April 9, 1954.

Bricklayers' Union journal. [12] "His work endures and stands the gaff of years . . . I have worked with a certain bricklayer who takes great pride in telling you one of his ancestors used to take his son to Buckingham Palace and point out some of the stately arches which he himself had built. . . . When a bricklayer has finished with a day's work there is something real to compensate for it. He can go home feeling that he has created something that will last longer than he will."

Employees resent any implication that they can be easily replaced by untrained workers. Partly, of course, such an implication threatens their job security. But there is more to it than that: If anybody can do your job, what can you say that you have accomplished in your working life? What more significant sign of utter failure? True, many workers feel that they contribute nothing to their job that a completely untrained man could not contribute, but they are dismally discouraged by this realization. As individuals, they feel they are achieving nothing.

This sense of frustration helps explain the popularity of do-it-yourself projects, many of which involve no economic saving for the home craftsman but do provide a sense of skill and creativity. A worker may come home tired from the factory or office and "rest" by working hard in his basement or garden.

For the skilled craftsman the feeling of skill is particularly important. Many companies have discovered that it is harder to get employees to lower their standards of quality than to raise them. When management decides that customers will accept lower quality, and that looser tolerances can be maintained, skilled workers stubbornly resist the consequent reduction in skill required. Looser standards mean less sense of accomplishment.

It is for this reason that many companies are plagued by running battles between engineers and top management. The engineers insist on close tolerances and top quality; they try to delay a new model from being put into production until all the "bugs" have been eliminated. Top management regards this desire for perfection as financially ruinous.

Progress and completion. If an employee is to have a feeling of achievement, he must have some way of measuring his progress. Everyone wants to know "How am I doing?" People like "feedback" even when there is no reward or penalty attached to failure or success. Thus, when a man idly throws a piece of paper at a wastepaper basket, he is interested in whether it goes in (even if he doesn't have to clean up afterward). Only if he can set up some goal and know that he has reached it can he feel this sense of achievement. Many routine jobs are considered boring and monotonous precisely because they give the worker no way to check his progress.

Productiveness. Perhaps all that we have been saying adds up to one point: most people have a genuine desire to be productive, to keep busy. [13]

12 *The Bricklayer, Mason and Plasterer,* Vol. 30 (May 1927), p. 134.

13 One astute student suggests that once people have started to work they have a virtual compulsion to keep on going, an urge that he calls "traction." W. Baldamus, *Efficiency and Work* (London: Tavistock Publications, 1961).

Certainly our observations cast doubt on the common assumption that most workers prefer to "goldbrick" than to work. In fact, it is harder to look busy than to work. Time passes more quickly when a worker is absorbed in what he is doing than when he is trying to avoid work. In our society, a healthy individual feels lost without some sort of job or hobby. Normally, expending mental and physical energy is a pleasant, not a painful, experience.

But if all this is true, how can we explain why people often do loaf on the job and go to extraordinary extremes to avoid work? Usually such behavior is a sign of dissatisfaction with the job, with supervision, or with the company as a whole. Workers who feel that they have been treated unfairly direct their energies to beating the system and show high skill in doing as little work as possible. This response, however, is a sure sign that the organization is beset by severe problems.

The sense of productivity and achievement is particularly important to executives.

They conceive themselves as hard working and achieving people who must accomplish in order to be happy. ... They obtain continual stimulation from the pleasure of immediate accomplishment. They feel the necessity to move continually upwards and to accumulate the rewards from increasing accomplishments. [14]

Autonomy

"You know, it's a funny thing. I work all day at the plant and then I come home and what do I do? I work some more—I mean in the shop in the basement. I love to do things with my hands. Funny, that's what I do at work—only it's different.

"You see at work I don't have any freedom. That's the difference. The company tells me when to start working, when I get time to go to the john, when I get my lunch and how long (I get .7 hours—that's 42 minutes for anyone who isn't an engineer). They tell me how fast to work and exactly what motions to make. About the only thing I'm free to do is to think how damn lousy the job is.

"Now, at home I'm my own boss—and believe me, that's a wonderful feeling."

—*Autoworker.*

Most people like being their own boss. Yet in modern industry only a few employees really have this feeling. The process of specialization has deprived the individual worker of his freedom to plan and organize his own job and has transferred initiative and responsibility to management. As Frederick Taylor, father of the scientific management movement, once put it, "Each man must learn how to give up his own particular way of doing things, adapt his methods to the many new standards, and grow accustomed to receiving and obeying directions covering details, large and small, which in the past have been left to his individual judgment." [15] The effect of this approach has been to strip many jobs of every opportunity for spontaneity and creativity.

Sometimes the tall stories told by workers are indicative of their hidden desires to do things in their own way. For instance, there is the tale of the

[14] William E. Henry, "The Business Executive: A Study in the Psychodynamics of a Social Role," *The American Journal of Sociology*, Vol. 54, No. 4 (January 1949), p. 287.

[15] Frederick W. Taylor, *Shop Management* (New York: Harper, 1919), p. 113.

assembly-line workers who fixed their cars so that when you stepped on the accelerator the windshield wiper started flapping and the horn blew "honk-honk." Then there is the story about the skilled glass blower who for years had been making glass rabbits with straight ears. One day he decided to let the ears droop. "I thought it might be a nice change," he told an amazed management.

Initiative and imagination are essential to any sense of autonomy; yet too often management fails to use the creative abilities of employees. As a consequence, they display their initiative and imagination in forms of which management disapproves, such as sabotage, union activity, and horseplay. Often the creative individual is considered a troublemaker.[16]

We must not paint too black a picture, however, for on many jobs workers do have a good deal of freedom. We have all seen janitors who really felt they were kings of all they surveyed—and behaved accordingly. Skilled workers, guards, inspectors, and many production workers frequently have this same feeling of independence.

How a man feels depends on both the type of work he does and how he is supervised. Mineworkers, truckdrivers, and railroaders all have above-average job satisfaction, which has been explained by "the absence of close supervision" and the fact that "the contact between employees and supervision is so much less than in factory work."[17] Of course, no one can be boss of everything, but within limits an employee can feel that he is his own boss. This is particularly true if he can feel that what he does is determined by the objective requirements of the situation rather than by human orders. (From an objective point of view, the utility substation operator has almost no freedom; he must constantly make adjustments to meet the changing demands for power. Yet he feels quite independent, since he gets his orders from dials rather than from people.)

Many jobs demand such a high degree of teamwork that the individual worker is deprived of much opportunity to make decisions by himself. But in a situation like this it is often practicable to have the decisions made by the group as a whole. *Participation* in decision-making by the group is the equivalent of autonomy for the individual.

Knowledge

The desire for knowledge is a basic impulse in human beings. People like to know not only "what" is happening to them but "why." They want both to understand the present and to predict the future. Arbitrariness, caprice, and unexpected events all make it hard for us to fashion an orderly, reasonable explanation of the events that shape our lives. To be at the mercy of people and forces that we can neither understand nor control is a serious threat to our sense of security. Take, for example, the unrest that prevails in an office after a familiar, well-known supervisor is replaced by a new man with unknown preferences, attitudes, and idiosyncrasies.

---

[16] Some observers report that the trend toward conformity is causing the same thing to happen on the management level. W. H. Whyte, Jr., *The Organization Man* (New York: Simon and Schuster, 1956).

[17] Blauner, *op. cit.*, p. 348.

People want to know about things that are directly important to them, and also about those that are not. Satisfying idle curiosity is also a way of spending one's time. The village busybody and the bored receptionist have nothing better to do than to pry into other people's business. The desire for information is so strong that if the truth is not available, appropriate substitutes will be fashioned.

The quest for knowledge has more constructive elements as well. Many people find that learning gives them a sense of achievement. Being an expert on something—whether it is baseball, trout flies, the fine points of one's job, or the ramifications of union politics—gives the individual a sense of uniqueness and progress.

RELATIVE IMPORTANCE OF VARIOUS NEEDS

Obviously, all the previously mentioned needs are important, but which is most important? Which can be used most effectively to motivate employees to work for organizational objectives?

This question has been the subject of extensive research. The answer has been found to vary with the individual concerned, his job, the general economic climate, and a host of other factors. Several generalizations seem to be at least partly valid, however, as we shall discuss below.

Needs Hierarchy

According to the well-known Maslow "needs hypothesis," [18] human needs can be ordered into a hierarchy, with physical needs being the "lowest" and most basic, followed in ascending order by what we have called security, social, and egoistic needs—and finally "self-actualization." [19] In this hierarchy a higher, less basic need does not provide motivation unless all lower, more basic needs are "largely" satisfied; but once a lower-level need is largely satisfied it no longer motivates.

Thus, once physical needs for food, clothing, and shelter are reasonably well satisfied, individuals become relatively more concerned with other needs. First, they seek to satisfy their safety or security needs for protection against danger, threats, and deprivation. (As we have seen, physical and safety needs are usually satisfied through pay, seniority, fringe benefits, and the like.) When the standard of living rises so that security is assured, then social needs take first priority, followed by egoistic needs. Finally, according to this hypothesis, only when most of the less pressing needs are satisfied will individuals turn to the ultimate form of accomplishment, self-actualization, which has been described as

[18] A. H. Maslow, *Motivation and Personality* (New York: Harper, 1954), Chapters 6-8.

[19] The terms Maslow actually used are *physiological* (equivalent to our physical), *safety* (our security), *social, esteem* (somewhat equivalent to our ego), and *self-actualization*. In our previous discussion we have not considered self-actualization as a separate need, largely because we find it difficult to distinguish this need from such egoistic needs as accomplishment.

"the desire to become . . . everything that one is capable of becoming," to make the very most of one's potentialities.[20]

The message for management in this theory is that as long as employees' lower-order needs are unsatisfied, it will be difficult to motivate them with those of a higher order. But once those lower needs *are* reasonably well satisfied, management will have to shift its emphasis to the higher needs if it is to provide continued motivation.

This point is nicely illustrated by two studies of job satisfaction. In an investigation in Nashua, New Hampshire, workers were asked why they wanted to stay on their present job and were requested to list any reasons why they might like to leave it.[21] In a similar study in New Haven, Connecticut, workers were asked to give the reasons why they were satisfied or dissatisfied with their present work.[22] Notice in the chart that the relative importance of the various needs was the same whether the workers were responding in terms of staying or quitting, or in terms of being satisfied or dissatisfied. But between the groups there was a significant difference. In Nashua, half the workers emphasized economic reasons; in New Haven, only about one-quarter of them did. Why such a difference?

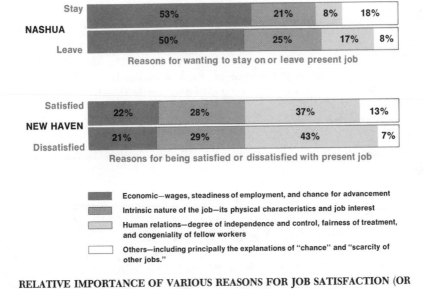

RELATIVE IMPORTANCE OF VARIOUS REASONS FOR JOB SATISFACTION (OR DISSATISFACTION) AS REPORTED BY TWO STUDIES

The answer can be found in the economic conditions existing in the two communities when the studies were made. New Haven was enjoying a period of

[20] A. H. Maslow, "A Theory of Human Motivation," *Psychological Review*, Vol. 50 (July 1943), p. 372.

[21] Charles A. Myers and George P. Shultz, *The Dynamics of a Labor Market* (Englewood Cliffs, N.J.: Prentice-Hall, 1951), pp. 130–131.

[22] Lloyd G. Reynolds and Joseph Shister, *Job Horizons* (New York: Harper, 1949).

full employment when jobs were plentiful and minimum economic needs were being met. Consequently, social and psychological factors gained importance. In Nashua there was substantial unemployment, created by the closing of a large textile plant. In effect, the men here were saying, "Better a bad job than no job at all."

The attractiveness of any one job factor (such as wages) . . . , is a consequence of the extent to which other job satisfactions or expectations are being fulfilled at the time. When a worker enjoys a steady job paying good wages, he is understandably more concerned about the treatment he gets from his supervisors, the degree of independence and control he has on the job, and whether the job is interesting. But when he loses his high-paid job he is more concerned about regaining steady, well-paid employment. [23]

The needs-hierarchy hypothesis has been subjected to a good deal of criticism. The two most telling points are the following:

1. People seem to differ greatly in the extent to which a need must be satisfied before they are willing to move on to a higher level. Furthermore, for some people egoistic needs may be more basic than social ones. A scientist's physical needs, for example, may be very easily satisfied, his social needs may be minimal, and his consuming passion for research may involve egoistic and self-actualizing needs. By forcing the facts, one might say that the scientist conforms to the needs hierarchy, but doing so does not help us understand his behavior.

2. As we have seen, the various categories of need overlap, and a given need may be fitted into more than one category. Money is perhaps the most important single source of need satisfaction; yet depending on the circumstances, it may satisfy any of the needs listed.

For all these reasons, it is very hard to put the hypothesis in operational form and to test whether or not it is true. Yet, despite its limitations it does present some useful insights into human behavior. Other factors must also be considered, however.

Personality differences. In recent years a theory of human motivation has come into prominence which challenges the place of the Maslow theory in organizational thought. According to this theory, which has been developed by McClelland and Atkinson, there are at least three major *positive* needs related to employee behavior in organizations: the need for *achievement,* the need for *power* (having control and influence over people), and the need for *affiliation* (to be accepted by others). There is also a negative need, the need to avoid *failure.* [24]

In contrast to Maslow's theory, the McClelland-Atkinson theory makes no provision for a hierarchy of needs. People differ in the strengths of their needs,

[23] Myers and Shultz, *op. cit.*, pp. 132-133.

[24] For example, see D. C. McClelland, *The Achieving Society* (Princeton: Van Nostrand, 1961). As defined, the needs for achievement, power, and affiliation bear some resemblance to self-actualizing, ego, and social needs, but the correspondence is not close.

and these differences are largely determined by the environment in which they have grown up. Only those with a high need for achievement will obtain a great deal of satisfaction from jobs that provide a feeling of accomplishment. Those with a high need for affiliation will prefer jobs that involve a strong sense of community.

Substitution of one need for another. To some extent, people will give up one source of need satisfaction for another. Once job security is obtained, workers will accept loss of social and egoistic satisfaction only in return for a significant increase in pay.[25] Conversely, many will accept lower wages in return for a more desirable job. As one worker put it:

"Sure this job doesn't pay much. But nobody pushes you and you are your own boss. I could get more in the mills, but I would hate myself for doing it: push, push, and bosses. Life is too short. I like the guys here."

Role of money. Management is sometimes deceived by workers' demands for money, because money has many meanings in terms of need satisfaction. If we looked solely at union demands on management and at the overt causes of strikes, we might well conclude that workers were interested in money alone. Yet, as we have seen, this is not the whole picture.

There are two reasons for this overemphasis. In the first place, workers may regard higher earnings as a partial compensation for the lack of other forms of need satisfaction. Second, money has a symbolic value. Money earnings are tangible; psychic earnings are not. If one is going to gripe, one seizes on something tangible to gripe about. Dissatisfaction with the job in general is often semiconscious and hard to put into words. If workers went to the boss demanding that he provide them with more interesting work, they would feel pretty foolish; but a demand for an increase of 10 cents an hour can be put in writing.

From the union's point of view, of course, the size of the paycheck is a measure of the union's strength and the officers' bargaining skill. Wage improvements can be obtained for everyone at one fell swoop around the bargaining table, but the union can improve human relations only piecemeal through the grievance procedure.

As mentioned earlier, money provides more than merely physical needs. For the high-need-achieving manager, the size of his paycheck provides concrete feedback as to the extent of his success.

Differences Among Occupational Groups

The types of satisfactions emphasized by various occupational groups will vary, depending on what opportunities for satisfaction are available to them,

---

[25] The overwhelming majority of employees in an automotive assembly plant indicated that they liked their pay but disliked the job as such. They took the job only for the extra income. Charles R. Walker and Robert H. Guest, *Man on the Assembly Line* (Cambridge: Harvard University Press, 1952), p. 143.

what they have come to expect, and which needs have already been satisfied. [26] Attitude surveys suggest that unskilled blue-collar workers, who have relatively little chance for autonomy or advancement, give relatively strong emphasis to job security and physical working conditions. Craft workers emphasize the *kind* of work they do, while white-collar workers are more likely to mention autonomy and the nature of their job. Service workers stress the social satisfactions derived from the people they work with and meet. Accountants have relatively less opportunity for being creative on their jobs than do engineers, whereas engineers, in many cases, are concerned with looking well in the eyes of their colleagues. Thus, we should not be surprised that one study shows engineers to be relatively more concerned with achievement, and accountants with advancement. [27] Along the same lines, another finds that "managers mention salary much more frequently than do professionals ... who stress the content of the job itself." [28] Finally, we have a study of executives which indicates that although executives at all levels are relatively well satisfied with their job security, lower-level executives are considerably more dissatisfied with their opportunities for autonomy and creativity than are those further up the ladder. [29]

HOW IMPORTANT IS JOB SATISFACTION?

How important is it for any person to have satisfying work? This question can be divided into two parts: (1) What does dissatisfying work do to the individual? And (2) what does it do to organizational efficiency and productivity? We shall deal briefly with the first question here. The second question will be discussed in later chapters, particularly Chapter 6.

The question of what role work plays in human life is a concern not only of management. It is a psychological, philosophical, moral, and even theological question, one about which scholars have debated endlessly. There is no clear answer, but let us state some of the issues in terms of a debate. [30]

The Case for Work Being Very Important

One group argues that mature human beings require high levels of egoistic and self-actualizing need-satisfaction from their jobs. The process of growing up involves accepting more and more challenge and autonomy and becoming more

[26] See, for example, Elizabeth L. Lyman, "Occupational Differences in the Value Attached to Work," *American Journal of Sociology*, Vol. 55, No. 2 (September 1955), pp. 138-144; Nancy Morse and Robert S. Weiss, "The Function and Meanings of Work and the Job," *American Sociological Review*, Vol. 20, No. 2 (April 1955), pp. 191-198; Blauner, *op. cit.*

[27] Fredrick Herzberg, Bernard Mausner, and Barbara Snyderman, *The Motivation to Work* (New York: Wiley, 1959).

[28] Morse and Weiss, *op. cit.*, p. 197.

[29] Lyman W. Porter, *Organizational Patterns of Managerial Job Attitudes* (New York: American Foundation for Management Research, 1964).

[30] For a more complete statement of the debate, see George Strauss, "Notes on Power Equalization," in Harold J. Leavitt, ed., *The Social Science of Organizations* (Englewood Cliffs, N.J.: Prentice-Hall, 1963), pp. 45-57.

independent. Those who do not have these opportunities (in particular those who are unable to express themselves meaningfully through work) never reach psychological maturity[31] Since the average man spends nearly a third of his waking hours on the job, if that job does not provide challenge and autonomy he may suffer real frustration, with results that are costly both to himself and his employer. Thus, the fact that many individuals have boring, meaningless jobs may lead to severe social problems.

Indeed, the very act of working satisfies basic human needs. Eighty per cent of those employees questioned in the survey of worker attitudes replied that they would continue to work even if they "inherited enough money to live comfortably without working.[32] "Working gives them a feeling of being tied into the larger society, of having something to do, of having a purpose in life."[33] The existence of the Peace Corps suggests that many seek meaning in their work and, indeed, through their work may seek a meaning in life.

The importance of work in modern life is indicated by the impact of unemployment and retirement on persons who have been active and productive for decades. Unless the retired employee can find some other kind of work (a hobby, for instance), the psychological effects of idleness may be extremely upsetting. All of us have heard comments of this sort: "After Dad was pensioned off he just fell apart. He didn't know what to do with himself." Unemployment can be even more demoralizing.

There is evidence that workers on unskilled (and presumably boring) jobs are significantly more likely to suffer from personality disturbances (as measured by interviews) and psychosomatic illnesses (as measured by dispensary visits) than are skilled workers.[34] Individuals who move from unskilled to skilled work tend to become better adjusted after the move, and vice versa.

In addition, as we shall discuss in later chapters, low morale and poor motivation may lead to inefficiency and low productivity. In sum, so the argument runs, the existence of unrewarding jobs creates an unhealthy situation, which is harmful to the individual, to the organization which employs him, and to society generally.

The Case for Job Satisfaction Not Being Important

The opposing argument is that many people adjust easily to dull work. They center life away from the job, expect relatively few satisfactions from it, and so are not disappointed when it offers them little in the way of challenge or sense

[31] For a classical statement, see Chris Argyris, *Personality and Organization* (New York: Harper, 1957). A later extension of this work is Chris Argyris, *Integrating the Individual and the Organization* (New York: Wiley, 1964).

[32] Morse and Weiss, *op. cit.*, p. 192 and p. 197. Interestingly, a substantial proportion (though not a majority) of middle-class employees mentioned "interest in work" and "accomplishment" as reasons for wanting to keep on working; by contrast blue-collar workers emphasized the importance of "keeping occupied."

[33] *Ibid.*, p. 191.

[34] Arthur Kornhauser and Otto M. Reid, *Mental Health of the Industrial Worker: A Detroit Study* (New York: Wiley, 1965); John R. P. French, Robert L. Kahn, and Floyd Mann, eds., "Work, Health and Satisfaction," *Journal of Social Issues*, Vol. 18, No. 3 (July 1962).

of creativity. Indeed, some suggest that many people would not want a high level of challenge and autonomy on the job, even were it available. Possibly such individuals are immature, but their immaturity is due far more to family environment than to the job; they have learned to be dependent in childhood, and are unlikely to change this pattern in later life.

It is claimed that most of the evidence designed to show the importance of need satisfaction is misleading, showing in fact that in our culture people want *some* sort of job (and preferably one with high status) but not that the job itself must provide higher orders of satisfaction. There is evidence, for example, that city (as opposed to country) blue-collar workers and those with a low need for achievement generally have little desire for intrinsic, through-the-job satisfaction, and they settle easily for jobs that provide plenty of social interaction (see our discussion in Chapters 7 and 9).

According to some studies, retirement in itself does not bring on the rapid deterioration of physical and mental health as was once supposed; health tends to improve after retirement. Further, evidence on the impact of unskilled work on mental health is still incomplete. Apparently, not everyone suffers equally from unskilled work, and some adjust more easily than others. And it is not clear whether mental ill health results from the intrinsic nature of unskilled work or from the fact that such work pays poorly and has low status both off and on the job. Insofar as mental disturbances are caused by economic and social pressures at home, higher wages may be a better solution than improved satisfaction on the job.

Attitude surveys suggest that most people expect relatively little from work, and so adjust rather easily to the demands of the job—though professionals and executives, whose work is more satisfying, find such adjustment easier than do factory workers. [35] Thus, a 1965 Gallup poll indicated that 80 per cent of manual workers were satisfied with their work (compared with 92 per cent of professional and business men). [36] On the other hand, other studies suggest that the proportion of those who would choose the same kind of work if they were beginning their career again varied from 91 per cent among mathematicians and 82 per cent among journalists to 52 per cent among skilled printers and 16 per cent among unskilled autoworkers. In other words, workers in general seem to have adjusted to their present jobs, though many would prefer other kinds of work, were it available.

Ideally, it would be better if everyone could lead a fully satisfying life, both on and off the job. Possibly job satisfaction would be greater were we to return to the idyllic preindustrial conditions pictured at the beginning of this chapter—if, for example, cars were made on a handcraft basis rather than on an assembly line. But the cost of doing so would be the abandonment of our modern technological efficiency and a substantial reduction in our standard of living. Few would be willing to pay this price. Or so the argument runs.

[35] The discussion which follows is adapted from Robert Blauner, "Work Satisfaction and Industrial Trends in Modern Society," Walter Galenson and S. M. Lipset, eds., *Labor and Trade Unionism* (New York: Wiley, 1960).

[36] But the same poll found only 48 per cent of nonwhites satisfied with their work, compared with 87 per cent of the whites.

Work and Leisure

Perhaps the issues will seem less confused if we step back and examine them from both a historical and a cultural viewpoint. Remember that our present attitude toward work is culturally based. Work has not always been so important as it is today, nor is it likely to be so important in the future. In centuries past, particularly when civilization was flourishing in Greece and Rome, work did not occupy an exalted position. In fact, those of higher social status did not expect to work, for work was primarily restricted to slaves and to free citizens who lacked independent resources.

During the Protestant Reformation, work took on many religious connotations. Work was clearly a duty, a duty to fulfill one's predestined "calling." It was also regarded as an ordained punishment for the sins of man. To fail to work was immoral. Our present feeling about the idle—that they are somehow not behaving morally—is a reflection of this religious emphasis. To maintain respect in our society, rich men must work.

Today, attitudes toward work differ greatly among occupational groups. For some, "work has now become the main business of life"[37] and the chief function of recreation is to recuperate to do more work. Certainly many professionals and executives feel this way. Indeed, some corporations seem to feel that their executives should behave as "Organization Men" twenty-four hours a day. But the central focus of other people's lives is not the job (which is merely a "way of getting a living") but the home or community. Such people find a large measure of challenge, creativity, and autonomy in raising a family, pursuing a hobby, or taking part in community affairs.

Further, in many occupations people spend less time on the job today than in the past. A half-century ago the six-day week (for, in some instances, ten to twelve hours a day) was the rule, and vacations and holidays were far from common. Today few people work more than five days a week, and the average worker has at least a two-week vacation and ten paid holidays a year. Not far over the horizon is the 30-hour, four-day week (already the New York City electricians' contract calls for a 25-hour week), while the Steelworkers' union may be establishing a new trend through negotiating a 13-week "sabbatical" for its members every five years.[38] In addition, our life span grows longer while the retirement age tends to come earlier. All these influences are eroding the key position held by work in our daily lives.

It has been suggested that work in the future will become increasingly routine and provide fewer and fewer opportunities for creativity and discretion.[39] On the other hand, as working hours grow shorter, there will be a new "bohemianism" off the job as people seek self-expression away from work.

---

[37] Charles R. Walker, *Modern Technology and Civilization* (New York: McGraw-Hill, 1962), p. 439.

[38] On the other hand, there are large numbers of moonlighters who seem to prefer work and its monetary rewards to leisure.

[39] Clark Kerr, John T. Dunlop, Frederick H. Harbison, and Charles A. Myers, *Industrialism and Industrial Man* (New York: Oxford, 1964).

Leisure will be the happy hunting ground of the independent spirit ... The new slavery to technology may bring a new dedication to diversity and individualism off the job.[40]

From such predictions, some conclude that perhaps the best use of our resources is to accelerate automation, shorten the workweek as fast as possible, forget about on-the-job satisfactions, and concentrate our energies on making leisure more meaningful. Certainly there are "dropouts" from our society who believe that there must be more "relevant" and "meaningful" things to do with one's life than to spend eight hours a day in a factory or office.

Others argue that it is impossible to compartmentalize work and leisure activities and that expanded leisure activities will never substitute for what is missing on the job. Indeed, it is suggested that work routines spill over into leisure routines, and that those who have routine jobs tend to engage in passive, routine types of recreation.

Nevertheless, the line between work and nonwork activities is drawn much sharper today than it ever was in the past. Prior to large-scale commuting, people lived and played with the same people they worked with, and a whole series of ceremonies and other social activities tended to integrate work, family, and community life into a seamless web. In those days, people felt little need to "get away" from work (and had less opportunity to do so). Today, since work and play occupy separate spheres in our lives, we feel under pressure to decide which is most important.

Two contrasting developments affect this decision. In the first place, the percentage of our population with some college training is growing rapidly. In many states, more than half our high-school graduates go on to college. In the past, college graduates have insisted on responsible, meaningful work. Today, however, a considerable portion of such graduates are alienated from business values; many of them reject conventional managerial careers. Thus, whether job satisfaction will become more or less important in the future is still uncertain.

Summary of the Argument

JOB SATISFACTION IMPORTANT	JOB SATISFACTION UNIMPORTANT
1. People want self-actualization.	Some people prefer unchallenging work.
2. Those who don't obtain job satisfaction never reach psychological maturity.	Individual personality becomes fixed before people start working. Work is not to blame.
3. Those who fail to obtain job satisfaction become frustrated.	Most people have relatively low levels of aspiration for job satisfaction and expect only routine work.
4. The job is central to man's life.	This is a professor's value. Many people focus their lives on family and community.
5. Those without work are unhappy. People want to work even when they don't have to.	Even though there are social pressures to have *a* job, this does not mean the job must be challenging, etc.
6. Lack of challenging work leads to low mental health.	Poor mental health may be due to low income or low status of routine jobs. Anyway, research findings are not conclusive.

[40] *Ibid.*, pp. 237–238.

7. Work and leisure patterns spill into each other. Those with uncreative jobs engage in uncreative recreation.

A new bohemianism off the job will make up for increasing boredom at work.

8. Lack of job satisfaction and alienation from work lead to lower morale, lower productivity, and an unhealthy society.

We can provide challenging work for everybody only at the cost of eliminating our mass production technology and high standard of living—and society is unwilling to pay this price.

9. The proportion of our society which has graduated from college is growing, and college graduates demand satisfying work.

College graduates are increasingly alienated from organizations and work.

CONCLUSION

Management can do its job only through motivating people to work for management's objectives. But it is impossible to understand motivation without considering what people want and expect from their jobs.

Since people spend about a third of their waking hours at work, it is not surprising that they should expect work to satisfy many sorts of needs—physical, social and egoistic—and that, further, these needs may be satisfied in a wide variety of ways—off the job, around the job, and through the job. Though there is some evidence that these needs can be ranked in a hierarchy, it is fairly clear that the various forms of need satisfaction can be substituted for each other.

There is considerable debate about the importance of satisfaction enjoyed on the job, as opposed to satisfactions derived elsewhere in life. Professors (and they are the ones who do most of the writing in this field) in general place high value on autonomy, creativity, and the quest for maximum self-development. As much as any other group in society, their existence is work-oriented; for them creative achievement is an end in itself and requires no further justification. As a consequence, they are inclined to equate true happiness with interesting work and assume that everyone should be as work-involved as professors are. Perhaps those professors who give such a major role for job satisfaction are right—but the case is not black-and-white.

As for the present authors, we hold a middle-of-the-road position. A man's work is one of the most important (if not the most important) activities in his life. Those who do not have satisfying jobs rarely have fully satisfying lives. As we shall discuss in future chapters, dissatisfying work can lead in many (but not all) circumstances to lower production and friction on the job, so that it may be in management's economic interest to reduce such dissatisfaction. But even where this is not true, management has a certain degree of social responsibility (as we shall discuss in our concluding chapter) to provide work opportunities which are psychologically meaningful. Regardless, we must bear in mind that work is not man's only objective, nor is work satisfaction the sole objective of management.

A safe conclusion is that there are substantial differences—determined in part by personality and culture—in the importance people assign to work but also, as we shall discuss in Chapters 2 and 3, that jobs differ themselves in the types of satisfactions they offer.

problem • ENGINEERING CONSTRUCTION COMPANY

This company designs and supervises the erection of chemical and petroleum processing plants. It employs a large number of engineers with college degrees, most of whom work in the Field Division or the Drafting Division.

The approximately 1000 engineers in the Field Division supervise the erection of plants throughout the world. As of 1956 (the date of this case), new college graduates received $425 a month. After five years they might reasonably expect $800 a month; after 20 years, $1500. However, few reach these higher salaries. By the end of two years over half have either quit or been discharged. Top management engages in frequent purges, weeding out those it thinks are incompetent. Fierce competition is encouraged for the top jobs. Men are often transferred from one part of the country to another with as little as one week's notice, a policy that creates particular hardships for children who must be constantly uprooted from school. Working conditions on the job are usually poor, with wind, rain, heat, and cold being common.

The Drafting Division contains approximately 500 graduate engineers. Prior to 1935, when the company was much smaller, high school graduates were hired to do drafting, but during the depression, men with college diplomas could be obtained for very little money and the policy of hiring them was started. Pay starts at $2.90 an hour and reaches $3.85 after two years, the highest drafting pay in the city. No one has been laid off for lack of work since the early depression days and discharges for incompetence are rare. There is one section head for every 20 men (salary $8500). Promotions to this job are normally obtained through seniority.

The drafting work on a single project may take as long as two years to complete, and prior to 1950 each project was given to a small group of men who would work on it from beginning to end. Beginning in 1950, substantial changes were made in organization. Individual offices were eliminated and all operations were placed in one large, well-lighted, air-conditioned room. Each man was given a specialty such as heating or wiring, and work now proceeds from one department to another on an assembly-line basis.

In both divisions liberal vacations, sick leave, and a retirement plan are provided. As yet neither division is unionized.

1. List separately for each division the needs which are and are not satisfied.
2. In which division will the engineers be easiest to unionize?
3. What recommendations would you make to management to improve morale and motivation in each division?

TECHNOLOGY AND JOB SATISFACTION IN THE FACTORY

2

The previous chapter explored what employees want from work and the meaning they give to work. This chapter and the next look at the other side of the coin: the impact of differences in work on employee need satisfaction. Many managers and students err in assuming that one job is basically like another or that the only important distinctions are those between managerial and nonmanagerial jobs. In this chapter we shall examine the impact of technology or work methods on employee satisfaction, and the informal adjustments made by employees, along with the formal modifications made by management, that seek to reduce the tensions created by technology.

Our focus will be on so-called "blue-collar" jobs (those involving manual labor), saving "white-collar" work for Chapter 3. The analysis contrasts three kinds of blue-collar work: (1) craft work (skilled tradesmen), (2) machine-tending and assembly line or mass production jobs, and (3) continuous processing or automation—recognizing that many jobs do not fall neatly into one of these categories.[1] The technology comparisons stress differences in

1. Variety of work activities, physical movement, and pace.

2. Opportunities to derive a sense of accomplishment (in both psychological and economic terms), of autonomy, and identification with the work.

[1] Some of our analysis is derived from Robert Blauner, *Alienation and Freedom* (Chicago: University of Chicago Press, 1964).

3. Job pressures and relations with management.

4. Social relations.

These categories, which are related to the physical, egoistic, and social satisfaction discussed in Chapter 1, will become clearer as we observe various examples of men at work.

CRAFT WORK

Craft work has a long history. The term craft work applies to certain tasks that resist mechanization and that require long and arduous training of their practitioners. Craftsmen still predominate in such industries as entertainment, transportation, construction, and printing, to name a few.

Variety and Movement

The craftsman's job provides abundant variety. Unexpected problems constantly crop up, the solutions to which cannot be programed by management. "Traditional skill thus involves the frequent use of judgment and initiative, aspects of a job which give the worker a feeling of control over his environment."[2]

In addition, unlike most factory workers, craftsmen generally move around a good deal, both to perform widely dispersed jobs and to obtain tools, instructions, materials, or assistance. This ease of movement gives a sense of freedom and diversity (also enjoyed by a salesman or a landscape gardener, both of whom prize their mobility). And since the employee is not "tied" to a machine or an assembly line, he can set his own pace. When he must figure out a difficult job problem, he can muse and putter for a time, taking breaks as he sees fit. On the other hand, when the work is going well he can accomplish a great deal quickly, whereby he gains both a little spare time and a sense of competence.

Accomplishment, Autonomy, and Identification

The craftsman has a rich sense of accomplishment; what he has done, he has done for the most part on his own. The machinist can see the model he has built; the plumber can point to his operating sanitary system. Each can be proud not only of his day-to-day work, but also of what he has made of himself. Most skilled jobs require lengthy training. In addition, in most craft work "age-grading," as the anthropologists call it, prevails. That is, an employee gains greater status and recognition with age.

[2] Ibid., p. 43.

Because his experience and knowledge accumulates, the old printer at the end of his career maintains his usefulness and is often the most respected man in the shop, unlike the old automobile worker, who may skid to the lowest job in the plant hierarchy. [3]

This sense of accomplishment is enhanced by community recognition. Whereas many factory jobs have no real identity outside the plant, such skills as those of electrician, machinist, and printer are widely recognized as skilled work and thereby accorded a certain status. The extent of craft identification shows itself in stronger loyalty to (and pride in) the trade than to any single employer, especially in industries where work is unstable and employees move from employer to employer.

A craftsman's ego-satisfaction has been well expressed by a toolmaker:

"As a tool and die maker, I feel that I have ability that the average man don't have. I can look at almost anything even in this room, tell you how it was made, and, if I had to, turn around and make the dies to duplicate it, I believe I could. ... In the apprenticeship training—you had to spend 9000 hours in the shop, 9000 hours to become a journeyman tool and die maker, and when you get a job say like on a big molding die, where you've already put say four or five hundred hours in it, just one slip and it's wrecked, so you got to stop and think. ... "[4]

Job Pressures and Relations to Management

There is a counterbalance to work autonomy—responsibility. Since a craftsman works on his own in a relatively unprogramed fashion, he can be held responsible for mistakes—from leaky plumbing to a wrecked train! Much anxiety can be generated by a job: "... where you've already put say four or five hundred hours in it, just one slip and it's wrecked ..." Of course, the ability to take pressures is a source of pride.

Management can have trouble in supervising craftsmen. Such men feel they know how their job should be done and are therefore reluctant to accept very much direction. They resist being rushed or taking shortcuts that violate their conception of correct method. This resistance to close supervision is often reinforced by strong craft unions that have their own work rules. Well-trained craftsmen who identify with their craft may require less supervision. They are used to accepting responsibility and being held accountable. Note that this arrangement reverses the traditional situation in which management imposes its rules on the worker.

Their independence is furthered by management's recognition that craft skills are scarce and that craftsmen cannot easily be replaced. Knowing and controlling the work, the methods, the pace, and the tools, the employee is not likely to feel dominated by management.

In short, craftsmen generally feel secure. Their only serious fears arise from economic instabilities and the threats of technological change which will render their skills obsolete (for example, computers that will do typesetting or automated machine tools).

[3] *Ibid.*, p. 53.

[4] Eli Ginzberg and Hyman Berman, *The American Worker In The Twentieth Century* (New York: Free Press, 1963).

Social Relations

Though craftsmen typically work alone or with a single helper, they identify with fellow employees who share the same training and job experiences. If you visit a construction site during work breaks, you will see clusters of men swapping stories of job problems met and conquered and sharing "tricks of the trade." Off-the-job social groups often consist of men who share a common trade. Where the craft involves unusual working hours (as with many newspaper printers or theatrical entertainers) almost all off-the-job friends may be fellow craftsmen (who share the same work schedules). These social groupings reinforce craft identification and are a significant source of job satisfaction. At the same time, the minimal need for interaction on the job makes it easier to get along with one's fellow workers.

Summary

One study of the craftsman's world concludes:

When work provides opportunities for control, meaning, and self expression, it becomes an end itself, rather than simply a means to live. ... Work for craft printers is a source of involvement and commitment. ... It is almost the expression of an inner need rather than the grudging payment of a debt imposed by external sources. [5]

In a real sense, craftsmen obtain the sense of involvement from their work that, as we shall see later, professionals obtain from theirs.

MACHINE-TENDING AND ASSEMBLING

Many blue-collar workers are machine-tenders or assemblers. Machine-tenders watch and facilitate the operation of semi-automatic equipment; assemblers combine parts by hand or with small tools. Assemblers are often tied together by a moving belt; each takes the partly completed work of the preceding worker as it comes to him on the line, attaches additional parts, and adjusts the unit on the line for passage to the next work station.

The way these jobs are now performed has been influenced by the scientific-management movement, best typified by the recommendations of its chief proponent, Frederick Taylor. Taylor believed in: (1) high specialization—breaking down jobs into very small parts, and (2) specifying in advance exactly how the job should be done—in a sense separating the physical work from the thinking. Taylor also favored payment by results or piece work. As Taylor himself put it:

Each man must learn how to give up his own particular way of doing things, adapt his methods to the many new standards, and grow accustomed to receiving and obeying directions covering details, large and small, which in the past have been left to his individual judgment. [6]

[5] Blauner, *op. cit.*, p. 53 and p. 56.

[6] Frederick W. Taylor, *Shop Management* (New York: Harper, 1919), p. 113.

This is what is now called "programing," and it is the primary characteristic of *mass-production* technology.

Variety and Movement

Machine-tending and assembly jobs provide little opportunity for initiative, ingenuity, and variability. By means of engineering studies, management carefully predetermines the exact motions and pace for each employee. This procedure insures that the work will be done quickly in a uniform, predictable fashion, and precisely coordinated with other jobs. The employee is confined to a fixed work station and is expected to leave it only with permission. What effects will such restrictions have on a man's attitude toward his job?

Short job cycle. An important determinant of job satisfaction is the length of the job cycle: how long it takes to perform a job operation before having to start it all over again. For a college professor the work cycle may be a semester; for a skilled craftsman, it may be several days or weeks. But for the man on a machine or assembly line the work cycle may last less than a minute. At the extreme, he may be simply tightening one or two bolts. Then he has to repeat the same cycle over and over again, with a deadening lack of variety.

"The job gets so sickening—day in and day out plugging in ignition wires. I get through with one motor, turn around, and there's another staring me in the face. It is sickening." [7]

On jobs of this sort all mental challenge has been eliminated, and in most cases only a few muscles are involved. Life seems one endless procession of bolts to tighten. A study of the automobile assembly line found a high correlation between the number of operations a worker's job called for and his level of interest in his job. [8]

Inability to control pace. Although some of these jobs allow an employee to stop and start machines, most give him little control over the work pace. For instance, in a textile factory the employee may tend dozens of machines which function automatically. He moves from one to another as they require attention: the mending of a break in the yarn, a maladjustment, the need for new supplies, and so on. His pace is a function of the number and type of machines he has been assigned and the frequency with which his particular skills are required, all of which depend on the engineering of the job—over which he has no control.

Most people like to vary their work rhythm; they may work fast for a while, and then slow down gradually as the day wears on. This variety in pace helps to reduce both fatigue and boredom on the job. The assembly line, however, makes no provision for the preference of individual workers. It sets the pace for him and never lets him change it. Thus the machine may be a worse autocrat than any foreman.

[7] Charles R. Walker and Robert Guest, *The Man on the Assembly Line* (Cambridge: Harvard University Press, 1952), p. 55.

[8] *Ibid.*, p. 54.

Fortunately, on most mass-production jobs workers do have a slight opportunity to vary their pace through "building a bank" or "getting into a hole." On some jobs a worker can hurry up a bit and build up a reserve or "bank" of completed work and then take a break for a few seconds while the work slides by. By pushing 15 seconds ahead and then falling 15 seconds "in a hole," an energetic worker can earn himself a 30-second break.

Limited attention required.   Another factor affecting the degree of satisfaction a worker derives from his work is the amount of attention it requires. A doctor enjoys his work because his job is constantly new and challenging and absorbs all his attention. Jobs like this are said to require *depth attention.* At the other extreme are the so-called *no-attention jobs,* which are so routine that the worker's mind is free to wander at will. Dishwashing is an example of such work; so, too, is driving over a straight highway with little traffic. Your mind is a thousand miles away, although subconsciously you are still watching the road.

The least-satisfying of all are jobs that require *surface attention.* Here the worker is obliged to perform a routine, unchallenging chore but at the same time to remain relatively alert. ". . . The mind, though not wholly absorbed by work, cannot free itself entirely from it." [9] Examples of this sort of work are watching control gauges, inspecting parts, grading exam papers, or adding up columns of figures. These jobs do not provide the challenge, interest, and sense of autonomy provided by depth-attention jobs; nor do they permit the employee to daydream as he can on a no-attention job.

These classifications, of course, are simply points on a continuum, for there are relatively few cases of, say, a purely no-attention job. Further, the attention demanded by a particular job depends largely on the abilities of the individual employee. A very bright employee may find that a job requires only surface attention, while a less able employee may find that the same job requires depth attention. (The implications for employee selection should be considered.)

Accomplishment, Autonomy, and Advancement

Inadequate sense of accomplishment.   "This job is endless. It just goes on and on. You don't feel that you are getting anywhere."

We all feel that we are accomplishing something when we can break our work down into units that can be completed successively. If we have two assignments to complete, we breathe a sigh of relief as soon as we finish one. When we are driving a long distance, we break the trip down into sections and feel great satisfaction as we pass by each check point.

Mass-production work characteristically fails to provide this sense of completion, or even a feeling of progress toward a goal. Each employee does only a small, specialized part of the total job. Rarely does he have a chance to look at the finished product and say, "Mine, all mine." Note the following comparison between an automobile assembly line and a steel mill:

[9] Georges Friedmann, *Industrial Society* (New York: Free Press, 1955), p. 146.

On the assembly line, only a small fraction of the "product" is ever seen or handled by most workers. In the (steel) tube mill, the whole product, from billet to finished product, as it moves through a series of machines, is worked on by everyone and can be followed by the eye of the members of the crew. Workers frequently go to the cooling and inspection tables to look over for their own satisfaction the job which they have just done. [10]

Excessive specialization deprives the worker of any real sense of skill. Work that has been so subdivided and simplified that it takes almost no time to learn provides little challenge or interest. Workers who exercise skill take pride in their achievement, but a man who has learned his job in a few hours knows that he can be replaced by almost anyone who happens along. This is one explanation of the tendency of mass-production workers to exaggerate the complexity of their jobs: It is just too humiliating for them to admit how simple their work actually is.

Lack of autonomy. These jobs are designed to eliminate all employee discretion; all his motions are preprogramed by management. He is told when and how to move each arm and perhaps even how to stand at his work place. Management does not want mass production employees making any decisions concerning how they do their job.

It should be noted again, however, and we shall return to this point later, that workers differ in their desire to exercise skill and autonomy. Some have no desire for creative challenge on the job—they are happy enough to daydream. Others are deeply disturbed because their work provides so little interest and meaning.

Little opportunity for advancement. Mass production jobs provide little opportunity for advancement. For one thing there are few promotional steps open; most jobs in the factory require almost the same skill level and provide almost the same pay.

In theory, most companies give outstanding workers an opportunity to rise to the top. Yet the technical requirements of modern industry mean that many supervisory jobs can be handled only by men who have had college training. In addition, pay grades have been compressed in many companies so that the range between the top- and bottom-paid jobs among unskilled and semiskilled workers is quite narrow. Skilled jobs, such as that of tool and die maker, are often filled through an apprenticeship program, and few men are accepted for such training after 30. Once a man reaches this age, his chances of rising out of the semiskilled class are slight.

Advancement redefined. Some opportunities for upward mobility are, of course, still open to the average worker, but these are somewhat limited (most, but not all, involve seeking off-the-job satisfactions).

1. Over the years he may come to regard seniority as a way of getting ahead. After all, unions emphasize seniority as a determinant in layoffs

[10] Charles R. Walker, "Work Methods, Working Conditions, and Morale," in Arthur Kornhauser, Robert Dubin, and Arthur Ross, eds., *Industrial Conflict* (New York: McGraw-Hill, 1954), pp. 353–354.

and promotions, and management concurs, with such symbols as long-service pins and testimonial dinners.

2. For some workers, the union provides a chance to "get ahead." Although there are few full-time union jobs with regular salaries, there are many part-time posts, such as steward or executive board member. Negotiating with management, handling grievances, and dealing with day-to-day union business offer many opportunities for creative expression and personal satisfaction.

3. Many workers feel they are advancing when they move to a job that may not be better-paying but that seems "better" in the sense that the work is cleaner, the pace is slower, or the location is away from the assembly line.

4. If the individual cannot advance by himself, the group to which he belongs may be able to advance the interests of its members. So long as his union can win him a 30-cent hourly wage increase each year, he feels that he has tangible evidence of progress.

5. Finally, many workers interpret "getting ahead" in terms of security and material possessions. As one man put it, "If you've got security, if you've got something to fall back on, you're getting ahead." They measure success not in terms of what they do, but in terms of what they own—a bigger car or a new TV set.

Job Pressures and Relations to Management

The factory employee has a carefully engineered quota of parts to finish or the requirement that he keep up with the line. Because his job is relatively simple and his methods and output readily observable, he is easy to supervise closely. Management exerts constant pressure to maintain a regular pace and thus maintain productivity. But what of the employee's view?

Assembler: You're always behind. When you get too far behind, you get in a hole. . . . All hell breaks loose. . . . The foreman gets sore and they have to rush in a relief man to bail you out. [11]

New employees, particularly, who find themselves falling behind, become anxious about their ability to keep up with the line or make the quota. Being replaceable they worry about being discharged, especially when there is no union or when, as new employees, they are on a *trial period*. Gradually, though, most develop those patterns of skill and coordination which enable them to meet the engineered standards.

Some workers even prefer machine-paced jobs or assembly lines. At least the "line" controls them impersonally; it keeps the foreman from breathing down their necks. Further, it eliminates the need to pay attention to how fast they are working and thus makes it possible for them to daydream. In effect, the machine sets a rhythm which their body seems to accept.

[11] Ginzberg and Berman, *op. cit.*, pp. 283–284.

Unlike craft jobs in which the worker maintains considerable autonomy, most machine and assembly-line work tends to pit workers against managers. [12] As we have suggested, it is tempting to supervise closely since both work methods and output are easy to observe. In mass-production factories, management is constantly trying to reduce labor costs and increase productivity by upping work standards and improving methods, thus forcing the employee to adopt new working procedures and perhaps to change his tempo. Although many engineering changes do *not* require additional physical effort on the part of the worker (in fact, they frequently reduce physical effort), the employee views the increasing output and the necessary changes in his work methods not only as burdensome but also as a threat to his job security. For some learning periods, the changes can also convert a no-attention job to one requiring surface attention.

Not only are job pressures maximized, but mass-production employees, in contrast to skilled craftsmen, tend to have rather formal relations with management, and little contact with anyone above their immediate supervisor. The status gap between workers and managers tends to be great since such employees, as we have seen, rarely become managers or have significant careers in the firm. Thus, they tend to see the world very differently from their managers who do have career possibilities, and whose success depends on their ability to maintain productivity levels for reluctant employees.

Adjusting to Mass-Production Work

How do employees adjust to mass-production work? Many learn to ignore the job through daydreaming or to modify the job by various "games at work." Others take more decisive action, either leaving or sabotaging the work.

Daydreaming. Daydreaming is a common means of escaping from the boredom of a no-attention job. As one observer notes, "The revolt against work is widespread and takes manifold forms in the United States. First and foremost it appears in the constant evasion of thought about work, the obsessive reveries while on the job." An employee told us: "If I thought about the job all the time I'd go nuts. I think about vacation and going hunting. You don't even know you are working."

The sort of daydream in which workers indulge varies with the individual and the situation. The man who is unhappy with his job and bitter over life in general is likely to brood over his miserable lot. If the work group as a whole is dissatisfied with the job and with the group's relationship with management, the workers tend to dream up grievances and engage in so called "obsessive thinking."

Almost all workers regard a job that requires surface attention as boring, mentally exhausting, and undesirable. (This is true even if the same work might

[12] A large-scale survey of British companies shows clearly that both labor relations and human relations are least amicable in the type of technology we are now discussing. Joan Woodward, *Industrial Organization: Theory and Practice* (New York: Oxford University Press, 1965).

require depth attention or no attention from someone else.) But there are some workers who can adjust moderately well to monotonous, no-attention jobs. These workers seem to have little need to derive satisfaction from the job itself and spend their working days in daydreaming. (These differences are discussed later in the chapter under "Job Enlargement")

In one study made by the authors, casual observation suggested that workers who daydreamed worked at a more constant pace than those who did not. Most of the complaints about being machine-paced and "tied to the line" came from those who reported they did not daydream.

Making a game out of work. In spite of its obvious inefficiency, some people like to mow their lawns in fancy figure eights. Making a game out of work provides variety, gives the worker a chance to show his creativity, and supplies goals to work toward.

On jobs that are not tightly machine-paced, the worker may experiment with various speeds and set himself various output goals. Workers on piece work are particularly likely to set goals for themselves (sometimes called "bogies") and to engage in elaborate calculations to make sure that they produce neither more nor less than the bogey (see Chapter 27). Although the primary purpose of these calculations is to avoid overproduction that might lead to a cut in the piece rate, they also provide a satisfying diversion from the monotony of work.

Social games provide a form of diversion. Gambling of various sorts is common in many factories, from flipping coins to see who pays for coffee, to World Series pools, to bookmaking, and numbers games. Horseplay (mock fighting, high jinks, and brawling) combines social activity and a chance to release aggression. (Accidents often result.)

Modifying the job. Workers can sometimes reduce the monotony of their jobs by introducing variations in their work that are unplanned by management. They may exchange work, modify parts of the job, and avoid others altogether. They drag out set-ups, find excuses to pick up parts more frequently than necessary, and perhaps let the machine break down in order to create a slight change in pace.

Absenteeism and turnover. Another means of adjusting to unpleasant work is to avoid it as much as possible. In practice this leads to absenteeism, frequent visits to the dispensary, excessive time spent in the washroom, feigned illness, and even quitting. Some have argued that employees may unconsciously seek an accident.

Walker and Guest found correlations between short absences and the "mass-production characteristics" of jobs on the assembly line. Absenteeism was highest on the jobs that required the least skill, were most repetitive, gave workers the least chance to express themselves, and so forth. [13]

[13] Walker and Guest, *op. cit.*, p. 120. Another careful research effort showed much the same thing: Absenteeism is higher on the less complex, less demanding jobs: Arthur Turner and Paul Lawrence, *Industrial Jobs and the Worker* (Boston: Division of Research, Harvard Business School, 1965), pp. 35-48. However, still another study indicates that repetitious work has no relationship to turnover: Maurice D. Kilbridge, "Turnover, Absenteeism, and Transfer Rates as Indicators of Employee Dissatisfaction with Repetitious Work," *Industrial and Labor Relations Review,* Vol. 15, No. 1 (October 1961), pp. 21-32.

Antimanagement activities. In a sense, antimanagement activities are an overt reaction to the frustration of mass-production work. Active union participation, for example, provides an opportunity to release aggression and to enjoy a sense of skill and accomplishment that is denied on the job. Similarly, sabotage and wildcat strikes enable a demoralized work group to let off steam. In Detroit, for instance, after long periods of overtime work on boring assembly-line jobs, employees appear pleased with the prospect of a strike!

Summary: Job Satisfaction in Mass-Production Work

Management pays a price for the work simplification, routinization, and ease of supervision inherent in mass-production work. The cost is largely in terms of apathy and boredom as positive satisfactions are engineered out of jobs. Being confined physically and limited socially to contacting his own immediate supervisor, the factory worker sees very little of the total organization and even less of the total product being manufactured. It is hardly surprising that there is frequently little pride in work or identification with the job. However, employees have put back some of the satisfactions they require by informal modifications of work methods (such as games and trading-off of jobs) and by concerted group activities (these will be detailed further in Chapter 4). Lacking satisfaction and identification, they also can develop a variety of aggressive and hostile patterns.

POSITIVE MANAGEMENT ACTIONS TO IMPROVE MASS-PRODUCTION JOBS

Since routine jobs (white- as well as blue-collar) are among the most common industrial jobs and represent the most serious problems in human relations, it is worth considering what steps management can take to ameliorate the situation.

Job Enlargement

Specialization in mass production has been pushed to the point where the smallest possible band of a worker's ability is being utilized. Already efforts are being made to reverse this process, and with some success in programs of job enlargement. These seek to expand job content: allowing employees to inspect their own work, to make minor repairs on the work or equipment, to select their own work methods and even to do "set-ups" (changing equipment or its adjustments). Note that these broaden the task to include more responsible and more demanding activities that were the province of non-production employees: inspectors, repairmen or maintenance workers. This *vertical* job enlargement (sometimes called *job enrichment*) can be contrasted to *horizontal* enlargement which simply adds a large number of somewhat similar tasks.[14] (For example, the assembler now doesn't simply put nuts and bolts together for a single component, but he bolts several such components together.) Horizontal enlargement lengthens the job cycle, reduces the repetitiveness and uniformity of work and may reduce monotony somewhat, but the additional complications are not intrinsically challenging and can convert a no-attention job into one requiring surface attention.

With vertical enlargement, on the other hand, the employee must become more involved in his work: the pace becomes less regular, a greater variety of skills must be employed (sometimes in a changing sequence), and he must assume more responsibility (for making decisions on quality or machine functioning and the like). We have already observed that many skilled craftsmen treasure this variability and sense of responsibility and job enlargement; thus it is a program for modifying the mass production characteristics of jobs in the direction of craft work.

Now for the results. Not unexpectedly there is disagreement over the efficacy of such programs. The example below is typical of the results reported by a number of researchers.

An example at the Polaroid Corp. involved operators and assistant operators who worked on a major film assembly machine. They felt that their work was repetitive, that they were in effect "chained to the machine." They also resented being told by the inspection and quality control departments when the film they produced did not meet quality standards.

The solution to relieving their frustrations was to change the operation so that they are now responsible for their own quality. In addition to feeding and controlling the flow of materials through the machine, they take photographs and make graphs to determine quality. It's possible for them to determine immediately if anything is not operating properly and take the necessary corrective action. . . .

Results have been impressive—as operators have taken more interest in the quality of their work, costs per roll of film have gone down and quality yields have gone up. It's also been possible to eliminate several inspecting jobs and transfer the inspectors to challenging jobs in the company.[15]

The critics argue not only that the data is not very impressive but also that there is a good deal of evidence that many employees who do not want to assume responsibility place little or no value on challenging work and are not seeking to gain psychological satisfaction from work. These researchers find many such employees who have not internalized the work norms of the middle class within the blue collar population of large cities. They are interested simply in pay and prefer simple, straightforward "no-attention" jobs (see pp. 21-22).

Job Rotation and Alternation

Some companies are seeking to reduce boredom through systematically moving workers from one job to another. This practice provides variety, lets the

---

[14] Cf. Frederick Herzberg, "One More Time: How to Motivate Workers," *Harvard Business Review*, Vol. 45 (Jan.-Feb., 1968), pp. 53–62.

[15] "Job Enlargement and Job Rotation," *Personnel Management Bulletin*, Report No. 157 (May 15, 1962), p. 1. Other strong proponents who summarize positive results include Chris Argyris, *Integrating the Individual in the Organization* (New York: John Wiley, 1964) and Robert Ford, *Motivation Through the Work Itself* (New York: American Management Association, 1969).

employee see more of the total operation, and gives workers a chance to learn additional skills. The company also benefits, since the workers become able to perform a number of different jobs in the event of an emergency.

Some workers object to being rotated from job to job and jolted out of their routine. They look upon their job almost as a piece of personal property; being an "expert" on one particular type of work gave them a feeling of status and importance that they lost when they were moved around. Our studies suggest that, in general, those who oppose job rotation work on no-attention jobs and enjoy daydreaming. Being shifted from spot to spot converts these no-attention jobs to surface-attention jobs and makes reverie more difficult. On the other hand, workers whose regular job prevent them from daydreaming endorse rotation as a relief from monotony.

Change of pace. Anything that will give the worker a chance to change his pace when he wishes will make him feel less like a robot and more like a human being—and will lend variety to his work. [16] Further, if workers are permitted to change their pace they can build "banks" and thus obtain visible evidence of accomplishment.

Rest periods. Extensive research on the impact of rest periods indicates that they may increase both morale and productivity. (1) They counteract physical fatigue. (2) They provide variety and relieve monotony. (3) They are something to look forward to—getting a break gives a sense of achievement. (4) They provide opportunities for social contacts.

Even where there are no formal rest periods, technology permitting, every worker takes a break once in a while, perhaps just by slowing down a bit, or going to the washroom or the coffee machine. If management tries to forbid this practice, workers will still "bootleg" breaks into the work schedule, although the value of the breaks in reducing fatigue will be impaired. Management must recognize that many of the rest periods workers take are minor goals that they set for themselves and rewards they give themselves for making certain quotas, rather than just the result of a desire to get away from work.

Scheduled rest periods seem to reduce the incidence of unscheduled ones. But on the other hand, as we have seen, many jobs fall into natural work units, and the natural time to take a break is at the end of a unit. Indeed, a few moments of relaxation at this point accentuate the feeling of accomplishment. Rest pauses scheduled for the whole department may tend to destroy these natural units, interrupt the work, and reduce the pulling power of the job. Further, when management *tells* workers when to rest, they have less feeling of autonomy than if they were to make the decision for themselves.

Giving a Feeling of Accomplishment

There are many ways in which management can give employees a feeling of accomplishment, though few are appropriate to every situation.

[16] One of the most insistent demands of the United Automobile Workers has been for the right to control the speed of the assembly line. This and safety are the two areas about which the union has had the right to strike at any time.

Setting goals. In order to satisfy the natural desire for specific assignments, and in order to provide definite goals toward which to work, some companies permit workers to leave early (without loss of income) when they have finished their job. Other plants set daily production quotas which are announced to the entire work force. When these quotas are "accepted" as being "fair," they may well provide motivation for higher production. In a sense, working to achieve a quota makes a game out of the work. On the other hand, employees may regard quotas as a form of management pressure. They will work hard for goals that they have set for themselves, but strongly oppose "unfair" goals set by management.

In any case, psychologists tell us that goals are much more effective (1) if they are realistic, if there is a reasonable chance of attaining them, and (2) if they can be achieved in the relatively near future. Finishing a chapter in an hour is a far more compelling goal than reading a whole book in an evening.

Breaking the work down into meaningful units. Earlier we pointed out that most people get a sense of accomplishment from completing a whole job. But just what constitutes a "whole job" and precisely what is meant by "completion" are matters that can be manipulated by management. By breaking the work down into units or batches, management can give the employee a feeling of completion every time he finishes one batch. The desire to finish a unit has a strong "pulling power" and also enhances the worker's efficiency.

Work units that are too large should be broken down and those that are too small should be lumped together. How large is the optimal unit? One study suggests that it should last for an hour or an hour and a half, depending on the situation. [17]

Maier reports an ingenious example of how the boring work of telephone maintenance in the central office was broken down into smaller units: [18]

There is no challenge of diagnosing trouble, and the job is very confining since a man can work for hours within the space of a few feet. There is never a real experience of progress. When the job is finished the worker starts all over again.

In one office the frames on which the men worked were subdivided by means of chalk lines. ... Each block required between one and a half and two hours to complete. The worker made his choice of ... unit. ... The benefits of this pattern of work were immediately apparent. ... Once a man selected a block he worked until it was finished.

Every time a man completed a unit he took a smoke or a stretch. Even lunch and quitting time found no untagged units. The men liked the plan and the supervisors reported that complaining decreased and the trouble with meeting work schedules was eliminated.

Avoiding interruption of natural units. A man who is engrossed in his work resents being disturbed and wastes a good bit of time trying to pick up his work again. Secretaries object to being asked to do something else when they are in the middle of a letter. It is almost a matter of simple courtesy to say, "When you get a break for a minute, could you do this?"

[17] D. Cox and K. M. D. Sharpe, "Research on the Unit of Work," *Occupational Psychology*, Vol. 25, No. 2 (April 1951), pp. 90–108.

[18] Norman Maier, *Psychology in Industry*, 2nd ed. (Boston: Houghton Mifflin, 1955), p. 489.

Similarly, workers object to starting a new job just before quitting time, although if they are behind schedule on an existing job they will spurt to finish it up. There is often trouble between shifts when one shift leaves unfinished work for the next shift to complete.

Other forms of goals. On some jobs the worker tends one or more machines and can see no visible accumulation of product. Here management may be able to provide other forms of goals, such as producing x amount per shift, reducing the time required for repairs by a given percentage, or avoiding breakdowns for an entire shift.

Providing information on progress. Even where production has nothing to do with incentive earnings or opportunities for promotion, employees like to know how they are doing.

In a plant that manufactured a large number of small items at high speed, management installed counters on each of the lines, just for supervisory purposes. Soon the employees were spending so much time sneaking a look that additional counters were installed at each work place. Informal competition developed both between lines and between shifts on the same line. Then the foreman brought in a blackboard and chalk and the men began posting their records. (*Question:* What might have happened had management deliberately tried to foster competition?)

Some companies post bar graphs showing the length of time actually taken to complete jobs as compared to the time planned. A telephone company circulates monthly indices of efficiency, particularly among its white-collar employees. [19]

Building career lines. Management can promote a sense of progress and commitment to the organization by fitting jobs together into promotional ladders. As we have seen, mass-production work typically provides "no place to go," and this lack of opportunity discourages those employees who may be most worth promoting.

Selection. A good deal of attention is already devoted to endeavoring to preselect those employees whose psychological dispositions are likely to be consistent with the available job satisfactions. More research, however, needs to be done in this area.

Providing Social Satisfactions

On jobs that lack other satisfactions, provisions for social relationships often produce very favorable reactions. Partitions can help identify a social group in what would otherwise be a huge amorphous department. Employees who work in isolation or among strangers (for example, mechanics who are "farmed out"

---

[19] Of course, such indices may be regarded as a method of exerting pressure. Or they may encourage quantity at the expense of quality. We shall discuss some of these factors later. See Peter M. Blau, *The Dynamics of Industrial Bureaucracy* (Chicago: University of Chicago, 1955), Chapter 3.

on a daily basis to engineering departments) can be given a home base by allowing fellow employees who share the same occupational status to get together first thing in the morning or at the end of the shift. Where this is impossible, shared relief time, access to telephones linking these workers, or group meetings may help.

Physical Context of Work

We have been concerned largely with the psychological and social setting of work, and the reactions of employees to this context. But there is also a physical context. Some craft jobs have to be performed in dangerous settings (consider the iron-workers who erect the superstructure of skyscrapers). Many factories (say, smelters) are hot and dirty. Some operations involving chemicals have acrid fumes; textile plants tend to be hot and damp (in part because thread doesn't break easily with high humidity). There are still many jobs which are physically exhausting on the auto assembly lines in Detroit. Many workmen have to be on their feet a good deal; cranemen sit in one place for long, fatiguing hours; and some generator assemblers have to crouch. We could extend this list, but it should be obvious that there are substantial sources of dissatisfaction to be found in the physical conditions under which jobs are performed.

Employees do like clean, comfortably cooled, light and airy workplaces in which they can sit and walk at will and where physical fatigue is at a minimum. Most managers know this, but some jobs are difficult to adapt to these rather universal desires.

Some observers who would argue that certain employees gain satisfaction from doing heavy—even dangerous—work under difficult circumstances. Their sense of "maleness" is enhanced and they poke fun at other men doing "women's" work.

AUTOMATION AND CONTINUOUS PROCESSING: NEW TECHNOLOGIES

Craft work represents an old tradition, extending back before the industrial revolution. Mass production work is associated with the factories of the nineteenth and early twentieth centuries. The new technology involves automated, continuous processing. What impact does it have on factory work and job satisfaction?

Perhaps a definition of automation is in order since the term has come into such widespread use. Although there is no single definition, most authors stress the following components: (1) use of high-speed computers for data processing or control, (2) use of "closed-loop feedback" techniques to facilitate self-control by machines themselves, (3) mechanization of transfer operations, (4) increased use of multiple-purpose equipment, and (5) the combination of jobs and work units in larger self-contained processes. [20]

[20] James Bright, *Automation and Management* (Boston: Harvard Business School, Division of Research, 1958); Floyd Mann and L. Richard Hoffman, *Automation and the Worker* (New York: Holt, 1960), p. 3; Charles R. Walker, *Toward the Automatic Factory* (New Haven, Conn.: Yale University Press, 1957).

Detroit Automation

Much "automation" leaves the intrinsic characteristics of jobs unchanged. Workers merely operate more productive machinery that positions the work, checks its accuracy, and transports materials from stage to stage automatically. But the operator continues to be a machine-tender, and a sharp status line continues to separate him from the engineers who install and maintain the equipment and the managers who supervise it. For the most part, this is what is called "Detroit Automation." Jobs may be somewhat less physically demanding, but there is also more pressure associated with the complicated, expensive and potentially very vulnerable processing techniques. [21] Should something go wrong, a great deal of production is lost. As a consequence, supervision may be even closer than before the changes.

Continuous-Process Technology

Something close to true automation does, however, exist today in some plants in the chemical and petroleum industries and in electrical power generation and steel manufacturing. Automation of this sort is most easily adapted to industries in which the product can flow continuously (particularly as a liquid or gas) from entering raw material to finished product through a number of interlinked stages. Continuous steel strip mills and modern electrical generating plants approximate the continuous flows of a chemical plant. In all such factories an employee spends much of his time monitoring gauges and control instruments, and his major work activities come only during breakdowns and start-up and change-over periods.

Such work contrasts sharply with that of craftsmen and machine operators. As we have seen, a craftsman utilizes manual, motor, perceptual and conceptual skills. He manipulates materials, his own body, and ideas. Engineers have eliminated the conceptual and perceptual element from the job of the semiskilled machine-tender and the assembly-line worker, though they must still develop some manual dexterity and motor skill, but far less than the craftsmen. Automated employees, however, need few physical skills, but they are expected to use their "heads." [22]

TYPE OF WORKER	SKILLS REQUIRED			
Craftsman	Manual	Motor	Conceptual	Perceptual
Machine-tender and assembly-line worker	Manual	Motor		
Automation worker			Conceptual	Perceptual

Variety and Movement

Most jobs in continuous-process plants require an irregular combination of surface attention and depth attention. The *job cycle* is a relatively long one.

---

[21] *Cf.* William Faunce, "Automation in the Automobile Industry," *American Sociological Review*, Vol. 23, No. 4 (August 1958), pp. 401–407.

[22] The table is adapted from J. Woodward, *op. cit.*, pp. 63–64.

Dials have to be checked and adjustments made when readings are "off standard." In one case in a chemical plant, 50 different instruments are monitored every two hours. [23]

The pace of work is uneven, but in part it can be adjusted to the comfort, convenience, and natural "rhythms" of the employees. Although the checking operations must be periodic, they need not be done precisely on time:

"Sometimes when it's close to the time for 2 o'clock readings, we might have soup on the stove. You can eat the soup first and do the work later or take the readings at 1:45 and then eat your soup." [24]

In utility generating stations and in some parts of a refinery, the operators may be confined to a control room. In a chemical plant, however, they must take lengthy walks through widely dispersed equipment.

Aside from monitoring operations, the other part of automated jobs consists of handling unexpected breakdowns (and sometimes assisting in regular starting-up and shutting-down activities). In this phase depth attention is called for, and time is of utmost importance. Because of the enormous costs involved in idle equipment, management expects everyone to pitch in energetically when there is trouble. But if there are going to be sufficient personnel available for such emergencies, when things are going smoothly, there is of necessity going to be a good deal of idle time.

Unlike a typical mass-production plant where a breakdown is a welcome relief, here a stoppage is a sign of failure. It is also a period of excitement, even drama. The unexpected breaks up the monotony. Locating, diagnosing, and fixing troubles can be absorbing, even though breakdowns also call for very hard work.

Accomplishment, Autonomy, and Identification

"Continuous-processing technology may serve to reverse the historic trend toward the greater division of labor and specialization." [25] It is this involvement in a tangible, complete activity (refining oil, producing electric power) that produces job interest and the satisfaction which grows out of meaningful activity. Employees feel *responsible* for keeping highly expensive technology going. Rather than concentrate on a small, essentially meaningless task, the employee develops a sense of commitment to the total process. Thus, he gains the satisfaction of knowing that in some measure he contributes to an observable, finished product:

The worker's role changes from providing skills to accepting responsibility ... the very definition of responsibility as a job requirement involves a meaningful connection between the worker's own function and the goals of the entire enterprise. [26]

[23] Blauner, *op. cit.*, p. 134.
[24] *Ibid.*, p. 138.
[25] *Ibid.*, p. 143.
[26] *Ibid.*

In contrast to the mass-production factory, there are not endless, impersonal rows of people repeating small tasks. Instead, relatively few men patrol and control a vast array of massive equipment, or they oversee a control room which is like a command post. Here employees accept some of the functions that supervisors exercise in simpler technologies.

Their sense of growth and development and importance is further enhanced by the career ladders that develop naturally. A refinery still or a production unit in a chemical plant is handled by a small crew which is differentiated in skill and experience; the lowest-ranking employee is usually called a helper and the top-skilled person can be a head operator stillman or crew chief. Because of the close interdependence of their jobs and the need to be familiar with a variety of complex tasks, new employees are brought in as part of general labor gangs and progress through a series of jobs as their experience increases and they evidence willingness to accept responsibility. Each successive job enables them to get a broader view of operations.

And here management, far more than in craft or mass-production industries, is willing to invest in continuing training. Hence, most employees experience a sense of steady progress in status and earnings. Highly important by-products are, for the employee, substantial job security and, for management, a work-force feeling identification with the company.

The top skilled crew-chief positions involve enormous responsibility and challenge in these industries. As an example, let us look at the chief melter in a newly computerized oxygen-furnace steel plant. Premixed, preweighed ingredients are transported to a huge pressure cooker (the furnace's converter), which heats them for about an hour and is then tapped. Here is a description of the work of the employee who handles the operation, Mr. Peral:

Mr. Peral directs operations with the computer from a control room several feet from the vessel. He is in touch with his eight men through a loudspeaker system. . . . To make a batch of steel, called a heat, Mr. Peral first has his computer figure out the ingredients, based on orders for specific grades of steel. Then the vessel is tilted to the "charging" side. The press of a button sets off 75 to 80 tons of scrap—. . . . How does Mr. Peral know when it's time to tap? "You've got to know your end points," he says. "You notice how the carbon flame above the vessel is dying? It's about ready." . . . Mr. Peral orders the vessel tilted again toward the charging side. Protected by a metal shield, two of his assistants insert a long pole called a thermocouple into the vessel. . . . If the mixture is not hot enough, the vessel is turned upright again and heated some more." [27]

Here, as elsewhere, machines do not completely displace employees; a number of critical jobs can still be performed more effectively by human beings.

Job Pressures and Relations to Management

Under automation the speed-up that occurs during breakdowns or change-over periods is not resented as efforts by management to get more work done. Here the employees can see for themselves when hard work is required, and the supervisor doesn't have to push them. Also, as we have seen, the technical

[27] *The New York Times*, March 18, 1965.

leadership in these situations often is provided by the top-ranking member of the crew, the chief operator. Since he works right alongside the other members of the gang and shares their values and difficulties, his demands are likely to be interpreted as reasonable. [28]

Mistakes can be terribly expensive, so employees cannot be rushed or excessively pressured by management. Although a craft worker can redo poor-quality work and an assembler's mistakes can be remedied by a repairman farther down the line, an error by a continuous-process employee may cost thousands of dollars before it can be rectified. Checking and repairing involve mental processes which cannot be coordinated by stop watch.

In many circumstances, management is pleased when employees are not working hard—this indicates that things are going well. If the employees work wisely and effectively, there are few or no breakdowns. Under these conditions both employee relaxation and company product are maximized!

There are other reasons why management seldom appears oppressive to employees under this type of technology. Since at least the top-ranking workers are highly experienced and well informed, their opinions are often sought out by supervisors and by engineers. Particularly when pilot-plant operations are conducted, employees are likely to have contact with levels of management above their immediate supervisor and with staff engineers. Thus, in a modern continuous-process steel mill, there is less status distinction between skilled hourly workers and management and more personal relationships than are found in an automobile assembly plant, where relationships are highly formal and primarily limited to order-giving by the immediate manager.

Since labor costs make up a much smaller percentage of total costs in automated plants than in nonautomated plants, management can provide more generous wages and fringe benefits. More important, since these plants are designed to operate with a minimum of employees, nearly all of whom are required no matter what the scale of operations, employees are less expendable during periods of recession. Furthermore, management as we have noted has a major investment in the career training of its workforce. The employees sense that they are not dealt with as a "variable cost," something that can be let go if business activity declines. Instead, they see themselves as having careers that will last their working life. [29]

Hours of Work

Many automated jobs require shift work and this is a source of dissatisfaction. To get maximum use of expensive equipment, it must be used round-the-clock. And, chemical plants and utilities operate day and night because their processes can't be turned "on" and "off" except at great cost.

---

[28] One article suggests that leadership exercised by "inside," working leaders was characteristic of man's earliest work groups: F. L. W. Richardson, "Managing Man's Animal Nature," *Pittsburgh Business Review*, Vol. 34, No. 11 (December 1964), p. 4.

[29] Of course, this assumes that the employee exhibits reasonable energy and learning ability. In recent years some oil refineries have had to cope with what they termed "obsolete" employees, often through early retirement.

Though a few employees like shift work, because it enables them to make alternative use of the daytime, most find that late hours interfere with normal family and social life. Many firms rotate shifts. This procedure avoids charges of discrimination and prevents jockeying for favorable schedules, but it requires employees to get used to constantly changing sleeping and waking hours, not an easy thing to do as anyone knows who has flown across a number of time zones. [30]

Social Relations

Most employees in automated industries work in teams. On some chemical operations there may be only two or three employees per shift; on others ten or more. The employees work closely together and must develop the ability to coordinate their efforts and help each other. In turn, close social relations develop on the team which may carry over into the community.

Whereas social-group boundaries are often ambiguous and vague in traditional industrial plants, they are more clear-cut here. Where hundreds of employees do similar operations under one roof or where an assembly line snakes for a mile or two past thousands working side by side, it is difficult for employees to identify with a specific group of fellow workers. The limited number of employees under automation and their specific relationship to a given process serves to unite a social group which has the same boundaries as the work unit.

We should not exaggerate the beneficial effects of automation on social relations, however. Some automated plants have only a small number of employees, widely dispersed, who rarely see each other. Isolated locations plus noise may make difficult all but limited conversation.

Summary: Automation and Job Satisfaction

It would be a mistake to assume that all job-satisfaction problems are solved by the introduction of continuous-process automation. For there is substantial monotony associated with watching and waiting: the "dial-watching" tasks.

Automation often requires a very high-level person for one hour a week and somebody who is capable of doing nothing for the other 39 hours. ... You are going to have trouble keeping people from getting a kind of "turnpike fatigue" running one of these machines. [31]

In addition employees are likely to feel substantial anxiety about making costly errors.

More than balancing these dissatisfactions, however, are the through-the-job satisfactions derived from the relatively long work cycles, flexible work rhythms,

[30] For a more complete treatment of the total subject of working hours see Clyde Dankert, Floyd Mann, and Herbert Northrop, eds., *Hours of Work* (New York: Harper, 1965).

[31] P. L. Cook, Jr., "Social and Economic Effects of Automation," *Twenty First Annual Midwest Conference on Industrial Relations* (Chicago: Graduate School of Business, University of Chicago, 1955), p. 10.

and the opportunities to work as a team in emergencies. In fact, the entire relationship between management and workers is improved over what obtained in traditional manufacturing: There is more two-way communication and mutual understanding. People handle problems as they arise and there is little need for management to impose quotas and work standards. Employees can see themselves progressing through a series of graded job steps. Relatively small numbers and management's investment in training give a sense of individualism which contrasts sharply with the impersonality of the traditional sprawling factory.

True automation is really the opposite of Taylorism and scientific management's mass-production methods. The former involves looking at work processes as a whole and giving employees a broader view and wider responsibilities. Mechanization and mass production foster a piecemeal approach: speeding up a machine here, eliminating an arm motion there, saving an operation some place else. It is hardly any wonder that employee reactions to these widely different technologies vary so dramatically.

CONCLUSION

While craft and continuous processing work provides much more job satisfaction than machine or assembly line tending, the picture is not a simple one. The former have associated dissatisfactions (e.g., increased personal responsibility) and the latter can appeal to employees who want to do a minimum of thinking. In order to assess the potential of any job to provide satisfaction (or dissatisfaction), it is useful to keep in mind the total array of technologically-based factors that contribute to employee reactions.

Often the alert manager can relate his observations of employee behavior and the sentiments they express to these various job factors. He is thus in a better position to interpret the underlying source of satisfaction or dissatisfaction. At times, as we have seen, the manager can go one step farther. He can make modifications at the margin of the job, so to speak, by changing the length of the cycle, the opportunity for social relationships, and so on. In a few cases the manager may actually be able to influence the over-all character of the job, whether it tends to fit toward the craft—continuous processing—or toward the mass-production end of the continuum.

problem 1 • THE HEADLINER GROUP

The headliner group is located in the Passenger Trim Department; it is their job to place the fabric covering on the inside of the car roof, stretch it to a fit, smooth out the wrinkles, and glue it into place. Though the job might, at first observation, seem to be rather simple, it is actually something of an art, for far more skill is required to handle the pliable fabric than is needed in working with unyielding metal, the major component of an automobile. To train a man to do the work with any degree of proficiency requires at least a week of constant instruction. For this reason, it is difficult to replace a headliner on short notice and few are trained to do the job.

The seven men who filled the job recognized the leverage inherent in even this modest skill requirement. They considered themselves superior to most of the assemblers who worked with metal parts, although their job, too, was highly repetitious. They also felt free to complain about anything and everything: heating, lighting, ventilation, the tools with which they worked, and supervisory prejudice.

Although each man performed the same job, the group did not actually work together on a car. Each installed the headliner on every seventh automobile. A worker would get into a unit, remain in it until he finished the work, and then go to the seventh unit back and repeat the cycle. Therefore, the work of a given man was not dependent on the work of any other. The amount of effort required might vary, however. For example, a station wagon would require more work, for it has more interior to be covered by the headliner than a two-door automobile. Although attempts were made to keep the proportion of each type of unit produced constant during each hour, it was indeed rare when no variation occurred. Difficulties in scheduling, errors, and problems in other departments made the maintenance of a constant "mix" almost impossible. Since these variations had an impact on the work time of the headliners, they were quick to seize on the smallest fluctuations, pressure the foreman for relief, and threaten the foreman with union action.

The major bone of contention of the workers was the time standard imposed on them. It was consistently argued that the job could not be time studied and that there was no "standard time" for the work. The group complained that there were too many variables to consider and even went so far as to aver that changes in the weather (humidity) would have noticeable changes on the material with which they worked. It was claimed that judgment was required for every unit was a little different. Resentment was also strong against their rate of pay. Although they were well-paid and within a few cents of the highest-paid jobs in the plant, the workers believed that their jobs required more effort than that of the door-fitters, the best-paid group. Because their work necessitated that they climb into the automobile, perform the operation with their hands above their heads, and remain stooped over in the unit until the headliner was installed, they contended that the task was the most tiring in the plant. It was also protested that not enough allowance was given for fatigue and contingencies, and that an extra worker should be trained and placed in the group to assist. Although the headliners had complained about the job and the work load, it was possible for them to give each other an extra break during some part of the day. While six men kept up the work, one could leave the job and go for a cup of coffee and a cigarette.

Since the foreman had to get the work from these men to maintain production, he had to have their cooperation. Checks were made on the cost which each foreman's area incurred as well as the quality of his production. Data were recorded daily on these two control items and were given to the foreman, the general foreman, and the department superintendent. Costs and quality were the determinants of the foreman's bonus and directly affected his chances for promotion.

If the foreman placed new pressure on the group to speed up, the quality would drop, the workers would slowly fall further behind, and the utility man would be required to help the men catch up, thus diverting him from his regular duties of relieving others and disrupting the whole relief schedule. Complaints were sure to arise from the others when this occurred. [34]

1. If you were instructing a new foreman in this department, what are the things you would tell him about the "headliners?"

2. What do you know about technology and job satisfaction that would be useful in managing such a group?

3. Do "gripes" and pressure provide any satisfaction? How?

[34] We are indebted to a former student, James T. Bennett, for this case.

problem 2 • DIRTY BOTTLES

The Milwaukee Brewing Company has been plagued with trouble among its *bottle inspectors,* whose job is to check each bottle carefully to make sure that it is absolutely clean as it leaves the bottle-washing machine. Though there have been many attempts to develop mechanical inspecting devices, none of these has worked with 100 per cent accuracy. As a consequence, each bottle must be visually inspected as it passes by the inspector on a conveyor belt. Although this job is highly paid, it is hard to find men to take it, and many quit after working on it a few months.

1. What seems to be the basic problem here?
2. What suggestions can you make for solving it?

problem 3 • CANDY WRAPPERS

All candy made by the Quality Candy Company is wrapped by hand. Candy is brought to each wrapper by chute. She wraps each piece and then drops it into another chute which leads to packers in another room.

Each girl handles a different kind of candy and their work locations are isolated from each other.

1. How will the girls react to this sort of work?
2. What can be done to increase their morale and output?

TECHNOLOGY AND JOB SATISFACTION IN THE OFFICE AND LABORATORY

3

In our description of blue-collar work, we have shown how employees seek to "wring out" of their jobs such satisfactions as reasonable interest and variety, a sense of accomplishment or status and autonomy. While many white-collar jobs are similar to production work, managerial and professional positions provide rich rewards in many job satisfaction "currencies." Indeed most students are drawn to work toward these careers and they occupy high positions on society's status ladder.

We shall begin by looking at those white-collar jobs that are most similar to factory jobs, but most of our emphasis will be on managerial and professional work. However, both the routine and the more challenging nonmanual jobs are becoming predominant in our advanced industrial society.

WHITE-COLLAR WORK

Economists have observed the following trend as industrialization proceeds. Primary industry (mines and farms) requires a decreasing proportion of the labor force as secondary industry (manufacturing) becomes more important. In its turn, tertiary industry (services) becomes increasingly significant. With increasing incomes, people want and can afford to pay for more services. And service industries (banks, hospitals, stores, and so on) tend to provide a high proportion of white-collar jobs. Even in our factories, the ratios of managers, engineers, clerks, and technicians (all white-collar workers) to production workers grow as more sophisticated technologies are utilized and as more attention is paid to research, design, marketing, finance, and other nonmanufacturing activities. The projected changes in jobs incorporated in the chart below show this increasing dominance of nonmanual work in the U.S. labor market.

White- vs. Blue-Collar

Prestige advantages. In almost every country white-collar work carries more prestige than blue-collar. In fact, some developing nations have great difficulty improving their productivity because the educated citizens all want to work in offices (as bank or government employees, lawyers, and so on) and not in factories. The reasons for the difference in status are not difficult to identify.

The names alone suggest an important difference. Blue-collar workers presumably get their hands and clothes soiled while working; the others can wear spotless clothing. White-collar jobs are thought to have individuality in contrast to the mass character of factory work, to be "middle class" as distinct from "working class"! They are also "closer," both physically and psychologically, to management, and it is assumed that promotions come easier and salaries are higher in office work than in the plant. For many people whose fathers worked on farms, in mines, or factories, just getting a white-collar job is a major step forward. Finally, the traditional difference in prestige between these two types of jobs reflects assumed differences in the relative difficulty and complexity of brain work as against manual work.

Some have said that white-collar "psychology can be understood as the psychology of prestige striving."[1] Managers have to learn that very substantial ego and social rewards are derived from what may appear to be unimportant differences between jobs. For example, a job title like "staff assistant" may provide a sense of advancement to an employee who was doing the same work when it was called "chief clerk."

Exaggerated differences. But it should be noted that the differences between blue- and white-collar work are declining. At least some factory work is as clean as office work, some much cleaner (for instance, the spotless, temperature-controlled manufacturing facilities where delicate instruments are made and tested). Some automated jobs (like the previously described chief melter in a steel mill) have a larger component of "brain work" than do most routine clerical office jobs. And there is some long-run tendency for the pay differential between blue- and white-collar work to disappear or reverse itself.

White-collar factories. The almost complete disappearance of differences between white- and blue-collar work can be observed in what could best be described as a white-collar factory. On a single work floor, there can be an acre

[1] C. Wright Mills, *White Collar* (New York: Oxford University Press, 1953), Chapter 4.

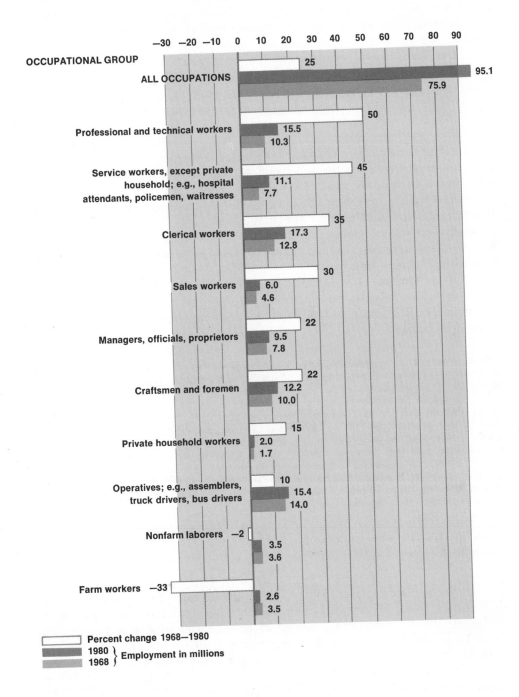

The chart shows the following data, read by occupational group with a scale from −30 to 90.

OCCUPATIONAL GROUP

ALL OCCUPATIONS
- Percent change 1968–1980: 25
- 1980: 95.1
- 1968: 75.9

Professional and technical workers
- Percent change 1968–1980: 50
- 1980: 15.5
- 1968: 10.3

Service workers, except private household; e.g., hospital attendants, policemen, waitresses
- Percent change 1968–1980: 45
- 1980: 11.1
- 1968: 7.7

Clerical workers
- Percent change 1968–1980: 35
- 1980: 17.3
- 1968: 12.8

Sales workers
- Percent change 1968–1980: 30
- 1980: 6.0
- 1968: 4.6

Managers, officials, proprietors
- Percent change 1968–1980: 22
- 1980: 9.5
- 1968: 7.8

Craftsmen and foremen
- Percent change 1968–1980: 22
- 1980: 12.2
- 1968: 10.0

Private household workers
- Percent change 1968–1980: 15
- 1980: 2.0
- 1968: 1.7

Operatives; e.g., assemblers, truck drivers, bus drivers
- Percent change 1968–1980: 10
- 1980: 15.4
- 1968: 14.0

Nonfarm laborers
- Percent change 1968–1980: −2
- 1980: 3.5
- 1968: 3.6

Farm workers
- Percent change 1968–1980: −33
- 1980: 2.6
- 1968: 3.5

Legend:
- Percent change 1968–1980
- 1980 } Employment in millions
- 1968 }

Source: U.S. Dept. of Labor, Bureau of Labor Statistics.

PROJECTED CHANGES IN VARIOUS OCCUPATIONAL GROUPS, 1968-1980

of desks and work tables stretching as far as the eye can see. Minutely described, mechanized short-cycle jobs, requiring such "tools" as card punchers or typewriters, are being performed by clerical personnel, all of whom receive very similar wages.

Identification with management has been much reduced on such jobs. Promotions to the supervisory level tend to be reserved for college graduates who come into special training programs that bypass the great majority of lower-skilled office jobs. As a consequence, many white-collar workers substitute the goals of security and prestige for personal advancement.

Of course, the introduction of computers is changing the office scene. Whether or not computers have increased or decreased the number of low-skilled, routine jobs is still being debated. Most modern, "automated" offices are really at a very primitive stage of automation; indeed, the stage is very like mass-production work. Employees who punch data onto computer cards or who place the magnetic ink numerals on the bottom of bank checks are doing finely divided, highly circumscribed, short-cycle jobs. To be sure, there are additional programmers, console operators, and maintenance personnel required, whose jobs are more interesting.[2]

Not unexpectedly, we find the reactions of many white-collar workers to their jobs very similar to those described in the previous chapter. Here below, for example, is a self-description provided by an office worker in a large insurance company:

"As an operator I had to complete 720 units in 4 hours with no more than 11 errors. This quota was often very difficult to meet, especially on nights when the packs were of more than average difficulty. The job was extremely boring.

"Each pack usually contained 180 policyholders' account cards. About 150 of these had to be billed on 'short forms.' There were two types of short forms—a #1 form and #4 form. The number of each type that was billed was recorded on a digital index on the machine. Usually, each pack had about the same number of each of the two types, and I played games of 'basketball' with each pack with the #1's vs. the #4's. Usually the scores were quite close, and on a couple of occasions the game went into overtime—that is, was continued in the next pack. Punching in the seven numbers that made up the policyholder's account number was my way of 'dribbling the ball down the floor,' and pushing in the button that rang up the total was 'the ball going through the basket.' "

Thus, workers in white-collar factories make a game of routine work just as do machine-tenders in factories.

Distinctive "white-collar" jobs. While differences in prestige and the physical characteristics of the work may have been exaggerated, there are white-collar jobs which provide distinctive satisfactions because of their unique properties. These are the jobs which embody major elements of human-relations service activity or intellectual effort or managerial responsibility.

[2] For a good review of the impact of mechanization on office jobs see Floyd C. Mann, "Psychological and Organizational Impacts," in John T. Dunlop, ed., *Automation and Technological Change* (Englewood Cliffs, N.J.: Prentice-Hall, 1962).

Where Work Is Human Relations: Service Workers

The social satisfactions which blue-collar workers are able to obtain are enjoyed for the most part *around* the job; for receptionists, salesmen, waitresses, and others in similar jobs, satisfactory social relations are the essence of their work. Thus, these employees enjoy the opportunity to gain social satisfaction *through* work, but, as a consequence they are subject to much potential frustration when these relations become pressureful.

In these human-relations occupations, employees are often required to fit into closely timed relationships with other employees, many of whom may be under great stress just at the time they are asked for their cooperation. This problem can be most easily observed in restaurants where the waiter feels under great pressure to serve his customers quickly and thus earn more tips. Waiters struggle with bus boys to get their tables cleared and set up quickly to be ready for the next customer. The waiter also may compete with other waiters to get scarce silverware or particular food items in short supply. Conflicts also occur between waiters and personnel in the serving pantry, kitchen and the bar.

Obviously, the need to cooperate under pressure can provide human-relations conflicts where personalities are poorly matched. Many individuals break down under such severe interactional strain: the constant bickering and the need to accommodate to others. For them the relative peace and quiet of a factory job, where "if you do your job no one bothers you," may be far more appealing. Other employees thrive on the hectic pace and the demands of fellow employees and customers alike; for them, interaction under pressure is highly satisfying and only the idleness associated with a slow day is painful.

A case example: retail selling. Retail selling is typically a fast-paced, unprogramed, demanding occupation and the pressures often exceed those in production work. As in any activity involving a customer, who is not a member of the organization, we find the need to adjust quickly to the whims and fancies of the person who is spending his money and expects *service*.

An example of the human-relations pressures and satisfactions of retailing is provided by the following description of a women's high-fashion specialty store.

The downtown store is managed by Miss Stoler and her assistant, Sylvia. Frances, Ruth, and Betty are all salesgirls, working on commission.

Whenever Mrs. von Jones and her daughter appear in the store, everyone jumps to attention; they are very good customers. One afternoon, Frances saw them first, greeted them, and used the intercom to call Ruth since the von Joneses enjoyed having Ruth serve them.

At one point Ruth said to Betty, who now had a customer, too, "Betty, run to the [other] stockroom and get me that size 14." Betty answered that she couldn't right now, she was busy. Ruth, obviously irritated, turned to Sylvia with her request. Sylvia complied.

Ruth soon exhausted the stock of suitable dresses to show Mrs. von Jones. She slipped out to take the back elevator to the Receiving Room, and, peering through the wiremesh security wall, spied several expensive pieces just being unpacked. Upon asking, she was informed that they were destined for a branch store, and would not be ready for transportation until late in the day. She returned in a few minutes with Sylvia, pointed to them, and said, "See, those are the ones." Sylvia, declaring that Miss Stoler had OK'd their removal from the Receiving Room, picked several items for Mrs. von Jones from the rack for the East Side branch, obtained the cost of the dresses from the Receiving Clerk, and told Ruth what the price on each would be. Together they went back up the freight elevator.

Ruth used the phone to call to the main floor for some things to be sent up for the daughter. The floor manager promised help, but, since all her girls were busy, she was obliged to take some things up herself. Ruth called the shoe department, described what had been sold thus far, and told the department head to "get up here now, before she leaves. Your customer will wait," Next Ruth went to get an additional fitter, and became quite angry when the Cashier told her, "Your saleslip isn't completed, and I can't process these charges until you get Mrs. von Jones' signature." Ruth took them back to the floor to get her customer's signature.

Miss Stoler began "closing the sale" with both the von Joneses for several garments, and since they wished to take two items with them, had them packed at the Cashier's desk. The Cashier called to the Credit Department for the OK, and was informed to "hold everything." It seemed that the account was 90 days overdue, in a large sum. When Ruth discovered the garments weren't being packed, she called the Credit Department, and demanded that it be OK'd at once. "She's in a hurry and she'll be mad. Besides, she always pays." [3]

[Note particularly the large number of diverse, unpredictable, and stressful contacts handled by Ruth in response to her customer's demands. In turn, many people in the store must adjust their behavior to meet Ruth's job requirements.]

Where Work Requires Mental Effort

An increasing number of jobs demand intellectual rather than physical effort. Copywriters, laboratory personnel, and programers all require creative talents that cannot be programed. Almost all involve depth attention and a highly variable work pace.

When the work is going badly, deadlines are approaching, or an obstacle can't be overcome, tremendous internal tensions are generated. Even slight inconveniences or frictions cause blow-ups:

The three programers responsible for finishing the work were a month behind; they could not debug what had been written so far. Worse, the computer was always "over them"; it was perfection and it taunted them by finding even the slightest mistake they made. One night when a supervisor came into the machine room and simply asked, "How are things going?" one of the programers flew into a rage.

Such people usually have an enormous sense of possessiveness. The drawing or copy or program being worked on is "theirs." Although this attitude brings forth extraordinary effort, it can also make it difficult for such people to accept aid, ideas, and advice from others or to modify their work so that it better fits into the work of others. (Among such people one often hears: NIH, meaning "not invented here," as an explanation of why an idea is rejected.) In this type of work credit for successes and failures is often easy to assign. Completion of a difficult assignment leads to elation, even euphoria. Failure leads to depression.

The nature of their work means that these persons sometimes know much more about their subject than does their supervisor.

"When one of my people gets stuck on a problem, I know I can't provide them with technical assistance. A supervisor fools himself who thinks he can. They're prima donnas. Many of those guys have received so much praise that you have to handle them with kid gloves. So the only way I can help them is to get them to step back a little from what they are doing, by asking the

---

[3] We are indebted to our former student, Mr. M. D. Strickler, for this description.

right questions. Often they have just been so intensely immersed in the work that they have missed some little point. Once you get them to take a different tack or step back they find their own mistake quickly enough."

The most qualified, the most independent and the most highly paid white-collar employees whose work is mental effort are the professionals.

PROFESSIONALS

Professionals represent a distinctive category of employees, although their job demands and interests are also echoed by nonprofessionals, often in more muted tones. To understand their motivations and their reactions to management and the organization thus enables one to better predict the behavior of a wide range of employees.

Historically, professions developed independently of institutions; in fact they were a reaction to the constraints and confinements of the medieval world. Thus self-employed doctors and lawyers are good examples of professionals. However, given the increased technical complexity of modern business and government, professionals are being hired and expected to work within organizations as researchers and staff specialists.

But first, who is a professional? Not an easy question to answer these days when nearly everyone—from taxi drivers to realtors—claims this special status. Professional standing stems from unusual technical competence growing out of extended, prescribed training and often recognized in terms of special university degrees, licenses and certification. Many craftsmen may have apprenticeships and most managers have college training, but neither group has the intensive, systematic, and extended training program associated with becoming an architect, a physicist or a lawyer. In turn the professional lays claim to a variety of special privileges because he assumes an ethical code whose values exhort him to serve his clients and place their welfare above his own. Obviously this ideal is not maintained by all professionals, but there are procedures by which the professional group itself will discipline those who flagrantly violate their code of ethics:

Any occupation wishing to exercise professional authority must find a technical basis for it, assert an exclusive jurisdiction, link both skill and jurisdiction to standards of training, and convince the public that its services are uniquely trustworthy. [4]

Intrinsic Interest and Variety

The professional wants challenging work and he often seeks to pursue an interesting lead or project even though management wants him to accept a more mundane but perhaps more immediately useful assignment. He frequently wants

[4] Harold Wilensky, "The Professionalization of Everyone?" *American Journal of Sociology*, Vol. 70, No. 2 (September 1964), p. 138. The article is a good summary of the subject, as well.

to pursue a tantalizing question or lead to its ultimate solution; his manager would be pleased to have a more timely solution even though it wasn't a perfect or ideal one. In much the same fashion, the professional within the organization is often accused of "gold plating" his work (adding needless frills and quality elements) when commercial realities dictate a less costly, less fancy approach. In short the professional in the organization, whether lawyer or scientist, wants to do meaningful work which will be judged worthy by his colleagues in the profession. His professional pride is involved in maintaining professional standards of excellence.

These differences can be summarized as follows:

PROFESSIONAL	vs.	HIS ORGANIZATION
Challenging assignment to further knowledge, theory		Assignment based on organizational needs, practical realities
Elegant, even ultimate solutions; perfectionist		Timely solutions; compromises to meet competition or solve problems
Completion, closure		Rapid shifts to meet budget and schedule requirements; abandonment of projects where payoffs not assured

Accomplishment, Autonomy, and Identification

As members in good standing of a respected discipline, their satisfactions come from meeting the standards of the profession, not the organization. Advancement may require moving among organizations, but this is no sacrifice since one's primary loyalty is to the profession. Such recognition is often associated with giving papers at professional meetings and publishing them in appropriate journals. This, in turn, may conflict with management's belief in withholding new ideas from potential competitors and its policy of secrecy.

The professional also expects to be judged by his peers since they are the only ones with comparable training and expertise. Similarly professionals expect to receive direction from their senior, most expert colleagues rather than from "outsiders" who may simply have a management title. This expectation produces a dilemma for professionals themselves. Highly competent scientists, for example, will be encouraged by their organizations to take on managerial responsibilities in order to provide the requisite professional leadership. However, the research-oriented professional may be reluctant to give up doing his own work. Further, since management per se has little prestige among professionals, he may fear that his reputation will suffer if he becomes an administrator and stops producing.

Thus the professional seeks independence from managers who do not share his values. He also believes he should be exempt from the rules and procedures which govern others in the organization. For example, they can resent regular working hours, preferring the freedom to work weekends, to stay all night if necessary, but not to be bound by the 9 to 5 regimen. These and other privileges they justify by pointing to their high level of identification and commitment to their work. As one executive said about professionals:

It really shakes you up to see the sandals, the beards, the endless coffee breaks, but the good ones really work; time means nothing to them and they'll knock themselves out to solve a tough technical problem.

The professional has a "Ptolemaic" view of the organization—he is the center of the universe. Given the importance of his work, the relative ignorance of outsiders who don't share his expertise and his own commitment to high standards of performance, he expects that others will defer enthusiastically to his needs and wishes. When he needs a new piece of equipment, a trip to a convention or another technician, he expects his request to receive quick approval. In fact, in pure professional organizations (like universities and, in part, in hospitals and court systems) administrative personnel, rather than being the line administrators, are the staff service arm of the organization; everything revolves around the professional's job.

Professionals have their own standards of what constitutes advancement. To be sure, they are interested in higher incomes and status titles (though they sometimes deny this). Still, many professionals place less value on salary than on these other satisfactions.

PROFESSIONAL	vs.	HIS ORGANIZATION
Critical decisions and judgments made by peers, fellow experts		Decisions and appraisals by management hierarchy
Senior colleague guides		Manager orders
Status as a function of professional ability, knowledge		Status as a function of managerial level
Indifference to rules and procedures, often unorthodox		Emphasis on procedures, discipline, and rules and conventional behavior
Organization designed to facilitate your work		Your work designed to facilitate organization goals

Job Pressures and Dual Loyalty

It would be unfortunate if the impression given is one of spoiled prima donnas. True professionals do indeed work hard; they push themselves and they know they can't rest on past laurels. Their work is in fields which keep changing as new knowledge is discovered. The professional who stops learning, whose intellectual energies flag, quickly finds himself surpassed by younger, more vigorous and more recently trained colleagues.

Given their external-to-the-organization standards of performance, professionals are often called *cosmopolitans*, to contrast them to less worldly employees. The latter, *locals*, are more likely to see the organization as their world and expect to advance on the basis of meeting internal criteria and learning the nuances (e.g., the norms, the rules, the personalities) of the organization. In some ways, this internal learning and measurement process is more finite, and some managers, at least, can relax after they have achieved reasonable competency at organization politics and learned their jobs well. The professional can never relax; his world is always changing.

And, of course, many of the conflicts we have described above between the organization and the professional represent this difference between cosmopolitan values and local values. However, there are times when the conflict is more apparent than real. Some employees claim to be professionals to discourage the supervisor from interfering with their ways of working or to try to get service personnel to provide them with quicker or greater support.

The New Professionals

Many groups are striving to professionalize themselves and thus join the ranks (and get the privileges) of the older established professions. For example, security analysts, hospital administrators, purchasing agents, programers, and laboratory technicians are attempting to establish standards that will set themselves apart from, and hopefully, above individuals claiming some competence in these fields but who lack formal preparation or adequate experience. Understandably, these staff specialists, whose claim to authority is based on formal professional training, often come into conflict with line managers whose knowledge and skill derive primarily from long years of on-the-job experience, intuition, and good common sense.

At times, the claim to the title of "professional" may be a tactic in an intergroup struggle. Managers whose promotions have been blocked or who see themselves losing influence may take refuge in professionalism as a source of job satisfaction or power.

In some cases management may even encourage individuals who, for one reason or another, are unlikely to raise their organizational status through the normal route of promotions to conceive of themselves as professionals. As professionals, it is hoped, they will be more interested in technical expertise than increased managerial responsibility.[5] "We look upon you as a professional salesman, a real expert in your field. With your experience it would be a waste to put you in an office," a manager explained to a long-service salesman in passing him over for promotion to district sales manager. Many companies provide titles, such as senior engineer, to assuage the frustrations of those whose careers have, in fact, deadended.

The Organization vs. the Professional

It would be a mistake to exaggerate, however, the restlessness of the typical professional working in industry. Many possess scarce, respected skills to which both fellow employees and management are deferential. They often receive special treatment, and their requests for services and assistance are honored

[5] Fred Goldner and Richard Ritti, "Professionalization As Career Mobility," *American Journal of Sociology*, Vol. 72 (1967), pp. 489–502.

before the requests of less prestigious employees. The modern organization provides a wealth of interesting assignments, and many people feel that "real-life" problems, where stakes are great, are much more exciting than problems in a cloistered academic atmosphere. The professional's goals of increased knowledge and skill and the solution of difficult problems are often company goals as well. Thus, the professional may see little conflict between his needs and the company's needs. For professionals, relationships with like-trained supervisors are usually informal, approaching relations between colleagues, and thus more satisfying than those enjoyed by other occupational groups.

In contrast, many professionals such as engineers are often marking time in their professional roles until they can be recognized and promoted into a management job. We turn next to these critical positions.

MANAGERIAL JOBS

Although the jobs of no two managers are exactly alike, certain characteristics sharply distinguish managerial from nonmanagerial jobs.

Let's look at a typical series of activities constituting a few hours in the life of a manager:

When Henry came in at 9 A.M. there were already six telephone messages on his desk. He first called back the Employment Office and told them it was all right to hire two temporary secretaries to fill in for vacations. ... Then he called one of the supervisors in the plant and told him to hold back on the Pickney Order because a parts shortage had turned up yesterday that would delay final assembly work. As his secretary came in to indicate that one of the more nervous expediters was outside waiting to see him, he waved to her their standard signal which meant he was too busy to see anybody. Then he called up Engineering and told them in no uncertain terms that no matter what happened they had to get those drawings done by the afternoon. He ignored the other calls.

As a breather he began glancing at his mail which his secretary had arrayed on the right-hand side of his desk. He soon had picked up a dictating machine to answer those deserving quick attention; several others he handed to the secretary to answer with a "pleasant 'no.'"

To get ready for a meeting with the head of the Division he used a slide rule to work up some figures on comparative costs of contracting-out and doing internally several maintenance jobs. Then he telephoned the Art Department to have the figures placed on large charts for display at the meeting. (He was anxious to make a good impression, since the man responsible for his next promotion was going to be there.)

He remembered that at 10:30 he was scheduled to interview a new engineer and he walked out to escort him into his office. It took 20 minutes to learn something of his background and personality.

Next, another supervisor came in to request that the cost accounting department redo last month's "variance analysis" since he was sure that his group's costs were stated incorrectly. Henry spent ten minutes looking over the figures with the man before agreeing to have them checked. And in the next few minutes, he took a call from a vending-machine company that wanted to install some equipment in the cafeteria, agreed to meet with a union grievance committee at the end of the week, and told an employee that he could not change his vacation date since others were already scheduled.

Intrinsic Interest and Variety

Within the short space of two hours, this executive had been in contact with ten people, engaged in a variety of different types of activity extended from mathematical and mental tactical calculations to interviewing, negotiating, and order-giving. Although he had to respond to other people, the how and when he responded and how he scheduled his day were largely up to him. The unpredictable and ever-changing nature of his job required constant alertness. In that dizzy array of contacts and activities, there was a great deal of challenge and the requirement for real depth attention. For many managers this pace is maintained through a ten- or twelve- (not an eight-) hour day and there is no time to daydream or seek social relationships for their own sake. And yet managers get the same pleasure from the "fielding" of the ever-changing variety of problems that a baseball player gets from a championship game. Most managerial jobs are quite malleable, flexing with the pushes and pulls of the unique personality filling them, as he interacts with countless others.

Accomplishment, Autonomy, and Identification

Accompanying this pressure are numerous satisfactions derived from having the status of a manager. It is not just the secretary who comes when the buzzer is pressed, but the large number of people whom he can call and who will give him a respectful hearing and who are dependent on him. And, of course, there are his immediate subordinates who accept him as their leader.

Particularly at higher levels of the organization, the manager derives enormous satisfaction from power, knowing he can influence critical decisions and may control the expenditure of tens or hundreds of thousands of dollars. And indeed the success or failure of new ventures may well be dependent on his personal acumen and decision-making skill.

In addition, managerial work pays well. In our society, salary is an index of success, a measure of accomplishment. For the executive, salary is the score card that tells him how far and how fast he has moved ahead. What he does with money is less important than the mere fact of earning it.

Most managers anticipate regular promotions which mean more money, more responsibility, more status. Given the intrinsic interest of their jobs, the opportunities for advancement and their preoccupation with the central nervous system of the organization, it is no wonder that they are identified with and often strongly committed to their organizations. In the eyes of many higher level managers, they *are* the organization.

While it is not surprising, it is regrettable that, when holding such positions, it is easy to project one's own motivations and commitments upon less well-situated employees:

"These workers don't want to give a fair day's work; they're always looking for a chance to get out of work, to talk or loaf or fool around. They don't want to take responsibility and show what they can do, even though it could lead to a promotion or a raise."

What this manager is forgetting is that these other employees cannot obtain the same intrinsic satisfactions he obtains. They cannot see the same rewards for themselves in the future nor can they get so involved in and committed to the future of the company. Neither participating in the key decisions nor able to see their impact, they view the company as something separate from themselves. For many managers, in contrast, the success of the organization and their own success are inextricably interwoven. And this identification in itself is enormously gratifying.

Job Pressures

There is a price to be paid for these satisfactions: heavy responsibilities and anxieties. Mistakes are easy to make, in part because the manager has to please other people, particularly those above him in the organization. Further, the success of his activities depends upon many people he does not directly control (for instance, the staff departments within the company). Since so much of his job involves decision-making and human-relations skills, the evaluation of which tends to be subjective, most managers feel themselves especially vulnerable to criticism, even to severe penalties (such as demotion) for making decisions which higher management does not like. Further, there is fierce rivalry for promotion at managerial levels—by fair means and foul. Still, most managers thrive on competition.

Obviously for some personalities and in some positions, the pressures become unbearable, and managers, like production workers, escape to go into business for themselves (where they are their own boss) or seek out a less competitive environment.

Sure I liked the title and the big salary and the showy office, but after awhile the pressures just got too much for me. A day didn't go by in which my boss didn't call to find out where I was going to be able to squeeze out some costs and get sales up. I had to constantly harass my salesmen on their expense accounts and that kind of discussion is no fun. When one of them didn't meet quota two months in a row I had to discharge him and that is one of the toughest things a manager has to do. And just last week, after spending two months preparing our budget for next year and arguing for it with my boss, and his boss and the Comptroller, I had to come back to my people and tell them we weren't going to get the authorization to buy that new equipment they were so excited about. I felt I let them down and they would lose confidence in me and in my influence upstairs.

Naive outsiders often view managers as omnipotent, solitary decision-makers reading computer print-outs and problem solving. Instead their jobs are built around high levels of human interaction. Through human relations the manager seeks to coordinate the work of his subordinates, communicate his wishes, ferret out information and be responsive to the requests and needs of colleagues, bosses, and subordinates. He is a man on the move, and while the satisfactions can be substantial, only the highly energetic who relish human association and confrontation and negotiation are likely to be successful.

Entrepreneurs

Some executives and would-be executives are impatient with both the complexities of the organization (such as the need to convince a boss or a staff expert, or to follow procedures) and the prospect of slow but steady progression.

They want to be completely on their own, making their own rules and setting their own objectives. They are willing to risk their own savings and their regular incomes for this complete autonomy and for the excitement of possibly winning a great deal if their business succeeds. Theirs is a go-for-broke point of view, and they like being in the position of having no one but themselves to blame if the gamble doesn't pay off. Often they are motivated by an overpowering belief in the potential of one of their own ideas (for a new product or service) and make great personal sacrifices to prove that they are right.

Obviously these driven, highly self-confident risk-takers scorn those less energetic souls who seek security (fringe benefits and a steady salary). They often make authoritarian bosses, since they make the same demands upon other people that they make upon themselves. However, they can still attract good people to work for them when they are successful in communicating their own enthusiasm that they have a world-beating idea and their confidence becomes contagious.

Below are some brief vignettes of several young entrepreneurs interviewed by *The New York Times:*

Mr. Stein started out merchandising rock souvenirs such as Elvis Presley sweatshirts and bracelets with names of rock stars.

When he traveled with the groups, he met several promoters and saw unlimited possibilities for big money. In less than two years he was booking some of the biggest names in the business, such as Jimi Hendrix and Janis Joplin.

"I wanted to make a lot of money, but on my own terms. I want to be heard, felt, have power. And if you don't have money, no one listens," says Mr. Stein, "Money is a tool. I want it to give me freedom." . . .

To Stan Buchthal, 23-year-old founder with two partners of a company that makes jeans, pants and T shirts, loving your work is a key to success.

"I really didn't start out wanting to make a lot of money. I just wanted to have a business of my own. And now, every few months, the orders keep doubling."

Mr. Buchthal went to work in the garment district right out of college but found the 9-to-5 white collar routine dull. . . .

He pays himself only $12,000 a year in order to have more money to reinvest in his company. He lives in a cheap Manhattan hotel room or bunks in with friends when business gets too hectic. . . .

"It's ridiculous how hard we work," says Mr. Friedland, whose short, wavy hair and easy grin make him look younger than his 27 years. "But we enjoy it, especially the sense of power and accomplishment that comes from running your own business." [6]

Many entrepreneurs find it difficult to make the transition from starting their own business to operating an organization. They are too impulsive and impatient with procedures or learning managerial skills. They really want to be on their own with perhaps a small group of trusted subordinates. Therefore if the business grows and requires more routinization, they may have to move on to still newer ventures and challenges.

[6] Excerpts from Jurate Kazickas, "The New, Young Capitalists: Getting Rich on Their Own Terms," *The New York Times,* April 18, 1971.

In-Between Categories: The Engineer

In some ways, executives (organizational and entrepreneurial) and professionals represent extreme cases. The modern organization typically includes within its white-collar professional group a variety of specialists who fall in between. Some, like salesmen and consultants, have entrepreneurial drives and needs (for being unfettered, on their own, and for having the opportunity to earn as much as they can). Others bear a closer resemblance to managers or to professionals. For example, many staff specialists—in accounting, marketing, industrial relations—see themselves as being *both* a member of the management team and a professional in their own right; they have technical skills arising from extensive training and they identify with the organization.

One of the best examples of an "in-between" group is provided by engineers in large engineering development departments, who are part scientist-professional, part manager and part worker. [7] As the following excerpt describes, the engineer may thus be torn in three contradictory directions: [8]

The engineer's dilemma. To a greater or lesser extent almost every engineer is uncertain of his role. Is he professional? Is he management? Or is he merely a worker?

Certainly his training and his title make him a professional. As a professional he has a mission to push back the frontiers of knowledge. He is partly bound by values (professional standards) other than those of the organization for which he works. He seeks his rewards primarily in terms of approbation from other professionals, rather than from within the organization itself. He aims to set his own rules and to be judged by other professionals.

But the engineer also feels some identification with management, whether he is formally classified as management or not. His job permits some discretion (often less than he wants), and his middle-class upbringing leads him to seek material rewards. In most companies the only way to get ahead, in terms of both prestige and earnings, is to be promoted through the ranks of management.

Finally, in moments of discouragement, the engineer may feel like a factory worker. Often he works in a large drafting room, and he may be subject to factory-like discipline (sometimes he must check with his boss before leaving the area and may have his coffee breaks carefully timed). His discretion may be quite limited; he may work on a tiny part of a total project and feel that he is making little contribution to knowledge. He may recognize that as an employee he is dependent on management and that, to some extent, he has the same economic interests as other employees. And so he seeks salary increases, overtime payments, protection against arbitrary acts of management, and so forth.

Of course, many of the engineer's interests cut across several values. As a management man and a professional, he is competitive: he desires to get ahead on his own (although getting ahead professionally is not the same as getting ahead in management). On the other hand, as an employee he is equalitarian and seeks equal treatment for all. As a professional and as an employee he seeks to expand the status and autonomy of his group. However, as a professional his aim is to carry out his work more successfully, while as an employee it is to win greater job control and economic security. But both his professional and employee interests incline him to identify with a *group* (difficult as this may be for an engineer).

[7] A fine study of engineers in industry is R. Richard Ritti, *The Engineer in the Industrial Corporation* (New York: Columbia University Press, 1971).

[8] George Strauss's studies of professionals in industry are summarized in "Professionalism and Occupational Associations," *Industrial Relations*, Vol. 2, No. 3 (May 1963), pp. 7-31. The passage quoted here appears on p. 23 of that article.

CONCLUSION

Personnel policies and managerial skills must apply to diverse groups with widely differing motivations to work and sharply contrasting views of their role in the organization. There is no longer the sharp break between workers and bosses nor the trim pyramids in which most employees were at the bottom (as workers) and a few elite were at the top (as the bosses). Many organizations today, in fact, are quite top-heavy or distended in the middle.

Modern organizations employ a variety of professionals and would-be professionals as staff specialists and researchers (e.g., market researchers and chemists); they have relatively large numbers of managerial personnel. Thus, managing managers and professionals becomes a challenge as critical as (if not more critical than) the challenge of managing workers (as we shall see in Chapters 14 and 15.) In addition, many white-collar workers—clericals, administrative assistants, computer operators—have interests that somewhat separate them from their blue-collar counterparts. But insofar as their jobs become routinized, their reactions to the organization become more similar to those of factory workers.

Another distinctive group are the entrepreneurs and those who seek high risk ventures and complete independence from organizational constraints. The small businessman, the rock musician, and the independent consultant share these values. However, even within large organizations, such people can perform critical roles when they take on new projects or ventures which can be handled

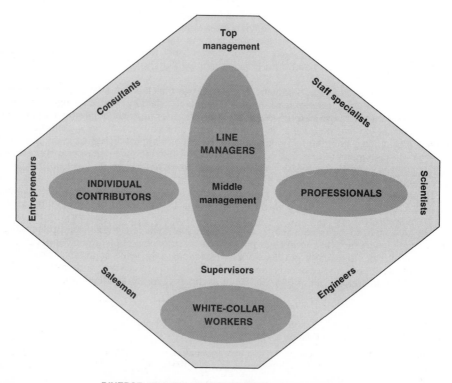

DIVERSE GROUPS IN THE MODERN ORGANIZATION

as though they really were an independent small business requiring the enormous enthusiasm and energy of an executive who feels it is "his" project or business.

The diagram (p. 66) suggests how these various white-collar job categories relate to each other. From one point of view professionals and entrepreneurs are very similar in their "distance" from management—they want independence. However, one group seeks it through economic self-sufficiency and the other through intellectual attainment. The central core of the diagram represents various levels of organizational power. The in-between groups are placed with reference to those with whom they most closely identify. Thus staff specialists perceive themselves as being part management, part professional. Engineers may be partially misplaced since (as we noted earlier) they can be part manager, part worker, and part professional.

With the exception of "white-collar factories" we have noted that all these hold forth the promise of significantly greater through-the-job satisfactions than many of the more traditional jobs associated with manufacturing. But as we have seen in our discussion of professionalization, these opportunities are more than matched by the rising aspirations of job holders. An increasing number of employees identify more strongly with their occupation than with any employer.

Thus, specialization does not inevitably lead to routine, monotony, and job insecurity. Modern industry calls for specialized persons as well as specialized jobs. The former, both highly trained and self-confident, bear little resemblance to the employees conceived by Taylor and his scientific management.

problem 1 • THE LIFE OF THE PROGRAMER

The Western Insurance Company, a large casualty insurance writer, had more than 5,000 employees. Several years ago it had established a separate computerized data-processing section. The center of activity in this department was the computer itself along with the programing group which developed new computer programs to handle the company's payroll, premium and policyholder records, billings, and so forth. In addition, the department stored computer tapes which contained great quantities of data that were relevant to these activities of the firm.

Unlike most of the clerical personnel in the company, programers did not have to punch a time clock, could take their lunch hour whenever they desired, and had no set coffee breaks. In total, there were about 25 in the group, most of them quite young. Almost all had college degrees, although a few were still attending evening classes. Even so, the programers had also been extensively trained by the company for their specialized work and continued to attend regular company training programs as new techniques and problems were introduced into their division.

The supervisor seemed to have the full confidence of the employees since he himself was an expert in their field. The more skilled and experienced programers were often sought out by the supervisor and other members of management for their advice on highly technical problems. Programing was the type of work in which some of the more routine tasks could be assigned to the youngest, least experienced workers (for example, the coding).

There was actually a good deal of work tension in the group. Although schedules could not be precisely set for the completion of a new program, because of all the uncertainties involved, the company was often in a hurry to finish the program so that data could be processed. Thus, there were pressures to meet deadlines. Further, large programs were divided up among a number of programers, and the work of each individual depended on that of his fellows. The computer itself was a source of tension because it demanded perfect work; and discrepancies or mistakes in logic would show up every time.

As a result, the successful testing of an important program was cause for general celebration throughout the group. Furthermore, a good deal of joking and light-heartedness was utilized to lessen the tension when one or more programers were having difficulties. There was an enormous sense of unity in the group since each man could understand exactly the problem another was facing and the tensions he was working under.

As we have seen the department was physically separate from the rest of the organization. While most of the company worked, particularly in the summer, under sweltering conditions, the programers, because of the needs of the computer, worked in refreshing air-conditioning.

Whereas most employees regarded Western Insurance as "a job," the programers thought of themselves as being specialists. They realized that their task was highly important to over-all company operations, and they had a sense of both responsibility and dedication. They were proud of the fact that they had successfully and jointly overcome a number of difficult schedules to develop the crucial programs that were the underpinning of the company's data-processing operations. This was a highly prestigious and strategic accomplishment. They felt the company could not operate without them.

Although pressure was often high and the work difficult, the constant impersonal push associated with factory work was lacking. And although there were set procedures underlying programing, much was left to the programer's skill, judgment, and discretion. There were no unalterable time tables or precisely defined methods that could be laid out for each project. The coordination came out of the closely timed human-relations patterns that the employees evolved as a means of working together.

Many of the programers often voluntarily remained overtime to complete a project; some worked right through a weekend when they were behind or felt that the work was going especially well. Some of the enthusiasm, of course, stemmed from having been instrumental in the establishment of an important new division and getting in, so to speak, "on the ground floor."

Recognition in the group was bestowed on the basis of ability and accomplishment—and a newcomer soon knew where every programer stood in terms of his ability. High-status programers got the desks enclosed by partitions, had both an "out" and an "in" mail basket on their desks, and enjoyed the privilege of keeping their graphic tools rather than having to return them to a central pool. [9]

1. List each of the elements in the job of the programer that appears to contribute to high motivation. Which may change for the worse?

2. How unique or distinctively related to programing are these and which might be found in most white-collar jobs?

3. Which suggest possible job modifications that management can make in other types of technology to achieve comparable motivational effects?

problem 2 • THE NEW WAITER

When I first came to work as a waiter for the Krautter Restaurant, I was sure I would not stay for very long; there seemed to be so much animosity.

Waiters were supposed to get "set ups" for their table (silver and glassware) from the pantry, but by mid-evening there were always shortages. Many waiters would take more than they needed in order to be sure they would not run out, and some would go into the kitchen to get things directly from the dishwashers, although this was against the rules. Many times there were arguments over hoarding of silver, and the dishwashers frequently chased waiters out of their area of the kitchen.

[9] This description was written by one of the programers at Western Insurance.

Busboys cleared tables, but I soon learned that one had to add something extra to the normal share of the tips received by the busboys if one expected to get fast service. Similarly, when customers asked for a special item (for instance, very rare beef) and the restaurant was busy, it was difficult to get the serving chefs to oblige. If you asked twice for something, they took this as an insult to their skill or intelligence, and giving something back to them could cause a mighty uproar. They seemed to have a real "chip on their shoulders."

I noticed that most of the old timers had "paired off" so that one waiter could ask his "buddy" for help when he fell behind. As a newcomer, however, I had difficulty getting anyone to cooperate with me. The result was that I often could not provide the service that customers expected and they would get upset and complain. Often this meant a very low tip and in some cases no tip at all, which is the worst insult a waiter can receive. However, at times I had the feeling that the hostess was sending people to my tables who had a reputation for being poor tippers. This, too, hurt my feelings.

All this was very puzzling to me. Waiting on table had looked so easy. I liked people and was willing to work hard, but this job was much more difficult than I had anticipated.

1. Which of the human-relations problems described here are typical of all service-industry jobs and which represent poor management?

2. What are the potential positive sources of need satisfaction that this new waiter is not describing and that may become more important when his "initiation" period is over.

problem 3 • EN ROUTE

Each newspaper delivery driver was required to make two trips each day with a jumper assigned to his truck as he left the paper's main garage. The stops were outlined on a sheet of paper along with the amount to be delivered at each stop. Drivers knew the time allotment for all routes and would never come back to the plant before that time allotment expired.

One of the most attractive aspects of working as a jumper or a driver was that usually at least six hours of the eight-hour day were spent away from the plant and immediate supervision. Invariably, the men would "pull the route" the quickest way, taking advantage of all short cuts, rearranging the list, and letting the waiting newsboys help them unload. Some did all this merely to prove that they knew routes better than the men who assigned them.

They would finish unloading all papers and then proceed to a place where the truck could be effectively hidden away from the prying eyes of an occasional newspaper executive who might happen by. The driver and jumper would then pass at their leisure an hour or more in a bar, poolroom, or lunchroom, until it was time to return to the plant. [10]

If you worked as a manager in this newspaper, are there changes you would make in these jobs? Justify your "yes" or "no" answer.

[10]We are indebted to a former student, Donald C. Waite III, for this case.

4 WORK GROUPS AND INFORMAL ORGANIZATION

We have seen that social needs are among the most powerful and compelling on-the-job motivations. The people who make up organizations behave as members of groups, and their membership helps shape their work behavior and attitudes toward the organization and the job. Groups may exercise far stronger control over their members than does management. Since management can achieve its ends only through working with people, it must also work through groups. But before considering the problems of supervising groups, we must first understand why groups develop and how they function.

WHY GROUPS ARE FORMED

Companionship

Psychologists may argue about whether man is born with this need or acquires it early in life; yet the need for relationships with other people is one of the strongest and most constant of human drives.

As we have discovered, many jobs call forth only a small fraction of a person's total abilities. To management he may be just another unit of labor or a time-clock number; to his friends on the job he is an individual. To these colleagues an employee can be himself and express his true feelings.

Research indicates employees who have no opportunity for close social contact find their work unsatisfying, and this lack of satisfaction often reflects itself in low production and high turnover and absenteeism. Many years ago Elton Mayo observed that employees in a textile plant who worked at isolated jobs were highly dissatisfied and consistently failed to meet production standards. Staggered rest periods helped a little. But when the company permitted these workers to take rest periods *as a group*, production and satisfaction both increased.[1] Similarly, researchers in hospitals have discovered that maids feel uncomfortable when they work only in the company of high-status personnel (doctors, nurses, etc.) with whom they cannot associate with ease. Several hospitals have found that when three or four maids are grouped together as a team, turnover falls and a much better job is done.

Identification

The difference may be subtle—but people want more than just to have friends, they want to *belong*. One can sense that he is part of a larger organization only by indirection, but the shared experiences of one's immediate colleagues are among the most meaningful and potent sources of job satisfaction.

Extensive studies during World War II indicated that soldiers' willingness to show bravery and make sacrifices was correlated not with loyalty to country or understanding of the war issues, but with loyalty to the immediate group. In other words, men committed acts of heroism that were motivated largely by the desire not to let their buddies down.[2]

Having learned this lesson, the army abandoned its system of bringing individual replacements into combat units and instead began rotating units as a whole.

Other studies indicate that smaller groups tend to enjoy higher morale. Employees working in large departments where everybody does the same job find it hard to form stable social groupings and often have low morale. Many companies with large secretarial pools are putting up waist-high barriers on the office floor to encourage the development of social groups and team spirit.

Understanding from Friends

The daily work routine is rich in opportunities for frustrations and tension. Whether we are harassed by an overbearing customer, an obstreperous typewriter, or a picayune inspector, we all seek a sympathetic ear, preferably from someone who has had similar experiences and can thus understand our troubles. Organizations that lack this outlet sometimes rely on the clumsy and expensive system of employee counseling, in which outsiders "hear out" employee troubles.

[1] Elton Mayo, *The Human Problems of an Industrial Civilization* (Boston: Graduate School of Business Administration, Harvard University, 1946), pp. 42–52. It should be noted that other factors were introduced that contributed to the improved morale and productivity. The work was broken up into self-contained tasks, and the rest periods themselves helped combat fatigue and monotony.

[2] E. A. Shils, "Primary Groups in the American Army," in R. K. Merton and P. F. Lazarsfeld, eds., *Continuities in Social Research: Studies in the Scope and Method of the American Soldier* (New York: Free Press, 1950), pp. 16–39.

Guide to Acceptable Behavior

Whenever we are thrown into a new social situation, we are uncertain about how we are expected to behave. Our work days are filled with ambiguous situations. How much time should I take for a coffee break? Must all copy be shown to the advertising manager? Even where there are established rules, one question remains: Is everybody expected to live by the letter of the law? Most employees don't want to violate the generally accepted "rules of the game"; at the same time they don't want to conform to restrictive rules that everyone else ignores. They want to know the "right" thing to do. The group fills an important need by providing all its members with a kind of "guide to correct behavior"— correct not in terms of any written policies, but in terms of what is actually acceptable.

Help in Solving Work Problems

A new sales clerk may not be sure about how to handle a complicated problem of returning some merchandise. A lab technician may be hesitant about asking his boss to repeat instructions, yet he is afraid that he may ruin the experiment without additional information. In each case the employee turns to his fellow workers for assistance, often preferring this source of help. [3]

The group's solution to a problem may differ from what management expects, and it may even be more efficient. Red tape is eliminated; shortcuts are evolved; informal channels of communication are established to cut across department boundaries. By the same token, work groups may also engage in featherbedding and work-restriction.

Many jobs which appear superficially dull and routine are made more interesting by the individual ingenuity and spontaneity encouraged and protected by the group. Although it may appear to the casual observer that management has defined a rigid series of job requirements, work groups provide a setting which spurs the individual to modify the job situation more to his own liking: for example, extra work breaks can be obtained because employees spell one another; unpleasant tasks assigned to one man can be rotated or shared by group agreement. The key point here is that all of these new activities take initiative and energy. Thus, on jobs which appear to require little of either, an outlet can be found in the informal modifications of the environment that are sanctioned by the group.

Certain jobs can be done by isolated workers, but working as a group often results in higher individual motivation and a faster work pace. Even schools are experimenting successfully with teaming students together rather than allowing each pupil to work alone or wait his turn to recite. Team members provide mutual help which increases the rate of learning.

---

[3] A study of government employees found that they consistently preferred getting assistance from fellow employees to going to the manager, and this ability to provide aid was a source of substantial prestige for the giver. Peter Blau, *Dynamics of Bureaucracy* (Chicago: University of Chicago, 1955).

Obviously, in most cases management must take the responsibility of making specific work assignments, but there are work situations in which a cohesive group can do a better job of fitting individual personalities to the work process and making expedient job assignment changes as new problems arise. The manager's decisions, since they must encompass a longer time period, are often less flexible and timely than the group's. And where the technology imposes extreme interdependence, and precise and instant coordination is required, for example in military fighting crews, the organization depends on the group to control and specify the individual's contribution to the total effort. [4]

Protection for the Membership

Groups help protect their members from outside pressures and authority. As we shall discuss later on, groups often resist management demands for additional output, longer work hours, and higher quality. Most dynamic organizations have a tendency to introduce changes in work methods and routines at a faster rate than the individual can adjust to them. The pace at which these changes are introduced can be materially altered by a determined work group.

Without a sense of group allegiance, individual workers may behave in ways that will injure their fellow workers. The work group often disciplines members who try to earn the supervisor's favor by "squealing" on fellow employees or by turning out too much work, or who fail to help their fellow workers on the job.

A market-analysis office was required to prepare reports for top management. As time passed, the men made these reports increasingly elaborate, using colored graphs, photographic reproductions, and ever-more detailed data. Some of this window-dressing had real value, but most of it was designed to catch the boss' attention. At last, the men realized that they were spending tremendous amounts of uncompensated overtime in their efforts to outdo one another. Finally, they got together and agreed on standards to limit their competitive efforts.

Group members often agree on the level of output each will put forth so that no one member will out-perform the others.

The most common target of group power is the immediate manager. Most managers are quick to recognize that although they have the authority, to make certain decisions would be downright foolhardy (see Chapter 8). The members of the group can express their displeasure by cutting down their work pace, sabotaging the work (discreetly, of course, so that blame will be hard to place), "working to rules," or making their boss look inept to his own superiors.

Multiple Group-Memberships

Rarely do participants in an organization belong to just one group. Take Adam Kopka, a mechanical engineer in the W Company. He has one group of

[4] It has been suggested that turnover of membership in an airline crew can increase the safety hazard since almost instantaneous collaboration is required in emergencies. Such collaboration can only result from working together as a team for a long time. Team members have to be trained as a group as well; it is less useful to train them as individual performers. William Karraker, "Teamwork and Safety in Flight," *Human Organization*, Vol. 17, No. 3 (Fall 1958), pp. 3–8.

friends whom he works with on a development project: two electrical engineers, a technician, and a chemist. In addition, he is identified with all those who report to Alex Fisher, the manager of the Special Projects Department, which includes two other project groups. He also feels close to other mechanical engineers who are scattered through the laboratory. His lunch group and after-hours bowling associates may include still other people. Now each of these groups has a different membership, although there may be a great deal of overlapping. For some purposes one group is the most important to Adam; for others, another. The mere fact that he belongs to several groups, however, may subject him to considerable stress when their respective interests come into conflict.

Suppose, for instance, that the mechanical engineers grow concerned that their jobs and point of view are assuming less significance in the laboratory. The engineers agree among themselves to exert greater pressure for higher mechanical-engineering standards in their design work. As long as Adam is in the company of his fellow mechanical engineers, he feels this is a fine decision. Back in his project group, however, he may find that this is a minority position and he is under pressure to emphasize other project goals. Now he feels under cross pressures; he can't be loyal to both groups.

HOW WORK GROUPS ARE FORMED

When an engineer designs the plans and technology for a new factory, and when an architect designs the office layout, they are also designing the social relations that will prevail within the organization. Management determines where men will work and what opportunities they will have to contact each other during the day. It also determines rates of pay, conditions of work, and the various symbols that are associated with each job. Given these basic elements, a sophisticated observer can predict the social relations that will exist within the organization long before the first employee enters the building.[5] Those in close proximity will begin interacting and friendship and solidarity will follow. Depending upon a variety of status elements that management provides, certain of these groups will begin to "lord it over" those whom they perceive as having lesser prestige.

But management decision-making also omits many factors that become part of the group dynamic. Most jobs are underdefined by management, and there certainly is little consideration given to differences in personality. Thus, at the outset, when a group of new employees is thrown together by layout and work location, there will be a good deal of clumsiness in achieving a harmonious intermeshing of people and jobs.

[5] For two such predictive studies, see A. Zaleznik, C. R. Christensen, and F. J. Roethlisberger, *The Motivation, Productivity and Satisfaction of Workers: A Prediction Study* (Boston: Graduate School of Business Administration, Harvard University, 1958); and Leonard Sayles, *Behavior of Industrial Work Groups* (New York: Wiley, 1958).

Bill, working next to Alice, wants to chatter constantly, while Alice prefers solitude. Henry sends over hand-written documents to Joyce which are undecipherable and expects Joyce to do the final checking of serial numbers. Both Joyce and Bill vie for the attention of the others in determining how the group will decide when to turn the thermostat up or down.

In a few weeks the rough edges and minor interpersonal frictions will have been worn away. Alice will have changed work locations with Joyce. Between them, Bill and Joyce will have convinced Henry to write more carefully and to do his own checking. Bill and Joyce will have worked out some way of dividing up the leadership role so that they don't come into direct conflict.

It is almost like pushing and pulling on the poles and strings controlling a big, amorphous tent in such a way that the tent eventually covers everyone comfortably, both big and small, tall and short. Thus, the crystallization of groups is also a process of filling in the blank spots and changing the inconsistent and incompatible elements that the organization originally provided.

The Group Becomes an Organization

Once these groups have been established, a dynamic, self-generating process occurs. Brought together by the formal organization, employees interact with one another. Increasing interaction builds favorable sentiments toward fellow group-members. In turn, these sentiments become the foundation for an increased variety of activities, many not specified by the job descriptions: special lunch arrangements, trading of job duties, fights with those outside the group, gambling on paycheck numbers. And these increased opportunities for interaction build stronger bonds of identification.[6] Then the group becomes something more than a mere collection of people. It develops a customary way of doing things—a set of stable characteristics that are hard to change. It becomes an *organization* in itself.

The Impact of the Group

What happens when the group becomes an organization within the organization? In effect, it contains in miniature the characteristics of the larger institution of which it is a part: goals, leadership, rules . . . and all the rest.

Every group requires an internal structure. "Structure" here means a set of unique characteristics that determine the members' relationships to one another and to supervision, the standards of conduct that are approved and enforced by the group, its system of rewards and punishments, and its system of communication.

All these aspects of group life are in balance with one another, or, as the social scientist would say, they are in equilibrium: (1) They are all interrelated, (2) a change in any one of them has an immediate effect on all the others, and (3) the members strongly resist changes in any part of this interrelated system.

[6] The best theoretical description of this process is George Homans, *The Human Group* (New York: Harcourt, 1950), pp. 48-155.

Suboptimization: Group Goals

Rather than having a commitment to the goals of the larger institution, groups evolve their own goals reflecting their own special interests. Engineers want a new high-temperature test facility; marketing wants to hire a social psychologist; and machinists want a more generous incentive scheme. These objectives evolve out of the process of working together and socializing. Here group members convince one another that they absolutely need to achieve these goals in order either to help the larger organization to accomplish its objectives or to help themselves achieve "fair" benefits. Obviously within such a "hot house" environment group members can grow very righteous about the fairness of their demands. And the result will be as predictable as when the wicked queen asked, "Mirror, mirror on the wall, who's the fairest of them all?" Group members tell themselves they're the fairest (and most needy) of them all!

The installation of a new computer in the Y Corporation was delayed two years by an interdepartmental struggle over who would control this new equipment. The Finance group claimed that it should be under their jurisdiction but Production and Sales both wanted a new "Computation and Programing" department to be created. Finance felt it would lose prestige if a separate department was created while Production and Sales believed that the new computer would not be as helpful to them if it was placed in an existing department. Thus, a very costly piece of equipment was wasted for two years, from the point of view of the total organization, because of these special interest groupings.

The organization thus pays a price in divisiveness for the help of the group in attaching and holding the individual. This has come to be called the *suboptimization* problem, where small group objectives tend to conflict with or take precedence over the larger organization's goals.

Leadership

Every group has informal leaders—individuals who have a special sort of status which results in their being followed by other members of the group. Someone has to take the initiative in getting people to recognize that there is a common problem to be solved. The leader circulates through the group to urge a united front in dealing with problems, or to devise punishment for an uncooperative fellow member. In the process of developing consensus on what needs to be done, a successful leader is careful to sound out the members and to smooth over internal differences of opinion by personal persuasion and suggested compromises. At times he serves as the group's representative in contacting the supervisor, or the union, or other work groups.

In summary, the leader performs vital functions that contribute to the group's ability to survive in its environment:

1. He initiates action.

2. He facilitates a consensus.

3. He provides a link or liaison with the outside world: managers, other work groups, the union.

There is a tendency to refer to *the* informal leader, as though a single leader could be identified in every group. Actually, unless the group is very small, the functions we have described are usually shared by several active individuals who together comprise the leadership of the group. Although the supervisor is most aware of the employee who contacts him as the group's representative, he must recognize that within the group, in less obvious positions, there may be other equally influential leaders adept in the use of human-relations skill as well as members who seek leadership but are rejected by the group. In fact some studies suggest that every stable group has at least two leaders, a task leader whose function it is to facilitate the group's attainment of its goals, and a human-relations leader who keeps the group from falling apart. The manager needs to be aware of these differences among the more active members of any group to be in a position to influence the group. Often, as we shall see later, it is easier to accomplish change by dealing with the group through its leaders than by attempting to persuade or order individuals to change.

Many studies have been conducted to determine the personality traits that characterize the effective group leader, but none of these studies has been altogether successful. It appears that each group requires a type of leadership suited to its own particular needs. These studies do suggest one important generalization, however: The group leader must live up to the group's idealized conception of what a group member should be.

Some members of a group may aspire to a position of leadership without ever winning group acceptance. Outsiders may assume that these men are more influential than they actually are, when they are outspoken and active in contacting others. It is important to distinguish between the two types of leader, since the false leader rarely represents the true feelings of the group he pretends to lead.

Group Standards of Behavior

The urge to conform to group standards pervades most social life. Boys must be careful not to act too differently if they want to be accepted by the gang, and girls must dress like the other girls in their crowd, even if their parents object. There are group standards in industry as well. Some of these standards exist for the sole purpose of making life more enjoyable for the group members: The accounts receivable department always goes out together for lunch; the maintenance gang spends its breaks playing gin rummy. If you don't do these things—you don't *belong*.

Other customs serve to make the job easier or to heighten the quality of workmanship. Waiters agree among themselves to share all tips equally and to help one another serve and clear tables during rush hours; if a college professor has to miss a class, his colleagues will try to stand in for him; retail clerks "spell" one another so that all the counters will be covered while one clerk is taking a break. All these customs reflect the expectations of group members with respect to one another's behavior.

Probably the most important group standards are those that protect the members of the group against real or imagined outside dangers, particularly from upper management. Production workers may agree on a level of output and exert pressure on those who deviate from it—especially on those who produce more than the accepted "bogey." "Eager beavers" in the classroom are frequently reminded that "C" is the "gentleman's grade."

Group standards of good workmanship and high quality often make management's task easier; for the group, by taking "troublemakers" in hand, reduces the need for management to impose discipline. A standard that a worker can be five minutes late also means that the group will prevent him from abusing this privilege.

A group of white-collar employees was frequently given the afternoon off when the ball team played a home game. Without any prompting from management, the employees agreed among themselves to 'come in an hour early to compensate for the short days. Employees who were unenthusiastic about this informal change in the schedule were pressured into conforming, and management gained the extra work time.

Larger groups, particularly in professional pursuits, often maintain ethical standards designed to further the goals of the over-all membership. Many a professional, whether he is an attorney, an accountant, or a scientist, undoubtedly is tempted to take short cuts that would save him time and money, and he may be absolutely certain that these short cuts would go undetected. And yet the standards that he has "internalized" during years of training and association with a professional group hold him to certain fixed patterns of behavior.

On the other hand such standards may make it harder for management. For example, they may be a handicap to an engineering administrator who finds it difficult to dissuade his staff from "goldplating" their work, setting higher-quality standards than are necessary. Many times groups urge their members to produce less than they might otherwise accomplish, to reject new assignments because they do not approve of the work, and even to coalesce in opposing the appointment of a new supervisor.

Group Attitudes and Values

In addition to group standards of behavior there are also group standards of attitude or values. People who work closely together naturally adopt common points of view that everyone is expected to share. "Most people don't realize how difficult our job really is." "Inspection is trying to make our job rough." "You've got to be a college man to make supervisor."

Many of these standards of attitude are without factual basis, of course. They are simply myths that have risen from the group's fears or wishes. Yet the group's acceptance of them *is* a fact—a fact that management must take into account.

As we have said, the individual becomes wedded to the group as a result of constant association and socializing. Members begin to think and act alike, not only in order to enjoy the fruits of group membership, but because the very process of living together reinforces certain feelings and attitudes in the mind of each member. These attitudes may have existed only weakly before, if at all. Before going to work in XYZ Company, for instance, a recently graduated chemical engineer considered himself only moderately well-trained and useful. After working in a research group composed entirely of chemical engineers, however, he decided that chemical engineers are the most skilled and valuable group in the laboratory. Through constant interaction with a group, certain predispositions are reinforced, or even distorted, in the minds of the members.

Pressures to Conform

Why is it that most people are so anxious to conform to group standards? In the first place, as members of the group, they look at things from the group point of view; they tend to identify with the group and, since it helps meet their needs, they accept its goals. Even those who have misgivings about the validity of the standards go along anyway, because they want to be well regarded by their fellows. Finally, the group has effective means of punishing those who insist on doing things their own way.

Ostracism is one of the most effective forms of group punishment for deviant behavior. A member who overproduces, who fails to share important information, or who is officious may find himself isolated from his fellow workers. In extreme cases, no one will talk to him or even acknowledge his presence. In less extreme cases, the deviant may be excluded from ordinary on-the-job social activities. When he has trouble, no one will come to his aid. Sometimes the group resorts to more direct techniques. Someone may "accidentally" let management know about some of the deviant's mistakes. His equipment or desk may be "adjusted" while he is away.

The punishments devised to enforce group standards are sometimes highly ingenious:

In one office, supervision was lenient in permitting employees to arrive late for work. When one man began to abuse this privilege by arriving very late every day, the group was afraid that management would start to crack down on tardiness. Whenever this employee came in late, his fellow workers applauded him warmly. This gesture served to emphasize their displeasure, and, it was hoped, would encourage management to deal with him on an individual basis.

It would be a mistake to assume that all group members conform. Not only do groups differ in their cohesiveness, in the "hold" they have over their membership, but individuals differ in their response to group pressures. Interesting experiments have been designed to assess the susceptibility of given individuals to group pressure. At one extreme are those who will deny what their own sense organs tell them to be consistent with group opinions. At the other end of the spectrum are those who are unshakable in their own beliefs, even in highly ambiguous situations when the group provides useful information that should cause them to modify their attitudes.

Status Systems

Just as soon as a loose aggregation of individuals develops into a genuine group, subtle status differences begin to arise. Roughly defined, status is a measure of a person's prestige within the group. It is an index to how important he is, to his position in the "pecking order," and, in fact, to how much he is accepted as a leader.

Status is generated by group interaction. It provides a sense of security, and failure to have one's status recognized generates insecurity. Think of the senior who is mistaken for a sophomore, or the professor who is introduced as a student. Moreover, status provides a reassuring guide to the members of the group in their contacts with one another. A man with high status expects and receives greater deference than a man with lower status.

How is status determined? What criteria do groups use in assigning higher standing to Mr. A than to Mr. B? Some status decisions are based on the attitudes and behavior of management; others are entirely the product of the informal organization of the group.

Status often depends on *job title*. Obviously a superintendent is more important than a general foreman and a general foreman outranks a foreman. Engineers outrank technicians, secretaries are "above" stenographers. In almost every organization the job titles are subtly graded according to levels of status, and the status of each individual depends in part on the job he holds.

Pay, of course, is one of the most important determinants of the status according to each job. Higher pay means higher status, and even a difference of a few cents per hour may have a significant effect on a job's status. The new manager may find this bewildering and unreasonable.

Take the case of the checkers and the loaders in one newly unionized plant. The checkers received $2.70 an hour, the loaders $2.60. The checkers insisted that since keeping records involved greater responsibility and required a high-school education, they should receive a pay increase of at least 30 cents. The loaders felt that since their job required considerable skill and physical effort, they should be paid as much as the checkers. The union succeeded in getting 20 cents for the checkers, but won 30 cents for the loaders—and the checkers were more unhappy than ever.

How one is paid also helps to determine status. Some companies have monthly, semi-monthly, and weekly payrolls. Being a salaried man on the monthly payroll may be less convenient, but it carries much more prestige than getting a weekly *wage* (which may be computed on an hourly rather than an annual basis). Sometimes, unskilled casual workers receive their pay by the day.

Work schedules are also a useful index. The hourly-paid man comes in at 7:30, the office clerks at 8:30, and the executives dribble in from 9:00 on—but the executives often work late at night. The freedom to choose one's hours, or being excused from punching the time-clock, is a mark of distinction. (Henry Ford once made all his executives punch the time-clock—thus lowering even further what was already rock-bottom morale.)

In which company lunchroom can you eat? Are tables reserved for you? Can you leave the building for morning coffee? Do you receive a daily copy of the *Wall Street Journal*? The allocation of these *special privileges* follows status lines.

Then there's the question of *where one works*. In the field or in the home office? In the new building where the important operations occur—or over in the "boneyard"? Working near the end of the production line carries more status than working near the beginning—for the finished product is more valuable and the job more responsible. In some offices, the closer a man works to the big boss the more status he enjoys. To be able to say "I work on the fourteenth floor" may be the pinnacle of prestige.

Among the job factors that affect status are: cleanliness, freedom from supervision, amount of training and skill required, and opportunity for promotion. A study of the restaurant industry even revealed substantial differences in the status enjoyed by employees who worked with various vegetables:

At the top were luxury or decorative items such as parsley, chives and celery. At the top of the regular vegetables were green beans. Next came spinach and carrots. Next to the bottom were sweet and white potatoes, and onions were considered the most undesirable of all. . . .

Comments of the workers showed that they valued highly in vegetables lack of odor, crispness, and cleanness in handling, whereas the vegetable that had an odor and that stained the hands or was sloppy to handle was held in low esteem. The low standing of potato peeling is too well known to require comment, but here at least the workers said they preferred potatoes to onions because they did not smell or stain the hands. . . . [7]

Most jobs carry with them certain *symbols* that bestow varying degrees of status. In the army, shoulder insignia denotes officer rank. Paratroop boots, berets, or wings indicate that enlisted men belong to elite outfits (and for this reason, during World War II, many men wore them without authorization).

In industry, too, there are countless widely recognized symbols. Take clothing, for example. Executives (and often, office people) wear coats. Foremen wear white shirts. Hourly-paid workers wear work clothes. The chef's hat and the machinist's apron are more specialized symbols of prestige.

Even though there was no plant rule in one company, only the higher-paid machinists wore white coats; the rest had white aprons. One lower-paid man wore a coat for a week, but social pressure forced him to discard it.

Some time ago, one of the authors conducted a series of interviews in a plant. Wanting to make it clear that he was primarily interested in studying the union and the work force and that he was not connected with management, he was careful to wear T-shirts whenever he was in the plant. One day he made the mistake of coming in with a regular shirt and tie. Several workers asked, "What's wrong—sold out to management?"

Among executives, the *type of office* a man has bears strongly on the amount of status he enjoys. Does he has his own office? How large is it? Does he have his own secretary? Does she have a separate office? What type of desk does he have? Does he have a phone? Or, even better, *two* phones? As one carpet company puts it, "A title on the door rates a Bigelow on the floor."

Status depends on *who one is* as well as what one does—that is, on the attributes or characteristics that the employee brings with him from his community and home. Among the qualities that confer status are education, age, seniority, sex, and ethnic background. A great deal of unrest in contemporary organizations results from the growing resentment against traditional status assignments nurtured by work groups. Covert discrimination against women, Negroes, Mexicans, Jews, Catholics—the list could be a long one—is being increasingly resisted, but the problems don't simply disappear (see Chapter 21).

[7] William F. Whyte, *Human Relations in the Restaurant Industry* (New York: McGraw-Hill, 1948), p. 36.

In many industrial plants, as management moves to correct past discriminatory practices—for example, in promotion of women or blacks—the company often meets resistance from other employees who are unwilling to accord them the higher status.

Individual behavior also seems to have some influence on status. People with pleasant personalities, specialized skills, or leadership traits ordinarily enjoy high status, as do individuals who conform closely to the behavioral standards of the group. The man who just doesn't know "how to behave" is likely to lose status—either in an exclusive club or on the factory floor.

It would be a mistake to conceive of status as merely a complication added by the members of an organization. Status systems facilitate the operation of any organization by:

1. Providing ego rewards and social satisfactions to people. As we have seen in Chapter 1, individuals will work hard and make sacrifices to obtain greater prestige.

2. Providing security and predictability by helping people know where they and others "stand."

3. Making contacts easier, particularly between relative strangers. Insofar as the relative status of each is known, individuals know who should defer or accommodate to whom. Symbols of status (such as insignia) can provide quick and unquestioning response to requests for action.

A progressive mental hospital endeavored to function by eliminating all outward distinctions in dress between patients and staff. The result was chaos; important identifications could not be made, particularly when bizarre behavior was being manifested. In violation of the formal rules of the hospital, the staff began carrying their keys in easy-to-observe places on their persons so that they could distinguish patients from fellow staff members.

Status Inconsistency and Ambiguities

Thus, there are multiple indicators of status—title, pay, type of work performed, symbols, and others. In a sense, each of these is a thermometer which measures a different aspect of status. So long as all these status "thermometers" give approximately the same readings, status is not likely to cause trouble in the organization. But when they read differently, when the various indicators of status give inconsistent or ambiguous measures, personnel unrest and dissatisfaction occur (see table on page 83).

For example, more prestigious group members expect to occupy the more prestigious jobs.[8] The longer-service, better-educated employee in a restaurant

---

[8] George Homans of Harvard University has developed what he calls a "theory of distributive justice": First, there are certain elements that a member brings to his job from his past or puts into his work on the job. Examples are age, seniority, sex, ethnicity, responsibility, and education. Homans calls these "investments." Second, there are other status factors the worker expects to get out of his job. Examples are the material rewards (pay, etc.), the interest of the job, and status itself, the prestige accorded him by his fellows. These Homans called "rewards" or "returns."

According to Homans, when the "investments" of an individual member or of one subgroup are higher than those of another, *distributive justice* requires that their "rewards" should be higher, too. When "distributive justice" does not prevail—*i.e.*, when investment is not equal to reward—Homans predicts there will be trouble on the job. (George Homans, *Social Behavior: Its Elementary Forms*, New York: Harcourt, 1961.)

STATUS CONSISTENCY

Individual Characteristics	Level of Education Attainment	Status of Ethnic-Religious Background	Level of Position
MBA, "WASP," executive	High	High	High
High school graduate, Jewish, supervisor	Medium	Medium	Medium

STATUS INCONSISTENCY

Individual Characteristics	Level of Education Attainment	Status of Ethnic-Religious Background	Level of Position
Ph. D., Black, researcher, scientist	High	Low	Medium
Graduate student, Episcopalian banker's son, working for the summer as a sweeper	High	High	Low

kitchen would resent being assigned to onion-peeling, particularly if junior employees were chopping greens and celery. The violation of a group standard would produce a disturbing status inconsistency. The same problem prevails when an employee is promoted to a department manager's job but is not given the type of office usually assigned to men of that rank.

Often a supervisor is unaware of the subtle distinctions drawn by the group among various jobs, work locations, and types of equipment. Seemingly innocent changes in job assignment or work location may precipitate ill feeling and resentment.

The metal-drawing department had four kinds of machines. Though work on each machine paid the same wages, there were noticeable differences in ease of operation. From the group point of view, it was a promotion to move to a Z machine and a demotion to move to an X machine. This attitude made it much harder for management to transfer men as production needs dictated and led to many grievances, particularly when management tried to move informal leaders to "lower-ranking" jobs.

Thus, the group's conception of what is right and fair is of critical importance in understanding employee reactions to the work situation. We would anticipate that "status anxiety" would show itself where there was status inconsistency. An employee with a prestigious family background and education working on a low-status job would be uncomfortable and likely to demonstrate aggression. The engineer without a college degree working with colleagues who all have a degree would be less sure of himself and might interpret a critical comment by his supervisor as being much stronger than it was intended. Thus, "status anxiety" can mean hypersensitivity, a condition which explains many problems of communications and morale in organizations.

Ambiguous situations in which the status position of an individual or group has not been clearly established can be troublesome. In a sense, group relations are characterized by a "culture lag": Status relationships do not keep up with technological and organizational changes. Newly created groups obviously suffer status anxieties, which are demonstrated through aggressive reaching out for recognition and symbols of prestige (such as office space). Take this example:

The bookkeeping-clerical operations of a large bank always occupied a status position beneath that of the "front office" groups that dealt with the public (for example, in handling loans and deposits). With the addition of expensive, powerful computers the "back room" operations took on added importance. In fact, some of the key computer and systems specialists had to be paid higher salaries than the loan officers and other "front office" personnel.

When these computer people began requesting some of the special perquisites that had been enjoyed in the past only by the high-status officers (such as executive dining room privileges), there was resentment in the latter group. It took several years for top management in the computer area to attain accepted high status.

Cases like the bank example confront management with a dilemma. Management argues that each group should be treated "equally," but if status distinctions are ignored, this policy is bound to generate trouble. The manager's problem is complicated by the fact that "underdog" departments may be struggling to get ahead and raise their relative status in the organizational community. [9]

Though ignoring status distinctions may cause trouble for management, so can excessive status-consciousness. Status systems can be too static for dynamic organizations and thus cannot or should not always be observed. For example, employees whom the group ranks low in status may well be equipped to handle more responsible jobs. And undue emphasis on status may hinder communications between superior and subordinate. [10] (This problem will be discussed further in Chapter 8.)

GROUP COHESIVENESS

Just as work groups are internally differentiated, so there are also significant differences *among* groups. One of the most important is the degree of unity or cohesion within the group. All the elements of group behavior that we have mentioned are influenced by this factor. The more united the group, the greater the likelihood that all members will conform strictly to group standards (in part as a result of heightened pressures to conform) and the greater the likelihood that a small leadership core will represent without challenge the feelings of all members. By definition, cohesive groups are internally consistent in their measures of status and are more likely to act in unison when their expectations are violated, either by management, by one of their own members, or even by another group.

[9] Competition for improvements in working conditions and benefits appear to be most frequent among groups that are more than halfway up the status ladder. Their position is somewhat ambiguous; they are almost the best, but not quite. Members of these groups seem to be carrying a chip on their shoulders. They seize on real or imagined slights that they can protest through the grievance procedure, and never miss a chance to put pressure on both union and management.

[10] *Cf.* Louis Barnes, *Organizational Systems and Engineering Groups* (Boston: Harvard University Graduate School of Business, Division of Research, 1960).

New employees may find it difficult to get accepted by highly cohesive groups, and this can create problems for management endeavoring to fill a vacancy. There may be a "trial period"—not unlike a fraternity initiation—in which the newcomer has to prove himself. He must show that he is willing to live up to the norms of the group, that he has an acceptable personality, and that he accepts his status within the group. Exclusiveness can come as an unpleasant shock to the unprepared employee.

For management, it isn't enough simply to recognize that such differences among groups exist. It also wants to be able to predict the conditions that will produce either united or disunited groups. From our own research and that of others, the following factors emerge as some of the determinants of group cohesion.

Status of the group. Other things equal, people are more likely to feel loyalty toward a high-status group than towards a low-status group. Social climbers, for example, are more careful to conform to the norms of the group to which they aspire than to the norms of a group from which they want to escape. Indeed, there is a kind of circular process at work here: A high-status group elicits greater loyalty from its members, which in turn makes the group even stronger and more likely to gain increased status.

Similarly, employees working at the very bottom of the organization's promotional ladder seldom develop a strong attachment to their work groups. In fact, they sometimes regard themselves as only temporary members of their group.

Size. Small departments are more closely knit than large ones. Loyalty, as we have seen, is a product of constant, face-to-face contacts. Naturally it is easier to have close relationships with all the members of a small group than with all the members of a large one.

Homogeneity. Groups whose members have different interests and backgrounds are often less effective in promoting their own interests than groups whose members are more homogeneous. When, for example, people with sharp differences in rates of pay and job duties work near one another, the resulting informal group is seldom cohesive. This lack of homogeneity may reflect itself in the formation of competing subgroups or cliques, and conflict between these cliques may become so intense that any area of common interest is almost obliterated.

Communications. Groups in which the members can communicate easily with one another are more likely to be cohesive. Internal group unity can be thwarted in noisy steel mills or along assembly lines. Even scattered groups, like maintenance crews, may become tightly knit if the technology of work requires or permits them to interact frequently with one another. We have observed one highly cohesive group whose members never saw each other on the job and yet were sufficiently cohesive to dominate the union and win substantial wage increases: These were electrical utility substation operators whose jobs required them to communicate by phone. Indeed, one of the determinants of group cohesion is the speed with which rumors or other messages can be transmitted through the group, for rumors contribute to the feeling of common identity.

Isolation from other groups.   Physical isolation from other groups of workers tends to build cohesiveness. Employees on night shifts find it difficult to make nonwork friends. Miners among others have demonstrated in countless lengthy strikes that they will stick together more stubbornly than workers who are more socially integrated with the rest of the community. [11]

Where there is no sharp line between one group and another, cohesion is difficult to achieve. For example, on the assembly line, *B* may interact with *A* on his left and *C* on his right, while *D* may interact with *C* on his left and with *E* on his right. Thus, a chain of interactions develops but little group solidarity. [12]

Managerial practices.   The customary behavior of the manager has a direct influence on the degree of cohesion that exists within a group. By fostering competition, and by constantly comparing one employee with another, he may make close relations impossible. On the other hand, he can build solidarity by rewarding cooperative behavior. Among members of management, where there is often sharp competition for promotion and recognition, there is less cohesion than among hourly-paid employees who look to the union for protection against management and have much less expectation of promotion.

Outside pressure.   Group members draw together when they are threatened by a common danger. A group of employees may forget their personal differences and close ranks against a new supervisor who is regarded as a threat to the group. The speed with which long-standing feuds are healed under pressure from a common enemy is sometimes wondrous to behold. Excessive pressure, on the other hand, may eventually weaken the group, particularly if the group loses the battle.

What happens when the pressure is removed? Group solidarity may diminish somewhat, but the cooperative patterns that arose during the time of crisis may well persist. Thus, the supervisor who inadvertently produces a strong anticompany clique may find that it survives long after the original grievances have been eliminated.

Changes in accustomed ways of doing things and sudden cancellations of prerogatives may also draw employees together. Management opposition to their new solidarity may serve only to strengthen the group.

Success.   A group is likely to be stronger and more cohesive if it has engaged successfully in cooperative action in the past. This is the familiar circular pattern: Cohesive groups are more successful and successful groups are

[11] Clark Kerr and Abraham Siegel, "The Interindustry Propensity to Strike—An International Comparison," Arthur Kornhauser, Robert Dubin, and Arthur Ross, eds., *Industrial Conflict* (New York: McGraw-Hill, 1954), pp. 191–193.

[12] Zaleznik *et al., op. cit.*, pp. 120–121.

more cohesive. Success depends on many other factors; for example, whether the group occupies a strategic position in the flow of work.

Naturally, when members find that their own group is not successful in protecting them or winning benefits for them, they are unlikely to abide consistently by group standards. In fact, members may begin to seek other affiliations that offer more security and status. This defection further weakens the group, and it becomes less and less successful.

The Agony and the Ecstasy

Clearly, individuals require group supportiveness and seek to develop group structures where they don't exist. In the process relationships become easier and more regularized, and commitments and identification intensified. All of this can produce gains—but also losses—for the larger organization.

Highly cohesive groups particularly can be unadaptive and intolerant of change. The norms that helped to eliminate interpersonal frictions can also inhibit acceptance of new procedures, equipment, and people. An organization can become frozen in the status system and work standards evolved within the group.

Particularly where the organization faces a dynamic environment and where change is imperative, management may have to consider methods of reducing the "culture lag" introduced by rigid groups. The increasing use of task forces, special projects and teams, and interdepartmental committees all reflect an effort to unfreeze group-based attitudes by intermixing diverse people in "temporary systems."

... the creation of changes in persons involves, essentially, a changing of the cultures in which the person finds himself. Isolation from the ordinary environment tends to shear away the person's or group's preoccupation with, and allegiance to, "things as they are." [13]

The commitment to group goals and values can also produce a strong momentum that can overcome efforts to change direction or reduce the size or status of a given program. Long after technology or markets have changed, the members of a well-entrenched group can keep insisting that their work is as useful and productive as ever. While in the early stages of any new development, such loyalties and enthusiasms might have been most useful; now they are a handicap.

CONCLUSION

In this chapter we have sought to analyze one important component of every organization: the aggregations of employees we have called groups. Although the boundary lines that determine group membership are affected by

13 Matthew Miles, "On Temporary Systems" in M. Miles, ed., *Innovation in Education* (New York: Bureau of Publications, Teachers College, Columbia University, 1964), p. 454. An excellent survey of research on temporary groups.

management's job assignments and supervisory practices, each group develops a momentum of its own. As a result, there is a constant elaboration of informal organization which does not appear on any chart or plan of the company's operations.

People seek membership in existing groups and form new groups for a wide variety of reasons. But at the bottom there always seems to be a search for satisfactions that are not provided directly by the job or by the supervisor—satisfactions such as companionship and protection.

Informal groups have a life of their own; they have customary ways of doing things and of looking at things; they have their own leaders and a minutely defined status hierarchy. These are the stable, enduring components of group life. In other words, informal organization is a *reality* that management can ignore only at its own peril.

Management sometimes tries to evade this reality by emphasizing the organization as a whole, even to the point of trying to break up what it regards as destructive cliques. Yet loyalty to the face-to-face group, to one's fellow workers, is much stronger than loyalty to the larger entity. Indeed, management can develop over-all loyalty only by encouraging teamwork and informal relations. The group may exercise far stronger control over its members than does management itself.

Other managements seek to by-pass the group by telling supervisors they should concentrate on dealing with each employee as an individual. It is certainly true that the supervisor must spend much of his time dealing with the personal needs and idiosyncrasies of his subordinates, yet he is completely missing the realities of the situation if he fails to see that the group is something more than the sum of the individuals concerned.

A good supervisor must understand the social organization with which he works, just as he must be familiar with tools, materials, and technological processes. If he is to avoid making unwitting mistakes, he must know the status structure of the group, its informal leaders, its standards and values. This knowledge will strengthen his tools of leadership immeasurably.

problem 1 • THE FRUSTRATED SALESMEN

Over the years, salesmen in the ABC Company had developed the habit of perusing office records. Management was anxious to discourage this practice for fear that a salesman who had become intimately familiar with company costs and customers might go over to a competitor. The problem was intensified when new offices were constructed separating the salesmen's quarters from those occupied by the office staff. The salesmen were now expected to request necessary information from the office staff over a four-foot counter, and were never to enter the new premises. Here is the way one observer described the salesmen's determination to preserve the practice of looking at the records:

"At first the salesmen would try to think of every conceivable way to 'break the barrier.' It became a matter of pride to see if they could enter the office and walk around. They said they had to speak to the accountant, to consult with the president, to check an order with a clerk, to pick up some clean towels—almost any excuse."

Management reacted by making the rules against infiltration even more rigid. All salesmen were absolutely forbidden to enter the office except for exceptional reasons. This time the reaction was even more severe. The salesmen began to complain about every sort of petty detail in the office. Their favorite complaint was that the switchboard operator was not giving them all their messages. Next they began to find all sorts of fault with their new quarters. The ceiling tile was installed improperly, the phones were on the wrong side of the desk, the lighting was inadequate, the floor was not cleaned regularly. Fights broke out between the salesmen and the sales manager, and the salesmen began to make aggressive remarks about the office force. They became more clannish and selfconscious. [14]

1. Basically, the changes management introduced were modest ones, and they did not "hurt" the salesmen. Why, then, were they exhibiting such aggressive behavior?

2. What group factors were affected by the change?

3. To what extent were these predictable reactions and of what value would such predictions be to supervision?

problem 2 • THE "OLD GIRLS"

Every summer, the Children's and Infants' Department of Hackett's Department Store had been plagued by friction between the regular full-time clerks and the temporary summer replacements.

The regular clerks had developed close social ties in the years they had spent together. They had a common ethnic background and all but two were unmarried or widowed. Whenever possible, they took their coffee and lunch breaks together and often saw each other after work. Further, the department had frequent slack periods when the clerks could sit around and talk together.

The replacements were drawn either from a "flying squad" of full-time employees who were assigned to different departments as need dictated, or from young high-school girls who took the jobs for the summer. Both groups were extremely unhappy at being sent to the Children's Department, and two of the high-schoolers asked for transfers after a short stay. The reasons became quickly evident. The independent work-structure evolved by the regulars had resulted in a department pattern which violated the store rulebook. There was, for example, a definite "pecking order" governing who could take coffee breaks when, and there were frequent unexplained disappearances and early preparations for departure at closing time. The regulars made little effort to assist or advise the newcomers, and criticized them constantly behind their backs. There were seldom more than two part-time girls in the department at any one time, and since they were unlikely to have known each other before, there was little opportunity for them to develop any relationship.

The major difficulties occurred in the area of commission sales. Although the full-timers had an unspoken agreement not to "push hard" for sales achievements, they bitterly resented any commission earned by replacements. They argued that as senior workers they deserved the lion's share of the commission income. The part-timers didn't need it as much as they did, nor had they worked to build up the department. Furthermore, the full-timers thought of themselves as embodying all the sales know-how in the department; the part-timers "didn't know how to sell." Catastrophe occurred when one of the part-timers made a substantial sale and "sabotaged" the commission of one of the regulars. The high-school girl came to the assistant buyer in tears; she had sold a crib when the full-timer in her area was absent from the department, and had been roundly berated for making the sale! She was told that she did not understand the merchandise, and that the other clerk could have made a larger, more profitable sale.

[14] We are grateful to a former student, J. J. Nerenberg, for the outline of this case.

The part-timers were naturally anxious to build up a good sales record. They were motivated to do a good, capable job—either with a view to winning permanent employment, or, in the case of the "flying squad," to convince management that they were worthy of promotion.

As a result, the "old girls" gave either misleading or incorrect information about merchandise or department policies to the part-timers, in order to slow them down and make their job performance less impressive. When a replacement turned to a full-timer for help while serving a customer, the full-timer would frequently take over and consummate the sale. Part-timers were often sent to the stockroom for more goods or were asked to rearrange displays. The full-timers were directing their energies into undermining the part-timers instead of into trying to improve their own sales records. [15]

1. How do you explain the behavior of the full-time clerks in this department?
2. Was management gaining any compensating advantages from the increased cohesiveness of the full-timers?
3. Is it realistic or typical to find employees doing average or below-average work and still viewing themselves as top-notch salesmen, as in this case?
4. What would you do if you were the buyer (department head) in this case?

problem 3 • NEW AGAINST OLD

The old "standard" spinning machines in a large manufacturing plant were operated chiefly by high-seniority men paid on an hourly rate. For nine years the company had been experimenting with new machines that were faster and easier to run. During the experimental period, the machines had been operated by younger men with low seniority. After a two-year tryout, these operators had been put on incentive rates.

To obtain the union's approval, management granted a "loose" rate (one on which it is easy to obtain high earnings). The union readily accepted, believing that unless the long-run productivity of this particular department was improved, the company would move its operation to another plant.

The old spinners, however, who were politically powerful in the union, resented the incentive system. They feared that it would set a precedent for working too fast and perhaps even reduce the amount of work available to them. Eventually this could mean fewer jobs.

Even before the incentive plan was accepted, the men on the old spinners derided the younger men as "damn fools for working themselves to death." In turn, the younger men were resentful of the old spinners' "creamy jobs" and were upset that the seniority system forced them to take what was then less desirable work, with little chance of obtaining jobs on the old machines.

After the incentive plan was put into effect, the men began to compare their paychecks in neighborhood bars. It became obvious that the younger men, on incentive, were earning a great deal more than the older spinners on their hourly rate. Since the two types of machine were located right next to each other, the old spinners were able to watch the ever-increasing production on the other line. With growing anxiety, they saw the differential in earnings grow larger and larger.

Some of the high-seniority spinners considered these jobs as rightfully theirs:

"Why should some young guy that has been in the plant less than a year be taking home 30 dollars more a week than guys like us that have been here more than 15 years? We'll be the laughing stock of the plant."

The two lines had never been friendly, but now they began to exchange angry threats. An informed leader among the top-seniority spinners told the "youngsters":

[15] We are indebted to a former student, Eben W. Keyes, II, for this case.

"You guys better save what you are earning because you're not going to be on these jobs very long. We're coming over to take them. They're ours because we're the oldest men in the department."

His counterpart in the young spinner group answered:

"Don't start anything because if you try to bump us [use the seniority provisions of the contract to take their jobs] we're going to fix those jobs so no one wants them.

"We took these jobs when no one else wanted them. We stuck to them through a two-year trial period when everyone else was laughing at us, and you fellows have no right to come over and bump us off."

Three of the more vocal old-timers submitted a formal grievance to their steward outlining their right to the new job and demanding that the union do something about the threat of the youngsters to use production increases to "ruin the new job."

In the meantime, the incentive workers made good their threat to accelerate production, hoping thereby to discourage the older men from any further interest in the job. Their logic was this: if they worked very hard, management would expect much more production than the older men, who had been "spoiled" by their hourly rates, would be willing to put out.

The older men responded by calling a departmental meeting, as authorized by the union constitution. The younger men boycotted the meeting but learned of the results the next day. They, too, submitted a formal grievance in writing, enunciating their claims to the incentive jobs. [16]

1. Analyze the sources of this conflict in terms of the type of group factors involved.

2. Assess the likelihood that struggles between employee groups will be an important personnel problem in most organizations.

3. Where these intergroup problems exist, to what extent is management also a participant? Why?

[16] This case is adapted from the authors' earlier book, *The Local Union* (New York: Harcourt), pp. 31–33. The case may be more meaningful after you read Chapter 5.

5 UNIONS AND LABOR RELATIONS

More than 18 million Americans belong to unions. This simple fact has profound implications for management. Although we cannot treat union-management relations in depth in this chapter, we will consider why employees join or don't join unions, how unions function within the organization, and their impact on management. First, however, let us note that labor relations do *not* represent as distinct a problem in relationships for the organization as we might first assume.

WHY UNION PROBLEMS ARE NOT UNIQUE

Occupational Associations Are Common

As described in Chapter 4, when employees work together and share common experiences they tend to develop into a group and to acquire goals of their own, which may differ sharply from the goals of the total enterprise. These groups are usually informal (with informal leaders and unwritten objectives). Sometimes, however, where there is a great deal of common occupational identification, employees form occupational associations. There are such associations for purchasing agents, nurses, industrial engineers, and the like. These groups may begin largely for social reasons, then move on to aid members to advance themselves and the status of the occupation. Eventually, some begin to consider bargaining directly with the employer for improved salaries and working conditions. The American Nurses Association (for example) took on aspects of a bona fide union when it decided to engage in collective bargaining.

Bargaining

It is easy to believe that without unions everyone would work together in harmony for common organizational objectives. Actually, bargaining is a way of life in nearly all organizations, even where there are no unions. As we shall see later, supervisors often exchange favors or make "deals" as a means of gaining cooperation from their subordinates. Large organizations include many different specialized groups even within management itself, and these groups negotiate with one another, "trading off" one advantage for another (see Chap. 15). Purchasing bargains with engineering almost as much as labor bargains with management.

Outsiders

The union, interested primarily in its own survival and growth, appears to management as an outside force with goals different from those of the firm. But companies have become accustomed to dealing with many "outsiders": government officials who insist upon special accounting or quality control procedures, outside contractors who work inside firms, and countless others who penetrate an organization's boundaries.

Differing Perceptions

Management often argues that there are no real conflicts of interest between workers and the company. Both stand to gain if profits and productivity improve. This is often true, but the significant point is that employees believe that there is a conflict of interest, say, between profits and wages. Although their overall interests may not always be in conflict, workers and management tend to see problems from a different vantage point. To the manager, a new machine may represent a saving in labor cost, which will strengthen the company, but to the employee it will appear as a threat to his job.

It is now a well-established uniformity of organizational behavior that wherever groups of people occupy widely differing positions in a hierarchy (vertically arranged organization structure) and carry out different activities, they are bound to see their interests as being different. [1]

Conflict

At one time it was believed that a harmonious consensus within an organization was normal and that only unions introduced intergroup conflict. Yet given

[1] William F. Whyte, "Models for Building and Changing Organizations," *Human Organization*, Vol. 26 (Spring 1967), p. 25.

the inevitable differences among groups within an organization (between production and sales, for example), conflict and differing objectives permeate modern organizations. Of course, these internal conflicts do not result in the actual breaks in relationship that occur in strikes, but they are similarly obstructive to organizational effectiveness. (Under many circumstances, conflict can be healthy, too, as we shall see.)

Appeals

Many supervisors fear that with the advent of the union all their time will be consumed handling grievances and that their power will be slowly whittled away. Yet many nonunion companies have established regular procedures that permit subordinates to appeal to a higher level when they feel that their boss is treating them unfairly. In fact, as we shall see in Chapter 14, some progressive companies pride themselves on their "open door" policies, which formalize the right of an employee to carry problems over his boss's head.

THE COURSE OF UNION DEVELOPMENT

Scattered efforts to form trade unions were made early in the nineteenth century; and by the close of the century, the American Federation of Labor was well established in a number of skilled crafts. Yet until the 1930's union membership outside these crafts was highly unstable. Though unskilled workers sometimes joined unions in times of prosperity, they abandoned them when hard times returned. This pattern began to change drastically during the Great Depression of the 1930's, when a relatively large, permanent trade-union membership emerged not only in the traditional crafts where workers had found it easier to organize, but also in mass-production industry.

Certain changes in the American economic and political environment coincided with this growth.

1. The Depression cost American business a great deal in prestige and employee confidence. Unions, on the other hand, gained prestige. Many observers regarded them as a healthy check on business power (a check that might help to moderate the business cycle). Gradually, unions began to escape the stigma of being somehow un-American.

2. Government at the state and federal levels, which had traditionally handicapped union organization (for example, by unfavorable court decisions and the use of injunctions), became more favorably disposed to labor. New legislation like the Wagner Act (1935) actively encouraged union organization.

3. A substantial segment of the working population began to accept as permanent the role of wage earner, realizing that it was not just a temporary stop on the road to owning one's own business. As we observed in Chapter 1, the American dream of moving constantly along to

better jobs had lost its luster for some and was replaced by a desire to protect the present situation. With this acceptance came an interest in improving one's lot as an employee through union membership.

4. The decline in immigration and the rise in educational standards tended to make our population more homogeneous. Relatively high standards of education raised the level of employee aspirations. No longer satisfied with just having a job, they demanded more and more from their jobs. And they regarded the union as a valuable ally in getting what they wanted.

5. Communities more readily accepted unions, and their participation in civic and governmental affairs increased union prestige. Membership became even more attractive as unions were given credit for the dramatic rise in wages, which occurred during and after World War II.

UNION MEMBERSHIP IN THE UNITED STATES SINCE 1900

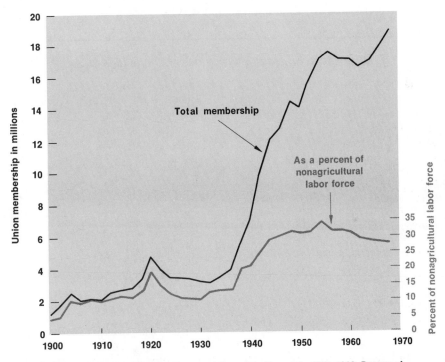

Sources: 1900–1952, National Bureau of Economic Research: 1952–1968, Bureau of Labor Statistics. Note: data from these two sources disagree to some extent.

Slowdown in growth

After World War II, union growth began to slow down. As indicated by the graph above, membership (in both absolute and relative terms) reached its peak in the mid-1950's and then began to decline. A number of factors explain this phenomenon.

By 1950, most easily organized employees had already been unionized. Union strength was concentrated in manufacturing, mining, transportation, and public utilities, and in these industries 80 per cent to 90 per cent of the blue-collar workers were already organized. The bulk of the unorganized factory workers were in difficult-to-organize areas such as small towns or the South, or they were employed by small companies or by companies such as Eastman Kodak or IBM which had the reputation for paying liberal salaries and fringe benefits.

Equally significant, as the table of manpower statistics reveals, the proportion of workers in easy-to-organize industries began to decline. From 1953 to the early 1960's, the economy slowed down while technological change occurred at a rapid rate. Manufacturing employment as a whole fell off. Although white-collar (nonproduction) employment within manufacturing increased quite sharply, blue-collar employment declined even more rapidly. Similar declines occurred in mining, transportation, and utility employment, leaving construction as the only expanding highly unionized industry.

SELECTED MANPOWER STATISTICS, 1953–1970 (in millions)

	1953	1961	1970	Increase 1953–1970
Total labor force	66.6	73.0	85.9	19.3
Military	3.5	2.6	3.2	−.3
Agriculture	6.2	5.2	3.5	−2.7
Unemployed	1.8	4.7	4.1	2.3
Nonagriculture employees	54.9	60.5	75.2	20.3
Manufacturing	17.5	16.3	19.4	1.9
Production workers*	(14.0)	(12.1)	(14.1)	(.1)
Nonproduction workers	(3.5)	(4.2)	(5.3)	(1.8)
Mining*	.9	.7	.6	−.3
Transportation and utilities*	4.3	3.9	4.5	.2
Contract construction*	2.6	2.8	3.3	.7
Wholesale and retail trade	10.2	11.4	15.0	4.8
Finance, insurance, and real estate	2.1	2.7	3.7	1.6
Services	5.9	7.7	11.6	5.7
Government	6.6	8.6	12.6	6.0

*Largely unionized sectors.

Source: Bureau of Labor Statistics.

The major growth in employment in recent years has been in industries with a predominance of white-collar work—trade, finance, insurance, services, government, and others—but for several reasons, white-collar workers are difficult to organize. Since union membership is associated with blue-collar work, many white-collar workers fear that joining a union would lower their social status. Many of these employees work in close proximity to management and hope to move into management positions themselves. Further, the fact that they are separated in small uncohesive groups makes it difficult for them to develop the kind of consensus needed for union organization.[2] Professional and technical employees tend to believe that they can get along on their own and that their individual chances for advancement should not be tied to the status of the whole group.

The slowdown in union growth (particularly in the late 1950's) can be attributed also to the exposure of corruption in a small number of unions. As a result of such disclosures, unions lost some of their reputation as crusaders for improvements in the lot of the comman man. On the other hand, management had done much to eliminate the tyrannical supervision that often contributed to unionization in the 1930's.

Another barrier to union growth was the passage of two laws, the Taft-Hartley Act in 1947 and the Landrum-Griffin Act in 1959. Though neither had the disastrous effect on unions that their opponents feared, both made unions' organizing campaigns more difficult, especially through restricting the use of a traditional organizing weapon, the secondary boycott.

Recent growth

Since 1965, union membership has begun to turn up again, at least in absolute numbers. Here, too, a number of factors seem to be at play.

1. Growing prosperity meant increased employment in the easily organized industries, especially manufacturing.

2. There have been some slight breakthroughs in two generally unorganized sectors. Led by Cesar Chavez, the Farm Workers have won some notable organizing victories in California. And a small amount of progress has been made in organizing traditionally white-collar industries, such as banks (and even stock brokers' offices). But as of 1970, the percentage of white-collar workers organized in private business was no higher than it was in the mid-1950's.

3. The big change was in the government sector. From 1956 to 1968 membership in government employee unions more than doubled: from 915,000 to 2,155,000. And this figure does not include independent associations (such as the million-member National Education Association) which in recent years have gone on strike, negotiated contracts, and differed from real unions only in name.

The growth of government unions is due to a number of interrelated factors: the very rapid increase in government employment generally (see table);

[2] Interestingly, sometimes engineers join unions when they work closely together in large undifferentiated groups, as in some huge aircraft and electronics plants.

a series of executive orders by Presidents Kennedy and Nixon, which made union organizing and bargaining easier at the federal level; another series of similar laws in many states; a number of successful strikes (particularly in New York City) which won unionized government employees salary increases far larger than they had been offered prior to the strikes; and the civil rights movement, which brought black workers into government unions, especially in the South (it was during an organizing campaign that Martin Luther King was murdered).

WHY EMPLOYEES JOIN UNIONS

Almost every union member is also an employee and has joined his union because he hopes it will better his relationship with his employer. Why does he feel this move is necessary? Many managers have two oversimplified explanations of why workers join unions: The first is that the company has been foolish or selfish, or both. By providing unsatisfactory working conditions and wages, by permitting supervisors to play favorites, management has actually encouraged its employees to seek out a union. Such conditions undoubtedly stimulate the growth of unions. But what about the many well-managed organizations that have been unionized? What has motivated the workers of these companies to join unions?

Here is where the second explanation comes into play. Unionization, it says, must be the result of outside agitators, rabble-rousers, and radicals, who by lies and deceit stir up an otherwise satisfied work force. This reason also is an oversimplification. To be sure, professional organizers from the outside have a great deal to do with bringing workers into the union fold. And they often make use of a small number of strategically located insiders who are willing to take on the task of agitating for the new union. But this is only a small part of the total explanation. Below we have summarized the opinions of many careful observers of union organization.

Desire for Better Economic and Working Conditions

Most people want to increase their income—even in top-paying companies. Seldom do we find a man who is convinced that the economic returns and physical satisfactions provided by his job are perfect and quite beyond improvement. In the United States, the greatest growth period of unions coincided with a rapidly rising income level for workers. Whether the unions have really obtained higher wages and better pension, insurance, and other benefits for their members, or whether these would have come anyway through normal economic and social processes, is not the point. The point is that an impressive number of employees *believe* that unions are responsible for improving their economic lot. Certainly they realize that the bargaining power of the individual employee is not very great. He can accept the wage or salary the company offers, or he can look for a job elsewhere. With other employees in a union, however, his economic clout is considerably greater.

Desire for Control over Benefits

In our society, many employees are unhappy when they are completely dependent on someone else for the satisfaction of their needs. Even when that "someone else" is very good, as many managements have been, and provides good wages, steady employment, and desirable working conditions, workers tend to be uneasy when they have no power to control the benefits received. In fact, management makes matters worse by emphasizing how much it has "given" its employees (that is, benefits provided at the discretion of the company, not offered because they *had* to be). In telling people that they should be thankful for what has been voluntarily given them, a company is also saying that what it has given can also be taken away.

Even in organizations where employees have always been treated with complete fairness and justice, stories circulate that John Jones over in Department 16 has been severely penalized for something he didn't do because a supervisor "had it in for him." In any situation where we lack the power to control what happens to us, we are more than ready to believe these "atrocity" stories and think, "Next time that could happen to us." The truth or falsity of the rumor may be unimportant.

In small companies, management is often able to maintain close relations with its employees; the company president may even know each man by name. But as organizations grow bigger, such communications tend to break down. In a large company, where top management is several levels removed from the individual employee, the individual's sense of dependency and lack of control over what happens to him can be very great.

Desire To Be Heard

Many an employee feels that, as far as his company is concerned, he is nothing more than a time-clock number. Though many would not want the responsibility of management, they would like greater opportunity to express themselves. In part, this is just the desire to complain when hurt. But more importantly, as individuals we all have a need to express our point of view—not just to "get more" for ourselves, but to enjoy the feeling of being a whole person instead of a pair of hired hands.

Despite the existence of an appeals procedure, most employees feel that without a union they have no means of safely going over the head of their boss with a problem. After all, they must rely on the boss to do many things for them. There are a hundred and one ways in which a supervisor can make their working life unpleasant and unrewarding. Discretion is frequently the better part of valor; when the supervisor says "No," most employees accept it as final.

This feeling of helplessness is particularly acute when the immediate supervisor is unsympathetic to their demands, either because he has no decision-making authority of his own (a point that will become clearer when we discuss communications problems in Chapter 14), or because he has a natural unwillingness to reverse his own decisions. If only they can gain access to higher levels in the organization, employees reason, they may find someone with the authority to satisfy their requests.

The union promises a worker an opportunity to protest inequities, to believe that if something goes wrong he will have a chance to be heard. The union offers a direct road to participate, for its leaders have access to the top decision-making levels of the organization.

The Union Shop

Many employees, of course, do not have a choice about joining a union. Approximately nine-tenths of unionized blue-collar workers labor under a union shop agreement; that is, they are required to maintain their union membership in their present employment.

Precipitating Causes

We have been describing some of the underlying reasons for the growth of unions. But how can we explain why a union is organized in a particular company at a specific time? Here are some typical precipitating causes:

1. A change in the top management of the plant. Employees fear that the new management will be less friendly and will not preserve the favorable conditions they are used to.

2. Specific problems arising from incentive-payment systems, particularly new standards or new work assignments.

3. The cutting off of promotional ladders—for example, requiring that all new supervisors have college degrees.

4. Sudden cutbacks and layoffs.

LEGAL FRAMEWORK

In the United States the basic labor law is the National Labor Relations Act, which covers most large companies (specifically those engaged in interstate commerce). The NLRA is based on the Wagner Act (passed in 1935), but it has been modified by the Taft-Hartley Act (1947) and the Landrum-Griffin Act (1959). Most provisions of this Act are administered by the National Labor Relations Board (NLRB).

The NLRB has two main functions: In the first place it administers the procedure by which unions become certified as *collective bargaining agents*. How does this procedure work? Suppose a union seeks to unionize a nonunion plant. Once it begins to get some support from the workers, it asks them to sign cards that authorize it to represent them in negotiations with the employer. As soon as 30 per cent of the employees sign these cards, the union is free to petition the NLRB to hold a *representation election*. The NLRB must then determine whether the group of employees whom the union wishes to represent is "appropriate" to form a bargaining unit. After that determination is made, the board holds a secret-ballot election in which employees can choose among the union which filed the petition, any other "intervening" union that has the support of 10 per cent of the employees, and no union. If a union wins this election, it is certified as the collective bargaining agent, and it now has the legal right to bargain with the employer, on behalf of the employees, for wages, hours, and terms and conditions of employment.

The NLRB's second major function relates to the prevention of *unfair labor practices* by either labor or management. For example, the act prohibits management from refusing to bargain with certified unions, from discriminating against employees because of union activity, or from establishing company-dominated unions. Similar provisions pertain to unions. Perhaps the most important of these outlaws the secondary boycott (a strike called against one employer to force it to cease doing business with another employer).

The act also provides for the Federal Mediation and Conciliation Service, a neutral middleman to help labor and management resolve their disputes (acting in much the same way as a marriage counselor trying to settle family disputes). Finally, the act permits the President to obtain a court injunction requiring an 80-day "cooling-off" period before a strike that would affect the national health and safety.

It should be emphasized that the law only sets the ground rules for bargaining. The terms of the contract which arises from bargaining are completely up to the parties. If the parties cannot agree, the union is free to go on strike, or the employer may engage in a lockout (that is, he can shut his doors and refuse to provide employment).

INTERNAL ORGANIZATION OF THE UNION

The Local Union

Now let us look at the rather complex structure of the unions themselves. Some employees are organized on the basis of the company or plant in which they work—for example, all the blue-collar employees of the Carter Chemical Company's Atlanta plant are eligible to join a local industrial union whose membership is restricted to Carter's employees. Frequently the white-collar clerical employees of such a company, or its most highly skilled maintenance employees, may belong to separate local unions. Industries that employ several clearly defined trades are usually not organized by unions on a plant or company basis. Rather, all employees in a given geographic area, usually a community, who have the qualifications to practice the trade, are eligible for membership in a local craft union—for example, all unionized bricklayers in Rochester, New York, belong to the same local, regardless of which employer they work for. Community-wide locals are also found where the employer unit is relatively small (for example, all the dry-cleaning plant employees in town might belong to a single local of the Teamsters), or where employees are likely to shift from one employer to another (for example, in the needle trades).

Why do we emphasize this difference between unions that are organized on the basis of an employer unit and unions that are organized on the basis of a geographic area? Because the governments of these two types of local union are quite different. Where the membership is derived from many different companies in a clearly defined geographical area, the union is likely to vest a great deal of authority in an elected business agent, who works full time on the negotiation of contracts, grievance problems, and the protection of the union's job jurisdiction.[3] Since these agents service many widely dispersed members who work for a variety of employers, they are very powerful, and management must be willing to deal regularly with them. Unfortunately, most of the corruption mentioned above has arisen in this type of union, and because of the growth of so-called service industries in the United States, this type is expanding at the expense of unions organized by employer units.

By contrast, in unions organized on a company or plant basis, authority usually is dispersed among a number of leaders, many of whom continue to work at their regular jobs and handle union business on a released time basis.

The Local Leadership

The local union has two types of officer: *Executive-board members* handle the union's internal business—finances, administration of election procedures, appointment of committee members, social functions, and so forth.[4] *Grievance officials* handle relationships with management—the union's collective-bargaining business. Grievance officials have a variety of titles, depending on the union and their rank—business agents, committeemen, stewards, grievancemen, chief stewards, and so forth. Most of these officials continue to work for the company in their regular jobs while they are serving in their union capacity, and the company often pays for the time they spend handling employee grievances. Larger and wealthier locals, however, may engage full-time elected officials to handle their grievances and negotiations.

The Membership

The most active union members—the elected officers—are employees who have more energy and ambition than they can expend on their jobs. Essentially discontented and anxious to get ahead, they often turn to the union when their drives are frustrated elsewhere.[5] Many of these men may also be excellent

---

[3] Unions organized on the basis of an employer unit are usually not active in getting jobs for members, nor are they concerned with making sure that no job in the community for which one of their members is qualified is filled by a nonmember.

[4] In some unions, the executive board is involved at some stage of the grievance procedure as well.

[5] Leonard Sayles and George Strauss, *The Local Union* (New York: Harcourt, 1967), pp. 56–70.

workers, and management frequently finds that leadership in the union may provide a clue to supervisory ability.

This active group, together with members who do not hold office but who attend union meetings and participate in the local's political life, is likely to include no more than 5 per cent of the membership, and frequently a good bit less. Most of the members prefer to "let George do it" when it comes to taking an active role. They pay their dues as they would pay premiums on an insurance policy, and they have little to do with organization except when a grievance arises or when a strike takes place.

Few members seem to feel that union membership conflicts with their obligation to the company that provides them with jobs and wages. Indeed, many workers feel what has been called "dual loyalty" to both company and union; for them the union is a way of "making the company better." Of course, unions also attract members with deep-seated hostility toward management, workers who seek to embarrass their supervisors through union activity. Such persons are likely to be most active in the original organization of the union. Organizing a new union typically requires stronger emotions than accepting it after the union has become established. However, many of the "firebrands" who helped bring in the industrial unions during the 1930's and 1940's are nearing or have reached retirement. Newer members may feel less commitment to an organization they did not help or observe get started.

The International Union

Most local unions are affiliated with an international union that provides them with certain services.[6] You are probably familiar with the names of many of these organizations: The Steelworkers, the Autoworkers, and the Teamsters,[7] (each with over a million members). Primarily, the internationals deal with union problems that are out of reach of the local, such as company-wide bargaining problems, government relations, and organizing the unorganized.

The international union usually hires "international representatives" to help the local union get established and to present local bargaining problems directly to management. These officials often participate in the later stages of the grievance procedure (which is described in the next section). Their most important job, however, is usually the handling of contract negotiations. The decision-making body for the international union is the convention, which is held once every year or two, or even more infrequently.

A large number of American international unions have joined together in the AFL-CIO, which serves as a general trade union organization.[8] It has almost no direct power over collective-bargaining matters, for most of its activities

---

[6] Many a national organization is usually referred to as an "international" union in recognition of the fact that it may have members in Canada.

[7] These are not the formal names of these international unions, but the unions are commonly referred to in this fashion.

[8] However, several important international unions are not included in the AFL-CIO. As of 1971 this group included the West Coast Longshoremen, the Teamsters, and the Mineworkers, and the Autoworkers.

concern problems of the labor movement and relationships with government. There are other units in the union movement, such as city councils and state federations, which are organized to represent union interests in dealing with various levels of local and state government.[9] The international union, however, is by far the strongest unit.

The Union as a Political Body

If management is to deal with a union successfully, it must recognize that the union is a *political* body. Most union officials—both at the local and international levels—are elected, and many union decisions—particularly at the local level—are made by direct vote of the membership. Therefore, decisions do not necessarily flow from top down as they do in management; officers cannot guarantee that the members will do as they are told, particularly in democratic unions, and members can always engage in wildcat strikes. Consequently, in order to win elections, officers must always win something in their negotiations with management. For this reason, they sometimes go through the motions of pressing grievances in which they do not believe.

Still, there is widespread apathy among union members—for example, the local union meeting, which is the major decision-making forum for the local, is usually very poorly attended. And yet, in spite of this apathy, management must recognize that what the union leaders do must at least appear to the members as satisfying their needs. Failure to recognize this fact may lead to a serious miscalculation of the behavior of union leaders. Whereas a top-management official in a negotiation may be able to make firm decisions on his own, a union negotiator may have to get membership approval before he can make a binding commitment. Unions are certainly not models of pure democracy, but in most unions an aroused membership can turn out its leadership in favor of another group. Discontent of this sort contributed to the defeat, in 1965, of David McDonald and James Carey, long-time presidents of the Steelworkers and the International Union of Electrical Workers, respectively. Indeed a continuing problem all through the 1960's was the tendency of rank-and-file union members to vote not to ratify contracts that had been negotiated by their leadership.

Intergroup Conflicts

An important component of the political life of the union is struggle *between* groups within the rank and file: Each wants improved benefits for itself and each wants to protect itself from the encroachments of other groups. Members of each group feel the union is theirs. It is easy to be misled into thinking that the local union is a single, cohesive unit with a leadership that can speak for all members. But look at the kinds of issues on which there can be coercive comparisons leading to internal disagreement:

[9] In sharp contrast to unions in most other countries—where unions are frequently highly active in politics and even dominate political parties—unions in the United States and Canada have only a mild interest in politics and seek to obtain their objectives primarily through economic means.

Younger employees want their leaders to get higher wages, while the older employees want negotiating efforts to go into improving pensions.

Higher-paid workers want "percentage" wage increases, and lower-paid workers want the same hourly increase to go to everyone "across the board." [10]

Management adds a new finishing process. Workers in Department 35 claim jurisdiction over this work while the employees in Final Assembly insist that the new work ought to become part of their department.

Such conflicts are not surprising when we reflect on the degree to which job satisfactions or dissatisfactions are felt in relative, not absolute terms (see Chapter 1). Thus, the leadership must balance off the claims of one group against those of another in the light of their relative political strength as well as the real equities. For example, some groups, if they don't get their way, will be able to defeat the officers at the next election or even to mount an illegal wildcat strike that will embarrass the officials in their dealings with management. Other groups put up no resistance if they lose their demands.

Varieties of Work-Group Pressure

Work groups seem to react to problems in different ways, depending on the kinds of jobs they do. At least four varieties of groups may be identified:

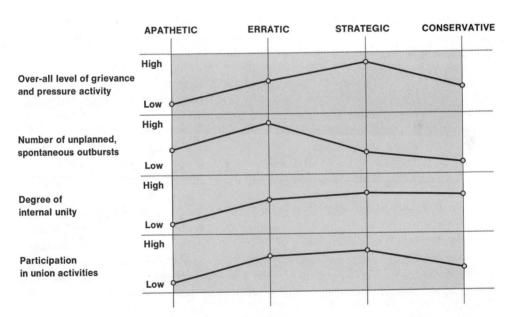

From Leonard Sayles, *Behavior of Industrial Work Groups* (New York: Wiley, 1958), p. 39.

SUMMARY OF WORK-GROUP DIFFERENCES

[10] For example, with a 5 per cent increase, employees earning $2.00 per hour would get 10¢ and those earning $3.00 per hour would get a 15¢ increase.

Apathetic Groups are least likely to pressure the union into fighting for them. They are often made up of men with low-status, relatively unskilled jobs who lack internal cohesion and leadership.

Erratic Groups at times exhibit very bellicose behavior, even walking off the job. Other times, with just as important problems facing them, they seem to be uninterested in any union actions on their behalf. These groups often include assembly line and crew workers, where there is a great deal of interdependence in work operations.

Strategic Groups are the most calculating and self-conscious groups within the rank and file and frequently exert pressure for more benefits for themselves. They are never satisfied, always feel "relative deprivation" and know how to exert effective political pressure on the union leadership. The most typical workers in such groups are individual machine operators who work independently, not in crews. They also hold jobs near, but not at, the top of the plant's status ladder.

Conservative Groups are seemingly content with their high-status position. These groups only occasionally feel the need to pressure the union to do battle for them. When they are dissatisfied, they are restrained and very rational in their approach. Often, maintenance workers and other skilled craftsmen demonstrate this pattern.

UNION-MANAGEMENT RELATIONS

Contract bargaining and grievance handling are the two main aspects of union-management relations.

The contract, the basic document that regulates relations between the parties, generally runs for at least a year; and in recent years, two- or three-year contracts have become common. Some contracts cover only a single plant or even a small group of workers in that plant. Others may cover a multi-plant company, such as General Motors (when this happens, "supplemental agreements" are often negotiated on a plant-by-plant basis to deal with special local problems). Where craft unions prevail, as in the construction industry, the contract typically covers all the workers within a particular craft and a specific geographical area (such as all the electricians in Hinsdale County). In a few instances, notably coal mines and railroads, essentially a single contract covers the industry throughout the country.

The tendency in recent years has been to broaden the area of bargaining. Small employers have banded together in employers associations to form a united front against their common union or to provide "strike insurance," as the airlines did, to protect a company that may be singled out for union pressure. And because one company may deal with a number of unions, as General Electric does, "coalition bargaining" has become increasingly common; that is, the various unions cooperate closely with each other during the bargaining period.

Regardless of how it is reached, the contract is usually a lengthy document (particularly when it includes special agreements on topics such as fringe benefits). The contract deals with not only wages, hours, and fringe benefits, but also with promotions, layoffs, discipline, and transfers (all subjects to be discussed later in this book).

It should be emphasized that even with a union, management continues to make most of the personnel decisions: who shall be hired, disciplined, promoted, given a pay increase, have his working conditions improved, and so forth. Very few decisions are made jointly. But *after* a manager takes action, the union can challenge the decision and file a grievance claiming that management is acting in violation of the contract or of past practice (which becomes the equivalent of a contract). Thus the grievance procedure is, in effect, a judicial process that determines the rights of the parties.

The typical grievance procedure moves in steps; at each the problem is discussed by union and management people on their respective levels. For example, the first step may involve the foreman and the steward, the second the superintendent and the chief steward, and so on. Most contracts provide that if no agreement is reached at these lower steps, the matter will be referred to an impartial third-party arbitrator (often a lawyer or a professor) who is selected jointly by the parties. After the arbitrator holds a hearing in which both sides present their case, he writes a decision based on his interpretation of the contract. Normally, his decision is final. [11]

John Jones Has a Grievance

Let us examine a hypothetical case to illustrate the operation of the grievance procedure and the ramifications of what may appear to be a simple grievance. Notice especially the number of people who are involved and their diverse points of view. [12]

The employee's problem. John Jones works as a laboratory assistant in the animal experimentation station of a large drug company. His work involves feeding, washing, and weighing animals, building cages, and occasionally cleaning them. Recently, Jones has noticed that he is required to spend much more time cleaning cages than are the other assistants. Since this is the least pleasant and lowest-status of all his tasks, he thinks it is unfair that he should have to do so much of it.

The supervisor's reaction. When Jones discusses his problem with the supervisor, Brown, he is told that job assignments are arranged in order to use the work force most efficiently. All assistants are hired with the understanding that they will be doing one or all of the tasks noted above. Brown feels that some of the other men are more skilled in handling the animals and doing minor

[11] In 1969, General Motors and the United Automobile Workers processed a total of 256,000 grievances, 2,500 of which were appealed to arbitration. The General Motors situation may be more prone to grievances than most, however.

[12] This case does not describe the exact procedure by which every employee complaint would be handled. The number of steps and the union and management personnel who become involved at each step vary greatly from one labor contract to another. But this case is typical. Many "grievances," however, do not get written down and processed through a formal procedure; they are handled verbally in the regular, day-to-day contracts of union and management officials.

construction work. So it seems a better use of manpower to have Jones spend more of his time cleaning cages.

Enter the union. Unsatisfied by Brown's answer, Jones considers calling in the union for help. He hesitates for a while, for fear that such a step may antagonize his supervisor and win him the reputation of troublemaker. Then he decides that, after all, help is what he pays dues for. So Jones talks to the union steward for the laboratory, who happens to work in an adjacent building. The steward discusses the problem with Brown and reports back to Jones the next day:

"Brown refuses to do anything. He says it's his job to make decisions like this one, and he is not trying to discriminate against you. I'm not satisfied with his answer. I'll see the chief steward tonight at the union meeting and see what he says."

Note what has happened: The steward has tried unsuccessfully to represent the worker and now has turned the case over to a higher level in the union, which can reach higher management.

The union's reaction. The steward goes to the chief steward and describes the case. Here is the chief steward's reaction:

"This is not a simple case; we have to be careful. In the first place we have to consider the reaction of the other men in the department. Jones is the newest employee; they may get pretty sore if more of this cleaning work is thrown at them. Secondly, the whole thing may backfire. Our present contract is weak on this point. There is actually nothing to prevent the company from changing a man's work, and if they start giving him a lot of the dirty jobs if they want to be mean about it, they might be able to justify paying him less money since his work may now be less skilled than before. Our only chance to win would be if we could show that the supervisor was doing this to Jones because he didn't like him. That would be covered by Clause 14. Discuss it with Jones, and if he has some evidence on this, get him to sign a grievance."

Note the implication behind this reaction: The union is not only the representative of the individual worker. It also has to think of its total membership. Actually, as you have already learned, many grievances and worker demands are directed against other employees, not against management. The union depends on the support of its total membership; dissatisfied members may succeed in ejecting officers or in overthrowing the union itself. Clearly, the union must consider the over-all implications of each grievance and demand.

Moreover, the union has to consider its strategic position vis-à-vis management. The union has certain institutional objectives. For example, it is seeking to strengthen its own position in the company somewhat independently of particular employee or group needs. Creating a fuss about Jones' complaint might lead management to insist on its contractual right to change jobs as it sees fit. Of course, the members might be aroused to seek a stronger contract at the next negotiations.

The middle steps of the grievance procedure. Jones agrees to sign the formal grievance papers charging Brown with discrimination. He notes on the printed form that his assignment to excessive cleaning duties followed an argument with Brown over new coveralls. "When I complained that my coveralls (supplied by the company) were too torn, Brown said I was always complaining and ought to have something to really complain about for a change." The grievance is also signed by the steward; the supervisor himself signs it, but only after adding this note: "Grievance refused—employee has not been discriminated against." Then the chief steward sends the grievance to the laboratory manager, asking for an appointment to talk over the matter.

Management's reaction. After the manager receives the grievance, he calls in the supervisor, Brown, to get his version of the case; he also checks with the personnel director to see whether similar cases have established precedents in this area that would affect the settlement.

The manager is at first concerned that this might be a case of discrimination. The company has a firm policy that no supervisor is to allow personal feelings to enter into personnel decisions. Having satisfied himself that Brown was right, the manager feels that he cannot grant the grievance. To do so would be to open the door to a stream of union challenges of work assignments. The manager tells the chief steward that even though a man may feel he is getting more than his share of the unpleasant jobs, it is up to the supervisor to make such decisions in accordance with his own work requirements and the available manpower. So while he will caution Brown to make sure such assignments are dictated by work needs and not by his personal feelings toward particular employees, the grievance will have to be refused. The manager's answer to the grievance is, "No contract violation, supervisor was acting within normal management prerogatives."

Higher levels of the grievance procedure. The next move is clearly up to the union. The chief steward and the steward explain to Jones that he has a weak case. No one has heard the supervisor threaten Jones, and even if the supervisor admitted using threats, that would not prove he was discriminating. Well, yes, there are some other steps that might be taken. The union's business agent could take the case up with the division manager of the drug company. If the company still refused to agree to divide the work up more equitably, the case could then be taken to arbitration.

The chances of winning, however, are not good, Jones is told. The chief steward advises Jones to be alert for other evidence of discrimination that would enable the union to reopen the case. He promises that the union will also try to obtain a contract clause next year to prohibit, without specific union approval, changes in work assignments that are equivalent to job transfers.

Even though the chances of success were very slight, the chief steward might have decided to push the case anyway. Grievances provide interesting, challenging work and relieve the monotony of his highly routine job in the company. And yet most union leaders are not anxious to build up a reputation for pressing weak cases too vigorously. They want their opposite numbers in management to believe that they are sensible men who can tell the difference between just and unjust claims—but that they are also tough, of course.

IMPACT OF THE UNION ON MANAGEMENT

What over-all effect does the existence of a union have on the organization as a whole and on the management of personnel? The following discussion, which goes beyond the specific grievance problems we have described, will also suggest some of the reasons why many companies have resisted unionization.

Challenges to Management Decisions

The existence of a union means that all personnel decisions are subject to close scrutiny and, perhaps, active challenge. In a nonunion situation, employees may grow dissatisfied and harbor a sense of injustice or injury, but they are not necessarily willing to express their attitudes. The union gives them a means of taking action, not only by approaching the immediate supervisor, but also by reaching higher in the management structure with their demands. For the manager who relishes unchecked authority, this is an unpleasant experience. Almost any manager would prefer to have his orders and decisions go unchallenged.

Competition for Loyalty

Furthermore, the union is in a strategic position to compete with management for the loyalty of employees. For example, it may try to claim credit for any improvement in wages or vacations—even implying that these benefits had to be wrung from an unwilling management. Particularly in the organizational stage, when the union is trying to establish itself, it may caricature company executives and their "desire to sweat labor." Such changes of dishonesty and high-handed tyranny come as a rude shock to executives, particularly to those who think of themselves as benevolent, thoughtful employers.

Review of Personnel Policies

The awareness that the union is ready to challenge its actions stimulates management to exercise more care in shaping personnel policies. Mistakes can be costly, not only in terms of the time and goodwill lost through grievance-processing, but also in terms of the new contractual demands that are likely to spring from employee dissatisfaction.

In one company, the supervisor gave overtime work (at time-and-a-half extra pay) only to workers who he felt had done a better-than-average job. The union claimed that this was outright favoritism and demanded that overtime be distributed with absolute equality among all employees. To avoid such an ironclad rule, the company quietly passed down the word to its supervisors that overtime should be distributed at least roughly equally and that monthly reports on how this is done should be submitted to the personnel department (thus somewhat restricting the power of the supervisors).

Over-all, the growth of unions has been an impetus to the development of better personnel policies. Certainly it has forced management to consider carefully the impact of such policies on its employees.

Rigidify Rules

Unions demand that personnel policies relating to pay, promotion, transfers from job to job, discipline, vacations, fringe benefits, and the like be written into the contract. Although this ensures that everyone is treated alike, it also greatly reduces management's discretion. Of course many nonunion plants have standard rules covering such matters just to preserve some uniformity in policy and to prevent obvious inequities from developing. (Further, in some unionized plants where foreman-steward relations are good, the inflexibility of rules may be reduced by informal agreements to waive contractual provisions. A rule preventing foremen from working may be ignored in a production crisis if the foreman himself is not strict in enforcing discipline.)

Threats to Efficiency

Management fears that the union may want to introduce barriers to efficient work methods, reduce work loads, and in general hold back productivity. For example, the union usually wants to introduce rules that prevent a man from working "outside his job classification"; that is, from doing work other than that listed in the description of his job. If a manager is prevented from assigning work in a way that will take advantage of the employees' aptitudes and experience, management reasons that labor costs are bound to go up.

Some observers argue that the increased costs that result from union pressures "shock" management into finding more efficient work methods.

Centralization of Decision-Making

A manager who fails to understand the contract may inadvertently prompt an embarrassing grievance. It may set a precedent that will be very costly to the company for a long period of time in other departments and strengthen the union's argument that the company is "unfair." For example, in our hypothetical case above, the laboratory manager was anxious to avoid establishing the precedent that work assignments were not a management prerogative. Fearing such contingencies, many companies have withdrawn from lower-level supervisors the authority to make certain personnel decisions. This authority has been delegated to higher levels of management and, in many cases, to staff departments with specialists trained in labor relations. [13]

[13] The problems created by the changing organizational position of the supervisor and the growing importance of staff departments are analyzed in Chapter 15.

Introduction of "Outsiders" into Labor Relations

As we have seen, an "international" union usually embraces members from a number of different firms.[14] Not only does the union have institutional goals distinct from those of the company (it wants to grow and prosper and its officers want to be re-elected), but it is also concerned with more than one employer. The union seeks wage increases in one company to set a precedent that will make it easier to negotiate a favorable contract elsewhere. Frequently, arbitration decisions set precedents affecting labor relations in many companies. As a result, many company officials feel that the problems to which union officers force them to devote time are not restricted to the interests of the particular organization and its employees.

Business agents and international representatives are not employees of the firms with which they negotiate. Although in principle many managers resent the fact that the union brings "outsiders" onto the scene, in practice they often find that the outsiders are more dispassionate and better able to understand the company's side of a grievance than their own employees would be.

EVOLUTION OF SOUND UNION-MANAGEMENT RELATIONS

There is little question that the introduction of a union may prove a traumatic experience for management. At the outset, the union may try to dramatize every company mistake, and the early days may be spent in destructive warfare rather than in the constructive solution of problems. In many firms this period may drag on for years in a kind of armed truce, with both sides trying to capitalize on the other's mistakes. While grudgingly accepting the existence of the union, managers may seek to limit its influence in the company and they may compete actively with the union for the loyalty of the membership. Yet many companies and their managements develop a more harmonious relationship and admit that the union can have a beneficial effect on the organization if dealt with properly.

Opportunities for Improved Human Relations

The most important factor contributing to sound labor relations is the recognition by management that its own actions and policies have a major impact on union behavior. To some extent "a management gets the kind of union it deserves."

To the management that is willing to explore new techniques, the introduction of a union into the organization need not be a catastrophe. The union can actually help management improve employee relationships.

Labor relations involve a problem that every company must face, whether or not its workers are unionized: this is the problem of adjusting the needs of the

---

[14] Many independent unions, however, which are not affiliated with international unions, have no organizational relationships beyond the company in which they are organized.

individual to the needs of the organization. Without a union, employees may find other means of protesting what they think is unfair: slowdowns, sabotage, or quitting. The union provides a peaceful means of resolving such disputes or differences in a way that will maintain productivity and preserve the work force intact.

Increasingly, managers are recognizing the merits of informal discussion of common problems. Even on subjects solely within the area of management prerogatives, they are learning that the union can serve as a channel of communication with the work force and can provide an aid in discovering and correcting weak spots in the plant. Thus the union provides a form of feedback.

Supervisors who are sensitive to human relations prefer to obtain group agreement before initiating changes in work procedure. Rather than deal with a large number of individuals with diverse points of view, they realize that it is far more efficient to sit down with a responsible union leader. He is the single spokesman who presumably represents the unified opinion of the entire work group and can subsequently sell his analysis to the group. In a sense, strong local unions are a guarantee that agreements will be honored. By obtaining agreement with the union, management, in effect, legitimates its own actions (a subject we will discuss at greater length in Chapter 8).

Unions are sometimes described as "managers of discontent." As such they often bring to the surface vaguely felt dissatisfactions and even magnify them. (Managers sometimes say "unions create trouble." Mostly, they merely identify and dramatize trouble that is already there.) Yet, as managers of discontent, unions also help to keep discontent in bounds and to channel it, so it can be dealt with in an orderly fashion.

Management learns that it can introduce changes in working conditions with much less friction if it consults with the union beforehand. Rather than sit back and wait for the union to raise problems, the company can make the first move and involve union officials in clearing up potential trouble areas.

"We knew we were going to have a lot of squawks over new job assignments when we brought automation into the department. This could have meant a hundred grievances and months of wasteful talk. Instead we went to the union and told them what our plans were, how many of what kinds of jobs there would be after the change. We got them to work with us in deciding who was going to stay in the department and how transfers would be arranged. We also negotiated the rates on the new jobs."

Consulting with the union prior to the development of grievances often produces a valuable by-product. As we have seen, union officials are typically active men who want to keep busy. If they can be involved in handling constructive questions, they are less likely to seek out problems and grievances.

The Manager's Role

The chances of converting hostility-ridden, destructive labor relations into a constructive pattern depend largely on the manager's ability to adapt to the existence of the union. When a union is first established, the manager may have difficulty dealing with subordinates who can speak to him as equals. At the outset, he needs to distinguish between the outspoken rabble-rouser and the genuine informal leader. The free-wheeling organizer may be motivated by deep-seated personality problems or personal grievances. Often he does not have the confidence of the group as a whole.

The manager should recognize that most employees experience no serious conflict between loyalty to the union (which they see as a sort of insurance program to protect them against future contingencies) and loyalty to management (which they see as a source of jobs and economic well-being). So if the manager rejects or becomes suspicious of everyone who expresses pro-union sentiments, he may alienate a number of very capable employees who, were they accorded responsibility and trust, might have identified themselves strongly with the company.

The manager also should be alert to the special problems affecting the union leader's behavior: He may be under conflicting pressures, one group wanting him to do one thing, another group insisting on something else. The manager should recognize the political position of the union leader and learn how to cope with him intelligently rather than bemoan the fact that unions are political institutions. [15]

Management representatives quickly learn to differentiate between the grievances on which the union leaders face strong political pressures and those which they are merely "going through motions" of pressing. . . . A shrewd management learns not to embarrass union officials before a close election. . . .

We have observed many episodes such as the following telephone call by a union leader to a personnel director:

"Look, Bill, we'll admit that Charlie Jones was drunk last week. Frankly we don't have a leg to stand on. If you'll take it easy on him—after all this is his first offense—we'll waive the formal hearing. And that'll save you a lot of time and money. . . ."

These are not collusive dealings but rather part of the flexible process by which both sides adjust to new problem situations which could not have been foreseen when the contract was written. [16]

Thus, as time passes, the union abandons its role as a *competitor* for the loyalty of the worker. It takes on the role of a *policeman* who calls "halt" when a company representative makes a mistake, but who also keeps the member-employee within the bounds of legal decisions and practices. In some companies, this evolutionary process advances to the point where the union becomes a genuine *collaborator*, sharing with management the problems of improving efficiency and productivity.

CONCLUSION

The problems of labor relations are not distinct from other human-relations problems that arise in an organization. The existence of a union reflects employee needs and dissatisfactions. Although the union cannot eliminate manage-

[15] Some management observers believe that it is easier to negotiate with an undemocratic union than with a democratic one, since the leaders of the undemocratic unions are less subject to membership pressures. Indeed it has been argued that the Landrum-Griffin Act, which was supposed to ensure union democracy, has actually contributed to labor-management strife.

[16] Sayles and Strauss, *op. cit.*, pp. 18–19.

ment's responsibility for the conduct of personnel administration, it can become an integral part of the employment relationship. Some human-relations problems, particularly in larger organizations, may be almost beyond the ability of management to solve, and the manager need not feel that the establishment of a union is evidence of his own failure. Thus, it is unrealistic to think of personnel administration as an *alternative* to unionization.

Union-management relations provide another challenge for management. In many companies, the necessity of working through these problems is just as much a part of the managerial job as developing budgets and work schedules, and issuing orders. While negotiation and consultation are time-consuming, frequently frustrating, and certainly threatening, they require some of the same supervisory skills and persistence that are necessary to carry out other management functions. These responsibilities cannot be avoided, nor would it be healthful for the organization if they could.

problem 1 • WILDCAT STRIKE

During the 20 years Harold Keller has worked for the Ridge Lee Company, he has risen to the top of his promotion ladder: a machinist first-class and one of the highest-paid nonsupervisory employees in the company. About five years ago, the workers in the company were organized by a union; Keller played no active part in the organizing campaign. About a year ago, Keller developed an illness that was difficult to diagnose; although he lost strength and energy, he was able to continue at work. Because of his good record and long service, the company found a number of special assignments for him and maintained his wages until he regained his health.

Just recently, the men in the machine shop in which Keller worked staged a wildcat one-day walkout that did not have the formal authorization of the local union. Employees in other departments were not involved. The men in the machine shop claimed that their wages had declined relative to wages in many other departments because they had had no opportunity to work more than 40 hours a week. Men in many of the other departments were working 45 hours and 50 hours a week.

Much to the surprise and disappointment of the machine-shop supervisor, Keller not only participated in this protest demonstration, but actually appeared to be one of the leaders.

1. Does Keller's action seem reasonable in light of the consideration management accorded him during his illness?

2. What should the supervisor do with Keller now?

3. How typical do you think this case is?

4. What is your reaction to the complaint of the men in the machine shop?

problem 2 • A CHANGE IN SCHEDULE

The company guards at the Elmwood Company were among the last groups to join a union, but they had always expressed a great deal of dissatisfaction over their work schedules. For many years there had been charges of favoritism in the assignment of work hours. Guard work had to be carried on around the clock, and employees who were assigned to the less desirable shifts or to week-end duty complained that they should have better working hours.

The issue of "fair working schedules" was plugged hard by the new union in signing up new members, and it was one of the first questions raised by the union leaders when they met with management to negotiate their first labor contract. In fact, this issue took up the first two weeks of negotiation.

When the issue was finally settled, management discovered that the agreement with the new guard union specified a work schedule that was almost identical with the one that had existed prior to unionization. Nevertheless, the union and the membership seemed satisfied with the agreement, and there was no longer the heavy stream of complaints about work assignments.

1. How do you explain this strange development? Were the employees dissatisfied before and, if so, why did they appear satisfied after the agreement was made?

2. What scheduling difficulties may the union leaders have become aware of during their two-week discussion with company representatives?

problem 3 • WHAT PREROGATIVES FOR WHAT MANAGERS?

The following item appeared in the *Daily Californian,* the student newspaper of the University of California, Berkeley.

In response to demands by black athletes that certain of their number be moved to the first-string Cal team, Coach Willsey replied, "I believe there are certain prerogatives that belong solely to the head of the team, and these include determining the relative abilities of various members of the team and placement of athletes in the various positions; simply the determination of who will play and where. I do not believe these prerogatives are negotiable. I cannot ignore these responsibilities and violate the ethics of my profession."

1. How justified is the coach? Would your answer be very different were he president of General Motors and replying to a newly organized union of executives? Why?

2. From the point of view of the team's playing efficiency, what would be the advantages and disadvantages of a system in which college football players were organized into a union that would negotiate with the coach regarding the terms and conditions of their playing? Is your answer affected by the fact that big-league college football is no longer purely amateur?

3. Should students as a group negotiate with their professors? About what?

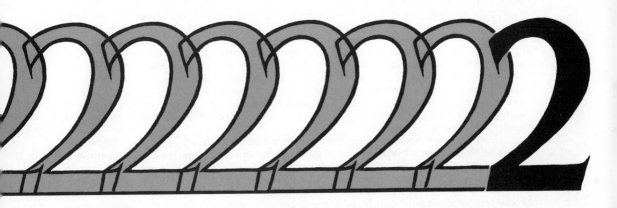

2

Motivation
and
Leadership

Up to this point we have been dealing with the "ingredients" of the business organization: people and their needs, technology and its impact, groups, and unions. In the following chapters we shall talk about the manager, the person whose job it is to blend all these ingredients in such a way as to enable the organization to satisfy its basic needs for effectiveness and efficiency.

What is a manager? A manager is one who is responsible for getting a job done that is too big to do by himself—a job that he can accomplish only through other people. True, he must have some technical ability. But it is the fact that *he must get his work done through others* that sets him apart as a manager and that creates the problems that we shall discuss in this section.

Clearly, management is not just a matter of giving orders or overseeing subordinates to make sure they follow rules. Management means building an effective work force and motivating each member of it to turn in his best performance. This is the job of every manager whether he is president, a regional manager, or a first line supervisor.

To be sure, managers have other functions besides dealing with subordinates. Depending on their level in the hierarchy, they may have to make decisions relating to finance, marketing, research, scheduling, quality control, or public relations. Technical, analytical, and imaginative skills may be as essential as human-relations skills. The manager may have to deal with customers, suppliers, the government, superiors, staff, and other supervisors on his own level. Yet one of the most critically important skills of any manager is skill in *leadership,* and in this section we shall emphasize the manager as leader.

What is the difference between a good leader and a bad one? Styles of leadership vary greatly from one situation to another. The techniques used by "a maid to control her man" are very different from those used by a drill sergeant. The political demagogue, the parish priest, the president of the senior class, the father of a family—all are leaders. And so are the unofficial, informal leaders we met in an earlier chapter. Each uses a style of leadership appropriate to his own situation. As we shall see, in organizations there can be a wide range of leadership behavior.

Every manager, however, faces the problem of motivation. When a man works for himself, either at his job or at a hobby, he works with enthusiasm and energy. How can we get him to work in the same way in our complex mass-production society, where men work not for themselves, but for others, and where the satisfaction derived from the work itself is often meager? As we shall see in Chapter 6, there are various means of "Motivating People to Work," some appropriate to one situation, others to another. Nevertheless, the most generally positive form of motivation, in circumstances where it is applicable, is what is called internalized motivation.

The effective manager has three tasks: he must decide how much to delegate and in what manner; he must exercise his authority in such a fashion as to maximize acceptance of his orders; and he must act as leader of his work team.

1. The manager should delegate decision-making authority to subordinates to the maximum extent the subordinates' abilities and the needs of the organization permit. Instead of issuing detailed instructions, he will lay down rules, set goals, and seek to indoctrinate subordinates in organizational objectives. All this is involved in "Delegation" (Chapter 7).

2. In "The Exercise of Authority" (Chapter 8), the manager must develop effective day-to-day relations with his subordinates. He must also take into account their conceptions of what they feel to be the legitimate use of authority.

3. The manager and his subordinates are members of the same work group. The effective manager is in effect a team leader. His job is to strengthen the group (provided the group's objectives are not opposed to those of management), to consult with group members, both formally and informally, and to work through the informal group structure (Chapter 9, "Manager-Group Relations and Participation").

Before we go on to discuss these three aspects of leadership, we must emphasize again that no one form of leadership is equally good in all situations. Factors involved are: the type of work; the cohesiveness of the group; the group's attitude toward management; the individual needs and personality of the subordinate; and the personality, experience, and technical ability of the manager. The best manager is the one who is sensitive to the needs of each situation and adjusts his style of management accordingly.

MOTIVATING PEOPLE TO WORK

6

One of the basic problems in any society is how to motivate people to work. In a modern society this is not an easy task, since many people derive only slight personal satisfaction from their jobs and enjoy little sense of accomplishment or creativity. In large organizations people must work together, follow orders they may neither understand nor approve, and obey instructions from superiors whom they had no part in selecting and may never see. Few have the opportunity for self-expression or the freedom from control enjoyed by the farmer or the independent business or professional man. How can we create a situation in which employees can satisfy their individual needs while working toward the goals of the organization? In particular, how can one motivate people who have boring jobs, little freedom to make decisions on their own, and the normal human quota of laziness and stubbornness?

In this chapter we shall consider five alternative methods for motivating people: (1) the "be strong" approach, (2) the "be good" approach, (3) implicit bargaining, (4) competition, and (5) internalized motivation. (We make no claim to have exhausted the list of possible forms of motivation, and in practice most managers use combinations of all five.)

BE STRONG

The traditional form of motivation in industry (and the one that seems to come easiest to most managers) emphasizes authority and economic rewards. At its crudest, this method consists of forcing people to work by threatening to fire

119

them or to cut their economic rewards if they don't. The assumption behind this approach, of course, is that the only reason people work is to earn money, and that they will work only if driven to it by fear of losing their jobs. It ignores the fact, mentioned in Chapter 1, that people also want around-the-job satisfactions. Off-the-job, economic satisfactions are not enough once a minimal standard of living is obtained.

This approach further assumes that since no one likes work, people will try to get away with doing just as little as they can. To prevent them from doing so, there must be close supervision. Management must tell every worker exactly what he is to do every minute of the day; it must spell out every rule and give the worker the narrowest possible range for discretion. Often rules are promulgated just "to show who's boss." Individuals are kept busy "to keep them out of trouble."

This thinking is inherent in some of the less sophisticated versions of scientific management: Men are hired to work rather than think, and the smallest possible segment of human ability should be used on the job. It is also related to what has been called the "commodity" or "contractual" theory of labor, which holds that labor can be bought and sold just like material supplies—and can be treated in the same way.

This approach paid off fairly well in the early days of the industrial revolution when workers and their families were so close to starvation that the material, off-the-job needs for food, clothing, and shelter were paramount. In recent years, however, people have begun to expect more from their jobs than sheer punishment. As a consequence, the "be strong" policy has become less effective as a motivating device. There are three major reasons why this approach has become less appropriate.

1. We discovered in Chapter 1 that as our standard of living has gone up and our physical needs have become better satisfied, people have begun to look for social and egoistic satisfactions higher up on the need hierarchy. This is particularly true in times of full employment. (Or to put it another way, we have used part of our increased productivity to provide ourselves with more material goods, such as bigger houses, better cars, and fancier cuts of meat; part to provide us with more leisure off the job, shorter hours, and longer vacations; and part to provide ourselves with a more decent work environment, which means among other things a slower work pace and less tyrannical supervision.)

2. Fifty years ago children were taught, both at home and at school, to show strict obedience to their elders. And so the child-grown-man found little difficulty adjusting to stern discipline in the office or factory. Recent years have seen a revolution in the way children are brought up. Freedom and self-expression are encouraged in the home; schools emphasize spontaneous discussion and individual expression. Youth culture today emphasizes self-expression, doing "your own thing." As a consequence, the young worker finds it hard to accept autocratic leadership on the job.

3. Basic to the philosophy of "be strong" is the expectation that if a man doesn't do what the boss tells him to do, he will be fired. Unions, however, have made it more difficult to fire a man; in effect, the minimum a worker can get by with is lower then it ever was before.

Application to White-Collar Workers

We all know how the bullying foreman uses "be strong" techniques. But others with authority apply the same policy to executives, supervisors, and white-collar workers. With no union to protect them and with a keen interest in advancement, these people may be effectively motivated by the fear of punishment (either through discharge or denial of promotion).

It is common practice for top management to set goals (increased sales, lowered costs, and so forth) for their executives, and then to exert constant pressure to ensure that these goals are met. The penalty for not meeting them is usually the withholding of promotions or salary increases, if not outright discharge. Some companies deliberately set their goals too high. Every time a goal comes close to being met, management raises it even higher, hoping as a consequence to stir employees to work harder and harder. As one supervisor remarked, "My philosophy is, always give a man more than he can finish. That way you can be sure you are getting the most out of him."

This is one reason we hear so much about "pressure" in many business offices. A top executive described his use of the "be strong" approach this way:

As soon as we examine the budget results and see a fellow is slipping, we *immediately* call the factory manager and point out, "Look Joe, you're behind on the budget. What do you expect to do about it?" True, he may be batting his brains out already on the problem but our phone call adds a little more pressure. [1]

The consequent feeling of frustration is intensified because the white-collar employee typically does not have the channels of redress or the opportunities to express aggression that are available to his blue-collar brother.

Impact on People

The trouble with "be strong" as a form of motivation is this: It ignores the fact that people are not passive, inert machines and that they often react in ways not intended by management.

1. This policy normally provides no incentive to work harder than the minimum required to avoid punishment.[2] The minimum may be fairly low for unionized workers who are promoted on the basis of seniority and who have a union to protect them if they are fired. On the other

---

[1] Chris Argyris, *The Impact of Budgets on People* (New York: Controllership Foundation, 1952), p. 5.

[2] Piecework does provide such motivation; but as we discuss elsewhere, the effectiveness of piecework is reduced by group-imposed "bogeys" (output restrictions).

hand, the minimum may be relatively high if the work is closely programed and if it is easy to see whether a man is falling down on the job. Applied to executives whose chances of promotion and winning substantial salary increases are great, the policy of "be strong" may seem effective. However, as mentioned above, executives often find it difficult to work creatively when subjected to pressures that "be strong" involves.

2. The essence of "be strong" is the application of pressure. But when subjected to *too much* pressure, employees fight back. When they can, they fight through their union. Even if they have no union, they engage in slowdowns, sabotage, and spoilage. As one worker commented, "In my shop there is an undeclared war of nerves. If management won't treat us like men, we aren't going to show much respect for them."

   Part of this "war of nerves" consists of workers' efforts to get away with doing as little as possible; there is no incentive for doing more than the minimum, but there is a great deal of satisfaction in making management look silly. Naturally, management reacts by deciding, "We have to watch these men like hawks if we are to get anything done at all." Both sides spend a tremendous amount of energy trying to outsmart the other. Production is lower than it might otherwise be, and management, in frustration, often strikes back irrationally, perhaps by imposing needless restrictions or by firing alleged ringleaders. Thus, a vicious cycle is set in motion, a cycle of restraints and evasions, more restraints and more evasions.

3. To protect themselves from pressure, employees organize groups and cliques, as we saw in Chapter 4. Existing groups may be drawn closer together and take on the new purpose, that of protecting themselves against management pressure. As we have seen, work groups frequently establish "bogeys" or standards of output that no member is expected to exceed—in spite of what management wants. Group members may even conspire to cover each other's mistakes and to punish squealers. As a result, higher management is kept ignorant of what is happening on subordinate levels and therefore cannot inflict the discipline that is necessary if "be strong" is to succeed.

   This policy of self-protection is openly practiced by hourly-paid workers; even executives, however, often band together in an implicit alliance to protect themselves against their own superiors.

4. Probably the most serious trouble with "be strong" is that it ignores a basic factor in human behavior: When people are put under too much pressure they become *frustrated*. (Note: we say *too much* pressure. Most of us respond well to some pressure, but all of us have a critical point— which differs from one person to another—beyond which frustration sets in.[3])

When people become frustrated they react in strange ways that tend to reduce the effectiveness of the organization in its main task of getting out

---

[3] Evidence suggests that, up to a certain point, anxiety facilitates the performance of all tasks, but that anxiety is more effective with simple than with complicated tasks.

production. Often their behavior seems quite irrational, in the sense that it cannot be understood in terms of the apparent stimulus.

Superintendent Jones' secretary usually does a fine, conscientious job. Today she forgot to type an important letter. Jones bawled her out unmercifully.

Jones is normally a kind man. Why did he act this way today? Certainly his behavior was not designed to get the letter out more quickly, or even to prevent his secretary from making mistakes in the future. The fact is that he had been trying to meet an important deadline with an inadequate staff of men, and his boss had just called him up to spur him on.

One response to frustration is *aggressiveness*, which expresses itself in many ways. Instead of bawling out his secretary, Jones might have picked a fight with another supervisor, had a hassle with his wife, or whammed a small, defenseless white ball around the golf course. If his frustration became too intense, it might have led to psychosomatic illnesses, such as high blood pressure or ulcers:

Once we observed a group of working supervisors who had been strongly pressured to increase production under difficult circumstances with no backing from management. There were nine men regularly assigned to the day shift. One had a nervous breakdown, another had a fatal heart attack that was generally attributed to overwork and fatigue. Of the remaining seven, five had serious illnesses and in most cases no organic cause could be determined. All this happened during a period of twelve months. Meanwhile, the men on the night shift, where pressure was much less, had an almost perfect health record.

There are many other reactions to frustration. Some people *repress* their feelings for a long time and then suddenly blow up without notice. Others *regress* to less mature levels of behavior. Everyone is familiar with the three-year-old who reverts to thumb-sucking when a baby brother arrives on the scene. Similarly, adults who are frustrated by excessive pressure may find it difficult to make decisions or react intelligently and may engage in juvenile (and aggressive) activities such as horseplay. Though employees may be dragooned into submission by the "be strong" approach, the consequent frustration may lead to a serious reduction in the quality of their decision. Under extreme frustration, they may simply fall into *resignation* and give up trying altogether.

Frustration may also lead to *scapegoating*—that is, picking on those who are weak and defenseless. It is not accidental, for instance, that racial tensions in plants are higher when times are bad and layoffs are pending. Another response is *fixation*, in which the individual persists in some fruitless activity, such as Lady Macbeth's handwashing, even though it obviously accomplishes nothing. When assigned a difficult problem, some managers spend their time shuffling papers rather than trying to work out a realistic solution.

Finally there is *sublimation*, in which the individual seeks to satisfy his frustrated needs in some more effective fashion. Thus, the executive who has been denied promotion may become active in a social club, just as the girl who has been jilted may seek to express her love in nursery school work.

The collective reaction of a group of workers to frustration may have a devastating effect on the entire organization. It may disrupt group solidarity and cooperation, turning departments, groups, and individuals against one another. It may lead to rumor, mistrust, and suspicion. It may result in unexplained wildcat strikes or a general state of snarling irritability. In most cases, the basic objective of the organization—*production*—is bound to suffer.

The Value of "Be Strong"

Thus, the effectiveness of the "be strong" technique of motivation is subject to significant limitations: (1) It motivates employees to do only enough work to keep from being fired (except where there are significant opportunities for promotion); (2) it motivates them to "get away" with as much as possible (often making a game of it), thus leading to a vicious cycle of further management restrictions and employee evasions; (3) it motivates them to band together in self-protection; and (4) it leads to frustration and in turn to a whole series of deleterious side reactions that jeopardize production.

And yet, as we shall see, there are times when "be strong" works fairly well. It works better in the short run than in the long run. It generally works better with white-collar workers than with blue-collar workers. It is most effective in nonunionized situations, during depressions when men are desperate for work, with members of minority groups who find it a difficulty to find work elsewhere, and in highly programed work where deviation from rules may be easily spotted. Even in these situations, though, there are undesirable side reactions.

BE GOOD

As a substitute for "be strong," many managements have adopted the philosophy of "be good." They have sought to raise employee morale by providing good working conditions, fringe benefits, employee services, high wages, and decent, fair supervision. By contrast to "be strong's" heavy emphasis on physical needs, "be good" also caters to security and social needs.

We may distinguish between two forms of "be good," which may be called *paternalism* and *hygienic management.* The argument for paternalism holds that if management is good to employees, they will work harder out of loyalty and gratitude. The argument for hygienic management ignores the question of gratitude; it holds that liberal benefits, good working conditions, and friendly supervision develop satisfied employees, and that satisfied employees work harder.

Paternalism

Paternalism is pretty much outdated, having had its heyday in the 1920's. In part, its wide adoption at that time was the result of genuine interest by employers in their employees, as well as the belief that "be good" was a more effective form of motivation than "be strong." In part, too, its popularity was a reaction to the rise of unionism during and immediately after World War I. In any case, under the banner of the "New Industrial Relations," management became interested in a wide variety of projects, varying from cafeterias and recreation programs for employees to cooking classes for their wives. Some of these programs were designed to change the employees' personal lives as well as their on-the-job performance. The Sociology Department of the Ford Motor Company of an earlier day went further than most programs. Headed by a Protestant minister, this department was manned by 30 investigators.

In what amounted to a brief reign of benevolent paternalism, these gentlemen and their house-to-house canvassers imposed . . . a set of rules which blended good sense with Ford whims and Puritan virtues.

On the positive side, the men . . . behaved like the home visitor of the modern public welfare agency. They doubtless helped to "Americanize" Ford's vast body of immigrant workmen. Their charges were encouraged to start savings accounts and to budget their incomes. They were given elementary lessons in hygiene and home management. . . .

At worst . . . its agents became, to some extent, collectors of tales and suspicions. . . . Hearsay as well as fact found its way into a card catalogue where a record was kept of every worker's deviations. . . . Frittering away one's evenings "unwisely," taking in male boarders, sending funds to the "old country"—these things came to be regarded as earmarks of "unwholesome living." The use of liquor was forbidden . . . as was marital discord that resulted in a separation or divorce action. [4]

Ford's program was shortlived, but similar patterns of paternalism were developed in other companies. There is little evidence that any of them were particularly successful in eliciting gratitude, in motivating workers to do a better job, or even in staving off the development of unions. In fact, some of the companies with the best-known histories of paternalism later became scenes of bitter labor-management strife.

There are good psychological reasons for believing that if management expects employees to work harder out of gratitude for benefits, then paternalism will fail to accomplish its purpose. What actually happens may be this:

1. Paternalism may engender resentment rather than gratitude. People don't like to feel dependent on someone else. They prefer to decide for themselves what they want. Letting others decide what is good for them makes them feel infantile and lowers their sense of importance. In spite of stories to the contrary, most people prefer earning things for themselves to having everything handed to them by others. Unearned rewards given out of the kindness of the employer's heart often are regarded as slights to the employee's sense of self-esteem. Instances of "biting the hand that feeds one" are quite common.

2. As time passes, the novelty of being given free "hand-outs" wears off, and employees begin to take their benefits for granted. Once they come to regard benefits as part of their regular compensation, management is obliged to provide increasingly impressive gifts. Otherwise the workers will turn resentful, and management will get no credit at all.

3. Paternalism incorporates some of the basic assumptions of "be strong." People are expected to be docile in return for their gifts, and work is

[4] Keith Seward, *The Legend of Henry Ford* (New York: Holt, 1948), p. 59.

still regarded as a form of punishment that people undergo only in return for a reward. Moreover, many of the rewards must be enjoyed *off* the job. Little effort is spent on making the job itself more rewarding.

Although paternalism emphasizes the positive nature of the gift, it also carries with it a negative threat: "If you don't do your job as ordered, your gifts will be taken away." In most instances, since the rewards are distributed without discrimination to everyone on the payroll, there is little incentive for the individual worker to do more than the minimum required to keep from being fired.

Hygienic Management

Today paternalism is seldom resorted to, except by smaller companies. Hygienic management, which, in a sense, is a more subtle version of paternalism, is quite common, however. Management showers workers with high wages, fringe benefits, good working conditions, good supervision, and all the rest, in the hope that they will have higher morale and *therefore* work harder. The only trouble with this assumption is the *therefore*. Since everyone shares equally in these benefits, there is no reward for good work and no incentive to increase output.

The term *morale* has been used in many different ways; but if morale means the employees' attitude toward the company as a whole, there is little evidence that high morale leads to high productivity.[5] Just the reverse may be true. Morale may be very low in a concentration camp, yet production very high. Similarly, workers may be well satisfied to "goof off" in a department where the work pace is extremely slow. Apparently, efforts by management to raise morale do not necessarily raise productivity.

A significant, but controversial, study has given us a new insight into the effectiveness of the "be good" approach.[6] In this study, accountants and engineers were asked to "think of a time when you felt exceptionally good or exceptionally bad about your job" and then asked to describe what happened and why they felt as they did. Interestingly, the factors which made people

---

[5] One careful scholar concludes that there is little convincing evidence that individuals, within any group, who have more favorable attitudes toward the company do a better job. See Arthur H. Brayfield and Walter H. Crockett, "Employee Attitudes and Employee Performance," *Psychological Bulletin,* Vol. 52, No. 5 (September 1955), pp. 396–424. For a study which lists some of the conditions in which low morale and high productivity may go together, see Harold Wilensky, "Human Relations in the Work-place," in Conrad Arensberg, *et al.,* eds., *Research in Industrial Human Relations* (New York: Harper, 1957), p. 25.

[6] Frederick Herzberg, Bernard Mausner, and Barbara Snyderman, *The Motivation to Work* (New York: Wiley, 1960). There have been a number of attempts to replicate this study with various degrees of success. The research techniques have been subject to quite serious (and we think justifiable) criticism. Victor Vroom suggests that (1) the findings are inconsistent with other evidence and (2) people are "more likely to attribute the causes of satisfaction to their own achievements and accomplishments on the job. On the other hand, they may be more likely to attribute their dissatisfaction, not to personal inadequacies or deficiencies, but to factors in the work environment." *Work and Motivation* (New York: Wiley, 1964), pp. 127–129. The authors of this present volume feel that despite the drawbacks of the research technique, the Herzberg study does point to a suggestive new way to examine the problem of motivation. See Robert J. House and Lawrence A. Wigdor, "Hertzberg's Dual Factor Theory of Job Satisfaction: A Review of Evidence and a Criticism," *Personnel Psychology,* Vol. 20, No. 4 (Winter 1967), pp. 369–389.

satisfied with their jobs were not the same as (or the opposite from either) those which made them dissatisfied. Apparently, the presence of so-called satisfiers would increase an individual's satisfaction, but their absence would not make him actively dissatisfied, only apathetic. Similarly, the presence of so-called dissatisfiers made people feel they had a "bad" job; but the absence of dissatisfiers did not make a "good" job.

What were these satisfiers and dissatisfiers? The satisfiers were: achievement, recognition, work itself, responsibility, and advancement. Note that all these forms of satisfaction arise *out* of the *content* of the work itself. The dissatisfiers were: interpersonal relations (both with one's superiors and peers), the technical ability of the supervisor, company policy and administration, physical working conditions, and the individual's personal life off the job. Note that all these factors relate to the *context* or the *environment* within which the job is performed, but not to the job itself. (Interestingly, salary ranked both as a satisfier and a dissatisfier. In general, when a man indicated that salary helped make his job a bad one, he was referring to the system by which salaries were set; when salary was mentioned as making a job a good one, salary was looked on as a sign of achievement and recognition.)

What is the relationship between these factors and productivity? The evidence is quite tentative, but Herzberg suggests that the presence of satisfiers leads to higher productivity (and for this reason satisfiers have also been called motivators). Dissatisfiers, on the other hand, do not lead to lower production nor does their elimination tend to raise it. Their elimination may reduce active resistance to the job, but promote only a passive acceptance of it. This attitude is illustrated by an interview we once held with a blue-collar worker on a routine job. This worker said:

"I got a pretty good job."
Q: "What makes it such a good job?"
A: "Don't get me wrong. I didn't say it is a *good* job. It's an OK job—about as good a job as a guy like me might expect. The foreman leaves me alone and it pays well. But I would never call it a *good* job."

The experimenters called the factors that led to this rather sterile, noninvolved attitude "hygienic factors" (since they are used to avoid discontent). We shall accordingly call management that emphasizes these factors "hygienic management" (and we shall discuss the characteristics of such management at greater length in Chapter 8). Such a "be good" policy may provide a pleasant environment in which to work and a considerable amount of around-the-job satisfaction, but little satisfaction through the job and little sense of enthusiasm or creativity. The emphasis is on job *context* rather than job *content*.

The Value of "Be Good"

We have applied the term "be good" to the philosophy which holds that high wages, good treatment, and so forth will automatically motivate employees to work harder. And we have suggested that this is an oversimplified theory of human behavior. Does this mean that it is a complete waste of money to try to make the company a better place in which to work? Of course not. Properly presented, fringe benefits and employee services are an important part of any personnel program. Such benefits bolster the company's reputation in the community and attract better workers. They also help to reduce turnover. Further, a feeling of security serves to reduce tension among employees and thus, to some extent, contributes to higher productivity.

"Be good" tends to make the job more tolerable. Without question, efforts to make the company a better place in which to work do pay off in terms of better workers and more harmonious relations on the job. But they provide little *direct* motivation for workers to contribute more than a minimum effort. Thus, they provide only a partial answer to the problem of how to motivate workers most effectively.[7]

IMPLICIT BARGAINING

One of the most common forms of motivation today (though some managers may hate to admit it) is bargaining. In this approach, management encourages workers to put out a "reasonable" volume of work by making an agreement to provide, in return, "reasonable" supervision (though the bargain is usually a matter of implicit "understanding" rather than any explicit agreement on terms).[8] In a sense, management agrees not to use all the pressures at its command if the employees will agree not to restrict output unduly. The chief difference between this approach and the two forms of motivation already discussed is that the terms of the bargain (namely, what constitutes *reasonable* supervision, and what constitutes *reasonable* output) are agreed upon more or less voluntarily by both parties.

Thus, in practice the level of output and the conditions under which men work are not determined unilaterally by the manager, but through unwritten agreement between manager and subordinate. There is an assumption that the parties are more or less equal in power, so that the terms of the "effort bargain"[9] or "psychological contract" are agreed upon voluntarily. Just how favorable the final agreement is to each of the parties is determined by their respective bargaining power. Let us look for a moment at the weapons in the possession of each party.

The employee's major weapon is this: Either they can display cheerful cooperation and maintain high production or else they can indulge in excessive clumsiness, misunderstanding, or overt slowdowns or strikes.

The manager's most obvious weapon is his power to discipline workers who fail to produce. In practice, in the typical unionized situation, formal discipline is

[7] In terms of organization theory, "be good" provides motivation "to participate" but not motivation "to produce." James G. March and Herbert A. Simon, *Organizations* (New York: Wiley, 1958), Chapters 3 and 4.

[8] At times, of course, management does engage in explicit bargaining with the union over the level of production.

[9] Maurice D. Kilbridge, "The Effort Bargain," *Journal of Business*, Vol. 33, No. 1 (January 1960), p. 12.

difficult to impose unless the worker's production is completely out of line. Still, the manager has at his disposal a whole arsenal of minor weapons: small but highly prized "plums," minor concessions, and petty but very real punishments. He can assign easy jobs or hard ones. He can make concessions in terms of time off and accept obviously false excuses for absenteeism or tardiness—or he can nag employees for minor offenses. He can provide the help that makes a job easier—or he can make work almost impossible (this is a particularly telling weapon where piecework is involved).

Sometimes the immediate manager permits minor violations of rules as part of the bargain. Superintendents in one gypsum mill allowed workers to punch the clock a little early so they could make more overtime, and to take limited amounts of material home with them for their own repair work.[10] In other situations, employees are permitted to take coffee breaks, make personal calls on the company phone, or take home company pencils. In return for this "indulgency pattern,"[11] they implicitly agree to work harder. Although such agreements are never put into words, they are tacitly understood by everybody concerned. They become group norms of behavior. As one worker put it:

"Our policy is to live and let live. We give the foreman reasonable production. He protects us from the time-study man who tries to jack up the output rate and looks the other way if we take a smoke. We look out for each other."

These privileges are extended only so long as the supervisor feels that the subordinates are doing a satisfactory job. Otherwise they are withdrawn.

A case in point was the "no-floating around rule" which specified that workers must stay at their workplace, except to go to the washroom or eat. When foremen felt that things were going smoothly in their group, that their men were "doing a day's work" and were friendly and "cooperative," they would allow their workers to "sneak off" for a smoke, and they would make no caustic remarks if they wandered over to talk to a friend. If, however, a man or a group was felt to be "goofing off," or was being "snotty," foremen were more likely to invoke the "no floating" rule.[12]

An analogy may be drawn between the indulgency pattern and bank deposits. Both subordinates and supervisors build up credits by doing favors for the other party, and both expect to draw on their account when they need a favor for themselves.

In many situations this policy of "live and let live" is the most realistic approach available to the supervisor. For all its disadvantages, it does make possible a reasonably satisfactory level of production and reasonably harmonious worker-supervisor and labor-management relations. Employees enjoy a sense of independence that they are denied under "be good" and "be strong," even though they are motivated in part by the fear that if they fail to produce the supervisor will withdraw their petty benefits. Probably equally important is the feeling that since the supervisor is "fair" to them, it is only proper that they put

[10] Alvin Gouldner, *Wildcat Strike* (Yellow Springs, Ohio: Antioch Press, 1954), pp. 19–20.

[11] *Ibid.*

[12] Alvin Gouldner, *Patterns of Industrial Bureaucracy* (New York: Free Press, 1954), p. 173.

out a "fair day's work." (In Chapter 8 we shall point out that when a supervisor is considered "fair," his orders acquire greater legitimacy.)

The picture we get from this point of view is not that of the worker crushed by the organization, but of one who fights it, copes with it, and retains his autonomy—making deals with it which satisfy both the individual and the organization. Yet unless bargaining is coupled with more positive forms of motivation, it suffers from many of the disadvantages of "be good" and "be strong." At best, "fair supervision" is a form of hygienic management. Implicit bargaining provides little egoistic satisfaction (except in the sense of outwitting management.) Work is still considered a punishment that one endures only for the sake of receiving the benefits that may accrue from living up to the agreement. Each side does something unpleasant in return for something pleasant. From management's point of view, bargaining offers little opportunity to raise production. Indeed, production is often stabilized at a fairly low level. Furthermore, change becomes very hard to introduce (see Chap. 8). On the other hand, as we shall discuss later, in some cases this may be the most that management can realistically expect.

COMPETITION

Another form of motivation is competition for the pay increases and promotions that go to the men who do outstanding jobs. Competition furnishes several forms of need satisfaction. The prospect of winning a promotion or a pay increase provides a meaningful goal to work toward. And actually attaining the goal means that the employee enjoys an economic reward, as well as a sense of accomplishment and completion, a sense of progress, and added social prestige. Less supervision is required on jobs where competition provides a reasonably satisfactory source of motivation, since each man is on his own to do the best job he can. There is no need to push him.

Competition is not particularly successful as a motivating device among factory workers, however. In union plants the principle of seniority substantially decreases the possibility of winning a promotion on the basis of hard work alone. The trend to reserve foremen's jobs for college-trained men has further reduced the factory worker's chance of rising into management. In theory, the incentive (piecework) system does provide an opportunity for workers to compete with one another. In practice, however, they usually cooperate to restrict output and prevent competition.

Among blue-collar workers (or white-collar workers in mass-production offices), competition is often more effective among *groups* than it is among *individuals*. We have observed numerous incidents where competition has arisen almost spontaneously between groups to see who will put out the most work, make the biggest reductions in scrap losses, and so forth. Workers seem to enjoy the increased sense of group belonging, the excitement of the game, and the thrill of winning.

Competition among individuals is much more widely accepted on the white-collar and managerial levels. Indeed, among salesmen, it is the traditional form of motivation. Yet even among nonfactory employees competition as a means of motivation suffers certain limitations and undesirable side-effects:

1. Not everybody is equally interested in advancement. Some people are highly ambitious, but others—who may be just as competent and hard-working—seek to avoid situations where they have to "cut the other man's throat" to get ahead. And many people, reasonably satisfied with their present jobs and earnings, do not want to expend the extra effort necessary to win a promotion.

   Many engineers and scientists are more interested in professional advancement than in promotions, particularly if the higher-rated job takes them from their laboratory and saddles them with administrative chores. In a sense, these men are competing, but they are competing for professional recognition rather than for the goals management has set for them.

2. Excessive competition has been known to disrupt an entire organization. "A football team may compete successfully with other teams, but it does not follow that it will compete best if its members are in competition with one another." [13]

   As we shall see in Chapter 15, the modern industrial organization is becoming more and more specialized; but activities such as credit, sales, advertising, engineering, product development, and so forth cannot be carried on without continuous cooperation from people who are performing other activities. There are fewer and fewer one-man operations, particularly at the higher levels of management. As a consequence, cooperation is vital to sustained productivity.

3. On many jobs it is difficult to measure who has been most successful, since it is impossible to identify the output of each employee. Even when objective measures are appropriate they are hard to formulate, and using them as the primary basis for distributing rewards may itself lead to a distortion of effort through an overemphasis on the factors being measured (see Chapter 14). Yet unless there is some purely objective way of determining who should receive promotions and rewards, competition may make subordinates overly dependent on their boss. They may be more anxious to look good than to do a good job.

   Overdependence tends to transform the subordinate into a "yes man" and "apple polisher" who is so fearful of making mistakes that he never has a chance to learn from them. The supervisor who is constantly looking upward toward his boss rather than downward toward his subordinates is likely to do a poor job of supervision, and he is certain to inhibit upward communication. But more of this in Chapter 14.

---

13 Harold J. Leavitt, *Managerial Psychology* (Chicago: University of Chicago Press, 1958), pp. 258–259.

4. Efforts to encourage competition are often regarded as pressure, and as we have seen, excessive pressure is frustrating. Aggression and regression are common by-products of the contests conducted by sales organizations. *Time* magazine writes that:

Many firms have ... enlisted salesmen's families in ulcer-building campaigns to spur the breadwinner on. One company regularly sends cards to the home showing the salesman's standing in the current company contest, gives wives tags to hang on furniture around the house to remind their husbands of the furnishings they can earn. Some firms have even sent buzzers and shrill whistles to salesmen's children; when dad asks what the noise is all about, the kids are instructed to tell him it's only a reminder to straighten up and sell harder. ... Such constant pressure from home and office is bound to take its toll on even the strongest salesman. ... "You can carry this business of pounding away at a salesman too far," says Republic Steel's General Sales Manager L. S. Hamaker. "It can be too demoralizing." [14]

Excessive emphasis on competition is particularly frustrating to the loser. Since most promotional hierarchies are shaped like a pyramid, with fewer jobs at the top than at the bottom, there are always more losers than winners.

Many work groups actually band together to protect themselves from attempts to encourage competition, either by formulating group standards of "fair competition" or by banning competitive practices altogether. (For examples, see Chapter 4.) This response is most common among hourly-paid workers, but employees at all levels apply pressure on the "eager beaver."

In conclusion, excessive competition may do more harm than good. In its pure form, the philosophy of competition as a motivating device seems to assume that work is itself uninteresting. When used in moderation, however, and in conjunction with other forms of motivation, competition among individuals may be useful, particularly with certain groups (salesmen, for example), and in situations where teamwork is not essential.

INTERNALIZED MOTIVATION

A fifth approach to the problem of motivation is to provide opportunities for need satisfaction *through doing the job itself,* and thus internalize motivation so that people will enjoy doing good work. Here, the better job an employee does, the higher his level of job satisfaction will be. This approach requires management to discard the assumption that work must be objectionable. It also de-emphasizes economic motivation and off-the-job and around-the-job need satisfactions.

Note how this approach differs from "be good." In that method the employee is *given* need satisfaction; here he *obtains* satisfaction *through his own work*—work that he enjoys and work that helps management. In "be good" it is assumed that greater satisfaction leads to harder work. Here the relationship is reversed: It is assumed that the harder work is the element which leads to greater satisfaction.

[14] *Time,* Vol. 72, No. 2 (July 14, 1958), pp. 75–76.

We have seen that in informal groups people work together and accept the orders of their leaders in order to achieve group objectives. In the same way, it is management's task to create conditions under which people "will willingly and voluntarily work toward organizational objectives" [15]—because they enjoy their work and feel it important to do a good job. This desirable attitude has been called by various authors "spontaneous cooperation" [16] and "Theory Y." [17]

The preceding chapters have already given some hints about how these opportunities can be provided. Later chapters will make other suggestions, but we shall list the major themes here.

1. We have already seen how intrinsic job satisfaction can be increased through redesigning the job, particularly through job enrichment.

2. We have also considered the importance of participation. Opportunities can be provided to work together as a team. When members of the group can participate in solving work problems, they may become more involved in the job itself so that their productivity rises.

3. Equally, if not more, important is the style of leadership shown by management. In the next chapter we shall suggest ways in which the supervisor may engage in "general supervision." Workers may be given an opportunity to enjoy a feeling of accomplishment in their work and, as far as possible, to be their own boss. Under such circumstances supervisors conceive of their job as a way of helping their subordinates rather than as a means of pushing them.

The Limits of Internalized Motivation

For all its merits, internalized motivation is not a panacea, though some observers are more optimistic about it than the authors are. To our minds, those who are most unreserved in its praise tend to overestimate the possible gains from its use and to underestimate the costs involved in making it work.

As we have just discussed, the policies of "be strong," "be good," and implicit bargaining provide little motivation to produce more than a minimum amount of work. Yet on many routine jobs this minimum may be enough, since management may have no need for outstanding performance. What is outstanding performance in the case of the assembly-line worker? That he work faster than the line? That he show creativity and imagination on the job? Management needs none of these. *Adequate* performance (as set by implicit bargaining, perhaps) is all that can be used on the assembly line and on many other jobs in our society. Here the conforming, dependent worker (who is not *dissatisfied*) may well be the best.

Further, as we have seen in Chapter 1, many people center their lives off the job and have little desire for the challenge internalized motivation provides.

[15] Douglas McGregor, *The Supervisor's Job*. Mimeographed; undated.

[16] See Elton Mayo, *The Social Problems of an Industrial Civilization* (Boston: Graduate School of Business Administration, Harvard University, 1945).

[17] Douglas McGregor, *The Human Side of Enterprise* (New York: McGraw-Hill, 1960).

There are those who argue that such people are immature and that they have adjusted to techniques such as hygienic supervision or "be strong" by becoming apathetic and dependent: Were the organization environment healthy, were internalized motivation available, the argument goes on, these people would react differently. But in many cases, these people's limitations stem from childhood or from the general culture. Even if the argument is valid, such persons may be too far gone to react well to internalized motivation, and their attitude is not likely to be changed short of intensive psychotherapy.

In addition, the reliance on internalized motivation can be quite costly to the organization. To increase intrinsic job satisfaction may require the use of job processes which are technologically inefficient. Increased teamwork may not be useful to the organization if employers unite to keep production low. To make general supervision work, many of the old-time autocratic supervisors must be retrained or replaced; this is an expensive process which may result in the demoralization and elimination of the organization's technically most competent employees.

Since it is extremely difficult to develop internalized motivation on many routine jobs, once the traditional, external sanctions (implicit bargaining, fear of discharge, and so forth) are removed, *net* motivation may, on balance, fall. Freedom may result merely in workers "goofing off."

Furthermore, it is fairly meaningless to talk of permitting exercise of discretion to assembly-line workers or girls on punch-card operations; the very nature of technology requires that all essential decisions be centrally programed. There are those who suggest that such programed jobs should be redesigned to permit job enlargement, and thus greater challenge and discretion. Yet, such technological changes can be made only at a substantial cost in terms of productivity.

Internalized motivation works best where the nature of the job permits the employee to enjoy autonomy (there may be little opportunity for it on the assembly line, but a good deal in professional work); where employees accept the organization's objectives (it might work better with managerial than blue-collar employees); and among those who make the job their central life focus (it might work poorly with women whose primary interest is finding a husband or bringing up their children).

In any case, the philosophy of internalized motivation is somewhat idealistic. It assumes that somehow the needs of the organization and needs of the individual can both be maximized at the same time, so that what is good for one will be good for the other. Clearly, this is rarely if ever, the case. Normally there must be some sort of trade-off, that is, if organizational needs are to come first, the individual will suffer to some extent, and vice versa. The most the manager can expect to provide is a reasonably satisfactory level of satisfaction for both parties. Conflicts of interest will continue to exist between management and employees, and it is totally unrealistic to expect to eliminate them altogether. Employees will want more satisfaction, management will want more production, and where the balance is to be poised between the two "is a matter to be solved by bargaining, not by scientific evidence." [18]

[18] Herbert A. Simon, "Authority," in Conrad Arensberg *et al.*, eds., *op. cit.*, p. 114.

A new approach helps put the previous discussion in context.[19] Called paths-goals analysis, it suggests that employees will be motivated to produce only if they perceive that production is a *path* toward a *goal* that they value, or more explicitly, that high production will lead to a reward that will satisfy a need important to them—and further, that the satisfaction from this effort is sufficiently great (equitable) to make the effort worthwhile (see chart).[20] Let us more closely examine this approach.

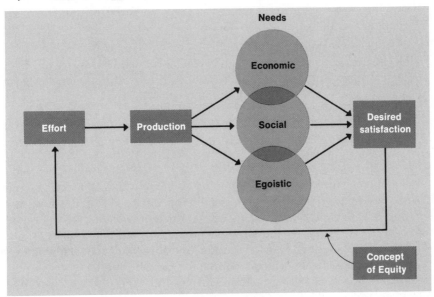

PATHS-GOALS ANALYSIS

1. Let us start with effort. Greater effort must lead to higher production. Normally it does. But if the job is such (as on some assembly lines) that effort is perceived to be unrelated to production (or some other organizational goal), then paths-goals analysis is irrelevant.

2. Production must be perceived to lead to some sort of reward. For convenience we have listed three forms of reward: economic, social, and egoistic. Obviously, rewards could be categorized in many other ways.

3. The reward must satisfy needs that are important to the employee. The reward may be social approval; but if the employee wants money, social

---

[19] Two notable contributors to this approach are Victor H. Vroom, *Work and Motivation* (New York: Wiley, 1964) and Lyman Porter and Edward Lawler, *Managerial Attitudes and Performance* (Homewood, Ill.: Irwin, 1968).

[20] Early human-relations theory was not well worked out, but it seemed to suggest that high morale would lead to harder work. (Certainly this is the basic assumption behind "be good.") Paths-goals analysis reverses the direction of causation: it suggests that where motivation is effective, work accomplishment leads to high morale.

approval will be less motivating. Naturally, personality variables enter here. Egoistic rewards may not be motivating unless the employee has a fairly high need for achievement.

4. The amount of satisfaction must make the gain worth the effort. As we have seen, employees have strongly held concepts of *equity*; i.e., what are the "fair rewards" (economic and noneconomic) which should accompany effort. Often these concepts of equity have been developed through implicit bargaining. Certainly any one employee's concepts will be heavily influenced by the attitude of his peers; but if the reward and resulting satisfaction from effort are believed to be inequitably low, the employee is unlikely to exert himself.

5. Finally, there must be feedback. An employee's motivation is likely to decline if he is uncertain whether his efforts will lead to payoff. Psychological theory suggests that motivation is greater the sooner the payoff is seen to come after effort. If payoff is long delayed, motivation will be reduced.

How does paths-goals analysis help us understand individual situations? Let us look at a few examples.

Assembly-line workers. Here effort has relatively little impact on production, since production is largely determined by the speed of the line. In the typical case it is difficult to reward higher production economically, since wages are uniform for everyone on the job, and promotions are determined by seniority. The foreman may praise a good worker (social reward), but the worker may not value this praise highly, at least not highly enough to induce him to put out extra effort. The job is boring, and it permits little sense of accomplishment; therefore, egoistic rewards are not forthcoming.

Thus the job provides little positive motivation. As long as the foreman engages in hygienic supervision, however (for example, he gives the worker as much relief as he can), the worker's concept of equity may make him feel that he should put in a "fair day's" work—which might mean keeping up with the line but not making any special effort to maintain quality.

Piece rate workers. Presumably, here effort does lead to higher productivity, and high productivity leads to economic rewards in the form of piece rate earnings. The motivational impact of piecework, however, may be reduced by other factors: (1) the worker may believe that if he increases his output, his piece rate will be cut (that is, he will be paid less money per item produced), and so his total earnings will be reduced; (2) by increasing output he may violate group standards (see Chap. 4) and thus be stigmatized as a "bogey breaker." If he has what McClelland-Atkinson call high need for affiliation, group approval may be a more valuable reward for him than the somewhat uncertain possibility of higher earnings. Thus the limited satisfaction to be gained from working harder may not be viewed as worth the effort.

Increased production that results from a worker's efforts may give him an egoistic sense of accomplishment, but he will value the feeling only if he has a high need for achievement. (As we shall see in Chapter 27, he may gain an even greater sense of achievement by restricting output.)

Management. Usually, increased management effort pays off in more effective performance (though, of course, the effectiveness of an organizational unit is a function of many factors other than its manager's efforts). Presumably, too, higher productivity is rewarded through promotions, salary increases, and bonuses. Yet, as we shall see in Chapter 25, managerial compensation schemes are often poorly designed; as a consequence, pay is frequently seen as being only vaguely related to performance. Indeed there is reason to believe that in practice the most effective motivator for management is egoistic—the sense of achievement derived from the fact that one's own decisions (efforts) have led to higher production, thereby demonstrating one's skills as a manager. [21] By and large, egoistic motivation works better for managers than for blue-collar workers, because the managerial job provides a greater sense of discretion and because managers generally are strongly achievement-oriented.

Job enrichment. When will job enrichment work? Normally, job enrichment provides the employee with greater opportunity to plan his own work. Very likely this will mean that there is now a closer relationship between effort and productivity. Higher production, in turn, may be a visible sign that the employee's efforts at self-direction have been successful. But does this form of success provide motivation? This depends on other factors:

- Does the employee in question have a high need-achievement motive?
- Does the employee value the skills that job enrichment permits him to exercise? A wrapping clerk is unlikely to be motivated by greater freedom to do his job if his real interest is in being a musician. Though job enrichment may permit him to produce more, this higher production may give him little feeling of real achievement.
- Is the task at the right level of difficulty (it should be neither too hard nor too easy), so that the possibility of success in fact appeals to this employee's achievement motive?

CONCLUSION

One of the central problems of any organization is to motivate its members to work for the organization's over-all objectives. Traditionally, management has resorted to "be strong." With the growth of unions, a rising standard of living, and changing patterns of discipline in home and school, this approach has become less effective. It motivates people to produce only the minimum necessary to keep a job (though in some cases this minimum may be adequate). Moreover, it creates frustration and other undesirable side effects. In practice it is often tempered with a large dose of implicit bargaining.

"Be good" removes some of the harshness of the authoritarian approach. It may help recruit employees and make them more willing to accept their jobs. As a consequence they may not be dissatisfied. But "be good" alone provides little

[21] See particularly Lawler and Porter, *op. cit.*

motivation to do more than the minimum amount of work to avoid being discharged.

Implicit bargaining, like "be good," relies on hygienic management. At times it is the most realistic approach, particularly where there is a union. It provides an atmosphere of live-and-let-live, but it rarely furnishes any motivation to *increase* production.

Competition has only limited effectiveness as a motivating device on jobs where there is little opportunity for promotion or where seniority prevails. Excessive competition may actually disrupt teamwork and lead to frustration and a host of undesirable side effects.

From many points of view, internalized motivation is the best form of motivation, since it provides the greatest opportunity for individuals to satisfy their needs and to develop their personalities. In fact, as paths-goals analysis suggests, internalized motivation is considerably more appropriate with some sorts of people and jobs (for example, jobs that require individual discretion and commitment) than it is with others.

In practice, most managers use a combination of approaches. If bullying is avoided, the external pressures and economic rewards of "be strong" may reinforce the internal pressures and egoistic rewards of internalized motivation. Hygienic management emphasizes job context; internalized motivation emphasizes job content; but the two approaches can be used in tandem. Only one thing seems sure: there is no simple all-purpose answer to the problems of motivation.

(Since all chapters in this leadership section are closely related, we have grouped all the relevant problems together at the end of Chapter 9.)

DELEGATION

7

A manager makes decisions by himself in some areas; in other areas he delegates to his subordinates. In this chapter we are concerned with the means by which the manager delegates and with the conditions under which delegation is feasible. Our next chapter will deal with how the manager may exercise authority in the areas where he makes decisions on his own.

Delegation on the face-to-face, supervisor-subordinate level is often called *general supervision;* on the organization-wide level it is called *decentralization.* General supervision involves giving increased autonomy to individuals; decentralization involves giving it to organizational subunits. The discussion in this chapter is primarily concerned with the face-to-face level, but much of what we have to say will apply to organization-wide decentralization as well.

THE MEANING OF DELEGATION

Delegation is, above all, a means of internalized motivation. Delegation is really a form of job enlargement, for it gives each subordinate a sense of being his own boss and exercising control over his work environment. As such, it seeks to offset the monotony and lack of autonomy that technology has built into many jobs. In paths-goals terms, it attempts to restructure the job so that harder work is in fact rewarded by greater satisfaction.

In applying delegation, a manager makes relatively few decisions by himself and frames his orders in broad, general terms. He is interested primarily in results, and he permits his subordinates to work out the details for themselves. He sets goals, tells his subordinates what he wants accomplished, fixes the limits within which they can work, and (if the subordinates are adequately trained) lets them decide how to achieve these goals. Instead of rattling off a list of orders, he is likely to communicate helpful information or make suggestions. He explains *why* he wants things done and points out how the subordinate's contribution fits into the over-all plan. In other words, he gives each subordinate the maximum freedom he can handle consistent with the aims of the organization. A successful plant manager exaggerated only a bit when he said:

"I never make a decision by myself. Oh, I guess I have one or two since I have been here. If people know their job, I believe in letting them make their own decisions. Of course, if there is anything which affects the entire plant, I bring the staff in to discuss it. But I don't believe in saying, 'This is the way it is going to be done.' "

Other managers seem to be unable to take this approach. They are inclined to give detailed instructions telling subordinates exactly how, and in what sequence, they want things done. They "were found to check up on their employees more frequently, to give them more frequent instructions, and in general to limit their freedom to do their work in their own way." [1]

Compare, for example, the difference in approach used by two office managers as they handed out the same assignment.

Office Manager A: "Call Jones Office Equipment and the Wilson Supply Store. Get them to quote you prices on all the office dictation equipment they will. Ask them to give you a demonstration. Invite two managers to the demonstration, Ellis and Conrad, and let them try it out. Get them to put their reactions on paper. Then prepare me a report with the costs and specifications of all the equipment. Oh, yes, be sure to ask for information on repair costs. . . ." (And so on.)

Office Manager B: "I'd like to do something about our stenographic system. A lot of the executives who don't have secretaries of their own are complaining that it takes them too long to get a girl who can handle their dictation. Could you check up on some of the various kinds of dictating machines, find their prices, advantages and disadvantages, and give me a recommendation as to what we should do? I think we can spend $2,000. Possibly you could talk to some of the executives to get their ideas."

Office Manager A tried to think of all contingencies and in doing so gave his subordinate the feeling that she was little more than an errand girl. Moreover, he took so much trouble in trying to think of all the possibilities that he might as well have done the work himself.

The Advantages of Delegation

What are the advantages of delegation?

1. Few supervisors have the time to handle both their own job and the jobs of their subordinates. The close supervisor who tries to make every

[1] Daniel Katz and Robert L. Kahn, "Human Organization and Worker Motivation," in L. Reed Tripp, ed., *Industrial Productivity* (Madison, Wisc.: Industrial Relations Research Association, 1951), p. 157.

decision by himself frequently exhausts himself physically and mentally. Furthermore, his decision may not be as good as those of his subordinates, since the man who is closest to a problem usually understands it better than anyone else.[2]

2. A subordinate can take pride in results that are directly attributable to his own judgment. He feels little involvement in his work when someone else makes all the decisions.

3. Delegation helps to develop the talents and abilities of subordinates. It is hard to train people to take the risks of decision-making without putting them in a position of making decisions on their own. Over-close supervision makes it difficult for people to learn, even by making mistakes.

Use of Pressure

One difference between what might be called delegation and close supervision lies in the use of pressure. Note how these managers "push" their men:

"I handle the amount of work given each clerk, watch the dates and time the work so that everything gets out on schedule. If a letter comes in late, we have to speed up handling it— give it special attention. It has to be rushed along—handled in a different fashion than the usual run. I have to watch this to see that we make up time lost in other departments."[3]

"A factory is not a kindergarten. We've got schedules to meet and my job is to make sure that we meet them. ... If you start babying the men, they will take advantage of you. They expect you to be tough."

Apparently, the managers quoted here have little trust in their subordinates' initiative or judgment, and feel that they have to check up on them constantly to make sure that they carry out instructions.

Note the difference in attitude reflected by this comment made by a manager who did exactly the same job as the first manager quoted above.

"If you keep your employees from feeling hounded, they are more likely to put out the necessary effort to get the work done on time. ... I tell them, 'if you feel the job is getting you down, get away from it for a few minutes.' "[4]

It should be emphasized that the absence of pressure does not mean that subordinates are free to set their own standards. As we shall discuss shortly, delegation is rarely possible unless subordinates are given some sort of direction. High standards are essential if the organization is to be effective. They are also important from the standpoint of morale, since most people derive satisfaction

---

[2] As we shall discuss in Chapter 14, the spread of computers has somewhat reduced this advantage of delegation. Provided information can be translated into computer language, electronic data-processing makes it possible to communicate the information quickly and accurately from subordinates to the data-processing center, and the computer itself never becomes exhausted from making too many decisions.

[3] Daniel Katz, Nathan Maccoby, and Nancy C. Morse, *Productivity, Supervision, and Morale in an Office Situation* (Ann Arbor: University of Michigan, Institute for Social Research, 1950), p. 18.

[4] Rensis Likert and Daniel Katz, "Supervisory Practices and Organizational Structure as They Affect Employee Morale," in Schuyler Hoslett, ed., *Human Factors in Management,* 2d. ed. (New York: Harper, 1951), p. 92.

from completing a difficult task. By setting exalted standards the leader indicates that he has confidence in his men. Throughout history, effective leaders have inspired their followers to strive for seemingly impossible goals.

In one sense, the general supervisor does apply pressure when he sets the goals he expects his subordinates to achieve. This is a very different kind of pressure, however, from the nagging, "breathing down a man's neck" type of pressure exerted by close supervisors. If subordinates accept the goals of the organization as valid, they tend to feel that the pressure to do a good job *originated* from the goals themselves, rather than from the supervisor. But we shall discuss this point later on.

Managerial Assumptions as to Subordinates' Abilities

The extent to which managers delegate may depend on their faith in their subordinates' abilities. The manager who feels that his subordinates are essentially lazy and untrustworthy is likely to exercise close supervision. He follows the precepts of "be strong" and in effect says, "Men will shirk their task whenever they can. If I were to leave the shop, everyone would stop work" (and no doubt, in his case, exactly this would happen).

Other managers may believe that their subordinates are loyal and dependable but incapable of initiative or judgment. Such managers may engage in hygienic management and may even permit participation in fairly trivial areas; however, they are unlikely to delegate extensively. Only when the manager has confidence in his subordinates' abilities is he likely to delegate to a significant degree.

SUBSTITUTES FOR DECISION-MAKING BY THE BOSS

Effective delegation does not mean that subordinates are permitted to do exactly what they want. Quite the contrary. Delegation is feasible only when there are means available (other than the superior's making the decision himself) which can insure that subordinates will make decisions which are at least "adequate" from the viewpoint of the organization. To use a fashionable term, subordinates must be "programed" (or directed) to insure that they conform to patterns of behavior which are consistent with organizational needs.

The extent of programing necessary, whether it is tight or loose, may depend on a number of factors which we shall discuss later. First, however, we shall consider four types of programing (or four means of avoiding direct orders) which are available to management. The first three are *rules, goals,* and *indoctrination.* The fourth, on a somewhat different level, is the influence of *technology and work-flow.* Let us look at these in turn.

Rules

Rules are a means by which the decision-making activities of subordinates are programed so that it is unnecessary for every decision to be referred to the supervisor. Thus, rules save time for the executive. His subordinates do not have to consult him on routine matters, for the rules lay down principles in advance. Decisions can, therefore, be made more quickly and at lower levels.

Rules set up standard operating procedures. They may be written or unwritten; they may be established by supervisory edict, by training, by implicit bargaining, or through consultation. The significant points are that rules (1) restrict subordinate behavior, and (2) are enforced, in one way or another, by management (and, as we shall see in Chapter 9, sometimes by the subordinate's peers as well). Though many people disparage rules (particularly written rules) as "red tape," they are essential if an organization is to operate effectively.

Rules serve to limit the freedom of subordinates. Naturally, the greater the area of freedom given the subordinate, the greater the feeling of autonomy he will have. Unfortunately, the subordinate cannot be given authority to do *everything* he wants: Well-understood limits or rules make it possible for him to exercise freedom within these limits. Sometimes, of course, these rules are implicit and need not be spelled out in detail.

Suppose you are the office manager and the Big Boss tells you: "Go ahead, use your discretion in redecorating the office. Anything you say, goes!" Beware! He doesn't really mean that. There are certainly clearly understood rules within which you must work. You must abide by the city building codes and the union contract. You cannot exceed your budget. Further, you must go through the purchasing department, fill out the proper forms, and so forth.

Also, if you are smart, you know that redecorating must play second fiddle to keeping production going. Unless you are on Madison Avenue, the office better wind up looking like an office, not a ladies' lounge or a Japanese garden.

Where there is room for doubt, the supervisor should state the rules clearly, sometimes even in writing. As we shall note later, it often seems that people are objecting to responsibility, when they are really objecting to uncertainty.

Rules have both advantages and disadvantages, as the following sections discuss.

Establish consistency. Particularly in large organizations, rules serve to make the behavior of the parts consistent with the needs of the whole. They reduce the possibility that personal feelings rather than organizational objectives will predominate in decision-making. For instance, in an effort to achieve uniformity, management frequently promulgates standard lists of penalties for disciplinary infractions. Thus, excessive absenteeism will result in the same penalty in every department, even though managers may not agree about the seriousness of this offense. The alternative would be to have one man handle all discipline.

Reduce personal dependency. Rules are impersonal and, in effect, reduce the power of both the boss and the subordinate. This makes it easier for the subordinate to obey and for the boss to exercise authority. An office manager put it:

It sure helped me when top management put in a rule that everyone must fly tourist class. This way when I turn down expense accounts with first class fare, the men know it isn't my fault (and almost no one puts it in any more).

Rules also protect the subordinate from arbitrary actions on the part of his boss. They are useful in defining employees' duties and responsibilities. They enable subordinates to predict the consequences of their actions—an ability that is essential to personal security. Well-thought-out rules establish limits within which employees are free to act on their own. Persons on higher levels step in only when one of these limits is violated, or when a question comes up which is not covered by existing policy. As a result, the position of employees is strengthened all down the line.

Permit routinization. Rules require the manager to initiate orders only once—when he lays a rule down. Most people prefer not to receive constant initiation, particularly when they cannot return it. But once rules are established for how a man should do his job (and once he is adequately trained in the meaning of these rules), then the job can be reduced to a routine. And "routinization protects the ego of those who would otherwise be continually ordered around."[5]

The value of rules in establishing routine was brought sharply to our attention in a training class for telephone supervisors. We asked a chief operator if she found it hard to delegate or give autonomy to operators since the nature of their job provided them little opportunity for discretion. "Oh, no," she said, "once a girl is trained, I let her completely alone. She knows her job and knows what she is supposed to do. She has complete freedom as long as she does her job."

Many employees apparently do experience a feeling of autonomy under such circumstances. Usually it is a situation characterized by constant change that requires most direction:

In their drive for change and progress, many executives overlook the stabilizing nature of work routines that can be built up and carried on by workers without constant attention from their supervisors. They fail to see that frequently imposed changes not only upset work habits of individuals, but also have a disturbing effect on the pattern of human relations that ties workers to each other and their supervisors.[6]

Excessively rigid rules. Rules may be too specific and detailed, however, and they may be applied too rigidly by subordinates who fail to use good judgment in handling specific cases. This is one symptom of what some people call "bureaucracy" (though the sociologists' definition is much more technical).

Unnecessary rules are difficult to enforce, and inadequately enforced rules may lead to a general breakdown of discipline. Even when they are enforced, if there are too many rules, men may live up only to the minimum requirements of the rules, feeling they have done all the company can reasonably require. Particularly when the reasonableness of the rules is neither self-evident nor well explained, they tend to make a man feel restricted, to breed resentment and aggressiveness, and at times to provoke a desire to break the rules just to prove one's independence.

[5] Henry Landsberger, "The Horizontal Dimension in Bureaucracy," *Administrative Science Quarterly*, Vol. 6, No. 3 (December 1961), p. 309.

[6] William F. Whyte, *Human Relations in the Restaurant Industry* (New York: McGraw-Hill, 1948), p. 263.

Excessively rigid rules also discourage individual discretion and initiative, and make it difficult for an organization to adapt to changing conditions. They give the petty tyrant a shield behind which he can vent his vindictiveness. They provide the inept supervisor with a crutch to lean on and enable him to avoid the conflicts and uncertainties of making decisions on his own. They subject the able supervisor to endless frustration and make it impossible for him to operate with the flexibility required for peak efficiency. At the very least, they lead to red tape and wasted effort. Here is the way the personnel director of a small branch plant described the effect of excessively rigid rules:

"The company employment procedures require us to check all references. This may be OK for some of the big plants with operations different from ours. But in this community with our type of work it is silly. We have written the top office a dozen times asking for an exception to be made for us. All they say is that it has to be uniform throughout the company. Why? Well, we go through the motions, but it really is a waste of time. *And in my job this kind of thing happens again and again.*"

Rules give the insecure supervisor a means of "passing the buck" for unpleasant decisions: "The office just issued a strict new policy—no more days off unless a man is sick; my hands are tied." The supervisor hopes, by blaming higher managers with whom the subordinate does not have any regular contact, to maintain his own good relationship with his subordinate. The result is a general weakening of the immediate supervisor's leadership position as well as damage to the employee's respect for the organization.

Rules have a tendency to become ends in themselves, particularly if those who carry them out forget the reasons for which they were promulgated in the first place. Consider this case:

In order to prevent salary increases from getting out of hand, top management decides that one per year is the limit for any employee. An exceptional employee does an outstanding job. To prevent him from accepting a better offer from another company, his supervisor tries to offer him an extra salary raise. The personnel department automatically turns the supervisor's request down, and the man quits.

We have no way of knowing, of course, whether this particular man should have been given an extra increase; we would need additional facts before deciding that. But it is clear that further investigation was called for before a decision was made.

Rebellious employees can cripple an organization by following every rule to the letter. For example, "follow-the-rules" campaigns have been successfully used by employees of the British Post Office and the Long Island Railroad as alternatives to the strike as means of putting pressure on management.

Correct use of rules. Rules are designed to set a general direction, to insure some measure of uniformity and consistency. But the basic reason for rules is not to restrict the individual, but to further the general welfare of the organization and the attainment of its goals. When a particular rule prevents this organizational objective from being attained, then it must give way, an exception must be made.

In summary, intelligently devised rules grant the individual in a large organization considerable freedom to make decisions on his own. To insure that his decisions are not completely unfettered, however, his actions need to conform to the goals of the total organization. This insurance is provided through setting limits—that is, through establishing rules. These rules or policies can free higher-level managers from the necessity of handling many time-consuming details. Subordinates do not have to check back with their boss each time an action or a decision is called for—they know the limits within which they can operate. The higher manager need step in only when one of the pre-established limits has been violated by a subordinate or when a case comes up that is not covered by existing policies. The danger is that the existence of rules makes it possible for the inept or autocratic manager to avoid his responsibility for making difficult decisions by interpreting rules in an excessively narrow fashion and "passing the buck."

Goal-Setting

By setting goals the manager can avoid the necessity for either making specific decisions or laying down detailed rules. This approach, which is in sharp contrast to detailed, minute-by-minute supervision, is often called "management by exception." It permits the subordinate to experiment, to adjust to novel situations.

Definite assignments. The manager who practices close supervision gives his subordinates detailed orders but sets no over-all goals toward which to work. As soon as the subordinate finishes one task, the manager gives him another. The manager's only goal seems to be to "keep the men busy." Few practices can be so destructive to morale.

The engineers studying a factory operation said the men could produce 500 units a day. The men said this was impossible. But one day, under the plant manager's urging, they really made an effort and reached their quota 30 minutes before the end of the shift. While they were congratulating themselves on their accomplishment, the plant manager saw them "loafing" and sent them back to work, saying that if they could complete 500 units in 7 hours, they ought to be able to get up to 550 or 600 tomorrow. And that is what he was expecting! Next day, production went down to 350.

When employees have the experiences of this sort day after day, they develop attitudes that have disastrous effect on output. "Work hard and what rewards do I get? More work. I might as well just *look* busy."

Delegation can be more effective when subordinates can be given definite assignments in terms of results expected. If an employee knows exactly how much he is expected to do, he has a goal to work for. He knows if he works hard now, he will have the reward of an easier time later on. He won't have to look busy just to keep out of trouble. (Once an employee told us, "I'm always in trouble because I work hard and finish up, so the boss sees me doing nothing. The man next to me has no trouble with the boss; he's slow and it looks like he is always working.")

On jobs which provide little satisfaction, leisure may be a strong reward. Some organizations allow employees who have finished their days' work to go home and still collect eight hours' pay. In England this practice is known as "job and finish." In America, electric-meter readers, postmen, and garbage-men often work on this basis. In all these occupations close supervision is almost impossible. (Of course, if a man finishes much too soon, the supervisor has an indication that the work has been assigned inequitably. Still, management must be careful not to kill incentive by using a few free minutes as an excuse to give a man extra work.)

On managerial levels, goals are also used. Thus, in many companies each department is considered a "profit center" for accounting purposes, and the departmental manager is given the goal of making the "planned profit" or of not exceeding "planned costs." Sales quotas are, of course, frequently assigned to salesmen. In each of these cases management must be careful not to destroy incentive by raising the goals too quickly after they have been reached.

Naturally, many assignments cannot be as specific as "Process 150 forms a day" or "Sell $500 worth of toothpaste a month." Some must be more general, such as "Wait on all customers who come to your counter" or "Handle all union grievances which come to your level." The latter sort of assignment does not, in itself, constitute a definite goal to work toward (unless it is put this way: "Take care of all these customers or grievances and you will have a few minutes break till the next group comes.") Still, a general assignment (such as "take care of all customers") provides more autonomy than does a host of specific instructions. There is real satisfaction in knowing "This is my job. Here I am in charge. As long as I do it adequately, no one will interfere with me. I will be judged on how well I do."

A number of companies have experimented with goals which are jointly set by the boss and his subordinates or by the subordinates themselves (see Chapter 9.) There is considerable evidence that goals set in this fashion are at least as high as those set by the boss alone—and that subordinates are more likely to feel such goals are fair and to be motivated to meet them.

Supervision by results.   Typically, when supervision by goal-setting is practiced, management interferes very little, so long as the goals are met, except perhaps to give subordinates praise, promotion, or some financial reward. Only when serious trouble develops does higher management step in. The establishment of standards has advantages from the point of view of both management and the individual employee.

1. The very fact that employees know their efforts are being measured may stir them to work harder. Statistical measures are sometimes more effective in insuring high output than are specific rules. To require each supervisor to make a monthly report on scrap loss may be more effective than a whole series of regulations or exhortations on avoiding waste. Such controls may also provide a swift means of altering the behavior of subordinates. Notice how this approach worked with interviewers in a public employment agency:

   Formerly, statistics were kept only on the *total* number of interviews carried on per month by each interviewer. This system motivated the interviewers to make a large number of *interviews,* but it gave them no incentive to find *jobs* for applicants. There was an immediate change in their behavior when statistics were also kept on the percentage of applicants who actually got jobs. In a two-month period the percentage of jobs filled jumped from 55 to 67. As one interviewer put it: "There is no tendency to get rid of an applicant as there was before. ... Since they are measured by placements, everybody tried to get a job for every applicant." [7]

2. Supervision by results makes each man feel that he is his own boss. He understands what is expected of him and is encouraged to show initiative and develop his potentialities. He has a goal to work for and a feeling of completion when he reaches it. This approach encourages competition between individuals and groups—though excessive competition has certain disadvantages, particularly when individuals are expected to work together.

3. The existence of a clear-cut set of performance standards makes it easier for superiors to criticize the shortcomings of their subordinates. Employees are often resentful when their boss talks about their personal failings: It is quite another matter when the criticism is couched in terms of helping them improve their record. In fact, the mere existence of such records tends to reduce the need for the supervisor to prod employees; they know automatically when they have fallen down on the job.

4. This approach to supervision makes it possible for higher management to discover when departments are having trouble and to take remedial measures quickly. As we shall discover in Chapter 14, this is a form of feedback, or upward communication.

5. Similarly, supervision by results makes it possible to evaluate the effectiveness of employees and supervisors and to decide who should get promotions or pay increases.

On the other hand, supervision by results can be attacked as over-emphasizing the individual at the expense of the group; as encouraging competition and passing the buck rather than fostering cooperation; as substituting for the single boss the more pervasive control of a number of "auditing departments" (such as accounting and quality control—see Chapter 15); and as placing excessive emphasis on immediate measurable results, as opposed to significant but immeasurable intangibles such as morale, good will, and employee development. Some of these problems, particularly as they relate to statistical controls, are discussed at greater length in Chapter 14.

Indoctrination

When employees fully accept the goals and values of the organization for which they work, they are said to be indoctrinated. Such persons are willing to subordinate their personal views to the higher interests of the organization as a whole. Indoctrination, in a sense, is a means of establishing organizational loyalty and commitment. Indoctrination makes it easier to delegate authority, since highly indoctrinated individuals all think in roughly the same terms and make

[7] Peter M. Blau, *The Dynamics of Bureaucracy* (Chicago: University of Chicago Press, 1955). p. 37.

their decisions on the basis of the same premises as their superiors. In other words, if a manager's subordinates are indoctrinated, he can feel sure that they will solve their problems in roughly the same way that he would himself. As a consequence, he has little need to be specific about rules or goals which his subordinates know as well as he does himself. They also know which goals are important and which can be broken when they conflict with others of higher priority. Ideally, then, with indoctrination, an organization can permit innovative flexibility as to *means*, knowing that there will be uniformity as to *ends*.

Many of the most effective organizations—such as the Marine Corps or the Catholic Church—rely on indoctrination to a high degree. A well-trained Marine can be relied on to "fight like a Marine" even in situations where he cannot be supervised by his superior officer. The Catholic Church operated for centuries on a decentralized world-wide basis, long before the advent of modern communications, largely because the strength of its priests' faith made it unnecessary for them to receive constant instructions from Rome. To a lesser degree many large corporations try to train their employees so that everyone in the organization can take a more or less consistent point of view towards their job. (Large corporations develop characteristic modes of operations and ways of thinking among their employees, and a General Electric man may well approach problems in a very different fashion from that of a man from Jersey Standard.)

As we pointed out in Chapter 3, professionals are also indoctrinated, but in terms of professional, not organizational, values. As long as the two are consistent (for example, as long as the company wants the scientist to engage in pure research or the company doctor to do his best to maintain employee health), decision-making power may be delegated to professionals with little need for external controls. But when professional and organizational objectives conflict (for example, when a scientist oriented towards pure research [8] is told to work on applied research), then some sort of closer control may be necessary. Skilled craftsmen are indoctrinated in much the same way. Their internalized sense of pride in craft motivates them to maintain high standards of workmanship as well as to put out a fair day's work.

Indoctrination usually requires a long period of hard training: The Catholic Church has its seminaries, the Marine Corps has boot camps, many companies have management training programs, [9] professionals, for the most part, learn their values in universities, and craftsmen in apprenticeship. Indoctrination is usually most effective, however, in organizations with high purposes and long traditions.

Indoctrination is far from being a universal cure-all for every management problem. Indoctrination can be really effective only when individuals internalize

[8] We do not subscribe to the myth that every scientist wants to do pure research. Many find considerable satisfaction working in the applied area.

[9] The function of management schools in providing managers with a common point of view has been described by IBM President Thomas J. Watson, Jr., as follows: "These schools were not only to teach general management, but—most important—they were to give our managers a feeling for IBM's outlooks and beliefs. After a time we found that the schools tended to put too much emphasis on management, not enough on beliefs. This, we felt, was putting the cart before the horse. We felt it was vital that our managers be well grounded in our beliefs. Otherwise, we might get management views at odds with the company's outlook." *A Business and Its Beliefs* (New York: McGraw-Hill, 1963), p. 91.

management's objectives and make them their own. The Church, the Marine Corps, and other such noneconomically oriented organizations have ideological appeals which make it possible to demand almost complete loyalty from their members; but business firms will rarely, if ever, win such perfect dedication. [10] Religious zealots may be willing to sacrifice their personal ambitions to advance the True Faith. But the typical corporate manager seeks to advance only *himself;* faced with a choice, personal success is more important to him than are corporate profits. And the typical worker has less interest in advancing the company's interests, particularly when he sees them as conflicting with his own. Thus, indoctrination in business may have a meaning considerably different from what it has in nonprofit institutions.

Still, indoctrination may be useful for instilling in organization members a common approach to problems which may reduce the need for restrictive rules. It is more effective, however, on the management level than among rank-and-file white- or blue-collar workers.

Technology and Work Flow

The nature of the work to be done restricts subordinates in much the same way as do direct orders, rules, and other supervisory techniques. The auto assembler's pace is set by the speed of the assembly line; the bank teller's, by his customers; the tool crib attendant's, by his fellow workers. In none of these cases does the superior have to tell his subordinates *how fast* to work; in each case controls are very simple: It becomes immediately obvious when a man falls down on the job.

Also, customers, fellow workers, and the demands of the work situation may tell the employee *what* to do; there is no need for the supervisor to initiate orders. This is true, for example, in a hospital operating room.

Although innumerable orders have been precisely responded to, most of them have flowed from the dictates of the patient's presence and condition. In a very real sense, few of the directives during surgery are arbitrary decisions on the surgeon's part. Rather, in the last analysis, the patient's needs have been the controlling element in the entire situation. Thus the person who seems to be the least capable of exerting authority—the supine, unconscious object—has in fact assumed the star role and preponderant influence in the course of the drama. [11]

Electric utility substation operators, who often work completely by themselves, report feeling that they are completely their own bosses, when in fact they have to respond to "orders" issued by dials and meters. In the same way, factory maintenance men work only when equipment breaks down, and how they do their work is normally determined by the nature of the emergency, not by the boss's instructions. As long as the subordinates are adequately trained and the technology remains relatively constant (two determining constraints), the boss

---

[10] In addition, the Church and the Marine Corps are able to isolate their members from conflicting pressures and values in a way which most businesses cannot. However, frequent transfers may reduce the strength of the business executives' loyalties to relatives, community, and social organizations.

[11] Temple Burling, Edith Lentz, and Robert Wilson, *The Give and Take in Hospitals* (New York: Putnam, 1956), p. 262.

intervenes only when there is obvious trouble. The most important problems involve lateral rather than boss-subordinate relations (we shall discuss lateral relations in Chapter 15).

When a man knows his job well, the mere giving of information serves as a substitute for an order. Note the difference between these two statements: "Bill, bring some parts over to Machine 16," and "Bill, Machine 16 is down to six parts." The second provides Bill with the information he needs to make his own decisions—and it assumes that he will make the correct one. It enables him to serve Machine 3 first if it has fewer parts than Machine 16. In addition, providing a man with abundant information has a positive effect on morale, even if he doesn't need all the information to do a good job.

Jobs can be rearranged to reduce the number of "human orders." We once observed a factory in which there was constant friction between operators and inspectors; the main trouble was the operators' resentment of what they felt was the inspectors' constant badgering to keep up quality. Only one inspector was able to keep up good relations. The secret of his success was that he rarely *told* a man he had made a mistake; instead, he showed him the offending part with the proper dimensions marked in chalk.

It should be emphasized that the various forms of programing just discussed are, in effect, substitutes for one another and for close supervision. As one form is strengthened, another may be weakened. For example, in times of rapid change, close supervision may be required, since goals are no longer well defined, the requirements of technology are not clearly understood, and new rules have yet to be devised and accepted. If indoctrination breaks down, then new rules must be enforced. When work becomes routine, then there may be less need for elaborate measurement of results because bottlenecks become immediately obvious, and perhaps just as immediately straightened out by those involved without need for intervention by higher management.

GENERAL SUPERVISION IN PRACTICE

By our definition, general supervision involves a high degree of delegation of authority and, in most cases, requires some indirect means in insuring that employees' behavior conforms to management's needs. We have emphasized that the general supervisor does not give constant orders nor does he spend a large part of his time checking up on employees or putting pressure on them to keep working.

What does the general supervisor do with his time then? As we shall discuss in Chapter 16, spending less time giving orders to each subordinate may permit a general supervisor to manage larger numbers of subordinates (in terms which we will discuss later, he can expand his *span of control* and have a *flatter organization*). Even where this does not occur, the activities of the general supervisor may differ substantially from those of close supervisors. General supervisors are more likely (1) to do work different from that of subordinates, (2) to concentrate on long-range rather than short-range problems and, (3) to engage in training. Let us look at these activities in turn.

Different Work from That Done by Subordinates

There is an old tradition that the good supervisor is the one who rolls up his sleeves and works alongside his subordinates, often setting an example by his efforts. The evidence suggests that this is a myth. Of course, in an emergency the good supervisor will always pitch in to help. And there are certain supervisory jobs that require close technical coordination, jobs such as that of orchestra conductor or engineering project manager. With these exceptions, however, research indicates that the high-productivity supervisor devotes much of his time to activities that pay off only in the long run, such as planning, improving human relations, and co-ordinating activities with other departments.[12] The low-productivity supervisor is more likely to do the same sort of work as his men, and to concentrate on paper work and short-term activities such as checking up on his subordinates or arranging for materials.

How can we explain these differences? In the first place, the close supervisor may seek to avoid the personal contacts required for effective leadership. He may feel more secure working with his hands or mind than trying to cope with human-relations problems. This is particularly true of the man who has come up through the ranks and to whom the supervisory position has been given as a reward for hard work, technical competence, and seniority rather than as a recognition of leadership abilities. Faced with an entirely new and confusing set of problems that he is ill-equipped to handle, he retreats to a behavior pattern in which he feels secure. The following account describes what happened to head nurses in a hospital—but it applies equally well to business situations:

In some hospitals women were raised to positions of authority over nursing floors because they had worked there the longest and had proved to be excellent craftsmen. Sometimes they had no experience whatsoever in organizing the work of others. Such a person, since her field of competence lay in the art of nursing rather than in supervision, tended to do what she was best at, which was to give direct bedside care. She put off the other parts of her job, resenting the time spent on paper-work, supervision and teaching. Sometimes a head nurse would have so much pride in her command of nursing skills that she found great difficulty in accepting the less perfect work of subordinates. She would follow each student or auxiliary around, picking up where they left off and finishing the job for them. . . .

Another type of retreat was that taken by the head nurse who centered all her attention on paper work. Sometimes this was an older woman who looked upon her promotion to this post as a graduation from hard labor, a kind of semi-retirement from the strains of bedside nursing.[13]

The very fact that the manager works alongside his men means that he must engage in close supervision. His presence provides a form of "pacesetting," and his men may well feel that his directions and example are a reflection of his belief that they cannot be left to do the job on their own.

True, it is difficult for a manager to avoid close supervision of this sort. Every manager feels a strong temptation to fix up a subordinate's mistakes

[12] Much of the most interesting work in this area has been done by the Institute for Social Research, University of Michigan. For summaries of this work, see Robert L. Kahn and Daniel Katz, "Leadership Practices in Relationship to Productivity and Morale," in Dorwin Cartwright and Alvin Zander, eds., *Group Dynamics, Research and Theory* (New York: Harper, 1953), pp. 612-627; and Rensis Likert, *The Human Organization* (New York: McGraw-Hill, 1967).

[13] Burling, Lentz, and Wilson, *op. cit.*, pp. 113-114.

himself rather than explain what should have been done. Doing something oneself is usually easier than teaching. As a supervisor in an engineering laboratory put it:

"Frankly, I've had a lot more experience than anyone in my section. Most of the time when I hand out a problem I can get the solution very easily. It requires superhuman control to let those guys take three times as long as I would to get the answer. But how else can they learn?"

The close supervisor either keeps nagging his subordinates, feeling that constant pressure is the best way to get results—or does the work himself and thus tries to avoid personal contacts.[14] The general supervisor, however, tries to provide explanations and motivate his employees to improve their performance. Instead of rushing in and taking the job into his own hands, he is patient enough to help a subordinate who has failed.

Concentration on Long-Range Problems

There is a significant difference between the way the general supervisor and the close supervisor spend their time on their job. The close supervisor is a man who runs from crisis to crisis putting out fires. He is concerned exclusively with the here and now (or perhaps checking on the past). He has no time for anything but short, specific instructions. Often he dispenses even with these, and pitches in to do the job himself. The general supervisor, on the other hand, looks to the future. He spends more time on planning, working to improve relations with other departments, setting goals, and training subordinates so they can meet emergencies without coming to him. In a sense he is making a capital investment of his time from which he will derive gains in time saved over the long run.

When employees are well trained and when work is delegated, the supervisor has time to concentrate on the over-all problems of his department and to develop new, more permanent solutions rather than just to cope with each crisis as it comes along. For instance, how does the supervisor react when a severe problem suddenly arises that calls for several men to work overtime? Does he go to each man in the department to ask him whether he is willing to stay late? Or does he develop a method of getting people to indicate in advance when they want extra work? The time the supervisor saves by adopting the second approach can be used for many useful purposes, including the improvement of relations with his boss, with staff sections, and with other departments with which his own department has to cooperate.

A study at General Electric reported this observation:

The least effective foremen spent the greatest percentage of their time finding immediate solutions to short-range production problems, while the most effective foremen spent the greatest percentage of their time on activities which involved planning and organizing the longer-range aspects of the job. The less effective foremen spent more time checking on work progress or status, securing materials, supervising materials or production movement, and similar activities which successful managers apparently delegate. Probably because of their greater emphasis on training employees, their belief in their abilities to carry out their assigned

[14] The term "close supervision" may seem inappropriate when applied to the man who avoids personal contacts and shuns supervising. Yet when this man does supervise, he is likely to supervise in detail.

tasks without checking, and greater success in organizing the work of their groups, better foremen did not find it necessary to continuously check the conditions in their area. [15]

Here is a summary of the findings on how the two groups of GE foremen spent their time. [16]

	FOREMEN	
Activity	Effective	Ineffective
Production	20%	40%
Personnel administration	23%	12%
Equipment and methods	14%	8%
Quality	6%	6%

There were similar differences in the pattern of communication between supervisors and their work groups: [17]

	FOREMEN	
Type of Communication	Effective	Ineffective
Giving *specific* work orders	3%	15%
Giving *general* work orders	5%	1%
Passing information to the group or engaging in two-way discussions with members of the work group	67%	47%
Receiving information from workers	25%	37%

The study comes to this conclusion:

When the more effective foremen found it necessary to give direction to the work of their employees, they would do so in a general way, giving explanations and suggestions, but leaving details of method and sequence up to the worker. The less effective foreman, on the other hand, gave a far greater number of direct work orders, without explaining why a job should be done, or how the specific order related to the over-all work pattern. [18]

General supervisors seek to develop an atmosphere in which workers feel free to bring their problems to them. In this atmosphere subordinates ask for help and information when it is needed, thus reducing the supervisor's need to give instructions. As one foreman told us:

"As far as getting action is concerned, it doesn't make much difference whether you *tell* a man what to do or he *asks* you. But it makes all the difference in the world in how he feels. So I try to be available for questions instead of telling people."

The GE study found that effective foremen were aware of this difference: "The lower-rated foremen spent more time seeking information from others, while the

[15] General Electric Company, Public and Employee Relations Service, *The Effective Manufacturing Foreman* (processed, 1957), p. 47; see also Quentin D. Ponder, "The Effective Manufacturing Foreman," in *Proceedings of the Tenth Annual Meeting* (Madison: Industrial Relations Research Association, 1957), pp. 41–54.

[16] Ponder, *op. cit.*, p. 47. The percentages do not add up to 100 because a number of miscellaneous activities are omitted.

[17] *Ibid.*, p. 52.

[18] *Ibid.*, p. 52.

higher-rated foremen spent more time answering requests for information," [19] as well as in improving their relations with their bosses, staff sections, and other departments. Here is a summary of how these supervisors spent their time.

FOREMEN

People Dealt With	Effective	Ineffective
Staff and service people	32%	20%
Own subordinates	19%	17%

This distribution is consistent with other findings that one of the most important functions of the supervisor is to represent his work group to other groups in the organization.

What picture of the general supervisor emerges from all these observations? The picture of a man who is abreast of his job, who gives his subordinates a broad range of freedom, and who is regarded by them as being available for help rather than being a source of pressure. In the studies cited, the supervisors who exhibited these characteristics were also the ones who had the most effective, productive subordinates.

Training

We have already mentioned that the manager who engages in general supervision places considerable emphasis on training his subordinates. Well-trained men have no need for detailed instruction. It has been said that the test of a good manager is what happens when he is away from his department. If his men have been trained well, everything goes so smoothly that he is hardly missed.

The close supervisor and the general supervisor adopt very different approaches to training. The close supervisor tends to equate training with the never-ending issuance of specific instructions; to him training and detailed supervision are identical. He has no interest in helping his subordinates learn so they can do without close supervision.

The general supervisor explains the *why* of his instructions; he gives his subordinates the theory, the over-all framework within which this particular instruction fits. Provided with this framework, subordinates can cope with unusual problems without having to run to their boss for new instructions every time a problem arises. Patient explanation and demonstration by the manager is frequently an essential first step. But in many areas it is more effective if the trainee is given an opportunity to think out his problems by himself—under guidance. For instance, when giving a new assignment the manager should try to avoid saying, "I want you to do it this way." Instead he might ask, "Do you have any ideas how this should be done?" and then encourage the subordinate to work out the problems involved. Possibly the manager can listen to the subordinate as he thinks through the problems out loud. If the subordinate cannot arrive at a satisfactory solution on his own, of course, the manager offers suggestions. But he is careful to give the subordinate maximum opportunity (consistent with his ability) to figure things out by himself.

[19] *Ibid.,* p. 51.

WHEN DOES GENERAL SUPERVISION WORK BEST?

We have spent our time so far contrasting close and general supervision, but with the exception of the GE study, we have said very little about what sort of supervision is most effective, principally because this is still a highly uncertain area. There has been a good deal of research in the area, but much of it is inconclusive and the most we can say is that there is no simple answer.[20] It does seem that a broad range of people (but not everyone) finds delegation satisfying. But this does not mean that delegation necessarily results in higher productivity. About all we can say is that the extent to which delegation will be effective varies with the circumstances. What are the circumstances? Here, the research data is very scanty, and the best we can do is to offer some hypotheses only partly supported by evidence.

It seems that general supervision works best (1) where the work provides intrinsic job satisfaction; (2) where the work group accepts management's objectives; (3) where worker and union-management reactions are harmonious; (4) where consistency and coordination are relatively unimportant; (5) where technology permits individual discretion; (6) where subordinates desire responsibility; (7) in the long run rather than in the short run; and (8) where the delegation is consistent with organizational climate.

Where the Work Provides Intrinsic Job Satisfaction

According to paths-goals analysis, general supervision is not likely to lead to higher production unless general supervision increases the sense of achievement that the employer gets from such higher production. Greater freedom to do a boring job may provide very little sense of achievement. General supervision seems most effective when a job is challenging, the work cycle is long, and there is an opportunity for intrinsic job satisfaction. In contrast, where there is little opportunity for creativity and internalized motivation, employees are less likely to perform effectively when left by themselves. One study suggests that, compared to unskilled workers, skilled workers feel more involved in their jobs and are more anxious for an opportunity to participate in making decisions relating to it.[21] Another study indicates a less positive relationship between general supervision and productivity on jobs where the work is machine-paced than on jobs where the men pace themselves.[22] Thus, in some cases, job enrichment may be a precondition for effective delegation.

General attitudes toward work are relevant here. Journeymen printers, for example, are very proud of their craft. They have internalized management's objectives of putting out high-quality work, and have a long tradition of self-

---

[20] One reason for caution in this area is that the relationship between cause and effect is rarely clear. A study may find that close supervisors have less efficient departments, but this does not prove that close supervision *causes* low efficiency. It may be that in departments where efficiency is low, close supervision is the most intelligent way of getting it back to normal.

[21] Howard Vollmer, *Employee Rights and the Employment Relationship* (Berkeley: University of California Press, 1960), Chapter 4.

[22] Michael Argyl, Godfrey Gardner, and Frank Cioffi, "Supervisory Methods Related to Productivity and Labor Turnover," *Human Relations*, Vol. 9, No. 1 (1958), p. 38.

regulation. With such a group anything but general supervision would be resented. On the other hand, relatively less benefit might be derived from general supervision in the textile industry, where workers generally have low aspirations, place little value in self-expression, display an "indifferent attitude toward the meaningfulness of work,"[23] and do not have work as a central life interest.

As mentioned earlier, the fact that a given job may offer *some* people intrinsic job satisfaction is not enough to motivate *everyone* to work hard at it. If a man does not feel his job offers challenge to *him*—if he does not value the skills the job requires—then delegation is not likely to lead to higher productivity.

Where the Work Group Accepts Management's Objectives

The general attitude of the work group toward management's objectives is also significant in determining whether delegation is realistic. If the group is indoctrinated to support these objectives, then a high degree of delegation may be feasible. But, as we shall discuss in Chapter 9, if the group does not support these objectives, then more autocratic techniques must be used to get the work done. A higher degree of delegation is possible in a hospital or a social agency, where presumably the organizational objectives are highly valued by the participants, than might be possible in a jail or concentration camp. In general, too, delegation works better where employees have become professionalized.

Where Worker and Union-Management Relations Are Harmonious

Obviously, general supervision is difficult to practice in the face of a militantly antimanagement union or where subordinates are bitterly divided on ethnic or other grounds. Similarly, it is hard to elicit cooperation in communities or in cultures where there is a long tradition of hostility to management and where everything a "boss" does is automatically looked upon with suspicion.

Where Consistency and Coordination Are Relatively Unimportant

In many instances the nature of a job requires that subordinates follow a uniform pattern of behavior, for example, where the job permits outsiders to compare behavior among employees. Thus, in a firm that deals with hostile unions, responsibility for labor relations is far more likely to be centralized than is training (which is a purely internal matter). Similarly, internal revenue agents are checked closely by top management in the Treasury Department to insure that there is a common, nationwide policy toward interpreting the law.

The nature of internal work-flow is another important factor. More delegation is feasible where there is "parallel" specialization than where specialization is "interdependent." Parallel specialization occurs where work activities are assigned so as to minimize the amount of coordination required, that is, where there is relatively little work-flow among individuals and departments. Inter-

[23] Robert Blauner, *Alienation and Freedom* (Chicago: University of Chicago Press, 1964), p. 176.

dependent specialization exists where the day-to-day functioning of the job of one individual or department is closely related to that of other individuals or departments. For example, in the programing of computers there may be a number of programers who each do part of the job. Since their respective activities must fit perfectly into one another, the manager must specify in great detail how each is to proceed.

An automobile assembly line, with its closely coordinated work flow, is a prime example of interdependent specialization, whereas a university represents parallel specialization. Indeed, academic freedom is possible largely because each professor can proceed on his own in research or class with only a minimum of coordination with others in the university.

Where the Technology Permits Individual Discretion

Technology often limits the amount of discretion which subordinates can be given. Some equipment can be operated only in one way; once it is put in place employees have no choice but to follow the prescribed routines. In some work, mistakes can be so expensive that higher management feels obligated to check subordinates constantly.

The need for decisive decision-making on many jobs leaves little room for delegation. The conductor of a symphony orchestra must exercise strong leadership and there is little opportunity for delegation or participation (a jazz combo on the other hand may practice considerable participation). Decisive decision-making is also required of a surgeon in the operating room, an aircraft pilot, and a ship's captain. In each of these cases subordinates are likely to get their satisfactions from the excellence of their performance as a team rather than from the opportunity to exercise discretion. As we shall discuss in Chapter 8, in these cases human-relations ability may well be subordinate, in the eyes of subordinates, to technical ability.

Technology also determines how managers might best interact with subordinates. A study of parcel delivery service indicated that drivers, who see their boss only for a few minutes each day, are more likely to prefer bosses with strong authoritarian attitudes, whereas positioners, men who handle parcels on the dock and who work in close contact with their boss all day long, prefer those who are not authoritarian. Since drivers spend only a short time with their boss, apparently they prefer someone who is decisive. [24]

Where Subordinates Desire Responsibility

There are substantial differences in the amount of responsibility people are willing to accept on the job. [25] One person may flourish under supervision that

[24] Victor H. Vroom and Floyd C. Mann, "Leader Authoritarianism and Employee Attitudes," *Personnel Psychology*, Vol. 13, No. 2 (Summer 1960), pp. 125–140.

[25] People may also differ in the areas in which they wish responsibility. Some individuals may accept a great amount in their home life and in community organizations, yet not wish much on the job.

another might find extremely restrictive. One of the authors learned this lesson the hard way when he was working in a government agency some years ago and was assigned an elderly secretary. Imbued with the principles of good human relations, he explained in detail the background of every letter he dictated, asked for her comments on style, and even suggested that, if she wished, she could draft some of the letters herself. At last she burst out. "I'm not paid to do that kind of work! That's your job."

Psychological research provides evidence that the nature of a person's personality affects his attitude toward supervision. Employees with a low need for achievement and high fear of failure shy away from challenges and responsibilities. Many seek self-expression off the job and ask only to be allowed to daydream on it. (For example, women who look upon their job as only a brief interlude before marriage may have relatively little desire for autonomy.) One study, for example, suggests that people who have a high need for independence and weak authoritarian attitudes are likely to respond to consultation with their supervisors by being more satisfied with their work and turning out a better performance; those with low needs for independence and strong authoritarian values are much less likely to respond in this manner. [26] In addition, there are many who have become so accustomed to the authoritarian approach in their culture, family, and previous work experience that they regard general supervision as no supervision at all. They abuse the privileges it bestows on them and refuse to accept the responsibilities it demands.

Consider the case of two hospital floors supervised by two very different head nurses. [27] The first head nurse (Miss Smith), though extremely courteous, was strict and uncompromising with nurses who violated regulations. She insisted that conversations be kept to a minimum and handed out detailed, unambiguous work assignments to her nurses.

The second head nurse (Miss Rogers) had a much more informal, almost kidding relationship with her subordinates and patients. She consulted with her nurses about problems and changes and succeeded in developing a strong feeling of camaraderie on the floor.

Now you might suppose that all the nurses would have preferred Miss Rogers' floor to Miss Smith's—but they didn't. The hospital let nurses choose which floor they wanted to work on; both floors were quite popular, but with different groups of nurses. In general the older women liked the security of Miss Smith's floor, where everything went according to predetermined routine. As one older nurse put it:

"I honestly feel I need a responsible person nearby to supervise me. I need guidance and therefore I prefer to work where there is fairly close supervision. . . . I like to do things in an orderly way. . . . (on Miss Rogers' floor) things are done too sloppily."

Most of the younger girls preferred the independence allowed them by Miss Rogers.

26 Victor H. Vroom, *Some Personality Determinants of the Effects of Participation* (Englewood Cliffs, N.J.: Prentice-Hall, 1960).

27 This case is based on the research of Edith Hamilton.

Why these differences? For one thing, nurses' training in recent years has become less strict than it once was, and the younger nurses have never experienced close supervision. More important, these differences may reflect an attitude toward authority that the younger girls developed in their formative years at home and at school, an attitude influenced by the wide range of freedom permitted to modern children. Indeed, subordinates' feelings toward their boss are often colored by the relations they had with their parents and the emotional maturity and security they developed as children.

Different groups develop different attitudes toward work. College graduates, for example, expect a great deal of responsibility and freedom. Certain ethnic groups, on the other hand, have trouble accepting the concept that people should make decisions for themselves, particularly decisions concerning work.[28] The Chippewa Indians are brought up in a cultural tradition which teaches one not to take the initiative. "In their passivity, restraint and expectation of immediate results . . . there is scant evidence that the average adolescent, once he leaves [the reservation] will acquire the inner ambition that helps to produce a high standard of living."[29]

Americans have often run into trouble trying to apply general supervision abroad. According to recent studies, Peruvian culture is characterized by rigid status distinctions and low levels of interpersonal trust. The concept of leadership (as opposed to domination) is unknown in the language. In contrast to most American findings, close supervision is positively correlated to job satisfaction.[30]

Several studies in the United States have compared reactions of urban and rural blue-collar workers to various degrees of challenge on the job.[31] In general, rural workers tend to react positively to work requiring greater skill and greater acceptance of job responsibility. Urban workers, on the other hand, seem either to have no preference or actually to prefer simpler, less challenging tasks. This surprising contrast is hard to explain. Possibly work and achievement (the so-called Protestant ethic) are more central to the life interests of those with a rural background than they are to those from certain ethnic groups in the city. Certainly those brought up on a farm are introduced to chores (now a rarity in city families) at an early age. For them, work and discipline are easily taken in stride. The city workers, on the other hand, seem to value more highly social satisfaction on and off the job. For them, the job is merely a means to an end.

[28] For examples from various countries see Heinz Hartmann, *Authority and Organization in German Management* (Princeton: Princeton University Press, 1959); James Abegglen, *The Japanese Factory* (New York: Free Press, 1958); and Frederick Harbison and Eugene Burgess, "Modern Management in Western Europe," *American Journal of Sociology*, Vol. 60, No. 1 (July 1954), pp. 15–23.

[29] Frank C. Miller and D. Douglas Caulkins, "Chippewa Adolescents: A Changing Generation," *Human Organization*, Vol. 23, No. 2 (Summer 1964), p. 159.

[30] William F. Whyte, *Organizational Behavior* (Homewood: Irwin, 1969), Chap. 32.

[31] This area is still quite controversial, with some of the controversy relating to methodology. Among the studies that find differences between rural and urban workers are Arthur N. Turner and Paul R. Lawrence, *Industrial Jobs and the Worker* (Boston: Harvard University Graduate School of Business Administration, 1965) and Charles L. Hulin and Milton R. Blood, "Job Enlargement, Individual Differences, and Worker Responses," *Psychological Bulletin*, Vol. 69, No. 1 (January 1968), pp. 41–45. For different findings, see Jon M. Shepard, "Functional Specialization, Alienation, and Job Satisfaction," *Industrial and Labor Relations Review*, Vol. 23, No. 2 (January 1970), pp. 207–219.

In the Long Run rather than the Short Run

Even under close supervision, a work group may be highly productive, particularly in times of widespread unemployment when men are fearful of losing their jobs. In fact, management has often found that the best way to get an immediate increase in production is to increase pressure and to impose close supervision. In the long run, however, close supervision may well lead to a deterioration of morale and productivity and to what one author calls "a liquidation of human assets."[32]

One experiment involved four divisions of a large company, each of which had about 100 clerical employees.[33] In two of these divisions managers and supervisors were trained in the principles of general supervision. In the other two divisions management cut the number of employees by 25 per cent without reducing the work load and systematically intensified the pressure and closeness of supervision. By the end of twelve months both groups had increased productivity. But the closely supervised group had increased theirs by 25 per cent compared with a 20 per cent increase for the group under general supervision. The employees under general supervision, however, showed significant improvements in measures showing loyalty, feeling of responsibility, and involvement in work. In the other group these same indices declined dramatically.

Of course, lowered morale need not lead to a decline in production. But increased pressure may well result in resistance on the part of individuals, informal work groups, and the union; in restriction of output; and in all the familiar symptoms of aggression that we discussed earlier. Under these circumstances management is often tempted to enter into the vicious cycle of closer and closer supervision, to which the employees reply by sabotage, wildcat strikes and ever-tightening output restrictions.

On the other hand, the sudden introduction of general supervision is unlikely to lead to an immediate increase in production where the individuals involved have become accustomed to close supervision. If, because of their previous experience, workers expect to be pushed into work, chances are that they will abuse any relaxation of pressure unless the process is handled with great skill. They may look upon the manager who tries to apply general supervision as weak and flabby. At times the manager who is being trained to use general supervision is regarded by his subordinates as threatening because his behavior is unpredictable. Employees sometimes find it easier to work for a hard-bitten so-and-so whose behavior is more predictable than one who seems to be changing his behavior every day.

Where Delegation Is a Consistent Pattern

The *over-all pattern* of supervision is more important than any one aspect of it. There is a danger that managers may adopt certain features of general

---

[32] Rensis Likert, "Measuring Organizational Performance," *Harvard Business Review*, Vol. 16, No. 2 (March-April 1958), pp. 41–50. See also Nancy Morse and Everett Reimer, "The Experimental Change of a Major Organizational Variable," *Journal of Abnormal and Social Psychology*, Vol. 52, No. 1 (January 1956), pp. 120–129.

[33] *Ibid.*

supervision and disregard others. A manager who delegates authority but neglects to train his subordinates to exercise it intelligently may well have worse results than the manager who retains all authority for himself.

More important than any particular manager's style of leadership is the general pattern of human relations that prevails in the organization. It is very difficult for a supervisor to practice general supervision if his boss and his fellow managers all practice and expect close supervision, particularly if the boss fails to back him up and show tolerance for his mistakes. Similarly, general supervision is more difficult if there are rigid rules that prescribe every step or statistical controls that immediately report to top management every deviation from planned performance.

CONCLUSION

General supervision is an approach to management which is based on giving subordinates wide authority to make decisions. It assumes that people will work harder if they are given freedom to make their decisions, and it relies on internalized motivation, the satisfactions people get from being free to do a good job more or less in their own way.

Delegation is rarely absolute. Delegation is possible only when management can be reasonably sure that subordinates will behave in a relatively satisfactory fashion and, if they make mistakes, that these will not be too dangerous to the organization. To insure that subordinates do behave adequately, management must provide some sort of guidance. Ruses, goals, indoctrination, and even the requirements of technology tend to provide such guidance.

There is a good deal of research which suggests that general supervision results in higher productivity. As we have indicated, this is not always true. The feasibility of delegation depends on a number of factors: the nature of the work, individual personality and background, over-all management practices, employee acceptance of management goals, union-management relationships, and the organization's needs for coordination and consistency. Unless these factors are favorable to delegation, delegation may not increase motivation substantially. Even if it does, the cost to the organization in terms of impaired coordination, and so forth, may be greater than the gains in terms of motivation.

Clearly, there is no one best method of supervision applicable to all situations. There are a number of means of delegations, some of which are applicable to routine work, for example, and others of which work best where a high degree of initiative is required. Only in rare instances is delegation enough in itself. Even the general supervisor must exercise authority. The problems this involves will be discussed in the next chapter.

THE EXERCISE OF
AUTHORITY

8

The manager must make many decisions on his own. He must do so when he sets the rules and goals previously discussed. And if the rules are violated or the goals unmet, it is the manager who must somehow restrain or reprimand the subordinates responsible for falling short. In some cases, subordinates may not be competent to make decisions because of lack of information, training, or understanding of over-all organizational needs. In other cases, as we have seen, subordinates may not be motivated to make the proper sorts of decisions or to exercise freedom in a manner consistent with organizational objectives. Often the manager must arbitrate disputes among subordinates.

In all the above situations the manager must exercise authority. But being given the right to do so doesn't mean that he will be effective. To get subordinates to respond to his authority requires that the manager both skillfully handle his relations with subordinates *and* establish himself as a legitimate source of authority. These are two separate considerations. The manager must have effective day-to-day relations, but more than this is required. Based on previous experiences, subordinates have developed perceptions of what leadership should be like. They expect that anyone to whom they give their allegiance will have characteristics and behave in a fashion consistent with this image.

Thus, this chapter will approach the exercise of authority from two points of view. First, we shall look at the day-to-day relations or interaction patterns between bosses and subordinates. Second, considering the problem from a longer-run point of view, we shall examine the conditions under which subordinates will view the manager's exercise of authority as legitimate.

DEVELOPING EFFECTIVE RELATIONS

Subordinates can hardly be expected to forget that their boss (or someone at a higher level of management) has the power to discharge them or withhold benefits and promotions. Regardless of how effectively the relationship between subordinates and superior is cloaked in democratic procedure, no one forgets for a moment that there are very real differences in power between them. In every work situation, problems of reward and discipline inevitably arise, and these problems often lead to frustration and bad feeling. One of the manager's goals should be to minimize this frustration and to try to create conditions in which people will accept authority with the maximum of enthusiasm and the minimum of resentment. The fair exercise of authority is one of the elements of an implicit bargain. It is also a form of hygienic management; in fact, it is the major form of motivation where opportunities for internalized motivation are slim.

Ambivalence toward Authority

The manager's job is always complicated by the fact that people feel a certain ambivalence toward authority. As Eric Fromm has suggested, most of us have complicated, mixed feelings toward independence and dependence. We value freedom but sometimes feel lost and anchorless when we have too much. We like protection but we don't like interference.

If management fails to provide enough independence on the job, employees will exercise independence on their own by resorting to absenteeism, union activity, slowdowns, and the like. On the other hand, employees find it difficult to adjust to too much independence, for no one can stand completely by himself. Most of us like to be assured that we are doing the right thing and that we will receive help when we are in trouble. On occasion we even like to have people make tough decisions for us.

To put it another way: People are generally willing to tolerate, and may even be anxious for, a few areas of their life which are unpredictable and exciting, but they insist that most events occur as expected. A research scientist, for example, may relish the novelty and uncertainty of laboratory work, but he insists that his secretary be always on call, that his technician give predictable responses, and that his car start with complete regularity.

Working in a large-scale organization requires that every subordinate be to some degree dependent on the organization generally and on his supervisor in particular; individual independence must be sharply restricted.

We shall now consider some of the ways in which the manager can exercise authority effectively, but without being unduly restrictive. The kind of personal relations he develops, the way he gives orders, his fairness in handling problems, and his manner in handling mistakes—all have a significant impact on subordinates' attitudes toward authority.

The personal, man-to-man relationships between a boss and his subordinates have a lot to do with the way subordinates view their jobs. Since employees are dependent on their boss, it is all-important for them to feel that he approves of both their work and themselves as individuals.

Creating a Feeling of Approval

The supervisor can foster a feeling of his approval of subordinates in many different ways: taking an active interest in subordinates, listening to their problems, giving praise when justified, showing tolerance when mistakes are made, and so forth. Notice that we say *feeling* of approval. We are talking about the over-all supervisory pattern rather than about any one specific act. In fact, the existence of such a feeling helps determine how individual acts are interpreted. *If* such a feeling exists, employees may tend to excuse their boss's mistakes; if it does *not* exist, they may exaggerate his mistakes out of all proportion. For instance, in the absence of a feeling of approval, a boss's attempt to show interest in his employees may be seen as meddling.

When the supervisor is interested in the welfare of his subordinates and is accepted by them as a member of their "team," then his close attention to what his subordinates are doing is welcomed by them. When the supervisor is around and showing interest in what they are doing, subordinates may be eager to please him and win his approval. On the other hand, when the supervisor is held by subordinates as indifferent to their welfare, or even as a hostile outsider, then his close supervision will probably meet with apathy and resentment. [1]

Thus, the over-all pattern of the supervisor's behavior is infinitely more important than any specific gesture. Take kindness and courtesy as an example. Obviously, saying "please" and "do you mind" is important, but employees soon see through superficial gestures if they conflict with the rest of the supervisor's behavior. In some situations cusswords are better evidence than icy courtesy that the boss likes you. Although most human beings like approbation, they are suspicious of indiscriminate praise. Further, praise for good work is not enough. People have bad days as well as good; a real feeling of approval assures the individual that his boss will show tolerance for an occasional mistake.

In short, the existence of a feeling of approval means that the supervisor has demonstrated a personal loyalty to his subordinates. Until he has done so, he cannot expect loyalty to flow the other way.

Note, though, that approval means different things to different people.

We once interviewed two lacquer-mixers who worked pretty much by themselves at opposite ends of a long factory floor. They did the same job and were under the same foreman (who said both did a good job). The first mixer said: "I've got a good boss. He knows I know the job so he leaves me alone, he never bothers me." The second mixer said: "My foreman doesn't care whether I'm dead or alive. He's a bum foreman who doesn't show any interest in his men or how they are doing."

[1] Martin Patchen, "Supervisory Methods and Group Performance Norms," *Administrative Science Quarterly*, Vol. 7, No. 3 (December 1962), p. 290.

Obviously, these two men looked upon supervision very differently. The first saw supervision as restrictive, to be avoided if possible. The second expected help and reassurance from his boss. Both men were anxious to win approval and acceptance, but what came through clearly as acceptance to one man seemed outright rejection to the other. The manager must be alert to these subtle differences in the manner in which his behavior—however well intentioned—is interpreted.

Developing Personal Relations

A feeling of approval is more likely to result if the boss shows personal interest in his subordinates. Consequently, an effective manager "makes" time to get to know his subordinates and to help them with their problems both on and (to a limited extent) off the job.

Need for personal relations. People like being treated like individuals. Yet, as far as the typical company is concerned, the average employee is nothing more than a time-card number or a job specification. The company is impersonal; only the immediate boss can make management personal. Particularly to a new employee, the immediate supervisor *is* the company, and what he does helps mold the individual's conception of the company as a whole. An insensitive manager can easily counterbalance all the company's efforts to create a good impression through public relations and fringe benefits.

Home problems affect efficiency on the job. So a good manager listens to his employees' problems, and in some areas actually offers assistance. Ordinarily, all he can do is listen, but even this interest provides some relief to an individual in distress. In any case, the more the manager learns about the people who work for him, the better he can understand their behavior and how to deal with it. (Of course, the manager should not seem to pry or meddle, as we shall discuss in Chapter 11.)

Even more important, good informal relations on matters that are not directly related to the job set the stage for better communication between manager and subordinate on problems related to work. Any social barrier will create a communications barrier. An employee rarely feels completely free and easy when talking with the boss about the work in hand, for he is quite aware that the boss is the one who hands out rewards and punishments. But when they talk about the employee's fishing trip, the employee is an *expert* for the time being, even if there is no true feeling of equality between them. Some of the air of permissiveness and informality created in discussing baseball or the weather may carry over to on-the-job affairs. Once the manager and the subordinate know each other as individuals, both will feel freer to bring up mutual problems.

To put it another way: The good manager tries to reduce the number of orders he gives by encouraging people to ask him questions rather than by telling them what to do. For this approach to succeed, however, the subordinates must feel confident and secure enough to go to their boss when difficulties arise.

Setting the tone. Obviously, it is the superior who sets the tone of the relationship, not the subordinate. First, the manager must make himself available to all comers. The boss who barricades himself behind a wall of formality or is always "busy, busy, busy" is not likely to develop satisfactory informal relationships. Nor is it enough to be a good fellow a few times a year. In most companies the permissive atmosphere of the annual Christmas party stands out in sharp contrast to the distant relationship that is normal for the rest of the year.

The manager must take the initiative by maintaining regular and frequent contacts with subordinates. Some managers make periodic "howdy rounds," talking to each employee in turn. Even if these encounters consist only of idle chatter, still they provide an opportunity for employees to bring up problems that are bothering them. In other words, the manager opens up the contact and lets the subordinate decide what topics should be covered.

But, there is more to being a good boss than being a nice fellow. Although many employees respond favorably to the "glad-hand" approach, most are suspicious of insincerity. After all, the manager must develop a *long-term* relationship, and over a period of time it is easy for subordinates to detect whether his apparent interest is sincere. It is better for an introvert to be naturally reserved than artificially friendly. In today's cynical world, people are highly suspicious of overfriendliness: They are constantly afraid of being manipulated. Unless the manager combines good informal personal relations with good job-oriented relations, he will be judged a hypocrite: "He'll try to butter you up. But watch out, he'll stab you in the back."

JOB-ORIENTED RELATIONS

Some early studies of managerial behavior contrasted "job-centered" with "employee-centered" supervision. The job-centered manager is interested almost exclusively in getting his job done; the employee-centered manager is interested chiefly in satisfying the needs of his subordinates. In the terms used in some studies, the job-centered manager is high in what we call "initiating structure" (running the job), whereas the employee-centered manager is more concerned with "consideration." Regardless of what terms were used, it was believed that these two qualities are on opposite ends of a continuum. Later research suggests that these characteristics are not mutually inconsistent. An effective manager is interested both in his employees as individuals and in the work they do. An interest in one does not preclude an interest in the other. A good manager, then, has effective job-oriented relations with his subordinates.

In one sense, this entire volume is concerned with job-oriented relations. At this point we wish to stress that, where feasible in directing the job, an effective manager will keep open the lines of communications with his subordinates, both upward and downward. He will provide them with information, consult with them, and listen to their suggestions. Let us consider each of these points in turn, although we have already seen something of the over-all pattern in our discussion of the General Electric study in the previous chapter.

Providing Information

Few of us are content to be at the mercy of forces we do not understand. We all tend to feel insecure in poorly defined situations. Research indicates that high-production supervisors tend to give their subordinates as much information as possible about what is expected on the job and what is likely to happen to them in the future. This information helps subordinates do better work by enabling them to make wiser decisions; moreover, it heightens their sense of security.

Understandably, employees are keenly interested in knowing what they are required to do on the job. For some, this need is satisfied only when they receive explicit direction in every aspect of their work. You will remember the nurse who said, "I need guidance and therefore I prefer to work with a fairly strict supervisor."

The older girls on Miss Rogers' floor complained because they did not receive enough detailed instructions; the younger girls on Miss Smith's floor felt insecure because Miss Smith failed to provide enough information for them to make decisions on their own, and had a habit of issuing unexpected and seemingly arbitrary orders.

Even those who value the freedom to make decisions themselves feel more self-confident in a well-structured situation. When they are given an order, they want some explanation of what is to be done, why it is to be done, and what limits will be set on their freedom—as well as any background information necessary to help them do a better job or to satisfy their natural curiosity. They prefer that the boss be easily available to answer questions or to provide assistance when asked.

The subordinate is especially curious to know *where he stands with his boss.* For white-collar workers in particular, "getting ahead" is of paramount importance. The subordinate constantly asks himself, "How am I doing?" and tries to divine from the boss's tone of voice or facial expression whether his performance is finding favor. The subordinate is directly dependent on his boss, he wants to please him, and he wants some sort of feedback or evaluation to indicate how his efforts are being received.

Finally, employees are keenly interested in knowing about anything that will have an effect on their future prospects or their work. "What's the production level likely to be next week?" "Are the rumors true that this department will be automated?" "How will this affect me?" "How bad are the squawks down the line about the bum job I did yesterday?" To the employee who is deprived of this sort of information, the future seems uncertain and sinister.

Consulting with Subordinates

The way a manager issues an order influences the way it is received. With routine orders there is usually little trouble. But before a manager issues an order that will have a major impact on his subordinates, or an order that they are likely to resist, it is better for him to discuss it with them than to impose it unilaterally with no opportunity for questions or objections. Even if the manager may wish to make the final decision himself, he may wish to increase the subordinate's sense of involvement through permitting him to influence the final decision.

The wise manager explains such "critical" orders orally at first, though later he may put them in writing for permanent reference. To be sure, it may take more time to issue instructions orally than in writing. Yet, as we will see in Chapter 10, voice communication is often more effective than the written word. It permits the manager, if necessary, to present a detailed explanation of what he wants and why he wants it—and in a way that is tailor-made to the subordinate's needs.

The effective manager also permits the subordinate to comment and to ask questions (at least within the limits set by other demands on the supervisor's time). This gives him a chance to judge how the subordinate is reacting to the proposed order and enables him to answer objections, explain points that are not clearly understood, or make arrangements for exceptional circumstances that may require special procedures. Moreover, the subordinate may come up with suggestions that will make the proposed order more workable—or he may object so strenuously that the supervisor will decide to withdraw the order altogether.

Doesn't the manager lose respect when he modifies or withdraws an order in face of his subordinate's objections? Yes—if his original instructions were stated in terms of "this is what I order you to do." No—if he has said, "I have been thinking about this and would like your reaction." There is a gain even if the manager eventually decides that he must impose an order over his subordinate's objections, for at least the subordinate has had a chance to be heard and to let off steam.

Finally, a subordinate is more likely to carry out an order if he has specifically agreed to do so, for he is then committed to take some action. If the manager closes the discussion with the question, "Are you willing to give it a try?" he is likely to get assent. Even though this assent may be enforced, there has been an explicit agreement to go along. Suppose the subordinate refuses to assent? In most instances it is better to bring the resistance out in the open at the outset than to assume that the order will be carried out when in fact it will be sabotaged.

Listening to Suggestions

Although there are many areas in which the manager cannot give his subordinates freedom to make decisions by themselves, he can encourage them to make suggestions. This practice provides the manager with many useful ideas and a more accurate feeling for what his subordinates are thinking. It provides subordinates with an opportunity to express themselves and to feel that they have made a valuable contribution.

Many of the suggestions made by subordinates are remarkably valuable. Understandably, the man who works close to a job day after day often knows more about it than his boss.

The manager should not only listen to the suggestions that are brought to him; he should actively seek them out. There are many areas in which the manager doesn't have all the facts that he needs to make important decisions. Asking for suggestions may certainly result in better acceptance of the decision, and it may improve its quality as well. There is no obligation for the manager to accept all the ideas presented, so long as he considers them seriously. If he rejects all suggestions out of hand, however, his subordinates will soon see through his pretense.

But what happens when management is obliged to reject a suggestion? Even here the suggestion has served a purpose. First, the subordinate did have a chance to express himself and to be heard. Second, by explaining why the suggestion was rejected, the supervisor can improve the subordinate's understanding of the problem and perhaps stimulate him to produce better suggestions in the future.

FAIR TREATMENT

Since subordinates are directly dependent on their bosses, they are understandably anxious to receive fair treatment from them. The boss can demonstrate his sense of fair play by letting each employee know exactly what is required of him, and by exercising consistent discipline. He can base his decisions on grounds that are accepted as legitimate by his subordinates, he can provide an appeals procedure (see Chapter 14), and, above all, he can make an all-out effort to treat them equally, so that the rewards he dispenses seem proportional to their contributions.

"Treating people equally" is not as simple as it sounds. The conscientious manager is torn between two conflicting, though universally accepted, platitudes: "Avoid favoritism" and "Treat people as individuals, in accordance with their special needs." He can never forget that each individual has special needs, but at the same time he must realize that what appears to be inconsistent treatment will create endless bad feeling within the group.

With all the good will in the world, the manager may begin to play favorites unconsciously and to follow the normal tendency of either favoring the passive, dependent, "good" employee or paying the most attention to the aggressive individual who fights for his demands, to "oil the wheel that squeaks the loudest." The manager must avoid both extremes.

Making exceptions. What about making exceptions in special situations? Obviously, treating people fairly does not mean treating everyone in exactly the same way. It does mean that when an exception is made, it must be accepted as legitimate by all members of the group. There is a general rule, for example, that vacations must be taken during the summer months. Bill Lawrence's wife is sick, so the boss lets him have February off to take her to Florida. Is this favoritism? Only if Bill Lawrence's fellow employees think so. An exception of this sort will be accepted as fair if the group (1) knows why it was made,

(2) accepts it as justified, and (3) is confident that another employee in the same situation would receive the same treatment.

Granting special favors when the circumstances permit not only lessens a subordinate's feeling that the organization is arbitrary and "heartless," but it may also lead to an "exchange of good turns." In a sense it is a form of implicit bargaining. As a worker in an assembly plant described it:

"My foreman knows the traits of human nature and acts accordingly. . . . He came in one morning and it was bitterly cold. He went out to the cafeteria and bought two big cans of hot coffee and gave it to the men. While we can't be bought the thought was there and we appreciated it. As a result the men picked up lots of jobs that ordinarily they would have let go through to be picked up by the repair man." [2]

The assumption behind this approach is that if the manager does more for his men than is absolutely required, they will respond in kind. It means, for instance, that if Jack comes to work with a sprained ankle, the foreman will find him some work that he can do sitting down; if a waitress is suddenly deluged with customers, the hostess will relieve some of the pressure by setting up tables and pouring water. The hope is that when an emergency arises the subordinates will reciprocate by doing more than is normally required, by working overtime or by producing more than the usual "bogey." Thus, an atmosphere is created in which both supervisor and subordinate exhibit a flexible attitude toward their mutual obligations.

HANDLING MISTAKES

In the previous chapter we suggested that managers should set realistic goals for their subordinates, train them to do the best job they are capable of doing, and then give them a wide margin of freedom. But this does not mean that management should sit idly by when employees violate rules, turn out sloppy work, or fail to do their job. Quite the contrary. Not only is such laxity bad for production (after all, the company exists to make a profit); it is also unfair to the conscientious worker who carries out his assignments effectively, and it even serves to encourage the "culprit" in his bad work habits.

The manager cannot ignore mistakes. But the manner in which he handles them may determine whether his subordinates will resent his use of authority or will come to look upon him as a source of help.

Blame or Help?

Research studies reveal that the difference between high-production and low-production managers lies not in their interest in eliminating mistakes, but in their *manner* of handling mistakes. Note the difference between these two comments:

[2] Arthur N. Turner, "Foreman—Key to Worker Morale," *Harvard Business Review*, Vol. 35, No. 5 (September 1956), p. 77.

"My boss thinks that whenever anything goes wrong it's always my fault. ... He never says what he can do to help you, but he always picks your job apart."

"My boss is the best man I have ever worked for. He finds out what's troubling you before he tells you what to do, and he'll ask why. ... Other supervisors come down here and start yelling at you before they find out what's wrong. But not him." [3]

When something goes wrong, the low-production manager is interested above all in fixing blame and bawling out the person responsible. ("Well, what sort of excuse do you have?") He has a tendency to look to the past, to "cry over spilt milk," and to assume that all negligence is deliberate. What is the effect of such an approach? The subordinate denies responsibility, tries to pass the buck to someone else, or at least to find some sort of excuse to show that he really wasn't at fault. This approach encourages the "stool pigeon" and tends to make the development of harmonious groups almost impossible. If the group *does* succeed in working together in such an atmosphere, it directs its efforts *against* the manager.

The policy of blame-placing often defeats its own purpose: It makes employees so tense and insecure that they make even more mistakes. And it motivates them to cover up errors and spend their time trying to avoid *looking* wrong. As a result, upward communications is impaired and higher management can never get a clear picture of what is really happening below. A kind of game develops: In an effort to uncover the deceptions of subordinates, higher management sets up inspection systems and elaborate control reports, while the subordinates become increasingly adept at hiding mistakes.

In contrast, high-production managers tend to look forward, rather than backward. They are interested in discovering what happened, why it happened, and what can be learned rather than in fixing responsibility. They look upon mistakes as an opportunity to provide training.

Mistakes as a means of learning. If the manager insists that subordinates must never make a mistake, he is also insuring that they will never assume any real responsibility. Not that the subordinate should be encouraged to make mistakes. Far from it. But if he feels that one mistake is disastrous, he will be completely inhibited from taking any responsibility or initiative. The boss who feels that every mistake is a calamity must abandon all hope of improving the performance of his subordinates.

In effect, when mistakes are punished by severe criticism, people learn not just to avoid *specific* behavior, but to avoid *any* situation where a mistake is possible. Actually, doing something wrong is often the most effective way of learning to do it right. Getting "burned" a few times may be the only way for us to learn that some of our pet ideas really won't work. In effect, a subordinate should have freedom to fail. A superior should weigh very carefully the cost of a mistake against the value of having the subordinate learn both (1) that he has the freedom to act on his own, even to make mistakes, and (2) that the particular

3 Charles R. Walker, Robert H. Guest, and Arthur N. Turner, *The Foreman on the Assembly Line* (Cambridge: Harvard University Press, 1956), p. 45.

way he has chosen was wrong. Overprotection by the superior means underdevelopment by the subordinate.

Some managers react to a subordinate's mistake by taking the job over themselves because they find this course easier than training the subordinate so he won't make the mistake again. Obviously, with an approach like this the subordinate will never learn, and he will become increasingly reluctant to take on responsibility on his own.

Calling Mistakes to Subordinate's Attention

When to call a mistake to a subordinate's attention depends both on the situation and on the subordinate's personality.

"Many times workers recognize their own mistakes and take steps to remedy them before the supervisor steps in. If, then, the manager pushes his criticism anyway, the worker becomes resentful. It is only when workers are unaware of their mistakes or seem not to be profiting from them that the supervisor should step in." [4]

On the other hand, it is clearly foolish to let a subordinate continue to make mistakes when he is obviously making no progress in solving them or when they are causing great harm to the organization. Leaving a subordinate in the dark when he is doing a poor job is unfair both to him and to the organization as a whole.

Some managers find it temperamentally difficult to correct their subordinates. They are unsure of the soundness of their own judgment; or they resist accepting the responsibility of "playing God" and judging other men; or they are reluctant to risk injuring the personal relations they have established with their men. As a consequence, one often hears managers defending their failure to offer constructive criticism: "You shouldn't correct anyone until you are 100 per cent sure you are right. You have got to get all the facts." But this is an exaggeration of the problem. There is no need to prove the other man *wrong*. The question of guilt is irrelevant. What *is* relevant is to discuss the trouble in terms of "What happened? What can be done about it?"

Investigating mistakes. Some observers say that a manager should never try to correct a subordinate unless he can offer a better alternative. The caution implied in this approach is commendable, and yet little harm is done when the manager says, "There seems to be something wrong here. Frankly, I don't know the answer, but perhaps we can work it out together." Certainly this is better than letting anger and suspicion mount until one has "all the facts." Lack of frankness between superior and subordinate cannot help but generate tension and misunderstanding.

When a mistake is made, ask the worker how it happened. *Let him tell you.* If his explanation is weak, he'll recognize it in telling the story, and so will you. You won't have to rub it in, in most cases, because he knows what is expected of him and is willing to recognize his own failings—when he isn't pushed and prodded with them.

4 William F. Whyte, *Human Relations in the Restaurant Industry* (New York: McGraw-Hill, 1948), p. 270.

Then ask him to *tell you* how the mistake can be avoided in the future. You don't have to accept his solution but, with this approach you are more likely to get him to accept responsibility for his actions and to try to do something constructive. [5]

Often the problem involves the entire group and can best be handled by group discussion. But there, too, the manager can refrain from trying to pin the blame on one or two individuals and concentrate instead on working out a solution for future activities that is satisfactory to everyone.

Criticism

Most mistakes are due to ignorance or lack of skill, and can be handled through training without resort to overt criticism. Some mistakes, however, are clearly due to negligence; here the manager has no choice but to let the subordinate know that he is dissatisfied with the subordinate's level of performance. But unless the manager is tactful in making his criticism, he will jeopardize his relationship not only with the subordinate but with the whole work group as well. Whyte suggests some useful rules:

1. The criticism should be voiced in a matter-of-fact manner. Emotional heat on the part of the critic seems to beget a defensive reaction on the part of the subordinate. Only when the subordinate refuses to act on the criticism does it seem advisable to apply the heat.
2. The criticism should be focused on the job operation and should, as much as possible, avoid placing of personal blame.
3. After it has been stated, the criticism should be dropped—unless the mistake has not been corrected. Men speak of the emotional tensions they have been under when working for a [supervisor] who would not only criticize you but would then seem to be "down" on you for a long time thereafter. One man described the more effective approach in this way:

"Ed will tell you right to your face how he wants it done. Oh, sometimes we might have a little argument about it, but when the argument is over, it is really over and forgotten. He never gets down on you. You like to work for a fellow like that."

4. Criticism should be balanced by giving credit for good work. No matter how skillfully a man makes his criticism, if he has only critical remarks to make, he destroys cooperation. [6]

It should be added that criticism of this sort is best offered in private.

Some mistakes, of course, are due to improper training, failure to understand instructions, or severe problems at home. In situations of this sort, the manager may be able to get at the root of the trouble only through skillful interviewing. And he may have to resort to formal discipline if the subordinate fails to respond to criticism and training. The problems of interviewing and discipline will be discussed in Chapters 11 and 13.

In our discussion to this point we have dealt with day-to-day manager-subordinate relationships. But in doing so, we gave a somewhat oversimplified picture. Having read this far, you might well conclude that there is one sort of boss-subordinate relationship which is best for all conditions. Obviously this isn't

[5] *Ibid*, p. 269.

[6] William F. Whyte, *Leadership in the Work Team* (mimeographed, 1956), pp. 12–13.

so. Let us look at the exercise of authority from a broader perspective and examine why subordinates follow their superiors in the first place. In so doing, we will gain some insight into how the means by which authority is effectively exercised may well differ from one situation to another.

LEGITIMACY

From a purely formal point of view, the manager receives his authority from above, from his superiors, who define his powers and responsibilities and who sometimes put a statement of these in an organization handbook. Another view is that the manager receives much of his *real* authority from below, from his subordinates, and that the statement of authority which he receives from above is merely a hunting license; for in spite of his statement of formal powers, if his subordinates are not willing to obey him, then he has no real authority.

How can the manager induce subordinates to obey him? Of course, he can use bluster, force, and the policy of "be strong." If enough pressure is applied, then his subordinates will comply. But as we saw in Chapter 5, their compliance may well be grudging and resentful.

Alternatively, subordinates may wish to comply because the organization is doing what they want to do themselves. Individuals lost in the wilderness gladly take directions from a leader who seems to be taking them back to civilization. Orchestra members exercise little autonomy, but they follow their conductor willingly because they want to create good music. Similarly, a junior research scientist will obey his boss with enthusiasm if he sees his boss's directions as helping him solve his own research problem. Note that in all these cases the subordinates would have followed their boss's instructions even if he didn't have the formal title. They obey because their ends are identical with those of their leader.

Relatively few cases involve either sheer coercion or the boss telling subordinates to do what they really wanted to do in the first place. Most situations occupy a middle ground: Subordinates obey their boss because they respect the legitimacy of his order, that is, because according to their norms and values it is expected and proper for the boss to give his particular order and for them to obey it.

Thus, the leader must establish a series of relationships with subordinates which support his legitimacy. But he must also recognize that the process of legitimization occurs in a group and cultural setting, for what any one individual perceives as legitimate depends largely on the views of his associates. The group makes it easier for the boss, though, for it often informally disciplines those who violate group expectations by not obeying legitimate orders.

As we mentioned in Chapter 4, every group has customs, proprieties, and expectations that its members believe are proper. A manager who violates these standards acts in an "illegitimate" fashion, and does so at his peril: Subordinates can retaliate in numerous ways, ranging from refusal to do more than their normal share in time of emergency, to wildcat strikes and sabotage. In contrast, the manager who respects the group's standards often wins its cooperation and, at times, finds that the group will modify its standards in management's favor. To take an example of the impact of such standards:

Train crews in a marshaling yard were handling 150 trains a day. Through short cuts (often violating safety rules) they were able to finish their work in six hours. The rest of the time they could sleep or read.

We can identify several standards in this situation: (1) 150 trains a day represent a proper work load; (2) the remaining time can be spent as the men wish; and (3) certain rules will not be enforced.

Then management decided that since the men had so much free time they could handle 200 trains. Immediately the men began to follow all the rules. They would never move a train even a few feet without having someone to go to the rear and wave a red flag. As a result, the men put in a full day's work, but productivity fell to 50 trains a day. Soon management gave up its demands for 200.

Here management violated group standards, broke the implicit contract, and acted in what the group felt was an illegitimate fashion, and the men retaliated in a way that left management helpless.

In the remainder of this chapter we shall consider what the group views as the legitimate use of authority. First, however, a word of warning: though we shall use the word "group" rather freely here, you should remember that social groups tend to overlap and that any given employee may belong to several groups with varying expectations (see Chapter 4).

How can a manager exercise power legitimately? The answer seems to depend on at least three factors: (1) his job legitimacy, that is, on his right to hold his power in the first place; (2) the way he behaves on the job; and (3) the demands he makes on subordinates. These three factors are obviously interrelated; for example, the manager can ask more from subordinates if his right to hold his job is legitimate, and if he makes his demands in a legitimate fashion.

Job Legitimacy

To some extent people obey leaders just because they are invested with the symbols or titles of authority. Soldiers are trained to obey those who wear officers' insignia, regardless of the individual merits of the wearer. Royal coronations and presidential inaugurations are ceremonials which symbolize the transfer of a certain "magic" to kings and presidents.

Nevertheless, every group has definite expectations about what qualifications their leader should possess. If the leader fails to live up to these expectations, then his subordinates feel that he is not "fit for his job"—and this holds true whether he is a foreman or President of the United States. The important thing is that the leader be respected. [7]

[7] Respect need not mean liking. As Machiavelli advised his Prince, it is often better to be feared than to be loved.

Background. Certainly there are expectations about the leader's background. He may be expected to belong to a certain ethnic group, to be a graduate of a certain college, or to have a certain degree (thus a Dean without a Ph.D. or a hospital director without an M.D. can find it harder to win support from subordinates).

The nature of the qualifications subordinates expect in their leaders will, of course, vary substantially from job to job. Thus, in many American companies the fair-haired boy who is promoted solely on the basis of family connections will find it hard to win cooperation. On the other hand, family connections are almost essential if one is to be considered a legitimate king (and, in some European firms, a legitimate company president). In some organizations a man is expected to work his way up through the ranks, and an outsider who is brought in over the head of someone subordinates feel deserves the job will have to face strong resentment (though "proper" behavior may ultimately win him respect). In other cases, it is traditional for leaders to be brought in through special channels; thus, for a long time in the army, officers won greater respect if they started their careers in West Point, rather than as privates. But traditions can change: In recent years the army has made it easier for enlisted men to become officers; on the other hand, many large companies have increasingly reserved management ranks for college graduates.

Technical ability. It is important for the supervisor to be technically skilled in his work, even if he rarely practices his skill on the job.[8] Indeed, subordinates often subject a new supervisor to a period of testing and initiation to determine whether he measures up to their standards. If subordinates feel their supervisor is master of skills they themselves regard as important, then in a way he has beaten them in a fair race—he has earned his job and is respected for doing so.

The feeling that the boss should show technical skill is particularly strong among men who take pride in their work and closely identify with their occupation (building tradesmen, for example, or college professors). Supervisors who do not possess the relevant skills have a hard time, indeed.

Technical skill is very important in certain types of work where close coordination is required between members of the work team—as in flying a plane, conducting an orchestra, or operating on a patient. In such cases, "unpleasant personal characteristics are often overlooked if competence is high enough. The irascible surgeon who is, nevertheless, highly respected for his skills is almost a legend. Colleagues and nurses judge doctors according to the mastery they exhibit."[9]

---

[8] The leader's technical skill need not duplicate that of his followers. A pilot can't overhaul an engine; perhaps a conductor can't play all the instruments in an orchestra; yet both derive status from their technical ability.

[9] Temple Burling, Edith Lentz, and Robert Wilson, *The Give and Take in Hospitals* (New York: Putnam, 1956), p. 266.

To summarize, we are discussing here what Herbert Simon calls the "authority of confidence."[10] To put it another way, the manager will find his authority more easily accepted if he is an authority *on*, as well as an authority *over*.

Managerial Behavior

Subordinates normally have well-defined expectations about how a "good" manager should behave, both on and off the job, though these may vary greatly from one situation to another.

In the giving of orders, for example, authority may be emphasized or underplayed. As we discussed earlier, North Americans tend to resent the outward display of authority, and often feel it proper that their bosses go through the forms of consulting with them. Engineers, scientists, and professors seem to hold this expectation particularly strongly. But there are many other cultures in which a boss is expected to be firm and to know his own mind.

Of course, all supervisors are expected to be fair and to treat people in a "nice way." But the nice way in the university would be very out of place in the army. An officer, for example, is expected to have a "military bearing," and a professor to display a "scholarly attitude." Some groups expect their supervisor to "act like a boss," and the men take advantage of him if he doesn't rule with an iron hand; in other groups it is a great compliment to say that the supervisor "doesn't act like a boss." In some situations a good boss is expected to "let his men alone"; in others he should be available every minute of the day—that is, he should be "in there pitching and providing leadership."

This much is clear: A manager should become familiar with his subordinates' expectations as soon as possible. The manager may eventually wish to change these expectations, but he must recognize the likelihood of resistance (see Chapter 12).

Social distance. Perhaps the most subtle of these expectations about managerial behavior concern the social distance (or status differentiation) which the boss should keep from his subordinates: Military officers should be aloof from their men; deans should invite all new faculty to dinner; plant managers are expected to make "howdy rounds" in the plant and to be good fellows at the company picnic (but perhaps only there); supervisors should show interest in their subordinates' home life (and in some plants go out drinking with their men on pay day). In most situations a boss is expected to "be friendly" (and this is particularly true where the American tradition of equality prevails), but the meaning of friendliness varies greatly from one situation to another. To violate these expectations may well lead to trouble.

A wide variety of factors is relevant here. At sea there has been a traditional social gap between officers and men. This distance is maintained by means of separate uniforms and separate eating and sleeping arrangements. Yet, on smaller ships this traditional formality tends to break down. Moreover, there is more formality in the navy, where men are subject to danger, than there is in

---

[10] Herbert Simon, "Authority," in Conrad Arensberg, *et al.*, eds., *Research in Industrial Human Relations* (New York: Harper, 1957), p. 106.

the merchant marine. And there is a decidedly different attitude in the American merchant marine, where most men rise from the ranks, than on European ships, where officers and the men they supervise usually come from different social classes.

When businessmen and government officials go to foreign countries they run into all sorts of unanticipated problems of social distance. An anthropologist describes how: [11]

"British respect for rank and maintenance of formal distance seems to have fit well with chieftainships and aristocracies in some parts of traditional Africa and the caste system in India. American equalitarian biases, on the other hand, have seemed to fit poorly in some parts of Oceania, where rank and social distance seem important. ... With secularized Hindus, nationalist change-oriented Africans and others sensitive about the possible social connotations of superiority in the maintenance of social distance, American informality—even "backslapping"—have been seen as desirable traits in the relationship. Some Latin Americans have even felt Americans to be cool and remote by their standards—more like the image we would have of the stiffly correct Britisher."

The question of expected social relationship is closely tied in with technological considerations. In a scientific laboratory a premium is placed on widespread communication of information and widespread participation. Here status differences are expected to be played down, and social relations are close. But in military organizations where the "technology" requires instant obedience, social relations are kept distant. Indeed, it is feared that if enlisted men become socially close to their officers and learn of their personal inadequacies, they may begin to question the officers' orders. [12]

Social distance is intimately connected with the manager's style of leadership. If he maintains informal, permissive relationships off the job, it will be hard for him to exercise autocratic supervision on the job; on the other hand, if he avoids all social contacts not directly connected with work, he will find it difficult to develop a free-and-easy relationship in discussing job-related problems. Certainly, snubbing people, particularly those with whom one has frequent work contacts, violates our democratic standards.

Work customs. A manager should also be sensitive to the indirect effect of his actions on work customs. Take status, for example. Assigning younger workers to the newest equipment may enable them to earn higher bonuses than their seniors, thereby splitting the work force into two hostile groups. Innocent decisions about parking lots or the arrangement of tables in the cafeteria may upset delicate social relations and may lead to turmoil and antagonism.

Time-honored work customs sometimes conflict sharply with management's formal rules. In a gypsum board plant, for example, it was a well-established

11 Robert N. Rapoport, "Some Notes on Para-Technical Factors in Cross-Cultural Consultation," *Human Organization*, Vol. 23, No. 1 (Spring 1964), pp. 8–9.

12 Technological change, however, has largely outmoded the brave infantrymen of Tennyson's day, whose job was "not to reason why," and put in his place a technician who is expected to make decisions on his own. Along with this the social aloofness of the officers has tended to decline. See Morris Janowitz, *The Professional Soldier* (New York: Free Press, 1960).

practice for workers to take "extra" boards home with them for personal use. When a new manager decided to enforce the rules against "stealing," he helped precipitate a wildcat strike. [13]

Work Demands

On most jobs there is felt to be an implicit contract between boss and subordinates which governs what the boss may legitimately demand in the way of work. If he restricts his demands to those that are believed legitimate, then obedience is almost automatic. On the other hand, if he makes demands that are felt to be excessive, he must be prepared for resistance. Implicit bargaining plays a very important role here.

Most employees realize that they assume certain obligations when they accept a job, and acknowledge that the boss has a right to insist on a "fair day's work." In effect, they feel, "Since I work here I must obey orders and try to do a job. I realize that it is the boss' job to get work out and the company's job to make money. So I'll do my *fair* share."

But employees have definite expectations of what constitutes their "fair share," a notion often embodied in a "bogey." They resent what they regard as "being taken advantage of." As we saw in the train marshaling case, they resist doing more than their bogey, and those who do so are subject to punishment by their peers.

Employees generally question working outside the limits of their customary job description (whether written or not). Regardless of the union contract, for example, a group may consider it unacceptable for a maintenance man to be asked to do production work—or vice versa.

A manager's instructions are more likely to be accepted if they seem to be concerned with getting the job done, rather than with the arbitrary exercise of authority for authority's sake. Employees object to being given busy work after their "fair day's work" is done. In general, subordinates reject orders as unfair if they are not reasonably related to the purpose for which they were hired.

Indoctrination leads men to resist inappropriate assignments. The more strongly an individual is indoctrinated in the organization's objectives, the more willing he is to accept work assignments which he feels are helping to achieve those objectives, and the more strongly he resists assignments which he feels are irrelevant to them.

On the other hand, technical instructions concerned with the job are considered legitimate—unless the individual making them is felt to be incompetent. Similarly, subordinates accept orders which are obviously required by the situation. They resent rules that are imposed for no apparent reason. Thus, no-smoking rules are hard to enforce unless employees are convinced there is a real fire hazard. The manager must be able to justify rules as essential to getting the job done, maintaining plant safety, and so forth.

[13] Alvin Gouldner, *Wildcat Strike* (Yellow Springs, Ohio: Antioch, 1954).

Conversely, subordinates often feel that their boss is remiss when he fails to enforce legitimate regulations. Mine workers in one situation placed the blame for accidents on a foreman, since it was his job to see the rules are followed.

[Employees] know that, as a group, they are incapable of making quick decisions; if the organization is to function effectively, there must be leadership in making decisions and putting them into effect ... They have no respect for the supervisor who gives orders timidly and with uncertainty. And, strange as it may seem, they like discipline—when they see that it is important in getting the job done. [14]

Employees often expect the boss to show *leniency,* to ignore minor or technical violations of rules as long as the job is getting done. As we have seen they also expect that under unusual conditions (say, when they have bad days) the boss will give them a break and not insist even on the fair day's work. As we have seen, this expectation involves a form of implicit bargaining, for in exchange for this "good turn" the employee may feel some obligation to work extra hard in genuine emergencies.

A System in Equilibrium

To conclude, we have seen that legitimacy is largely determined by subordinate expectations, and that these expectations in turn are established and enforced *in part* by the various forms of implicit bargaining discussed in Chapter 6. At first, the bargain established in this fashion may be little more than an armed truce, but over time, expectations arise that the bargain *should* be observed by both parties. Gradually, expectations "harden" and acquire what anthropologists have called the "crust of custom."

Thus, the manager-subordinate relationship can be conceived of as a system in equilibrium: There are strong forces operating against all parties to restore them to equilibrium should they ever stray away. The manager is confined and restricted by his subordinates' expectations. As long as he is content to accept them, his job is rather easy. The manager who ignores or flouts these expectations does so at his risk, though sometimes—if the organization is to deal successfully with external challenges—the risk must be taken. Before doing so, however, the manager should pause and consider what he intends to do, or perhaps devise an approach that will achieve his objectives without a frontal attack on what subordinates feel to be right and proper.

It should be emphasized that expectations arise through other means besides implicit bargaining. Some expectations are established by the culture generally and efforts to change them solely through the group are doomed to failure. The manager's task is made even more difficult because his subordinates may belong to a number of different groups, each with its own set of expectations. Indeed there are times when expectations are quite difficult to determine. Certainly a manager is misconstruing his function if he is trying to win a popularity contest.

[14] William F. Whyte, *Human Relations in the Restaurant Industry* (New York: McGraw-Hill, 1948), p. 259.

CONCLUSION

Although delegation may reduce a manager's need to exercise authority, he cannot abandon it altogether. The boss remains a boss. In fact, there are some people who, because of personality or background, expect their boss to provide firm, detailed leadership, and there are situations where delegation is not enough to get the job done. Knowing *when* (and when not) to use firmness is one of the critical criteria for effective leadership.

It is also important to know *how* to use authority: The manner in which it is used may spell the difference between resentment and acceptance. The effective supervisor maintains good communications with his subordinates. He develops personal relations which indicate that he accepts and values them as individuals. Although he may make decisions which his subordinates don't like, he endeavors to consult with them, to listen to their suggestions, to provide them with wanted information, and to treat them fairly. Even the handling of mistakes may provide an opportunity to strengthen supervisor-subordinate communications. Such methods may not generate positive enthusiasm for management's objectives, but will reduce resistance to authority. At the minimum they provide the hygienic management discussed in Chapter 6.

Subordinate acceptance of authority (though not necessarily enthusiasm) is facilitated when the manager's right to a job, his behavior on the job, and the demands he makes on subordinates—all are accepted as legitimate. His claim to legitimacy is judged in a group and cultural setting, however, and expectations may vary substantially from one situation to another.

Though subordinate expectations (or concepts of legitimacy) do place limits on a manager's discretion (limits which he may at times wish to expand), within the "zone of indifference" he often has a considerable degree of freedom. Certainly a manager should not show exaggerated concern for what his subordinates think. Effective leadership requires an understanding of social pressures, but a true leader does not become a prisoner within them; instead he makes use of them to work toward organizational objectives. In the next chapter we shall consider the relationship between the manager and the subordinate work group within which many of these social pressures are generated.

MANAGER-GROUP RELATIONS AND PARTICIPATION

9

Our discussion so far has been concerned primarily with the relationship between the manager and individual subordinates. But as our analysis of legitimacy demonstrated, boss-subordinate relations do not occur in a vacuum. Men belong to groups, and these greatly influence their expectations and behavior. Thus, this chapter will consider some of the problems involved in developing the work group into a team which works effectively for management objectives. We will consider the desirability of building cohesive groups and the methods by which this can be done, the development of group participation (and the controversial question of group decision-making), and how the manager can work through the informal organization.

BUILDING A WORK TEAM

Not long ago a nationally known concern distributed to its supervisors a pamphlet entitled "Deal with Individuals, not Groups." Its message was simple: Individuals, if properly handled, will work for management's objectives; groups will inevitably oppose management. Cater to the worker's competitive spirit, reward his individual efforts, and break up his attachment to the group, the argument ran, and you will be surprised how much work he puts out.

The fostering of competition is not the only means that management can use to break up group cohesion. As we saw in Chapter 4, groups can be made so large and heterogeneous that "team spirit" becomes difficult to develop. Similar effects can be obtained by modifying technology and work arrangements. In restaurants even the height of the counter separating waitresses from countermen affects their ability to work together.

But is it wise for management to try to splinter the informal organization? There is no absolutely clear answer to this question. To be sure, cohesive groups show greater teamwork. Its members gain greater social satisfaction from working together. Morale is higher. Turnover and absenteeism are frequently lower. Further, it may be easier to supervise a closely knit group, since the supervisor need not repeat information and orders to every member; the informal leader will act as an effective channel of communication to and from the supervisor. A quarreling, disorganized group finds it hard to work together and may direct its aggressiveness against management in the form of poor workmanship, sabotage, grievances, and wild-cat strikes.

On the other hand, certain dangers arise when the work group becomes too tightly knit. Such a group may be reluctant to accept new employees as members and, though there may be more cooperation within the group, cooperation with outsiders may suffer. Thus, competition and ill feeling may develop among rival groups.

But does cohesion increase productivity? Several studies suggest that cohesive groups produce either substantially more than the average or somewhat less.[1] Particularly where the job requires close cooperation among the members of a work team, the mere existence of cohesion makes work more efficient. In general, however, cohesion results in higher productivity only if the group accepts management's demands for higher production as legitimate. If the group is unified for the purpose of protecting itself against management, then greater cohesion will mean less production. All cohesion means is that the members will adhere more closely to the group standards, whatever they are.

Where management finds that there is no possibility of developing groups with goals that are compatible with the objectives of the organization, it may become necessary to resort to measures that will weaken or eliminate informal groups. Continuous movements of personnel, particularly those showing leadership potential, and supervisory patterns that stress dealing with the individual are two possible ways of keeping strong groups from developing.[2] In most instances, however, given a sound over-all program of human relations, it is in management's interest to promote teamwork.

What can the supervisor do to develop teamwork? Most important, he can develop a sensitivity to the facts of group life discussed in Chapter 4. He can familiarize himself with the social geography of the group he supervises and

---

[1] Stanley Seashore, *Group Cohesiveness in Industrial Work Groups* (Ann Arbor: Survey Research Center, University of Michigan, 1954); Daniel Katz and Robert Kahn, "Human Organization and Worker Motivation," *Industrial Productivity*, L. Reed Tripp, ed. (Champaign, Ill.: Industrial Relations Research Association, 1951), pp. 161–162; Morton Deutsch, "The Effects of Cooperation and Competition on Group Process," *Group Dynamics*, Dorwin Cartwright and Alvin Zander, eds. (Evanston, Ill.: Harper, 1953), pp. 319–353.

[2] These were among the techniques used by the communists during the Korean War to break down the morale and cohesion of American prisoners.

learn to identify the patterns of status, leadership, friendship, and cliques that exist within it. Understanding relations can help in a host of ways. He can:

1. Avoid putting enemies together by carefully assigning men to work positions—thus reducing the possibility of personal friction.

2. Put friends together. True, this arrangement may lead to more talking on the job, but a number of studies suggest that production is higher when employees are permitted to pick their own work teams—and this is particularly true where the work requires cooperation. (On the other hand, sociometric selection of work teams may be inconsistent with an organizational policy of racial integration.)

3. Provide special help and attention to isolates—the lonely workers who make no friends. Careful recognition of the position of such employees and the use of clique leaders to help them win acceptance may do much to improve their performance and to prevent them from quitting.

4. Assign men in a way to avoid the growth of competing subgroups.

> A study of social organization in the merchant marine suggests that watches (work teams) were most effective when (a) the entire group came from the same social background, or (b) every member of the group came from a different background. When two sharply different cliques formed, efficiency was impaired. [3]

5. Cut down on excessive transfers *between* departments, within the limits of union seniority rules.

6. Rotate jobs within the group in order to strengthen each employee's identification with the team as a whole rather than with his individual job.

7. Try to set up situations in which the employee can make his job easier by cooperating with others.

> In restaurants we studied, management trained the waitresses to work together and help each other. They were taught to consider two, three, or more stations as a unit and to divide the work among themselves in the most efficient manner.
>
> ... The waitresses are told to help only those girls who will return the favor. ... The girl who helps nobody can get nobody to help her, and she drops behind and has trouble with her service. The girl who gives help gets help in return. [4]

8. Provide financial incentives: Group incentives may do more to encourage cooperation than individual bonus plans.

9. Make sure that new workers are carefully introduced to the group. Many companies have a "big brother" system in which every new employee is assigned an older employee to help him become familiar

---

[3] Stephen Richardson, "Organizational Contrasts on British and American Ships," *Administrative Science Quarterly*, Vol. 1, No. 2 (September 1956).

[4] William F. Whyte, *Human Relations in the Restaurant Industry* (New York: McGraw-Hill, 1948), p. 214.

not only with the formal requirements of the job but also with the informal mores of the group. In his social contacts with the group, the supervisor should be careful not to exclude the new employee.

10. Provide employees such as maintenance men or internal auditors, who are constantly moved from department to department, some opportunity to work together as a common group and to feel they have a home.

DEVELOPING GROUP PARTICIPATION

Many high-production supervisors have discovered that they can obtain better results by giving a group an opportunity to participate in decision-making, either through consulting with the group or by allowing it to make and implement decisions by itself.

Industrial engineers in a metal-plating department had been trying for a long time to figure out an equitable way of dividing up the girls' work. The operation was unusually complex and erratic, and every time the engineers made a suggestion the girls were quick to prove that it was unfair to someone. The engineers were about to give up in disgust when the girls asked, "Why not let us decide?" In a short while they had worked out job allocations that even the engineers agreed were superior to theirs.

Naturally everybody gains from this sort of participation. The girls win the satisfaction of exercising greater control over their work environment, as well as the feeling of success from having accomplished something by themselves. Management gains in that better decisions are often made by people close to the job. There is less need for the supervisor to exercise authority or to follow the philosophy of "be strong"; individual employees are more likely to obey rules they themselves have established.

Employees who are given the freedom to regulate themselves are far more capable of making sound decisions when emergencies arise. Since they make the decisions by themselves, there is less need for them to refer every problem to the manager. As a consequence, he can concentrate on long-term planning and handling relations with other departments.

When subordinates are given the necessary freedom, they often do an impressive job of working out their own methods of scheduling, quality control, and so forth. They may even set production goals for themselves and discipline those who fail to live up to expectations. Sometimes these goals are surprisingly high.

Groups that participate in setting goals for themselves often make higher demands for themselves than supervisors and methods engineers consider practical. A furnace cleaning job was cut from four to two days; tardiness was set at less than 3 per cent when formerly it was 10 per cent; service calls were reduced from one in 14 to one in 21 . . . repairs per man per day rose from 8.5 to 12.5 when the crew planned the service; and over a period of three years men worked more days when they decided whether or not the weather was inclement than when the supervisor made the decision. [5]

[5] Norman R. F. Maier, *Principles of Human Relations* (New York: Wiley, 1952), p. 172.

The mere fact that the group is given the power to enforce and implement rules increases the likelihood that they will accept the rules, even rules to which they might otherwise object. In other words, whether or not a group accepts management's objectives depends not only on *what* is demanded but also on *how* it is demanded.

The superintendent of a machine operation was convinced by his Safety Department that long-sleeved shirts were a safety hazard even when rolled up. So he posted a notice that beginning the next Monday morning wearing long-sleeved shirts on the job would be prohibited.

Monday morning four men showed up with long sleeves. Given the choice of working without shirts or cutting off their sleeves, they refused to do either and were sent home. The union filed a sharp grievance, asking for back pay for time lost.

Then the Personnel Department stepped in. The rule was suspended for a week and a special meeting was called with the union grievance committee. The safety director explained that if a worker got his sleeve caught in a machine his whole arm might be ripped off. The union agreed to the rule provided that it was extended to include management (who originally had been exempt on the grounds that they didn't get close enough to the machines).

Next Monday the rule went back into effect. A few men, forgetfully, arrived in long sleeves. The other men handed them a pair of scissors and insisted that the offending sleeves be cut off on the spot. Later in the afternoon a union vice-president and a company time-study man were treated in the same way.

Summarizing, these examples suggest that permitting the group to participate in decisions—through actually making the decisions, enforcing them, or being consulted about them—may result in genuine advantages for management. Employees take more responsibility for minor problems without constantly running to the supervisor with questions, they set production goals (at times at higher levels than would be set by management), they enforce their own rules, and they even modify their group standards in a way they might not otherwise do. In addition, of course, members of the work group gain many satisfactions from participation: a chance to be creative, to feel a sense of accomplishment, to show leadership, to let off steam, and so forth. To a large extent these are egoistic needs. Furthermore, there are situations where the group expects management to consult with it; if management fails to do so, subordinates may feel that management is behaving illegitimately.

How can the manager stimulate participation of this sort? To some extent he can permit it to develop naturally, merely by refraining from close supervision. However, if he goes too far, and simply says "Take over," fumbling and confusion are bound to result. In the following two sections we shall see that managers can encourage the group to develop effective participation through (1) holding meetings with subordinates to consider mutual problems, and (2) working through the informal organization of the group.

HOLDING MEETINGS

Many an effective manager calls his subordinates together whenever he has a problem of common interest. Of course, individual problems can be discussed and worked out in private conversations, but *group* problems require *group* discussion. Such meetings need not be formal. Indeed, meetings range all the way from a regular session of the board of directors to an informal discussion between a foreman and a couple of mechanics around a machine that has been causing trouble.

Meetings of this sort may be used for three different purposes:

Information-giving. This meeting is simply a substitute for posting a notice or speaking to subordinates one by one. Obviously, taking the whole work force away from their job is an expensive procedure, but it insures that everyone will be notified of new directives or information which are important to the whole group. Furthermore, such meetings give subordinates a chance to ask questions, raise objections, and discuss the implications of the announcement.

Consultation. Just as a manager can ask individuals for suggestions on how to solve a problem (see p. 169), so he can call a meeting for the same purpose. Though the manager will make the final decision on whether or not the suggestions are accepted, people derive great satisfaction from knowing that their ideas are being considered and even more if they are used. A group of individuals exchanging opinions and experiences often comes up with better suggestions than any one person working alone. A suggestion that has evolved from the contributions of many members of the group is more likely to be implemented with enthusiasm by the entire group than is a suggestion that is the brain child of one person, whether he is the manager or an individual subordinate.

Group decision. Just as a supervisor can delegate authority to individual subordinates to handle problems that involve them alone, so he may call a meeting and delegate authority to a group to handle problems that involve the group as a whole. Of course, there is little difference between a meeting called to solicit suggestions and a meeting called to enable the group to make decisions on its own. But, by waiving its veto power, management thrusts upon the group the responsibility for choosing between alternatives.

Group Decision-Making: Subject for Controversy

Most business meetings are called for the first two purposes mentioned above—for information-giving or for consultation. Yet, the greatest amount of interest and conflict about group meetings centers on the third purpose, group decision-making. Some observers seem to feel that group decision-making is almost a cure-all for every business ill. There are books on human relations and supervision devoted almost entirely to this one process. The controversy revolves around three basic questions: (1) whether group decision-making will lead to decisions which from management's point of view are proper, (2) whether group decision-making is a form of unfair manipulation, and (3) whether group decision-making is more effective than individual decision-making.

Can meetings be trusted? Critics make this objection: "Very well, group decision-making has some value, but can you be sure the group can be trusted to make what is from management's point of view the right decision? Won't subordinates avoid responsibility and try to get out of work? If given the power to make decisions, won't they wander over into areas that are none of their business?"

Actually, there are many areas in which management does not care what decision is made, so long as there is no excessive dissension. For example, management is unconcerned with how men divide up the dirty work so long as the work is done—or how rest periods or vacations are scheduled, so long as the time allotted is not exceeded. Since no vacation schedule can satisfy everybody, hard feelings are bound to result. The manager who can pass the responsibility on to the group saves himself a major headache.

In other areas the manager's objectives coincide with those of the group—in matters of accident-prevention or avoiding jam-ups in the parking lot, for example. Possibly management should reserve a veto power over decisions in such matters, although it is unlikely that the group will make decisions that are, from management's point of view, far wrong.

The manager, of course, is interested not only in getting a sound decision but also in getting one that is accepted by the group. An *adequate* solution that is enthusiastically implemented by the group may well be better than a *perfect* solution that meets with stubborn antagonism. Thus, the group-decision process is of particular value when management is more concerned with getting *acceptance* of a decision than with its *quality*.

How can a manager keep a meeting from encroaching on areas of decision-making that are not its proper concern? One way is to set clear *limits* to the group's area of freedom. (These limits are similar to the authority-delegating limits we discussed in Chapter 7.) Suppose management is interested in refurnishing the ladies' lounge. The experienced manager might say, "We have $500 allowed us. How should we spend it?" rather than "What should be done?" or, even worse, "How much should we spend?" Similarly, instead of asking "How much vacation time should you get?" the manager might ask, "How many people can we spare at any one time during vacation and still maintain production? Who should go when?"

If there is no agreement on basic objectives, however, even the setting of limits provides no absolute safeguard against what management might regard as irresponsible decisions. Children balk at being asked, "Which do you want, milk of magnesia or castor oil?" and their parents also object to being asked to make that sort of choice. Normally a group will refuse to make a decision on "We've got to lay off 20 men. Who should they be?" unless there is some previous agreement among the parties that *someone* will be laid off. There must be a mutual acceptance of objectives before a group decision is possible.

Ideally, management provides broad areas of freedom in which subordinates can regulate their own behavior (this is simply teamwork). However, there are bound to be areas of basic conflict between superiors and subordinates, between the organization and its members. In approaching these areas, the most a manager can do is explain why he has made a particular decision and perhaps ask for questions. At one time or another, every supervisor must face the inevitability of making and announcing distasteful decisions.

Manipulation?   Some observers feel that group decision-making is nothing but manipulation or even brainwashing—a device by which management imposes its will upon the group without the group's realizing what is happening. Certainly, many managers look upon participative techniques as a means of getting subordinates to accept decisions which are not in the subordinates' interest, or as a way of making them feel that there is no real conflict between their interests and those of management.

Much of the argument is exaggerated. Group decision-making works best in those areas where management is really willing to accept the group's free decision. True, management may pretend that the group has more freedom than it really has. And it may try to manipulate the discussion process so that employees seem to agree when they really do not. But experience suggests that subordinates quickly see through "mock democracy" of this sort. Such attempts at brainwashing may be successful at first, but in the long run in a free society they are likely to backfire, giving rise to mistrust and resentment.

It must be remembered that group decision-making is a form of delegation and is subject to the limitations we discussed in Chapter 7. It works best on jobs which are of intrinsic interest to those who do them, and it works much less well with those whose central life interest is away from the job. Similarly, it works best where participation is encouraged consistently throughout the organization and less well where the objects sought by participation are inconsistent with the subordinates' basic values.

For example, since academicians, professionals, and members of higher management are likely to have roughly the same objectives as do their bosses, participation with these groups may well be effective over a wide range of subjects.[6] On the other hand, among workers who lack intrinsic interest in their work, participation may be effective only over a narrow range. Thus, group discussion among secretaries about when to hold a coffee break may lead to acceptance of the agreed-upon time and perhaps to fewer breaks at other times. It is more problematical, however, whether such a discussion will lead to their working harder.

Group vs. individual decision-making.   Even apart from possible differences in objectives, is group decision-making more effective than individual decision-making? The answer seems to depend on the nature of the group, the problem being considered, and what is meant by "effective." Groups sometimes turn out higher-quality solutions than do individuals, although this isn't always the case. In solving problems where there is one definite solution, a group is more likely to be accurate than an individual. Furthermore, group problem-solving has the advantage of enlisting a variety of backgrounds and experiences; thus, the range of solutions is usually greater, and the group solution is more likely to represent a balanced point of view. Meetings are particularly useful when the participants represent various departments whose coordination is required to implement the final decision, for the discussion tends to force the

---

[6] Participation may be particularly effective for academicians and professionals, since these groups value highly the concept of "colleagueship."

departmental representatives to look at the problem from an organizational rather than a departmental point of view.

Individual decision-making, on the other hand, is more likely to be firm than to represent a compromise. Individuals are more capable than groups of handling subtle relations—whether in threading a needle or in developing a complex theoretical formula. Thus groups may be more efficient than individuals in solving crossword puzzles, but individuals are better at devising them. Great works of art are almost without exception the products of single individuals. "Could *Hamlet* have been written by a committee," it has been asked, "or Mona Lisa been painted by a club?"[7]

In addition, meetings are awfully time-consuming. Decisions reached in them take longer than do those of individuals, particularly if time is computed in terms of total man-hours expended. Sometimes, of course, the higher quality and easier acceptance of decisions reached through meetings makes them worth the extra time involved. On the other hand, managers on occasion pass the buck to meetings when they are psychologically unprepared to make decisions themselves. Meetings under these circumstances accomplish little.

There is the risk, too, that presenting a problem to a group to discuss may lead to greater conflict than existed before—and skillful leadership is required to prevent this. The danger of conflict is particularly great where vested interests are involved (for example, when a group is deciding whether "soft jobs" should be rotated or assigned on the basis of seniority). The less cohesive the group, the greater the difficulty in reaching agreement, though experience in making decisions of this sort may help cohesion develop.

The advantages and disadvantages of group decision-making through committees are effectively summarized in contrasting remarks by well-known executives from two companies with vastly different attitudes toward the use of committees:

"If you can name for me one great discovery or decision that was made by a committee, I will find you the one man in that committee who had the lonely insight—while he was shaving or on his way to work, or maybe while the rest of the committee was chattering away—the lonely insight that solved the problem and was the basis for the decision."[8]

"It stands to reason that if you get five men together and one man is wrong, the mistake will be picked up. Or if one man has a good idea, the others will contribute to it and develop it. And if they have good ideas, what comes out may be better than the separate ideas added together."[9]

Group Consultation on a Day-to-Day Basis

The preceding discussion may have given the impression that the use of meetings involves a drastic change from traditional management practice. Quite the contrary. In some companies most major decisions have long been made by

[7] Donald W. Taylor, Paul Berry, and Clifford H. Block, "Group Participation, Brainstorming, and Creative Thinking," *Administrative Science Quarterly*, Vol. 3, No. 1 (June 1958), p. 27.

[8] Ralph J. Cordiner, former Chairman of General Electric, as cited in Justin G. Longenecker, *Principles of Management and Organizational Behavior* (Columbus, Ohio: Merrill, 1964), p. 206.

[9] Frank Abrams, former Chairman of Standard Oil of New Jersey, as cited in *ibid.*

committees, particularly at the higher levels of management. And at lower levels it is now accepted practice for supervisors to hold regular meetings at which subordinates can raise questions, discuss common problems, and consider new developments. Increasingly, such meetings are being held even on the hourly-paid level, though they are still probably more common in organizations such as restaurants, hospitals, stores, schools, and libraries than in manufacturing plants.

Some organizations require that regular meetings be held as a standard practice at all levels. Unfortunately, supervisors may call these compulsory meetings merely because they are told to do so: They go through the motions but never become involved in the spirit of consultation. An office girl once described her experience to us:

"We have meetings once a month. The office manager asks us if we have any questions or suggestions. Sure we have lots of complaints, but no one has the courage to bring them up. Once in a while one of the girls who is looking to make a good impression asks some silly question, although she already knows the answer."

Actually, the mere act of holding formal meetings is less important than the manager's willingness to consult with subordinates informally when problems arise. Status differences create less of a barrier to communication when consultation takes place around the drawing board, over the machine that has broken down, or in the cafeteria—than at a formally called meeting.

WORKING THROUGH THE INFORMAL ORGANIZATION

It would be impractical for a manager to call a meeting every time he has a problem to solve. Often he can work out a solution by himself, taking into account the standards and expectations of the group. But at other times the successful manager will make use of the informal organization of the group.

Informal Leaders

As we mentioned in Chapter 4, groups evolve their own leadership. Informal leaders play key roles in every organization, and without their cooperation management must face an uphill battle against sabotage and apathy.

W. F. Whyte tells the story of two settlement-house recreational directors who handled the same problem in different ways. The problem was this:

The younger boys were to use the play center till 9 o'clock, then they were to leave and make room for the older boys. But, instead of going home, the younger boys would hang around the door, bang on the windows, and generally create a nuisance.

Again and again the first recreational director asked the boys as a group to go away—but with no results. Faced with the same situation, the second director turned to one member of the group and merely said: "Listen, Joe, the time's up. Be a good fellow and take your gang out of here." Joe, who was the informal leader, complied immediately and the group left. [10]

[10] William F. Whyte and Burleigh B. Gardner, "The Man in the Middle: Position and Problems of the Foreman," *Applied Anthropology*, Vol. 4, No. 2 (Spring 1945).

Why was the second director so successful? He recognized the informal leader's special status, and gave him an opportunity to gain still more status through proving his power to the director. Under the first director's approach, the informal leader could exhibit his power only by opposing the director's will; had the group obeyed the director, the informal leader would have lost status.

The situation is very much the same in business and industry. A manager can either fight the informal organization and its leaders or work with them. If the informal leaders fail to win recognition by working *with* management, they will get it by working *against* management.

Management is often heard to complain, "All our trouble is caused by a few ringleaders. If we could only get rid of them, our trouble would disappear, morale would rise, and our employees would be loyal once again." Unfortunately, these "ringleaders" are often informal leaders; the trouble they cause reflects the desires of the group. In dealing with them, a certain amount of bargaining is often required. Eliminate the informal leaders, though, and the group may become still more antagonistic to management, morale may fall even lower, and new ringleaders will step to the fore. In a nonunionized situation it may be possible to eliminate ringleaders one by one till finally nothing is left but a cowed, disorganized mass of individuals who docilely obey orders. However, such individuals never show a gleam of initiative or teamwork.

What is the alternative to firing ringleaders? Working with them. There are numerous ways in which a manager can build up good relations with the informal leaders working under him. Among other things he can pass information along to them first, ask their advice on technical or human-relations problems, and assign them to train others.

There are, however, several dangers that the manager must guard against:

1. The informal leader is often hard to identify. The outstanding man who does the best work and cooperates most readily with management may *seem* to be the informal leader, whereas these characteristics may actually make him a social isolate. On the other hand, the "loud-mouth" may serve as the group's *spokesman* rather than its actual *leader*. The group may even have different leaders for different purposes. Sometimes the members of the group will follow one individual when they act in cooperation with management and another when they are antagonistic. Finally, there may be no identifiable informal leader at all.

2. The very fact that the informal leader works closely with management may result in his losing status with the group: He will be known as a "company man." This danger is particularly acute when there is antagonism between the manager and the work group generally and the informal leader is asked to do things that the group does not accept as legitimate.

3. Carried too far, cooperation becomes favoritism. It is one thing for the manager to give the informal leader information and to ask for his advice. It is quite another to give him easier work or special favors. Nothing could be more effectively calculated to drive him from his leadership position.

The Working Supervisor

The working supervisor is a group member to whom a manager may show special attention without giving rise to charges of favoritism. There are two kinds of working supervisor. The most obvious is "the straw boss," sometimes called the working foreman, leadman, keyman, or group chief. He is the leader of a group of men who do roughly the *same* sort of work. He shares their work and performs certain quasi-supervisory duties as well.

The other sort of working supervisor exercises his authority by virtue of his technical position on the work team, because his work is *different* from that of the others and requires more skill. Working supervisors are common in process industries and also in some of the older, more traditional industries in which craft skills still prevail. For an example from a traditional industry:

In glass-blowing shops where high-quality crystalware is manufactured for the luxury market, each work team is headed by a gaffer. The gaffer, the top man in a six-step hierarchy, is a craftsman of considerable skill and long seniority in his trade who does more intricate work than either members of his team. He is accountable to management for the quality and quantity of the ware produced by his team and has almost complete authority over their work performance.

The supervisory power of these top-status crew members rarely receives such formal recognition from management. Instead, it exists because of tradition and because supervisors have found these men to be effective assistants in running the department.

Since the working supervisor often gains status because of his seniority and technical proficiency, subordinates will be more willing to accept orders from him than from the foreman himself. This is particularly true where the foreman has not come up from the ranks himself, where coordination of the work force requires a high degree of technical skill that can be acquired only through years on the job, or where constant attention and order-giving are required, as with a fast-paced steel-mill crew.

We have observed situations in which management has impaired output and demoralized the work group by deliberately or inadvertently taking away some of the working supervisor's power and prestige. This often happens when a college-trained foreman pays too much attention to the formal organization chart and not enough to traditional relationships between workers and management.

Actually the relationship between foreman and working supervisor is a highly personal one and cannot be established simply by top-management edict. In many cases, the foreman can substantially increase his effectiveness by consulting with the working supervisor and channeling orders through him.

The Union Steward

The union steward is ordinarily an informal leader who commands respect outside union matters. Provided the over-all union-management relationship is friendly, the manager may wish to pass on information to the steward first, use him as a sounding board for proposed changes, and even ask his advice. Again if relations are good, this consultation can be handled outside the context of formal collective bargaining and in a way that will not lead to the loss of the manager's power or the establishment of precedents that management may later regret. Such consultation has the great advantage of permitting the steward to participate in solving technical and human-relations problems in a constructive, positive fashion; otherwise, in order to display his status, the steward has to resort to the essentially negative activity of processing grievances. In a strongly unionized situation, the supervisor will never be able to develop cooperative relations with his subordinates if he bypasses or ignores the union.

CONCLUSION

The manager rarely interacts with his subordinates in isolation. Usually this occurs in a group setting. In handling group problems the effective manager will consult with subordinates before taking action and in some areas will encourage them to make their own decisions. He may meet with the group as a whole or channel his activities through the group's informal structure. He may work with informal leaders, working supervisors, and union stewards.

A strong case can be made for participative management, in which the manager makes a practice of encouraging his subordinates as a group to discuss a wide variety of significant work-related problems. Ideally, participation of this sort will lead both to greater cohesion and to greater acceptance of management's objectives. To the extent that such a cooperative relationship can be established, the gains are substantial for both employees and for management. An atmosphere of cooperation provides essential need satisfactions for subordinates: the social satisfaction of working together, a feeling of identification with the group and the over-all organization, and a pride in accomplishment.

For the manager, such cooperation, if achieved, makes life a lot easier. There is less need for him to check on his men, for they make their own rules, take care of emergencies by themselves, and may even discipline their own team members. Participation is particularly useful during periods of change.

There is a danger of being Pollyanna-ish, however. We have tried to suggest the limits of participative management. There are many areas in which there are conflicts of interest between subordinates and management. Subordinate acceptance of the legitimacy of management's demands and behavior does not necessarily mean that these subordinates will "internalize" and work enthusiastically for management's objectives. It may only mean that they will put in a "fair day's work." What is such a fair day's work is largely determined through implicit bargaining and may be fairly low. To the extent that subordinates expect to be consulted, participative techniques may provide merely hygienic management (see Chapter 6) rather than positive motivation to work.

In a sense, strengthening group cohesion through participation may make management's task harder, for the group will now develop expectations that its acquiescence is required for what management does. Meetings take up a lot of time. If they are given genuine freedom to make important decisions, there is no guarantee that the decisions will be those which management wants (and the very process of discussion may lead to internal friction among group members). If the meeting is manipulated so as to come to the "right" conclusions, the members will eventually see through such mock democracy. In fact, many of the benefits of participation can be obtained without formal meetings, merely through working with subordinates on an informal basis.

Leadership: A Last Word

In our discussion of leadership we have tried to emphasize that there is no one pattern of management that is universally appropriate. Instead, the pattern of management that is most appropriate to a given situation depends on a number of factors:

1. Personality and background of the manager. *Example:* A manager who is brought in from outside the organization will almost of necessity maintain a greater social distance from his new subordinates than will one who has risen from the ranks.

2. Personality and background of the subordinates. *Example:* Professional engineers expect and require a higher degree of delegation than do older nurses with a rural background.

3. Type of work. *Example:* Assembly-line workers, who have relatively little opportunity to obtain need satisfaction from their work, may require closer supervision than do maintenance men.

4. Urgency of getting results. *Example:* If quick results are required, there may be no time to develop a cooperative, cohesive work group.

The sensible manager will take all these factors—and many more—into account before he decides how to behave in a particular situation. Even in a given situation, however, there is a broad range of leadership approaches that will be successful if properly implemented. For instance, in Example 1, a manager brought in from outside might very quickly develop close social relations with his subordinates and thus increase rather than decrease production. Or, in Example 3, a maintenance supervisor might get excellent production in complete violation of the principles of general supervision.

It is important to remember that many successful businessmen have violated all the principles discussed here. They have been successful in spite of their human relations—or perhaps because they have so inspired their subordinates to identify with the company and its success that employees have given their all in spite of supervisory actions that would be resented in almost any other context. (We are talking here about what some sociologists call the difference between "instrumental" and "expressive" leadership.)

In fact, the ability to supervise is only one of the many characteristics of a good manager. The company president, for example, must be effective in dealing with his subordinates. But this is only one part of his duties: He also makes plans, evaluates the recommendations of others, represents the company to outsiders, and so forth. He must have technical and administrative as well as human-relations abilities. In fact, as we shall discuss in later chapters, getting along with still higher management may be more important for him than getting along with subordinates. Perhaps the primary function of any top executive is to adjust the goals of his organization to the needs of his times. The ability to sense the main current was the central genius of Washington, Lincoln, Franklin Roosevelt, Queen Elizabeth I, and Churchill. It is also the genius of the business executive who decides at the opportune moment to switch his company's operations from wholesaling to direct sales—or the man who steals a march on the market by making plans for the mass production of a new chemical though the laboratory tests are far from complete.

Certainly we would admit that the executive's ability to make critical decisions of this order is more crucial to the survival of the organization than his particular skill in dealing with people.[11] An organization permeated with inappropriate[12] human-relations practices, however, is unlikely to remain profitable for long, regardless of the personal brilliance of the man at the top. An organization can be successful even if some of the individuals in it, even those at the very top, lack important skills, *provided* there are others in the organization who can fill in for them. The president may be inadequate in dealing with people, but the organization will be little harmed provided he channels his contacts through someone high in the management hierarchy who is skilled in this area. Available evidence suggests that the quality of supervision in itself is often relatively unimportant in determining levels of productivity—particularly where production rates are determined by technology or by group standards.

Similarly, on lower levels it would be unrealistic to expect management to promote men entirely on the basis of their leadership abilities. What is important is not that every manager be a good leader, but that the structure of the organization and management policies be such as to encourage sound human-relations practices.

At this point you may complain, "A few chapters ago you seemed to state a strong preference for delegation. Now, many hedges later, haven't you worked yourself into a position where it doesn't seem to make much difference what kind of supervision is used?" By no means. We think that the healthiest, soundest, most profitable organization will be the one in which delegation can be used effectively. But to make it possible to use delegation effectively, it may be necessary to revamp the whole organization through changes in organization structure, delegation, improved communications, and even, as we suggested in Chapter 2, substantial changes in the technological processes of production. Changes of this sort may well create cumulative changes in the over-all organization that will make general supervision possible.

As a consequence, the face-to-face relationship between supervisor and subordinate cannot be considered in isolation from the other factors that we will consider in later chapters. First, however, we should define more closely some of the skills required by the supervisor.

---

11 Though we would argue that major critical decisions must be made in the field of personnel administration just as frequently as in such fields as marketing, production, or finance.

12 Note we use the term *inappropriate*. The appropriate practice for the given situation may be the unrestrained use of authority.

problem 1 • THE PRESIDENT'S LETTER

The following letter was sent to the *Harvard Business Review* by the president of a medium-sized insurance company. The president is explaining why his company has so few immediate personnel problems in its Home Office (which, we may assume, houses about 500 employees, most engaged in routine, clerical operations.) [13]

The reason lies not in the attitudes of workers but in the attitude of management. It is true that lavish offers of fringe benefits give no assurance of mollified workers. This company has gone far in the fringe area, but I have never felt that what we did accounted for the remarkable *esprit de corps* our people show. I feel it is how we do it.

By that I mean that for eleven years since I came to head this company my first objective in dealings with our people has been to dignify them as individuals and to express a feeling of pride in them which quickly won their recognition. This is the pattern followed by my staff. Supervisory attitudes—management's real intent—are quickly observed and evaluated by employees. My company takes this seriously.

Alex Osborn of B.B.D.&O. is an old friend of mine. You may have seen his two recent books, one captioned "Your Creative Power," and the other more recent one entitled "Applied Imagination." These books have been widely circulated among our officers and supervisory people, and many things have come out of them. For example, we took a longer look at our suggestion plan and approached it on the basis that whatever the quantity or quality of suggestions, the Suggestion Committee must deal, not only with an open mind, but liberally, with suggestions in the first year. While we get many suggestions that cannot be given dollar awards, we make sure that occasionally a good suggestion gets a walloping return. We now invest a rather substantial sum in suggestion awards, and I submit we get a great deal of genuine interest and benefit. Our plan works well and it costs us about the same as one qualified clerical person.

I am interested in the local orchestra, and a few years ago it was brought to my attention that there were several unsold boxes. I hit upon a plan evolved from Osborn's thinking that pays off three ways, and it has been most successful. Our people are encouraged to bring flowers from their garden to decorate the lobby of our building. They are given a credit line for so doing and feel good about it; secondly, our lobby is as attractive as any you will find; and thirdly, those who add to its beauty are rewarded by pairs of tickets to the concerts. The orchestra benefits as do our people. The plan appealed to every bank and insurance company in this town, save two, and there are no unsold boxes. Parenthetically, I maintain a box adjacent to that purchased for the employees. I am usually there and find an opportunity to visit either before the concert or during intermission with my people and their husbands and wives and friends.

Perhaps the most significant thing we have done is one which has given dignity to every person in the building and it happens to be in the field of philanthropy. In 1947, I was General Chairman for the Community Chest Campaign, and the slogan adopted by the company's employees committee that year was "PAR FOR E.A.R." [E.A.R. is the president], and in that year there was 100% giving. The company became pleasantly notorious throughout the city for this 100% accomplishment; and believe it or not, with a constantly changing personnel, the record of 100% giving—every officer, every employee, every cafeteria and building maintenance worker—has been maintained through the years since. Every year the drive is completed on the first day and a telegram sent to the general chairman. In the public meetings which follow, our people are photographed and feted. Every individual feels personally responsible for the result.

Our pay scales are measured by objective job analysis and careful performance rating. Our hours are the best, our working conditions as good as any, and there is a constant effort to be humane in all matters.

We have had interesting conversations with the group acting as the Board of Governors of the "Employees' Club" over the years, and we have met every reasonable request they have made. Biweekly pay was one of the requests which we adopted costing us about 8% more in salary, smoking in work areas which we permitted, music in work areas which we maintain. We are always willing to listen to our people. If they want something that will help them in their work and in their happiness here we will go far to supply it.

Ours is not a perfect shop, and I may be lulled into thinking it is happier than I suggest,

[13] Vol. 32, No. 6 (November 1954), reproduced by permission of the author and publisher.

but of one thing I am sure, while most of our officers have had collegiate experiences, there isn't one who came into the world with a gold spoon in his mouth, and that may account for their interest in people and their problems.

I have a great feeling of intimacy with our employees. I write dozens of longhand letters to those who do me and this company favors, and I write a specially dictated letter to each person on his reaching a fifth, tenth, etc., anniversary.

We make a good deal of a Christmas Party that is a really a family affair. There is no drinking in connection with it, though we are not opposed to drinking as such. We bring in the families and children of all people who wish to come. It is a very successful affair.

Similarly we take an interest in our retired people and annually give them the finest dinner and entertainment in the best place available. We encourage them to visit the office and to attend the functions held by active employees.

If our people should become upset about anything I am prepared to say it would be my fault, because there is nothing reasonable they could urge that we could afford to do, that we aren't doing, or be willing to do. If we could not do it my experience with them has been that we could spell out the reasons convincingly and acceptably.

We take good care of our older people and pay an extra service allowance for length of service which is quite considerable in the case of the older and in some cases, less productive people. We have meetings in which the dignity of the individuals is advanced with deliberate care.

Morale cannot be won in a day or purchased at any price. It takes a long time to develop good morale and it takes constant planning to preserve it. On the other hand, I could lose it all in one day's misbehavior. All I would need to do would be to walk through a work area and complain about the posture of a couple of people and ask whether it was necessary to burn as many lights. It would help to turn on lights but it would never do to turn one off.

The important thing is that the work be congenial; and if that is not so, liberal rules and wage scales become of less importance. Care must be taken in the employment of people and more care in the treatment of them later. We try to take that care and that I think is why we apparently do so well in our company.

1. Evaluate the effectiveness of this company's program.

2. How are the various forms of motivation, which were discussed in Chapter 6, utilized in this company?

problem 2 • THE TOOL CRIB ATTENDANT WHO READS

Bill Smith works as a tool-crib attendant at the Acme Company. A tool-crib attendant has a fairly responsible job: He has to keep tabs on who gets what tools, keep the tools in order, make minor repairs, and order new tools when the stock runs low. At the beginning and end of each shift there is a lot of work to do, but most of the time the men have relatively little to do, especially on the night shift. Nevertheless it is one of the highest-paid nonskilled jobs in the plant. (To work up to a skilled job, a man has to start as an apprentice in his twenties.)

Until last year Bill held an important union office and used his free time and the strategic location of the tool crib for political purposes. Last year he was defeated; those who opposed him felt his aggressive attitude toward the company was merely provoking trouble.

Shortly thereafter Bill was caught by his foreman reading a newspaper on the job. The following exchange took place:

Foreman: You're supposed to be working now. We're not paying you for reading.
Bill: I'm doing my job. I've got nothing to do now. How does it hurt you if I read?
Foreman: If I let you read, then the men on production will want the same privilege. If I stop them, they will say I'm discriminating against them. You pushed a grievance case just like that yourself. In fact, since I'm dealing with a legal eagle like you, I'll give you a written warning just to cover myself 100 per cent.
Bill: Why do I get the warning? I'm not the only one who's been reading papers. You're picking on me just because I made you eat a lot of dirt when I was a union official.
Foreman: No, I'm warning you because you're the first man I caught. I'll warn everyone else I catch too.

Bill: You can't give me a warning. There's nothing in the plant regulation about reading newspapers. We've never received any notice, and you're punishing me for a rule you've just set up. That's poor personnel policy.

Foreman: OK, I'll post a written order too—and this warning is just to make double sure you know about it.

Bill: OK, I'm filing a grievance. By posting the notice you're admitting this is a new order. I don't want any warning in my file that you can hang over my neck from now till doomsday.

Bill filed his grievance, but his steward, who was a political opponent, never "found time" to push it. Shortly afterward, Bill's wife got a job as a night telephone operator on the 11:30 P.M.-7:30 A.M. shift. Bills's own shift ran from 8:00 A.M. to 4:00 P.M. Bill's plan was to pick his wife up after she finished work, then drive down to the Acme Company, where he would turn the car over to her and go to work himself.

Acme and the phone company were on opposite sides of town and Bill began to come in late for work. After this occurred several times, his foreman gave him a written warning that if he came late again, he would be fired. From then on, whenever he saw he couldn't get to the plant by the starting whistle, he went home, reported sick, and took the rest of the day off. Technically, management could have required a doctor's certificate from him, but this was never requested unless a man had been out of work for several days.

Finally, the situation got to be too much for Bill and he requested a transfer to the midnight shift in accordance with the seniority provisions of the union contract. The foreman turned him down on the grounds he did not possess sufficient "fitness and ability" to work the night shift since there was provision for only one tool attendant on the night shift and Bill's poor tardiness, absentee, and newspaper-reading record would mean the company would often be caught short.

Bill did not explain the real reason for his absenteeism, fearing that it might bring him punishment. Instead, he caught the plant manager at the plant gate and said to him:

Bill: Mr. Struthers, I just asked my foreman to give me a transfer to the "mid" shift and he turned me down. I got the seniority, but he said I couldn't make the move because I've been absent too much. That's true: My wife's been sick once in a while and I've had to stay home to take care of the kids. If I can work the night shift, my sister can take over when my wife's not feeling good.

Mr. Struthers: OK, Bill, I'll see what I can do.

Next day Struthers had the following phone conversation with the foreman:

Mr. Struthers: Is it true you turned down Bill's transfer application because of his absentee record?

Foreman: Yes I did. I don't think he can be trusted on the job.

Mr. Struthers: Well, I'm willing to take the chance.

The following day Struthers told Bill his transfer would go through shortly.

Meanwhile the day-shift foreman told the night-shift foreman, "You're going to get a guy named Smith who will give you a pack of trouble. Watch him like a hawk."

Six o'clock the first morning of Bill's new shift, the foreman dropped in on him, sure that Bill would be asleep. Instead Bill had spent the whole evening washing down the walls and building a new cabinet for his equipment. Since that time the foreman has checked on him only at infrequent intervals. Bill is fairly satisfied with the new work:

"Of course, it is just as boring as can be. I hand out about ten tools a night. I've repainted and completely straightened out the crib, but you can't do that forever. I can't read my paper in the spare time, so lots of times I go to sleep, often for six hours. I have an arrangement with the fellows in the shop that if anybody from management comes they'll make some noise and wake me up."

1. Was management wise in instituting the no-newspaper-reading rule? List the arguments that could be presented *for* and *against* this course of action. (Assume management may not increase Bill's job duties.)

2. What was wrong with the way the order was issued? What would you have done?

3. Suppose you were night-shift foreman and word came to you through the "grapevine" that Bill was sleeping on the job. Would you have done anything? What? Why?

4. Go through the rest of the case and point out other mistakes made at different levels of management.

problem 3 • FILLING A VACANCY FOR FOREMAN

Management has been having a great deal of trouble in the cone-making department in the Ashford Plant. Cone-making used to be done entirely by hand and required considerable skill. Today much of the skilled work is handled by machinery, though there is still some work for skilled cone-makers left. The majority of men in the group do relatively unskilled but physically taxing work feeding the machines. The work process involves heat and fumes, and the department is isolated from the rest of the plant in an older, rather dilapidated building.

For years management has pretty much let the cone-makers have their own way, though on occasion there have been wildcat strikes or slowdowns over petty grievances or to prevent the introduction of technological change which might threaten their jobs. Their foreman, Mike Malone, has looked upon his job chiefly as that of protecting his men from management pressure. In recent years, productivity has tended to fall, and costs in this department are considerably higher than in comparable departments in other plants, especially since the wages of the unskilled workers are almost as high as those of the skilled workers—and the skilled workers are among the best paid in the industry. In part because of anticipated employee resistance, management has been reluctant to install new production methods and is giving some thought to shutting down the department altogether and buying cones in the open market.

Malone, who has come up through the ranks, is ready to retire and management must find a successor. Among the possibilities are:

a. *John Callahan,* age 50, who has been with the department for 33 years. He knows cone-making backwards and forwards, is well liked by the men, and has been union steward for years.

b. *Gus Nowak,* college graduate, age 32, who has done an outstanding job in cutting costs as foreman of the assembly department, a department of low-skilled workers which includes many women and has always had considerable turnover.

1. Is this a cohesive group?

2. Why might it resist change?

3. What are the relative strong and weak points of each candidate for foreman? Which one would you select?

4. Assuming Nowak is selected, what advice would you give him?

5. Assuming Callahan is selected, how should the plant manager try to handle him?

problem 4 • INFLAMMABLE MATERIAL

Through the years your company has had a no-smoking rule that has been largely ignored. Recently some of your departments have begun working with rather inflammable material, though there is still almost no fire danger in most of the departments. You are plant manager.

1. Describe the steps you would take to handle the danger of fire and yet maintain sound human relations.

2. Why would you take these steps rather than others?

problem 5 • THE SAFETY GUARD

While walking through your department, you notice that one of the operators a couple of aisles over seems to be working with the safety guard up. However, as he catches your eye, he fumbles with a piece of stock and knocks the safety guard into place—at least that is how it looks to you. This is a serious offense. When an employee commits this violation (often in order to speed up his operation and make it a little easier), the usual penalty is a three-day layoff. Several people have been seriously injured by failure to use the safety guard.

1. How would you approach the employee?

2. What would you say?

3. What would your objectives be in your discussion with him?

problem 6 • TIME TO SLEEP

The Merrimac Corporation sells, rents, and services electronic data-processing equipment and employs a large staff of servicemen to keep its customers' equipment in order. The 30 service-men who work out of the St. Louis district office (which covers most of the Midwest) all live in the St. Louis area and are often required to travel to customers in distant locations; usually they travel by air. A given trouble call may take several hours or even days of work.

A problem has arisen from the fact that, when an assignment is completed, the men fly back to St. Louis and often arrive home late in the evening or even after midnight. Under these circumstances management has always allowed the servicemen to take a few hours extra sleep and not report to the office the first thing in the morning. Recently there have been signs that the men have begun to abuse this privilege. A few men have developed the habit of taking the entire morning off after every out-of-town trip, even if they arrive back at their home by 5:00 the previous evening. And other employees are beginning to wonder whether they might do the same.

Management has considered imposing a hard-and-fast rule that all servicemen must report for work at 9:00 A.M. regardless of what time they got in the night before. But in some cases this would impose an obvious hardship, and it might encourage the servicemen to spread their work out so that instead of finishing their job in the afternoon and returning home late they would slow down and work through the next morning, returning home in the afternoon.

Above all, management is anxious not to disturb the employees' high morale and interest in their work. These servicemen are paid a salary, receive liberal fringe benefits, being treated almost like members of the management.

Advise management on how to handle this problem.

3

Managerial
Skills

In this section we shall look more closely at some of the skills that the effective manager must possess. Obviously, before a manager can supervise his subordinates he must be able to communicate with them. Yet communication is not a simple matter. The words uttered by the sender of a message may have a different meaning for him than for the man who receives them. Particularly when subordinates are insecure, hostile, or suspicious of their superiors, they may ascribe unintended meanings to messages from above. To prevent misunderstanding, the senders of messages, at all levels of the management hierarchy, must be careful to fashion them so that their meaning is clear to the receiver. This is the problem we shall discuss in Chapter 10, "Communications."

Effective communication is a two-way process. The good manager must also be a good listener. Interviewing, which is merely deliberate listening, is an essential skill if the manager is to get to know his subordinates. In addition, merely by listening, the manager may help subordinates solve their own problems or at least induce them to become more receptive to what he has to say (Chapter 11, "Interviewing: The Fine Art of Listening").

Chapter 14, "Introducing Change," considers a problem that is directly influenced by the quality of communications within the organization. As we shall see, it is the meaning that is communicated by a proposed change that most often leads to resistance. Effective use of communications, interviewing, and conference leadership—as well as of some of the managerial skills discussed earlier—helps insure that change will be readily accepted.

What happens when change is rejected? When subordinates refuse to obey new rules—or, for that matter, old rules too? Then discipline is required (Chapter 13, "Discipline"). In a way, discipline is also a form of communication: The message management is trying to transmit is that it really intends to enforce certain rules. To make discipline accepted and meaningful, the rule and its penalty must be carefully communicated, and the offender must be made to understand that the reason for his being disciplined is the fact he broke the rule, not personal animus on the part of the manager.

Considered together, these are some of the skills that an effective manager uses in implementing the philosophy which we discussed in the preceding section of this book.

COMMUNICATIONS

10

Almost everything a manager does involves communications, and yet it is only too easy for him to assume this involves no problems. After all, he has been communicating all his life; ever since he learned as an infant that to get something or to make his feelings known he had only to speak up. We all have the power of speech: to communicate. But . . .

I thought you wanted me to start that new job *after* I finished what I was doing.

How did I know he was *serious* about quitting?

I *discount* almost everything I hear from those guys in Corporate Communications!

But I was sure you meant London, *Ontario*.

The steward thinks I am *bluffing* and won't fire Jones.

On the surface, face-to-face communications would seem to be simple. Have you ever listened to two old friends talking together? Rarely do they use complete sentences; often a single word, a grunt or a groan, or a raised eyebrow communicates as much meaning as lengthy speeches would convey between casual acquaintances. A few syllables go a long way.

But successful communication does not necessarily take place automatically whenever two people get together. Let's examine a situation more typical of business life. The shop-clerk tells his boss with pride, "This is the heaviest day we've ever had." But the boss thinks the clerk is lazy and looking for an excuse not to unload new stock. So he answers angrily and the subordinate concludes that the boss is an overbearing, ungrateful so-and-so.

The basic problem in communications is that the meaning which is actually received by one person may not be what the other intended to send. The speaker and the listener are two separate individuals living in different worlds; any number of things can happen to distort the messages that must pass through these stages:

SPEAKER			LISTENER	
Intent →	Expression ⟶		Impression →	Interpretation
(Motive)	(What is said)		(What is heard)	(Meaning assigned)

The human sensory apparatus does not transmit an exact duplicate of reality from the outside world into the mind of the observer. Our needs and experiences tend to color what we see and hear. Messages we don't want to accept are repressed. Others are magnified, created out of thin air or distorted from their original reality. [1]

What are the causes of breakdowns in communications? What can be done to overcome them? We shall consider each of these questions in turn.

WHY COMMUNICATIONS BREAK DOWN

Hearing What We Expect to Hear

What we hear or understand when someone speaks to us is largely shaped by our own experience and background. Instead of hearing what people tell us, we hear what our minds tell us they have said. These may be the same things— or very different. We all tend to have preconceived ideas of what people mean; when we hear something new we tend to identify it with something similar that we have experienced in the past.

The manager tells an employee that the company has lost some important orders. Now this employee has had other jobs, and whenever a company has lost business he has been thrown out of work. So he "hears" the manager's statement as, "You can expect to be furloughed in the near future." When the man announces that he has quit to work elsewhere, the manager may be surprised to learn that the man thought his job was in danger.

An extreme form of letting expectations determine communication content is *stereotyping*. For example, we may expect athletically inclined, big-muscled people to be rather dull, and when they say something we say to ourselves, "Well there is another typical remark made by someone who is all brawn and no brain." We grow up believing that Rarutanians (or some other group) are shiftless and lazy. Bill Jones is a Rarutanian. When Jones comes up with an intelligent short cut on his job which took a great deal of time and energy to develop, we take it as proof that "he's always looking for a chance to loaf, just

[1] Our discussion is greatly influenced by Alfred Korzybski, *Science and Sanity* (Lancaster, Pa.: Science Press, 1933).

like all the rest of them." Though ridiculous, such stereotypes are stubbornly preserved even in the face of conflicting evidence.

Although this is short-cut thinking, "one of the most time-consuming pastimes of the human mind is to rationalize sentiments and to disguise them as logic." [2] This is another aspect of the human need for predictability in daily living.

Ignoring Information That Conflicts with What We Already "Know"

Most of us resist change. We tend to reject new ideas, particularly if they conflict with what we already believe. In some ways our communications-receiving apparatus (sense organs and brain) works like an efficient filter. When we read a newspaper or listen to a political speech, we tend to note only those things that confirm our present beliefs. On the other hand, we tend to ignore anything that conflicts with our beliefs; sometimes our filters work so efficiently we don't hear new information at all. And even when we do hear it, we either reject it as a fallacious notion or find some way of twisting and shaping its meaning to fit our preconceptions. Because we hear and see what we *expect* to hear and see, we are rarely disappointed.

Communications sometimes fail to have the desired effect because they run counter to other information that the receiver possesses. Statements that hard work leads to promotion are ignored in a company where promotions, in fact, often are made on the basis of seniority or favoritism. A guarantee that "the company never cuts an incentive rate because employees are earning too much" is disregarded if rates have, in fact, been cut as a result of minor engineering changes. Below is a dramatic example of the problem.

During February, 1971, the National Emergency Warning Center (an arm of the U.S. Office of Civil Defense) transmitted a coded message to all civilian radio stations warning of an impending nuclear attack. Although the message was sent in error, its form and content were precisely correct, and nearly all civilian stations were supposed to go off the air after announcing that "the President has directed an emergency action notification." Even though every station knew the correct procedure, and each had been drilled in its response, all but a small number ignored the message. Apparently most station managers found the coded alert inconsistent with what they believed to be reality.

Cognitive dissonance. In recent years a great deal of psychological research has been conducted on the mechanisms by which human beings cope with what they perceive to be irreconcilable communication inputs, or *cognitive dissonance.* [3] This research suggests that one can predict very strong differences in the "receiver's" reaction to information he hears which is consistent with what he already believes, compared to his reaction to new information which is inconsistent with his established beliefs. (These differences are summarized below.)

[2] Fritz Roethlisberger and William Dickson, *Management and the Worker* (Cambridge, Mass.: Harvard University Press, 1939), p. 88.

[3] Its foremost scholar is Leon Festinger. See his *A Theory of Cognitive Dissonance* (Stanford, Calif.: Stanford University Press, 1957). How various cultures differ in their responses to this dissonance is described in Cedric Clark, "Cultural Differences in Reactions to Discrepant Communications," *Human Organization,* Vol. 27, No. 2 (Summer 1968), pp. 125-131.

COMMUNICATION IS CONSISTENT WITH EXISTING BELIEFS	COMMUNICATION IS INCONSISTENT WITH EXISTING BELIEFS
Seeks additional exposure, more "information"	Avoids exposure
Accepts information as valid	Rejects validity
Remembers what is heard	Easily forgets
Memory is accurate	Memory distorts information

Not only does the receiver evaluate what he hears in terms of his own background and experience, but he also takes the sender into account. How reliable is he as a source of information? Does he have an axe to grind?

Often the receiver ascribes nonexistent motives to the sender. This is particularly true in labor-management relations. Many union members, convinced that management is trying to weaken the union, interpret every company statement as an attempt to deceive them. Similarly, management often regards every union grievance as a political maneuver designed only to win votes. Both sides are sometimes right, of course. But this mental set makes mutual understanding and agreement more difficult.

One experimenter clipped a cartoon from a union publication illustrating "The Four Goals of Labor" and pasted it up with a caption indicating that it had come from a publication of the National Association of Manufacturers. When the clipping was shown to union members, they were overwhelmingly critical of it as an unfair, biased representation of labor's goals. Having accepted the source as antilabor, they automatically drew the "obvious" conclusions.[4]

This sort of bias is one of the reasons why company newspapers (so-called "house organs") find it difficult to gain worker acceptance. Once employees become convinced that the paper is just a management mouthpiece, many will believe nothing it prints, no matter how objective or verifiable. So, too, with pamphlets and other give-aways. If these are tagged as propaganda, all the information they contain becomes suspect, even useful information about health and household safety.

Similarly it is hard for a manager to shed a reputation for being hardboiled or unfair. Suppose he goes through a training program and emerges with every intention of turning over a new leaf. Subordinates may well be suspicious of his motives and assume that his new approach is just a trick. If so they will distort and misconstrue every move he makes. He is now unpredictable. (Chapter 24 discusses management training.)

A manager who receives a suggestion from a colleague or subordinate may assume one of two things: (1) Here is an alert, intelligent employee who is anxious to make a contribution to the efficiency of the organization, or (2) here is somebody who is trying to show me up by suggesting something he figures I was too foolish to think of myself. And which of the two motivations he attributes to the subordinate will have a substantial effect on what he actually "sees" in the suggestion.

In short, it is extremely difficult for us to separate what we hear from our feelings about the person who says it.

[4] William H. Whyte, Jr., *Is Anybody Listening?* (New York: Simon and Schuster, 1952), p. 223.

Halo Effect

One aspect of stereotyping and evaluating the source is the tendency to ignore the "greys" and to react in "black or white" terms. Thus, when someone is speaking who has gained our trust or who begins a speech by saying something with which we agree, we will hear nearly everything he says as good and correct. On the other hand, someone we distrust will be ignored or heard to say nothing worth attending to. The failure to make appropriate discriminations between the "good" and "bad" that may be intermixed both within a single person and his comments is often called the "halo effect."

Influence of Reference Group

Clearly, the group with which we identify ourselves—the "reference group," as psychologists call it—creates some of this bias. As advertisers discovered long ago, an individual rarely changes his mind by himself. His attitudes toward politics, music, recreation, work pace, and all his other activities and interests are largely colored by the group with which he identifies. As we mentioned in Chapter 9, the manager is wasting his time trying to convince an individual employee to work harder when there is a strong group standard to the contrary. The employee would be risking ostracism if he went along with the manager's request. Management often uses slogans and posters to indoctrinate workers with the importance of promoting safety, cutting scrap losses, making suggestions, or engaging in good housekeeping. They even send personal letters to employees' homes. The trouble with these efforts is that they are directed to the *individual*, whereas the basic attitudes and convictions are determined by the *group*. Thus, if an employee's fellow workers see the supervisor as harsh and unfair, chances are he will feel the same way.

Even the categories of thought used by different groups may be widely divergent. It may well be that trying to convince an hourly employee to improve his *industriousness* will be less effective than trying to convince him to improve his *skill*. Employees can distinguish differences in skill but can't always distinguish differences in industriousness. [5]

In a large organization, the difficulties of perception are compounded. An announcement may go to dozens of groups with different occupational and status interests. What each group "hears" depends on its own interests. An announcement that the company has purchased the patent for a product that will be manufactured in a new plant on the West Coast may be heard in these different ways:

Design engineer: "This may be an indication that the company prefers to go outside the organization for new ideas, and that is bound to hurt our status."

Production engineer: "This new product will mean more work for us. Some of us may have a chance to move out West."

Worker: The new products aren't going to be manufactured in the home plant. That means if business should get slack, we're likely to get laid off. A bad trend."

[5] Harry Triandis, "Categories of Thought of Managers, Clerks and Workers about Jobs and People in Industry," *Journal of Applied Psychology*, Vol. 43, No. 5 (1959), pp. 338-344.

Or take this example.

The head of marketing has recently spent a great deal of time convincing the company president that they are losing business because competitors' prices are lower. Thus, when the president requests new cost-saving efforts, the marketing manager hears the news as a significant policy statement. On the other hand, the production manager, who does not contact customers, "hears" this as another platitude.

This is one of the most serious sources of friction in industry. With all the sincerity in the world, we try to frame a message that will break the communications barrier and carry an appropriate meaning to those to whom it is directed. But in many instances we know too little about their point of view, and our efforts miscarry.

Effective communications depends upon shared experiences and common frames of reference. Where these are lacking, it is not surprising that a great deal is not heard or believed.

Words Mean Different Things to Different People

This is the so-called "semantic" problem. Essentially, language is a method of using symbols to represent facts and feelings. Strictly speaking we can't convey *meaning;* all we can do is convey *words.* And yet the same words may suggest quite different meanings for different people. The meanings are in the people, not in words.

When management says that profits are essential if the business is to survive, it is thinking of profits as a means by which the company can buy new equipment, expand, and provide more jobs. To management, profits mean a successfully operated, growing enterprise. But to employees, the word profit sometimes suggests a picture of excess funds piled up through paying inadequate wages.

We find this problem arising in the "economic education" programs conducted by many companies. Here again the difficulty is that the management which sponsors these programs and the employees for whom they are produced live in different worlds. Abstractions like "profits," "capital," and "productivity" have real meaning in the world of management, but they may have little meaning to the employee (or very negative associations).

This problem is especially acute with abstract terms. But even simple concrete words and phrases often lead to trouble; again because the sender and receiver live in separate worlds. For instance:

The foreman spots oil on the floor and tells a machinist, "Get that oil wiped up as soon as you can; it's a real safety hazard." The machinist nods that he will. Ten minutes later an inspector slips on the very same spot.

The supervisor is enraged by this needless accident. When he prepares to penalize the machinist for failing to follow instructions, he is told, "But I was going to do it *as soon as I could,* as you told me. I thought you could see that I was working on a delicate cut, and I had to finish that first."

To the supervisor "as soon as you can" meant immediately; to the operator it meant as soon as it could be done without endangering his work. It is foolish to try to decide who was right. Here we see the fallacy of the simple "tell them what you want them to do" approach. Simply telling people isn't enough when the sender and the receiver give the words different meanings.

Symbols. For some people, a particular word or phrase may have a symbolic meaning that others overlook. When we use words of this sort, we may find ourselves communicating things we had no intention of saying.

When the manager tells a new supervisor that the parking lot is too crowded for him to have a parking sticker, something more is being communicated than simple information on parking conditions. What the new supervisor hears may be this, "You are not accepted as a member of management, and everyone will soon know it."

An Afro-haircut, a flag decal on an auto windshield, a campaign button—all communicate a great deal more to those who see them than does their objective reality. And often it was not what the wearer (or sender) anticipated.

My son gave me this peace button to wear on my sweater. When I got to work I was surprised at the funny looks I was getting. When I asked what was up they said that they had always thought I was a reasonably conservative, level-headed person, but now they wondered if I was turning into a hippie. When I defended my desire for peace, one worker said, "Sure, we all want peace, but it looks to me as if you're joining those pot-smoking radical groups!"

Thus, symbols are powerful communicators, and the message often exceeds what the sender intended. To take another example, observers of collective bargaining have noted that violent antagonism develops in discussions about "management prerogatives" or the "union shop." Again, these are terms that have great symbolic significance. While the manager is talking about prerogatives to the union, he is really trying to say that the very basis of the managerial function and perhaps of the free-enterprise system is involved. Similarly, the union leader arguing for the union shop feels that acceptance or rejection symbolizes the real place of the union in the plant—is it a permanent, accepted institution or merely a temporary nuisance that is being tolerated? Compromise on such issues is difficult, for both parties feel that their vital interests are at stake.

Argot

Occupational groups and sometimes social groups tend to develop their own special language, called "argot." Sometimes group members forget this when they are talking to an outsider who doesn't share these "insider" meanings.

The new supervisor was dismayed when a subordinate told him that a customer's shipping request had been "pickled in oil." The men used this term to mean giving an order extra-special treatment.

Although argot simplifies in-group communication and provides a sense of belonging and sometimes status to those who use it, there may be other motivations involved in its use. Individuals may seek to impress people with their complex technical knowledge by using complex technical terminology—sometimes called jargon.

Similar to argot is the use of special techniques of speaking and acting that only insiders understand. For example, Americans often tease each other, feigning extreme criticism when it is not meant seriously.

Of course, teasing and joking perform another function in communication that is often forgotten. Many people learn to impart in this fashion delicate or sensitive information that would be unacceptable (or cause an antagonistic reaction) if it were said straightforwardly.

Nonverbal Communication

In trying to understand what another person is trying to say to us (and thus to predict their future behavior) we use many *cues* beside language—what has come to be called "body language." Looking at the eyes, the shape of the mouth, the muscles of the face, even bodily posture may tell us more about what the other person really thinks than the words he uses. The reverse is that we ourselves often communicate things unintentionally. Arriving at the office angry because of a traffic jam, a disgruntled manager may be "telling" his subordinates by his general appearance that he is dissatisfied with their work, although that was never intended.[6]

Styles of dress, tone of voice, even our manner of speaking often communicate a good deal about us. The noncollege-trained employee may have a difficult time adjusting to a company in which most employees have degrees because he always seems "different." He must learn a number of subtle bits of behavior that are assimilated during college and that communicate to others that one is sophisticated, or well-educated, or reasonably high in status. It is not easy to learn all these hidden cues, which communicate even more than what we think we are saying. (This is also a problem for minority group members; see Chapter 21.)

Emotional Context

When we are insecure, worried, or fearful, what we hear and see seems more threatening than when we are secure and at peace with the world. Rumors of all sorts spring up when management makes a change of any kind without adequate explanation, even a change as simple as moving desks around the office. This is particularly true during an economic recession. Then statements and actions that under less trying circumstances would have passed unnoticed become grounds for fear. "Yes, Joe might be right, they are going to double the work load." "I saw the foreman looking at the seniority list; I guess the rumors are right, a lot of men will be laid off because of the new equipment."

By the same token, when we are angry or depressed, we tend to reject out of hand what might otherwise seem like reasonable requests or good ideas. Our

[6] A summary of the best work in this field is presented in R. L. Birdwhistell, *Kinesics and Contexts* (Philadelphia, Pa.: University of Pennsylvania Press, 1969).

gloom and despair color everything we do and see. And while we are engaged in arguments, many things said are not understood or are badly distorted. Similarly, when elated, we may not "hear" problems or criticisms.

Noise

Living in a world of words and being deluged by sounds all the time, individuals learn to "tune out" many things. While a mother usually hears her child crying, the father often sleeps through, although he would hear his wife call. Many things a manager says are ignored, actually never heard, because they sound so much like what he always says: "Work efficiently," "This order is very important," "Save materials," "The company is depending on us." Thus, before individuals can hear a message, they must learn to discriminate between background noise (timeworn cliches) and what is significant and relevant new information, worthy of attention.

There are many types of "noise" interfering with accurate reception. In addition to the noise with which we're all familiar—that is, irrelevant, distracting sounds that make hearing difficult—there are also other types of noise covering up or muffling the receiver's words. Here are some examples of noise:

I get a dozen announcements a week from all our staff departments; changes in this policy or that procedure. There are pages and pages of minutiae there to digest. How do they expect me to ferret out what is really important?

Barger is some talker! It takes him an hour to spit something out, and most of us are exhausted or tune him out before he gets down to the heart of his story.

The boss just told us that jobs and salaries depend upon our costs being lower than those of our competitors. My reaction is, "So what else is new?"

Thus, when the noise level is high, the listener simply hears *unmeaningful* sound that contributes no new information.

Summary

Barriers to communications among members of an organization cause breakdowns, distortions, and inaccurate rumors. They plague the daily life of the manager who must depend on accurate transmission of orders and information for efficient operation. The implication is clear: Don't assume that every message that you send will be received in the form you intended it to be.

DEALING WITH BARRIERS TO COMMUNICATION

Up to this point we have purposely presented a discouraging, one-sided picture: pervasive problems and no solutions. But the picture need not be this bleak. We now know many techniques for improving communications, even though—it should be emphasized—none is a cure-all. Perfect understanding between people is impossible.

Among other things, good communications requires solving simultaneously two quite different problems. The manager must learn to improve his *transmission*—what words, ideas and feelings he actually sends to the other person. At the same time he must cope with his own *reception*—what he perceives the other person's reactions and statements to be. We shall devote the rest of this chapter to a discussion of several methods by which a manager can maximize his success in communicating. At first glance, these techniques may appear mechanical substitutes for mutual trust and understanding. However, a wide variety of research confirms the efficacy of considering communications as both a psychological and technical problem.

Adjusting to the World of the Receiver

In communicating, the temptation is to adjust to *yourself.* You have the need to say something and to say it in a particular way. In fact, often you communicate when your emotional needs to speak are strongest and the odds of being understood the lowest.

I was just boiling with rage. He had done it wrong again, so I explained why we needed to keep this particular customer: how much they had purchased in the past, who else would be impressed with their being a steady customer, their tie-in with the consolidated buying syndicate and all the rest. But I could tell that salesman wasn't understanding!

Of course he wasn't! The manager was gaining satisfaction by venting his feelings and not trying to get through to the other person.

How does the speaker adjust to the *receiver?* Several passive techniques are available, as well as more dynamic ones. The passive involve thinking ahead and endeavoring to be aware of the listener's needs, the possible symbolic interpretations he will give, and the right time to communicate. Dynamic techniques revolve around *feedback* and reinforcement, to be discussed later.

The Receiver's Expectations

It is extremely difficult to get through to a listener when what you are trying to communicate contradicts his expectations and predilections. If your typist has been in the habit of preparing only a single carbon, you must *stress* a request for two carbons. If being sent to the front office is regarded by employees as a sign of impending discipline, you must take pains to communicate that this is not the reason, if in fact it is not.

In short, you must be sensitive to the private world of the receiver, try to predict the impact of what you say and do on his feelings and attitudes, and tailor your messages to fit your receiver's vocabulary, interests, and values. Managers who work with a variety of groups in the organization must learn techniques of "simultaneous translation" to avoid misunderstandings. The greater the gap between your background and experience and that of the receiver, the greater the effort you must make to find some common ground of understanding.

Awareness of Symbolic Meaning

As we have seen, symbols play a vital role in the "private world" of the listener. Here is a case in which effective communication was blocked until symbolic meanings were taken into account:

To help in the preparation of market analyses the District Sales Manager asked the salesmen to compute correlation coefficients from their records. These coefficients could be calculated quite simply and painlessly by use of a simple formula. But the salesmen refused to do what they were asked. One excuse followed another: The computations were too complicated, it was clerk's work and not part of their job description, the coefficients were really useless, and so on. There seemed to be no way to convince the men to perform this simple task, and their persistent refusal seemed out of all proportion to the issue at hand.

Why was this modest request greeted with such stubborn resistance? The very degree of the salesmen's reaction was the key to the problem. Investigation revealed that coefficient correlations had been tried three years earlier, when the department was headed by an inept supervisor who had earned the universal dislike of his subordinates. Among other things, he had tried to revamp all the departmental procedures and in the process had introduced this statistical technique. Ever since, the salesmen had associated the term "coefficient correlation" with autocratic supervision. To them it had become a symbol of oppressive management. Once the company had plumbed this seemingly irrational attitude, it was a simple matter to develop a different terminology for the operation, to conduct training in how the computations should be carried out, and to gain ready acceptance for the whole activity.

The moral of this story is clear: If there is extraordinary, unexpected resistance to a proposal, try to find out whether some symbolic meaning is associated with it.

Often the would-be communicator must prepare the way for effective listening by taking the time to prove that he shares certain symbolic values which he presumes to be of importance to the other person.

(A supervisor describing some new work procedures to his department): Here is the way we are going to handle Eastern Division Receivables. The procedure grows out of that hassle we had with the Comptroller's office and the computer people. We're always the forgotten ones in these new procedures, and the computer people get their way. This time we took "first place" in the final agreement on procedures, and we aren't going to have to handle those silly blue forms any more either, the ones that took us all so much time. Now, here is how we'll have to handle the. . . .

The speaker is showing his solidarity with the group and with some previous issues that have riled people: the status of the computer, the blue forms, the position of the Comptroller's office. These have nothing directly to do with the new procedure he wants to communicate, but if his listeners feel that he shares their values and needs, they are more likely to listen with alertness and sympathetic understanding and accept him as a credible source of new information.

Where these common symbols do not exist, the sender may have to build up systematically some shared experiences, and, thus, shared symbols, before he can expect to communicate on more difficult, more controversial subjects.

Critical Timing

Messages can come too early and too late; theoretically there is an ideal time when the odds are greater that the message will get through.

Communications are too early when they presume to deal with problems or subjects which the listener hasn't experienced: "I didn't understand a word they were saying about human relations problems because I had never worked and certainly had never been a supervisor." On the other hand, when an employee has a problem which frustrates him he may be highly receptive to new ideas.

Similarly when an individual is away from his neighborhood or work group (assuming he is not frightened), he may be more receptive to materials which conflict with his prejudices and predispositions, his "conventional wisdom":

(An engineer describing his experiences as part of a company task force): I've never learned so much so quickly. Part of it was being thrown in with finance and marketing types from other parts of the corporation, and also working as a team overseas. Everything was new to me; I had never done this sort of work before and there was nobody there to tell me what I expected to hear. [7]

Thus, it may be useful to wait until there is time available to get people to another location (e.g., taking executives to a resort "retreat" to rethink corporate policy) or away from their normal associations.

A manager can also make the mistake of asking a subordinate to communicate his results or findings prematurely. At least, when the manager wants the subordinate to continue to be open-minded and alert to new possibilities (say in R & D), he may find that too-early communications rigidifies expectations; once having verbalized what one is doing, new data are seen as confirming these early predictions. Don't get people to take a stand too early, in other words, until you are sure they have as much information and data as they need to draw sensible conclusions.

Communications come too late when opinions have already hardened or the subject has become a battleground between groups or individuals. One way of limiting the amount of noise or distortion is to communicate your message before those other beliefs or attitudes come into play. Then the communication will meet less resistance and your chances of getting it accepted will be greatly increased.

Management announced that Foreman Green would retire in a few months and would be replaced by a man named Williams from another department. One of the men felt that Williams had done him an injustice years ago, and spread the word among his fellow employees that Williams was a tyrant who played favorites.

Long before Williams set foot in the new department, a petition was sent to top management requesting that a different foreman be assigned. And once Williams showed up, everything he said and did was fitted into the picture the employees had already established. Every job assignment he made was scrutinized for favoritism. Even harmless statements were often interpreted as threats.

A situation like this is an ideal breeding-ground for misunderstanding and unrest. Yet management could have minimized the problem by taking positive action before the picture of the new supervisor got established, perhaps by having the employees meet him as soon as the announcement was made.

---

[7] A harsh, devious form of this principle is involved in "brainwashing," which involves separating the individual from all familiar supports (friends, home, etc.) so he will be more receptive to the constant haranguing of his captors. Less devious is the value of foreign travel in stimulating learning.

It is a waste of time to try to communicate during an argument or bitter debate, when the person has to defend his preconceptions. During such acrimonious discussion, to concede (or even to "hear" accurately) would mean admitting that you are less worthy than the other person.

When issues have become polarized in an organization, informal groups pressure their members to hold only orthodox views and not to concede anything to outsiders:

"There was no use talking with the Shipping people about anything after that battle over who was to blame for the loss of the Krystar business. Anything you said to them about procedures, or even a minor problem, they interpreted as being just a continuation of the arguments. And no one from Shipping would dare agree with anything we said in Production or even listen to us—he would be massacred by his colleagues for heresy."

These group processes (discussed in Chapter 4) color everything that an individual has heard and introduce impossible rigidities in the communications process.

Utilizing Feedback

Perhaps the single most important method of improving communications is *feedback*. This term, adopted from engineering, refers to the ability of certain complex machines (technically, systems) to check on their own performance and to correct it if necessary—often called cybernetics.

We all use this principle of feedback in our human communications—perhaps without realizing it. Even in casual conversations we are constantly on the alert for cues to whether we are being understood (such as attentive nods from the other person). Similarly, a good teacher is always interested in audience reaction among his students. If they seem confused or drowsy, he knows his lecture isn't getting across. The good manager is equally conscious of the need to determine his subordinates' reactions to what he is trying to communicate.

An interesting study illustrates the importance of feedback. Two students were placed in different rooms and one was asked to communicate to the other the position of an interconnected series of dominoes placed on a grid. Both had identical grids in front of them. The sender was permitted to explain to the receiver, in any way he saw fit, the relative positions of the dominoes. Yet it was impossible to complete the task successfully when the receiver was forbidden to respond—that is, when communications were entirely one-way. No matter how painstakingly the sender explained the pattern, the receiver never understood all of it. Apparently some opportunity to ask for further information, at least to answer "yes" or "no" to the questions of the sender (e.g., "Did you understand what I said?"), is essential if complex information is to be communicated. Without feedback, false perceptions creep in, and even a small error that goes uncorrected may become magnified into a major distortion.

This experiment also revealed that communications gain in speed and efficiency as more and more feedback is permitted. Limiting the receiver to "yes" or "no" responses is less effective than allowing him to expand his comments to whatever he deems appropriate.

Using Face-to-Face Communications

Face-to-face communications are superior, under most circumstances, to written orders, printed announcements, or business letters. Only when the sender is able to experience direct feedback from the receiver can he really know what the receiver is hearing and what he is failing to hear. How else can the sender become aware of the hidden meaning—the symbolic significance the receiver is ascribing to his words? How else can be bring out into the open contradictory information already in the receiver's mind that may cause him to reject or ignore the communication?

Another reason for the greater effectiveness of personal confrontation is that most of us communicate more easily, completely, and frequently by voice. Probably the greatest advantage of such communications is that they provide immediate feedback. Merely by looking at the audience, the skillful speaker can judge how it is reacting to what he is saying. If necessary he can modify his approach or vary the intensity of his voice. (The human voice can provide a wider variety of emphasis and pace than any printed page, regardless of the number of type fonts used.)

Even better feedback is possible if the recipients of the message are allowed to comment or ask questions. This gives the supervisor an opportunity to explain his meaning or to consider unexpected problems. (Printed material can provide explanations, but few writers can anticipate all the questions that might be asked.)

For example, it is almost impossible to criticize someone's performance in writing without his taking serious offense. The cold type or words always sound more harsh and condemnatory than they may have been intended, and such written criticisms often provoke strong emotional counterreactions. The result is that the recipient tends to reject the entire message as having come from a hostile source. The same criticism discussed in a face-to-face exchange can be made much more acceptable and thus will be heard.

Furthermore, we usually ascribe more credibility to what we hear someone say than to words attributed to him in print. Employees conditioned to the "slick" releases of public relations offices tend to discount many of the printed announcements they read. Actually hearing the boss say that the company is in serious trouble, however, may carry a great deal more weight than would a statement in the house organ, particularly if employees have an opportunity to ask the boss direct questions.

A Secretary of State explained why he frequently left Washington:

"Well, I fly because I go to meet heads of government, foreign ministers of other countries, and in a few minutes or at most a few hours of personal consultation you can achieve a much better understanding than you can possibly achieve by working through notes and writing to each other." [8]

Does all this mean that written messages have no place in the organization? Not at all. In fact, they are often indispensable. Lengthy, detailed instructions must be put in writing so that the person to whom they are addressed can have

[8] Dana Adams Schmidt, "Instant Diplomacy and the New Diplomats," *Columbia University Forum* (Fall 1958), p. 36.

a chance to study them at leisure. The spoken word exists only for an instant, and then vanishes. The written message provides a permanent record to which the receiver can refer to make sure he understands what has been said, and to which the sender can refer as evidence that he has in fact said it. Frequently, too, the relative formality of written communications gives the message greater weight than it would have if it were delivered orally.

For very important messages, both the spoken and written word may be used in combination. For instance, if a new procedure is to be introduced, the supervisor might call a meeting of his subordinates to give them a rough outline of the change. At this point he could (1) explain why the change is necessary, (2) answer their questions, and (3) perhaps make adjustments to meet objections. Once general agreement has been reached, the new procedure can be reduced to writing for future reference.

Adjusting rate of speaking. To facilitate face-to-face communications it is important to become aware of differences in speaking patterns. Some people, for example, speak with long-drawn-out pauses between thoughts or sentences. If such speakers are interrupted by someone who becomes impatient sitting passively so long, they will often fail to reveal all of their original ideas. Also, interruptions can cause anger, which impedes communication, as already noted.

In conversation, a listener's attention is often lost by a speaker who insists on talking too long a time without allowing the other person to respond. Many individuals have such verbal energies that the words come out like a torrential downpour, and, in the process, they lose their audience. On the other hand, the natural style of speaking for some people is in short bursts. These people are only comfortable and able to say all that they want to if the other individual replies each time they stop.

Failure to adjust, to synchronize, to the speaking patterns of the other person causes breakdowns in communications because of lost ideas as well as the discomfort and emotional reactions associated with interruptions or long silent periods. [9]

Using Many Feedback Channels

How do we know if the person to whom we are communicating understands, agrees, or sympathizes with us, or is indifferent, hostile, or confused? There are several techniques for maximizing feedback.

Observation. In a face-to-face situation, we can observe the other person and judge his responses by his total behavioral set. We can watch for nonverbal cues—the expressions of puzzlement, anger, or comprehension that flicker across the face of the listener, or the subtle body motions that reveal impatience, animosity, or agreement. These cues give eloquent expression to attitudes that the receiver may be reluctant or unable to express in words.

[9] A more precise explanation and description of how people differ in the physical pattern of their interaction is provided by the researcher who has done most of the studies in this field. *Cf.* Eliot Chapple and Leonard Sayles, *The Measure of Management* (New York: Macmillan, 1961) pp. 114-141.

Indeed, by their posture and facial expression, the set of their lips, the movement of an eyebrow, people often tell us more than they do in hours of talk or scores of written memoranda. A subordinate is seldom eager to challenge the orders of his superior. But in the course of informal, face-to-face discussion, an alert supervisor can detect the subordinate's lack of enthusiasm by his tone of voice and his general physical behavior.

Few of us appreciate just how much valuable information these nonverbal cues transmit. As many have observed, "when communication is at peak efficiency, words are often superfluous. Good examples of this are the hospital operating room, the jazz band, and some small interdependent work teams in industry. The close coordination necessary for these groups to achieve their goal is attained largely through small bodily movements and expression changes.

Listening with a "third ear." We must listen carefully if we are to discover what a person is trying to say. Though few of us can qualify as psychiatrists, we can learn to listen with a "third ear" by asking ourselves such questions as: "What did Joe really mean when he told me he was 'fed up'? Was it his assignment? His family? His chances for promotion? Me, as his boss? Why did he remain silent when I asked him for details?"

There is a hidden content in many communications that can only be inferred by the listener. (This underlying element is frequently referred to as the *latent* content as distinct from the *manifest* content.) Although the listener should keep his imagination in check, he should try to go beyond the logical verbal meaning where there is some evidence that emotional feeling is involved. Most communications are, in fact, a combination of fact and feeling.

A good example of this hidden content is provided by the word "communications" itself. An office manager complains to the personnel director that all his human-relations problems stem from "poor communications." If the personnel director wants to be of assistance, he will try to get behind the manager's use of the word "communications." The manager might mean that there are divisive cliques that tend to distort his orders or that he, the boss, never hears the "real truth" about what is going on in the office. He might be using the word communications to mean that cooperative teamwork is lacking, or to mean many other things. The point is that the words used by a speaker may not be very informative until we have an opportunity to question him on what he really means in terms of actual observable behavior. The listener must try to get back to the *referents* of the speaker and to avoid the easy assumption that both people are attaching the same meaning to abstract terms like *poor communication*.

Reinforcing Words with Action

Words by themselves are suspect. Employees are more likely to accept new propositions when they observe an actual change in behavior or participate themselves in the process of change. For example, supervisors in one company were told that they would have the final say in granting individual pay increases. This was a radical departure from past practice. Most of the supervisors were skeptical about whether management really meant what it said. But this feeling disappeared when they began filling out recommendation forms themselves and sending them to the personnel department (a minor clerical job that in the past had been done in the superintendent's office). The consistent reinforcement of verbal announcements by action increases the likelihood that the communication will be accepted.

Employees learn that their supervisor, not the personnel department, controls pay increases when they see him taking this action and hear directly from him that they are to receive the increase. Where Personnel does the notifying, they perceive otherwise.

Management must be careful not to allow supersalesmanship techniques to dominate its thinking in communicating to employees. Because employees are able to judge for themselves the quality of the relationship they enjoy with a company, sustained repetition of slick slogans will not be effective. One cannot advertise one type of personnel program and deliver another. In the same vein, low-pressure statements are probably more effective than high-pressure pronouncements. Instead of telling workers how generous their pension benefits are, it may be more effective to give them the facts (comparative data on pension plans for the industry or community) and let them draw their own conclusion. It is difficult if not impossible to communicate "values"; facts can be transmitted with some success, but even facts are subject to distortion.

Once management has acquired a reputation for accuracy and credibility in its communications, it can do a more effective job of communicating information on new problems. The British learned this lesson during the war.

Early in World War II, when the radio stations of most countries were widely suspected of distorting the war news, the British Broadcasting system adopted a policy of frankly reporting Allied setbacks. This gave the British an advantage in morale and tactics over their enemies when the tide turned in favor of the Allies, for Europeans of all nationalities were ready to believe the news of the German rout—simply because it came from a source that had proved itself trustworthy.

Using Direct, Simple Language

Written communications should be as intelligible and readable as possible. Every manager must insure that his announcements, public statements, and directives are couched in simple, direct language. Government agencies have been the favorite butt of jokes about "gobbledegook," but many private organizations also are guilty of torturing simple statements into complicated puzzles, and of using specialized and complex jargon. Low readability is undoubtedly a factor in the breakdown of communications. (And since most people talk more simply than they write, it is another reason for using face-to-face communications whenever possible.) High readability, however, is not an answer in itself to the fundamental barriers to communication that we have discussed.

In a similar vein, emotionally charged rhetoric should be left to debating teams. Strong adjectives and expletives, innuendoes and exaggerations cause most listeners to turn off, not on, and raise questions concerning the credibility and balance of the speaker. Crowds, particularly in political gatherings, can be aroused by demagoguery, but most reasonably intelligent listeners, alone or in small groups, reject the inflated statements of the silver-tongued politician.

Introducing a Proper Amount of Redundancy

Communications engineers have developed techniques for measuring the amount of "redundancy" in a message—roughly the amount of repetition it contains. The supervisor who wants to give a direct order or transmit technical information should make sure that his message includes substantial redundancy. Then, if any word or phrase is misunderstood, there are other elements in the communication that will carry his point. To give a very simple example:

A firm manufacturing several thousand varieties of chemical compounds used a numerical coding system to refer to each of the products. Increasingly, management found that mistakes were creeping into the ordering system. When a supervisor requested a shipment of compound #28394, a clerical error would occasionally result in a wasted shipment of #23894. Each digit was crucial, and the slightest mistake was costly. Eventually the firm adopted individual names for each compound and these words had a great deal of built-in redundancy, as do nearly all words. If a clerk ordered "calitin" instead of "calithin," the shipping department knew what he meant.

If each word is crucially important, it pays to say the same thing in several ways. In giving complicated directions, for example, it is wise to repeat them several times, perhaps in different ways, to guarantee successful transmission.

At times, however, a manager may want to avoid redundancy and concentrate instead on introducing novelty or originality into his communications. We tend to ignore many of the messages we receive simply because they sound so familiar. Most of us are guilty of repeating our favorite clichés to the point where people no longer listen to what we say because it is all so predictable. ("I know what the boss is going to say the minute he starts on that line about us all being one big happy team.")

There is some need for surprise, in modest doses to be sure, if we are to gain the attention of those with whom we wish to communicate. This is particularly true when our message contains something that contradicts expectations. For instance, to repeat our previous example, if your typist has been in the habit of preparing only one carbon, you must stress your request for two carbons.

Thus, the supervisor needs to balance carefully the redundancy and surprise elements of his communication.

CONCLUSION

The swiftest, most effective communication takes place among people with common points of view. The supervisor who enjoys a good relationship with his subordinates has much less difficulty in explaining why air-conditioning equipment cannot be installed for another year than does the supervisor who is not trusted by his men. When people feel secure, they can talk to one another easily. Where discontent is rife, so is misunderstanding, misinterpretation, rumor, and distortion. In this sense, communication is a dependent variable. Where there is mutual trust and human relations are good, it is easy; where there is distrust, it is almost impossible. Therefore, the communications area is *not* the place to start improving supervisor-subordinate relationships.

Nevertheless, the problem of communicating accurately and effectively in

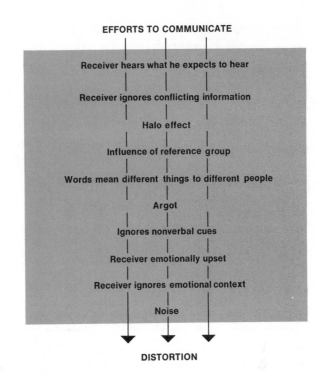

EFFORTS TO COMMUNICATE

Receiver hears what he expects to hear

Receiver ignores conflicting information

Halo effect

Influence of reference group

Words mean different things to different people

Argot

Ignores nonverbal cues

Receiver emotionally upset

Receiver ignores emotional context

Noise

BARRIERS TO SUCCESSFUL COMMUNICATION

DISTORTION

each contact makes a supervisor's job more difficult. He must guard against the natural inclination in our highly verbal society to assume that simply *telling somebody* is enough to insure successful communication. Fortunately, as we have seen, the supervisor can resort to a number of techniques to facilitate the transmission of understanding between people in their day-to-day activities.

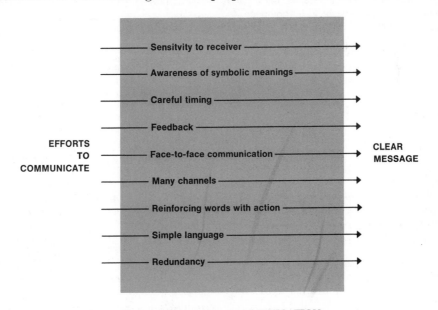

Sensitvity to receiver

Awareness of symbolic meanings

Careful timing

Feedback

Face-to-face communication

Many channels

Reinforcing words with action

Simple language

Redundancy

EFFORTS TO COMMUNICATE

CLEAR MESSAGE

TECHNIQUES FOR IMPROVED COMMUNICATION

One must be careful not to draw the conclusion that "the more communication the better" is always true. There are limits to how much an individual can absorb and be responsive to. Needless information can overwhelm important data. Also, there may be private fears, hopes, and hostilities within an organization that ought not to be communicated because they would only engender adverse reactions.

Many managers regrettably conceive of communications as a selling job, persuading the wary and the unconvinced by an overwhelming array of facts and arguments. They conceive of feedback in terms of having an answer for every objection, and they believe that as long as their words are comprehensible to subordinates, they will go along with what is said. [10] This is a highly naive view of the problem of communications that can only lead to further misunderstanding. Communications is a matter of both transmitting and receiving.

This chapter has emphasized transmitting. In Chapter 11 we will consider one of the most useful techniques for receiving information: interviewing.

problem 1 • "WELCOME ABOARD"

This was Joe Phelan's first day on the job, and he was anxious to learn as much as possible about what was expected of him and what kind of company he was going to be working for. He had been hired as a technical writer primarily to prepare manuals to help customers operate the complex industrial equipment the company manufactures.

He was somewhat apprehensive since this was the first time he had ever worked for a large corporation, and this company had a reputation for being impersonal and bureaucratic.

No one greeted him when he came in a few minutes before nine this Monday morning, but remembering the man's name he was replacing, he found the office that he assumed was to be his. The desk still contained a few candy bars and a rather worn blotter. There was also a note to call his supervisor, Cal Thompson.

He followed instructions, and in a few minutes Thompson appeared:

"We certainly are glad to have you aboard, Phelan. Hope you like your new office. By the way, here are half a dozen manuals we issued during the past few months; I think if you read them you'll learn a lot about the work we do. Later this morning my secretary will bring over a lot of background material on the new Series 18 machine which you'll be working on, and tomorrow you'll meet the engineer in charge of the project. Oh, yes, don't forget to go down to the Medical Office sometime today; they want to complete your records. If you have any questions don't hesitate to call me, but I've got to go to a meeting now myself.

Joe thanked him and said he looked forward to getting into the project. "Also, I wonder if I could meet some of the sales people who work with the kind of customers I will be writing for?"

Although Thompson thought that Phelan seemed a little over eager to make a good impression, he only replied, "In due time," and left the room. Thompson's tone of voice convinced Phelan he had spoken out of turn.

Just then Thompson's secretary called to tell him that the normal lunch hour for the department was from 12:30 to 1:30 and that if he had any typing to do he should send it to her and she would transmit it to the typing pool. Phelan, without thinking, replied, "I thought lunch was at noon and I've already agreed to meet an old friend then. And, by the way, could I see the Series 18 file?"

[10] *Cf.* Douglas McGregor, *The Professional Manager* (New York: McGraw-Hill, 1957) p. 153.

Secretary: "I assure you, Mr. Phelan, I am correct when I say 12:30, but whether or not you wish to observe that, of course, is up to you. I am not your secretary, by the way."

Phelan: "Yes, I know that, but Mr. Thompson said you would have those materials."

Secretary: "If he said that, he must have forgotten to give them to me. When he does, I assure you that you will get them immediately."

1. Note all the communications breakdowns that occurred and in each consider what misconceptions each party received.

2. How much of this could have been avoided if Joe Phelan had been less apprehensive?

problem 2 • DISAPPEARING FURNITURE

Carlin Mailaway specializes in reproductions of New England antiques and sells them by means of a nationally distributed catalog. The company, located in Great Barrington, Massachusetts, has won a dominant position in the market it serves.

Recently, Carlin instituted a more formal inventory system. The results were appalling to the General Manager, James Coffin. According to the second quarterly inventory, at least $2,000 worth of merchandise had disappeared "mysteriously" during the preceding three months. Almost simultaneously the warehouse supervisor found several pieces of merchandise wrapped as trash in a refuse barrel—as though they had been placed there by someone who intended to retrieve them later.

As soon as the figures were confirmed by a sample rechecking, Coffin dictated a letter to the Warehouse Supervisor, and sent copies out to every one of the 28 employees working in the warehouse. The letter read as follows:

Our auditing procedures have just disclosed a shocking loss of goods in our warehouse. In the future, no unauthorized personnel are to be allowed into the warehouse section of our building and all employees working in the area will be expected to refrain from carrying packages in or out of the department and permit close scrutiny of their persons as they leave work.

In no sense should any of our loyal, faithful employees interpret this as a slur against their characters. We know that they would want these stern provisions to be introduced to eliminate any possibility that they might be implicated.

We will appreciate your cooperation and thank you for your help in the past.

1. As a long-service employee in this department, how would you "interpret" this letter? Would others interpret it differently, do you think? Which ones and why?

2. What would you think the General Manager's motives were in writing this letter?

3. What alternative procedures might have been considered? What would their shortcomings and advantages be?

4. How might the Manager's letter have been better conceived and written?

problem 3 • FAIR EMPLOYMENT POLICY

For many years the Brace Machine Works had employed blacks only in menial jobs. After deliberation, and in part as a result of the passage of new state legislation, top management decided to adopt an unambiguous policy of offering equal employment opportunities for members of all nationality, racial, and religious groups.

The president of the company called in the personnel director for his counsel on how to announce this new policy in a way that would not only assure blacks of equal employment opportunities but would also guarantee that they would not be discriminated against in opportunities for promotion to better-paying, more skilled positions.

1. If you were the personnel director, what advice would you give the president?

2. In helping him frame his approach, what questions would you ask, what information would you need, and what knowledge about the company would be useful to you?

11 INTERVIEWING: THE FINE ART OF LISTENING

"My boss doesn't give a hoot about me. As far as he is concerned I am another piece of machinery."

"I'll say this about my boss: No matter what your problem is, he'll hear you through."

Effective communication requires effort both by the sender of the message and the receiver. The last chapter was devoted largely to the sending of messages. In this chapter we shall be concerned with an important aspect of receiving them—with listening.

Listening is one of the most important of all management tools. Yet even though people learn to listen before they learn to talk, relatively few listen well—few have learned the art of *interviewing*.

What do we mean by "interviewing"? Most people think of interviewing in the sense of the formal interviews connected with getting a job. By interviewing we intend much more than this: we mean deliberate, active listening whose purpose is to draw the other person out, to discover what he really wants to say, and to give him a chance to express himself fully.

HISTORICAL BACKGROUND

Management first became aware of the value of interviewing in industrial relations during the 1930's as a consequence of studies conducted at the Hawthorne plant of the Western Electric Company. These studies were primarily concerned with the determinants of morale and productivity. However, in their attempts to uncover basic feelings regarding these factors, the researcher found that direct questions designed to find out how the subjects felt about specific aspects of their jobs resulted in superficial, "lifeless" answers. Even worse—or so it seemed at the time—instead of giving "straightforward" responses, some of the people interviewed tended to talk about what interested them most at the moment.

Following this clue, the interviewers tried a radically new experiment: They sat back and decided to let the interviewees direct the interviews. Now they discovered that people began to express their *feelings* as well as give factual answers. Employees launched into long tirades (to which the interviewers patiently listened) revealing attitudes that might otherwise have been kept carefully guarded. In fact, some employees expressed attitudes that they had not been consciously aware of themselves. As a consequence, the interviewers discovered surprising relationships about which they would never have learned by asking direct questions.

More important: The employees benefited greatly as well. Just by talking freely in the presence of a sympathetic listener, they got their problems off their chests and felt better. They experienced what psychologists call *catharsis* (from the Greek: to make pure). In addition, merely by talking things over, the employees began to gain insight into the nature of their own problems. Once they had relieved their feelings by speaking openly in a receptive environment, they were able to look at their problems more objectively. And their clearer understandings, supplemented by further discussion, often enabled them to work out solutions (at least to those problems that they were in a position to solve themselves).

Impressed by the value of the Hawthorne experience, Western Electric instituted a program of formal counseling. Specially chosen counselors were trained in the use of *nondirective* interviews. (By nondirective interviews we mean—as we shall explain later—a type of interview in which the interviewer encourages the interviewee to express his own thoughts with considerable freedom—as contrasted to directive interviewing, in which the interviewer asks direct questions and tries to keep the discussion within predetermined limits.)

These "free-floating" counselors were given no regular supervisory duties; they were completely separate from the normal management hierarchy. Their function was merely to listen to employees' problems without giving advice or taking action. Other companies rapidly followed Western Electric's example. Particularly during World War II counseling was very popular. Many employers assigned "free-floating" counselors throughout the company, especially to help women workers.

The counselors faced a tough ethical problem of what to do with the information they received. If they repeated to management what they had been told, the workers would no longer trust them. On the other hand, if they could use their information in a discreet manner, they might be able to eliminate the causes of trouble. Often the counselors compromised by giving management general reports without revealing details that might identify individuals.

In recent years the use of such counselors as a personnel tool has declined.

It was discovered that this technique has many drawbacks, including the following:

1. Although counseling might help an individual make a better adjustment to a poor environment (say to an inept supervisor), it didn't improve the environment itself. Employees often began to feel that they were wasting their time talking to a counselor who could do nothing for them, and ended up almost as frustrated as before.

2. Counseling is directed almost entirely toward changing *individual* attitudes and behavior, in spite of other evidence from the Hawthorne study itself that group attitudes are often more important than individual attitudes.

3. The counseling system gave subordinates a chance to bypass and tattle on their supervisors. Naturally, the supervisors objected.

4. In some cases employees began to compare the "good" counselor with the "bad" supervisor. Supervisors felt they were entitled to the undivided loyalty of subordinates.

5. The counselors discovered that they were spending most of their time with a few disturbed individuals who really needed deep psychotherapy rather than counseling.

The basic trouble with "free-floating" counseling was its separation from line management. Line management emphasized downward communication. Counseling provided upward communication. But the two forms of communication went along different channels.

Management began to learn that effective communications must go both ways. Upward communication and downward communication, listening and order-giving, are both more effective if done by the *same* person. Furthermore, if they are merged into the same process, something new and better emerges. Thus, there has come the realization that counseling or interviewing or listening (which are really all the same thing) is not a special technique for use by personnel experts only, but a vital aspect of good management generally.

LISTENING AS A MANAGEMENT TOOL

To list the circumstances where interviewing is useful would be almost like listing the functions of management itself. Indeed, all through our discussion of general supervision and methods of correcting mistakes we constantly emphasize the importance of listening. The following example indicates what might happen when this approach works at its best.

Suppose you are a division manager and you want to introduce a new system of quality control. Although you have not as yet consulted with the production supervisor, you have heard through the grapevine that he has strong objections to the new system. Yet his cooperation is essential if the system is to succeed.

You feel pretty certain that your plan is good and that the production supervisor's objections are not well grounded. You are the boss, of course, and you could give him a direct order to put the plan into effect. (Question: How would the supervisor react to this order? How loyally would he carry it out?)

Instead, you decide to listen to his point of view. In spite of the grapevine you can't really be sure you know what his objections are until he has spoken to you personally. If you are at all sincere, you must admit to yourself that his objections may have some merit. (Question: What would happen if you had already made up your mind and just went through the formalities of listening?)

So you explain the proposed change to him, being careful to emphasize that you still have an open mind, and ask him to comment. You listen attentively and encourage him to express himself fully. As he speaks, he relaxes and explains his point of view with more balance and restraint than he would if he felt he were on the defensive. Instead of trying to answer his arguments, you encourage him to tell you everything he thinks and feels about the change. When he finishes, you briefly summarize what he has said to make sure you understand—and also to indicate *to him* that you have understood.

After speaking his piece, the production supervisor feels free to listen to your point of view—which may have changed since you heard his objections. You fill in some of the areas where you feel he was mistaken, indicate the points on which you have changed your own thinking, and explore with him any adjustments that seem necessary. Even if he is still not fully convinced of the wisdom of your plan, he is more willing to try it out and probably feels pleased that you consulted him and listened to his objections.

The above example suggests the flexibility of the interview technique (though we must emphasize that the results are frequently not as good as we have pictured). It is obviously well suited to formal interviews, such as those used for hiring, exit, and requests for transfer. But it is also appropriate in less formal situations, such as the following:

Low morale: finding out the cause of employee dissatisfaction, turnover, or absenteeism.

Discipline: discovering why employees are performing unsatisfactorily and helping them to evolve means of correcting themselves.

Order-giving: getting reaction to and acceptance of orders, to see that the person who receives the order really understands it.

Resistance to change: gaining acceptance of new techniques, tools, procedures.

Merit rating and evaluation: helping an employee correct his weaknesses.

Grievance-handling: finding out the real causes of a union grievance and getting the union officers to agree to a constructive solution.

Settling disputes: finding out the causes of the disputes between employees and getting them to agree to settlement.

The interview approach is not something to be applied only when dealing with specific problems. It is a general attitude which the manager can apply day in and day out in his dealings with fellow supervisors, subordinates, and his boss. In a nutshell, it is a matter of always being ready to listen to the other fellow's point of view and trying to take it into account before taking action oneself. If this attitude is absent, then communications may become blocked, as they did in one company:

The most frequent complaint was that although orders and instructions about work traveled easily enough, it was difficult to take up ordinary feelings, especially if they were critical about the job or about life in the factory. The main stumbling block in getting such feelings resolved was the reticence about communicating them upwards. The reticence was said to be due to the fact that if a person tried to express to his superior his feelings about the job, or about the superior himself, it was all too likely that the superior would argue with him and try to show him that his feelings were unreasonable and that they did not tally with the facts. Having the existence of one's feelings denied in this way only made things worse. The person was not only left with the original feeling but in addition had a resentment against his superior for not understanding him and not helping him get at what was disturbing him. [1]

Establishing Confidence

The manager must take the initiative in encouraging subordinates to come to him with their problems. He must show that he is willing to hear them out. Otherwise minor irritations may grow to tremendous proportions, even before the manager has become aware of the danger.

If the initial interview is a pleasant experience for the subordinate, he will come back more freely and more regularly when new problems arise. If it has been an unpleasant experience and if he feels he has been "put on the spot," he will be reluctant to reveal what is on his mind in the future.

The manager should be aware that some of the men who report to him will be easier to get to know than others. Some will talk to him quite freely and easily. Others will hold back because of fear or natural timidity. The manager must be careful not to spend all his time with those to whom it is easy to talk.

To avoid the charge of favoritism, and to insure that he is able to deal with the problems of all his employees, the manager must go out of his way to make contact with employees who are reluctant to come to him. The manager must recognize that there is an invisible barrier which separates him from his subordinates. For some, this status difference is of little importance, but for many it makes effective upward communication much harder.

Off-the-Job Problems

Managers sometimes use interviewing to help employees solve personal off-the-job problems. Normally stable individuals may have unexpected trouble and seek to use their supervisor as a wailing wall. However, the manager should be careful not to give advice or get himself saddled with the responsibility for running his subordinates' personal lives.

The manager should be particularly cautious when sensitive areas are reached in the course of an interview. In situations like this, what most people want is a sympathetic, understanding listener rather than an adviser. They may ask for advice, but actually they want only a chance to talk. Even when advice-giving is successful, there is the danger that the employee may become over-dependent on his manager and run to him whenever he has a minor problem.

The manager should be still more careful when deepseated personality problems are involved. In such a case it is wise to refer the person to a professionally trained specialist rather than to play amateur psychologist. The average manager is not equipped to do counseling, nor is this part of his job. The patient-psychiatrist or client-counselor relationship is just not consistent with that of subordinate and boss. And the subordinate may resent being conned by the nondirective technique into blurting out confidences which he later regrets having revealed.

[1] Elliot Jaques, *The Changing Culture of a Factory* (London: Tavistock, 1951), p. 133.

THE USE OF THE NONDIRECTIVE APPROACH

In understanding how the nondirective approach should be used, it is helpful to think of the interview as running through three stages: feelings, facts, solutions.

1. *Feelings.* The interviewee is encouraged to release his feelings; the interviewer is concerned with helping the interviewee express himself. This stage is the most purely nondirective, for the interviewer still has little idea where the discussion will go.

2. *Facts.* Having blown off steam, the interviewee is now ready to look at the facts rationally. In this stage the interviewer can be more directive and may even use "probes" (to be discussed later) to bring out information that the interviewee has not already volunteered. In fact, the interviewer may contribute additional information on his own.

3. *Solutions.* Once the facts have been assembled, the interviewee is in a position to weigh alternate solutions and pick the best one. As we have mentioned frequently, it is preferable to help the interviewee work out his own solution; however, the supervisor may have to be rather strongly directive to make sure that the solution is consistent with the needs of the organization.

These, then, are the three major stages of the interview, although it may switch back and forth from one stage to another as different problems are considered. Still on a given problem the interviewer should stick to the order indicated: feelings, facts, solutions. Certainly he should avoid the common human tendency to jump to a solution before getting all the facts.

Equally important, he should not waste his time trying to isolate the facts before the interviewee has had a chance to express his feelings, to blow off steam. Why? Because feelings color facts, and as long as a man is emotionally excited he is unlikely to approach problems rationally. Furthermore—and the point is subtle—the feelings of the people concerned in the situation are themselves facts that must be considered. For instance, the office manager has been having trouble getting Mary to do a full day's work. The most important fact in this solution may be the manager's intense dislike of Mary as a person. Until the manager's feeling is recognized as a complicating element, "facts" he presents will be distorted by his antagonism toward Mary.

Does this mean that the interviewer should never express himself—that he should never try to correct the other person if he is wrong nor try to change his opinion? Of course not. It may be enough for the psychiatrist or the professional counselor merely to listen. The manager must also take action. But in most cases, before he takes action he should wait until he has heard the interviewee's whole story.

The nondirective approach is not a magic solution to all human-relations problems, of course. There are times when a supervisor may have to be quite firm and directive in the solution stage of the interview to make sure that the solution is consistent with the needs of the organization. For instance, the supervisor may listen patiently to the subordinate's objections to a new system; the subordinate may persist in his resistance; and the supervisor may still have to overrule him, explaining why, and insist that the system be used. However, the subordinate will have had the satisfaction of being consulted, of knowing that he had his day in court to present his side of the story.

INTERVIEWING TECHNIQUES

Skillful interviewing is an art, and like all arts it requires training and experience. It can be learned better by practice than by reading a book, especially when the practice is supervised by an experienced instructor. Fortunately, one can gain unsupervised practice every day of the year.

Each interviewer must develop a system that is comfortable for him and that fits his personality, but he should avoid using the same technique with all people and for all purposes. An interview held for disciplinary reasons will naturally be different from an interview held for the purpose of order-giving.

Regardless of the form of the interview, here are a few hints that may prove useful.

Encouraging the Interviewee to Talk

Your primary objective is to get the interviewee to talk freely, *not to talk yourself.* The best way to find out what the other person wants to say is to listen, and the best interview is usually the one in which the interviewer talks least.

But listening is not easy, for our natural impulse is to talk. This is particularly true when we feel threatened by what is being said to us—for instance, when we are being criticized. Under these circumstances our normal impulse is to defend ourselves rather than to listen.

Listening is more than just not talking, however. It requires an active effort to convey that you understand and are interested in what the other person is saying—almost that you are helping him say it. A friendly facial expression and an attentive but relaxed attitude are important. A good interviewer also makes use of phrases such as "Uh-huh," "I understand," "That explains it," or "Could you tell me more?"

Even silence can be used to keep a man talking. When he pauses in his discourse, he is either being polite and giving you a chance to talk, or else he wants you to comment, to evaluate what he is saying. Merely by not taking up his challenge, by waiting through his pause, you indicate that you have nothing to say at the moment, that you want him to continue talking.

Even if you plan to use the nondirective approach, it is vital to set the stage properly, to indicate to the interviewee what you want the interview to cover. For example, if you wish to talk to a worker about sloppy work, you might start with, "Bill, you seem to be having a little trouble with the blue-edge gadgets."

Reflective Summary

One of the most effective devices to encourage the other person to talk is the *reflective summary*, in which you try to sum up the feelings a man has expressed, disregarding the factual details and incidentals. For example: "The reason I want to quit is that so-and-so foreman keeps pestering me. He won't give me a chance!" Then he stops, wondering whether he has got himself into trouble by saying too much. Your response, "He won't give you a chance?" encourages him to tell the rest of his story, but it does not commit you in any sense. Such a summary serves a number of purposes:

1. It shows the worker that you are giving his ideas careful consideration and that you understand him—in other words, that you are being fair.

2. It gives him a chance to restate and elaborate his attitudes if he feels that you haven't quite grasped his point.

3. It serves to highlight what he has really been saying. Often people are surprised to learn what their words have meant to someone else, and are rewarded with deeper insight into their own attitudes.

The reflective summary is particularly effective if you reflect not only what the man has actually said, but can somehow put into words what he has tried, unsuccessfully, to express. Be careful, however, not to hear more in his words than he intends to put into them. For if he finds you reading things into his words that he did not mean to be there, he will be doubly careful to watch what he says.

Your summary should indicate neither approval nor disapproval of what the interviewee is saying. It should simply indicate that you are listening attentively. For instance, he says, "It's got to the point where I may lose my temper and take a poke at the foreman." If you were to say, "Well, that's quite understandable," you would almost be inviting him to carry out his threat! A more satisfactory response would be "You are sore at him because. . . ."

Probes

The "free-floating" counselor is interested primarily in getting at the interviewee's underlying feelings. And as a manager you too are interested in the feelings of your subordinates. But if you know that you must act on the basis of what you learn in the interview, you will also want to get all the facts, the whole story.[2] This means that after the feeling stage has passed, you should to some extent direct the interview. Tactfully and calmly, you should steer the conversation, but without forcing the interviewee into an area he does not want to enter, and with no hint that you have already made up your mind.

One way to direct the interview is to build on what the interviewee has already said. By repeating certain words selected from what he has said, you can

[2] In other words, your interviewing is "organization centered," not "client centered."

indicate that you would like him to talk more about this particular area. This device is called a "probe." For example, in explaining how a fight started between himself and another employee, the man being interviewed says, "Joe was always riding me. When he picked up my lunch bucket, that was the last straw." Now if the supervisor wants to find out more about what Joe has done to arouse this man, he has a good chance to insert a probe: "You say Joe was always riding you?" Then he stops and waits for the man to go on. Notice that the interviewer does not say: "What did Joe do to make you so sore?" Rather, he simply repeats the employee's own words. Chances are this approach will encourage the man to tell more about the "riding" than he would if he had been asked a direct question.

Less subtle probes are: "Could you tell me more about . . .?" or "I am interested in what you said about. . . ."

Weighing Alternatives

Sometimes it is enough if the interview helps you find out how the employee feels about the situation and what the essential facts are as *he* sees them. In other instances, however, you may wish to help him devise a solution. How can you do this without seeming to impose your own ideas on him? The following approach may be useful both in individual interviews and in group meetings:

Let us assume one of your managers wishes to discipline severely one of his employees who has been a troublemaker. The manager's first suggestion, for example, may be that he should go right out to the shop and fire the troublemaker. If you keep asking for additional suggestions, he may suggest lesser penalties. Finally, he may even come around to suggesting certain changes in his own behavior.

Now, after the manager has offered all these suggestions, you would attempt to get him to examine each one:

What would its probable effect be?
How would the men react?
How would it help him solve his problem?

By helping the interviewee think through his problem, you may succeed in having him come to a conclusion that is *his*, not yours. And if it is his, he will be much more likely to act on it with enthusiasm.

THINGS TO AVOID

Too Much Warm-up

Many people feel that before getting down to the subject of an interview, particularly if it is an unpleasant one, they should try to place the interviewee at ease by discussing some irrelevant topic—baseball, fishing, traffic jams, or what have you. Thus, a foreman calling a man in to lay him off may chat about the Dodgers for a few minutes before settling down to the nasty task.

This approach may relieve the foreman's anxiety, but it intensifies that of the worker, particularly if he has some idea of why he has been called in. While he is on the "hot seat," he may be thinking, "Why doesn't this character get down to business? Why does he have to play cat-and-mouse? What's this building up to?"

Such "warming-up" is useful at times; however, the interviewer should be careful to use it only when it actually reduces anxiety. Often when the manager initiates the interview, "beating around the bush" merely increases the suspense. Similarly, if the employee comes to the manager with a problem, he probably wants to get down to business without delay.

Premature Judgment

The interviewer should avoid giving any indication that what the subordinate says either pleases or displeases him. In other words, he must refrain from passing judgment before all the facts are in. This restraint is extremely important because subordinates look for verbal or facial cues that will tip them off to what the superior wants or does not want to hear. (Of course, unconsciously we are always forming impressions, even on the most meager facts. However, the supervisor should be aware of his predispositions and try to keep them from warping his judgment or his communication.)

Criticizing or moralizing puts the interviewee on the defensive. Even if he does not argue back, he will begin to edit what he says in order to win the interviewer's approval. He will concentrate on proving that he is right rather than on giving an honest explanation. Certainly putting a man on the defensive makes it harder to find out what he really thinks.

Even praise or sympathy should be avoided until the end of the interview, for it makes the interviewee think his present approach is correct and encourages him to avoid the hard work of thinking the problem through.

Direct Questions

One of the most frequent errors made by inexperienced interviewers is transforming the interview into a game of "twenty questions." A man has fallen into the habit of coming to work late and his supervisor is anxious to straighten him out before discipline becomes necessary. Having had some training in human relations, the manager suspects that a home problem is involved. His end of the conversation may run something like this:

"Do you have trouble starting your car?"
"Is there any trouble at home?"
"Does your alarm clock go off on time?"
"Did you have a drink too many last night?"

To each question Bill replies, "No, it isn't that." And to himself he says, "That's none of his business." And then another question is shot at him.

Here the manager, not Bill, is directing the interview. Note that every one of these questions is phrased in such a manner as to put Bill immediately on the defensive and make him over-cautious in what he says. Some of the questions, such as, "Did you have a drink too many last night?" he may feel are insulting.

The interviewer rarely knows the right questions to ask; if he did, he would probably know the answers as well. The interviewee's problem is usually more complex than it seems at first glance, and direct questions tend to narrow it down too quickly.

To complicate matters, most subordinates try to say what they think will please their supervisor. Direct questions often imply the kind of answer the supervisor wants, or at least give the subordinate an "out." For instance, the question "Did you have trouble starting your car?" provides a ready excuse for a tardy worker.

If the supervisor wants to find out what the subordinate really has on his mind, he should leave the situation as free as possible to permit the subordinate to emphasize the things that are important to *him*.

If possible, the interviewer should avoid questions that can be answered with a simple yes or no. "Well, do you like your job?" "Do you think the tools are in bad shape?" Questions of this sort shut off discussion because they can be answered by a relatively meaningless "Oh, I guess so," "I suppose you might say that."

Arguing

Little is gained from argument, at least in the early stage of the interview. Yet everyone has a strong human tendency to correct the other person when he says something that is obviously wrong. Moreover, if the interviewer himself is attacked personally, he must exercise tremendous restraint not to answer back.

For example, an employee says he is having trouble doing the work because the stock has been changed. "The company must be buying cheaper material these days." Now if you know that there has been no change whatsoever in the materials, you will be strongly tempted to "set the employee straight" on this point, although his complaint may be a symptom of something much more basic. If you give way to this temptation, you may simply transform the interview into a fruitless argument. If you just continue to listen, however, the employee may move on to more basic problems and difficulties that he finds more troublesome to discuss.

Excessive Psychologizing

Sometimes managers abuse the nondirective technique by shifting the discussion from the technical aspects of the question at hand to the subordinate's motives in dealing with it.[3] Such abuse occurs most commonly when the manager has a psychology or social work background. For example, a subordinate may have a sound practical objection to something his boss may want to do. Instead of listening to the objections themselves, the excessively psychologically-oriented boss may look upon the subordinate's attitude as an example of hostility and may seek its emotional basis. Obviously such an approach often adds to the hostility it is designed to alleviate.

[3] For a good discussion, see Peter Blau and W. Richard Scott, *Formal Organization* (San Francisco: Chandler, 1962), pp. 188–189.

Advice-Giving

When you finally get the complete picture as the employee sees it, you may be able to provide advice or information that has not previously been available. But again it is often better to help him work through his own problems. In any event, you should hold off giving advice until *after* the interviewee has told his entire story—until you have all the facts.

Masterminding

Many people go through the motions of the nondirective interview but violate its spirit. They hope by asking shrewd questions to manipulate the interviewee into believing that he is thinking through his problem by himself, though the way questions are worded inevitably forces the interviewee to arrive at the interviewer's own predetermined conclusion.

Masterminding is used with various degrees of sophistication. One of the less subtle forms makes constant use of the leading question, the "don't you feel?" approach: "Don't you feel it would be better for the company and your own future if you came to work on time?"

Questions like this usually permit only one answer. They are thinly veiled forms of advice, judgment, or just plain bawling out. They are even more directive than an overt, straightforward statement. The interviewee is often free to reject outright advice, and even if it is clear that he must accept it (in other words, when the advice is really an order) he may be unhappy about it, but willing to be a good soldier. Masterminding, however, not only requires the interviewee to do what the interviewer wants, but also to say that he likes it. The interviewee is treated like a child and the alleged interview degenerates into a form of brainwashing.

There are subtler forms of brainwashing in which the interviewee may actually feel convinced of something at the time of the interview, only to realize that he has been duped after he has had a chance to think things over. Conversion at a forced rate seldom lasts. As the poet Robert Burns once said:

> He who is convinced against his will,
> Is of the same opinion still.

People change their attitudes slowly, and only when they are ready to do so.

CONCLUSION

Interviewing is a form of communications, and like other forms of communications it is most effective when it is two-way. A good interview is more than a one-way process in which the interviewee tells his story to the interviewer; the interviewer must in turn be constantly communicating his interest in the interviewee as a person and in what he has to say.

It is not enough for the manager to understand his employees; he must also give them the feeling that he is sincerely trying to help them. The manager must not only listen, but must also communicate the feeling to his employees that they are being listened to.

The basic purpose of nondirective interviewing is to enable the interviewer to find out how the individual sees the problem or situation at issue, and then to help him think and, above all, *feel* his way through to a solution. The goal of this whole philosophy is for the supervisor to be perceived as a source of help—as a man who can assist the subordinate to develop and do a better job.

It has been argued that the interview approach would be fine if a manager had nothing else to do all day except serve as a wailing wall, but that in practice he just doesn't have time to do much listening. Realistically, pressure and other demands may make him abrupt and unsympathetic in his dealings with subordinates. And yet the manager who "makes time" to listen may find not only that his human relations are better, but that in the long run he will save time by having fewer personnel crises to deal with.

The nondirective interview is not a cure-all for every situation. Effective interviewing requires considerable skill, and even a good interviewer discovers that many people find it difficult to discuss their problems. Moreover, many problems involve several people and require group discussion. Finally, certain problems cannot be decided at the manager-subordinate level. Still, in spite of these reservations the interviewing technique is a general-purpose tool for every manager.

problem 1 • INTERVIEWING DRILL

In each of the following cases, which of the responses suggested would be more likely to lead to a constructive solution of the problem? Remember that these represent the opening of the interview.

1. You have come home from a hard day and your wife greets you with:
   "What a day I've had. The baby was crying all morning. The washing machine broke down and I had to do the things by hand. Then I went downtown to buy a hat and had to wait twenty minutes for a bus. I couldn't find a thing I liked and everybody was so pushy and the store was so crowded. When I got back the baby-sitter had let the stew burn—and I'd worked on it so hard. I'm so mad I could cry. And I've got to go downtown tomorrow again to look for a hat."

   a. "You must have had an awfully hard day."
   b. "Your old hat looks pretty good to me."
   c. "I'm tired too. You should hear what happened to me. First. . . ."
   d. "Don't say another word. Put on your glad rags and I'll take you out for dinner and don't mention it."
   e. "You know, maybe we ought to get another baby-sitter."

2. A worker has been late three times in the last two weeks. You ask him why and he replies:
   "I just can't seem to get up in the morning. Frankly, I've lost my enthusiasm for the job. It doesn't interest me any more. So when I do get up I've got to rush like mad to get here."

   a. "Don't you think you are letting the company down?"
   b. "Do you have an alarm clock?"
   c. "You've got to lick this problem or I've got to lay you off and give you some time to think it over."
   d. "The job doesn't interest you any more?"
   e. "Are you having any trouble at home?"
   f. "Have you thought of going to bed earlier?"

3. A worker who has been making little progress tells his boss:

"I just can't seem to get the hang of things. I try to find out what I'm supposed to do, but no one tells me. The other guys don't pay any attention to me and I can't figure it out by watching. Maybe I ought to quit."

a. "Why don't you give the job a chance? Most people take a while to learn it."
b. "Why don't you try harder? You can't get ahead without hard work."
c. "If I were you I would ask the other fellows to help you."
d. "Do you have any ideas why the other fellows don't help you?"
e. "I'll assign one of them to instruct you."
f. "You feel that the other fellows don't pay any attention to you?"
g. "Let me show you how to do it."

4. A toolmaker tells his foreman:

"I've had ten years' experience and no one ever told me I did a bum job. Sure I make a few mistakes, but why do I get all the blame?"

a. "All I want you to do is be a little more careful in your work."
b. "You feel the standards are too high?"
c. "I'm not saying it is your fault. I am just asking you to please do the piece over."
d. "You feel you are unfairly blamed?"

problem 2 • THE EXTRA HALF PLUM

Scene I

Mary, a salad girl, is seated at a table backstage by herself, thumbing through a magazine. She is off duty. Miss Jones walks on stage from the right and stops at Mary's table.

Miss Jones: Mary, may I speak to you for a moment?

Mary: All right.

Miss Jones. It's about your work. I feel that you're a hard worker but there are times when you seem to grow a bit careless. I've noticed lately that sometimes your salads are a trifle sloppy in appearance, and you don't always check your recipes carefully enough. For example, the fruit salad calls for two halves of plums. I saw you putting three on some of the salads today. If you just check up on things like this, you'll do the job I think you're capable of.

(Mary does not answer. She shuts the magazine, gets up, and walks away. Miss Jones looks startled, then walks toward the office of Mr. Black, the manager, downstage left, and knocks on the door.)

Scene II

Black: Come in. (Miss Jones walks in and sits down.) Hello. What is it, Miss Jones?

Jones: I'm worried about Mary Stevens. I thought maybe you'd want to talk to her.

Black: What seems to be the trouble?

Jones: Well, she's a hard worker, but sometimes she just doesn't seem to have her mind on her work. Now that wouldn't be so bad if she'd let us correct her, but the girl won't take criticism. I just asked her to be a little neater in putting up her salads and I checked her on putting an extra half plum on the fruit salad. I put it just as tactfully as I know how, but she wouldn't even answer me. She just sat still until I was finished and then walked right out on me. It was a deliberate insult.

Black: Yes, that's bad. . . . Do you think she is quitting?

Jones: Well, I don't know. But I don't see how I can use her when she behaves that way.

Black: Do you want to get rid of her?

Jones: Well, you know how short we are at that station. I can't really spare her and she can do a very good job when she wants to. Maybe it's some trouble at home. I don't know. But I thought you might be able to help her.

Black: I'd be glad to talk to her for you. She'll be coming in for her paycheck tomorrow. I'll see her then.

Jones: Thanks. That'll be a big help to me.

(Black's office. Black at desk; Mary comes in.)

Black: I was hoping you'd come in to see me. Won't you sit down, Mary?

Mary: (hesitates, then sits down) Well, I suppose you know all about it.

Black: Miss Jones told me something about it, but I want to get your side of the story. After all, we want to be fair with you. I've always done my best to see the employee's point of view. We want you to feel satisfied with your work here, and if there is some problem I can help out on, I want you to feel free to talk things over with me.

Mary: Well, I don't suppose I should have walked out, but I just couldn't take it.

Black: You mean, you can't take criticism?

Mary: Well, not exactly. But this is such a nerve-wracking job. And Miss Jones is always picking on you. She doesn't seem to appreciate the work you do.

Black: Mary, don't you think you're being a little unfair to Miss Jones? Now, I happen to know that she thinks very well of you. She wants to help you.

Mary: She doesn't act that way. I mean—well I know she has to see that the work gets done right, but it seems she's always looking over your shoulder to catch you or something. And such little things, too, she—

Black: Mary, you have to remember that the little things add up together to make something pretty big. If we neglected the little things, we wouldn't be in business very long. Now that extra half plum—it may seem like nothing at all to you, but we have to work out the prices and portions to make a small profit on that salad. If we put in an extra half plum, we're really giving it away. If we sell 100 of those salads a day, that mounts up. We're doing all the work for nothing. Now, I'm not criticizing you, but I just want you to understand the importance of these things. Do you see what I mean?

Mary: Well, if I did put on an extra half plum, it was only on 2 or 3, not 100. I don't remember every one, but I know it was only 2 or 3.

Black: Sure, that's what I'm getting at. You were just a little careless. That's all. Miss Jones was trying to correct you. Now, you don't blame her for trying to see that the work is done right do you?

Mary: Sure, she wants it done right, but she doesn't realize what we're up against. It's one thing to know just how to make a salad. It's another thing to have to make hundreds of them in a rush, like I have to. If Miss Jones had ever worked behind the counter like the rest of us, she'd know what it's like.

Black: But Miss Jones did work behind the counter when she was getting her training.

Mary: That's different. You weren't so rushed then like we are now.

Black: Yes, that's true. But I'm not trying to defend Miss Jones to you. I'm just trying to help you to get this thing straightened out. Now, you didn't like the way Miss Jones criticized you. But let's look at both sides of it. Do you think you were fair to her?

Mary: I know what you think. You think I wasn't polite to her. All right, I wasn't. I lost my temper. If I had said anything, I would have told her what I thought of her. So I thought it would be better not to say anything. Well, what of it? It's done, and I'm through now. Give me my paycheck and let me out of here.

Black: Your check is here for you, Mary, but let's not be hasty about this. Remember your aunt has worked here a long time. She hoped you'd fit in too. If you just walk out this way, it'll be quite a blow to her.

Mary: I don't care about her or Miss Jones or you either. I've got my own life to live. I'm tired of having people always pick on me and tell me what to do. I know what I want to do now. I want to get out of here. Give me my check!

Black: Well, if that's the way you feel about it—(hands her the check). [4]

1. Comment on how Mr. Black handled his conversation with Mary.

2. How should he have handled it?

3. What mistakes did he make?

[4] We wish to express our thanks to Professor William F. Whyte for permission to use this case, which was prepared by him.

INTRODUCING CHANGE   **12**

We live in a world of change. We Americans in particular have learned to expect change as part of our everyday life. We pride ourselves on being modern and up-to-date in our habits and behavior. Still we may be more traditional than we think. To be sure, we accept and even welcome changes in terms of material things, such as household gadgets or cars. But we tend to resist changes in our interpersonal and job relations, because these changes threaten the security of the orderly and familiar ways we have known in the past, and often our status as well.

One of the most important measures of an organization's strength is its ability to change. In fact, it *must* anticipate environmental changes by altering its own policies and structure in time to meet these new conditions as they arise. In this chapter we shall discuss (1) why there is resistance to change and (2) what can be done to deal with it.

TYPES OF RESISTANCE TO CHANGE

Of all the types of resistance to change, perhaps the one most commonly recognized is the resistance of many employees to technological change—to automation, for example. Such resistance is readily understandable. In some instances, technological change means that employees must agree to work on faster machines with increased workloads. In others, it requires the acquisition of new skills and even a new approach to work; for example, the worker must learn to watch and adjust equipment rather than to operate it manually. In still others, as in the case of locomotive firemen and flight engineers, it may mean the loss of work altogether.

But there are many other forms of change which are also resisted: changes in organizational structure, methods of compensation, and so forth. Take the case of a clothing store, once famous for its high-quality merchandise, which is located in an area from which high-income customers have moved. A new owner resolves to introduce a lower-priced line and to induce his salesmen to engage in high-pressure salesmanship. The salesmen are likely to react violently to changing well-established patterns.

Resistance to change is sometimes as deep-rooted at the managerial level as it is at lower levels. In many companies one hears constant complaints about "old fogies" who are hampering progress. As we explore elsewhere, there are problems involved in re-educating managers to improve their supervisory practices, to give higher priority to accident prevention, and so forth. Indeed, managers tend to resist the introduction of almost any new personnel practice. They may regard a new system of job evaluation as a threat to existing status relationships, or the introduction of tests in hiring as a threat to their traditional prerogative to hire whomever they wish. Similarly, as we will discuss, managers may object to the new patterns of relations which may be imposed by the introduction of the computer.

Resistance to change may show itself in unexpected ways, for instance in aggression, regression, and in all the negative reactions discussed in Chapter 6. It may appear as absenteeism, resignations, requests for transfer, and as "the expression of a lot of pseudo-logical reasons why the change will not work."[1] One clear sign of resistance is a series of apparently "emotional" or "irrational" objections to minor changes; these often indicate that more deep-seated problems are involved.

It should be emphasized that not all change is resisted. Some forms of change are welcomed (such as new typewriters). Aerospace companies, for example, engage in constant technological and organizational change with relatively little resistance. It is not change itself which causes the resistance, but the meaning of the change for the people involved. Thus, one should expect greater resistance to change in a company which is contracting or stationary in size than one would in a company which is expanding, even though the expanding company has a larger number of changes—the reason being that in the expanding company the changes are less likely to threaten employees' social or economic status.

WHAT CAUSES RESISTANCE TO CHANGE?

Economic Factors

The most obvious reason is economic. Workers resist automation when they fear they will lose their jobs; they are unimpressed by arguments that in the

[1] Paul Lawrence, "How to Deal With Resistance to Change," *Harvard Business Review*, Vol. 32, No. 3 (May 1954), p. 49.

"long run" there will be more jobs in other parts of the country. What concerns them most is the economic welfare of themselves and their families.[2]

Similarly, a craftsman may fear that new developments will reduce the economic value of his skill. In the same way, managers themselves oppose a change that helps the company as a whole but hurts their individual promotional opportunities.

Sometimes the economic factors underlying resistance to change are obscure and not immediately apparent. In one plant the employees began to damage parts they were sending to a new plant overseas; formerly the parts had been shipped to a domestic plant. Was this blind resistance to change? Not at all. Investigation revealed that the employees were afraid the company was shifting more and more of its operations to the overseas plant and feared that eventually they would lose their jobs.

We must, however, guard against the common misconception that workers generally—and particularly their unions—blindly resist all forms of technological progress. The Hat Workers and Clothing Workers unions, for instance, have developed special programs designed to encourage management to introduce such changes. They recognize that only through rising productivity can their wages be raised. Similarly, the United Mine Workers cooperated with coal-mine owners in an extensive mechanization program which has resulted in substantially fewer jobs in the coal fields, but higher earnings for those who remained. Foreign visitors to this country express surprise at the extent to which American workers have learned that technological change redounds to their benefit. There is, however, a significant gap between the intellectual recognition of this relationship and the acceptance of change in a particular case.

Inconvenience

Equally understandable is the resistance to change that threatens to make life more difficult. A worker fights the assignment of extra duties; he has learned his old job so well that it requires no attention any more, while the new job requires surface attention. Similarly, executives dislike the inconvenience of being reassigned from one location to another. Even if the company pays their expenses, there is the bother of buying and selling houses, packing, and readjusting to new work and a new environment.

All of us develop a vested interest in our usual way of doing things. Our everyday habits provide us with a certain security in our life. Some of these are quite trivial: We drive to work by a fixed route every day, even though other routes are equally good; when our usual route is temporarily blocked, we are annoyed by the inconvenience of having to change our pattern.

Learning new ways requires the expenditure of energy, and human beings are generally lazy. Even for the simplest job there are "tricks to the trade" that take time to learn. When a man is thrown into a new situation his tricks no longer apply and he loses the security of the familiar.

[2] For similar reasons, workers may object to bigger workloads, even when there is no demand for greater physical effort. They reason that they may work either themselves or their friends out of a job or that management is getting "something for nothing."

Uncertainty

The new way is always strange, threatening, and laden with uncertainties—even if it is an improvement over the old. We have a chance for a new job at higher pay. Should we take it? Maybe not. How hard will it be? How long will it take to learn? Will we be able to meet the challenge? Who will our friends be? The opportunity may be very good indeed, yet there is a strong tendency to let well enough alone.

One reason for this fear is the lack of factual information. We know our present circumstances; we don't know what the new ones will be. Some people are gamblers by nature, but the average person hesitates to venture into uncharted waters. The uncertain is always threatening.

New equipment is introduced into the plant. What will it mean to our job, our status, our security? A new boss is assigned to the department. What will his policies be? How will they affect us? Often the rumor mill exaggerates the potential threat of a change. Until management clarifies the impact of the change, such rumors can panic a group of employees.

Uncertainty caused by lack of information may be corrected simply by providing answers to questions—assuming that management is aware of what questions are being asked. But there is another kind of uncertainty that cannot be dissipated by providing information: the anxiety that springs from the individual's fears about how *he himself* will react to the new situation. Every draftee is assailed with doubts the night before his induction. What will army life be for me? Every veteran is delighted to provide information, but one one can predict how *I* will react. For this sort of uncertainty there can be no quick remedy.

Symbols

Symbols raise special problems. Remember that a symbol is something which stands for something else. The flag symbolizes one's country; the Bastille, pre-revolutionary oppression in France; the supervisors' parking lot, their special status; the restaurant's white table cloth, its general excellence. A symbol cannot be eliminated without threatening in people's minds the things for which it stands. Note, for example, the widespread emotional reaction to the change in the Canadian flag, or the following case from industry:

The new manager of the Integrity Insurance Company had little difficulty with his "modernization" program until he decided it was a waste of money to print policies on high-quality parchment paper. His proposal to substitute a cheaper but still durable paper led to a storm of protest from the company's insurance agents: The new paper wouldn't look or wear well, it didn't look right, the customers would think it cheap. Investigation revealed that to the agents the parchment paper was a symbol of Integrity's reputation as a leader in the industry. They began to fear that these changes would mean that Integrity would be just like any other insurance company.

Small changes may symbolize big ones, particularly when employees are uncertain about how extensive a program of change will be. When a situation begins to shift, subordinates search for indications of what lies ahead. A symbol represents a whole framework of treasured relationships and values; subordinates unite to protect it against attack just as if everything it represented were actually in danger.

Threats to Interpersonal Relationships

As we mentioned in Chapter 4, anything that disrupts the customary social relationships and standards of the group will meet with strong resistance. In particular, employees oppose changes which threaten their status or their painfully acquired, socially valued skills.

For example, vests and coats in one clothing center are made by separate groups of tailors, though to an outsider their skills seem readily interchangeable. Over the years the demand for vests has fallen off while an acute shortage of skilled coatmakers has developed. Yet in spite of the combined urging of union and management, the vestmakers refuse to transfer to coatmaking. As a result the vestmakers lose over $30 a week. Why do they persist in this apparently illogical attitude?

The vestmakers are a small, tightly knit clique of friends who are proud of their skill. They have a long-established union local of their own. They fear that if they were transferred to coatmaking their clique would be broken up, they would become the *least*-skilled coatmakers rather than highly skilled vestmakers, and they would lose the protection of their local. Thus, the change is a threat to their prestige, their ability to meet their social needs, and their union protection.

Even when no change in physical location is involved, most changes tend to upset interpersonal relations. Take the situation in a small firm that had just hired a new purchasing agent.

Previously each department head had ordered his own supplies. Now the department head merely filled out a purchase order and the purchasing agent decided on the supplier and negotiated the price. Though this policy saved the department heads from being pestered by salesmen and saved the company money, the department heads were highly antagonistic. They missed the feeling of importance that came from dealing directly with salesmen; the purchasing agent was far less obsequious to them than the salesman had been, and he threatened their authority by suggesting at times that they might use cheaper, lower-quality material. This fact may help explain why they began complaining about red tape and about how the purchasing agent made their jobs harder, not easier.

Every supervisor develops patterns of informal relations with his subordinates. And every new supervisor requires a long period of initiation before he is accepted by his subordinates as their legitimate leader (see Chapter 8), in part because they fear that he may not follow his predecessor's patterns of informal relations. In fact, *any* new member of a group has a hard time until he develops satisfactory relations with his colleagues—and one of the reasons why people resist being transferred to new jobs is that they dislike the disruption of old relations and the work of establishing new ones.

Other changes may threaten a man's opportunity to provide leadership. For instance, before automation a crew chief on a press directed the men who worked with him; after automation there was less need for teamwork and less opportunity for him to issue orders. Or the change may mean that the man who used to call the signals waits passively for someone else to take the initiative.

Under the old scheme the maintenance man scheduled his own work; under the new scheme he must wait until someone calls him, thus reducing his discretion and status and substantially changing his social relationships with others.

Individuals adjust their pattern of social relations to fit their own special personality needs, just as they adjust other elements of their life in the formation of habits. Over a period of time, assuming an employee is not anxious to quit his present job, he has probably developed a good fit between his personality needs and the requirements of the job. The man who wants to boss others around, even if he is not officially a supervisor, has probably found a position in the work group that permits him to initiate activity; the worker who wants to avoid social pressures has probably found a job where no one can push him, not even the man who works next to him. Changing work procedures and systems, and introducing new equipment, upsets these convenient, pleasant job patterns. The sequence of work may be so drastically changed that the man who was formerly isolated must now work with a high-pressure colleague, and the leader is left with no one to lead.

Resentment toward New Orders and Increased Control

Whenever management institutes change, it must substantially increase the number of orders it gives to subordinates. This results in a change in interpersonal relations, and this second change, in turn, may well lead to resistance.

Some people resent taking any orders at all. Others have become accustomed to a certain level of control from higher management but resist any attempt to strengthen this control. On routine jobs or on jobs where employees are used to being their own boss, direct orders from management are relatively rare. When change occurs, they become subject to all sorts of unusual pressures from supervisors, staff people, and the big boss. Suddenly they find that someone is checking up on them and barraging them with far more orders than usual. This sharp increase in control reduces their feeling of autonomy and self-reliance. It emphasizes their dependence on management.

Similarly, members of management often resist change when it is initiated by staff people who normally have little control over (or even contact with) the line people who must carry out the change. Staff people have a strong incentive to promote change because it increases their prestige and influence; for almost these very reasons, however, line people have a tendency to resist change.

Resistance of this sort occurs also in the relations between staff groups. Engineers, for example, often resist suggestions by purchasing agents to utilize new materials which have come to the purchasing agents' attention through salesmen. Engineers feel that they should have exclusive authority to specify the material used, and that they should tell the purchasing agent what sorts of material should be used—not vice versa. So when purchasing agents try to influence the engineers, they are reversing the usual channel of communication. (We shall discuss this problem at greater length in Chapter 16.)

It has been argued that one of the main problems in introducing change is to keep it from being introduced in an intermittent fashion. The organizations that have greatest difficulty are often those that make changes only once in a while. The trick, it is claimed, is to make change almost continuously, to make change for the sake of change, even if there is no compelling reason for change at the moment. Perhaps this suggestion is too extreme. Still it does emphasize the point that living under change is very different from leading the same placid existence day after day.

Rather than distribute the disruptive impacts of change throughout the organization, some companies have established separate departments that specialize in change and uncertainty. In this way they protect the routine efficiency of regular departments from being disturbed.

Union Attitudes

Unions are also likely to resist change unless management consults with them, either formally or informally. It is not enough to inform individuals or consult with them. Every union has certain institutional needs that must be met if it is to retain its members' loyalty. If management makes a point of working with the union, the union may cooperate in introducing the change. If management ignores the union, the only way the union can preserve its status is by opposing management.

What happens when management decides to introduce new equipment that will require men to learn new jobs and assume new responsibilities? The typical approach in some companies is for the industrial engineer to make all the necessary plans, perhaps in consultation with the foreman. When the equipment arrives, the foreman assigns men to the new jobs and the personnel department computes the new pay rates. Almost inevitably, the union will find something wrong with the change and will file a grievance—and perhaps even sponsor a slow-down or wildcat strike. Why? If the union were to accept management's action passively, it would in effect be abandoning what it regards as its proper role. The only way to save face is to fight the proposed changes.

In other companies, management customarily informs the union of proposed changes long before they are made, asks for suggestions on how the seniority clause should operate when men are transferred, and bargains over wage rates for the new job. The union's status is preserved, and it assumes responsibility for resolving what might be a bitter dispute over who will be assigned to the new jobs. Of course, in bargaining over wages the company may have to make concessions, but the over-all cost may be less than the expense of trying to force the change over the union's objection, for workers are in an ideal position to insure that unwelcome change will prove unsuccessful or costly.

The Computer: An Example of Resistance

Workers are not the only group to resist change. Some of the most clear-cut examples of stubborn resistance to change have involved the reaction of managers to the "computer revolution" of recent years. Though computers have been widely installed, many managers have strongly opposed the use of the management science techniques that the computer makes possible. Though these techniques have undoubtedly been oversold, there is little question that their full potential has not been realized.

Why has there been such resistance? In the first place, management science techniques often require that records be kept more accurately than ever before, thus making the line manager's life more difficult. More important, many managers believe that computer systems reduce their discretion. Information that they need is "locked up" in the computer where they can't get at it; further, they believe that computer-processed reports are often inaccurate.

Computer language frequently baffles line managers, thus making them heavily dependent on computer experts. In some cases computers actually make decisions that line managers once made themselves (for example, regarding line balancing and inventory control). In addition, many managers fear that the computer will reduce their status or even cost them their jobs. Part of this fear arises from the fact that these managers are often unable to understand what the computer does; regardless of the cause, however, the fear is very real.

The introduction of computer-oriented techniques is often hindered by poor personal relations between computer specialists and line managers. The typical computer man (who is often young) is convinced that he has mathematical proof that his proposed change will result in greater efficiency. He is prepared to explain his method of analysis to line people, but if they cannot understand it, he insists they accept his word as an expert:

"I've developed a program that should save the company thousands of dollars in terms of reduced inventory, will eliminate stock-outs, and greatly speed up customer delivery. Though I've simulated the organization and know my program will work, I just can't get them to accept it. They tried a bobtailed version of my plan on an "experimental" basis, but they didn't use it right. They said my plan wasn't practical. I know it would have worked had they given it a chance. Instead they sabotaged it."

Line managers, on the other hand, tend to be antagonized by this cocksure attitude. To them management is more art than science: "He hasn't any experience doing what we do," they say. "And he doesn't take the human equation into account." Given this attitude it is understandable that they often, consciously or unconsciously, sabotage efforts to introduce computer-oriented changes into management practices.

The hostility shown to management science techniques is only an extreme example of the resistance that line managers frequently show to proposals initiated by staff departments. This kind of resistance to change will be discussed further in Chapter 15.

Change and the Over-all Organization

So far we have dealt with change as if it involved only two groups, one seeking change, another resisting it. Obviously, this is not so. "Since every group is a social system, any change in one of its component parts is likely to require or result in alteration or rearrangement of other parts."[3] Apparently simple changes may involve a host of people who at first may not seem concerned. For

[3] Paul C. Agnew and Francis L. K. Hsu, "Introducing Change in a Mental Hospital," *Human Organization*, Vol. 19, No. 4 (Winter 1961), p. 199.

example, a change may appear to affect only Mr. A, but it affects his relationship with Mr. B, who becomes upset, thus hurting his relationship with Mr. C. Mr. C in turn deals with Mr. A in a less friendly fashion than usual, which further upsets Mr. A. Eventually, a comparatively minor change touches off a major crisis.

Change must be seen in organizational terms. Rarely are a manager and his immediate subordinates the only ones involved. Very often the need for change develops first: Profits decline, competition adopts new products or production processes, equipment begins to wear out and get out of date, and so forth. Management may cling to its traditional ways at first, even though to an outsider the need for adjustment may be obvious. Eventually, one group within management (usually a staff department) may become aware of the problem and propose a solution. Now it must sell its solution to other groups within management. Line personnel may resist because they have the difficult task of implementing the change. Other staff men may resist also: the controller, for instance, because the change is too expensive, or the personnel director because it would disrupt a tricky union relationship.

While the plan is under consideration, rumors fly, restlessness increases, and sometimes exaggerated fears arise. When the plan is finally tentatively adopted at higher levels, management must now try to win the acceptance and cooperation of those at lower levels, and sometimes from the union. Often the change may have widespread and unexpected ramifications and may disrupt precariously balanced relationships.

The process should not be considered entirely a one-way street which runs, for example, from staff to line to subordinate employees. Line management will seek additional information from staff, it will raise objections, and it will suggest modifications in the proposed plans. Staff people may now be the ones who are resisting the changes proposed by line. Subordinates will react in the same way, openly if they are permitted to speak out, otherwise on an undercover basis. (For example, they may "modify" management's plans through outright sabotage.) Often subordinates propose change which higher management will "resist" in turn.

In organizations where human relations are sound, however, change is usually taken in stride. But in organizations where tensions and dissatisfactions are high, changes will be more difficult to accomplish. For example:

The high degree of [social] integration, the relative lack of conflict, and the level of job security in the chemical industry provide an atmosphere in which technological change is more accepted by workers and management than in the automobile industry, where, because of its history of labor-management strife and its irregular employment patterns, workers are naturally suspicious of the motives and effects of technological innovation. [4]

In some situations, stresses which are not obvious in ordinary circumstances become evident when change is introduced, almost as if the change is the straw which breaks the camel's back. Consider the following ingenious study conducted at General Electric: [5]

[4] Robert Blauner, *Alienation and Freedom* (Chicago: University of Chicago Press, 1964), p. 153.

[5] Stanley Schacter and others, "Emotional Disruption and Industrial Productivity," *Journal of Applied Psychology*, Vol. 45, No. 4 (August 1961), pp. 201–213. The above description of the experiment is somewhat oversimplified, but gives the essential picture of what was done.

The experiment was concerned with two sets of groups of workers, all doing repetitive, no-attention work. First these employees went through a "manipulative period" of several weeks. One set of employees, the "Favored Groups," received praise and friendly help from their bosses and were protected from disruption. The other set, the "Disfavored Groups," were nagged and pestered by management in a number of annoying ways. As might be expected, the Favored Groups developed positive attitudes toward their treatment while the Disfavored Groups expressed feelings of considerable aggravation. Nevertheless, neither treatment seemed to have a significant effect on the various groups' output rates.

At the end of the manipulation period, all special treatment stopped, except that shortly thereafter slight changes were made in each group's production methods. In both sets of groups both quantity and quality of output went down but the effect was very significantly greater in the formerly Disfavored Groups than it was in the Favored Groups.

The lesson for management here is that, although morale may have little impact on productivity under normal conditions, it may well have the effect of making change more difficult. The impact of change upon an existing organization is always difficult to predict.

Violation of Expectations

One concept may help summarize much of what we have said about resistance to change. In previous chapters we suggested that in most well-established groups there are generally accepted (legitimate) norms about the rights and responsibilities of both managers and subordinates—and that the nature of both these rights and responsibilities are established by implicit bargaining. Change, however, violates the implicit bargain. Unless the manager is careful in how he introduces change, his action is likely to be regarded as illegitimate, and subordinates, through resisting the change, will seek to restore the previous equilibrium.

REDUCING RESISTANCE TO CHANGE

Let us examine the problem of introducing change in still another framework. Take a situation in which workers are producing at 70 per cent of the efficiency that might be expected on the basis of purely technical considerations. Obviously, certain forces are operating to hold the rate down. For instance:

1. Dislike of work.
2. Fear of working oneself out of a job.
3. An informally set "bogey."
4. Dislike of the supervisor.

Yet another set of forces must be operating to keep the rate *as high as* 70 per cent. These may be:

1. Fear of losing one's job—or at least fear of losing special privileges.
2. Pressure exerted by the supervisor.
3. Financial incentives (if there is piece work).
4. Fear of being caught idle.

Presumably, at the 70 per cent rate of production, the two sets of forces have reached a balance which has been called a quasi-stable equilibrium.[6] That is, a system has been established in which one set of needs is balanced off against the other. (See A in the diagram.)

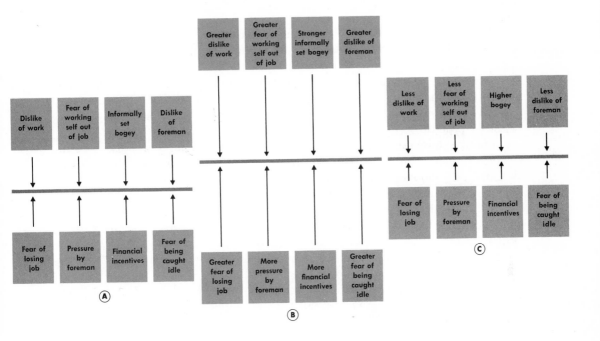

A: Quasi-stable equilibrium
B: Higher equilibrium with strengthened upward forces
C: Higher equilibrium with weakened downward forces

Now, if management wants to increase production, the typical approach is to strengthen the upward forces (B in diagram), perhaps by having the foreman apply even more pressure or by installing piece work. This method of introducing change we shall call *overcoming resistance*. Of course, the higher production climbs, the more workers' resistance is raised, until finally a new equilibrium is reached where the two sets of pressures are once more in balance. However, and this is a crucial point, at the new equilibrium, stronger forces are operating on each side, and tension is at a higher level. Frustration is greater, and employees are more likely to devise techniques to insulate themselves from the pressures acting on them. From management's point of view this is an inefficient way of doing things. It is like trying to stop a car by using the brakes without taking one's foot off the gas.

Fortunately, there are more efficient ways of accomplishing the same objec-

[6] This concept of quasi-stable equilibrium was developed by Kurt Lewin. See his "Frontiers in Group Dynamics," *Human Relations*, Vol. 1, No. 1 (1947), pp. 5–42.

tive. Instead of strengthening the upward forces, management can weaken the downward forces (C in diagram), perhaps by making the work less disagreeable, or by inducing workers to change their bogey, or by reducing their dislike of the foreman. This method we shall call *reducing resistance*. Here, too, a new equilibrium will be reached at a higher level of production, but at a lower level of tension. It is like stopping a car by taking one's foot off the gas, but by not using the brake.

Though method 2 (reducing resistance) frequently cannot be used without some of method 1 (overcoming resistance), the former places the least strain on human relations.

In overcoming resistance, management seeks to apply enough pressure on a man to induce him to do what is expected. For instance, the most obvious way to overcome resistance to change is simply to threaten to fire a man if he doesn't adjust, or promise to pay him more if he does.

But this threatening approach leads to all the problems we discussed in Chapter 6 under "be strong." A man may respond to threats either by quitting altogether, by sabotaging the change once it has been introduced, or by implementing it in a half-hearted manner.

What about trying to deal with resistance by promising a man an economic reward if he will accept the change? If the reason for resistance in this case is largely economic—and in many cases it is—obviously an economic reward is a good answer, for it helps reduce the cause of resistance and thus helps get the change accepted with less tension.

On the other hand, economic rewards are less successful if the reason for resistance is noneconomic. For instance, an executive may be offered a salary increase to move to a new location. Let us assume that the executive's immediate reaction to this offer is that the new location is very unpleasant and that he has misgivings about the type of work he will be doing and the type of men he will be associating with.

Confronted with such a choice, the executive will probably experience painful indecision. Indecision is always frustrating even between attractive alternatives. He may even try to get the salary increase without leaving town, perhaps by going to work for another company. And regardless of what he decides, for years to come he may resent having been forced into the decision. If he stays, he may deplore his economic sacrifice every time he pays a bill. If he goes, his attitude may make it difficult for him to adjust to the new situation.

A large chemical company used quite a different approach in manning a new laboratory in a remote section of the country. Their approach emphasized reducing causes of resistance. First, the company publicized the importance and challenge of the new laboratory's work and hinted broadly that assignment there would offer great opportunities for promotion. Then it invited a small core of experienced engineers to accept positions in the new lab and told them that they could invite less-experienced men to join them. However, management made it clear that those who were invited were free to reject the invitation. The potential candidates and their families were brought together from all over the country at the site of the new lab and were given a chance to get to know one another and to investigate housing possibilities. As a consequence, the firm had little trouble recruiting able men to work in the new location.

In the discussion that follows, we shall seek to emphasize methods of reducing, rather than overcoming, resistance.

Through Economic Incentives

As we mentioned earlier, much of the resistance to change has an economic motivation. Either men hear that the change will result in an immediate loss of job or earnings, or else they fear that it will affect their long-run job security or chances for promotion. The easiest solution in such a case is simple but expensive: Guarantee that these fears are groundless. For instance, if a man refuses to work on a new machine merely because he fears a loss of piece-work earnings, management might guarantee him that his earnings will be no lower on the new machine. It is quite common in union contracts today for management to guarantee that no one will be displaced by technological change. Certainly, too, if new equipment is to be introduced that will displace men, the change should be made in a period of expanding employment when the displaced employee can be offered another job that offers equally good security and pay.

Such guarantees are extremely useful in smoothing over change. The difficulty is their expense. The very reason for change may be the desire to cut costs because of economic necessity. Even in such a case management may reduce resistance if it can truthfully show that the change will be an improvement in the individual's own (not just the company's or the other workers') economic prospects in the long run.

Though the bulk of this chapter is concerned with noneconomic means of handling resistance, you should not draw the wrong impression from our allocation of space. *Economic motivation is very important in our society.* And when the cause of resistance is economic, all the noneconomic techniques that we are about to discuss will be meaningless. True, an employer may successfully manipulate an employee into acquiescing to a change that is not in the employee's best interest. But in the long run, in a free society such attempts at brainwashing tend to backfire against their instigators. We emphasize this point because there are employers who feel that if proper "human relations" are applied, employees will be willing to do without a fair wage. Such misuse of human relations is, in our opinion, highly immoral; fortunately, it is rarely successful.

Through Two-Way Communication

Resistance to change that springs from fear of the unknown can be reduced simply by providing appropriate information. This information should explain not only *what* is to happen but also *why.* And it should be sent to the whole organization, to those both directly and indirectly involved.

This question of communications raises all the problems that we discussed in Chapter 10, particularly: (1) Is the information really understood? And (2) does it answer the questions actually being asked? Here, as in most areas of human relations, only *two-way* communication will serve the purpose. When major change is contemplated, superiors and subordinates should sit down and discuss the proposed plan in a way that will bring doubts and questions out into the open where they can examine and answer them. After all, even though management's ideas may work in theory, employees may have the know-how to make them work in practice. Indeed, what management diagnoses as *employee* resistance to change is sometimes really management resistance to listening to employee suggestions.

Through Group Decision-Making

We have seen that most people have a strong desire to participate in decisions that affect them directly. Group decision-making involves subordinates actively in the process of introducing change and enhances their sense of control over the environment.

One group-decision experiment was made with girls who were learning machine-paced work and who were failing to keep up with the required pace.[7] In discussions with their foremen, the girls requested that they be allowed to determine the pace themselves. A dial was installed that allowed them to set their own speed. It was discovered that the girls set up a work pattern which varied with the time of day, but that the *average* speed was considerably higher than the *constant* speed previously set by engineers. Yet the girls reported that their work was easier, and their total output was between 30 and 50 per cent higher than expected.

Unfreezing attitudes. People often resist change because they hold certain fixed attitudes or stereotypes to which they adhere in spite of all evidence to the contrary. Group decision-making helps them *unfreeze* these attitudes so that they can be re-examined.

An example occurred in a pajama plant.[8] During World War II the company's staff psychologist tried to persuade management, in view of the general manpower shortage, to abandon its policy of not hiring workers over 30. The top-management group immediately opposed this suggestion, insisting that older women took too long to train, had a higher absenteeism rate, and never worked at top speed. When the staff psychologist mentioned the good performance of older women currently employed, management dismissed them as exceptional cases.

Shifting to another approach, the psychologist tried to involve management in a minor research project to find out how much money the company was losing through employing older women. Management itself determined the criteria to be used (production rates, turnover, absenteeism, and learning speed) and also decided how the data were to be gathered. In short, management became actively involved in the project. To management's surprise, the data showed that older women were better on all counts. Highly excited by these findings, management changed its policy and even spread the word of its shift to other companies.

Notice that the psychologist failed when he tried to attack management's stereotypes head-on. But he succeeded when he induced management to unfreeze its old attitudes by engaging in the research study. By doing this, management opened its mind to objective evidence. In a sense the approach used was like double-clutching. Instead of shifting directly from one attitude to another, the group went first into "neutral" before taking up its final position.

Establishing new group standards. In Chapter 4 we mentioned that groups develop certain standards of proper conduct and that individuals who fail to live up to these standards are subjected to pressure to conform. When an individual member of a group decides to accept a change imposed from above, he fears

[7] William F. Whyte and others, *Money and Motivation* (New York: Harper, 1955), Chapter 10.

[8] A. J. Marrow and John R. P. French, "Overcoming a Stereotype," *Journal of Social Issues*, Vol. 1, No. 3 (1945), pp. 33–37.

that his fellow workers will criticize him for playing along. But when the entire group is involved in the decision leading to the change, just the opposite occurs: The man who *refuses* to accept the change is pressured into accepting the group decision. In effect, group decision-making may lead to the establishment of new group standards that are rigidly enforced.

Commitment and refreezing attitudes. Group decision-making commits each member of the group to carry out the decision that is agreed on. It refreezes the group. Even if a member has reservations or second thoughts, he is under strong pressure to implement the decision. Providing employees with information and arguments may influence them one way or another, but they themselves must decide whether to accept or resist a proposed change if they are to experience any commitment to the ultimate decision.

Though group decision-making may serve as a useful tool in reducing resistance to change, it is by no means a cure-all for management's problems. It works effectively in areas where management is relatively indifferent to what the group decides; for instance, management may not care how the work is divided up so long as the job is done. Group decision-making may also prove effective when management and employees have overlapping but not conflicting interests. But when no community of interest exists, or when participation is foreign to a group's experiences, group decision-making is of little use in reducing resistance to change (see Chapter 9).

Through Bargaining

How does bargaining differ from group decision-making? In group decision-making, management gives the group freedom to make its own decisions (though within limits). Bargaining implies a willingness to talk things over and to make compromises in an effort to get the group's approval of proposed changes. However, management does not agree in advance to accept any decision made by the group. Normally, it accepts only some of the group's proposals and only as a *quid pro quo* in exchange for the group's accepting the rest of what management wants.

Sometimes bargaining is implicit (as we mentioned in Chapter 6)—that is, unspoken understandings are reached on how much management will demand in the way of change, and subordinates in effect agree to accept a limited amount of change as long as management is "reasonable" in its demands.

Often, explicit and open bargaining is more useful, particularly in a unionized situation. As we have seen, unions insist on being consulted on every matter that affects the welfare of their members. Some changes, such as pay cuts, may clearly require union approval. In other instances, management may have the power to make a change on its own, but may be caught up in a swarm of grievances if the union does not approve of what was done. When workers are transferred from one job to another, for example, the union may charge that the seniority clause of the contract has been violated. When workloads are increased, the union may charge that there is a violation of the health and safety clause of the contract or of established past practices.

Many managements insist on their "prerogative" to make all decisions by themselves. When the union attacks their actions, they try to limit the discussion to the strictly legal question of whether the contract was in fact violated. They feel that once the union is given a say, it will be difficult or impossible to operate efficiently or to make any decisions at all.

There are times when management probably should stand on principle, particularly to show that unrelieved obstinacy on the part of the union can provoke equal obstinacy on the part of management. But management should set an example of reasonableness—at least to the extent of listening to the union's point of view.

Management loses little of its essential power when it informs the union well in advance of proposed changes and shows a willingness to listen to objections. But these gestures may not be enough in themselves. The union is seldom satisfied just to be informed or to be given an opportunity to air its objections, if these objections always prove fruitless. If management wants to win the union's support in introducing change, it must give careful open-minded attention to grievances brought up by the union. And it may even let the union participate in the decision-making process itself.

Regardless of whether management lets the union participate in decision-making, management must be prepared to make concessions and to accept union suggestions that it may not feel fully desirable, on the theory that a reasonably adequate solution enthusiastically supported by the union is better than a perfect solution strongly opposed by the union.

Many of these same principles apply to dealing with nonunion groups. The interests of management and subordinates often conflict. Regardless of how assiduously management uses the techniques of consultation and group decision-making, there will be occasions when subordinates are unwilling to accept everything management wants. Under these circumstances it is only common sense for management to make some concessions to the subordinates' strongest objections, if only as a means of winning more complete acceptance of other aspects of the proposed change.

Collective bargaining is difficult with nonunion groups, for there is no established mechanism to rely on. With small nonunion groups, however, it is at least possible to discuss problems with the group as a whole, and with larger nonunion groups management can deal with informal leaders or specially selected committees.

Management is under no obligation to bargain over every change it wants to initiate. On occasion it must push proposals through without regard to the objections of subordinates. But whenever management acts this way, it should be fully aware that it may be preparing the way for costly resistance later on.

Handling Symbols

How can management minimize resistance when it becomes necessary to change or eliminate some feature that has acquired symbolic meaning? First, management should indicate clearly that changing the symbol is not the same as attacking the values for which the symbol stands. Thus, in switching from parchment paper for insurance policies (see case on p. 244), the sales manager might emphasize that the change will help create the modern, up-to-date atmosphere that customers of the Integrity Company expect.

Sometimes it is possible to replace one symbol with another: When a new state is added to the Union, the old flag is discarded, but a new one takes its place. Similarly, if it becomes necessary to move foremen's cars from the front to the rear parking lot, special areas might be reserved for them, marked with special signs.

We have been told of an interesting example of this technique used by the administrative staff of a hospital. Members of the resident medical staff often had guests in the hospital cafeteria for Sunday dinner. Due to crowded conditions they often found it impossible to find a whole table for themselves. They had the cafeteria director place a sign on a group of tables: "Reserved for Medical Staff." Immediately several other high-status groups asked for similar consideration. To avoid the inflexibility and embarrassment that would arise if a majority of tables were specially reserved, the director changed the notices to read: "Medical Staff Are Requested to Use These Tables." This request could be justified on the grounds that it would make doctors easier to reach in case of emergency calls—and it also minimized the feeling that this was an additional symbol of the doctors' higher status.

Making Changes Tentative

When the individuals concerned are permitted to participate in making the final decision on whether or not to accept a change, it is sometimes useful to ask the group to go along with the change on a tentative, trial basis at first. This approach has two advantages:

1. It enables employees to test their own reactions to the new situation, and provides them with more facts on which to base their decision.
2. It helps to "unfreeze" their attitudes and encourages them to think objectively about the proposed change. A change introduced on a trial basis is less threatening and generates less resistance than a permanent change.

However, where the individuals concerned do not participate in making the final decision, tentative changes may be unwise. They prolong the period of uncertainty and tension and the length of time in which the group is supervised closely. And there is always the chance that employees will in effect "participate" in the final decision—by resisting it or sabotaging it.

Slow Change or Quick?

Should change be introduced slowly or quickly? The answer is not clear. Many people believe in "making haste slowly," on the grounds that slow changes are less disruptive than fast changes and provide greater opportunity for adjustment. Given time, the new will blend with the old—as, for example, in the British constitution.

Fast changes, if forced on people, may lead to violent resistance, and the resulting shock may disrupt the entire organization. There may be some resistance to slow change, but it will be less intense at any given time. Indeed, if the change is introduced slowly enough, it may not even be perceived—or else the organization may become accustomed to constant, gradual change as a natural process, as the fashion industry has.

Slow change entails certain dangers of its own, however. Every change has widespread ramifications, and it is bound to be less effective if it is just patched onto the existing set of practices. In introducing change it is far better for management to consciously re-examine the entire process to determine what adjustments should be made. Unfortunately, however, when management introduces slow change, total re-evaluation is rare (often because management wants to avoid "trouble"), and practices are continued that become increasingly inappropriate to the changed situation.

The story is told of how during World War II the British army ordered a time study of their standard procedure for firing artillery. [9] Most of the operation seemed efficient enough, except that just before the gun went off two men came to attention. When the time-study man asked why, he was told, "We've always done that." Only after considerable research did he discover that the original purpose was to keep the horses from jumping (though horses had not been used for years).

When change is so gradual that people do not recognize that it has occurred, they may well continue to behave in a way that was appropriate only to the old situation. If change is to be made slowly, management would be wise to give everyone concerned an over-all picture of what is eventually intended. Otherwise employees will begin to wonder, "Something is happening, but we don't know what," and exaggerated fears will arise about where the change is leading.

Actually, if employees fully understand and accept the change, there is little reason not to make the change rapidly. Adjustment is required only once, and there is small likelihood of anachronistic holdovers from a former period. Fast change eliminates the need for the constant series of adjustments that are required by slow change and which leave the organization in an endless state of turmoil.

Other Techniques

One of the most common and most difficult problems in introducing change is that of bringing in a new manager to head up an existing department in an established company. Ordinarily, if the old manager has been well liked, the new one will have two strikes against him, for none of the employees will believe that he can be as good as his predecessor. At the outset, everyone wonders what changes the new man will make. His most inconsequential acts are carefully examined for clues to his future policy and may be exaggerated into foreboding of future disasters. His subordinates may resent him as an outsider and prepare themselves to reject everything he does.

[9] Elting Morison, "A Case Study of Innovations," George Shultz and John R. Coleman, eds., *Labor Problems: Cases and Readings*, 2nd ed. (New York: McGraw-Hill, 1959), p. 264.

Let us examine this problem and how it was handled in a specific situation; our example will illustrate several techniques that may be helpful in introducing change in a wide variety of situations. W. F. Whyte describes how a new supervisor was introduced into a large restaurant: [10]

Since the old supervisor had developed warm relations with her subordinates, the restaurant manager was afraid that her departure might have a bad effect on the morale of the whole organization. Consequently he prepared the way for her successor with great care. First, he discussed the problem of a replacement with both the old supervisor and the chef, her chief assistant. The chef proposed a candidate for the job; though this candidate had to be rejected, the reasons for the rejection were fully explained to the chef.

When the new supervisor was finally selected, she was introduced to her subordinates at a general meeting. The manager announced that the old supervisor was leaving and went on to say how much she meant to the restaurant. The old supervisor spoke with great emotion about how sorry she would be to leave her associates. Then she introduced the new supervisor, extolled her virtues, and asked her employees to show the new woman the same cooperation they had given to herself. Finally, the new supervisor promised to do her best to follow in her predecessor's footsteps.

For the next few days the new supervisor followed the old one around, getting to know people and trying to learn the supervisor's routine and methods of dealing with people. On the old supervisor's last day, the whole kitchen staff gave her a farewell party.

Although the new supervisor decided that she would eventually make certain changes in the operation, she spent her first few weeks trying to follow the human-relations pattern established by her predecessor. Only after she was fully accepted by the group did she begin making changes.

What techniques were used here to win acceptance for the new supervisor? How might these techniques be used in other situations?

Consultation. The manager respected the key position of the chef in the informal organization and requested his opinion on the change. When he felt the chef's opinions had to be rejected, he was careful to explain why.

Other organizations may use similar techniques to involve key subordinates in the selection process and thus substantially increase their acceptance of the final decision. Universities, for instance, typically appoint faculty members to the committees that choose presidents or deans.

Induction. The old supervisor was careful to introduce the new supervisor to all key personnel and to explain the customs of the organization. Doubtless this did much to save the new supervisor from making a social *faux pas*, to help integrate her into the social pattern of the organization, and to minimize the amount of disruption caused by the change in command.

Ceremony. The meeting at which the new supervisor was introduced, and the farewell party for the old supervisor, both served a ceremonial or symbolic function. They formalized the fact of change and helped the old supervisor pass on some of her prestige to the new.

[10] Adapted from *Human Relations in the Restaurant Industry* (New York: McGraw-Hill, 1948), pp. 319-331. For another example of a successful handling of what sociologists call a "succession crisis," see Robert Guest, *Organizational Change: The Effect of Successful Leadership* (Homewood, Ill.: Dorsey, 1962).

There is a tendency in our cynical society to play down the importance of ceremony. Yet it is no coincidence that throughout history every strong, stable institution—be it church, state, university, or company—has been noted for the ceremonies by which it helped focus individual loyalty on the organization as a whole.

Ceremonies are particularly important in time of change. Take, for example, the traditional ceremonies observed at the crucial moments of our life: birth, graduation, marriage, and death. The presence of relatives and friends and the giving of gifts and flowers help symbolize friendship and the unity of families. By involving ourselves in the formalized rites of the ceremony, we somehow protect ourselves from some of the fears and pains of moving from one stage of life to another. The heightened emotional atmosphere helps prepare individuals for major changes in their relationships with others. Indeed, we have learned to expect really important changes to occur in this way.

Probably more important, the use of ceremony is a public proclamation that in spite of apparent change the basic values remain the same; the new pays obeisance to the old. The English cry, "The King is dead; Long live the King." The French say, "Plus ça change, plus c'est la même chose." In primitive countries, oil companies may hire medicine men to sprinkle holy incense on new oil wells—thus showing their willingness to come to terms with the other culture.

Avoiding change until acceptance is assured. The new supervisor avoided making changes until she had developed informal, social relations with her subordinates. This is in conflict with the old adage that a new broom should sweep clean—or that a new manager should make all his changes at once. True, as we suggested earlier, it is sometimes (but certainly not always) desirable to complete change quickly rather than to let it drag on. Even so, it is usually wise for a new manager to wait before taking action until he knows more about the organization and the people with whom he is dealing.

In earlier chapters we distinguished between the supervisor's formal and informal authority, pointing out that the first arises from his official position, the second from the respect accorded his technical and leadership skills. The man who has both informal and formal authority can win acceptance of his ideas more easily. But the new manager has only formal authority and in effect must force his ideas on his subordinates. After a few months he begins to accumulate informal authority; as he becomes trusted as an individual, his ideas meet with less resistance.

Building on the past. In the restaurant case cited above, the new supervisor made it clear that she had no intention of throwing out past practices wholesale. As anthropologists and missionaries long ago discovered, it pays to learn the customs of the people with whom one works, particularly their ceremonies, symbols, and expected ways of doing things. Changes can be introduced more easily if an adjustment is made to the past. There are times, of course, when one may wish to cast out all the old patterns of behavior and start completely from scratch. However, in doing so one also casts out the good with the bad, the baby with the bath.

Change is among the most common of management problems. Yet management suffers from selective perception: Too often it is so concerned with the technical aspects of change that it fails to recognize that even a seemingly small change may have profound ramifications and that people sometimes resist change even when it is in their economic interest. They have vested interests in the old ways; they fear the uncertainties of the new. They give strange meanings to change, and dislike having their traditional customs, symbols, and patterns of dealing with people violated. People seldom resist change just to be stubborn; they resist it because it hurts them economically, psychologically, or socially.

Management often regards resistance as something essentially irrational, forgetting that apparently irrational attitudes or behavior may be symptoms of deep-seated problems. Or management may seek to overcome signs of resistance without knowing why the resistance exists. Too often management assumes that winning acceptance of change merely requires good salesmanship or one-way communications. Just as management plans the technical aspects of change, so must it consider in advance the impact on human relations.

The first step in dealing with resistance is to bring the real problems out in the open, to establish genuine two-way communication. After all, management has the responsibility not only of generating new ideas, but also of getting them accepted. Those who are seeking to initiate change would be wise to listen carefully to questions, objections, and suggestions for modification. Questions should be answered. Some objections and proposed modifications may be useful and their acceptance will improve the over-all quality of the proposed change. Other objections and modifications may not be of high quality themselves, but their acceptance in the spirit of bargaining may make it easier to win acceptance for the over-all change. Symbolic meanings must be considered and an intelligent judgment made on whether change should be introduced quickly or slowly.

This chapter has dealt with change from only a fairly narrow viewpoint. In later chapters we will point out certain staff departments (of which the computer group is only an example) that specialize in seeking to get others to accept change. To do this successfully requires some very special skills (see Chapter 15). Change, moreover, can be facilitated or made more difficult by the very way the organization is structured (as we shall see in Chapter 16). Finally, management and organization development programs (Chapter 24) seek to change the entire pattern of human relations within the organization.

problem 1 • SMALL FASHIONABLE STORE

A small, fashionable clothing store with about 25 long-service employees has always catered to the wealthy classes. Traditionally it has closed at 5:00 P.M., but a new manager is considering whether it might be more profitable to stay open two nights a week until 9:00.

He is concerned about how he would distribute evening work, particularly since each salesclerk has her own clientele. Also, he is far from sure whether any of his present customers would prefer to come in during the evening. The salesgirls work on commission.

Advise him on what he should do about the employee-relations aspect of his projected change. In particular, discuss why the employees might resist this change and what might be done to reduce each form of resistance.

problem 2 • NEW MARKETING MANAGER

You have recently been hired by the Winspear Corporation as Marketing Research Director with instructions to rejuvenate the entire research program. When your predecessor started the program 30 years ago, he had advanced ideas, but in the years prior to his retirement he seemed to slow down both physically and mentally. He handled a few projects himself, but the rest of the staff (12 employees) gradually began to look for guidance to Heath Bailey, Assistant Marketing Research Director. Bailey ran the department in a competent but unimaginative manner.

Your talk with your new subordinates indicates that they are quite capable, and in general get along together well. However, two of the youngest men in the department, Bob Hertel and Jim Delevan, seem restless and anxious to try out new ideas.

At present Bailey handles all administrative matters himself. Following the practice developed under your predecessor, the staff reports to him, he hands out assignments, makes decisions, and then at long intervals tells you what he has done.

By now you have a number of research projects that you would like your research staff to begin. Some are quite different from anything the staff has done before, and several require a good deal of travel—which is also new.

1. Are the human relations in this department sound?
2. Should you try to change Bailey's key position in the organization? Why? How would you go about making the change?
3. What sort of relationship would you like to develop between yourself, Bailey, and the rest of the staff?
4. How should you handle Hertel and Delevan?
5. How do you intend to introduce the new research programs?

problem 3 • AN MBA's STORY

I finished my MBA in May and was hired by the Brown Company (Boston, Mass.) in June. I worked in corporate headquarters in the Comptroller's Office with a small group of newly hired MBA "types" knowledgeable about accounting, systems, and computers. Our little group was given the assignment of converting the accounting groups located in the various plants to a new corporation-wide computerized cost system that would provide top management with much better information concerning plant performance.

My boss was Henry Froman. Froman had a pretty good reputation in the company, as far as I could learn, although he had little formal accounting training. He had been hired 25 years previously as a clerk (after two years of business college) and gradually promoted up through the company to Assistant Comptroller. I first developed doubts about his abilities when I came in to see him on some work I had been doing on the accounts at the Seattle plant. It seemed to me that before moving toward computerization, the entire Seattle system had to be changed, and I had a number of suggestions to make.

I had carefully prepared my presentation so that it was concise but logical. When I had finished the presentation upon which I had worked several weeks, he just thanked me, and that was all; no appreciation, no comments. I guess I might have thought this was just a bad day for him or I had said something wrong, but I had the same experience many times. I was discovering all sorts of problems, not only at Seattle, but in other parts of the corporate accounting procedures. Further, I discovered a way we could cut down on the amount of time-sharing we would require in our new computer set-up, and I presented these ideas to him at various times. Each time he was polite, but it seemed as though the more I went in to see him, the less appreciation I got.

Anyhow, I was anxious to get out into the field and away from the rarified atmosphere at "corporate." The biggest job was going to be Seattle. It was an old plant, and they were set in their ways. My first job was to dig out information about the relationship of their accounting to their actual production, inventory, and shipping processes. The man I was to work with was the head of the plant's accounting group, Eli Phillips.

When I met him, I explained that the corporate computerized set-up would begin handling a good deal of their work load as soon as we were able to program what top management would need in the way of information. He said he would be happy to be of help.

Over the next couple weeks, however, I experienced a good deal of difficulty getting data. It was like "dragging it out of them." In fact, I discovered that it was easier to spend my time looking at the data itself rather than trying to get Eli or his staff to help me. I stayed there nearly a month, going back over nearly five years of records.

Some months later, my report on Seattle and other material our little group had collected was incorporated in the new system. It was time to begin testing and debugging the program. The plan was that for some months we would be running parallel accounts at corporate (with our computer) and at the plants (with their manual methods). Both corporate and plant would then be able to evaluate how the new system was working, and we could improve it as we went along.

Well, when the Seattle people began getting the print-outs, they screamed bloody murder. They said a number of key parameters had been ignored, we didn't understand what they did there, and the computer-processed data was useless. Froman called them and said that problems were to be expected, and I would be down to talk with them about changes.

When I got to Seattle, it was a repeat of my previous encounters. I met with Eli and the plant manager there. I first presented again the rationale behind the whole program and what we hoped to accomplish in better control by centralizing this data analysis. When Eli said it would never work at Seattle, we got into a long, emotional argument over how different they were from the other plants.

When I got back to Boston, I made a number of modifications based on what I had learned. However, the following week there were the same screams from Seattle: it was not providing a true picture of their operations, they argued.

Froman decided to push the work ahead at other locations and let Seattle lag behind. Over the next few months the installation was completed at the other three plants but was not finished at Seattle. When I decided to leave for another job, Seattle was still left out of the system.

A good deal of blame can be placed on Froman—he's too easygoing and not forceful enough—and on Eli Phillips. Phillips just made up his mind it wouldn't work; and being stubborn, he wouldn't change his mind.

1. Comment on the MBA's view of his job and his problems.

2. What are the processes at work here that he doesn't comprehend?

3. What changes in his behavior might have improved the situation?

13 DISCIPLINE

We have purposely left discipline to the end of this part so that we could discuss other problems first. Discipline is required only when all other measures have failed. Suppose you have clearly instructed an employee on his duties, have listened to his problems, have tried to help him to do better, and have tactfully criticized his performance (as discussed in Chapter 8)—yet he still fails to meet standards. Then what? Then, reluctantly, you are forced to resort to discipline.

But can discipline be made consistent with what we have said about general supervision? We think it can.

In the first place the best discipline is self-discipline, the normal human tendency to do one's share and to live up to the rules of the game. Once people understand what is required of them, they can *usually* be counted on to do their job effectively and with good cheer. Yet some people (perhaps most of us) find that the possibility of discipline lurking in the background helps our "better selves" win out over our "lazier selves." As one man put it:

"If you can get away with small things you keep trying to get away with bigger and bigger things until, finally, you are caught and you are in trouble. Just for example, if you can sneak nuts and bolts out of the plant in your lunch box, you start trying to take spare parts and accessories out next ... It's much better if you know that they are going to check your lunch box every night and you can't even take out the smallest thing. Then ... you don't get into bad habits." [1]

[1] Daniel M. Colyer, "The Good Foreman—As His Men See Him," *Personnel*, Vol. 28 (September 1951), p. 142.

Ordinarily, if employees feel that the rules by which they are governed are reasonable, they will observe them without question. That is to say, they will respect the rules not because they fear punishment, but because they believe in doing things the *right* way. Coming to work on time; following the supervisor's instructions; avoiding fighting, drinking, and stealing at work; punching the time clock—all these are accepted by a majority of employees as reasonable rules, as necessary conditions of work.

Standards accepted by the group are frequently enforced by the group. (See p. 187, for example, our story of how machinists enforced the rule against long-sleeved shirts.) Still, it is useful for management to back up the group when it is seeking the same objectives as management. The following quotation from a worker on an automobile assembly line illustrates a common feeling:

"If a man is late all the time, the guys just try to avoid him. They have no use for a guy like this. He just makes it hard for us all because the utility man [the substitute for all jobs on the lines] cannot do the work as well as the regular man, and so we have to work harder just to keep the work up. Of course, if a guy is just trying to give a smart aleck foreman a hard time, we are all for him. . . . But if the fellow is just a slacker, the foreman should straighten the man out for the sake of everybody." [2]

Most employees are tolerant when a man has an occasional off day, provided he does his part the rest of the time. But they resent seeing someone else "get away with murder" while they are doing a full day's work. As one man said:

"[Management] should be able to trust men, not have to watch them all the time. But you don't like to do your best and work hard while the other guy goofs off, loafs, and is always busy while you swing the job. It burns you." [3]

In fact, unless the culprit is disciplined the rest of the group may adjust to his low level of performance.

Thus, consistent proof that all rules are being enforced serves to strengthen the informal group's efforts at correction. Clearly, good managerial practices will vastly reduce the need for discipline. But if employees realize that infractions of rules will be disciplined, good management will become even better.

When new rules are introduced, management must make every effort to convince employees of their reasonableness and legitimacy. For instance, as we mentioned in Chapter 8, management should avoid introducing too many rules or rules that seem unrelated to doing the job at hand. No organization would survive if its only means of winning acceptance of correct procedures was to discipline all violators. Our disastrous experience with Prohibition shows the futility of trying to enforce a law that the majority feels to be unreasonable. In other words, management should try to establish what has been called "positive discipline," an atmosphere in which subordinates willingly abide by rules which they consider fair. In such an atmosphere the group may well exert social pressure on wrong-doers and reduce the need for the "negative" punitive discipline discussed in this chapter.

[2] *Ibid.*, p. 143.
[3] *Ibid.*

TYPES OF DISCIPLINE

How severe should the penalty for wrongdoing be? In recent years many companies have provided what is called "progressive" or "corrective" discipline, which calls for increasingly severe penalties each time a man is disciplined. Except for very serious wrong-doings, an employee is rarely discharged for a first offense. This is particularly true if the firm is unionized, since arbitrators insist that a man be given a second chance unless the offense is particularly bad. Frequently they will insist that the employee receive a warning about the nature of the punishment he will receive if he violates rules in the future. Before sustaining discharge, some arbitrators insist that evidence be provided to show the supervisor made an effort to rehabilitate the rule violator. Progressive discipline implies that some effort be made at rehabilitation.

Ordinarily, the sequence of penalties under "progressive" discipline is as follows:

1. Oral warning.
2. Written warning.
3. Disciplinary layoff.
4. Discharge.

Oral warnings, as a form of correction, were discussed in Chapter 8. When a man fails to maintain standards, or has broken a rule, a clear oral warning that repetition may eventually call for discipline is in order. The supervisor should, of course, concentrate on helping the subordinate figure out ways to prevent his troubles from recurring.

Written warnings are the first formal stage of progressive discipline. Psychologically, perhaps, they are not different from oral warnings, but they are made part of the employee's record—and they can be presented as evidence if more serious penalties follow, or if the case is taken to arbitration. Written warnings, sometimes called "pink slips," are often prepared in four copies—one each for the foreman, steward, personnel department, and the disciplined individual.

Disciplinary layoffs (to be distinguished from layoffs caused by lack of work) are next in severity. Usually they are for several days or weeks; layoffs in excess of a month are uncommon. Some companies skip this stage of discipline altogether, particularly when it is hard to find a trained replacement, on the grounds that it is too cumbersome to replace a man for just a few weeks. Moreover, the disciplined employee may return from his layoff in an even nastier mood than when he left.[4] On the other hand, there are some employees who pay little attention to oral warnings, but to whom actual punishment, such as loss of income, is convincing proof that the company means business. A layoff may shock them back to their sense of responsibility.

Discharge remains the ultimate penalty, but one that is being used less and less commonly. The expense of training a new employee makes the loss of an

---

[4] For the argument in favor of eliminating layoffs as a step between warnings and dismissal, see John Huberman, "Discipline Without Punishment," *Harvard Business Review*, Vol. 42, No. 4 (July 1964), pp. 62-68.

experienced man very costly to the company, and the hardships that face a man who has been discharged make arbitrators and unions increasingly unwilling to permit its use. Many arbitrators, indeed, refer to discharge as "industrial capital punishment"—and for good reason.

Consider the impact of a discharge on a man of say 55, with 30 years' seniority. In the first place, he may lose pension rights which would eventually be worth $30,000 or more, plus substantial vacation benefits. Few high-paying employers would be willing to hire a man of his age, especially after they check his references and discover his discharge. Certainly he can expect less pay than he was getting from the job to which his 30 years' service had carried him. Further, as a low-seniority man, he is now fully susceptible to all the winds of economic misfortune. Assuming he loses $2.50 an hour for the rest of his life, his financial loss may be as high as $75,000.

No wonder one arbitrator told us: "I am very reluctant to let a man be fired unless I feel the company's grounds are justified, both morally and legally. I think the employee should have every chance to mend his ways." Faced with this attitude among arbitrators, companies are forced to place greater emphasis on their selection and training programs. Workers who are discharged today are often individuals who simply don't care for their jobs, younger employees with no family responsibilities, or persons with severe behavior problems, such as alcoholics or psychotics.

Demotion is seldom used as a disciplinary measure; it is ordinarily reserved for situations in which an employee has been mistakenly promoted or is no longer able to perform his job. As a disciplinary measure, demotion has a number of disadvantages. Losing pay over a period of time is a long, slow form of constant humiliation, as compared with the sharp slap of a layoff. Also, if a company is going to retain a trained man in any capacity, it makes more sense to use his highest skill.

Managers whose performance is below standard are rarely given layoffs or formal demotions. Instead, they are often quietly transferred without cut in pay from responsible jobs with substantial promotional opportunities to dead-end jobs with little or no opportunity for salary increase or promotion. Or, in some companies, they are requested to "resign."

Most firms find that it is best not to treat either managerial or hourly paid employees so harshly that they give up hope or lose motivation.

THE "RED HOT-STOVE RULE"

Inflicting discipline puts the manager in a dilemma. How can he expect his subordinates to continue to regard him as a source of help, when discipline is by nature painful? Can he impose discipline without generating resentment? We think so—through what Douglas McGregor called the "red hot-stove rule." This rule draws an analogy between touching a hot stove and undergoing discipline. When you touch a red hot stove your discipline is *immediate*, with *warning*, *consistent*, and *impersonal*.

Let's look at these four characteristics as applied to discipline. When you burn your hand you are angry with yourself. Sometimes you are angry with the stove too, but not for long. You learn your lesson quickly, because:

1. The burn is immediate. There is no question of cause and effect.

2. You had warning. If the stove was red hot, you knew what would happen if you touched it.

3. The discipline is consistent. Everyone who touches the stove is burned.

4. The discipline is impersonal. A person is burned not because of who he is, but because he touched the stove.

In short, the act and the discipline seem almost one. You are disciplined not because you are bad, but because you have committed a particular act. The discipline is directed against the act, not against the person. There will still be resentment against the source of the discipline, but the more automatic the discipline becomes, the more this resentment is reduced. As one worker put it: "I really had it coming to me. I was looking for trouble. I can't blame the foreman. His job was to enforce the rules. That's what he is paid for."

Put another way, "the purpose of discipline should be to obtain compliance with established rules of conduct—that is, to correct improper conduct. It should not be punitive in nature, that is, to discipline solely for the purpose of getting even with the employee." [5]

Let us see how the "red hot-stove rule" works out in practice.

Immediate Discipline

The supervisor should begin the disciplinary process as soon as possible after he notices a violation of the rules. (Of course, if he has lost his temper he should wait until he has cooled down.) Note what happens if he delays action:

Joe Jones has a bad tardiness record. He comes in a half-hour late, but thinks the supervisor hasn't noticed it. By noon, Joe decides he has nothing to worry about.

The supervisor *has* noticed it, but he is busy on another problem and he figures it might be a good idea to let Joe "stew awhile." Late in the afternoon, just before closing time, he calls Joe into the office to give him a two-day layoff.

Naturally, Joe feels he has been treated unfairly and resents both the discipline and the supervisor. He assumes the supervisor has been saving his grudge instead of "having it out like a man." In the future, he will never feel secure with the supervisor and will always wonder, "What's he going to pull on me next? Why does he have to play this cat-and-mouse game with me?"

Further, the more quickly the discipline follows the offense, the more likely it is that the offending person will associate the discipline with the offense rather than with the person imposing the discipline—that is, the more automatic the discipline will seem.

[5] H. D. Garrett, *Building a Responsible Work Force* (Ann Arbor, Mich.: Bureau of Industrial Relations, University of Michigan, 1955, multilith).

Of course, immediate discipline does not mean that a man should be judged without full investigation. But it does mean that the supervisor should take notice of the offense as soon as possible and push the investigation with all due speed.

For instance, a man comes in to work after two days' absence. According to your records, he never called in to report sick, and, therefore, he is subject to discipline. "Immediate discipline" requires that you call him into your office for an explanation as soon as he gets to work. However, if he claims he was unconscious under a doctor's care during this period, you obviously are not going to discipline him until you have a chance to investigate. Even here you should push your investigation as rapidly as possible.

When the facts of a case are not clear, and yet immediate action is necessary, many companies provide for suspension. The employee is told that he is "suspended" and that he will be informed later about what discipline will be imposed. This technique may be used where tempers are so high that calm appraisal is impossible, or where the guilt is obvious but the amount of penalty can be determined only after further investigation. Suspension also makes possible a consultation among various levels of management before the final penalty is determined. Since suspension is a form of layoff, however, it should not be used unless the offense calls for at least a layoff. If the suspension is longer than is justified by the offense, arbitrators will usually order back-pay.

Advance Warning

If discipline is to be accepted without resentment, both the man who is being disciplined and his fellow workers must regard it as fair. And *unexpected* discipline is almost universally considered unfair. This means that (1) there must be clear warning that a given offense will lead to discipline, and (2) there must be clear warning of the amount of discipline that will be imposed for a given offense.

Assume that a rule has been posted for several months but that the supervisor has never disciplined anyone who violated it. Clearly, no one expects that the rule will be enforced in the future either. Now the supervisor grabs one man and makes an example of him. The victim might well cry, "Why me?" Discipline without warning violates the workers' expectations of fair supervision. Further, if the case were taken to arbitration the company might lose.

Does this mean that once an order is laxly enforced the company can never again enforce it? Perhaps, in a unionized situation, for an arbitrator may rule that a *precedent* of no enforcement has been established. If, however, there has been at last some enforcement of the rule (that is, if the company has not given clear evidence of its acquiescence to nonenforcement), the company can begin strict enforcement once it has issued clear warning of the change in policy.

Suppose, for instance, the company has been very lax in requiring men to be at work on time. Before starting to penalize tardy workers, the company should give clear warning that it is tightening up on enforcement. The supervisor might call the men together and, after appropriate discussion and explanation, say "From now on I'll expect you to come to work on time. Anyone who is more than five minutes late without adequate excuse will receive a written warning. If you receive more than two written warnings in any 30-day period, you will get a day's layoff."

We have already discussed the need for effective communications within the organization. Once more, let us emphasize management's responsibility to make sure that all employees really know what the rules are and how they are to be enforced. A failure to communicate such information deprives employees of clear warning. A communications program might include, among other things, the following:

1. Upon induction, the immediate supervisor can explain the rules to all new employees, perhaps with the help of the personnel department.
2. Notices can be posted on the bulletin board, and handbooks distributed to employees.
3. In some cases, lists of penalties can be included in the union contract.
4. When rules are changed, the immediate supervisor can call a group meeting or notify individuals informally.
5. When a rule is about to be violated, or actually is violated (provided it is a minor, first offense), the supervisor can issue an informal warning.

Many arbitrators, interpreting the legal meaning of the contract, might say that posting a notice on a bulletin board constitutes clear warning. But from the point of view of human relations, this is not enough. Written communications should be supplemented by oral communications. The better job management does of explaining a new rule and why it is necessary, the easier it will be to enforce it—simply because workers will be more likely to accept it as reasonable. Regardless of the legal requirements of arbitration, management is clearly to blame if the men unwittingly violate rules because they don't know what is expected of them. Good communications pay off by significantly reducing the amount of discipline that must be imposed.

Consistency

If two men commit the same offense and one man is more severely disciplined than the other, naturally there will be cries of favoritism. One of the quickest ways for a manager to lose the respect of his subordinates and to lower the morale of the work group is to impose discipline in a whimsical, inconsistent way.

Management must always keep in mind the educational function of discipline (and also of nondiscipline). Consistent discipline helps to set limits (that is, to inform employees what they can and cannot do); inconsistent discipline inevitably leads to confusion and uncertainty. When some rules are permitted to go unenforced, employees may either (1) decide to ignore all rules, or (2) become confused about what is really required of them.

For instance, one day the boss lets Mary , his secretary, get by with handing in a report that is full of erasures. The next day he bawls her out for a sloppy report that is actually less sloppy than the previous day's. Under the circumstances, it is hard for Mary to know what standards are expected of her. She may well decide that the discipline has nothing to do with her act and "learn" only that the boss has a personal grudge against her. Not only won't she learn the rules, but she will be resentful as well.

Every individual wants to know the limits of permissible behavior, and one way to establish these limits clearly and dramatically is to punish those who exceed them. We all tend to be unhappy and insecure in a situation where we are not sure what is expected of us. Child psychologists, for instance, have learned that children are not necessarily happier when they are given absolute freedom. One reason they get into so much mischief is that they are trying to find out how much they can get away with, at what point Daddy will spank. Grown-ups are the same way. They want to know "How far can I go? What can I do? What can't I do?"

The rules of fair warning and consistency require that discipline be neither greater nor less than expected. If the degree of discipline comes as a surprise, the company may have failed to give adequate warning; if it is less than expected, the company will have difficulty in gaining acceptance of a more serious penalty in the future. When there is uncertainty and misunderstanding about whether the offense is to be punished and how much the punishment is to be, then the policy is inconsistent. If the rule-breaker sees the supervisor as wielding arbitrary discretion, then he may blame the supervisor for his discipline rather than himself.

Consistency is hard to maintain. Some people we like—others we don't. Sometimes we see a rule violation as a personal insult, a direct challenge to our authority. Other times, prompted by our natural instinct to be understanding and kindhearted, we are tempted to tell the rule-breaker, "Well, I'm going to let it go this time, but don't do it again."

Dissatisfaction may arise over excessive leniency as well as over excessive harshness.

The office had a rather strictly enforced rule that employees could not leave without permission until the end of the work day. Braden was caught by his supervisor in the hall heading for the exit about ten minutes before quitting time. Upon review the normal penalty of a two-day layoff was suspended because the following week was Christmas. However, a petition was signed by the other employees protesting this decision as showing favoritism and thus being discriminatory! They felt that since he was obviously guilty, he should receive the same penalty others had received.

One source of inconsistency is management's tendency to be stricter in slack times and to ignore rule violations when manpower is short.

Crawford had a terrible absenteeism record. He missed work for two days without a legitimate excuse. Normally, given his record, his offense would justify an immediate two-week layoff. However, Crawford's services were badly needed on a rush job. No one else could take his place. So the supervisor added the incident to Crawford's personnel record and warned him that a further violation would lead to discharge.

Keeping Crawford on solved the immediate problem of maintaining production. But the long-term effects might have been more serious. What did Crawford and the other workers learn from this incident? One of several things: (1) The absentee rule was not to be enforced strictly, (2) the supervisor was playing favorites, or (3) strict discipline in time of slack work was merely a dodge to get around the seniority provisions of the union contract. In any case, the employees' respect and trust for their supervisor probably took a nose dive.

Often a supervisor finds it easier to transfer a problem employee to another department than to face the hard task of disciplining him. In one case a man who had consistently failed to live up to company rules had been transferred 11 times without any record of disciplinary action appearing in his personnel folder. This employee could hardly be blamed for not knowing what standards of behavior were expected of him. No one had taken the trouble either to help salvage him or to rid the company of a constant expense.

Consistency in enforcing discipline may be expensive in terms of lost production, but inconsistency may be even more so. Although the evidence is incomplete, it would appear that automobile plants that are most hesitant about enforcing rules against wildcat strikes (work stoppages not officially authorized by the union) have had the worst record of such strikes. Yet if a whole department goes on strike, it may be very costly to discipline everyone. Not only will the company lose the production of that department, but the men in other departments may walk out in sympathy.

Wildcat strikes are set off by a variety of causes (frustration with the work or slow handling of grievances, for instance). Obviously it is better to eliminate the causes than to punish the symptoms.[6] Still, if no discipline is imposed, the men "learn" that they can engage in such strikes with impunity. Companies that have been willing to sustain the short-run costs have found that wildcat strikes have decreased. Further, when management takes a firm stand, the union finds it easier to discourage its members from taking matters into their own hands. Many union leaders have told us candidly that they find it hard to observe the "no-strike" provisions of their contracts when management doesn't take the initiative in disciplining violators. "We can't be more against strikes than management."

Consider another problem involving consistency of discipline. We have heard foremen say, "I can only catch a small proportion of the rule violators, but those I catch I punish severely." Is this fair? Many men consider it a form of "Russian roulette." Adventurous souls may make a game of this procedure and try to see how much they can get away with. Furthermore, scattered instances of discipline hardly constitute clear warning.

If a rule is on the books, the manager should make an effort to enforce it (and enforce it uniformly). If he finds it impossible to do so, the rule may have to be revised or dropped altogether. Sloppy enforcement of one rule encourages employees to disregard other rules.

In some situations, of course, 100 per cent consistency is impossible. For instance, unless everyone is searched as he leaves the plant, stealing may be impossible to stamp out. However, such searches are expensive and deeply resented by employees. The company may have to rely on stern punishment of anyone who is accidentally caught stealing. Since workers generally accept antistealing rules as reasonable, there will be little resentment of this policy, inconsistent though it seems.

---

[6] Indeed, if workers are prevented from wildcatting, they may release their aggressions in other ways—through slowdowns and absenteeism, for example.

Does consistency require that the penalty should be determined entirely by the offense, regardless of the personal history and background of the person who committed it? Of course not. We have already said that it is common industrial practice to be more lenient on first offenses. Arbitrators are reluctant to let "industrial capital punishment" be imposed on a man unless a reasonable effort has been made to rehabilitate him. Certainly each case should be considered on its own merits. As a top industrial-relations executive put it:

"There is no precise mechanical formula. . . . Each instance of misconduct must be viewed . . . individually. . . . This, of course, is a matter of judgment, but . . . four principal factors should be taken into consideration . . . first, the seriousness and circumstances of the particular offense; second, the past conduct record of the employee and his length of service; third, the lapse of time since his last misconduct for which disciplinary action was taken; and fourth, the plant practice in similar cases." [7]

For example, three employees are caught gambling. One has been disciplined for the same offense before, the other two have not. The first man is discharged, the other two are given written warnings. This, we would argue, is being consistent as it may first appear. Although each case should be considered on its own merits, the over-all disciplinary program must be kept consistent. Certainly if two individuals with the same personal histories commit the same offense, they should be treated equally.

How long should a rule violation be held against an employee? Current management practice tends toward disregarding offenses committed more than a year or two ago. Thus, an employee with a poor absenteeism record would start afresh if he maintained a good attendance record for a year.

There has been considerable discussion in industrial-relations circles about whether or not good personnel policy requires the posting of all rules and the setting of standard penalties for violations. For example: "Rough-house: First offense, warning. Second offense, one-day layoff. Third offense, one-week layoff. Fourth offense, discharge."

Those who favor such lists argue that they provide effective warning and greater consistency. Those who oppose them feel that they make it harder for management to distinguish between various degrees of guilt. Mandatory discharge for stealing would mean that the employee who is seen taking a box of safety clips would receive the same penalty as one who was caught robbing the safe. One company with a rigid series of penalties was obliged to impose only a one-week layoff on an employee who had altered his output records—this was the standard penalty for inaccurately reporting production figures. Actually, the employee had been doctoring his records for years and had received hundreds of dollars in unearned incentive payments as a result. Had the company not set up a specific penalty in the rule book, it could have imposed a far more severe penalty.

Some companies insist that unless they maintain a uniform list of penalties they are unable to justify discipline to the union. Others say that such lists enable the union to force the company into excessively legalistic decisions on discipline. For instance, if the company had no specific rule against loafing, legally it couldn't discipline a man no matter how lazy he was.

[7] Garrett, *op. cit.*, p. 5.

Impersonality

We have said that a good supervisor encourages his subordinates to express themselves freely and tries to play down differences in status. He tries to build up the feeling that he and the worker are on the same team. Doesn't the imposition of discipline seriously endanger this relationship? It may. In fact, the disciplined employee might easily murmur, "That so-and-so. I thought he was my friend. I'd rather have a boss who wasn't such a hypocrite and then you'd know where you stand."

It is not easy to impose discipline without causing the person disciplined to feel resentful and aggressive. But the manager can minimize the danger to the relationship by imposing discipline in as impersonal a way as possible.

Discipline is most effective and has least negative effect on individuals, if the individual feels that his behavior at the particular moment is the only thing being criticized and not his total personality. [8]

In its opening stages, the disciplinary interview is not much different from most other forms of interview. First, state the problem as you see it; then encourage the subordinate to state his point of view. Let him tell you his story. Ask *how* it happened, not *why*. Give him every chance to explain himself. Try to avoid this sort of exchange:

Supervisor: Late again, I see. Didn't I tell you yesterday, if you were late once more this month, I'd give you a layoff. . . .
Employee: But . . .
Supervisor: (ignoring him) Well, you've had your last chance. You better go home.
Employee: But I did get here on time—only the superintendent called me in to his office to discuss the Savings Bond drive.

Instead, do your best to draw the man out and try to discover the real story. Use the interview technique. Don't ask him for his excuse, but concentrate on the *basic* reasons for his rule violation. Has he been poorly instructed on the job? Has he lost his motivation? Is he having trouble at home? Why? (Of course, you should have asked yourself some of these questions long before the employee's misconduct led to discipline.)

Sometimes your interview will give you all the facts you need. In other cases you may need to investigate further, perhaps by checking with other members of management. Avoid making a decision until you have the whole story, but reach your decision as soon as possible.

Once you have decided what discipline is appropriate, impose it quietly and impersonally. For example, suppose in a lateness case that the employee shows general irresponsibility, and that his only excuse for his latest tardiness was that he forgot to set his alarm clock.

Supervisor: Well, I can see how it happened. But from the company's point of view, not setting your alarm clock is not an adequate excuse, particularly since this has happened three times this month.
(Pause—in which to listen to objections.)
You have already received two written warnings this month and the rules now require that you receive a day's layoff.
(Pause—again for objections.)

[8] Chris Argyris, *Executive Leadership* (New York: Harper, 1953), p. xiii.

Jim, you've got to figure out a way to get here on time. You do a fine job when you are here, but the rule (and I think it is a fair one) is that if this occurs again within 30 days you will receive a week's layoff and if it occurs again you will lose your job. I don't want this to happen. Now what can be done about it?

(Then discuss positive means of avoiding trouble in the future. Try to get him to suggest a workable plan—or suggest one yourself. Even if this doesn't work, end with:)

Jim, will you try harder to get here on time in the future?

(The answer is bound to be "yes" and you have, for what it is worth, a positive end to the interview and a positive commitment to do something.)

Note that the discipline here has been imposed impersonally and the employee has been given every chance to express his objections. After imposing discipline the supervisor reverts to his role of *helping*. The interview ends on a positive note.

After disciplining a subordinate, you may understandably tend to avoid him or to alter your attitude toward him in subtle, hardly noticeable ways. But these shifts in attitude are particularly dangerous, for they generate corresponding alterations in the subordinate's attitude. He concludes, "You hurt me and you know it." Eventually, the whole relationship may be destroyed. By contrast, if you treat the man as you always have, you indicate that by-gones are by-gones, that it was the act that was punished, not the man.

Simple as this advice may seem, it is hard to carry out in practice. Both parties are upset by what has happened. It is easy to understand why the person who has been disciplined is resentful, but the act of imposing discipline is also emotionally distasteful to the person who imposes it. Most of us feel guilty when we hurt other people—even when such a feeling is not justified. To protect ourselves from guilt feelings, we have to build up a feeling of anger. But, since we fear the anger of the person we have disciplined, we become unapproachable and cold after we have imposed the penalty. As a result, we seem to be disciplining the other person *as a person*, rather than as the violator of a specific rule. Naturally his response is, "He doesn't like me."

Two mistakes are common in imposing discipline: the supervisor either apologizes or bawls the offender out.

APOLOGETIC DISCIPLINE

Supervisor: Jim, I'm sorry I have to do this, but the rule says I must. How would the other fellows feel if I didn't do something?

Subordinate: (to himself): Even the boss doesn't think it's a good rule. Boy, I sure have tough luck. *Or:* He doesn't have guts enough to back up his own rules. *Or:* Why does he worry about the other fellows? I know they won't care if I get off. *Or:* Who's he kidding?

PERSONAL BAWLING OUT

Supervisor: I've given you every chance, gone out on the limb for you, and you haven't helped at all. You told me last time that you would really make sure you'd leave home early, and you broke your promise. Well, I've done all I can for you. You are letting the company down. You aren't being fair to them or to the other men. You've got to wise up or you'll really be in trouble, and I won't bail you out.

In the second case, the superintendent is being overpersonal, possibly because he feels a little guilty. There is no need to remind the employee over and over again of what he has done, to rub his nose in the dirt. Instead, it is much better for the supervisor to make it clear that he wants to let by-gones be by-gones and that he assumes the man will mend his ways.

It requires a great deal of maturity to approach discipline without a sense of guilt or hostility, particularly if you feel that a man's disregard of the rules is a reflection on your own managerial abilities.

THE ROLE OF THE UNION

As yet we have said little about the role of the union in matters of discipline. We have observed in our research that unions rarely object strongly to discipline provided it is applied consistently and provided the rules are clearly publicized and generally considered reasonable. Of course, union officers may go through the motions of filing a grievance at the request of a disciplined member, much as a lawyer defends a client even though he is wrong. But in doing this, they often feel as this union officer did:

"I've got to go to this grievance meeting and fight for that so-and-so. He had it coming to him and got what he deserved. How can he think he is so much better than anyone else he doesn't have to follow the rules?"

Management should not expect the union to discipline members who violate the contract.[9] When the union does impose discipline, it is abandoning its traditional role as the worker's defender, and management is failing to assume its responsibilities. A management spokesman makes this point:

"The union cannot maintain its proper function of representing the employee and protecting his interests if it assumes any part of management's function of setting disciplinary penalties. If the union agrees with management as to what a proper penalty should be in a particular case, it forecloses its right to protest the penalty. Union representatives should be in a position to protest any disciplinary action taken by management against an employee on the grounds that the discipline is unfair, unjust, discriminatory, lacks cause, or is too severe.[10]

Management must also be realistic about the union leader's political position. Often union leaders feel obliged to defend members whom they themselves think are guilty; to do otherwise would be to risk defeat at the next election. Once management recognizes that union leaders must often perform what is for them an unpleasant job, life becomes a good bit easier for both management and the union.

Management may be able to reduce the number of grievances prompted by disciplinary action by bringing the union into the earlier stages of the disciplinary procedure.

Bill Jones has been absent frequently. According to accepted plant practice, after five no-excuse absences, he can be laid off for a month. Jones' foreman informs the department steward that he intends to enforce the rule against absenteeism and that the steward might try to "straighten Jones out" before he gets into real trouble. Where the foreman-steward relationship is a good one, the steward will often warn the man informally that continued violations may lead to a penalty that the union will find difficult to get reduced.

In this way the union is given an opportunity to play a constructive role without being burdened with the responsibility for applying discipline.

[9] There are a few exceptions in the building and clothing trades, where powerful unions may discipline members who violate the contract.

[10] Garrett, *op. cit.*, p. 1.

Quasi-Legal Procedures

The presence of a union need not impair management's efforts to maintain a satisfactory disciplinary policy. But it may force management to adopt what might be called a "quasi-legal" procedure.

Most union contracts require (1) that the company may discipline employees only for "just cause," and (2) that any employee who feels he has been unjustly disciplined may appeal to higher management through the grievance procedure, and, if management's answer is unsatisfactory, to arbitration. The arbitrator makes the final decision on whether the discipline was for just cause. He may sustain the company's action completely, or reduce the penalty, or decide the penalty was entirely unwarranted and eliminate it altogether.

The grievance procedure provides a valuable protection to the individual worker, awkward though it may be for management. Management has the right—one might even say the *duty*—to establish the rules under which the organization shall operate. But a channel of appeal must be kept open from management decisions on whether or not these rules have been violated. Thus, the grievance procedure operates as a means of enforcing consistency.

In our Anglo-Saxon tradition, a man is assumed innocent until proved guilty, and in establishing guilt the burden of proof is almost entirely on management. For instance, to prove that a man has been loafing on the job, more than the supervisor's unsubstantiated word is required. Management must be able to produce objective, factual data which show that other employees on comparable jobs consistently produce more than the alleged offender. And it must show that the worker's low production was not due to poor material or faulty equipment. Similarly, the union may challenge any rule that has not been clearly communicated to the employees or consistently enforced.

As a consequence, disciplinary matters must sometimes be handled in a legalistic, courtroom manner, particularly when they reach the arbitration stage. Unfortunately, both union and management may find themselves devoting more energy to legal intricacies than to dealing with the human problems involved. Each side tries to build up an air-tight case and to poke loopholes in the case of the opposition. The billowing clouds of legal technicalities often serve as a smoke screen that obscures the underlying human problems. Fortunately, the company that maintains a generally fair disciplinary policy as part of its standard procedure is less likely to become involved in the legalisms of arbitration.

The existence of the grievance procedure means that the supervisor's disciplinary penalty may be reduced or eliminated, either by higher management or by an arbitrator. It is even possible that a man, who the supervisor is sure has flagrantly violated the rules, may be totally exonerated. Under these circumstances the supervisor naturally may feel frustrated when his decision is not "backed up." However, such possible miscarriages of justice are the price that must be paid for development of a judicial system which permits every accused employee to have his "day in court." A basic tenet of our society is that it is better for a guilty man to go free than for an innocent man to be convicted.

The reason why "guilty" employees are acquitted at higher stages of the grievance procedure is usually that the supervisor has failed to gather evidence, to be consistent in his application of discipline, or to communicate the requirement of the job to employees. Hence it is important for higher management to train and advise supervisors on the requirements of a sound disciplinary policy.

CONCLUSION

Basically, discipline is a form of training. When disciplinary problems arise, it may be as much management's fault as the workers'. Many disciplinary problems grow out of management's failure to inform employees what is expected of them.

On the other hand, effective discipline depends on more than one-way communication in which the supervisor tells employees what to do and punishes them if they don't. Employees may be aware of a rule, yet refuse to accept it. For instance, if there are large numbers of employees taking extra-long lunch hours or using sick leave as a vacation, the problem is not to punish the guilty but to get group acceptance of a new standard. We must initiate discipline by winning acceptance of the standard. Once this has been accomplished, discipline will be provoked only by the small minority of recalcitrants.

For discipline to be accepted, the rules must be effectively communicated and the penalties inflicted must be consistent. Discipline helps employees learn the requirements of their job; and if discipline is applied impersonally, without personal animus, the respect shown the supervisor by his subordinates may actually be increased.

problem 1 • DISCUSSING MISTAKES

Suppose an employee has been making a series of small mistakes. Is it better for the supervisor to (1) discuss each mistake with him as it occurs, or (2) discuss his *over-all* record with him from time to time?

problem 2 • THE DRUNKARD

Dave Thatcher comes to work drunk. The foreman sends him home with another man, intending to speak to him when he is sober. As soon as Dave comes in the door the next morning, he drunkenly picks up a high-pressure hose and squirts the foreman in the face. The company discharges him for insubordination, assault with a deadly weapon, intoxication, and violation of company rules. There are no posted rules or penalties.

The union doesn't deny that Dave was pretty high. However, it alleges that (1) he has been having trouble with his wife, (2) his record has otherwise been excellent, (3) he was sent home but not otherwise given a warning on the first day, and (4) in other cases of drunkenness that occurred this year the men were referred to Alcoholics Anonymous.

The company answers: (1) The wife trouble is irrelevant, (2) Dave's work has not been good, even though he has not received previous formal discipline, (3) he was in no condition to appreciate a warning on the first day, and (4) the men referred to Alcoholics Anonymous were quiet drinkers who hadn't committed major violations of company safety rules. It adds that Alcoholics Anonymous is for alcoholics and, aside from the two-day spree, there is no evidence that Dave is an alcoholic.

1. Was the company's position correct?
2. What sort of penalty should be imposed?

problem 3 • THE AUTO THIEF

The company's employment application says "Falsification of this form will be grounds for immediate discharge." Among the questions on the form is this one: "Have you ever been convicted of a crime?" Howie Bowman was employed three years ago and has a perfect record. Suddenly the company finds out that 15 years ago, when he was 17, Howie was convicted of stealing an automobile and given a suspended sentence. He had not mentioned this fact on his application.

1. Should Howie be disciplined?
2. How long should the company hold this rule violation against him?

problem 4 • FIGHT

The foreman catches two men fighting. Smith had been kidding Jones about his hillbilly background. Jones took a poke at Smith. Smith hit back. Both have had a good record in the past.

While some companies try to determine who really started a fight, others feel they will get nowhere trying to settle personal feuds between workers, but should exercise discipline only when one party resorts to his fists to settle differences. What do you think? Should both men receive equal punishment? Should Jones be punished more severely for starting the fight—or Smith for provoking it?

problem 5 • NO GAMBLING

A foreman says, "We have rules posted against gambling. Of course, we don't enforce them against small bets and there is some card-playing for money in the washroom at lunch break. However, we have the rules posted as a standby measure if things get out of hand."

Do you agree with this foreman's approach?

problem 6 • THE BOOKIES

A company has a posted rule against gambling. Six months ago two men were given written warnings about shooting dice. One day the local police arrest two other men on plant property for bookmaking. There is evidence that they have been collecting bets on horses in the plant. The men plead guilty before the judge, who gives them a suspended sentence. When they return to the plant they are discharged. To date, both men's records have been perfect.

If this case were carried to you as an arbitrator, what would you decide?

problem 7 • BEARDS

The Crosby Bus Company has a rule: "All drivers shall report to work neatly shaven and in a clean, neatly pressed uniform." The company is proud of its employees' appearance and believes that it improves customer relations. The rule has been generally observed without trouble, although in the last three years three men were orally warned about sloppy dress, and one man was given a two-day layoff. Mustaches have been allowed.

The company's efforts to improve the appearance of employees were encouraged by what they heard about a new policy instituted by the Brightline Bus Service in a nearby city. Brightline had posted these rules covering their garage employees:

No goatees, beards, or sideburns extending below the ear lobes; no Afro haircuts. Mustaches must be neatly trimmed and must not extend beyond the corner of the mouth.

Hair must be trimmed so that it does not cover the collar, and shirttails must be tucked into trousers.

When these rules were posted, Brightline justified them on the basis of public relations and safety: garage employees wear uniforms with the company's name, and they are frequently seen on the streets and in restaurants; long hair is a safety hazard around machinery and when an employee is welding.

Norton Foster, a Crosby driver, returned from vacation with a well-trimmed beard. His boss asked him to remove it. Foster refused, on grounds that his personal liberty was being violated.

1. Should Foster be disciplined? If you were the arbitrator under a union contract, what would you decide?

2. Brightline's employees were outraged, and the union claimed that these were arbitrary and unreasonable rules that violated the basic rights of employees. *Are* Brightline's rules reasonable and appropriate? Can you propose more reasonable rules? Is there any way to avoid so much detail in prescribing dress and appearance?

3. Do your answers for Crosby's drivers differ from your answers for Brightline's mechanics?

4

Organization

Up to this point we have been talking about some of the components of the organization: individual workers and their jobs, supervision, informal groups, and unions. Each of these is an integral part of the organization, but there is a missing element still to be considered: the organizational system itself, within which all these components interact. In this section, therefore, we consider the impact of organization structure on human behavior.

As long as people work in small groups and see each other almost continuously, little thought need be given to defining in advance how they are to relate to one another. They develop patterns of relationship almost spontaneously: few formal plans need be made except to insure a high quality of supervision.

As more and more people are added to the organization, however, the management of personnel becomes more complex. For work to be done efficiently, an orderly pattern (or system) of human relationships must be evolved. This pattern is commonly referred to as *organizational structure.* In large organizations, merely giving consideration to the needs of *individual* workers and the requisites of face-to-face supervision is not enough.

Our primary questions, then, are these: What patterns of human relationships enable an organization to function most efficiently? What problems arise in the attempt to establish these patterns? What type of organizational structure is most likely to motivate people to work toward management's objectives? How can structure be evaluated in human-relations terms?

In a very real sense, an organization is a set of human relations. Every organization has a hierarchy of authority. The men at the top give orders to the men beneath them and so on down the line. The purpose of the hierarchy is to make it possible for a large number of people to work under the over-all control of a relatively small number of managers.

Organizations also spread out horizontally. Rather than having one person do the total job—for example, designing a new machine—many people are brought together, and their activities are coordinated so that, although each does only a small part of the total job, finished engineering drawings are produced. This is the familiar principle of division of labor. By assigning only a limited number of tasks to each specialist, the organization hopes to attain greater productivity than it could if each person were to do the whole job by himself.

These two principles—(1) control exercised from the top down through successive levels of hierarchy and (2) specialization of function—are the source of a host of challenging human-relations problems that management must somehow solve. Indeed, failure to develop an adequate organizational structure may nullify the benefits of effective supervision. Careful planning in this area must precede any other management program.

A number of answers have been proposed to the human-relations questions associated with large organizations. These proposals are analyzed in Chapter 16, "Minimizing the Human Problems of Larger Organizations". We shall devote particular attention to efforts to provide greater decentralization, whereby lower levels of the organization are assigned self-contained tasks that limit their need for contact with other levels of the organization.

HIERARCHY **14**

Heretofore our discussion has concentrated on a two-level organization: an employee and his supervisor in direct face-to-face contact with one another. However, it should be apparent that as the size of an organization increases, there will have to be more than two levels. No longer can a single manager supervise everyone. With the addition of a number of managers comes the need for supervising and coordinating the work of the managers themselves: managing the managers. Thus, another level is introduced into the organization, and with it relationships which do not involve face-to-face contact. More and more levels will be introduced as the organization grows in size.

In this chapter we shall be looking at the human problems associated with multi-level organizational structures. First we shall consider what these organization structures look like. Then we shall examine in turn the distinctive problems of leadership and communication in this type of organizational setting.

CHARACTERISTICS OF HIERARCHIES

The term hierarchy refers to this multi-leveled, vertical structure. A hierarchy tells us who outranks whom within the organization, who must defer to whom; in other words, the formally prescribed status differences. The result can be summarized in the familiar organization pyramid.

For coordinating the activities of large numbers of people, some form of pyramidal organization is inevitable, simply because there will always be fewer people with very high status than with moderate or low status. Only in this way can order be maintained.

Those students of management whose views have been labeled "scientific management" or "bureaucratic theory" conceive of a very regularly shaped pyramid. The table of organization or organization chart that is so familiar represents this pyramid. The actual relationships among members of organizations are presumed to be consistent with this structure with the results that:

1. Nearly all contacts take the form of orders going *down* and reports of results going *up* the pyramid.
2. Each subordinate must receive instructions and orders from only one boss.
3. Important decisions are only made at the top of the pyramid.
4. Each superior has only a limited "span of control," that is, he supervises only a limited number of individuals.
5. An individual at any level (but the top and bottom) has contact only with his boss above him and his subordinates below him.

Under the impact of recent research, this traditional view of the organization pyramid is undergoing modification, which is often called *contingency theory*. Let us look at each characteristic of the pyramid theory and compare it with contingency theory.

Up and Down Contacts

Traditional view. The only significant contacts in an organization are those between superiors and subordinates: giving orders (downward) or reporting back on results (upward) or requesting information (up or down).

Contingency theory. Researchers are becoming much more aware of the importance of horizontal or lateral contacts in activating organizational goals (see Chapter 15). For some time, organization theorists referred to these horizontal contacts as the "informal organization," implying that they were not really required or anticipated by management when it designed the "formal organization" (or the pyramid). To be sure many lateral relationships are primarily social contacts that take place largely within informal groups (Chapter 4), yet other lateral contacts are work-oriented, such as work-flow contacts among people who must collaborate to get a job done, as well as so-called staff-line relationships.

One Source of Orders

Traditional view. The manager is viewed as the sole source of power. Other sources (such as informal groups) are viewed as illegitimate.

Contingency theory. Since staff groups are in a position to reward friends and to make life less pleasant for enemies, they too exert power. Though staff's requests may be called "advice," line learns that this is advice which it is perilous to ignore. In addition, fellow employees with roughly the same status in the organization exert pressure and even give orders. For example, when an engineering group requests some drawings from drafting, engineering is giving what amounts to an order, even though the two departments may be of equal formal status.

Decisions Made on the Top

Traditional view. All important decisions are made by top managers since these are the best informed and most competent people in the organization and so can set broad policies for the organization as a whole. The policies they make are passed down through successive levels of the organization and, as they are passed down, are spelled out in increasing detail and transformed into operating instructions.

Contingency theory. The traditional view may have been realistic when companies comprised a small number of trained (and educated) managers and a large number of relatively unskilled, untrained workers. Today, organizations hire many managerial, professional, and technical personnel. Since they are often better informed on technical subjects than their superiors, the latter must abdicate certain key decisions to them. This view has been expressed as follows:

... the business enterprise of today is no longer an organization in which there are a handful of "bosses" at the top who make all the decisions while the "workers" carry out orders. It is primarily an organization of professionals with highly specialized knowledge exercising autonomous, responsible judgment. And every one of them—whether manager or individual expert contributor—constantly makes truly entrepreneurial decisions which affect the economic characteristics and risks of the entire enterprise. He makes them not only by "delegation from above" but inevitably in the performance of his own job and work. [1]

Limited Span of Control

Traditional view. An effective organization requires tight control. The supervisor is responsible for coordinating the work of his subordinates. To do this he must have a very limited span of control. The fewer subordinates, the better the management. This point of view results in quite steep pyramids. In large companies it is not unusual to find ten levels separating the hourly employees from top management.

Contingency theory. As we have already seen, under many circumstances subordinates perform more effectively with limited supervisory order-giving and controlling. Also, coordination can often be enhanced if employees contact one

[1] Peter F. Drucker, "Long-range Planning, Challenge to Management Science," *Management Science*, Vol. 5, No. 3 (April 1959), p. 242.

another directly (that is, through lateral not hierarchical relationships). "Flatter" organizations, involving broad spans of control, thus are often desirable.

Whereas traditional management theorists assumed that there were fixed maximum numbers of subordinates who could be supervised effectively, research now suggests that the desirable number varies, depending on the basic technology of the enterprise. A study of 90 English companies showed the following differences: [2]

KIND OF TECHNOLOGY	MEDIAN SPAN OF CONTROL OF FIRST-LINE SUPERVISORS
Unit of small-batch production (fabricating "one of a kind" products such as custom-designed suits)	23 subordinates for each supervisor
Mass-production and assembly-line work	49 subordinates for each supervisor
Automation and continual process production	13 subordinates for each supervisor

No Bypassing

Traditional view. Contacts in the organization are supposed to follow the table of organization. An individual restricts his relationships to his immediate boss and his immediate subordinates. As a result every manager has full information about the activities and people he is responsible for.

Contingency theory. For reasons that will become clear in the latter parts of this chapter, timely communication often requires bypassing certain steps in the hierarchical chain. Also, every organization needs an *appeal channel,* a mechanism by which subordinates can go over their boss's "head" when they feel a serious injustice has been done to them.

EXTENDED HIERARCHIES

Although we have been critical of the simple, traditional view of organizational hierarchies, it would be a serious error to ignore the importance of rank differences. There clearly are successively higher levels in the modern organization, with fewer occupants of the levels as one moves upward. And clearly, too, status differences make leadership and integration possible and promise rewards that encourage employees to seek advancement.

We shall first want to look at the impact of the hierarchy on the position and problems of the immediate supervisor and on his relationship with subordinates. Secondly, we shall assess the impact on the efficiency of operations and communications.

[2] Joan Woodward, *Industrial Organization: Theory and Practise* (London: Oxford University Press, 1965), p. 69.

The Manager as a Man in the Middle

Our emphasis in earlier chapters—and the emphasis in current research, training, and management thinking—has been on the relationship between managers and their immediate subordinates. In actual day-to-day activities, however, many managers spend less time with their subordinates than they do with superiors, staff, and others at their own level. And as we saw in Chapter 7, there is evidence that the effective manager spends a greater proportion of his time on upward and horizontal contacts than the ineffective manager does.

Every manager, except for the company president, belongs to two groups: the work group of which he is the leader, and the higher-management group of which he is the immediate representative. The manager is thus a man in the middle, endlessly beset by conflicting loyalties and demands. The ineffective manager allows himself to be squeezed by these conflicting pressures; the effective supervisor resists them and serves as a communications link between those above and those below him.

Transmittal of supervisory styles. Supervisory styles are "handed down" from level to level; good supervision at the top is reflected by good supervision at the bottom. The evidence suggests that those who receive general supervision are more likely to practice general supervision themselves, and that those who are supervised closely will supervise their subordinates closely.

It is perfectly natural for a manager to reflect the supervisory style of his boss, for the boss is the one who hands out rewards. His actions are looked upon as clues to the behavior he expects from his subordinates. If a manager is subjected to pressure by his own boss, he has a strong tendency to pass it on to those below. Transmitting pressure—and perhaps increasing it a bit in the process—is a time-honored way of relieving frustration and soothing a wounded ego. As a consequence, many managers decide:

"I can't afford to have any mistakes made in my department or my boss will get me in trouble. He's likely to quiz me on everything that happens. So I better check up on everything and have all the facts and explanations at my finger tips. This means I have to keep close tabs on my men."

Furthermore, no manager can permit his subordinates to exercise freedom in areas in which he does not have freedom himself. Some top managements, for instance, issue strict rules which describe in detail what they want subordinates at all levels to do in almost every conceivable situation. Under such circumstances the supervisor has little discretion to delegate.

On the other hand, the supervisor who receives general supervision from above feels free to let his subordinates make decisions by themselves. Knowing that he will be judged by over-all results, he encourages his subordinates to experiment and does not penalize them for making unintentional mistakes. He recognizes that as long as he produces results his boss will back him up and refrain from meddling with petty details.

Representing subordinates. Employees are quick to recognize that their immediate supervisor has limited powers. The levels above make many crucial decisions that will affect their welfare.

Therefore, the effective supervisor must act as a spokesman and protector for his subordinates, and must represent their interests to higher management. (You will remember that, in our discussion of informal leadership in Chapter 4, we mentioned that the informal leader functioned as "an outside contact man" for the group. The effective supervisor fills a similar "linking pin" role.)

In a sense, the effective supervisor serves as a shock-absorber, shielding his men from outside influences that jeopardize their welfare and productivity. As one foreman put it:

"If I treat a man right and he figures a way of doing a job which gives him a little rest, then so much the better for him. My boss doesn't understand that, so that you might say I am a concrete wall between the general foreman and the man. I have to take it one way, but not give it out the same way."[3]

Moreover, he speaks out for the interests of his men when he thinks that management has made a wrong decision. He acts as spokesman for subordinates who have little opportunity to contact higher levels of authority. Note what one worker said:

"My present foreman is the nicest guy I ever worked for. The other foremen respect him also. I saw him stick his neck out with the general foreman over work loads. ... He'll argue a point with the general foreman if he thinks he is right."[4]

Much depends on the supervisor himself, of course. Being a spokesman for the group is not enough. The supervisor must be successful in getting results. Thus, the effective supervisor has what has been called influence;[5]—that is, other levels of management respond to his requests. When the supervisor is successful, the confidence of his men is reinforced. When he is perpetually turned down, his men become disillusioned with his effectiveness in exerting influence.

In fact, general supervision *without* influence may lead to poorer results than close supervision *with* influence (or at least to more dissatisfaction).

Conflicting loyalties. Do effective supervisors feel greater loyalty to their subordinates or to their boss? Often members of management complain, "We've got to make our supervisors feel they are company men. They're always taking the employees' point of view." This may not be too regrettable a situation. There is evidence that at least on the first level the good supervisor identifies as closely with his subordinates as he does with management.[6]

Still, the employee-oriented supervisor's loyalty is not undivided. He is also loyal to upper management—or, to be more precise, as a linking pin, he is motivated to carry out the assignments that have been delegated to him. As a

[3] Charles R. Walker, Robert Guest, and Arthur N. Turner, *Foreman on the Assembly Line* (Cambridge: Harvard University Press, 1956), p. 26.

[4] *Ibid.*, p. 27.

[5] Donald Pelz, "Leadership Within a Hierarchical Organization," *Journal of Social Issues*, Vol. 7, No. 5 (1951), pp. 48-55.

[6] Daniel Katz, Nathan Maccoby, and Nancy Morse, *Productivity, Supervision, and Morale in an Office Situation*, Part I (Ann Arbor: Institute for Social Research, University of Michigan, 1950), p. 27.

result, he may sometimes find himself in conflict with the men he supervises and have no choice but to act restrictively. And yet he must somehow manage to keep his dual role intact, for he will sacrifice his effectiveness if he becomes too interested either in meeting management's production demands or in safeguarding the interests of his men.

If management fails to recognize this duality and attempts to enlist a supervisor's undivided loyalty, he may lose his ability to act as a representative of his employees and eventually his effectiveness in helping management gain its objectives. [7]

The special problem of the first-line supervisor. First-line supervisors probably suffer more from being men-in-the-middle than do the members of any other supervisory group. Their subordinates, whether they are production workers, office girls, or engineers, do the actual work of the organization. These subordinates have no one to supervise and often little chance for promotion. As a consequence, even if they are paid salary or commission, they are less likely to identify with management.

The first-line supervisor can ignore this potentiality for revolt only at his own peril. His subordinates, as a group, are in a strategic position to embarrass him. By following his instructions too literally and by failing to use common sense, they can spoil work, damage equipment, and waste materials. By slowing down in unison they can prevent him from meeting schedules; through a hundred different subterfuges they can increase his costs. Thus, though the first-line supervisor is subject to many pressures from above, he cannot pass these pressures down to lower levels; if he tries to do so, he will only make matters worse.

The inevitable result is that the first-line supervisor must somehow come to terms with his subordinates. He must be particularly careful to insure strong, continuing motivation. Often, too, he must make deals with the union steward involving special concessions to the men in return for their implicit agreement to keep production high.

As might be expected, expedient arrangements such as these are rarely acceptable to higher management. Consequently supervisors sometimes become "two-faced," turning one face to management and another to their subordinates. Caught inescapably in the middle, they must cope with all the problems of higher levels of management and at the same time resolve all the problems that are peculiar to their own position in the hierarchy.

Personal Contact between Levels

Even with effective representation, there is evidence that employees like to have some personal contact with higher management. Some such contact facilitates identification with the total organization.

We are all familiar with generals, kings, and presidents who on occasion mingle with the "people." An actual view of the leader, perhaps hearing his

[7] F. C. Mann and J. K. Dent, "The Supervisor: Member of Two Organizational Families," *Harvard Business Review*, Vol. 32, No. 6 (November 1954), p. 112.

words directly, even touching his hand or coat, is meant to impart confidence in his human or organizational qualities. Particularly if the head of the organization has a strong personality, he can impart a sense of identification with himself; he in turn personifies the total organization. In an effort to recreate the personal intimacy between hierarchical levels that characterizes small organizations, many managers try to cultivate the feeling of "one big happy family." They resort to such devices as:

Personal appearances by top management before employee groups.

Special, personal letters from the company president to employees on anniversaries with the company, or after special accomplishments (*e.g.*, a new patent).

Christmas parties, bowling teams, golf tournaments, and other events at which various levels of the organization meet informally.

All these efforts are designed to give the feeling that top management consists of flesh-and-blood individuals who are genuinely interested in the welfare of their subordinates. As we noted in our discussion of communications, subordinates often suspect or distort management's motives. As with other aspects of managerial behavior, personal contacts by higher management cannot be evaluated in isolation; they take on meaning only in context. If the president's "personal" birthday card fits into the employee's previous perception of his relation to the president, fine. If not, the birthday greeting may seem hypocritical. Similarly, it is waste of effort for the boss to be a mass of smiles at the annual picnic if he is completely unapproachable at other times of the year. Under such circumstances, gestures that are intended to be warm and personal may well be perceived as merely hypocritical.

Multilevel organizations have certain advantages over smaller organizations in reducing tension over the exercise of authority. Depending upon an individual's needs, upper levels—far removed from his immediate experience—can be seen as composed of either saints or sinners. If immediate supervision is unsatisfactory, subordinates can say: "If only the old man (the president of the company) really knew what was going on he would straighten things out." On the other hand, many blame unpopular decisions on top management rather than the immediate boss. (However, the manager who maintains good relationships with subordinates by always blaming his superiors is not doing his job effectively.)

PATTERNS OF DOWNWARD COMMUNICATION

If we turn from the impact of hierarchy on leadership to day-to-day operations and communications we shall discover still other human-relations problems.

At the beginning of the chapter we concluded that a hierarchical form of structure is necessary to move directions and information efficiently through a large body of people. Unfortunately, when we draw boxes in an organization chart and connect them with lines, we have a tendency to believe that the system we design will function like a physical model—that is, we think of an organization as though it were a system of interrelated pipes and reservoirs. Water starting at the top always reaches the bottom in exactly the same quantity and quality as when it started out—if everything is connected correctly, that is. Thus, the model suggests that someone at the top issues an order or makes a policy decision, and the next person in the hierarchy passes the instructions along to the men who report to him, and so on down the line. Similarly, significant information from "down the line" is reported upward through the same system of "pipes" so that those at the top will have at their finger tips all the information they need to administer the affairs of the organization.

But an organization is not made up of mechanical parts or pipes. It consists of *people*, whose attitudes and behavior are affected by the system of human relations in which they function. These people upset the simple mechanistic working of the hierarchical model. They introduce distortions in both the downward and upward transmission of information. Here we shall concentrate our attention on these distortions and on the human-relations problems they create.

Distortion in Downward Communications

Let us start with an example. Top management decides that racial discrimination in employment shall be eliminated. What happens as this policy is passed down the line through successive stages of the hierarchy? By the time the policy reaches the individuals who do the actual hiring, it may have been transformed almost beyond recognition, for example: "Hire *some* Negroes at each location, so that the company appears to be nondiscriminatory."

In part, this sort of distortion is caused by the communications problems we discussed in Chapter 10. People may "hear" the new policy in ways unintended by top management. But the organization itself complicates matters further. The order-giver is a long way from the final recipient. You may have played the game in which a story is passed from person to person in a group. Each person alters the facts slightly to fit his own needs and preconceptions, often without intending to do so. When the story finally re-emerges, it has been distorted beyond recognition. Information passing through many status levels can be more confused.

Complex statements of policy, whose accuracy depends on subtle shades of meaning, are particularly vulnerable to distortion. A fairly simple company decision to grant every employee with more than six months' service a two-week vacation with pay could probably be communicated down through several levels without major alteration. But an announcement of policy on union matters, or on promotions, is often badly mangled or downright misleading by the time it filters down through the levels of the organization.

Two sorts of distortion are particularly common. The first is *exaggeration*. Every subordinate is dependent on his boss's goodwill, for the superior has countless ways of making his job either easier or harder. Consequently, most subordinates are highly sensitive to the boss's every whim and seek to anticipate his desires, sometimes before they are expressed.

Many a subordinate asks the boss's secretary, "What is he gunning for today? Is it safe for me to mention . . . ?" The authors once observed a personnel department hectically preparing to run a morale survey (though the department doubted that it was a good idea) purely because a top official had read a short article in a popular management magazine and had remarked to the personnel director, "This looks like a good idea for us."

The second common type of distortion is just the opposite: the *playing down* of directives. Lower management drags its feet in carrying out an order, or follows the letter but not the spirit. For example, we once observed the reaction of middle and lower management to a top-management directive to install a supervisory performance-evaluation program. This program required each superior to rate his subordinates every six months, and then to discuss his ratings with them. With few exceptions, the managers were reluctant to adopt this new program, which they felt would breed more antagonism than good will. So they procrastinated, in the hope that the program would gradually be forgotten by all concerned.

In short, employees frequently receive mystifying directives that have been passed down from higher levels of the organization. For example, managers are told costs must be cut. But how should a priority be placed on this order compared to other instructions that have been issued? Should other objectives that have been established—for example, smooth labor relations or safe working practices—be ignored? Or modified? Or given a lower priority? When directives appear to conflict, as they often do, or priorities are unclear, as they often are, employees spend a great deal of time and energy "researching" the problem: What is top management really thinking now and what group has the most influence on the president's thinking?

To summarize, the larger the organization, the more difficult communications are, and top management finds it harder and harder to maintain firm control over the lower levels of the hierarchy simply by issuing orders. Top executives are never really sure of what is happening below, and those at lower levels become uncertain about what is expected of them. As a result, management's decisions often become vitiated or distorted as they move down the line.

Short-Circuiting the Lines of Communications

Going through channels: the red-tape problem. The typical large company has not one but a number of separate hierarchies with parallel lines of upward and downward communication. Each hierarchy represents a specialty. Since, in theory, these specialties are completely independent of one another, except for coordination at the top, one might think that there would be little need for contact between them. Nothing could be further from the truth.

Take a typical problem: A group of plumbers are working on the airconditioning equipment in the accounting office. The men stop work a half-hour before quitting time and engage in extensive "clean-up" operations. After this has been going on for several days, the clerks begin to grumble that they should have the same privileges.

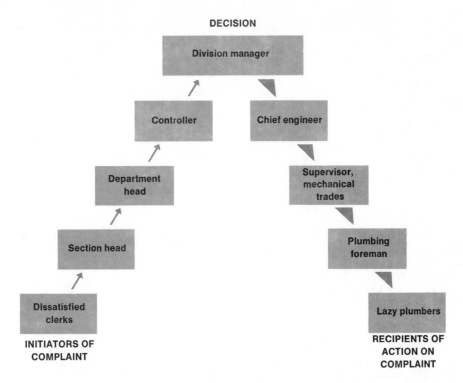

DECISION

Division manager

Controller

Chief engineer

Department head

Supervisor, mechanical trades

Section head

Plumbing foreman

Dissatisfied clerks

Lazy plumbers

INITIATORS OF COMPLAINT

RECIPIENTS OF ACTION ON COMPLAINT

ACCOUNTING AND MAINTENANCE HIERARCHIES

How can the accounting supervisor handle this problem? In theory, he must report the matter to his supervisor and so on up the line until it reaches the common boss over both accounting and maintenance. Then the matter descends down the maintenance chain of command till it hits the plumbers.

In this case it might take six supervisory contacts before the problem could officially come to the attention of the supervisor who is directly responsible. If there were a need for frequent adjustments between the accounting section head and the plumbing foreman, the number of contacts would soar astronomically.

In one sense, this cumbersome procedure is desirable. If the accounting supervisor were to start giving orders directly to the plumbers, the plumbers would be subject to all the evils of "too many bosses." A clearly defined sequence of supervisory contacts, by contrast, helps to bring order into interpersonal relations.

But in emergencies the need to go through channels can be costly in terms of managerial time and may only complicate the problem. Days and weeks may pass before a serious problem can be attended to. Think what would happen in a hospital: "... Suppose a piece of oxygen equipment goes out of order. If the nurse were to report it to the head nurse, she to the chief engineer, and he to the repairman, the patient would probably be dead before the equipment was fixed." [8]

[8] Temple Burling, Edith Lentz, and Robert N. Wilson, *The Give and Take in Hospitals* (New York: Putnam, 1956), p. 323.

As you can see, it becomes more difficult to move swiftly and effectively on challenging problems within the specialized organization. Particularly in large companies, the burden of going through channels, in terms of the sheer number of interactions that must take place for every problem, tends to slow the organization and creates endless frustrations and conflicts. It is under these circumstances that one hears that "red tape" or bureaucracy is defeating the purpose of the company.

As a result, there is a widespread temptation to short-circuit the chain of command. In the case above, the accounting supervisor might go directly to the plumbing foreman. But those who are left out—those who get "short-circuited"—are understandably resentful of such violations of the chain of command and feel their leadership position threatened.

Bypassing. A manager may become so frustrated by the time-consuming process of going through channels and the apparent inability of subordinates to carry out instructions precisely as they were intended, that he bypasses intermediate levels and goes straight to the men involved. Here is a description of a top executive (former President of Curtiss-Wright) who was particularly well known for taking direct action and cutting through red tape:

Hurley is chief expediter at C-W and chief executioner of good ideas with bad cost records. He seldom "moves through channels." He figures that the division manager doesn't have any more idea than he has of what is wrong or the figures would not have been negative in the first place. So instead of waiting for a briefing, Hurley moves directly to the spot, right down to the machine on the floor if that is the heart of the problem. Many a division manager has discovered hours later that the boss has been in his department and long since moved on. And many department heads have discovered that an important job has been given to an employee they hardly know, and without consulting them. Hurley spots a man who seems bright and says, "You do it." That the job may be completely unrelated to the employee's work is of no concern to Hurley. [9]

Attractive and dramatic though bypassing may seem, we must remember that sticking to the formal channels has one great advantage: It insures that everyone who is supposed to be informed actually is informed.

Mass communications. In many companies the word *communications* refers not to the transmission of information through normal hierarchical channels, but to what we would call mass communications: the company newspaper ("house organ"), bulletin-board announcements, direct mailings to employees, fillers in pay envelopes, movies, a loudspeaker system, and so forth. Most major companies have special staffs assigned to preparing material of this sort.

Mass communications are seldom used by themselves to convey messages that are really important. When management wants to raise production or cut costs, it sends clear, unmistakable orders down the line, and makes sure that every subordinate understands them. Mass-communications techniques are used chiefly in areas that are peripheral to management's main job of getting the production out—areas such as safety, personnel policies, suggestions, and the company's financial position.

[9] William B. Harris, "Curtiss-Wright Throws Away the Book," *Fortune,* Vol. 57, No. 1 (January 1958), p. 115.

Why are mass-communications techniques used so widely in these areas? There are several reasons:

1. Often the information to be transmitted is of a technical nature. If details of a new insurance scheme, for example, are transmitted by word of mouth from top management through the various levels of supervision, they are bound to be badly distorted by the time they reach the rank and file.

2. Since messages of this sort do not have A-1 priority, management wants to insure that they will not be distorted or forgotten by lower supervision. Lower supervision is chiefly interested in getting out production, and messages relating to "fringe" areas may be laid aside or given perfunctory attention. The supervisor tells his men at the end of a meeting, "And, of course, as you know, I'm supposed to tell you once a week to be sure to wear your safety hats."
Many of the messages sent through mass-communications channels are sponsored by staff departments, such as finance or personnel. And these departments have learned through sad experience that if they have to trust line management to carry their messages, the information will never reach lower-level employees.

3. Finally, in contrast to what we said earlier, some messages are so vitally important that it is essential that details not be distorted by transmission through channels.

A large, geographically dispersed corporation, recently made a number of vital changes in salary policy affecting every one of its 75,000 employees. To insure uniform and simultaneous reception, loudspeakers were installed in every location and work stopped for 15 minutes to permit the company president to address the entire workforce.

As is probably already clear, it is unwise for management to rely excessively on mass communications. With the exception of movies and loudspeaker announcements, mass communications involve the printed rather than the spoken word; they are always one-way rather than two-way. You will remember from our discussion in Chapter 10 that printed one-way communications lack flexibility and the opportunity for the feedback of the face-to-face spoken word. A man can't ask questions of a bulletin board, nor does a letter repeat itself if the reader is drowsy or inattentive.

If the message is of any importance at all, the use of mass communications tends to reduce the status of the immediate supervisor. In effect, top management is saying, "We don't trust you to explain complicated problems." Often, too, if the message is of importance, the subordinate has questions to ask about it. If his boss can't answer them, then the subordinate's respect for him will drop even more.

On the other hand, the fact that messages are sent through mass communications channels rather than through the line may indicate to the employees that the message is really not important. If the boss says "work faster" and the bulletin says "work safer," the subordinate will be more likely to pay attention to the boss than to the bulletin board.

Improved mass-communication methods. In order to overcome these difficulties, many companies are using mass communications with greater finesse. For example, top management may (1) give higher supervisors advance notice before relaying messages to lower levels, (2) urge the immediate supervisor to add a few words to supplement the formal message, and (3) encourage subordinates to address questions concerning these materials to their immediate boss. Such efforts preserve the advantages of specificity and uniformity, enable the immediate supervisor to retain his status, and encourage feedback from subordinates.

The grapevine. Though not consciously designed by management, the grapevine is frequently an extremely effective means of communication. "Being flexible and personal, it spreads information faster than most management communications systems operate. With the rapidity of a burning powder train, it filters out of the woodwork, past the manager's office, through the locker room, and along the corridors." [10] Often subordinates learn of top management's decisions through the grapevine long before anything is put into writing. And when formal messages are transmitted, rumor "helps" explain and interpret them. Since the grapevine is personal, spoken, and permits feedback, it often has a far stronger impact on the recipient than do other forms of communication.

Many times the grapevine is surprisingly accurate; in fact, exaggeration is less common than simplification and abbreviation. Of course, individuals in a position to initiate the process—for example, a key executive secretary—gain status and influence in the informal organization.

Many managers feel that rumors should be stamped out, on the grounds that they are often false, exaggerated, malicious, and even give away management secrets. Yet the grapevine performs a very useful function: It tends to correct some of the shortcomings of formal communication. Bill and Joe are in totally different divisions of the organization, but their work is closely tied together. A change is made in Bill's department that will vitally affect Joe. It may take weeks for the message to go up through the formal channels of communication and then reach Joe—possibly much distorted. But if Bill passes the word along to Joe on the job, the message is transmitted efficiently and accurately.

Actually it is unrealistic to expect that rumors can be stamped out. The grapevine fills a vital human need. Gossip gives people a social outlet and a chance to exercise their imagination. It gives an opportunity to relieve fears of the unknown by expressing anxiety in the form of stories. Above all, it allays curiosity.

Communication and Supervision

It is useful, for a moment, to look at the relationship between hierarchical communication and patterns of supervision. The aggressively authoritarian manager may have difficulty even in communicating *downward*. Sometimes subordinates seek to impress the boss by doing more than he has requested and thus

[10] Keith Davis, *Human Relations in Business* (New York: McGraw-Hill, 1957), p. 244.

exaggerate his orders. Alternatively, they may object to the boss's order, yet fear to express their objections openly. Instead, they "play down" the order and systematically sabotage it or give it only token compliance. Subordinates may be afraid to ask their boss questions even when they fail to understand what he has said. In the last two instances, it should be noted that the boss's failure to encourage upward communication makes downward communication more difficult.

Often, this type of manager has little confidence in his subordinates, so he discourages communication, particularly through the regular channels. He doesn't trust subordinates to convey information or orders and, not trusting them with information, he doesn't see why they need more than the minimum amount required to do their job. His idea of good communication frequently is in terms of what we have called mass communications.

PATTERNS OF UPWARD COMMUNICATION

A healthy organization needs effective upward communications as much as it needs effective downward communications—and for two primary reasons:

1. Obtaining information. Top management depends on a steady stream of information from subordinates in order to make intelligent decisions. How well are we doing in Line 7? Is that new quality-control man working out OK? Are we going to have to hire some more junior engineers? Without some sort of reporting system, top management can never find out what orders are needed or how effectively its orders are being carried out. Effective upward communication furnishes management with quick and accurate reports on what is happening at lower levels.

Successful upward communication requires that management's questions be truthfully answered. More than this, it requires that vital information be transmitted upward even if management has never requested it; it requires that *management be willing to listen to unsolicited messages.* The men at the top do not always know the right questions to ask or the right instructions to give. Subordinates frequently have useful suggestions to make, questions to ask, or problems of which their supervisors are ignorant. Unless subordinates feel free to communicate these matters upward, management will lack some of the data essential to sound decision-making.

2. Maintaining morale. It is psychologically unsound for the initiation of contacts to run in only one direction—always from superiors to subordinates. No one is happy when he is always on the receiving end. We all want some opportunity to express ourselves, particularly to those who control our activities and welfare. When we are disturbed or under pressure from others—for example, when an earlier deadline has been unexpectedly imposed, or another department is demanding speedier service from us—the need to express ourselves becomes even more urgent.

Difficulties in Upward Communication

Effective upward communication is difficult to obtain, particularly in larger organizations. Indeed there is a certain amount of censorship at each level in a large organization. Let us examine this difference in detail.

Covering up. Subordinates have a natural tendency to withhold unfavorable information from their superiors, or to filter the information as it is passed up the line. Often middle- and lower-level managers conspire with subordinates to hide from higher levels serious mistakes, deviations from standard procedures, or unsolved problems. Sometimes these deceptions are deliberate falsehoods to avoid blame; sometimes they just take the form of failure to report self-incriminating information.

Status problems. In an effort to maintain his superior position, and to ration his scarce time, the manager may isolate himself from his subordinates by setting up barriers. An advance appointment, appropriate dress, passing the scrutiny of an officious secretary—all may be necessary before a man can ask the boss a modest question.

A department head calls in one of his subordinates to give him special instruction on handling an important project. The instructions are confusing, but the subordinate makes no attempt to ask clarifying questions. Why? Simply because he is afraid that the supervisor will interpret his questions as evidence of slowness or stupidity. He is not sure that the questions he will ask will be "good ones"—that is, the kind of question an intelligent, competent man is supposed to ask. So rather than risk hurting his reputation, he remains silent.

Strangely enough, this common cause of breakdown in upward communication is also one of the easiest to remedy. The solution is simply for the supervisor to encourage questions, indicating that they are expected and appropriate—in fact, giving the subordinate the feeling that asking questions indicates a high degree of alertness.

Pressures for Upward Communication

In a small organization the manager can see for himself how his decisions are being carried out. In the large organization, managers can "see" only through the eyes of others. Top management normally relies on "auditors" and the reports of managers at the next level in the hierarchy, who in turn must rely on those reporting to them, and so on down the line of command. But top management finds it very difficult to discover what is really happening on the levels below. One often hears executives asking, "We wonder what is really going on at the work level."

Quite revealing are the apocryphal stories about the efforts of navy captains to learn what is happening below decks. In the typical tale the captain disguises himself as a seaman and wanders through the ship, or invites a seaman to his cabin for drinks and talk.

On the other hand, employees are often anxious to bring their problems to the attention of higher management. Joe feels that his manager is discriminating against him and wants a fair hearing from someone higher up on why he has been denied a promotion. Jack has thought up a new fixture that he is sure will cut machining time by one-third, but his foreman brushes him off with a curt rejection. Bill feels at ease with his immediate supervisor, but realizes that it is pointless to complain to him about his salary when someone higher up makes the decisions. In effect, all these men are saying, "If only someone in top management would listen to us!"

Appeal Channels and Bypassing Techniques

Appeal channels. Most organizations have some form of appeal channel by which a member can challenge his immediate superior's decision. Some procedures are quite formalized, as with the establishment of a union in a company or with the use of the Inspector General in the armed forces. Since a superior has so much power over his subordinates, it is not surprising that these channels have been carved out. They give subordinates a greater sense of security and provide higher management with useful information.

However, organizations have also been successful in using less formalized procedures. Many companies have experimented with the "open-door" policy whereby every employee is guaranteed the privilege of walking into the office of any manager at any level in the organization to voice his complaints. In some companies this policy has succeeded in opening up a worthwhile channel of appeal. More often, however, subordinates take advantage of the privilege only rarely. Why? One reason, of course, is the deterrent of social distance—the fear that keeps the buck private from complaining to his colonel that he has been assigned to KP too often, even though the colonel makes himself available. More than this, the subordinate realizes that once he exercises the privilege of appeal, he will have jeopardized his whole future with his immediate superior.

A subordinate knows intuitively how his supervisor feels about the open door. He calculates that if he walks through this portal he has only a slim chance of winning anything and a good chance of losing a great deal. After all, the immediate superior controls many things that the complainant holds important—job, salary level, work assignments, and so forth. The risk is too great, so the open door is rarely entered. [11]

Understandably, a supervisor is upset when a subordinate decides to go over his head with an appeal. The supervisor begins to worry lest the subordinate reveal practices or mistakes that he has carefully tried to cover up. And he recognizes that if the top boss does decide to grant the complainant's demand, a

[11] In at least one very large and successful American corporation the formal open-door policy works. There is a well-publicized series of appeal steps, almost like a grievance procedure, that ends in the president's office, which is many hierarchical levels above the average employee. Each year a significant number of employees get to see the president with their personal grievances. He has so frequently supported them and reversed decisions of lower levels of supervision that, not surprisingly, there has been a morale problem among supervisors! This is not the typical case, but it does indicate what a management can do in creating a viable appeal channel.

steady stream of complaining subordinates may appeal his decisions and thus seriously endanger his leadership position.

What is a boss to do when the subordinate of one of his supervisors comes to him with a problem? If such bypassing is encouraged, the effect on the supervisors' morale may be disastrous. Yet if it is completely banned, the effect on the workers' morale may be equally harmful. Probably the best approach is to listen to at least a summary of the problem and then to suggest tactfully that the subordinate see his immediate supervisor.

Committees. Management sometimes sets up special conference groups or committees to find out what is on the minds of employees. These committees give lower-ranking personnel a chance to express their attitudes directly to top management, thus bypassing intermediate levels. For example, the first-line supervisory group may elect representatives to meet weekly or monthly with the general manager to discuss current problems. The representatives are encouraged to ask about the rumors floating about on their level, ask questions, ventilate gripes, and give management some ideas of the unsolved problems in their departments.

Some companies have used similar devices for hourly-paid personnel. Here caution needs to be exercised to insure that these committees do not conflict with existing unions or violate the provisions of the National Labor Relations Act, which prohibts employers from assisting in the formation of employee organizations with union-like functions.

Other techniques. Suggestion systems are used by many companies as a means of collecting specific ideas for improving company efficiency. In a sense, a union itself provides a very important channel of upward communication by bringing the average worker's problems directly to the attention of top management. Many cost-sharing union-management cooperation plans bring committees of workers face to face with top management in discussions of production problems (see Chap. 28).

Staff specialists provide another upward channel because of the ease with which they can contact higher management. They may hear of good ideas that have been smothered by unsympathetic superiors or good men who have not received adequate recognition. (Of course, their position as "spies" can be a source of conflict between these specialists and the line manager.)

STATISTICAL CONTROLS

Now let us explore what is probably management's most effective means of upward communication—statistical controls. Normally, management introduces statistical controls in order to further coordination, pinpoint responsibility, and find out what is actually happening at the operating level. Since figures are harder to distort than subjective reports, higher management insists on receiving a constant flow of data on production, sales, costs, quality, grievances, salary increases, turnover, and so forth.

Functions of Statistical Controls

Through cost accounting, for example, "standard costs" are developed for every item produced or service rendered. If the standard cost of an item is 35 cents and the foreman can make it for 33 cents, he is making a "profit" (part of which may accrue to him, personally, as a bonus). If he spends 37 cents to make it, he is incurring a "loss." These departmental profit and loss accounts, called *variance accounts,* provide standards by which higher management can measure departmental efficiency. Other standards may be set in terms of quantities produced, man-hours expended per unit, sales, scrap loss, turnover, and so on.

To insure that these data reach headquarters rapidly and without distortion, they are ordinarily collected by staff departments, such as accounting, quality control, and personnel. Because these departments operate at least semi-independently of the line, the data can be reported directly to the top without being filtered through intermediate steps of management that may have reputations to protect. Computers enormously increase the amount of data that can be assembled and the speed with which they can be transmitted to top management.

In addition to providing top management with the information it needs for decision-making, statistical controls serve many other functions.

Supervision by results. Statistical controls eliminate the necessity for close, detailed supervision, and provide the evidence needed for supervision by results. Through reports on profits, sales, and so forth, top management can evaluate the effectiveness of subordinate departments without checking on every detail of their work. Without satisfactory statistical controls, decentralization is difficult.

Standards. Statistical controls also make it possible for management to set standards for achievement and to emphasize areas that require special attention. For instance, if top management is anxious to focus attention on a scrap-reduction program, it will begin asking all subordinate departments to report each month how much they have reduced scrap losses over the preceding month. Thus, statistical *controls* are a means of downward communication and exerting pressure.

Personnel evaluation. In turn, they help develop goals and provide motivation and measures of success for those whose work is measured by controls. Statistical controls that measure individual performance provide a means for selecting, appraising, and compensating employees.

Difficulties in Measurement

Yet statistical controls should not be considered as a magic cure for all organizational ills. Improperly handled, they may create as many problems as they cure. Elements like department costs, efficiency, and productivity are difficult to measure fairly, while the very act of measurement may distort effort.

Naturally if employees are to be evaluated largely in terms of their success or failure in meeting these goals, it is important that the goals be fair and reasonable. Establishment of such goals is a highly technical and often inaccurate procedure. It is all too easy to set standards that are too "tight" or too "loose." (It should be obvious, too, that the greater the reliance on statistical measures of efficiency, the greater becomes the power of the staff departments which prepare them.)

Many types of work are so general and intangible that is is almost impossible to devise an adequate technique for measuring them. How is one to measure the effectiveness of the personnel department? [12] Surely not in terms of cost, because low cost may simply mean that nothing is being accomplished. Not in terms of turnover, number of strikes and grievances, productivity, and so forth, for all these things are related to over-all plant policy or the organization as a whole. Roughly the same sort of objectives can be raised against any direct rating of staff departments. And there are other departments, such as research, where meaningful results become apparent only in the long run.

In talking to engineering supervisors in a large organization, we heard this common complaint: Supervisors had a hard time evaluating their subordinates, and subordinates didn't know what was required to get a pay raise or promotion. One supervisor put it this way: "An engineer is constantly making decisions in which he is balancing time against efficiency against cost. It is practically impossible to know whether his judgment is good. Also, if a man doesn't get results, how are you to know whether he has been 'goofing off' or been up against a streak of bad luck?"

Even more severe problems arise in attempts to make a comparative rating of various departments. How does one rate costs in division A, which makes the same product year after year, against division B, where the product is always undergoing change? Some department stores try to measure departmental efficiency in terms of sales and profit, but the level of sales in any department may depend on its location in the store, the weather, and the business cycle more than on the individual efficiency of the department manager.

Unfortunately, the measures selected to evaluate performance may be a reflection of what is easy to measure, rather than the real criteria of effective performance. Because of the problems of dealing with short-run and long-run factors, situational exceptions, the combination of personnel, production, financial and marketing effectiveness, one often sees organizations using overly simplified controls, devices which are not much different from worker incentive plans that just measure raw output.

[12] Or how does one measure the efficiency of a university professor? By the number of students who take his courses? But this may depend on whether the professor makes it a "snap course" or on the nature of the subject matter. By student rating? Perhaps, but teaching ability is more than being a good showman. By relative scores on an identical exam, jointly graded and given to all students in the same course? Possibly—but note the motivation this gives the professor to cover only those points likely to be on the exam. In many colleges, promotion is largely based on the number of scholarly articles published, with an obvious effect on the relative time spent on research as against teaching. How does one compare the efforts of a classics professor with those of a chemistry professor? Obviously, direct measurement has its limitations in the university as well as in industry.

Distorting Behavior

If excessive emphasis is placed on statistical controls, compared to other forms of upward communication, the very act of measurement may lead subordinates to distort their efforts and work less efficiently.

Overemphasis on the items measured. Departments will normally concentrate on the items that are being measured rather than on the job as a whole. Successful banks realize that good customer relations are vital and that a very poor impression is created when a teller refuses to serve a customer until he has finished adding up his figures. Yet "the teller has found all his rewards in the past for careful balancing of the books. ... He has never been rewarded or punished for his treatment of customers." [13]

Supervisors are supposed to maintain both high morale and high productivity. Morale is intangible and difficult to measure, but productivity and costs can presumably be measured to a tenth of a decimal place. As a consequence, productivity comes first; good employee relations are a luxury to be enjoyed only when there is nothing wrong with output.

Token compliance. Supervisors may greet statistical control with token compliance—that is, by striving to *look* as if they were meeting their standards. Unfortunately, the effect of keeping up appearances may well be to lower overall performance.

As part of a drive to cut excess inventory, managers in one company were required to give a monthly report of supplies on hand. What happened? There was a scramble to use up all the stock before the end of the month and to insure that no new supplies were delivered until after the beginning of the next. But the average inventory over the month remained just about the same.

Inefficient scheduling of work. Sometimes the existence of standards results in a long-run deterioration of real performance, *even on the items being measured.*

Because management in one company paid so much attention to end-of-month efficiency ratings, department supervisors left no stone unturned to get as many units into finished stores as possible. They even resorted to such expensive and disruptive processes as "bleeding the line"—that is, stopping operations in order to complete more units by the deadline. This process is summarized by what another foreman said:

"For the last two weeks of the month we're driving hell out of the men. We have to get pieces out and we are always jammed up at the end of the month. . . ." [14]

Even where employees are not subjected to such hectic pressures, the mere existence of standards may induce them to schedule work less efficiently. A claims adjuster once told us, "Of course, some claims are harder to handle than

[13] Mason Haire, *Psychology in Management* (New York: McGraw-Hill, 1956), p. 17.

[14] Frank Jasinski, "Use and Misuse of Efficiency Controls," *Harvard Business Review*, Vol. 34, No. 4 (July 1956), p. 107. This problem is even more serious in Russia where "storming" (as it is called there) during the last week of every month is done at high pressure. David Granick, *The Red Executive* (Garden City, N.Y.: Doubleday, 1960), pp. 267-270.

others, but as far as the quota is concerned they all count the same. So I always try to keep a few easy cases aside to handle at the end of the month if it looks like I won't be able to meet the quota without them. I try not to turn in too many cases in any month or they'll always expect me to work that hard." Piece-workers also build up "banks," to equalize their earnings over the week.

Emphasis on short run rather than long run. The use of statistical controls often produces short-term results at the expense of the organization's long-term good. Managers often complain that supervisors are "department-centered" and show no loyalty to the organization as a whole. For instance, department managers in retail stores are rewarded for high sales and profits in their *own* departments. By pushing shoddy merchandise they can sometimes get high sales for themselves at the expense of the goodwill of the entire store. Yet under these circumstances, what other sort of motivation could be expected? Similarly, salesmen, conscious of the importance of an impressive sales record, may ignore the store's public relations—showing themselves unwilling to spend time with indecisive or dissatisfied customers—in favor of the easy, free-spending customer.

Covering-up. Faced with the necessity of having to look good on paper, the natural impulse of employees is to try to "adjust" the reported statistics. At times plain lying is sufficient, but sometimes it is necessary to hide the evidence. In one department the men put defective parts in refuse cans and covered them over—with the foreman's full knowledge. Ironically, the more reliance is placed on control measures, the less top management may find out about what is really happening.

In the midst of a safety campaign, one employee suffered a slight injury at the end of his shift which might have kept him home for several days. The foreman begged him:
"If you can possibly come to work tomorrow I will guarantee you will not have to do a lick of work until you really feel up to it. I'll pick you up at home and drive you back. But for the love of Mike, let's not have a lost-time accident on our record."

Passing the buck. Another unfortunate by-product of excessive emphasis on standards is an added inducement to pass the buck. If parts turn out defective, there is always an argument about which department should be charged with the cost of repair. Similarly, there may be endless haggling over whether time spent in training new employees, or in the handling of grievances, should be charged against the particular department or against the personnel department.

In a well-known national company, accident-prevention is so strongly em-phasized that regular tribunals have been established to determine whether an accident will be "charged" against the foreman of the department in which it occurred. In one case, all sorts of internal political pressures were used to influence the panel members in their decision. These tribunals seem more concerned with fixing responsibility than in determining and eliminating the causes of accidents.

Impaired teamwork. Statistical controls and supervision by results rest on the assumption that each individual supervisor should be held responsible for the efficiency of his own department. Within limits it is healthy to encourage individual responsibility. Yet overemphasis on individual performance may lead to excessive individualism and selfishness, particularly in departments that are highly interdependent.

Reduction in discretion. Insofar as statistical data are used as the basis for evaluating the success or failure of managers and departments, they serve to reduce the discretion of the immediate supervisor. As one researcher has noted:

The evaluation of subordinates is a major responsibility of supervisors. If this evaluation were based entirely on statistical indices, this responsibility would be reduced to a clerical task, the application of a mathematical formula to a set of data. This would not only make the job of supervisor less interesting for him but also undermine his authority over subordinates. [15]

Centralization. The introduction of electronic data-processing apparatus has a similar effect on the position of the supervisor. Such equipment makes available to top managers vastly more data than they have ever had before, and permits them to make detailed decisions affecting the smallest department in the company—thus completely bypassing middle management.

Standards as a form of pressure. Without question, management uses standards as a means to apply pressure. The techniques, of course, vary with the supervisor, as these contrasting quotations indicate:

"I go to the office and check the budget every day. . . . If it's OK, I don't say anything. But if it is no good, then I come back here and give the boys a little—well, you know, I needle them a bit."

"You know, it is a funny thing. If I want my people to read the budget, I just lay it on my desk and leave it alone. They'll pick it up without doubt." [16]

Notice that both approaches use standards as a form of pressure. Basic to both is the assumption that failure to meet a quota is prima-facie proof of falling down on the job. In effect, the standards are transformed into an extremely arbitrary boss. Many a supervisor says, "I don't want excuses, just get the job done." It does little good for the subordinate to reply, "But I did get the job done—only the profit figures don't give the complete picture." When standards are boss, all explanations are regarded as excuses.

Perhaps one of the [supervisor's] greatest criticisms of budgets was the fact that they never included the reasons *why* they were not achieved. . . . Supervisors disliked intensely the fact that their departments would look "sick" in the budget while the reasons for the "sickness" were never published along with the results. [17]

[15] Peter Blau, *The Dynamics of Bureaucracy* (Chicago: Univ. of Chicago Press, 1955), p. 41.

[16] Chris Argyris, *The Impact of Budgets on People* (New York: Financial Executives Foundation, 1952), p. 24.

[17] *Ibid.*, p. 11.

Improved Use of Controls

The use of control measures is an essential part of management's job in any large organization. No top manager can know everything he needs to know without quantitative data that summarize what is happening and that compare actual results with expected or planned results. When carefully presented, these data enable him to detect trouble-spots almost instantly, without reviewing every facet of day-to-day operations. All he need do is look for the variances, the departures from the quantitative limits that he has set for his subordinates—the number of units to be processed, the amount of permissible overtime, the number of merit increases, and so forth.

The challenge for the manager is also to develop methods of using control channels of communication that do not have the serious drawbacks described above. If he is successful, the rewards can be substantial—greater autonomy, job satisfaction, and better performance for subordinates at each level.

One test of good usage is the organization's response when a man fails to meet standards. Is his failure regarded as evidence of incompetence, perhaps meriting discipline? Or is it just a cue for management to find out how badly he has fallen down, to help him find out why, to stand ready to give him whatever assistance he needs? Management must decide whether to use controls as a means of "catching" people, or as a means of identifying problems and allocating the resources of the organization to provide assistance. Management's choice is dictated in part by its approach to setting standards in the first place. Standards are probably most effective when they are set by the supervisor and subordinate working together. They are least effective when they are imposed by staff officials or top managers who have relatively little understanding of the specific department. Standards are particularly troublesome when they are used as a basis for setting compensation (as in a bonus system) without appropriate appeal channels.

In summary, statistical data do not necessarily give a complete picture of "results." Failure to achieve "results" should always raise the question *"Why?"* "What has happened to cause this departure from what we anticipated?"

In the words of the old saw, "Figures don't lie." Maybe they don't lie, but that doesn't mean that they are capable of dictating action without the aid of managerial judgment bolstered by information gleaned from multiple sources. [18]

Such comments become even more important in an age of computers.

CONCLUSION

Organizational structure is more than a series of interconnected boxes and lines on a chart. It is a pattern of human relationships—planned and un-planned—that has evolved over a period of time in response to the human and technical problems of the firm.

[18] Jasinski, *op. cit.*, p. 106.

The manager of any large organization faces a difficult task of getting all employees (frequently including many levels of supervision as well) to coordinate their efforts and to follow his direction. To accomplish this objective he must make use of both downward and upward channels of communication—he must both give orders and assess their effectiveness. Yet the systems of human relations that he depends on for transmission are far from foolproof. Organizations often do not function as planned. Serious distortions are introduced by the necessity of communicating through many levels.

The individual supervisor also has his problems in dealing with the hierarchy. The leadership techniques he can use are limited by the methods of management used by his boss and his boss's boss. He must learn to balance the conflicting demands of those over him with those underneath. If he succumbs completely to either (for example, by failing to represent vigorously the interests of his subordinates to higher levels), his leadership position is weakened.

In an effort to duplicate some of the communication advantages of the smaller organization, modifications are introduced in the hierarchical structure. These include, among others, techniques for bypassing and short-circuiting, such as mass communications, attitude surveys, and special committees. Multi-leveled organizations have special needs for protected appeal channels by which those at lower levels who feel an injustice or believe they have been unfairly treated can get a hearing at key decision-making levels without depending on their immediate supervisor to represent them. Unions and open-door techniques help to fill this need. However, there is a danger that these modifications can be as injurious to the organization as the problems they are supposed to remedy. Usually they threaten the leadership position of the immediate supervisor.

Large organizations cannot depend upon the ability of management to oversee everything directly. Therefore, a variety of control measures are developed which serve to both measure and motivate performance. While they are supposed to communicate to upper management accurately and impartially what lower levels have accomplished they are susceptible to a variety of distortions.

problem 1 • BAD FIXTURE

Telephone Conversation—(Plant Manager phones, somewhat excitedly, to one of his superintendents)

PM: "Say, this morning when I was walking through one of your departments, one of the setup men, Joe Smith in Department X, stopped me and said the fixture he was using on his machine was no good. It had to have a couple extra clamps on it which slowed production down on his machine by 10%. What are you doing about this?"

Supt.: "I don't think I know anything about the situation you're talking about. I'll have to check into it."

PM: "But the setup man said that this has been going on for two days now. Haven't you heard anything about it?"

Supt.: "No, I guess I wouldn't hear anything about it unless it involved a problem that the foreman out there thought he couldn't handle."

PM: "Well, get on it as soon as you can, and let me know what you find out as soon as you do."

In Superintendent's Office

Supt.: (to Foreman) "I've called you in to ask whether we are having any serious trouble with the fixtures over in Joe Smith's area."

Foreman: "Well, I've been with Engineering on this. They're designing an entirely new-type fixture, so we're getting along with this the best we can in the meantime. I know it's costing us something to limp along this way, but I figured it was cheaper than ordering a replacement for the old fixture at a thousand dollars and have it become obsolete in the couple weeks it would take them to develop the new one. I feel this new design is going to really save us some money. Why, is there anything wrong?"

Supt.: "Yeah, the boss wants to know what we are doing to take care of it. Maybe this is something I should have known about since the boss was so interested."

Foreman: "Oh yeah, I remember yesterday when the boss came through; Smith and he started talking. I guess I should have gone over to see what was up. And the next time, on something like this, I'll check with you immediately."

Supt.: "Did the setup man know what was being done with Engineering about the fixture?"

Foreman: "Sure. I told him yesterday. He knows the whole story. I wonder what he's trying to pull—griping to the boss."

Supt.: "Well, I'll call the boss and you take care of Joe."

Foreman: "O.K."

1. Why was the PM disappointed that the Superintendent did not know about the malfunctioning fixture? Should he have been upset?

2. What effect did the PM's call have on the methods of supervision that would be used in the future? Describe the probable changes in the relationship between the PM and Superintendent, between Superintendent and Foreman, and between Foreman and setup man.

3. Did the Foreman handle Smith correctly? Is there anything the Superintendent can do to review this problem with the Foreman that will not discourage his taking responsibility and initiative?

4. Assume that the whole incident could be repeated. What should the PM do after learning about the operating troubles in Department X? Be specific in describing what should take place in the contacts between:

   PM and set up man
   General Superintendent and Superintendent
   Superintendent and Foreman
   Foreman and setup man

5. What might Smith's motives have been in this case?

problem 2 • THE ASSISTANT'S DILEMMA

Bill Adams was hired to fill a new job as assistant to Alfred Grozia, the laboratory head and research director. Adam's assignment was to handle all the administrative details for a very busy executive-scientist.

After about six months on the job, Adams was on good terms with nearly everyone in the lab. In the course of a conversation, Adams learned that one of the ablest metallurgists, Isaac Carroll, was seriously considering quitting. Carroll's boss, Felt, a project director who reported directly to the research director, had been giving Carroll a great deal of extra routine work to do. Not only was Carroll finding it difficult to complete his regular research activities and earn recognition for the quality of his performance, but he also found the additional work tedious and unsatisfying. Carroll had asked for a technician to serve as an assistant, but this request had been turned down.

Adams was unsure of what to do. He was convinced that Felt was unaware of Carroll's extreme dissatisfaction. Felt had a reputation for "pushing" people, although he was technically competent. But Adams was reluctant to broach the question to Felt; the two had never hit it off, and Felt had made it clear that he wanted no interference from the boss' assistant. Moreover, Adams was reluctant to speak directly to Grozia, for fear that he might be regarded as a "spy," and cause Carroll serious embarrassment. If word got out, Felt would feel that Carroll had gone over his head. At the same time, Carroll's resignation would be a serious and needless loss to the organization.

How would you handle this situation if you were Adams?

problem 3 • A LETTER TO THE PRESIDENT

The company president has received a long letter from an employee in the shipping department, complaining that he did not get a promotion to which he felt himself entitled. The reason, claims the employee, is that his supervisor has a grudge against him. Moreover, he claims, the supervisor's judgment cannot be relied on. In his letter, he discloses a number of violations of company policy that the supervisor has countenanced, and a number of private deals that have been worked out in the department.

What should the company president do with this information?

problem 4 • QUITTING TIME

Eggert is the general manager of a large Eastern department store, with responsibility for directing most of the operating departments. For years, two of these departments—packaging and merchandise-marking (ticketing)—have been afflicted by a high turnover rate, failure to meet deadlines, and employee grievances.

Recently the situation in marking has improved significantly, although it is still far from satisfactory. Apparently the present supervisor in the marking department, Elsohn, is doing a good job—at least the selling departments are no longer complaining about incorrect ticketing or failure to have merchandise ready for floor display on time.

Recently Colson, the head of the packaging department, complained to Eggert that all sorts of disciplinary problems were being created by the way Elsohn was running his department. The two departments were physically adjacent, and Colson's employees noticed that the people in marking consistently stopped work 15 to 25 minutes before the end of the day to freshen up, gossip, and relax. There was a clear store rule that all personnel were to work until the closing bell had rung; ample time was provided during the day for employees to take breaks.

Colson said he could hardly enforce this rule in his own department so long as it was being flagrantly violated next door. Eggert promised to "look into the situation."

1. What would you do if you were Eggert? What information would you need? What criteria would you use in evaluating new data?

2. What are the dangers here?

15 SPECIALIZATION

Seldom is an organization composed of people who all do the same type of work. The typical pattern is for individuals and groups to *specialize* in one function or activity, leaving other functions to their colleagues in other departments or divisions. In fact, specialization has become so common in contemporary life that we tend to take it for granted. In this chapter, however, we shall see that the use of specialization as a means of increasing output and efficiency has many repercussions on the patterns of human relations.

SPECIALIZATION AND JOB SATISFACTION

Actually, we can think of two kinds of specialization: specialization by task and specialization of people. *Task specialization*, the most familiar, involves breaking jobs down into their finest components (as suggested by Taylor and his disciples). Task specialization has these clearly recognizable advantages:

1. It reduces training costs, for a worker learns more quickly when he concentrates on a single function.

2. It avoids the waste of time involved in shifting a man from one kind of job to another and enables each man fully to develop his skills for a particular job.

3. It makes unnecessary the duplication of equipment that would otherwise be used on only a part-time basis.

4. It enables the company to purchase more specialized equipment.

5. It simplifies the problem of developing job controls.

6. It reduces wage costs by making it possible to hire less-skilled workers.

People specialization, on the other hand, involves hiring employees with high levels of training: product designers, reliability engineers, market researchers, and the like.

Task specialization, as we saw in Chapter 2, can create serious morale and motivational problems. In the typical white- or blue-collar factory, many employees have little sense of accomplishment, autonomy, or identification with work. People specialists, on the other hand, often work on depth attention jobs, identify strongly with their work, and may even enjoy professional status.

THE NEED FOR COORDINATION

Managers sometimes believe they can get something for nothing. They can get the advantages of increased specialization by dividing up more complex jobs into simpler jobs or by hiring additional trained specialists. But they ignore the possibility that the problems of coordination so created may more than outweigh the advantages gained. The purpose of any organization is to complete work: the production of goods or services. No matter how hard an employee works, his efforts are wasted unless they integrate with those of his fellow workers.

Acme Distributors used telephone operators to take phoned-in customer orders. The operators formerly typed up the forms for use by central billing and the warehouse. The company recently added a group of special typists to transcribe the operators' pencilled notes. Now there is conflict because some operators use abbreviations and have poor handwriting. Also, some operators fail to look up the serial numbers in the catalogs, thus requiring the transcribers to do extra work. None of these problems existed, of course, when one girl did a total job.

How specialization creates unproductive work has been described in a popular spoof on the internal working of large organizations, *Parkinson's Law.*

Parkinson's Law. Parkinson argues that the number of people employed in a given department has no relationship to the amount of work that needs to be done. In order to improve their own position vis-à-vis others in the organization, managers are motivated to expand their staffs needlessly: "An official wants to multiply subordinates, not rivals." However, this grand strategy for self-aggrandizement rarely reveals itself because the new personnel make work for one another—with the organization's strong propensities for division of labor. Parkinson describes how seven officials can keep busy doing work that was formerly handled by a single employee, Mr. A.

For these seven make so much work for each other that all are fully occupied and A is actually working harder than ever. An incoming document may well come before each of them in turn. Official E decides that it falls within the province of F, who places a draft reply before C, who amends it drastically before consulting D, who asks G to deal with it. But G goes on leave at this point, handing the file over to H, who drafts a minute that is signed by D and returned to C, who revises his draft accordingly and lays the new version before A.

What does A do? He would have every excuse for signing the thing unread, for he has many other matters on his mind. Knowing now that he is to succeed W next year, he has to decide whether C or D should succeed to his own office. He had to agree to G's going on leave even if not yet strictly entitled to it. He is worried whether H should not have gone instead, for reasons of health. He has looked pale recently—partly but not solely because of his domestic troubles. Then there is the business of F's special increment of salary for the period of the conference and E's application for transfer to the Ministry of Pensions. A has heard that D is in love with a married typist and that G and F are no longer on speaking terms—no one seems to know why. So A might be tempted to sign C's draft and have done with it. But A is a conscientious man. Beset as he is with problems created by his colleagues for themselves and for him— created by the mere fact of these officials' existence—he is not the man to shirk his duty. He reads through the draft with care, deletes the fussy paragraphs added by C and H, and restores the thing back to the form preferred in the first instance by the able (if quarrelsome) F. He corrects the English—none of these young men can write grammatically—and finally produces the same reply he would have written if officials C to H had never been born. Far more people have taken far longer to produce the same result. No one has been idle. All have done their best. And it is late in the evening before A finally quits his office and begins the return journey to Ealing. [1]

Technology and Human Relations

Buried here is an important principle of organizational behavior: The division of labor is responsible for a predictable pattern of human relations. Anything that changes the specialization is going to change human relations. For example, if we give A some additional assignment it is likely to change *whom* he sees, *when* he sees them, *how often*, and *what* he must do in relation to other people he contacts.

Managers are often insensitive to how profoundly rather small changes in technology, by altering jobs, can change human relations. Take, for example, the division of labor in a restaurant. Generally, a single bartender prepares drinks in response to the verbal orders of waitresses who have just come from their customers. The result is usually a group clustered around the hapless bartender asking when their orders will be ready. To complicate matters, there may be misunderstandings concerning what combination of drinks was ordered by a specific waitress. Is it the fault of the inadequately enunciated requests of the waitress or the poor memory of the bartender?

Now look at the changes in the pattern of relationships if the restaurant changes technology by insisting that all waitresses write their orders and place them on a spindle to await the bartender:

1. Contacts between waitresses and bartenders are reduced by the buffer action of the spindle and written orders.

2. The bartender can now exercise more initiative by rearranging and combining waitresses' orders in such a way as to make his own job easier or more pleasant (for instance, mixing all the Manhattans at the same time).

[1] C. Northcote Parkinson, *Parkinson's Law* (Boston: Houghton, 1957), pp. 5-6.

3. Waitresses no longer have to wait in line to place their orders; the spindle becomes a "queuing device" for holding their orders in place.

4. Disagreement over who ordered what can be resolved by written evidence rather than more fallible individual memories. Furthermore, differences in voice characteristics and in ability to demand service are cancelled and greater equality among waitresses is maintained.

Coordination among Specialists

Specialization has increased the relative importance of lateral relationships, as distinct from hierarchical (superior-subordinate) relationships. Both managers and nonmanagers alike spend a great deal of their time in contact with other people in the organization (and some outside the organization, as well, such as with government, unions, suppliers, customers) who are neither their boss nor their subordinate. Many of these relationships involve people at roughly the same status level. In one organization, for example, managers had to maintain close working relationships with as many as 70 or 80 people who were not superiors or subordinates.

BASIC PATTERNS OF LATERAL RELATIONS

But we can go further than noting simply the lateral-relations explosion that characterizes the modern organization. By watching the interaction of managers, professionals, technicians, and blue-collar people in large, complex organizations, we can identify certain recurring patterns of relationship. These patterns encompass the ways in which specialists in the organization come together, the recurring problems they face, and the feelings these problems generate.

Research suggests that there are at least five distinctive patterns: Work flows, service flows, advisory flows, audit flows, and stabilization flows. These relationships will be described in turn.

Work-Flow

Nearly every employee is in an intermediate position in the flow of work: He depends on those who precede him to prepare supplies, papers, or semi-finished parts for him to work on; those who follow him similarly depend on him. For example, a factory clerk may collect and summarize production data; he then sends it on to an accountant who processes the data further. Or, the waitress gives her order to pantry personnel; they in turn are served by runners from the kitchen; the cooks and their assistants in turn prepare the food for the runners. Each of these is an example of a work-flow sequence. Note that employees who must time their actions to coincide with the needs of others may not work near one another; they may not even have a common supervisor. Naturally these relationships generate problems.

Buckpassing. Friction is normal on any job, for work rarely goes as planned. And when things go wrong in a specialized organization, people are tempted to avoid accepting responsibility and to pass the buck to others involved in the work sequence. For example:

A shortage of material develops on the night shift. When asked why, the night-shift workers protest that the day shift failed to keep the material bins full. They insist the day shift never does its share; they just used up the stocks provided by the night truckers.

This natural tendency of each person to defend his own interests hurts the organization as a whole. This difficulty is accentuated when higher management pressures subordinates for results at any cost, and imposes heavy penalties. Thus, the system of rewards built into the organization frequently motivates its members to think only of their own personal interests. In so doing, they make it more difficult for others to do their job.

Status complications. Normally, higher-status employees give orders to lower-status employees, and not vice versa. This is true throughout life. We expect to have to respond to persons of higher prestige than ourselves; in fact, we are often very reluctant to try to approach them first.

Sometimes the work-flow patterns *reverse* this normal relationship. We have all seen situations such as this:

A clerk is sent to ask a skilled craftsman if it would not be possible to speed up on a particular job. The employee bristles when approached in this manner by a mere "clerk" and may, if anything, slow down his operation.

This is a critical source of human-relations difficulties in the restaurant industry. Whenever female waitresses give orders to male bartenders, or when young pantry personnel give orders to veteran chefs, periodic blow-ups hurt productivity as well as job satisfaction.

Uneven patterns. Most people want to achieve some equilibrium in their dealings with others: They don't want two people asking them to do something one day and 25 the next. Employees are willing to tolerate a certain amount of variation in this contact pattern from day to day as the work load varies; however, this range of tolerance can be exceeded only at the expense of much tension and discontent. Unfortunately, work rarely flows evenly through an organization. There are usually periods of crisis when everyone feels under tension, tempers are short or nonexistent, and normally suppressed conflicts break out into open hostility.

Some of the crises are periodic. At the end of the month clerks in the billing department work under high pressure; store clerks rush to spruce up their display before the monthly visit of the district manager. Other crises are unexpected. A vital piece of equipment breaks down, a rush order comes in from an important customer, the "brass" from the main office arrives on a surprise inspection trip.

In each of these situations the normal level of contacts is left far behind as members of the organization scurry around to get other individuals and groups on whom they depend to get their work out faster, cheaper, or more impressively. When work routines are interrupted, management becomes worried, and frequently many levels of the hierarchy descend simultaneously on some small group of employees, thus making matters even worse.

Design and development decisions. Sometimes problems between specialized departments arise not from the actual flow of work but from the need to coordinate decisions. Here we are faced with many of the problems we have already discussed, plus some others that we have not as yet considered.

Increasingly in modern industry, the work of each department is so closely coordinated with that of the other departments in the organization that each department's decision affects all the rest; and yet no department can make a decision without knowing what the others are doing. Problems of this sort resemble simultaneous equations, where no one part of the problem can be solved without solving all the rest. In industry, such problems often arise in large engineering laboratories that design new products, or in "job shops" that are constantly planning the production of items to the customer's special order. Each department or group controls a part of the "answer"—but these parts must be assembled before the organization's problem is solved.

To see these problems in action, let us look at the process of designing a new-model TV set, as we observed it in one company. The Engineering Department is, of course, the one most directly concerned, and it consists of five sections. *Electrical* determines in theoretical terms how the set will be made (technically: what the over-all "system" will be). *Mechanical* tries to fit the components together; it often finds that Electrical's theoretical plans are impractical or even that one Electrical engineer's theoretical suggestions are incompatible with those of another. *Chassis* designs the cabinet; close coordination is required if the components are to fit into the cabinet. This is not as easy as it sounds, since Electrical and Mechanical are constantly designing improvements which give better reception, but which conflict with the company's over-all goal of producing an ever-thinner, lighter set.

Automation designs the machinery which makes the printed circuits and attaches the tubes to it; in contrast to Electrical, which wants an ever-more "sophisticated" set, Automation wants one that is simple enough to be reduced to printed circuitry and put together mechanically. *Industrial Engineering* determines the techniques by which the set will be manufactured (other than the operations that are 100 percent automated). Like Automation, it seeks to eliminate what it feels to be unnecessary frills.

Further complicating over-all coordination are the pressures brought by outside departments: Sales wants an attractive product that will sell easily, and Manufacturing wants a set that is easy to put together. And management as a whole is interested in keeping costs low, profits high.

Note that in this case no one section can make modifications without affecting all the others. A change in cabinet, for instance, may require adjustments by every other section, yet each adjustment may in turn require further compensating adjustments elsewhere. Each section has its own vested interest. Electrical, with its goal of technical perfection, conflicts, for example, with Industrial Engineering's goal of manufacturing ease.

Since a new model must be designed each year, intergroup conflicts tend to reach a crescendo as the time for a final decision approaches. As the deadline draws near, an increasing number of compromises and adjustments must be made, tempers grow raw, and human-relations problems begin to complicate the technical ones. Each engineer likes to feel that he has *completed* his end of the job and hates to reconsider his position just to please another section.

Complicating all these problems are the changing status relationships between departments. When TV was new, the major problem was to design a workable set, and Electrical was the highest-status section. Today the emphasis is on sales appeal and manufacturing ease. Electrical still thinks its function is the most important one, but management seems to favor other sections when it makes critical decisions and hands out promotions.

We have gone into the problem of this TV engineering department at some length because we think its problems are typical of many in management. When an organization is small, and specialization at a minimum, the problem of coordination can be solved by one man who keeps all the details in his head and can predict by himself all the possible ramifications of each possible change. Once the organization passes a certain size, however, no one person can keep track of all the variables. At this point, good communication among the specialists becomes all-important.

Service Relationships

Often an organization centralizes auxiliary functions such as maintenance, purchasing, laboratory analysis, and computer processing. These "service relationships" between the suppliers of services and their in-company "customers" involve distinctive human problems.

Bottleneck operations. Intergroup competition may manifest itself in a struggle to corral as much as possible of a "scarce resource." The incident below involves interdepartmental competition to get priority in having maintenance work done—as described by a departmental supervisor in a large plant.

"Whenever we need equipment repaired, we put a tag on it saying what we think is wrong and send it to the Repair Department. We have a series of different-color tags which we can use. We use a white tag for a routine job. Yellow tags mean important but not top priority. A red tag means the repair is highly urgent and production will be held up until the piece is returned. Well, we suddenly burned out one vital unit and I sent it down with a red tag because we needed it back desperately. When I didn't hear from them for several days, I really got mad and decided to check on what was holding us up. Well, you can imagine how burned up I was when I entered the Repair Department to see that every piece they had down there was red-tagged."

This approach, of course, simply makes scarce resources become scarcer. When one supervisor decides that he may not have all the supplies or repair facilities available that he might need in the future, he takes steps to build up an ample reserve. When other supervisors follow suit, a potential shortage becomes an actual scarcity and the whole priority system breaks down.

Unbalanced pressure. In organizational terms, pressure springs from the efforts of *others* to originate action for you when you are unable to originate for others. Pressure is great when one person repeatedly and consistently attempts to do so (the supervisor who comes back constantly to ask why a certain job has not been completed), or when a relatively large number of people come to you with conflicting demands (as was the case in the repair department described above, and in most service departments).

In either instance, the endless pressure is bound to keep you in a state of unrelieved discomfort. Look back to the "Case of the Red Tags" from the point of view of the repair department. Imagine the pressure the repairmen are under who control the scarce resource! Here is an example of a job subjected to constant pressure, as described by the supervisor in charge:

"We are part of a special purchasing division that services the engineering department. It is our job to order parts and materials for the various research projects. Well, it has gotten so that nothing is routine anymore. The engineers are always engaging in rush projects—you know, someone gets a brainstorm and they want to get it under way immediately. So they come down with the orders they want filled. First they try to get you to tell them it will be done within an hour. By the next morning they're calling the boss to complain you are not working on it fast enough. They can't seem to understand that it all takes time and we've got lots of other rush jobs. It seems as though we are always under pressure; someone is always asking for greater speed than we can give them. Let me tell you; I have never experienced such tension."

Reaction to pressures. The tensions created by these pressures take their toll in departmental efficiency. The rate of personnel turnover is often high, while those who stay usually resort to one or the other of the following patterns of defense or adaptation:

1. Some workers affect an air of resignation, though they may be seething inside; they work off their tensions on their families, friends, or themselves (in terms of psychosomatic illness).

2. Others fight back. They give vent to their frustration by dealing with their tormentors in an aggressive fashion. One observer has related a classic case of how a group defends itself against excessive pressure from other groups:

The Ship's Store department on a large ship found that certain groups were always demanding rapid service on complicated requisitions. The Ship's Store workers, moving with speed and efficiency, merely announced that these offending groups would have to fill out in perfect detail the multicopy, excessively complicated formal requisition sheets that were required by an official, but rarely observed, rule. These same pressuring groups also were denied their share of the personal items that were distributed, in part, at the discretion of the Stores department: stationery, film, etc.

Unfortunately, this response may further reduce organizational efficiency and lead to additional pressure.

3. Still others develop a cordial personal relationship toward the offending groups. The expert at this approach uses a mixture of kidding, sympathetic listening, and sincere concern. This is the approach followed by the men's store that hires a delectable blonde to handle complaints.

4. Finally, some workers establish their own system of priorities and firmly resist all efforts to violate it. This is what the rushed butcher does when he asks his customers to take a number and wait until it is called.

Employees who work side by side day after day often work out their own systems for accommodating the demands they make on one another. These systems may be reinforced by group norms that forbid fellow members to push or pressure one another. Large, specialized departments, however, even when they are located close together, seldom develop such informal patterns of accommodation.

Advisory Relationships

Modern organizations employ many technical experts to provide advice. An internal advisor can help solve questions such as the following. To the plant engineer: "We seem to be getting more machine breakdowns on line 24 than on any of the others; what's wrong?" To the company lawyer: "Our largest customer is threatening to shift to a competitor; is it legal for us to give him a special price advantage?" To the packaging department: "We're getting a lot of breakage in shipments; what's wrong with our packing methods?" Note that most of these questions concern recurring problems that the normal organizational procedures have not been able to cope with successfully.

The personnel department has a typical advisory relationship (although it may have other nonadvisory functions, as well). Using this department as a case study, let us examine some of the human problems inherent in the advisor's role.

What is "advice"? Many theorists draw a sharp line between line and staff. The staff man is expected to provide technical information or advice and counsel (because he is an expert in the field), but he does not make decisions. In practice, however, these theoretical distinctions are blurred.

When providing *information,* the personnel manager simply furnishes the facts that will help the manager make sound decisions. For instance:

1. The disciplinary clause of the union agreement means thus and so.
2. The "going rate" for engineers like Jones in our present labor market is $850 per month.

Or he may play a more active role and furnish *advice:*

1. You are likely to provoke a wildcat strike if you give Bill Williams a disciplinary layoff.
2. On the basis of the record, Jones looks like a better bet for the promotion, since the man on the job will have to assume a good deal of initiative without close supervision.
3. If you hire Smith at that salary, you are going to have some dissatisfied older employees in your departments.

Finally, he can make *decisions:*

1. Don't discharge Brown; give him a warning slip.
2. Hire Green to replace the man who left.

Sometimes there is a very narrow line between providing facts and providing advice. Thus, by selecting his facts carefully, the personnel manager can actually sway the line manager's decision one way or the other. Also, what is given as "advice" may be interpreted by the recipient as a decision.

The temptation to exceed the advisory role. Historically, management has tended to turn over more and more functions to well-trained experts. When experts were first used to supplement the skills of line supervisors, the distinctions between information, advice, and decision-making were rarely made. Further, management showed a readiness to accept expert advice uncritically. Often, since management was very anxious to avoid trouble with the unions, for example, the industrial relations department actually *told* supervisors whom to hire, what to pay them, and how to answer their grievances. The result was often disastrous to the prestige and status of supervisors.

In practice, it takes a strong-willed personnel manager to resist the temptation to become a decision-maker. Once he has grown accustomed to providing advice and counsel, he may find it irresistible to take the next step and actually make decisions. Even when the personnel manager is careful not to usurp the line supervisor's responsibility, his actions may still be misinterpreted. The following case illustrates this problem:

A grievance was filed against Gus Homes, a departmental supervisor, for failing to divide overtime equally. Homes argued that employees who failed to meet production standards on regular work should not be given overtime. The union contract said nothing about overtime, although general plant practice sanctioned equal division. The personnel director of the company, anxious to avoid any union bargaining on the overtime issue, urged Homes to change his mind. Homes refused. Some weeks later, Homes was transferred to a less desirable job. The plant grapevine reported that the manager had "given him the axe" on the recommendation of the personnel director. The truth of the matter was that the manager had believed for some time that Homes should be removed from his department. The overtime situation was just one among many reasons that seemed to justify the move.

From this point on, other supervisors thought twice about refusing the personnel director's "advice." His recommendations had become cloaked with line authority; he had become another boss.

When the manager wants more than advice. Line managers, themselves, may encourage staff experts to broaden their range of activities. The willingness of the personnel man to help out on a difficult problem, for example, may provide the supervisor with welcome relief from burdensome responsibilities. In effect, he says to the personnel man, "Good, you handle the personnel and I'll take care of all the technical problems." Then, if a decision backfires, the line supervisor can simply point out that he was following personnel's advice. What a pleasant relief this excuse provides!

And so it is easy to understand the line supervisor's reluctance to question the expertise of the specialists whom top management has hired. The subordinate manager who challenges their ability runs the risk of making a bad decision for which he will have to bear all the responsibility. He may even prefer to interpret "advice" as a decision in order to avoid assuming responsibility and in order to pass the buck to the expert.

Paradoxically, a manager may resent an advisory group's power and at the same time grumble that it is failing to take responsibility for decisions. As one supervisor expressed it:

"We stay away from the industrial relations department as much as possible—they're always trying to sell you on some new program that makes more work for you. But then when you go to them with a problem you can't get a straight answer from them; they won't tell you how to handle it. They give you a lot of pros and cons and stuff that leaves you more confused than when you went in."

Broader contacts. Staff advisors are in position to short-circuit the chain of command and to communicate with people at all levels. Frequently they have *top* management's ear, and this fact increases lower management's reluctance to disregard staff's advice. Staff men may also develop close relations with men at the *lower* levels of the organizational ladder. For example, personnel people often provide a more sympathetic ear for the disturbed employee than does his own supervisor, and he may prefer to take his troubles to them. If this happens too often, the line manager will lose contact with his employees and their respect as well. For instance, a manufacturing superintendent once told us, "My foremen have learned that they can get action a lot faster if they go to staff than if they see me. Except when there is trouble I am pretty much a figurehead—and then I am the one who has to bear the blame."

Caught in this dilemma some managers take the easy way out—they pass the buck to higher management and to staff. In effect, they say, "Don't blame me. Blame the other guy."

Conflicting advice. We have simplified, of course, by implying that at one time only one advisor (the personnel man) is involved. In fact, in the modern organization, expertise is distributed among many specialized groups and a given problem can call for knowledge of engineering, standards, methods, personnel, and finance. The boundary lines are never clear and each group feels that theirs is the real "answer" to the difficulty. Thus, a manager may be deluged with helpers, many of whom are inclined to remind him of their associations with higher management in order to encourage his adoption of a particular solution to the problem.

Audit Relationships

In traditional theory a manager watches everything his subordinates are doing to be sure that they are not violating the rules or standards of the organization and that they are achieving their work goals. In large organizations, however, it is often difficult for the manager to make these observations directly. For one thing, where the work is highly technical, the manager may not be trained to evaluate its adequacy.

For example, even an engineering manager who is not a specialist in circuits may be unable to answer the questions: "How good is the new design for that circuit?" Lack of technical knowledge may also prevent the manager from assessing the adequacy of subordinates' financial and personnel skills.

Similarly, the rules, procedures, and standards of an organization may be so complicated and extensive that no single manager can administer all of them. Just imagine how many personnel, engineering, and financial procedures alone there may be in the typical large manufacturing company.

Finally, the manager has difficulty overseeing the observance of standards because of the tendency of subordinates to hide or distort unfavorable information (see Chapter 14). Not being able to evaluate everything himself and not fully trusting all that is told, the manager in the large organization must use specialists who help him appraise and evaluate the work of subordinates. Yet their work, in turn, creates a host of human-relations problems.

Standards are ambiguous.

The engineers inspecting a finished piece of electronic equipment claimed that it would not operate in a room kept at 100 degrees temperature. The department that built the equipment argued that the humidity was too high in the room and that if the air were drier, it would hold up, as the standards require, and operate at 100 degrees.

Standards conflict.

The production control department told the production supervisor to ask people to work overtime because output was falling below schedule. However, the accounting department has issued an ultimatum that all overtime work must cease, since the budgeted overtime allowance has already been exceeded. The supervisor spends a good deal of time going back and forth between these two "audit" groups, trying to get one or the other to concede.

Auditing generates suspicions and distrust.

Quality-control inspectors often say that bad work is hidden so that it won't be discovered and reported, thus making the job of checking quality that much more difficult. In trying to do a thorough job and overcome the hurdles that are put in their way, the inspectors appear to be overly eager to find trouble. Many operators and their managers assert, "Inspectors have to find a certain number of errors to justify their existence and their fancy budgets."

Stabilization Relationships

Somewhat similar to the audit pattern is the stabilization relationship, except that the contacts are more frequent and regular. These relationships grow out of the need to coordinate the separate parts of an organization, each of which pursues its own objectives. As with auditing, this function would have been performed by the manager himself before the age of specialists. Let us look at some typical examples:

A manager would like to reduce his output tomorrow because two machines will be down for repairs. He can't make this decision himself, however, because it will obviously affect other departments in the flow of work, departments that rely on those parts for their assembly requirements.

A manager wants to give an employee a large raise to keep another employer from bidding him away. The raise is an unmixed blessing for the particular manager, but it could hurt other managers who have to explain why their best employees are not getting comparable increases.

In the first case, the manager will have to have his production schedule checked with the production-control group. In the second case, a salary administrator will have to give approval. Thus, stabilizing relationships involve getting approval for certain critical decisions from experts who are supposed to keep the total organization's needs in view. As in auditing relationships, the needs are often not absolute and fixed; there is much room for differences of opinion. What will actually happen may be the product of the respective negotiating skills of the individuals involved.

A persistent problem is that both auditing and stabilization relationships force managers to contend with multiple sources of influences all pulling in various, often inconsistent directions. For example, the personnel department may urge managers to utilize lower-skilled employees because they are easier to hire in a tight labor market while at the same time the engineering department may be demanding more exacting work. The astute manager learns to sense which requirements are the most dangerous to ignore and adjust his behavior accordingly. At times, personnel considerations predominate, then engineering, and perhaps later on financial.

ORGANIZATIONAL IMPLICATIONS OF INCREASING SPECIALIZATION

As noted before, many people think of the organization as a pyramid with all decisions being made at the top to be obeyed by the subordinates below. But reality is more complicated. As specialization has increased, so has the need for obtaining effective cooperation and coordination between specialized work groups, if work is to move smoothly through the various stages of production, if service groups are to be spared overloading, and if advisors, auditors, and stabilizers are to be used properly.

With hierarchical relationships it is clear who is boss and who is subordinate; but lateral relationships are less clear since no one is clearly superior to another. Hence, lateral relationships lead to much intergroup friction and competition for status and influence.

Specialists often identify more with their respective groups than with the organization as a whole. One reason, of course, is that the group members interact with one another more frequently than they do with persons outside the group. This identification with an informal group provides an important need satisfaction for employees who might otherwise feel lost in the larger organization. These satisfactions can contribute to over-all efficiency, but, as we know, a price must be paid for these advantages.

What happens when groups of specialists concentrate on their own narrow interests rather than on the interests of the organization as a whole? Each seeks to impress its own point of view on the total organization. Each wishes to enhance its relative status or prestige. Though the competitive struggle may help keep each group on its toes, it may also get out of hand, leading to destructive friction between groups, and doing serious injury to the organization as a whole.

Department In-Breeding

As time goes by, each specialized group—the accountants, the production men, the engineers—will adopt a distinctive point of view that shapes its entire way of doing things.

The "in-breeding" that develops within these specialized units makes it difficult to hammer out common agreement on interdepartment problems. Since representatives of each specialty have been conditioned to think in a characteristic way, they find it hard to work together with others as a team. Here is a good description of what happens:

We've refused to recognize or admit that the various components of our industrial machine are driven by different people with different motives. Sales, for example, is always looking for something to add to the product in order to gain competitive advantage ... sales presses for changes to get an edge over competitors. Engineering wants changes too, but for an entirely different reason. They're always fighting for easier, cheaper production. Where Sales wants to add to the product, Engineering wants to simplify it. Production has a totally different idea. They know that their salvation lies in keeping the men at the machines doing the same thing over and over again. Any production man will tell you how and why repetitive work is the secret of mass production. And he'll fight changes at the drop of a suggestion.

Is it any wonder that we have friction? And, mind you, this friction exists when people are working together with the best intentions. [2]

A sociologist looking at the same problem draws a similar conclusion, but in somewhat different terms:

The over-all managerial problem has become more complex because each group of management specialists will tend to view the "interests of the enterprise" in terms which are compatible with the survival and the increase of its special function. That is, each group will have a trained capacity for its own function and a "trained incapacity" to see its relation to the whole. [3]

SPECIALIZATION AND THE FOREMAN'S ROLE

Earlier we noted some possible sources of conflict between advisory groups such as personnel departments and line management. This was but one example of a more general problem affecting the status particularly of first-level supervisors or foremen. Let us look at the impact of specialization on the foreman.

Fifty years ago. A half-century ago, the foreman had almost absolute power. He did all the hiring (there were no personnel departments in those days) and he expected his men to show gratitude for being selected. If he picked friends or relatives, no one was in a position to object. The workers were

---

[2] Bernard Davis, "The Pill's Grim Progress," *Esquire*, British edition, Vol. I, No. 3 (August 1954), p. 55; cited by Lt. Col. Lyndall F. Urwick, "The Span of Control—Some Facts about the Fables," *Advanced Management* (November 1956), p. 11.

[3] Reinhard Bendix, "Bureaucratization in Industry," in A. Kornhauser, R. Dubin, and A. Ross, *Industrial Conflict* (New York: McGraw-Hill, 1954), p. 170.

completely dependent on him and naturally catered to his every whim. Often they even felt obliged to give him Christmas presents. As one old-timer put it:

"In the old days the foreman used to be King—he really *was* a big shot—he'd walk down the plant floor like he really owned the place and you better do what he wanted fast—or you'd be looking for another job."

He had the sole power to discharge employees, for unions were rare and personnel standards nonexistent. Single-handed, he took care of all the activities that are now called scheduling, methods, safety, wage administration, and quality control (though many foremen of those days would not have known what the terms meant).

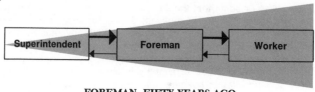

FOREMAN, FIFTY YEARS AGO

Scientific management. The first blow to the foreman's prestige was the scientific-management movement. The doctrine of specialization preached by its apostle, Frederick Taylor, meant that the foreman's job would be broken up into functional specialties. By 1930 many of the foreman's functions had been taken over by staff departments. *How* men worked was decided by the methods department; the *sequence* in which they handled products was decided by production control. Quality-control inspectors came into the foreman's shop to check on quality. A special organization arose to handle safety, and another was set up to take care of maintenance. In many cases even the hiring of workers—the foreman's traditional prerogative—was taken over by the personnel department, thus usurping one of the foreman's main sources of prestige and loyalty.

The union. During the 1930's the union made its first appearance in many plants. No longer was the worker obliged to humor the foreman in order to protect himself from being fired. Union membership sapped the loyalty of employees to their immediate supervisor, making it harder for him to make his orders stick. A radically new style of supervision was required, to which it would take the foreman years to adjust.

Worse, another official was added to those who could give the foreman "orders"—this official was the union steward, who was technically the foreman's subordinate.

Further, largely as a means of protecting itself against the union, management began to centralize the functions of discipline, promotion, and salary administration in the personnel department. Management's reasoning went this way: The union filed grievances whenever the foreman violated the contract or showed favoritism; and whenever a foreman in one plant made an unfortunate decision, the union regarded it as a precedent that could be used against the company in its other plants. Very well, said the company, we will centralize all these functions in the hands of experts, to insure a uniform, consistent policy. What little power the foreman had left was now restricted by specific rules.

As a consequence, the foreman was exposed to conflicting orders and pressures from all sides. His fall from power was almost complete.

Loss of opportunity for promotion.   The next blow fell when the foreman was deprived of his opportunity for promotion into higher management. More and more companies now began to recruit their future executives from among college graduates. In some companies the foreman was faced with a dead-end job.

The war.   Next came the war period, with its frantic pressures to perform miracles with untrained help. And then the final blow: The advent of wage controls meant that in many cases the foreman's wages fell below the wages of some of the men he supervised, particularly the men on piece work. By the end of World War II, foreman morale was at an all-time low.

The foremen join a union.   To protect themselves against this steady erosion of their prestige and power, a number of foremen decided to establish a union of their own. The Foreman's Association of America spread like wildfire. The foreman reasoned that if other workers could bolster their position by joining a union, he would be foolish not to do the same thing himself. He felt himself excluded from management, relegated to the status of a mere messenger boy.

Management rediscovers the foreman.   The rapid spread of the Foreman's Association came as a traumatic shock to management. It was bad enough to lose workers to the union; if the first-line foremen were to defect as well, how could management hope to control its men?

Management's first reaction was an all-out attack on the Foreman's Association. On a more constructive level, measures were taken to induce foremen to feel once again as though they were members of management. One measure was largely social: Management clubs, management dinners, and other activities were arranged at which foremen could mingle on a supposedly equal level with their superiors. Management also made an effort to improve downward communications by means of newsletters and meetings designed to help the foreman feel that he was "in the know" on company developments—hopefully, before the union learned of them.

But management's major efforts to rehabilitate the first-line foreman were in the area of training. At the least sophisticated level, the newly instituted training programs consisted of trite exhortations to feel and act like management (though, as one foreman put it, "it is more important to be treated as management than to be told that you are management"). The better-conceived programs helped to equip foremen with the attitudes and skills necessary to lead men rather than drive them.

More substantial than any of these measures was the decision taken by some companies to cut down on the power of staff and restore it to the foreman. In many instances foremen were given the final say over hiring, discipline, and promotion. Some of the safety and quality-control departments, along with much of personnel, became advisory, with the foreman exercising actual control in these areas.

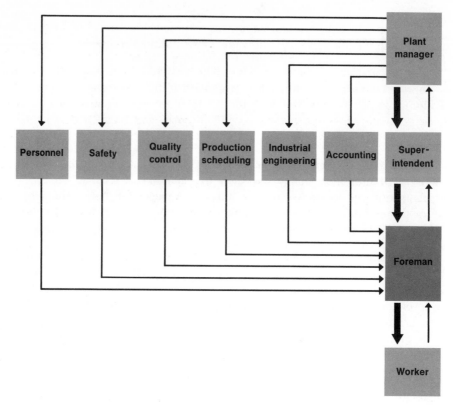

**THE GROWTH
OF STAFF**

A few large companies have experimented with creating a kind of superforeman. The number of employees reporting to the foreman have been doubled or tripled but he has been given a number of assistants and an advisory staff who report directly to him. Thus, for example, he has his own industrial engineer and personnel assistants. They assist him in setting work standards, dealing with grievances, scheduling, and so on. With his own staff the foreman no longer has to negotiate with outside staff departments.

All these efforts reflect a recognition that the foreman leadership role cannot be fractioned. If the foreman is to have the confidence, loyalty, and respect of his subordinates, he must have some significant control over those areas of decision-making that most affect his people.

CONCLUSION

Organizational human-relations problems often are mistakenly thought of solely as a by-product of autocratic supervision or uninteresting jobs. But normal frictions between specialist groups also contribute to human-relations problems. With increased emphasis on specialization in the modern organization and on "lateral relations" have come increasingly difficult problems of coordination.

We do not question the contribution of specialization to productivity. However, this chapter has emphasized that a manager's problems do not end when he has broken a single job into parts that can be handled by specialists. Managerial success depends on being able to put these parts together again and on developing coordinated cooperation among various individuals and subgroups so that the total organizational goals can be achieved.

We examined in some detail the relationship conflicts inherent in five different patterns of on-the-job relationship prescribed by the division of labor. These were the work-flow, service, advisory, auditing, and stabilization patterns. We noted that any given manager must spend as much, if not more, of his time and energy engaged in these lateral types of relationship as he does dealing directly with subordinates and superiors. Over the years, the position and status of the first-line supervisor has been endangered by these new specialists, and new organizational arrangements have become necessary to avoid further deterioration.

Employees learn to identify with their own specialty and frequently lose sight of the over-all organization. Employees who are supposed to integrate their work activities so that ideas, materials, or papers pass smoothly from department to department often engage in struggles for rewards and prestige. Very often these clashes are not resolved by fixed rules or by top management decision but by bargaining. The weapons used in these intergroup struggles are techniques that enable men to avoid responsibility, to pass the buck.

On the positive side, the increased emphasis on negotiations, the multiplicity of relationships that have to be maintained (compared to just dealing with superiors and subordinates) also gives much greater challenge to managerial jobs in the modern organization.

We have suggested certain "short-term" remedies that may help to ameliorate some of the pressures arising from specialization. In Chapter 16 we shall consider the possibility of making basic changes in the organizational structure designed to reduce the underlying causes of discontent.

problem 1 • THE DOOLEY CASE

You were just promoted from a buyer at headquarters to the job of Purchasing Agent of the newly acquired Dooley Division of the General Products Company. In most companies the job of P.A. is to negotiate for the purchase of needed equipment and supplies on the basis of requisitions submitted by user departments. Most P.A.'s feel that at the plant level they should report to the plant manager.

As you left your old boss in central purchasing, he cautioned you,

"Be careful now. Remember, that division was pretty much a one-man firm till we bought them out. Bill Dooley would never have sold out if he didn't need capital for expansion. His outfit is a big money-maker and as Division Manager he is still the boss there. As long as he brings in the profits, no one from headquarters is going to interfere with his decisions. He's never had a P.A., and you are the only man sent from headquarters except the controller. The Big Boss [company president] persuaded him that having a P.A. was the fashionable thing to do, but I'm not sure if Dooley knows what purchasing is all about."

You arrived at the new plant—miles away from the main office. Dooley turned out to be a likable bundle of nerves of about 45. He showed you around, or tried to, because it seemed that he couldn't take a step without someone running to him for a decision—mostly on technical questions. The administrative problems he seemed to push off on Bob Wallace, the manufacturing superintendent.

As you went around, you noticed a sanding belt that was not of the latest design. So you commented that one supplier had developed a new product that was both cheaper and better. Dooley seemed delighted: "Well, get us the new product. That's what we have you here for." Wallace seemed a little unhappy but said nothing.

You were shown your new office, next to Wallace's and personnel's in the factory building; Dooley, the accounting office, and engineering were in the new building.

When Dooley left, Wallace sat down with you and began to speak haltingly. "To tell you the truth, I'm not sure how we will be able to use you. We never had a P.A. before. Dooley brought you in because headquarters said you might help out here. We are really a very small outfit with only 200 people, and we just don't believe in paper work. We have always worked so well together that we really don't need it. Now as I see your job, it is to keep the salesmen off Bill's and my shoulders—except for the few with whom we have developed very good relations—and to buy our supplies at the lowest possible cost."

Before you could comment, he was off on an errand, having instructed a general foreman to show you around. You asked what you felt were shrewd questions about costs and output, some of which the general foreman seemed reluctant to answer. You noticed several parts that it would seem better for the company to buy rather than make. When you suggested this, the general foreman answered, "This is a small firm, mister, and a lot of people depend on this work."

You tried to talk to the chief engineer. He showed a lot of interest in your background, your family, your housing arrangements, but he seemed to freeze up when you mentioned his work.

"It's highly technical . . . making big advances which are hard for a layman to understand. . . . Yes, we make up the blueprints and tell the shop what to make. They're a good lot. All local boys, been with us a long time, take care of the troubles before they come up. . . . Specifications? Well, insofar as we have them, we draw them up with Dooley; he tells Wallace what to buy . . . I guess you'll be helping Wallace on that. He handles all the paper work. He needs help. Things have been getting pretty busy recently."

The controller gave you a different picture.

"I'm going crazy here. Been trying to get some sort of cost analysis, but don't make any progress because there are no records kept of anything. If I want specific information, I can usually get it from Dooley or Wallace—they keep it in their heads—but I can't develop anything systematic. If I try to pin Dooley down on a new system of some type, he seems to listen, but he's off on a new problem before I get an answer. I just can't get cooperation from anyone."

Next day Wallace started giving you instructions. "Get in touch with some of the coal firms in town and see what price you can get. Maybe we can buy cheaper. Call up Louhurst Bros. and ask them to send over 10 gallons of Sherman-Williams white paint."

You asked if a purchase order was needed. He answered, "No. When the bill comes in, Mary in the office will call Jack in receiving, and if it came in OK, she'll send out a check. . . . Oh, Bill or I sign it."

Just then the phone rang. It was Wallace again. "I'm sending over a salesman from the MM Company, who is going to make some widgets for us and it's a big order, so make up some kind of contract with him—he'll tell you what we agreed on—and send it to me to check over and sign."

1. How much could you realistically expect to accomplish during the next three months?
2. What problems would you face in getting acceptance of a real purchasing program?
3. How is your problem complicated by the personalities and vested interests of these people?
4. How do the various parties—Dooley, Wallace, the general foreman, the chief engineer, and the controller—view you?

5. What plans could you make for handling each of them?

6. What mistakes did you make at the outset?

7. How has the absence of specialization, rules, procedures, and so forth helped or hindered the Dooley Division?

problem 2 • TECHNICIAN POOL

The Bellows Chemical Laboratories were engaged in the development and production of a number of organic chemicals used in the printing and textile industries. As a result of the growing acceptance of the company's product line, the research laboratory experienced a major expansion.

In this company the job classification of "laboratory technician" referred to persons who performed routine tests at the direction of professionally trained employees. A variety of tests was involved, and many of the tests required considerable skill to execute. All the technicians had completed high school and several had attended college for one or two years. The professionals in the laboratory were all graduate chemists or engineers.

The work of the laboratory was organized under the "project" system. The work was authorized by management, as required, and assigned by the head of the laboratory to one or, at the most, two professionals for execution. When the work was completed, the chemists or engineers involved were given new assignments.

Until recently, the size of the laboratory (both professional and technician groups), was small enough so that frequent interaction among the entire staff was possible. Desks of all personnel were located within a single "conversational" area, and everyone had fairly accurate knowledge of the goals and work requirements of the various active projects. When a chemist or engineer had a series of tests to be run, he would ask the technician who seemed least burdened with work at the time to undertake the assignment. On the whole, this arrangement worked smoothly. Delays in the work and manifestations of discontent among the personnel were infrequent.

Recently the demands on the laboratory have increased markedly. The number of active projects has increased by a substantial margin, and the number of professionals employed has approximately doubled. Also, several additional technicians have been assigned to the laboratory.

When it became apparent that the informal arrangement for scheduling technician time would not function adequately with the larger group, a "technician pool" was created and put in the charge of a senior technician. Professionals who desired tests run were to route their requests through the head technician, who in turn would assign technicians from the "pool." [4]

[4] We are indebted to one of our former students, Mr. E. W. Coleman, for the outline of this case.

1. What problems will the new system create?

2. What will be the reactions of technicians and engineers to the new system?

3. Why is the new system more justified now than it was when the laboratory was smaller?

16 MINIMIZING THE HUMAN PROBLEMS OF LARGE ORGANIZATIONS

We have been looking at some of the problems that stem from extended lines of authority and the division of labor in the contemporary organization. By this time you may have decided that advantages of large-scale organization are hardly worth the cost. There are those who look back nostalgically to the "good old days" when companies were small, when the boss knew all his employees intimately, when everyone worked together and did a whole job, when problems of coordination and communication were at a minimum. Neither horizontal nor vertical cleavages were particularly significant, and the work group and the company were synonymous. Many studies have shown that employee morale is higher in small work groups than in large ones. Motivation and job satisfaction are all easier to achieve in the more intimate setting.

The technological and economic advantages that come with size, however, mean that large organizations are here to stay. Size makes possible many of the economies of specialization (*e.g.*, mass production) and the introduction of expensive equipment (*e.g.*, electronic data-processing machines). As the organization grows, it usually gains what economists call "economies of scale"—that is, money can be borrowed at lower interest rates, supplies purchased in larger quantities, and so on.

Even from a human-relations point of view, large organizations possess advantages. Larger companies have pioneered in introducing personnel programs designed to eliminate many of the sources of unrest common to smaller companies. They have sought to regularize employment, to develop training and promotion programs stressing merit rather than nepotism, to introduce equitable wage and salary administration programs that adjust income to job responsibility, and to provide retirement and insurance programs to reduce the fear of illness and old age.

The basic problem is this: How can organizations gain the advantages that come with size and specialization without paying a heavy price in terms of reduced employee and managerial effectiveness? In the small organization where face-to-face relationships predominate, a manager of goodwill who likes and respects people may prove highly successful. In the large organization, good intentions are not enough; human relations needs to be *planned* to insure an environment conducive to productivity.

How can organizational structure be designed to minimize human friction? In answering this question, we shall try to show that the manager who plans his organizational structure intelligently and realistically can:

1. Reduce the number of levels in the organizational hierarchy, even though he does not reduce the total number of employees.
2. Improve the efficiency with which the immediate work group solves the difficult work-flow problems of coordination and cooperation.
3. Improve cooperation between groups within the organization.
4. Relate personality variables to job design.

FEWER LEVELS OF MANAGEMENT

In Chapter 14, we mentioned that the existence of many levels within an organization complicates the problems of management. The individual employee feels lost because he is many steps removed from the key decision-makers who control his welfare, and both top management and the worker feel isolated from one another. Orders and information have to pass up and down through so many levels that there are countless possibilities for distortions in communication.

It is not uncommon for large corporations to have ten to twelve levels intervening between the hourly-paid employee and top management. And yet the number of levels required by the organization is *not* automatically determined by the number of employees. For instance, Sears Roebuck reported in 1950 that with 110,000 employees in their retail division, there were only four levels of supervision *between* the president of the company and the salespeople in the stores.[1] This "flat" structure was not accidental; it was a reflection of deliberate management policy to maximize the number of subordinates (the span of control) reporting to a given supervisor.

Flat vs. Tall Organizations

Fortunately, the Sears Roebuck Company has analyzed the effect of its organizational setup on human relations within the company. Sears operates many stores that have an almost identical number of employees doing highly

[1] James C. Worthy, "Factors Influencing Employee Morale," *Harvard Business Review*, Vol. 28, No. 1 (January 1950), p. 69.

similar jobs. In some of these stores, 32 department managers report directly to the store manager; in others, the department managers report to 5 or 6 division managers, who in turn report to the store manager. Obviously, the first is a relatively *flat* type of structure; the second, a *tall* type. What has Sears observed in the operations of these two quite different organization patterns?

The tall organization tended to encourage close supervision. With a relatively small number of subordinates, each supervisor, whether he was the store manager or the division manager, was able to give very detailed instructions to and exercise strong control over every one of the people in his unit. But in the flat organization, the relatively large number of subordinates made this type of supervision physically impossible. Each supervisor was obliged to rely on general supervision and good training; he just didn't have the time to keep a close watch on everyone. The delegation of responsibility in these stores encouraged subordinates to work on their own initiative and learn from their own mistakes. Since the supervisor could not make a decision on every problem that arose, subordinates achieved a high degree of self-reliance. The results showed themselves in the higher profits, better morale, and greater number of promotable executives produced by the flat organization.

Another obvious advantage to the fewer-leveled organization is the saving of managerial time: Problems are handled more quickly. Equally important are the better human relations associated with fewer levels. Communication is expedited; the individual employee finds it easier to identify with the work of his part of the organization.

Not every organization, of course, can arbitrarily increase the number of subordinates reporting to each of its supervisors. The ability of Sears to make use of a relatively "wide" span of control is a function of the following factors: [2]

1. It was possible to develop efficiency measures (controls) for the various departments so that a manager could be left to make nearly all his own decisions and only have to account for the final results: in other words, supervision "by results."

2. Department store personnel receive a good part of their compensation in the form of commissions and bonuses based on sales performance. These incentives provide them with a high degree of motivation and decrease the need for close supervision.

3. No great amount of coordination between department managers was required in these stores. In effect, each department could be operated relatively independently of the others, thus reducing the amount of supervision required by the store manager.

One other interesting facet of the Sears study is worth mentioning since it relates to what we shall say later about personality. The Sears organization found that certain managers *preferred* the "tall" organization and its attendant close

[2] Though the evidence is somewhat mixed, in general it supports the position that broad spans of control are associated with routine work.

supervision. Given their personalities, that was the way they wanted to manage. Others, if they were shifted into that kind of store, immediately set about to increase the number of people reporting to each supervisor. Their personality was such that they trusted people and didn't want to exercise close supervision.

BUILDING INTEGRATED WORK TEAMS: A SYSTEMS VIEW

Which jobs should be put together under a common supervisor? This is often called the *departmentation* decision. Naive managers assume that the answer is obvious:

The drill presses and the punch presses have *always* been in separate departments.

The sales engineers report to the manager of engineering; after all they're engineers, aren't they?

But, of course, such decisions are not obvious. Whereas many organizations rely on functional boundary lines (grouping together employees with similar job titles or "functions"), others are showing an increasing interest in a *systems view* of organization. In this approach, the manager looks at what people actually have to do in their relationships with one another if work is to flow smoothly. Those people who must coordinate their task are then placed together under a common supervisor. [3]

The significance of this approach was underlined by the problems associated with producing highly complicated military equipment like the Polaris submarine. A large number of separate tasks had to be integrated perfectly. If task No. 32 wasn't done, No. 33 couldn't begin—and there were thousands of these distinguishable design, manufacture, and assembly tasks. Further, the sophistication of the technology required that each task be done in such a way as to intermesh perfectly with the others in terms of dimensions and operating characteristics.

Given these kinds of problems, new organizational procedures had to be invented. New *control* techniques like PERT (Program Evaluation and Review Technique) were given to managers to enable them to watch the progress of the work through its various stages and to identify where bottlenecks threatened. More importantly, managers were given responsibility for the development of a total weapons system rather than being divided up according to functions (such as design, development, manufacture, testing, and so on). This was the same "task force" procedure that had been utilized in the Manhattan Project, which developed the atomic bomb.

In civilian work, this systems approach reflects itself in increasing emphasis on organization by *product* manufactured or service rendered rather than by *process* or function. But this distinction will be clearer if we look at an example.

---

[3] For a more complete and precise definition of these criteria, see Eliot Chapple and Leonard Sayles, *The Measure of Management* (New York: Macmillan, 1960), pp. 18-45.

The Ajax Company: Customer-Order Processing Department

To illustrate how this reorganization can be accomplished, we shall describe a case in which changes in organization substantially altered the human relations of the situation. Notice particularly that the original emphasis on functional specialization, a characteristic of modern organizations, as emphasized in Chapter 15, was the chief source of the difficulty. The division of labor employed *before* the change looked logical and reasonable on paper. Management's mistake was in assuming that people behave like the rectangles and lines of an organization chart.

Before

The Ajax Company manufactured small home appliances which it sold to retail outlets. Every order sent in by salesmen in the field had to be processed by four different groups of employees in the home office.

   a. *Customer contact clerks* communicated with the customer if the salesman's order was unclear, if the merchandise ordered was unavailable, or if price changes had taken place.

   b. *Billing clerks* checked the arithmetic on the order and entered correct charges and credits on the customer's account.

   c. *Inventory checkers* checked to make sure that goods ordered were available for shipment.

   d. *Credit approval clerks* examined the customer's credit status in order to authorize shipping.

The Ajax Company placed each "functional" group of employees under separate supervisors, as in the diagram below. Thus, each customer order passed through four distinct departments and two divisions. Each specialist belonged to the organizational unit to which his function was *logically* related.

WORKFLOW PROBLEMS BEFORE REORGANIZATION

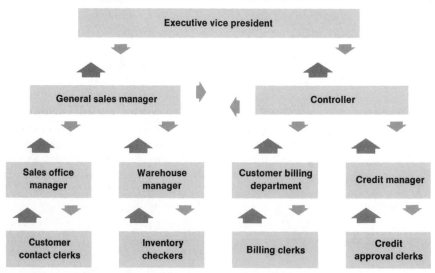

You can probably predict what happened. The design of the organization made no provision for the cooperation and communication required to complete the *total job* of customer-order processing. There was constant conflict among employees. Inventory checkers complained that they had to track down merchandise that might later be dropped from the order as a result of the discovery of a salesman's clerical error or inadequate customer credit. Responsibility for delays in processing orders were "passed" from one group to another. The billing clerks complained that the inventory checkers were always late with their information, and the inventory checkers retorted that their delays were the result of faulty information from customer contact clerks.

Higher management was always being called in to settle disputes. When conflict arose between an inventory checker and a customer contact clerk, for example, each would contact his superior, who in turn would take the battle up to the General Sales Manager. When the billing clerk complained that he couldn't get up-to-the-minute information from the customer contact clerks (and thus made embarrassing errors in customers' accounts), the problem might have to go to the Executive Vice President. Even the Sales Manager and the Controller were constantly blaming one another for difficulties in each other's departments.

After

In a reorganization of these functions, all employees processing customer orders were placed under a single general office supervisor, who in turn had first-line supervisors for the various geographic areas served by the company. The new organization looked like the following chart.

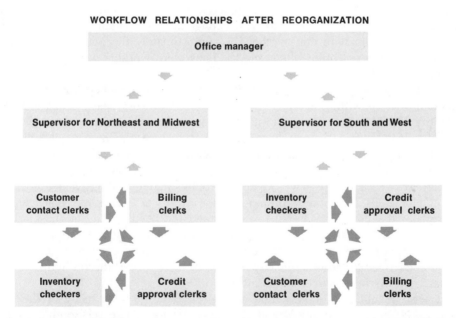

WORKFLOW RELATIONSHIPS AFTER REORGANIZATION

Under each of these supervisors, the specialists continued to do much the same job they had done before. Now, however, any dispute could be settled face-to-face within the immediate work group, or, in exceptional instances, by the first-line supervisor. No longer was it necessary to channel complaints up the line through two or three levels of management. The new scheme saved a great deal of executive time and made it possible to settle most problems by horizontal work-flow contacts between the employees themselves. The arrangement increased output enormously by eliminating many petty frictions.

The sales, warehouse, and credit managers now have a lateral, not a supervisory, relation to the office supervisor. Each was made responsible for establishing standards of performance for the clerical employees who did work involving their respective special interests, and for auditing to be sure that these standards of performance, that is, controls, were being observed.

Reduction in Number of Levels

Under the new systems arrangement, nearly every decision, and all information that has to be communicated, is handled either at the work level, among the employees themselves, or between them and their immediate supervisor: one of the two geographic office supervisors. The organization of this part of the business now consists of two relatively autonomous divisions, each of which can function almost entirely on its own.

In short, what happened at Ajax was this: (1) Management reduced the number of levels of supervision that had to participate in the solution of normal, daily work problems. And (2) it created more inclusive work teams that could handle problems on a face-to-face basis with a minimum of friction.

Improved Communications and Coordination

Recall the recurring struggle and frictions among the customer contact, billing, and credit approval clerks and inventory checkers. There was little of the mutual help, and loyalty, that we described as characteristic of the informal work group in Chapter 4. Why? The employees who had to interact with one another in order to complete the assigned work of processing customer orders did *not* belong to the same group. The billing clerks, for example, may have had a fine relationship with one another, but unfortunately the people they had to work with were not other billing clerks. They were working with employees in other departments.

The manner in which work activities are organized influences the quality of communications within the work group: People who work near one another and identify with the same group find it far easier to share the information they need to coordinate their jobs than do people who have infrequent contact with one another. In fact, much of our earlier discussion of flow-of-work problems could just as logically have appeared in a discussion of "communications problems." When two work groups have so much trouble understanding each other that communications are misinterpreted or go astray, or when top management complains that lower levels fail to understand the needs of the business—these are usually indications that the groups that make up the organization are too far apart. Because they report to different supervisors, they develop unique interests. Their separate worlds, their special skills, their special desires and activities create barriers to effective communication.

Vast quantities of information are required to perform many of the jobs within the large organization, and the superior-subordinate relationship cannot possibly carry the burden of communicating all of it. Students of organization are often surprised by the amount of work-oriented information that is communicated during what appear to be social contacts. During a coffee break it is not unusual to hear a conversation of this sort:

"Say, Joe, just out of curiosity, tell me what your guys are doing to mangle those parts we're supposed to put together in a minute and a half."

"Bill, you've got the wrong villain. Orders came down from the plant manager's office to loosen up on our tolerances. They figure we were rejecting too many out-of-limits parts and wasting money. In fact, they claim that you guys have been having it too soft with our perfect parts; now you'll have to just work a little harder to put 'em together."

These semi-social contacts, which are normally a product of membership in the same group, are an indispensable supplement to more formal channels of communication.

Research Studies of Organization Change

Mining. [4]   Let us examine what happened when a natural work team in a coal mine was broken up. At one time all the operations at the mine face were performed by a small team which worked together on a single shift. Since they were in close contact with one another, it was easy to devise solutions for problems as they arose. Each member of the group felt responsible for the entire operation.

In the mistaken belief that it would increase efficiency, management combined these small groups into much larger ones working over larger areas. For example, one crew did nothing but prepare the new "face" for blasting. Others handled the recovery of the coal that came down after the dynamite had been set off; another crew worked on timbering and moving rail lines. This new division of labor was carried out on a three-shift, 24-hour cycle: Each shift performed a different function. Each worker became a specialist. As a result, no single group of workers felt responsible for the total operation; as problems arose, each shift developed the habit of shrugging them off and passing the buck to the next shift. Communications, which at best are very troublesome in a mine, were further complicated by the workers' being separated from each other in time and space. Previously, the small groups were almost self-supervising (motivated as they were by a group incentive plan); now, coordinating the various individual workers, none of whom had much motivation, became a complex management task. Even new equipment did not compensate for production losses due to work-flow problems.

Textile mill. [5]   An Indian textile mill, which had undergone intensive "job re-engineering," did not attain satisfactory output levels. Each occupational group in the mill was assigned a work load based on a careful study of all the job components. For example, in one room containing 240 looms, the following assignments were made to the 12 types of specialist:

1. Each weaver tended approximately 30 looms.
2. Each "battery filler" served about 50 looms.
3. Each "smash hand" was assigned some 80 looms.
4. Each of nine different categories of maintenance men was responsible for from 120 to 240 looms.

All these occupational tasks were highly interdependent, and the utmost coordination was required to maintain productivity. But the assignment of work loads militated against coordination. In effect, each weaver came into contact

---

[4] E. L. Trist, G. W. Higgin, H. Murray, A. B. Pollock, *Organizational Choice* (London: Tavistock Publications, 1963).

[5] A. K. Rice, "Productivity and Social Organization in an Indian Weaving Shed," *Human Relations*, Vol. 6, No. 4 (1953).

with five-eighths of a "battery filler," three-eighths of a "smash hand," and even smaller fractions of the other nine workers on whom he was at least partially dependent to keep his looms operating.

When the work was reorganized so that all interdependent workers were made part of the same work group, production soared. Work groups were reconstructed so that a single group of workers was responsible for the operation of a given bank of looms. The new interaction pattern produced regular relationships and communications among workers and led directly to the increase in output.

An automated power plant. With good fortune a team of social researchers was able to study the introduction of automation into a large steam power plant. Automation, with its integrated controls, served to break down the organizational boundaries between the independent boiler, turbine, and electrical departments. These groups of men had been responsible separately for steam generation, turbine operation, and the distribution of the resulting electricity. Automated processing permitted management to put a single foreman over the entire operating force and eliminate intergroup problems. In the research, the employees also reported:

... being significantly more satisfied with the amount of information they got about both the plant and the company [than a comparable work force in a nonautomated plant]. Reducing the number of people between the top staff and the employees appears to have eliminated one of the communication barriers between these ... groups .... [6]

Summary of cases. The conclusion to be drawn from these studies is that in designing the organization the administrator should provide each work group with a relatively autonomous task. Only under such circumstances can competent *internal* leadership and group responsibility develop.

Ideally, the individual worker should be permitted to coordinate his activities by himself (that is, through job enrichment). If the same girl does both the typing and the filing, problems in integrating the two processes are unlikely to arise. The next best thing is to have the coordination take place within the immediate work group, where each individual feels loyalty and responsibility to his fellow workers and is willing to adjust his pacing, the quality of his work, and his over-all efforts to the needs of the others.

Developing Identification with the Total Job

The type of organization rearrangements we are considering have another valuable by-product. The new groups that are created are more likely to have high morale than are large, highly specialized work groups.

The structure of a work group has profound effects on the job satisfactions derived by its members. An employee who is just one of many, all doing the same operation, which operation in turn is only a small part of some larger activity, feels little sense of accomplishment or identification with the larger

---

[6] Floyd Mann and L. Richard Hoffman, *Automation and the Worker* (New York: Holt, 1960), p. 56.

unit. However, in the semi-autonomous groups we have been describing, in which people who do complementary tasks are brought together:

Employees have a much better opportunity to know each other, so that cooperation between individuals and departments can develop on a more personal, informal basis and not be so largely dependent on impersonal systems and administrative controls. Employees can see much more readily where they themselves "fit" into the organization and the significance of their jobs in the whole scheme of things. [7]

When large numbers of people doing similar work are brought together in a single department, particularly if their work is unchallenging, personnel difficulties are likely to multiply. Typing pools, departments filled with hundreds of draftsmen or engineers doing identical tasks, all are sources of serious morale problems. To be sure, such a scheme may mean that the work can be scheduled more efficiently and that complex and labor-saving equipment can be used to handle the work of the entire organization. Yet the concentration of a large number of people, all doing the same job, tends to isolate them from the total organization. These groups become conscious of areas where their needs conflict with the rest of the organization.

IMPROVING COORDINATION BETWEEN GROUPS

It would be unrealistic, however, to assume that completely autonomous work groups can be developed. In the modern organization, work groups and departments have to cooperate with one another if the objectives of the enterprise are to be attained. Consequently, management has a responsibility to innovate organization changes that further intergroup cooperation.

Layout and Contacts

Excessive physical distance among groups almost invariably reduces their opportunities to cooperate.

"As accountants, our job is to help department heads improve their procedures and records to make their jobs easier and the results more effective. Oftentimes, however, we are not called in early enough when a new project gets started or some change is contemplated. The fault lies in our location—the laboratory accounting office is located in a small rented building several miles from the nearest research or development group. Being far away they never get around to calling us until their plans are already fixed; it takes so much longer to undo things than to get in on the ground floor. When we used to be located in the same building, these problems never occurred."

One way to improve opportunities for contact between groups that need to coordinate is to revise office and work-floor layouts. At the same time, the manager may also want to separate groups that do not need such intimate contact. Too easy access between such groups may encourage them to make unnecessarily frequent demands on each other.

Where for one reason or another such physical shifts are impossible for the manager to arrange, he may be able to devise special procedures to bring groups

[7] Worthy, *op. cit.*, p. 68.

together that have to coordinate their activities but that are part of separate organizational families. We observed one company in which such procedures were hit on by chance. Two groups of engineers who reported to separate departments but who were working on interrelated drawings found that they needed to see each other more frequently than the normal flow of work allowed. Since there was no company cafeteria, the members of the two groups developed a car-pooling arrangement for traveling to and from lunch so that they could discuss their problems on the way.

Committees and Coordinators

Special committees are useful in facilitating exchange of information between groups that normally have little contact with one another:

The members of one department were upset by another group's habit of sending in requests for "rush orders" that put tremendous pressure on everyone. They couldn't understand why these last-minute needs could not be predicted earlier. It was only when cross-department staff meetings were held that they learned about certain inherent technical problems that made last-minute supplies necessary.

Under the direction of a skilled chairman, committee meetings provide an opportunity for systematic, face-to-face discussion of problems and dessemination of information.

Increasingly, large companies make use of coordination or liaison specialists. For example, *product planners* have the responsibility for getting development engineering, manufacturing, and sales to work together. They work between each of these groups, persuading them to modify their efforts for the common good, that is, the design, production and distribution of a new product.

Training

As we have seen, many of the problems of coordination in specialized organizations arise out of the fact that each group has its own "vested interest," its own typical point of view or approach to problems. The engineer is interested in quality, for instance; his training and the nature of his work give him little interest in cost reduction. The accountant has just the opposite point of view. Such differences are inevitable (in fact, properly utilized by management they contribute to organizational strength).

An effective training program can help the engineer put himself into the accountant's shoes. It can show each group how its own actions sometimes cause unwitting but unnecessary affronts to other groups. It can show each group how it can communicate with others in understandable terms.

Supervision

The good manager evaluates the status of intergroup relationships as part of his regular supervisory pattern. He seeks to identify potential and actual points of friction in the organization and to determine whether they are the result of poor organization design, personality problems, bad placement, or temporary operating problems.

Some of the types of reorganization we have been describing might approximately be called shifts toward greater *decentralization*. Large, amorphous organizations in which nearly every decision must go up through many levels are highly *centralized*. They are the ones cursed with the problems of many-leveled hierarchies and specialization described in earlier chapters (like the Ajax Company before it was reorganized).

And yet centralization is not just a product of a particular managerial or supervisory philosophy, such as: "Close supervision is useful because people can't be trusted." Centralization also results from the design of the organization itself. When operations are highly specialized and departments finely subdivided, decisions *must* be made by higher levels in the organization, and rigid rules *must* be employed. The reason, of course, is that no supervisor, any more than a single employee, is in a position to be "on his own." Because only a small part of the total job is done by any one employee or department, upper levels of management must step in to insure cooperation and coordination.

Where the work of the organization is broken up into so many functional divisions again, cooperation can no longer be achieved spontaneously. After all, each functional unit was set up as a distinct entity in order that it might achieve a more efficient system. Each unit, therefore, tends to operate primarily in terms of its own system rather than in terms of the needs of the organization as a whole. Each unit becomes jealous of its own prerogatives and finds ways to protect itself against the pressures and encroachments of others. Conflict develops on the employee level as well as the supervisory level, thus forcing an extra administrative load on higher levels of management because of the need for constantly reconciling differences. [8]

With a systems approach, by contrast, management often considers a very different set of variables in deciding on organization structure. Rather than grouping employees together because they do similar work, management assesses the number and type of contacts required to complete a total operation. When interrelated jobs are carefully grouped together, the supervisor can be left pretty much to his own devices. He can serve as an effective leader, since he has autonomy himself and can in turn delegate some autonomy to his subordinates.

The Vice President of Manufacturing in a large oil company has described the organization of one of the company's new refineries in systems terms.

In this refinery all the men except the accountants and laboratory technicians are part of a single operating team. There is only one department—the Operating Department. The men have been trained somewhat as the crew of a submarine, in that every man can fill almost any breach. They are not concerned whether someone is doing their work, or whether they are doing someone else's work. Their interest lies, as a team, in keeping the operation going. All of the operating work is their work.

There are ten on each shift. They run the entire refinery, including crude distillation, catalytic cracking and reforming, product testing, blending and shipping of products, and the utilities. [9]

[8] Worthy, *op. cit.*, p. 71.

[9] Clarence H. Thayer, Vice President in Charge of Manufacturing, Sun Oil Company, Philadelphia, Penn., "Automation and the Problems of Management" (address to the Wilmington, Delaware, Chapter of the Society for the Advancement of Management, delivered on October 14, 1958).

Under this philosophy of management some of the large concentrations of staff groups that create problems of coordination for the line manager are being dispersed. Middle managers and sometimes even first-level managers may be assigned their own staff specialists (to assist in methods work, personnel, tooling, and so on). That they can directly control the activities of the specialists makes coordination much simpler and helps train the manager to do his own control and planning. In turn, as a manager gains skill and experience in these tasks, his self-confidence and status are built up.

Decentralization means shifting "downward" the point at which all the employees necessary to do a complete job come together and report to a common supervisor. Again, this shift means that more responsibility can be delegated to the manager. Building the organization structure around the flow of work permits the large company to enjoy the human-relations advantages of the small company. All the operations that need to be integrated come under a common supervisor at the lowest possible level. This supervisor is able to communicate directly with everyone who has any impact on his ability to meet the goals assigned him. Workers and managers who must coordinate their activities are made members of the same team. Each employee is able to contact directly his real boss—the man who makes the important decisions.

Limitations of Decentralization

This technique of decentralization is not a cure-all for human-relations problems, however. While companies like General Motors, Sears, duPont, General Electric, and others are enthusiastic about its virtues, others, like Chrysler, have tried it and moved away.

One of the reasons for this difference in experience may be that decentralization requires unusually able personnel—managers and employees who can accept delegation and general supervision and the responsibilities these entail. This means that management must devise good selection procedures by which it can accurately identify managerial talent and must also provide for effective on-the-job training. Decentralization demands that all managers in the company share a common understanding of the methods and objectives of the organization; otherwise autonomy may lead to anarchy.

There are other limitations that make decentralization something less than a cure-all for organization ills. Decentralized organizations may not be as effective in making quick decisions or in adjusting to rapid environmental changes. For example, it may be hard to get separate units to agree to manpower cutbacks unless the change is imposed from above. Many organizations are composed of parts that are too interdependent to allow for a great deal of autonomy—the opposite of the Sears, Roebuck case described earlier. Interdivisional cooperation may prove deficient when each division concentrates primarily on its own objectives rather than on those of the organization. One division may be unwilling to share scarce technicians with another, although the needs of the latter are more pressing. A research laboratory that is completely autonomous may fail to coordinate its activities with the needs of the manufacturing divisions. In turn, the manufacturing divisions may fail to appreciate how they can make use of research. Finally, decentralization has many added hidden costs arising from duplication of specialized staff work and the costs of operating the necessary controls to keep top management informed.

PERSONALITY AND ORGANIZATION STRUCTURE

Another key influence on job performance is personality. Particularly on jobs with a high human-relations content, where most of the working day is spent interacting with other people, personality is a major determinant of what will be done and how it will be done. This statement holds for store clerks and superintendents and industrial engineers as well as many other white-collar jobs.

Let us first look more specifically at how personality shapes job performance and then consider what can be done about the personality factor in order to improve organizational performance.

How Personality Shapes the Organization

Traditionally, personality was ignored in organizational decision-making because jobs were dealt with in isolation. It was assumed that a job could be defined in terms of abstract "responsibilities" without giving much thought to the relationships between jobs, what behavior was expected of the individual in relation to other people in the organization. Thus, it should make no difference whether the position "Product Engineer for Special Fabrics" is occupied by Mr. Ross or by Mr. Jones. Each should do it in exactly the same way, because that is the way the organization is designed to function.

But practice differs enormously from theory. The organization will undoubtedly not function the same way when Ross has the job as it did with Jones. Each man's personality will reveal itself in the way he works with his colleagues, his boss, his subordinates, and other departments. As a result, when the incumbent on a job changes, everyone has to adjust to a whole series of changes in the way work is accomplished.

Thus it is naive to assume that employees fit themselves into the straitjacket of the job specification. As they try the job on for size they begin squirming a bit, pulling in here and pushing out there, until the job begins to fit their personality needs. The result is that the organization functions differently from the way the designers of the structure envisioned.

Brown as purchasing agent is supposed to spend about half his time analyzing sources of supply and negotiating purchases, and the other half managing the employees in the purchasing office. Brown enjoys negotiating, but is unhappy handling what he calls these "darn petty personnel problems." So he spends less and less time supervising and more time buying. Gradually the job of running the office is assumed by his chief assistant, since the employees need someone to turn to with their problems.

In contrast, Smith is supposed to spend his time drawing up engineering specifications. However, he has a flair for dealing with people, and he soon finds that other engineers are coming to him with their problems. He begins to represent them directly in contacts with the division head. As his reputation as a "fixer" grows, upper management uses him as a trouble-shooter. He does less and less engineering and more and more human-relations work. At the same time, his own boss, the section head who prefers puzzling over blueprints to worrying about employee relations, gradually loses authority.

What an organization *really is* reflects the personalities of those who hold key jobs. The personality of the chief executive permeates the entire company, and as we noted earlier, personal preferences of store managers at Sears determined whether "tall" or "flat" organizations evolved.

Similarly, supervisory styles, how subordinates are dealt with, are often reflections of personality make-ups. Here is one example: [10]

Berg believed that a good supervisor should delegate as much responsibility as possible to subordinates. He couldn't understand why he was always being criticized for failures to delegate. If one watched him supervise the answer was clear enough. Yes, he would give orders that would allow the individual to assume a great deal of responsibility. But he was very impatient and never took the time to train a subordinate thoroughly before giving a new assignment. Often the employee didn't know the background of the problem he was expected to handle and how it related to other activities for which he was responsible. Lacking complete information and adequate training, he either went very slowly or made serious mistakes. When Berg observed this behavior he hastily moved in and handled the job himself, always saying "It's easier to do it myself; no one wants to take real responsibility any more." Thus, his method of handling order-giving (arising from his fast-paced personality) frustrated his own intellectual belief in delegation.

Using Knowledge of Personality
to Solve Human-Relations Problems

When personality problems arise, a manager has three principal choices. He can endeavor to get people to modify their behavior to make their job performance more consistent with the needs of the job, or he can change the job, or he can replace the person. The last, of course, is the most drastic and frequently the most painful decision.

Modifying behavior. If the manager knows the proper behavior in a given situation, he may be able to persuade or train employees to adopt this pattern. In the Berg case, Berg's manager was able to get him to recognize that he, in fact, did not delegate. Berg became aware of his own propensity to "move in" too rapidly. He learned the importance of spending adequate time in giving assignments, to spend at least a half hour consecutively with a subordinate when a new project came in, and to wait several days before checking up on the subordinate after making an assignment.

Redesigning jobs. Many times it is easier to change the job than to change the person. Many behavioral attributes are too deeply ingrained to modify easily. Thus, parts of a job that are difficult for the individual to perform or on which he conflicts badly with other people may have to be removed. Jobs can, in fact,

[10] This and the cases following are adapted from Eliot Chapple and Leonard Sayles, "The Man, the Job, and the Organization," *Personnel* (March-April 1958), pp. 72-79.

be viewed as flexible packages of component parts, at least some of which are shiftable in order to tailor the job to the needs and competencies of the individual personality who will be manning it.

A large aircraft firm employed a training director who had long years of experience in designing both programs and materials. However, he lacked the ability to develop effective working relationships with the managers of other divisions. Nor was he able to put over his program in the face of opposition. Though management believed that training should be carried out at the divisional level, the training director found every excuse to stay in the central offices. Top management then evolved a plan to shift the "selling" parts of his job to an assistant and give the training director additional responsibilities for company publications.

Selection and rejection. Many times the types of problems we have been describing are avoided by considering the behavioral requirements of the job in advance and selecting an appropriate personality to fill the job. Of course, when the individual is unable to develop satisfactory relations with subordinates or colleagues, he may be shifted to another job or leave the company. This course of action can be embarrassing and costly to all concerned. Thus, changing people (personalities) changes the operating characteristics of organization just as does any structual change.

CONCLUSION

Unfortunately, some managers believe that the prime requisite for a smooth-running organization is a clear-cut, symmetrical organization plan which shows each man who his boss is and what his responsibilities are. Or they assume that the most logical scheme is to bring together under a common supervisor all employees who do similar work—that is, to organize personnel according to a "functional" pattern.

The results of such approaches to organization may have a disastrous effect on efficiency and human relations. They consume a great deal of managerial time simply because many levels of supervision are regularly involved in the day-to-day problems of getting work done. They encourage intergroup struggles. Further, managers are compelled by the difficulties inherent in the organization structure to resort to close supervision and rigid rules; they cannot afford to delegate much responsibility. But the mere piling up of pressures, rules, and controls does not guarantee that all the parts of the organization will do "as they are told" and coordinate their activities effectively.

We have endeavored to show how some of the problems stemming from large, impersonal hierarchical structures based on the principle of division of labor can be ameliorated or solved. Care needs to be taken to insure that both work groups and department jurisdictions encompass as many as possible of those jobs that are closely interrelated. Cooperation that arises spontaneously out of the structure of the organization is far easier to maintain than that which is imposed by rigid rules, control, and close supervision. Furthermore, such decentralization leads to an enormous saving in managerial time and energy. It means that more of the day-to-day work problems can be solved by the immediate supervisor, rather than having to be carried up through one or even several levels to a common supervisor.

In a somewhat analogous fashion the manager endeavors to build effective personality-job combinations. An effort is made to find personalities compatible with the behavioral requirements of the job and to modify ineffective relationships. This can sometimes be done by transforming elements of the job (for instance, the training director helping the individual to observe where his activities are inadequate—such as the manager, Berg.)

In short, organizations should be constructed from the *bottom up*, rather than from the *top down*. In establishing work-group boundaries and supervisory units, management should start with the actual work that must be performed, an awareness of who must coordinate his job with whom, when, and where. Making work groups as inclusive as possible discourages close supervision and fosters downward delegation. Rather than an amorphous institution in which people cannot understand the relationship of their jobs to the objectives of the business, the organization then takes on some of the desirable characteristics of the informal group, an organic human system.

problem 1 • CONTAINER COMPANY

Until a few years ago a nationwide container corporation had an organizational structure that looked something like the chart on the opposite page.

In the old organization, the departmental organization of the plastics, glass, and paper divisions was exactly the same as in cans. (There is no space on the chart to show it.) Not all departments are portrayed in either structure.

1. What are the relative advantages and disadvantages of the new organization compared to the old? Why do you think the change was made?

2. Which organization is more centralized? Why?

3. Which form of organization has greater need for computers? Why?

4. What changes are needed in the behavior and personality of the president to make the new system work?

5. Neither organization chart lists the staff agencies that report directly to the president. How are the old and new organizations likely to differ in terms of their staff organization? (For example, what sorts of departments—other than those already listed as reporting to him—are likely to report to the president under each form of organization?)

6. List the most important forms of adjustment required by managers at lower levels to make the new organization work.

7. Which form of organization will adjust more easily to technological change? Why?

8. Which sort of organization is more likely to engage in "far out" research?

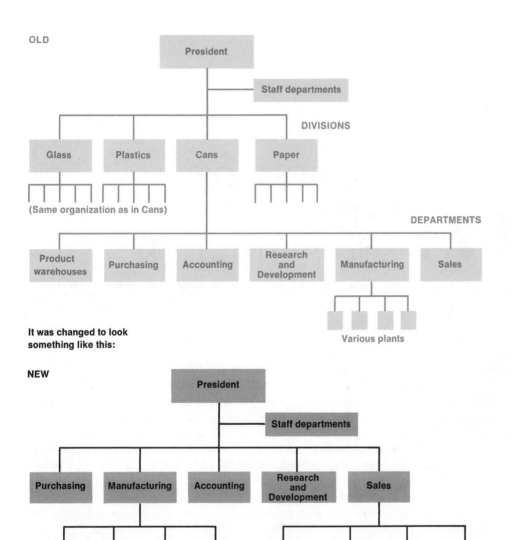

OLD

President

Staff departments

DIVISIONS

Glass   Plastics   Cans   Paper

(Same organization as in Cans)

DEPARTMENTS

Product warehouses   Purchasing   Accounting   Research and Development   Manufacturing   Sales

Various plants

It was changed to look something like this:

NEW

President

Staff departments

Purchasing   Manufacturing   Accounting   Research and Development   Sales

Glass   Plastics   Cans   Paper

Various plants

Consumer sales; e.g., paper towels   Food industry   Nonfood industry   Warehouses

17

THE ROLE OF PERSONNEL ADMINISTRATION

The massive growth of unionism in the United States both before and after World War II, the findings of social scientists like those involved in the famous Hawthorne Studies, and increased sensitivity to human relations convinced many corporate leaders that they did not understand the needs and strivings and complaints of their employees. Inevitably a hierarchy creates vast communication gaps between management and workers. Some staff group is needed to help management understand the employee point of view and to facilitate the building of durable relationships that preserve organizational integrity. This is the background of the contemporary personnel function.

The personnel function in management is especially concerned with the development of a highly motivated, smoothly functioning work force. True, this job is actually the responsibility of every manager, as is suggested by the oft-repeated phrase, "Management is people." Yet the *personnel department* has a special part to play in this field. And the fact that personnel is the responsibility both of the entire organization and of one special department makes the lateral relations between the personnel department and other departments particularly difficult.

In this chapter we shall be concerned with the unique contribution of the personnel specialist and the personnel department. First, we shall endeavor to provide some historical perspective. Next will come a brief description of the scope and organization of the functions of personnel administration. Finally, we shall examine the organizational implications of these functions, concentrating on those that pose the most difficulties.

The Period 1900–1930

Paternalism. One of the first manifestations of organized concern with the personnel function in management was the pre-World War I industrial welfare movement. Certain benevolent employers sought to improve the lot of the working man. The Industrial Revolution having brought with it many deprivations, life was often brutish for workers, particularly in congested cities. Incomes were too low to meet basic human needs. Supervisors were harsh, and many employees were recent immigrants who knew neither their rights nor the ways of this strange land. To alleviate these conditions, some employers developed a wide range of paternalistic benefit programs, extending from loans in times of adversity to lectures on thrift and homemaking. Such employers often hoped that their employees would be grateful for their benefits and, being happier, would work harder.

Some more foresighted employers hired social workers to help with these problems of adjustment and to provide sympathetic guidance for those who found themselves suffering from extreme pressure or discouragement. Others sought means by which workers' interests could be systematically represented within the organization. Since workers were afraid they would be punished if they complained to their bosses, the personnel department was a place to go for a fair hearing. In fact, personnel people served as an upward channel of communication between employees and production managers and represented the interests of employees in the councils of management.

Employment and records. Many personnel departments, however, made their first appearances as record-keeping departments. They maintained employment records (such as date hired, background information, successive jobs held in the company, and disciplinary penalties imposed), and also time- and production-records for the purpose of preparing payrolls. These were relatively routine clerical tasks that other members of the organization were probably glad to have taken from their shoulders. These functions are still important in view of the growing emphasis on pension and insurance programs, seniority benefits, and in-company promotion and management-development programs.

Response to new knowledge. The early decades of the twentieth century are associated with the scientific management movement. F. W. Taylor and his followers, dealing largely with production workers, showed that productivity could be improved through time study, the careful design of jobs and tools, and the use of incentives. Meanwhile, new psychological research made it possible for companies to improve employee-selection procedures by looking systematically at human differences. Similarly psychological principles of learning could be useful in training.

Both scientific management and psychology taught management to realize that human problems required analysis and systematic attention. To minimize *ad hoc* or expedient decision-making, specific *policies* were drawn up, particularly in regard to personnel (policies toward wages, employment, and retirement).

Governmental innovations and legislation. Government led the way in some personnel developments. The Civil Service pioneered in certain aspects of job evaluation, and private industry followed. In World War I, the U.S. Army experimented with a variety of selection and placement techniques that were later taken up by industry.

Government also contributed to the personnel field by legislation. Since the 1910's, there has been a growing stream of protective labor laws, both state and federal, that impose fair hiring practices, regulate wages, hours, safety and hygienic conditions, and provide social security.

Response to unionization. Employer opposition to trade unions helped increase the status of personnel departments, for many early benefit programs were looked upon as means of keeping unions out. The peak of the antiunion drive among large corporations occurred in the 1920's, when the so-called "American Plan" became popular. Under this scheme, employee-representation plans (ERP's) were established to provide a type of grievance procedure and to give employees a voice in decisions affecting the work force. Although many ERP's were but cynical efforts to provide the shell of representation without the substance, some employers sought to use these plans in good faith as a means of improving communications with rank-and-file workers. (Ironically, some of the leaders who arose in ERP later were active in starting unions.)

The 1930's

The personnel decision-making stage. During the 1930's there was another shift of emphasis: in many companies the personnel department (with its title often expanded to read "industrial relations department") was now expected to take direct charge of all employee and union relations. Often it was given full responsibility for hiring, firing, wage determination, handling union grievances, and determining who should be transferred or promoted.

Why did the personnel department suddenly gain so much power? Partly because of a widespread recognition by management of the importance of the human element, but probably the fear of unionism was the chief factor. Unions were on the offensive all through the late 1930's. They charged management with setting substandard wages, with discharging employees unjustly, with harboring foremen who acted as petty tyrants, with basing transfers and promotions purely on favoritism, and with paying little attention to human dignity. Faced with such charges, many companies felt that the best way to keep unions out was to eliminate the grievances that made workers turn to them. Management believed that inept supervisors were largely responsible for what observers conceded were haphazard personnel policies. So in many companies management gave the personnel department broad powers to establish uniform personnel policies and to police and administer them, as we discussed in Chapter 15.

Unions came into many large companies in spite of the personnel department's efforts. But this invasion only served to increase its status. Now it had the responsibility for negotiating the labor contract and handling grievances. And since unions constantly seek out chinks in management's armor and try to establish precedents in one department that can be used elsewhere, the personnel department was given still further centralized control over personnel activities throughout the organization.

Yet as the supervisor's standing as a leader declined, the question of the staff's proper role in the organization was asked more and more persistently. To the supervisor the enhanced power of the staff meant a usurpation of his authority, a weakening of his relationship to his own subordinates, and a forced dependence on a department that did not share his responsibility for meeting cost and production objectives. The demoralized supervisor complained that he was being asked to run his department without any effective power to select, discipline, or reward his subordinates. Furthermore, the industrial-relations department overruled his decisions so frequently that he often gave up all attempts to exercise supervisory judgment.

In many organizations, personnel departments gained the power to make final decisions concerning such matters as selection, wage and salary administration, and discipline. Other organizations, seeking to protect the supervisor's status, attempted to restrict personnel to a purely advisory role. These companies believed that staff groups, like personnel, should restrict their activities to advising and counseling supervisors who request their assistance.

The Present

In recent years the influence and prestige of the personnel function has expanded, for many reasons. Management no longer conceives of personnel work solely as a series of techniques to keep hourly workers satisfied or to meet governmental obligations. The members of management themselves constitute a growing work force (involving selection, remuneration, and promotion problems, to name but a few). There is also an increasingly large professional-specialist group within organizations, and these people have high expectations that must be responded to. Long-range manpower projections have become a crucial tool for management at every level of the organization, and training takes place at almost every level.

In addition, particularly in very large organizations, audit and stabilization functions that serve as a control on personnel-related decisions have increased in scope. Many of these are administered, as we shall see in this chapter, by the personnel department.

Wider use of social science. Management has also become more sophisticated about human relations. Management has learned that productivity is not simply a matter of getting the right man on a well-designed job and paying him an equitable wage (with perhaps an incentive rate attached).) Employees restrict output, informal groups oppose change, and status systems and personality problems complicate and distort communications.

In other words, the simple tenets of scientific management have come under question and the emphasis has shifted from individuals to groups, social systems, and communication networks. Increasingly, to solve productivity problems management has turned to supervisory-development programs, personnel research, and organization analysis (often bringing in concepts from sociology, applied anthropology, and social psychology). Further, computers now aid in these analyses.

Most recently, the onrush of automation, the rising costs of unemployment insurance and supplementary benefits, and demands from the community for more attention to the problem of minorities have caused management to rethink its manpower policies. New approaches have been made to the retraining of older or unskilled workers. Revised transfer policies, early retirement, and various techniques to stabilize employment levels have been tried.

Finally, there has been a growing appreciation of the effect of community attitudes toward the firm both on attracting suitable manpower and shaping employee behavior in the organization. In this connection, companies have explored methods of measuring community attitudes and public-relations programs to increase understanding.

THE SCOPE OF PERSONNEL ADMINISTRATION

The accompanying organization chart suggests the scope of functions performed by a typical personnel-industrial relations department in a large organization.

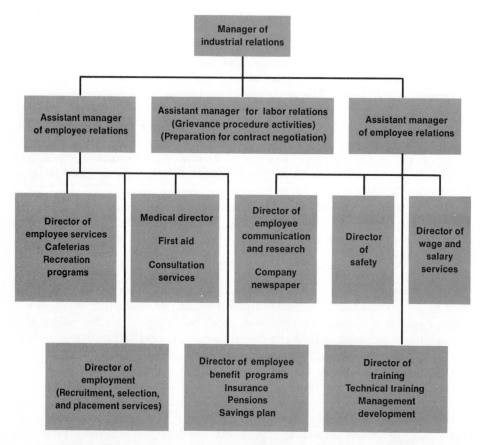

INTERNAL ORGANIZATION OF A LARGE COMPANY'S PERSONNEL DEPARTMENT

It is relatively easy to discern the historical changes in personnel philosophy and to sketch out the major functions of a typical personnel department. More difficult to explain is how a personnel point of view becomes a part of day-to-day managerial decision-making.

A typical company's organization manual will describe the personnel department's duties roughly as follows:

Personnel should provide the leadership required to formulate, recommend, and implement appropriate policies and procedures to ensure that the XYZ organization obtains and makes adequate use of the human resources required to accomplish the organization's goals.

How can this broad responsibility be fulfilled and Personnel's voice heard? It is not enough for Personnel to stand for "good" policies such as non-discriminatory employment, promotion based on merit or rational salary administration. Top management must give them support. However, even when such support is forthcoming, these policies are subject to conscious or unconscious distortion. Only if line and staff are able to work out a viable pattern of give and take will the organization's carefully contrived personnel policies become more than words in a manual (to be read once and only once by the neophyte manager).

Traditionally, personnel work has been conceived of as a *staff* function, that is, as secondary or subsidiary to the major *line* functions of business (such as manufacturing or sales). The staff category also meant a lack of authority and, of course, low prestige (and often low compensation as well).

But, as we have already seen, this dichotomy is an oversimplification, both because staff groups do have power and because there are various patterns of relationships associated with those functions of the business that go by the title of "staff."

As do other specialized staff departments, Personnel engages in audit, stabilization, advisory, and service relations with other managers and groups. We shall examine the problems involved with each in turn, observing how they contribute to the implementation of sound personnel policy.

AUDIT RELATIONSHIPS

Personnel's audit functions serve three basic purposes: (1) they help ensure that sound policies are being implemented; (2) they assist in evaluating the cost-effectiveness of alternative personnel techniques; and (3) they serve to alert top management when existing policies should be changed. Let us consider these objectives first and then examine the main auditing tools at Personnel's disposal.

To make sure policies are implemented. It is always easier to promulgate policies than to ensure that they are executed.

The Keller Company claimed with pride that all its promotions were based on merit alone, without regard for length of service. Top management was convinced that this was in fact the case until a recent personnel survey indicated that over 80 per cent of all openings were in fact filled by senior men.

Auditing procedures help indicate the extent to which policies are carried out. Top management normally takes action only when serious crises occur (for example, if the government threatens to cut off contracts because not enough blacks are being hired). But management generally is too engrossed with its day-to-day problems to identify a gradual erosion of standards which may cause serious harm over the long run. A regular program of auditing makes it possible to detect significant trends *before* they become crises (when problem-solving is much more difficult), and also makes the whole control process less threatening. When management steps in during a real crisis, tempers are short, executives are under stress, and everyone is likely to be fearful and resentful.

To maximize cost effectiveness. Personnel programs can be very expensive. Processing job applicants for management positions through a complete series of psychological tests may cost hundreds of dollars; the price tag on some training programs may run into the thousands. Too often organizations accept the value of such programs entirely on faith.

The American Computer Company had adopted a most liberal educational leave policy. All engineers with two years of service could obtain a one-year leave of absence from the company to take courses leading to an advanced degree. If their supervisor certified that such courses would contribute to their job effectiveness, the employees were paid full tuition and expenses and continued on one-half salary for the year. Personnel surveyed the costs and returns from the program after it had been in operation for five years. Much to the surprise of everyone, it was discovered that it was costing over two million dollars annually, and that of the more than 600 employees who had taken advantage of this educational leave policy, more than half had left the company. These findings caused management to reevaluate its program. [1]

As this case illustrates, the alert organization constantly reevaluates its personnel programs to make sure it is getting the most value for its money. Further, since most personnel objectives can be achieved by a variety of techniques (for example, less expensive recruiting may require that more money be spent on training), the personnel department must continually compare the costs and benefits of each.

To evaluate programs in personnel terms. Personnel has to counter the tendency for line managers to ignore the human relations' implications of their actions. Managers are always under multiple pressures from a variety of sources, especially their boss—to meet budgets, schedules, reduce waste, etc.—and under this pressure they find it easy to forget the potential reactions of employees or to neglect the longer run impact of today's decision.

Recognizing the growing technical complexity of supervisory jobs, management decided that all supervisors should have a college degree, thus cutting off the promotional opportunities for a group of black and Puerto Rican employees, many of whom had management potential. Personnel persuaded management to make an exception to its new rule for men who had come up from the ranks.

---

[1] Before adopting the simple solution of just dropping the program, management should first try to find out why these engineers left (another personnel auditing task). Conceivably, their jobs were not challenging enough to make use of these engineers' newly developed abilities. If so, management must compare the relative costs of losing these engineers against the costs of trying to enrich these jobs or changing the promotional ladder (see Chapter 18).

In the same vein, Personnel, given its unique perspective, sensitivities, and contacts, can identify trends requiring new or modified policies as illustrated here:

Unstated company policy required all men to wear "dress shirts and ties" to work. Similarly women had been discouraged from wearing slacks or pants. After a number of confrontations had occurred in various departments where bosses had criticized employee dress, the personnel department decided that "clarification" of existing practices was long overdue. Following discussions with top management, the following letter was sent to all supervisors:

"The Company should not in any way seek to prescribe styles of dress for any of its employees, supervisory or non-supervisory. The only criteria management should employ is that employees do not dress in such a way as to be offensive to their fellow employees or create a disturbance."

Audit Techniques

In accomplishing its auditing tasks—assessing implementation, cost-effectiveness, and new trends—Personnel has developed measurement techniques or *controls*. But as we saw in Chapter 14, critical choices must be made as to what will be measured. Further, information doesn't speak for itself: It must be interpreted with care and it can be used either to "catch" people, bludgeon them, or to help them solve problems.

The organization generates vast quantities of data which, properly interpreted, can be useful in measuring the effectiveness of personnel policies—absenteeism and turnover figures, records on illness and tardiness, scrap, incentive earnings, overtime payments, formal and informal grievances, and even unsolicited letters from former employees. In addition, Personnel itself can generate control data; attitude surveys are a good example.

Attitude surveys. Many companies use attitude surveys to find out how their employees feel about their job, their supervisors, specific policies, or the company as a whole. The making and interpretation of such surveys is a growing but specialized field. Psychologists in colleges, in management consulting firms, and in personnel research departments have become highly skilled in preparing, administering, and evaluating questionnaires.

Some experts argue that standardized surveys (which can be purchased from firms specializing in psychological services) are the best, for they make it possible to compare firms and departments and to point out significant deviations from "norms" that have been developed on the basis of experience elsewhere. Other experts argue that special questionnaires should be devised to meet the needs of each particular company.

Most surveys consist of written questionnaires that may be filled out on the job or at home. In either case, care is taken to preserve the anonymity of the respondent. Many questionnaires require the employee to indicate the degree of his feeling in regard to each point. For example:

I feel fairly well satisfied with my present job:

_____ strongly agree   _____ disagree   _____ undecided
_____ agree   _____ strongly disagree

Other questions may invite the employee to choose among various alternatives:

The following items describe different conditions that may be bothering you in your work. Check the ones that need to be improved:

Ventilation	( )	Unpleasant noise	( )
Lighting	( )	Faulty unsafe equipment	( )
Temperature	( )	Dirty work station	( )
Air cleanliness	( )	Other _____	( )

Some surveys try to elicit more detailed (and perhaps deeper) answers through so-called "open-ended" questions, such as, "What would you say are your most serious dissatisfactions with your present job?" A modification of this technique is the sentence-completion procedure, in which the respondent is requested to complete sentences like "The most serious complaint I have about my present job is _____." These and other more sophisticated forms of survey are far more expensive to score than the check-your-answer forms, and are less frequently used.

Once the forms have been filled out, the results must be tabulated and analyzed. Simple, so-called "straight runs" (e.g., 70 per cent of the men like their jobs) are usually less informative than cross tabulations, such as:

SUPERVISORY BEHAVIOR	JOB ATTITUDES	
Among employees who report that:	Like their job	Dislike their job
Foreman speaks to them often	85%	15%
Foreman speaks to them rarely	45%	55%

Interpreting data: turnover and absenteeism as examples. Most companies recognize that turnover and absenteeism are symptomatic of a variety of personnel problems. An employee who dislikes his work or his boss is far more likely to use a slight cold or the need to go to the dentist as an excuse for taking a day off. If his sense of alienation is great enough, he will quit altogether. Personnel watches absenteeism and turnover data closely, not only because both are expensive in themselves, but because they may be symptoms of deeper problems.

Some consideration will also have to be given to frequency of data collection. If the collection period is extended, significant trends can be hidden in the averages or await detection for too long a period. Thus, annual data is not timely enough and weekly may be too frequent (e.g., a bad snowstorm or transportation failure may distort the data); monthly figures may be most useful.

Ratios, such as those below, are used widely. Often these data are interpreted on a comparative basis: Absenteeism in Department A is higher than it was last year or higher than in Department B; or turnover in the Jones Company is 25 per cent higher than the nationwide average for its industry. But such simple comparisons are often misleading.

Typical Formulas Used to Calculate
Absenteeism and Turnover [2]

$$\text{Absenteeism rate (\%)} = \frac{\text{Number of employee days lost per month}}{\text{Average number of employees} \times \text{number of work days}} \times 100$$

$$\text{Turnover rate (\%)} = \frac{\text{Total number of separations per month}}{\text{Average number of employees on payroll}} \times 100$$

Manager A has a much higher turnover in his department than Manager B; what does that mean? Below are some of the possibilities:

1. A is a poor manager, and his people are more likely to quit.

2. A's department has many more new employees, many of whom are young and unmarried, and these typically are more likely to leave voluntarily.

3. The company has announced a cutback in the division in which A's department is located; many ambitious employees are leaving, fearing layoff.

4. A's department is located in a "tight" labor market and competitors are bidding for labor; B is located in an area of labor surplus.

5. B is reluctant to appraise critically his employees, while A has higher standards and encourages those who do not fit the job or are not suited to the work to seek other employment.

Although absenteeism and turnover are costly, remedial action cannot be taken without assessing the meaning of the data. But if Personnel develops its own diagnosis and then seeks to impose its solution, line management is likely to reject the data *and* the analysis. Not having been consulted, they may perceive the situation very differently and challenge the data (e.g., "But our department can't be compared with theirs; we have young women workers and new supervisors"). Much of this will reflect the resistance to change discussed in Chapter 12.

Personnel is responsible for directing higher management's attention to human-relations trouble spots and for helping to develop remedial actions. But it can do neither job unless it enjoys a good working relationship with the line officials who must institute changes. Unless this relationship exists, the staff can prepare any number of lengthy reports and analyses, but most will automatically be filed away and never referred to again. Successful industrial-relations person-

[2] Bureau of National Affairs, *Personnel Policies Forum, Absenteeism and its Control* (Survey #90, June 1970). It should be noted that most of this data as reported in national surveys includes days lost because of illness and injury as well as other excused absences. Of course, there is nothing to stop management from separately calculating excused from non-excused absences, but the distinctions may not be that clear. Medical excuses are not that difficult to obtain and injury can be feigned.

The BNA survey cited above suggests that the most frequently reported causes of absenteeism (in declining importance) are the following: illness and injury, family responsibilities (such as an ill child), transportation difficulties, marital difficulties, alcoholism. Companies surveyed during the first half of 1969 reported an average rate of absenteeism of 4.6%, with 5% of the firms reporting over 10% and 13% under 2.5% (*Ibid.*, p. 2). Other observers have noted much higher absenteeism on Mondays and Fridays.

nel have learned that they are more effective in improving line performance if they discuss the results of their evaluations with the supervisor involved *before* they send them on to higher management. This gives the supervisor a chance to improve his performance before the boss learns that he is doing a poor job. Rather than a pressure mechanism, the staff report then becomes a device to help the supervisor remedy defects in his operations and meet the standards established by top management. When most of the problems uncovered by staff investigations are remedied without recourse to higher levels of the organization, one usually finds that staff and line groups work together harmoniously.

Instead, Personnel is well advised to involve line managers in the data gathering and interpretation process from the very beginning. Line should be given a voice in deciding what data should be collected, and how it should be disseminated. At times Personnel may pass the data on to affected managers without comment, letting the numbers speak for themselves. Alternatively the data can be used as a springboard for supervisory training. Here the supervisors themselves are encouraged to give meaning to the data, and, of course, they are more likely to accept interpretations which they themselves have made. [3]

Line managers also will be more willing to accept a staff control report if they can see how its contents will help them achieve their objectives and if it is timely. As a personnel director described his technique for dealing with the salary increase problem:

"If we wait until the manager gives out his increases, we are in trouble because then all we can do is blow the whistle on those that have exceeded the percentage top management has established. Also we get into a dogfight over whether or not special circumstances justify more increases in a particular case. So we concentrate most of our efforts on working with managers and showing them how to get the most mileage out of their budgeted salary increases and how to handle those whom they've got to disappoint in such a way that they don't become problem cases."

Inevitably, line managers resent Personnel's power to rank their performance and affect top management's appraisal of them. The degree to which Personnel can develop impersonal, quantitative measures (in contrast, say, to subjective appraisals of supervisory leadership effectiveness) and can involve line managers in the design and interpretation of the measures reduces the staff-line tension associated with auditing.

STABILIZATION RELATIONSHIPS

Even more power is exercised by Personnel when it engages in a stabilization relationship (see Chapter 15). In many instances line managers must clear with Personnel before they can go ahead with their plans (presumably in order to assure that their decisions don't hurt larger organizational objectives). For

---

[3] For an interesting example of the use of feedback from morale surveys to change supervisory attitudes (as they learn what their subordinates believe and perceive), see Floyd Mann, "Studying and Creating Change: A Means to Understanding Social Organization," in Industrial Relations Research Association, *Research in Industrial Human Relations* (New York: Harper, 1957), pp. 146-167. A more complete analysis of the theory behind the use of survey data as a means of upward communication is contained in Rensis Likert, *New Patterns of Management* (New York: McGraw-Hill, 1961).

example, Personnel's approval may be required before pay increases are granted, union grievances answered, employees hired, or job offers made.

We needed to hire a programmer, and after we described the job, Personnel told us we could only offer $170 a week. You can't hire good programmers in this area for that, and when we told Personnel the rate had to be higher, they simply said that there was a company-wide salary plan and they couldn't allow a single job to distort the whole plan. I don't see why they should be the last word on this; after all the salary comes out of our budget, and we need one!

Problems When Personnel Wields Power

Impairment of line responsibility. Line managers resent these restrictions on their freedom when they emanate from groups such as personnel staff who appear to have excessive authority with no concomitant responsibilities.

Resentment may also arise if it is felt that Personnel is a lower-status group initiating action for a higher-status group.

And as another cause of trouble, see what happens when the supervisor is required to get the permission of the industrial-relations department before discharging an employee (part of a stabilization role). The supervisor now may be inclined to shrug off responsibility for the future performance of the man. "After all, I really wanted to get rid of him, but they made me keep him," reasons the supervisor. The supervisor has many difficult and risky decisions to make. This one may cause a work stoppage and that one may lose a valuable man. If management wants the supervisor to take responsibility for making difficult, unpleasant decisions, Personnel cannot "second guess" these decisions.

Who is the boss? Another serious ramification of staff decision-making is the potential erosion of the supervisor's leadership position. As employees begin to detect that the personnel department is determining their rate of pay, who is hired and who is fired, they find little reason for dealing with their direct supervisor as the "boss." He, in turn, will find it increasingly difficult to motivate or control the behavior of his subordinates, since he no longer controls the rewards and penalties or determines the basic decisions in his department.

Alternatively, the personnel department can become the "good boss" when employees discover that they can obtain relief from their supervisor's decisions by taking them "to Personnel." In other cases the supervisor "passes the buck" to the personnel department; he tells a subordinate, "I'd be glad to give you that raise, but they (the personnel people) won't let me."

Seeing only part of the picture. Further, most supervisory problems do not lend themselves to decisions by staff departments, largely because a single staff expert, by virtue of his job and his training, sees only part of the picture. Often a seemingly trivial decision concerning something like the change of one man's work schedule may involve questions of cost, production balancing, safety, quality, work-group stability, and a host of special circumstances that can only be known to the immediate supervisor in the department where the question has arisen. The supervisor can call on one or more experts like the personnel man for advice on parts of the problem, but rarely can the expert solve the whole problem.

"Passing the buck." Of course, we should not forget, as noted in Chapter 15, that many line supervisors *want* Personnel to make decisions in some of these difficult human problems of administration. The readiness with which line officials surrender responsibility for unpleasant personnel matters has been described by Mason Haire:

If we are assembling widgets we usually know just what to do. . . . However, at the next step up the hierarchy the job is very different. Now, although the superior is responsible for the number of widgets turned out, he can't assemble them himself. He must accomplish the production through a very uncertain medium that intervenes between him and the widgets themselves—the people on the production line. It is a medium that is changeable, unpredictable, and intractable. It is a little like trying to pick a cherry from the bottom of a tall glass with two wobbly straws. It is easy to see what you are trying to do, but the instrument with which you are working is very hard to control. In many cases it seems likely that it is because of the difficulty of the medium through which production must be accomplished that managers turn away from the medium itself, in an unconscious effort to escape the problem, and say, My job is production—I'll hire an expert staff man to worry about the people. [4]

The need for good working relations. Line management may look upon Personnel's control activities (i.e., audit and stabilization) as just another form of pressure designed to make its life more difficult. At the operating level, the supervisor has to cope with informal groups, he has to adjust to the demands of his subordinates if he is to get them to accept his demands—and this means that he must often depart from the plans, procedures, and policies that top management has established. Understandably, he regards Personnel's control activities as a threat to his established ways of doing things. Line managers are motivated to hide their methods of operation, to juggle figures or seek excuses or shift responsibility in order to cover up deviations from standards (see Chapter 14). In the process, they develop an antipathy for the "checkers" who "are just showing off their technical virtuosity . . . they don't understand the problems we face on the firing line."

Perhaps the most serious problem stemming from Personnel's power in the organization is the potential damage to what is often presumed to be its major function in the organization: providing expert advice. Is it reasonable to expect a line manager to reveal his problems and his department's shortcomings when Personnel is also in the position of auditing his performance and sometimes denying his requests for salary adjustments and the like?

Before answering that "loaded" question, we shall have to explore the characteristics of a staff *advisory relationship* in which this power is minimized, and the line manager retains full control.

ADVISORY RELATIONSHIPS

The ideal advisor waits to be called; his job is to provide help for the line manager when it is requested. He doesn't force his ideas or expertise on the line or threaten the line manager with sanctions unless his counsel is taken. Either type of pressure makes it unlikely that the line manager will feel like confiding

---

[4] Mason Haire, *Psychology in Management* (New York: McGraw-Hill, 1956), pp. 49–50.

in the staff expert or perceive him as a friend in time of need. Rather he will be perceived as another source of pressure, even another boss.

On the other hand, how does the advisor get himself called upon and his skills utilized? The realities of organizational politics require that he have reasonable visibility and be able to demonstrate that his skills and knowledge are being utilized by managers. Here then is a dilemma: The passive staff man may well be perceived as filling the advisory role, but in the process he may lose his department's budget and status. To make matters worse, if, as a result of not being utilized, managers make critical mistakes, and, for example, stimulate a "wildcat" work stoppage, Personnel will share the blame with those very same supervisors who didn't ask for help and counsel. It's no excuse to say, "My help wasn't asked."

When people seek help. A way out of this dilemma is to structure the situation so that managers want help. The existence of the control measures described above can motivate managers to seek out Personnel for assistance in improving their performance.[5]

(Personnel Manager) Our knowledge of training never got used until top management asked for an annual report on what each department was doing to upgrade the skills of its employees. Within a week of learning that this report would be part of the annual performance review, we had eight requests from department heads to consult with them on training.

Building and maintaining a sound advisory relationship is not simply a matter of using control data to prove to the line manager that he needs help. Rather, this relationship requires carefully patterned give-and-take. Personnel staff must learn to work with managers in terms of their needs and problems. An example should make this requirement clearer.

Chet Anthony; a case example.

The personnel department has noticed that turnover is very high in Chet Anthony's department. Chet's boss, the vice-president in charge of sales, urges the personnel director, Phillips, to do something to halt the loss of valuable personnel. What should the personnel director do? How should he approach Anthony?

What happens if he calls on Anthony to say that both he and the vice-president are worried about his high turnover rate? Chances are that Anthony will react this way:

"Here is someone representing the vice-president. Phillips carries the boss's authority. All right, what do they want me to do? If they're willing to put up the money for higher salaries or take the responsibility for putting in some new-fangled ideas, that's up to them; it's no skin off of my teeth."

Clearly, the battle is lost before it has begun, for Anthony has no intention of telling Phillips what his problems really are. From this point on, Anthony may cover up as much as possible and try to shift the blame for any future problems onto Personnel.

[5] *Cf.* Edward Gross, "Sources of Lateral Authority in Personnel Departments," *Industrial Relations*, Vol. 3, No. 3 (May 1964), pp. 121–133.

And if Phillips makes suggestions, Anthony may term them "too theoretical" or "impractical," or else accept them superficially (perhaps just to settle the issue), only to destroy them in practice through subtle sabotage. For example, he may agree to introduce some technique of general supervision and even hold meetings with his subordinates and ask for their advice, but continue to hold the threat of punishment over the head of anyone who does not immediately accept his point of view.

How then can the personnel director influence the department head without "pulling rank"? Primarily by persuading Anthony to regard him as a *source of help*. Anthony has certain objectives that he is trying to achieve. He may be anxious to establish a record that will earn him a promotion, or to win prestige in the eyes of his fellow managers, or to minimize the amount of administrative red tape. Phillips can exert influence by convincing Anthony that his skills and knowledge will help him reach his goals.[6]

The staff expert must keep in mind that Anthony's way of handling his department has evolved over a long period of time in response to his own particular needs. For any real change to take place, Anthony must discover for himself that his behavior is inadequate to the situation, and must be genuinely ready to accept help.

Phillips might start the discussion by commenting that he has noticed a rise in the turnover figure and is curious about what it signifies. Is Anthony having any trouble training replacements? Is there anything the personnel department can do to help? Using this as an opening, Phillips might encourage Anthony to explore the problem. While Anthony talks, Phillips should avoid seeming to judge him, or to be imposing a solution on him. Instead, Phillips should make it clear that he is merely trying to find out how the problem looks to Anthony and perhaps help Anthony view his problems and himself more realistically. Phillips should concentrate on creating an atmosphere that will permit a free and easy discussion of all the facts in the case and the possible alternative solutions.

In the process of working together on a variety of problems, Phillips can learn Anthony's attitudes toward his job and its problems. He also can present a picture of Personnel's role and position in the organization. He can make it clear that the goals of the personnel department are to help other groups and individuals help themselves to deal with their human-relations problems, and to provide specific skills and techniques when they are called for by the line managers.

Next Phillips might encourage Anthony to consider the alternative solutions to the problem, and the probable success of each. This is the most crucial point of all, for Anthony must work through for himself the ramifications of suggested changes. He must regard as his own any programs that are developed, and must assume responsibility for implementing them. For example, Anthony may have to make a presentation before his boss to get a new appropriation to assist in solving this problem. "Role-playing" (see Chapter 24) then can be used to try out various approaches to the boss. Such training, counseling, and try-outs should

---

[6] We are indebted here to the excellent analysis of the role of the staff expert first presented by Douglas McGregor in his article, "The Staff Function in Human Relations," *Journal of Social Issues*, Vol. IV, No. 3 (Summer 1948), pp. 6–23.

be designed not only to increase the line official's skill but also to bolster his confidence in himself.

In effect, Phillips should try to use all his knowledge of individual needs and informal group behavior, of supervisory skills (such as interviewing and discipline), and of labor relations *to help* the line supervisor make *his own* decision.

In this case, Anthony may decide that his own supervisors need a training program to improve their managerial skills. But he would prefer to have the whole program handled by the personnel department—after all, this is "out of his field" and personnel people are the experts. Phillips should be wary of such efforts to shift the responsibility to his department. Lacking responsibility for the program, Anthony would never be sure that it was exactly what he wanted; the supervisors participating in the program would not associate it with the "boss's" attitudes and desires.

Of course, Phillips must not be merely a passive listener. He must provide information and evaluations, when asked—though only as a means to help Anthony make a realistic decision. For example, he might reveal some of the dimensions of the problem by probing more deeply into the turnover statistics: Who is leaving—what age groups, from what occupational groups? How does turnover here compare with turnover in other departments? What are the possible causes: wages, supervision (including Anthony's), other factors in the work environment? Personnel, like any other specialist department, has analytical tools at its command—in this case, perhaps, a community salary survey or a review of department employment records.

Thus, a simple "yes" or "no" answer—a "do this" or "do that" response— by the personnel man to line problems wastes an important opportunity. Research in learning suggests that training is more effective and individuals more highly motivated to learn when they have immediate problems that they want to solve. The best time to help train a supervisor to make better decisions in the future is when he has an immediate problem.

Eventually, with the passage of time, subsequent discussions with the personnel department should enable Anthony to handle his personnel problems by himself, and to ask for help only when especially difficult problems crop up. The end result should be a better-informed supervisor with considerable skill in applying to his day-to-day problems the knowledge developed by personnel experts.

Characteristics of the advisory role. Let us summarize the elements that seem to characterize a healthy advisory relationship:

1. The manager turns to the personnel man for help with his problems largely on his own initiative, with a feeling that he can discuss them freely with a sympathetic listener who is not in the line of authority.

2. The manager comes to understand the role and to utilize the skills embodied in the personnel group, and, in turn, the personnel staff grows familiar with the special interests and needs of the managerial group it services.

3. The manager is helped by Personnel to understand the dimensions and alternative solutions of his problems, and is helped to develop skill in evaluating alternatives.

4. The manager increases his own ability to cope with the human problems of his group. He regards problems as means of developing new abilities and insights.

5. The personnel staff develops greater acceptance for its ideas and points of view, not through putting pressure on the line manager to change "or else," but through developing confidence in the staff's "helping" role and through proving in practice that it can contribute to the supervisor's effectiveness.

6. The line organization receives credit for any improvements that result.

You will have realized, of course, that we have been describing an ideal staff-line relationship, one that is difficult to achieve in practice.

Good advisory staff work is, in fact, like education—it slowly takes effect after there is some critical mass of knowledge built up in the mind of the student. Thus, the advisor is concerned with the longer-run impact of his "teaching."

SERVICE RELATIONSHIPS

In practice, it is impossible to draw a neat dividing line between Personnel's responsibilities for carrying out audit duties and responsibilities for carrying out *service* functions. The identification of a recurrent line problem often leads directly to the development of a new service program.

In performing a service activity, the staff department does something *for* the line department. Usually the relationship is quite amicable, for line departments have little interest or ability in these specialized areas and are glad to have staff relieve them of what they feel are "nasty headaches." For instance, the division manager is glad to have Personnel handle the writing of job descriptions or to undertake recruiting, testing, and training programs. Other times, the service function can lead to frictions.

Line asks for too many services. Even a service relationship can have frictions. At times line management requests services that staff believes are unnecessary, ill-advised, or that should be handled by the line. For example, a line department may ask the personnel department to run a training program for first-line supervisors, even though the personnel department is convinced that such a program will be useless until higher management itself participates in it. A manager may pass the buck to the personnel department in the handling of a ticklish disciplinary problem. Or the general manager may ask the already overburdened personnel director to edit a new company newspaper.

Some of the services requested may appear wasteful. A training program is not always the answer to employee-relations problems. A bigger and fancier house organ may worsen the problems of poor employee-employer relations.

Personnel staff should try to persuade line departments not to request unnecessary services. In the last analysis, however, staff may have to provide such services if the line authority insists—at least, if line is willing to pay for them out of its budget.

Conflicts over scarce services. When line's demand for services becomes too great, staff must ration its limited time and energies among rival claimants. Department A wants Personnel to devote more of its efforts to recruiting engineers; Department B thinks Personnel should concentrate on finding better accountants. The staff department must show great tact in setting priorities, for every time it turns down one department's request for services it hurts its advisory relationship with that department. Preferably line-management establishes standards for these priorities.

Resistance to staff performance of services. In contrast to the previous example, some line departments, imbued with the "do-it-yourself" philosophy, object to having staff perform certain services. Thus, the engineering department may feel that it should recruit its own engineers, since "the average personnel man doesn't know what makes a good engineer tick." Certainly when the line department has direct control over a service, it does not have to compete with other departments for scarce resources. Furthermore, line may feel that staff does not understand its special needs. Often, too, line supervisors are suspicious that Personnel wants to take over a service in order to increase its own importance and the size of its budget and its staff.

As in the case of stabilization activities, the line can be very critical of staff service activities that seem unduly complex, making work for its own sake—just red tape:

"Rather than preparing a useful guide for the man on the job that may fill a page, Personnel sends up a job analyst who interviews everyone in sight, types up a dozen complicated forms, and then issues a formal job description that no one will ever look at once it is filed away. Those guys are following some textbook procedure to the letter, when the whole activity accomplishes nothing."

Line's resistance is intensified if management charges the cost of the new service against the line department's budget, or if it requires line managers to spend time and energy on the new activity.[7]

We once watched the difficulties encountered by the personnel department in one company that attempted to introduce a new management-development program. Line officials tried to sabotage the program, even though it was designed to help them develop more promotable subordinates. However, in another company an almost identical program was welcomed by line managers. Why the difference?

In the second company, the firm's president had indicated that one of the new *controls* he would begin watching was the number of promotable executives produced by each department. Line managers asked the personnel department to *help them* create management-development programs. In the first company, the initiative had come exclusively from Personnel.

In short, line managers welcome staff activities that promise to help them achieve their own goals and resist those that do not seem intimately related to their needs.

[7] It is common accounting practice to prorate the cost of service programs to all line departments according to some criterion like number of employees or gross sales.

Personnel initiates programs. Personnel departments sometimes find themselves engaged in service activities that they feel should really be handled by line simply because line refuses to accept responsibility for them. At other times, staff throws its energies into service activities seemingly as a compensation for its failure to develop satisfactory advisory relationships with line. One personnel director told us:

"I handle grievances myself. I know you professors think this is wrong—it detracts from the supervisor's prestige and so forth. But I can't trust them to handle grievances properly—every time I let them try it I get into trouble. I've tried training programs, but I can't get them to change their ways. Some day our present supervisors will retire and I'll let the new men handle the responsibility. But for the moment I can't risk ruining my union relations just to back up a theory."

Staff often retreats into service activities because they do not require such close working relations with line management as do most advisory relationships. For example, a safety director may have tried in vain to get supervisors to attend a safety course, or to induce them to discipline employees who engage in unsafe practices. In despair he resorts to a safety poster campaign—not because he thinks posters can compete with a supervisor's order in changing employee behavior—but because he knows that no one will object to posters and at least he will have a sense of achievement and something to show management in the way of "activity."

Centralized Company Services

Personnel departments also carry out service activities that are far removed from the day-to-day problems of other parts of the organization. Examples of this include the processing of claims and records relating to company welfare programs, the operation of company medical facilities, fire and plant-protection units, manning reception desks, administering suggestion plans, and running cafeterias. Sometimes Personnel becomes almost a catchall for activities that don't fit elsewhere.

The numbers of people supervised can be very substantial and the administrative requirements demanding. Many times professional personnel skills are diverted from more profound challenges. A typical frustrating example is company food services, always a fruitful source of complaint and frustration. There is some trend toward the contracting-out of such functions, which are so unlike the normal "business" of the organization, on the grounds that a specialized outsider can do it more efficiently and with less drain on in-company administrative talent.

One of the earliest staff roles was that of a spokesman for or representative of the manager. The personnel man is often requested to serve as a *liaison* to various community and government groups. He may represent the company on fund-raising committees, at public hearings, or at high school Career Days. His experience with interpersonal relationships should enable him to be more effective than a typical line manager might be as an intermediary between the company and outsiders.

Personnel research. Increasingly, particularly in larger companies, centralized personnel departments are adding a research function. Such a department might:

Audit

1. Measure extent to which employees perceive that the company's promotion-on-the-basis-of-merit policy is working fairly and without discrimination. (Is existing policy working?)
2. Validation studies to assess whether selection tests actually predict superior performance. (Cost-effectiveness study)
3. Assess what changes in existing company practices will be required by fair employment practices legislation, including surveying percentages of minority groups now employed. (Changing policies)

Service

1. Respond to department head's request to ascertain employee preferences for layout of new offices.
2. Morale survey to assist division in identifying sources of discontent.

For these purposes, such research groups may employ social psychologists, human factor specialists, psychometricians, and sociologists, among other social scientists. [8] Other examples of personnel research are discussed in the next chapter.

BALANCING STAFF FUNCTIONS

Staff departments in decentralized organizations face special difficulties: Their immediate supervisor is usually the line manager who heads the branch operation, but they also have a "functional relationship" to the central-office staff group. Thus, a personnel man in the Akron office of the Superior Insurance Company takes his orders from the District Manager in that office, but his chances for promotion also depend on whether or not he pleases the Vice-President for Personnel in New York City. Conflict often arises when the central staff tries to get some new program adopted throughout the organization—for example, an employee-appraisal system. The local personnel man is urged by New York to lobby for the new program, but the management in Akron is far from enthusiastic about having New York interfere in local employee relations. The local staff man is caught up in a "role conflict," since he must try to satisfy the incompatible norms or standards of two distinct groups.

What is the right mixture of staff patterns? How do these various lateral-relations patterns fit together on a day-to-day basis? Obviously we can't be too specific because industrial relations departments differ in the scope of their functions. Some perform a number of service activities, others place greater stress on the advisory role. An excessive emphasis on the audit and stabilization functions is likely to make it more difficult for staff to develop an easy, advisory oriented give-and-take relationship with line.

---

[8] Human factor specialists are concerned with the design of instruments and the physical conditions of work to allow for maximum utilization of employee sensory functions. Psychometricians construct and evaluate testing procedures.

Personality and skill differences among staff personnel will also shape the mix that evolves. The temperament required to wait patiently for others to bring you problems, to counsel them without any form of pressure or use of power, is very different from that associated with administering large service functions or negotiating acceptance of stabilization responsibilities.

The distribution of functions and responsibilities may also vary, depending upon the level with which the staff personnel executive is interacting. To the top managers of the organization, staff is likely to enjoy an advisory relationship; service functions may predominate at middle levels (divisional and plant management); and audit and stabilization roles impact lower-level management.

Even within a given personnel activity, one can observe an intricate mixture of staff and line functions. The following list describes the staff and line contributions within a single *service* function: hiring new employees. Note particularly how closely line and staff must coordinate their activities.

*Division of Labor for the Employment Function ***

DEPARTMENT SUPERVISION (LINE)	PERSONNEL-EMPLOYMENT SPECIALIST (STAFF)
1. Prepare requisition outlining specific qualifications of employees needed to fill specific positions. Help create reputation that will attract applicants. [First step.]	1. Develop sources of qualified applicants from local labor market. This requires carefully planned community relations, speeches, advertisements, and active high-school, college, and technical-school recruiting. [Second step.]
2. Interview and select from candidates screened by Personnel. Make specific job assignments that will utilize new employees' highest skills to promote maximum production. [Fifth step.]	2. Conduct skilled interviews, give scientific tests, and make thorough reference checks, etc., using requisition and job description as guides. Screening must meet company standards and conform with employment laws. [Third step.]
3. Indoctrinate employees with specific details regarding the sections and jobs where they are to be assigned—safety rules, pay, hours, "our customs." [Seventh step.]	3. Refer best candidates to supervisor, after physical examinations and qualifications for the positions available have been carefully evaluated. [Fourth step.]
4. Instruct and train on the job according to planned training program already worked out with Personnel. [Eighth step.]	4. Give new employees preliminary indoctrination about the company, benefit plans, general safety, first aid, shift hours, etc. [Sixth step.]
5. Follow up, develop, and rate employee job performance; decide on promotion, transfer, layoff, or discharge. [Ninth step.]	5. Keep complete record of current performance and future potential of each employee. [Tenth step.]
6. Hold separation interview when employees leave—determine causes. Make internal department adjustments to minimize turnover. [Eleventh step.]	6. Diagnose information given in separation interviews, determine causes, and take positive steps to correct. [Twelfth step.]

* Robert Saltonstall, "Who's Who in Personnel Administration," *Harvard Business Review,* Volume 33, No. 4 (July 1955), pp. 75–83.

In every organization there is the danger that staff enthusiasms outrun practicalities. Many times these take the form of keeping up with the Joneses: seeing what other companies are doing in special personnel services and trying to duplicate or imitate these, regardless of the absence of a proven internal need or of procedures to measure the contribution. A recent example has been the proliferation of costly organization development programs (see Chapter 24).

CONCLUSION

Ideally, Personnel should be a lobbyist favoring managerial attention to human problems. Just as finance emphasizes costs and margins, and marketers stress the customer, Personnel is people-centered. Success here will depend upon the degree to which they are perceived as making hardheaded, realistic contributions to the solution of management problems.

Personnel work has had and continues to have status problems. Its historical association with social work and record-keeping, its frequent responsibilities for a miscellaneous collection of peripheral activities, and the fact that shortsighted top managements often transfer less-than-successful executives to a "safe" personnel position—all contribute to diminished status. On the other hand, few companies fail to recognize that the effective management of human resources is one of the most crucial factors associated with growth. Insofar as personnel managers prove themselves effective in contributing to this objective, their status and influence are assured.

The nature of the personnel function is often confusing and ambiguous. Personnel men engage in high- and low-status activities at the same time. Their roles as advisors may often seem inconsistent with their roles as auditors and stabilizers. Although personnel work is a separate speciality, it is also at the heart of every manager's job. Thus, a delicate balance must be kept between those aspects of personnel which should be handled by the line manager and those which should be handled by the staff specialist.

Close coordination must exist between Personnel and other functions of the organization. The successful personnel executive must gain the confidence and respect of his colleagues in other departments. He must persuade them that he is seeking to help them with *their* problems and to meet their objectives, that he is using techniques that are useful and valid, and that he is not seeking to embarrass or show them up. He is certain to run into trouble if he seeks credit for constant "victories" or is too concerned with status.

Further, the personnel man deals with complex and recalcitrant materials. Figures and materials are relatively manipulable; they "stay put" and there are reliable, highly workable theories by which they can be put to appropriate use. Despite much social research, the behavior of human beings is less predictable.

From one point of view, Personnel's chief job is to help line management learn to detect and solve its own problems. Line's motivation to learn is heightened when it is aware that it has a problem. As auditors, personnel men should be conscious of the difficulties which each manager faces in meeting the standards set for his unit by top management. By helping the manager think through his difficulties, and by providing him with new skills and techniques in coping with them, personnel can discharge its training responsibility.

Many managers who wish that Personnel would step in and take over their human-relations troubles still resent Personnel's interference when it stops them from transferring an employee or giving a raise.

Thus, personnel men require unusual personalities. They must identify organization trouble spots and work with line management without creating antagonisms and without using threats. Their job is sometimes made particularly difficult by differences in their own background and training and that of line officials.

Although we have examined a variety of tasks performed by, and alternative "philosophies" of, Personnel, the real role of the personnel expert will depend upon how he actually fits into the day-to-day functioning of the organization: who consults him, when, what activities and operations he is responsible for, what monitoring he performs, and what credence is given to his analyses and evaluations. [9]

Regarding the personnel function, one thing is clear: The problems tomorrow will not be those of today. The organization encompasses a wide variety of human beings; it exists in a cultural milieu including the life of a community. Thus, the mores of society and values of diverse social groups—in fact, most of the pressures of daily life—will have their organizational counterpart. At times, these pressures may involve the jealousy or suspicions of various racial or religious groups. Economic instabilities, the fear of unemployment, and the striving of women for new careers all complicate the personnel field. Growing public concern with pollution, with land usage and "corporate" citizenship, similarly, will shift the nature of the personnel problem.

The field of personnel resembles a lightning rod, attracting the tensions and human conflicts that abound in the organization and the community. If professionally handled, these challenges can be a constructive, not a destructive, force in the life of the organization. Just as, on balance, the need to deal with unions and their demands probably strengthened the capability of American industry, management's need to cope systematically with a new and unanticipated series of problems tomorrow can strengthen the firm.

Looking to the future of Personnel, it seems clear that a heavier proportion of time and effort will be devoted to planning and control functions. As companies have become much more planning conscious in other fields (marketing, finance, production), they have also sought to establish clearer policies as to their requirements and usage of human resources. Because manpower planning has become such a critical function, we shall devote the next chapter to this subject.

problem 1 • APPRAISING THE ENGINEERS

Growing out of a top management decision, the Development Division of Crowder Engineering has been required to implement an "obsolescence program." The policy that will be administered by the personnel department requires each unit head to rank all of his employees,

[9] For a summary of some of the inherent ambiguities in the role of personnel managers, see George Ritzer and Harrison Trice, *An Occupation in Conflict; A Study of the Personnel Manager* (Ithaca, N.Y.: N.Y. State School of Industrial and Labor Relations, 1969).

thereby identifying each group's lowest 10 percent. The policy states that this low-ranked group will be considered for discharge, transfer, or early retirement, depending on further individual evaluations.

The corporate personnel man is very enthusiastic about this program, and he helped sell it to top management. The head of Personnel for the Division has been less than enthusiastic about it, on the grounds that the Development Division has a select group of employees; he also believes an across-the-board dropping of 10 percent is a serious mistake. Further, in his efforts to explain the program to unit heads within the Division, he has encountered great resistance.

Under the corporate timetable, each unit head was to submit his rankings to his Division manager by July 1. As of June 30, only 6 out of the 27 unit heads had submitted their forms. On that day the Division manager received a call from the executive vice-president at corporate headquarters, reminding him that these would be due the next day. The following dialogue took place after the manager excitedly called his personnel man to his office:

> *Division Manager:* Harold, how come you let me down? Here we are just about overdue on those rankings, and you never alerted me that we were going to be in trouble on this. Your job is to keep me out of trouble with the head office on personnel matters. You are in contact with those unit heads, and if you spot that they are not doing something that they are supposed to be doing—come to me with it, and come quick. Now what the blazes can we do this late?

> *Personnel Manager:* This is one of the most unpopular policies that has ever come out of headquarters. I've been trying to convince our people to go along with it, but frankly I find it hard to be convincing! And, Joe, if I run to you and "squeal" on your people who may be violating some policy or other, they'll never have any confidence in me. They won't tell me things about their real personnel difficulties, and I won't be able to provide the kind of assistance you want me to provide for them, to keep this operation functioning smoothly.

> *Division Manager:* But you put me out on a limb when you don't keep me informed. I want you to "squeal" if you find someone who isn't doing his job in the personnel area; that's as much a part of your job as helping those guys. You're my eyes out there in the labs.

1. How can the personnel man reconcile the demands of his advisory and his audit responsibilities to the division manager?

2. The personnel man also has a "functional" relationship to the corporate personnel department. Evaluate that relationship.

3. What should the personnel man do when he has to enforce an unpopular policy that he himself has doubts about?

problem 2 • INFLUENTIAL PERSONNEL

The finishing department in a large paper-manufacturing plant has been the source of many grievances. The personnel director of the plant has evidence that the superintendent of the department is in part at fault. The superintendent, a member of the "old school," assigns heavy disciplinary penalties for the slightest violation of shop rules. The most recent grievance, which almost resulted in a strike, concerned a two-week layoff he had given to a man for "loafing on the job." Caught smoking in the washroom, the man had insisted it was common practice for workers to leave their machines for brief intervals when setup men were changing rolls. The union won its grievance, and the employee received two weeks' back pay for the "unjustified" layoff.

This was just one of a series of such instances. To date, the finishing department has had two wildcat strikes and several slowdowns.

It is common knowledge in the company that the personnel director has had several discussions with this superintendent about his handling of disciplinary problems and his dealings with the unions.

The plant manager is primarily concerned about maintaining output levels. Competition is severe and stoppages impair the company's ability to fill orders. For this reason the plant manager has decided to transfer the superintendent of the finishing department to a considerably less important job. In doing this, he points out to the superintendent that the transfer is a direct result of his failure to follow good personnel practices and that he has had ample opportunity to "mend his ways" with the help of the personnel director.

Word quickly spreads through the organization that the "word of the personnel director is law" and that supervisors violate his "suggestions" at the risk of transfer or discharge.

1. How can the personnel director, under these circumstances, retain his staff status and avoid "undermining" the authority of line supervisors?

problem 3 • A CASE FOR ROLE-PLAYING: DEALING WITH A SUPERVISOR ACCUSED OF DISCRIMINATION

Role for Personnel Director. You are convinced that the supervisor of the receiving and marking room is discriminating among his employees. There is now a union grievance on your desk charging that he has failed to equalize overtime in the department as required by the union contract. Two girls were passed over for Friday night work that involved an extra four hours (or pay for six hours), which amounts to about $10 lost wages for each girl, Miss Smith and Miss Jenkins.

The supervisor claims that he asked the girls on Friday whether or not they would like to work and they said they wanted to get an early start for a weekend trip. The union claims that the supervisor purposely waited until late Friday before announcing the opportunity in order to discriminate against these particular girls. In the past, the supervisor has indicated that he was dissatisfied with their work and attitudes.

In "playing" the role of personnel director, have clearly in mind the objectives you want to accomplish through your discussion with the supervisor.

Role for the Supervisor. You have been pressed to cut costs. Your department is a sort of "graveyard" to which women who have failed elsewhere are transferred. You don't like to admit this, however, because it lowers your prestige. In fact, you yourself may have been put in this department for the same reason! Where possible, you try to give the girls who do accomplish something a little extra break, feeling that it is the only way to encourage them, since all jobs pay the same. The work is unpleasant, though relatively easy and not fatiguing. The two worst shirkers are Miss Smith and Miss Jenkins. They are always baiting you, and you are pretty sure they are telling other people in the department false things about you behind your back.

You did wait until late in the day, hoping that they would refuse. You don't see how you can face them if they win the grievance and get back pay. You feel that would destroy any chance of improving the morale and efficiency of your department.

1. Role play the personnel director's interview with the supervisor.

2. Assuming that the personnel director is unsuccessful in his interview with the supervisor, what should be his next move?

5

Manpower and Employee Development

We are now ready to consider the core policy areas of personnel management. Since each supervisor faces almost identical problems in developing and maintaining effective employee relationships, and since the actions of one supervisor have an impact on all others within the same organization, progressive companies try to establish and maintain systematic policies to assure consistency in the handling of personnel questions.

A stream of qualified personnel must be kept flowing into the organization and through the various promotional, training, and transfer channels designed to allocate and develop scarce human resources. This is a continuing responsibility, for no organization is static: employees are always leaving, and shortages are always developing at certain points, surpluses at others. In this section we shall examine alternative methods for developing this "stream of manpower" and various criteria for judging the effectiveness of manpower policies.

The major requirements for an organization's manpower policies and their interrelationship as a total system are spelled out in Chapter 18, "Manpower Planning." This sets the stage for the more specialized policy areas that follow. All organizations must find methods of attracting suitable candidates and then selecting those who are most suited to the careers available, and this is the focus of Chapter 19, "Recruitment and Selection." Even well-selected personnel, particularly in a dynamic world, will require further training to aid their development, and the timing, methods and underlying theories of training are considered in Chapter 20, "Technical Training." The focus, however, is on the nonmanagerial components of the work force.

Selection and training programs both deserve special attention in the light of the challenges of improving the organization's performance in hiring and promoting minority group members, and these issues are analyzed in Chapter 21, "Minority Employment."

374

MANPOWER PLANNING 18

One of the hallmarks of modern management is the ability to plan. The skills management has developed to plan for new markets, new capital investment, and new development programs are now being applied to the personnel field. This new approach is called manpower planning.

Narrowly defined, manpower planning means forecasting: the prediction of the numbers of people whom the organization will have to hire, train or promote in a given period. Broadly defined, manpower planning represents a systems approach to personnel in which the emphasis is on the *interrelationships* among various personnel policies and programs. This contrasts with the more traditional "piecemeal" concern with selection, training, promotion, and the rest as separate, compartmentalized functions.

We shall look first at the narrower and more quantitative view of manpower planning—forecasting—and then we shall turn to the more qualitative, systems implications in this new approach to personnel.

MANPOWER FORECASTING

The first step in any planning effort is to get some picture of what has been occurring in the flow of people into and through and out of the organization. Obviously the past isn't going to repeat itself precisely, but some picture of the dynamic interrelationships among these personnel flows will help the organization predict its needs at least in the short run.

Haire's model, illustrated below, for example, gives a good over-all view of personnel movement within the management group of a single organization.[1]

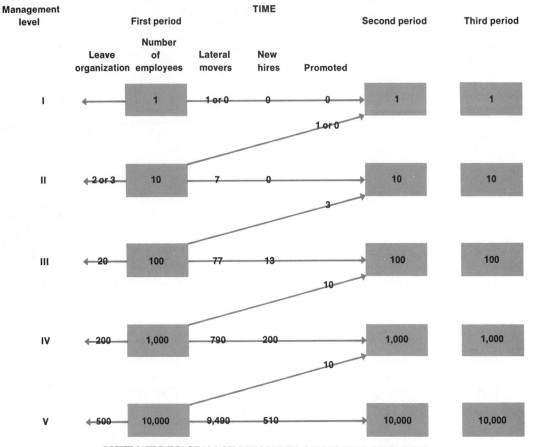

SCHEMATIC DIAGRAM OF PERSONNEL MOVEMENT OVER TIME

Given past experience with managers leaving the organization (e.g., 20, on the average, quit, retire, are discharged or become ill in management level III) and managers promoting (e.g., 10, on the average, will promote from level IV to level III), the model predicts how many new managers must be hired at each level to maintain a stable system. The model can be used to predict the consequences of other contingencies. If more management training and more promotion from within is practiced, the model shows how much additional recruitment must take place at lower levels and how much recruitment can be reduced at higher levels. Similarly, if turnover can or should be reduced, the implications for reduced hiring are spelled out.

Manpower inventories and computers. The application of new technology (particularly computers) to record keeping enables management to make more effective use of employee records in this regard. In addition to personal biographi-

[1] Mason Haire, "Approach to an Integrated Personnel Policy," *Industrial Relations*, Vol. 7, No. 2 (February 1968), p. 108.

cal information, such as age, previous education and training, work experience, and perhaps some psychological factors, such records contain a job history of the employee within the company. When such records are computerized, it becomes possible to answer quickly questions like the following:

How many employees in what jobs will be retiring in each future year? How many employees with appropriate backgrounds (education and experience) will be available for promotion to engineering management type of jobs next year? Who in our present work force is qualified today to be considered for an opening as a commercial underwriter?

Thus, skills and manpower inventories help to answer a range of questions extending from the broader planning type issue to immediate placement problems. The first requires a knowledge of the over-all profile of the current work force; the second needs specific, detailed information on individuals.

The profiles give management an "early warning system" for both bulges and shortages of people at certain points. (A bulge can result because large numbers were hired at the same time with comparable skills to meet a sudden expansion. The bulge will somehow have to be "digested" by appropriate transfers, training, promotion—even severance.) Since there is usually a relatively long lead time required to get people through the system to reasonably responsible technical or managerial positions, appropriate selection actions must be taken years before the need will develop.

Good forecasting, combined with the use of flow models like the one we have been describing, can alert management to upcoming manpower shortages or surpluses. On the basis of such warnings, management can take measures to handle problems before they become so serious as to inflict major damage to the organization. Below are two examples of the kind of problem that might be avoided were management given early warning:

The Delevan Company expanded rapidly during and after World War II, and few managers were hired during the 1950's and early 1960's. Thus, its managers are drawn from a relatively compact age group, and most of them are in their 50's and late 40's. There is little between them and the next group of managers, now in their late 20's and early 30's. Further, since the older managers "ran the show" by themselves for all these years, they have not developed the habit of delegating authority. As a consequence, to meet the needs of the 1980's and 1990's, and also to provide middle management in the interim, the company must (1) provide rapid development experience for the younger managers; (2) "pirate" qualified managers in their late 30's from other companies to fill middle management slots; or (3) use a combination of these.

Sometimes even more drastic measures must be taken:

As of 1970 there were a number of government laboratories which were in very much the same situation as the Delevan Company. A high percentage of their scientists were hired during and immediately after World War II. Since this was a relatively young group at the time, there have been few retirements or deaths. On the other hand, total employment has remained stable, so there have been few new recruits and most members of the work force are in their fifties or early sixties. Over the years a number of old-timers have declined in creative ability; some have narrow skills for which there is little need today. The newer skills are concentrated among the few young men recently hired. Now along come budget cuts and civil service requirements that heavy emphasis be given to seniority in layoffs. Given the age distribution of these scientists, even a slight layoff means that men with 10 or 15 years service are eliminated. Top management of the lab worries that if the cuts get deeper there will be no one left under age 55. With limited funds available, these laboratories do not have the options available to the Delevan Company to hire younger men. Instead, if government civil service regulations permit, they must encourage men in their late 50's to seek early retirement.

Dynamic Factors

Past trends often do not continue and new factors emerge which substantially modify the manpower flows. Then the more static Haire model we have been utilizing (see p. 376) is inadequate.

Changes in demand. Changes in the type of technology employed, in the range of products and services offered, and in over-all company policies will have an impact on future manpower requirements.

An insurance company begins making more widespread use of computers at the same time as it introduces job enlargement. Both have the same impact: a decreased requirement for unskilled clerical personnel. This, in turn, is bound to have an effect on hiring rates, promotions, and the costs of recruitment and training. But the precise impact is difficult to determine without the use of some sort of flow model.

Of course, such calculations are not easy to make. Equipment salesmen and technology enthusiasts often exaggerate the labor-saving results of new installations. Frightening predictions that computers would substantially reduce the need for white-collar employees proved unfounded. In part, of course, such predictions depend also upon sales forecasts.

As the Claridge Company shifts to a more technically sophisticated product line, it must anticipate that the proportion of college-trained salesmen will have to increase. However, the anticipated doubling of sales in these product areas in the next two years will *not* mean a doubling of manpower. The marketing manager for technical products will have to be consulted as to the relationship between sales volume and sales personnel.

Change in supply. Both a changing labor market and company policies can have a major impact on the supply side of the manpower equation. Perhaps college graduates are harder to hire or the government is placing pressure to hire more minority group members. Over the longer run, it may be realistic to prophesy greater utilization of women, minority group members, and even part-time employees. [2]

It will also be useful to observe how the skills profile of the work force is changing over time. For example, if newer employees are better educated than older employees, the company can make use of more internal promotion to fill higher level positions. However, such a change may also be accompanied by higher turnover, since such employees are likely to have more attractive alternatives than do less well-educated employees. [3]

Limitation of Forecasting

Forecasting is still far from an exact science. While advance planning is useful in seeking to anticipate personnel changes which are just beginning to

---

[2] An example of what we mean is provided by an analysis of predicted changes in the work force in the current decade. Almost half the growth in the labor force (15 million) will take place in the 25–34 age group. Only relatively small growth will take place in the younger and older age groups. Women will continue to increase their relative participation (see Chapter 21).

[3] For a good summary of current practice see Arthur Saltzman, "Manpower Planning in Private Industry," in Arnold Weber, Frank Cassell and Woodrow Ginsburg, eds., *Public-Private Manpower Policies,* (Madison, Wis.: Industrial Relations Research Assoc., 1969), pp. 79–100.

show themselves, management needs to remember that such forecasts depend upon the continuation of trends, which may easily change. A decline in the economy can change drastically both the need for manpower and even the number of voluntary resignations (because alternative jobs are not available). The result can be that a predicted shortage in certain jobs becomes a difficult surplus.

Given this discussion of manpower forecasting, let us now look at manpower planning in its broader sense. The manpower system consists of four elements: (1) job structures; (2) career paths; (3) policies to improve employment stability; and (4) policies covering work force reduction by means of attrition, layoffs, and discharge. (Later chapters will deal with related topics, such as recruitment, selection, and training.)

JOB ANALYSIS AND JOB DESCRIPTIONS

The job description is a source of basic information for all of manpower planning. In fact such descriptions are also essential for selection, training, work load, incentives, and salary administration, as will be discussed in forthcoming chapters. All these personnel areas require that the relevant duties, tasks, and employee requirements be made explicit for each organizational position.

Clearly, job descriptions are useful, even though individual deviations from them may be allowed. A new employee will want to know what is expected of him, and when the supervisor detects coordination problems between employees, he will need to know what each should properly be expected to do. Where such mutual role expectations are compatible, there is less likelihood of work flow friction.

(Men's furnishings salesman): I get so angry, I could burst. Those stock boys are supposed to place the new merchandise in the display cases; instead they just leave the boxes all over the counter for us to arrange. They say it's our job, but I know it's theirs.

What duties are required in a particular position? The actual job title may be misleading. Some have been inflated to provide ego satisfactions, e.g., the plumber who calls himself a sanitary engineer. Others have just become less accurate because of technological or organization changes, e.g., engineers who have become technical sales specialists. Further, various individuals perform the same job differently. Smith is an accountant who enjoys spending time with line managers, helping them analyze their cost variances; Jones prefers to stay with his own department doing analytical work.

Thus, there can be a number of ambiguities surrounding what is a *job*, but before dealing with the problems of definition let us look at the process of acquiring and analyzing the relevant information.

Job Analysis

Large companies have specially trained job analysts; in smaller organizations the supervisor develops the analysis, ideally in collaboration with the employees involved. The analysis itself consists of two parts: a statement of the work to be performed (the job description), and the skills and knowledge which must be possessed by anyone filling the job (the job specification).

Job or occupational titles in themselves often give a misleading impression of the actual content of a job. A "milk deliveryman," in addition to being able to drive a truck, must also handle customer accounts and sell the company's products. An engineer may have to spend most of his time *selling* department heads on the importance of using standard parts. Many so-called "clerk" jobs embrace a range of duties that are unrelated to the simple tabulating or recording activities one might associate with the job title.

Particularly at managerial and staff levels, the personalities of the key people with whom the new person will be dealing (especially his boss) become an important element in any realistic job specification.

Care needs to be exercised that excessively broad and ambiguous requirements are not established like "intelligent worker" or "hard working" or "good personality." These encourage discriminatory or foolish hiring practices.

Job Descriptions

Obviously there are a number of ways to group and organize duties and tasks, and these will vary somewhat, depending on whether we are talking about manual, clerical, professional, or administrative jobs. For purposes of simplification we shall simply list the major categories of analysis that might be included. [4]

FUNCTIONAL CATEGORIES	AND	EXAMPLES
Procedures, equipment, and subject matter with which job holder should be familiar; typical problems and requests he will receive		Develop new-product quality tests
Scope of responsibility; magnitude of discretion; "time span of control"		Responsible for approving claims up to $500, these decisions reviewed semiannually by Comptroller's Office
Standards of performance and work load		Undertake machining from blueprints to tolerances of .001 inch
Relationships; job interfaces		Calls set-up man to adjust equipment when tolerances can't be maintained
Supervision; reporting relationships		Reports to Purchasing Manager but also receives direction from Comptroller and Manager of Engineering for special assignments
Qualification, probationary and training period		After 90 days becomes permanent employee
Working conditions, hazards		Operators must stand through most of the work day and be able to lift up to 50 pounds of machine stock; work in hot, humid areas under cranes
Promotion and career opportunities		Secretaries can qualify for chief clerk and office manager positions

[4] For another approach to this area see Ormon Wright, Jr., "Developing Qualification Requirements—A Functional Approach," *Personnel Journal* (December 1966).

If properly handled, such descriptions could provide relevant inputs to computer controlled *employee information systems* that provide a variety of useful manpower data on, for example, the changing character of company jobs (as a function of changing technology and markets), similarities in tasks being performed in various departments that might suggest new promotional ladders or organization changes, and many others.

Ideally the description should distinguish between *prescribed* and *discretionary* content of each job. Thus, every salesman may be required to submit a field report weekly covering his customer visitations. More experienced and capable salesmen will be expected to use their *discretion* in providing management with information about changing conditions in the marketplace, its sources and possible remedies in terms of the company's product line. [5]

As noted, management must decide how broad to make jobs; whether, for example, there should be a different category of job for each type of secretary employed or a single job, "Secretary." This can have a critical effect on promotion and transfers.

In much the same vein a decision has to be made as to how specialized or broad the job should be from the point of view of both selection and promotion. Narrow jobs are easier to fill, but they do not build as much qualification for future assignments, and they discourage the employee from reacting to emergencies or changed conditions.

The Carlton Company found that it could not get employees to do even minor maintenance on their machinery (such as daily oiling), because the job description made no mention of any responsibilities other than production.

Management may be induced to keep the job narrow in order to reduce the evaluated wage rate that will be assigned (see Chapter 25). However, some supervisors will endeavor to collude with employees to upgrade the job in order to obtain a higher rating (by adding duties and responsibilities), thereby satisfying current employees and making it easier to hire new employees. [6]

Of course, in dynamic organizations, where tasks are constantly changing, it may be useful to keep job descriptions more general, more flexible, and less detailed, particularly when they are developed by central staff groups to cover broad areas of the business. [7]

An organization may wish to compare its job descriptions, or position guides, as they are sometimes called, with those developed for other organizations. The most comprehensive and widely cited reference in the field is the U.S. Department of Labor's *Dictionary of Occupational Titles,* which contains 22,000 separate titles. More specialized management and professional job descriptions from representative companies are published by the National Industrial Conference Board. [8]

[5] Wilfred Brown, "What Is Work?" *Harvard Business Review,* Vol. 40, No. 5 (September-October 1962), pp. 121–128.

[6] For this reason Personnel often exercises a "stabilization" function in checking job descriptions before they become the basis for job evaluation and selection decisions.

[7] *Cf.* Paul Lawrence and Jay Lorsch, *Organization and Environment* (Cambridge, Mass.: Graduate School of Business Administration, Harvard University, 1967), pp. 126–127.

[8] E.g., NICB, "Examples of Position Guides in 15 Companies," *Studies in Personnel Policy,* #165, 1958.

Job Specifications

Experience and judgment should enable the personnel specialist to help management translate job requirements into human requirements: the educational, experience, and personality requirements for anyone filling the job. This doesn't have to be a one-way street; knowing who will be available may exert an influence over how the job will be structured.

The danger here is the temptation to ask for too much background in the way of education and experience, particularly formal degrees and certifications. These requirements can unduly increase salary costs and employee expectations. Similarly there may actually be advantages in bringing in new people who do not have a specific background in the field.

We had always thought that a manager in consumer appliances had to have been in the business for at least four or five years. Now we find that if we take a bright employee from some totally different function of the business, he starts asking some very basic questions about how we do things, and doesn't take much for granted. Often those "dumb" questions of the apprentice are just the kind of perspective our tradition-bound department needs.

It is difficult to specify personality requirements because of the measurement problem (see Chapter 19). Clearly some distinctions can be made in jobs that require building and maintaining close working relationships with many different people from positions that involve only routine contacts with a small number of nearby colleagues.

Changing jobs to meet people's needs. Our discussion has assumed that job descriptions remain fixed and that people adapt in order to meet these requirements. While reasonable uniformity may be desirable in some situations, in others management needs to be flexible, as the following example illustrates.

We very much wanted to keep Miss Callaner. She had a number of attractive outside offers and wanted more responsibility, but we thought she just didn't have the math and statistics background to take over the Market Research manager's office. Then we finally decided to upgrade the department's statistician's job to where he became "Assistant to the Manager." Since she would have less to do with survey design and evaluation, we were able to add more liaison duties with our field sales departments to Miss Callaner's new position. In the process we think it's probably a better mix of duties for a Market Research manager than was the old job.

While this type of analysis is often used to reduce the skill requirements to make positions more suitable for minority group members (see Chapter 21), the same approach encourages managers to think creatively about the whole range of job-person relationships. Particularly within management there can be a number of alternative "clusterings" of duties to assist in the matching of people and jobs.

DESIGNING CAREER PATHS

Every organization is faced with such questions as: Should employees be promoted within relatively specialized (narrow) career lines or be given broad exposure to a variety of jobs? How much promotional opportunity is desirable?

Under what circumstances should openings be filled with an already trained outsider or by training an insider?

The answers depend upon an understanding of the dynamics of promotion systems, including organizational needs and employee expectations.

Employee Expectations

Within a given organization, its members come to anticipate a certain pattern of job progression based on what they have observed of the internal mobility of other employees. Below are some examples of quite different types of career ladders:

In police departments it is expected that everyone starts at the bottom, as a rookie, and moves up—even though there has been some recent discussion of bringing in college men at higher ranking status as "police agents."

The military traditionally has a two-career ladder system: an enlisted man starts as private and advances as high as warrant officer; an officer starts as second lieutenant or ensign and may end his career as a general or admiral. But there have been increasing opportunities in recent years for some enlisted men to become officers.

The hospital has an even more rigid caste system: nurses aides rarely become nurses (except through dropping out from their jobs and going to nursing school); nurses may aspire to be head nurses or even superintendents of nurses, but never doctors, etc.

The university for its academic staff has a well-known ladder: instructor, assistant professor, associate professor, and full professor.

Typical companies have at least four distinct ladders:

—manual workers are hired into unskilled or labor pool jobs and promote on the basis of seniority up to higher paying and/or easier machine-tending positions, or perhaps inspection.

—skilled tradesmen often start as apprentices, or "helpers," and move up to craftsman classifications.

—clerical employees move to more desirable locations and higher paying white-collar jobs.

—managers often start as trainees or as assistant supervisors and can, of course, move to top management (although most will not). Often there are separate ladders for sales, production, or engineering which converge for the last few steps in upper management. There may also be separate "professional ladders" in fields like accounting, law, and personnel.

Characteristics of Career Paths:
Length and Breadth

Very obviously the rookie patrolman can move up a much longer career ladder than a hospital medical records librarian, who, in most hospitals, will occupy a "dead-end" job—i.e., one that provides no promotional steps. Most industrial relations experts favor the formal structuring of jobs to provide reasonably long, orderly career ladders, because of the motivation and training they provide.

Where the career ladder leads up to jobs that are much different or much more responsible than those required at the *port of entry* (the bottom job), special care needs to be taken to be sure that hiring standards reflect this. Thus, petroleum refineries traditionally promote personnel from the labor gang up through many steps to the stillman post, a crew chief responsible for millions of dollars of technical equipment. There can be morale problems associated with new employees being *overqualified* for their port-of-entry job, marking time until they can be promoted to positions that call for more of their abilities.

On the other hand, in industries like advertising and in many research and teaching posts, while salaries and status go up with movement along the career ladder, there is little difference in the type of work performed at the higher, as compared to the lower, levels. In fact, in many engineering companies, an employee may shift from being a manager of one project to a staff technical person on the next project.

Some companies rely so heavily on the promotion-from-within policy that they cannot afford to keep people who do not qualify or are not desirous of moving ahead. Many universities similarly follow the practice of "up or out," which simply means that instructors and assistant professors must either earn a promotion or seek employment elsewhere.

Breadth of job or career paths vary substantially. In more craft- and professionally-oriented work, the paths tend to be "narrow" and the experience obtained is all in similar function. Many modern managements, on the other hand, pride themselves in providing very diverse exposures to rising executives (see Chap. 22). Managers shift laterally as they move upward, gaining experience in a variety of functions such as marketing, manufacturing, and finance. Other companies find that while this circuitous routing makes a well-rounded top executive, it tends to diminish the in-depth knowledge and competence of executives in the various functional fields. They, therefore, keep the lines narrow until close to the very top of the pyramid.

Broader career paths increase the likelihood that there will be few or no "dead-end" jobs, because a wide variety of promotional opportunities are made available. A more broadly and less parochially trained work force with wider perspective can be the result. Against these advantages must be weighed the costs of constantly retraining men for new jobs requiring different knowledge and skills.

Technology Shapes Career Ladders

The breadth and length of career ladders can be related to the technology of the industry; it is not simply a management judgment. The manner in which employees move from one job to another is largely determined by the industrial structure. The automobile, steel, and aerospace industries offer examples of quite different patterns.

In automobiles, movement is on a broad basis because production jobs are quite related in terms of training requirements, skills, and processes. Long narrow progressions from the lowest operation to the top are largely absent because the process does not require such training. Consequently, there is broad movement in the industry, even arrangements for plant transfers. . . .

The steel progression is quite different. It features long narrow seniority lines, with slow upward movement. Competence learned in one department—for example, blast furnaces—does not necessarily equip a person to work in another—for example, rolling mills. Once a worker starts up one roster, he has generally determined his type of work in the industry. This is especially important for blacks, for they have been traditionally placed in some departments (blast furnaces) and excluded from others (rolling mills). Given such a practice within a structure like that of steel, great difficulty is encountered in altering the pattern because an employee in the blast furnace department who desires to transfer must start at the bottom of the rolling mill hierarchy, and this involves loss of pay and seniority. In contrast, lateral transfers in the automobile industry are common because the extent of special knowledge or esoterica required there makes them feasible, whereas in steel it does not. . . .

In the aerospace industry, training is all-important for upgrading because, by the very nature of the business, new techniques, methods, materials, and processes must be learned in order to handle new jobs. Promotion depends more on competence and work mastery after special training than on automatic job progression with on-the-job training. [9]

Dead-End Paths

Many times employees are concerned that the promotion ladder on which they find themselves doesn't lead "upward" very far. "In this organization, if you get started in Packaging, you know you've had it."

The organization needs to guard against a situation in which pockets of promotable personnel build up in some areas where promotions are "sluggish"—and a dearth of promotable personnel builds up in other areas where promotional openings are more numerous. It is desirable to have "many roads to the top" so that no group is favored. Where technology is changing rapidly, this may be difficult to accomplish, and only a major retraining and development program can protect promotional opportunities.

When the computer industry shifted from vacuum tubes to solid state components, a large number of traditionally trained electrical engineers who had been qualified to move to high-level positions found themselves "disqualified" because of their lack of knowledge about solid state physics, just as several years before that, the mechanical engineers had been displaced by the electricals!

A seemingly innocent change in management policy within a given department sometimes wipes out the promotional opportunities of a whole group of workers. Whyte describes such a case:

In view of the rapid scientific and technical development of the company [the Vice President of the department] decided that only college graduates should be appointed as foremen. The new ruling hit the HI-Test plant particularly hard, for some of these men had been singled out as especially able and promising. . . . They were at the top now with no place to go. . . . It was common to hear them say, "We're just bumping our heads against the ceiling here." [10]

When management finds that there are dead-end jobs in the organization where promotions are unlikely, it should try to tie them to other jobs or else fill them with employees who have neither the capability nor the desire to move ahead. Without promotional opportunities, organization effectiveness may suffer.

A large English electrical manufacturing company noted that its small-appliance operations were very inefficient compared to its industrial-goods departments. A survey disclosed that promotions into top management always came from the latter area so that the highly motivated managers shifted out of appliances leaving that department with the less ambitious. [11]

[9] Herbert Northrup et al., *Negro Employment in Basic Industries* (Philadelphia: Wharton School, University of Pennsylvania, 1970), pp. 729–730.

[10] William F. Whyte, "Engineers and Workers: A Case Study," *Human Organization*, Vol. 15, No. 4 (Winter 1956), p. 5.

[11] *Cf.* Kenn Rogers, *Managers—Personality and Performance* (London: Tavistock Publications, 1963), p. 68.

Manpower hoarding.   Departments sometimes try to hoard more employees than they need, particularly employees with scarce talents; for example, engineers were hoarded during the shortages of the 1960's. Understandably, employees grow restless when they realize that the opportunity to advance is being blocked by the piling up of surplus manpower. Excess manpower can mean absence of job challenge; if there are too many people for too little work they get into one another's way.

Interdepartment competition may also be a factor in restricting promotional opportunities. For example, a department that was carrying on a full-scale training program for tool-makers refused to honor requests from employees who finished the course to accept a promotion to another department, claiming that the other department was "too cheap" to do its own training. On the other hand, there are situations in which everyone recognizes that certain departments will train workers for other departments. The important thing is to insure that the organization's control systems, such as cost accounting, reflect this contribution. Also if some supervisors are reluctant to let their trained workers move on to higher-rated jobs in other departments, serious inequities are bound to develop.

A means of minimizing some of these differences among departments is to require that job openings be announced throughout the organization and candidates be evaluated by some screening body that is *not* partial to those coming from a given area. This practice, sometimes called "open bidding," serves to tie together a number of individual promotional ladders.

Clarity of Career Paths

Some career ladders are sharply defined: the head teller is always selected from senior tellers working in her bank, who, in turn have moved up from trainee to teller. Others are less so: In Company X the most common route to the presidency has always been through sales, but the most recent top executive had a financial background and currently there are rumors that the Board will bring in someone from outside the company.

There is one obvious disadvantage of clarity in career paths. Some companies are able to transfer ineffective employees to less critical jobs or to positions which don't block others from obtaining promotions, without this appearing to be a demotion. Particularly in large organizations, it is possible to create reasonable ambiguities as to whether a man is going up, sideways, or down. Often salary levels are not known precisely, and even when they are, there is usually enough flexibility in most salary evaluation plans to allow for more generous payment to longer service employees who are no longer eligible for promotion. [12]

Whatever their "shape" or clarity, career paths must be integrated with other aspects of personnel administration. They must be related to the salary structure so that each promotion provides a significant salary increase. Also the

---

[12] The best view of this process is provided by Fred Goldner and Richard Ritti, "Professionalization as Career Immobility," *American Journal of Sociology*, Vol. 72 (1967) pp. 489-502. They find that companies often cover up these demotions by calling them shifts to more professional (and, therefore, less managerial) positions.

various lines must be compared with one another to be sure that there are equitable interrelationships. An assistant department head, which is two rungs up one career line, should have similar pay and responsibilities to other assistant department heads who are similarly situated.

INTERNAL PROMOTION VS. EXTERNAL RECRUITMENT

The above discussion of career paths assumes that the organization is intending to fill most of its job vacancies through internal promotion and employees will gain their qualifications through on-the-job training, perhaps supplemented by additional formal training. An alternative policy would be to recruit a candidate for higher level openings from outside the organization, someone already filling a comparable job in another firm or with the appropriate formal education. What criteria are available for choosing between *training* and *selection* as alternative means of filling job openings? A short case may highlight some of the issues:

Assume that there is a shortage of claim investigators in an insurance company. In the past many of these investigators have come from the ranks of two separate groups: claims clerks and general clerks (both do a variety of clerical and filing tasks with policy holder correspondence). The claims manager has requested permission to hire young college graduates as investigators directly, with the understanding that they would be given six months training to prepare them for these specialized positions. Most of the clerks do not have four-year college degrees, but they do not require formal training since they learn a good deal about the work as they perform a variety of clerical assignments through which they are rotated.

The manager argues, "We need college graduates in these claims jobs because they can be stepping-stones to middle management. If we continue to fill them with clerks, we shall eventually have shortages of qualified 'insiders' for management openings."

Thus, the filling of any single job has many ramifications. The proposal here would cut off promotional opportunities for some personnel and increase them for others. In addition, training costs would go up, at least in the short run, and conceivably the company would have to pay higher salaries to recruit college personnel. All of these factors would have to be weighed before a final decision was reached.

The Case for Promotion from Within

Providing better-qualified employees. No organization can rely on outside recruitment to fill all its requirements. True, certain jobs are similar from one organization to another, but most jobs require specialized knowledge that can be obtained only within a particular firm. Even jobs that do not seem to be unique require familiarity with the people, procedures, policies, and special characteristics of the organization in which they are performed.[13] As we have already observed, career lines allow for on-the-job training insofar as jobs are arranged in such a way that experience gained performing the lower job prepares one for the next rung up.

---

[13] There is evidence that blue-collar jobs in the middle range of the promotional ladder are most likely to be unique to a particular company. Unskilled work and highly skilled jobs are more likely to be similar from one company to another.

Internal recruitment is also a means of selection. We shall see in Chapter 19 that most selection procedures, such as interviewing and testing, provide a far from perfect picture of a new applicant's potential worth. Seeing a man in action, however, over a period of years, enables management to make a realistic assessment of his skills.

Promotion also provides a process of "selective socialization." Over time, those whose personalities and skills enable them to fit into the organization's human relations tend to stay on; those whose personalities conflict tend to leave—either voluntarily or involuntarily. This is called self-selection.

Providing motivation. People will work harder if they know this will lead to promotion. But employees have little motivation if the better jobs are reserved for outsiders. (Most managements want their employees to believe that promotions come automatically with hard work. But too many employees perceive this as a capricious process in which the instrumental factors are luck, being in the right place at the right time, and sponsorship by an executive who, himself, is rising rapidly.)

Providing job satisfaction. Americans want to keep moving ahead. Being given additional responsibilities is not enough; people want the tangible recognition that a higher-ranking title provides. In addition, most workers look forward to unbroken, continuous service. They like to feel that they can get ahead in their own company without having to turn elsewhere.

Cost. It probably is more expensive to recruit an outsider who has already demonstrated high performance and must be lured away from his present employer (and perhaps present residence).

The Case for Recruitment from Outside

Just as many organizations seek outsiders to sit on their boards of directors in order to introduce new perspectives, so they reserve certain lesser positions for newcomers. This infusion of "new blood" keeps the system from growing stagnant, repetitious, and overly conformist. This is probably of less importance in hourly-paid jobs than in staff and managerial jobs, however. (Actually, there needs to be an optimum "mix" of newcomers and oldtimers. Too many highly competitive, hard-driving executives can be almost as destructive as too many time-serving old fogies.) Recruitment from outside the firm can reduce the expense of training new employees, which can be very high, particularly for skilled craftsmen and technical personnel.

Different company philosophies. The recruitment vs. promotion decision (for higher level jobs) is partially one of economics: where do you invest your money? Recent research suggests that companies tend to adopt unbalanced strategies: Some invest a great deal in expensive selection testing techniques (particularly to hire executives and professionals), while others are more likely to have extensive on-the-job training and stress promotion from within. [14] Rarely do companies have what would seem highly desirable: a balanced program.

Unless expanding very rapidly, most companies are more likely to hire highly trained professionals from outside than to promote their managers from within. [15] However, if, as many observers suggest, management itself is becoming more professionalized (meaning that managers identify more with their occupation than with their firm), we would anticipate increased job hopping among impatient executives. Anxious to find challenge and increased responsibilities, they may seek out alternative sources of employment to climb a career ladder in contrast to moving up within a single organization.

ADMINISTERING CAREER PATHS

This has been a conceptual discussion; now let us move to some of the difficult day-to-day problems of administering these "lines" and "ladders."

Number of Promotional Steps

The number of promotions possible is not inherent in the technology; management makes the choice. For example, take a clerical department with 20 employees doing various telephoning, typing, filing, and copying tasks. By deemphasizing the differences in job duties, the company could place all jobs in the same salary grade. Contrariwise, by meticulously evaluating differences among the jobs, conceivably each employee could receive a slightly different salary. In the latter case there could be a 20-step promotional ladder.

What is the optimum number? Too few promotional steps may injure morale by eliminating the sense of personal progress and accomplishment. Too many promotional steps may mean that an excessive amount of time and effort must be spent in selecting candidates gaining acceptance for the choices, and shifting employees. The result may be chaos. In approaching this question of frequency of promotions, we must be careful to distinguish between promotion to a better job and periodic wage or salary *merit increases* (see Chapter 25).

There is a good bit of ambiguity, particularly on professional jobs, about when an employee has actually moved to a more important job, for job definitions are often quite elastic. An engineer, for example, may be required to work on a more difficult assignment for several months before the change is officially recognized by what we would call a promotion—that is, a job title with more prestige and increased income. When a man is officially promoted to a more responsible position may be simply a matter of supervisory judgment.

Varying attitudes toward promotion. People differ in what promotion means to them. Many managers tend to project their own feelings about promo-

[14] Research in this area is described in John Campbell, Marvin Dunnettee, Edward Lawler and Karl Weick, *Managerial Behavior, Performance and Effectiveness.* (New York: McGraw-Hill, 1970.)

[15] *Cf. Ibid.*, p. 23.

tion onto their employees, forgetting that not every employee wants to be promoted—at least not in the terms in which management typically conceives of promotion. Employees differ greatly in their "level of aspiration."

Management sometimes makes the mistake of using a highly unpopular job as the required stepping-stone to higher positions. As a result, serious shortages may develop in these higher positions because few candidates are willing to spend time on the undesirable rung of the promotional ladder.

Similarly, when an employee enters into an apprenticeship program, he is often required to accept a reduction in pay for a number of years before he wins a craftsman's rating. Management officials assume that employees should be willing to make short-run sacrifices in return for long-run benefits, but they forget that their own time perspective may be quite different from that of their employees.

What management regards as a substantial promotion may not seem like a promotion at all to the employee himself. The nurse or salesman may not want to be an administrator. The additional responsibilities or travel requirements of some jobs may more than outweigh the status associated with the new salary and title. As noted in Chapter 3, technical personnel may be reluctant to give up their specialties to become administrators. In order to motivate and reward these professionals, many companies establish "dual ladders" which allow them to move up through a series of steps without assuming managerial positions. Although this does alleviate some of the inequalities, it is doubtful that, given the present organization of industry, the same status and perquisites can be given to a "Principal Research Scientist" as to a "Divisional President." The promotion ladders are not really parallel.

Finally, there is always a group of employees who are quite content to stand still, who prefer the known to the unknown. Unwilling to risk what they have in hand, they want to stick close to the people they know and the responsibilities they are familiar with. To these people, *improvement* means regular wage increases, more security, and perhaps an easier job. Yet in some industries, technology has made it difficult to satisfy this last desire; the majority of jobs are fast-paced and demanding.

To summarize: Management must provide career ladders that will encourage promising employees to take the risks involved in moving upward. It must not discourage valuable employees from seeking advancement by making service in an unpopular job a prerequisite to promotion. It must provide for employees who do outstanding work but are unwilling to take on new and additional responsibilities. And it must provide alternatives for those who are reluctant to assume supervisory responsibilities.

SELECTING WHO IS TO BE PROMOTED

Having settled on a general promotion program, management must face the still more difficult task of deciding who to promote, since there are usually more candidates than openings. The choice usually revolves around evaluations of relative merit, ability, and length of service.

Merit and Ability

If promotion is to be an incentive, the best-performing (i.e., meritorious) employees ought to be advanced. However, since differences in *merit* may not be readily measurable, the man who was not promoted may feel that favoritism was involved. As a further source of discontent, on many jobs performance reflects the coordinated activities of many people or chance factors (for instance, selling a product that is in short supply)—thus making individual merit difficult to measure.

But there is also the question of *ability*—that is, *potential* performance on *other* jobs. Jones may be doing fine on his present job but lack the ability to do the work on a higher-ranked job. Smith, on the other hand, may be doing poorly at present because of inadequate supervision or the unchallenging nature of the work. Put him on more difficult work and he may blossom.

Long-term factors are also relevant. The individual best fitted for an immediate promotion may not have the greatest long-term potential. That is, the most deserving candidate at the moment may seem to be a senior employee who has the ability to move only one more step up the promotional ladder, but it may be better to promote a younger man who may eventually advance into higher management.

In addition, ability is as difficult to measure as merit. The specific traits, attitudes, personalities, and skills that make up ability are frequently ambiguous. For this reason companies often rely on objective measurements—years of education, for example.

To complicate matters further, some people may be given special opportunities to acquire valuable skills whereas others are not. Certain jobs give employees an opportunity to move about freely, bringing them into contact with high-level personnel whose opinions are crucial in promotion decisions. They "learn their way around the organization" and are on the spot when a promotional opportunity turns up.

What we are saying is that some effort should be made to reward both merit and ability, even though neither is easy to measure. Organizations that have failed to reward excellence in service, or that have relied too heavily on personal relationships or length of service, suffer in terms of both efficiency and morale.

Seniority

The extent to which promotions should be based on seniority is almost always an area of dispute between unions and management.

Arguments for seniority. The use of such criteria as performance evaluation, selection tests, and supervisory opinions leads many employees to feel that promotions are not made fairly. And charges of favoritism and discrimination may lead to declines in morale and productivity. Unions object that as long as managers have the power to select the most suitable candidate for promotion, it is a simple matter for them to discourage ambitious employees from speaking out against company policy.

To avoid this difficulty, it is often suggested that promotions be based on some objective criterion, and that the only truly objective criterion is length of service. When management knows that it is going to promote the employee with the longest service, chances are that the company will give him the training he needs to move into the new job. Management will also tend to perfect its initial selection procedures, for once an individual gets into the organization his future will be relatively assured. (Universities anguish over tenure decisions.)

In certain societies, the older men invariably occupy the highest positions; although we do not follow this practice rigidly, we still feel that it is appropriate for the senior people within an organization to occupy higher positions than their juniors. True, we make a good many exceptions: the long-time employee who is clearly incompetent, and the young man who is a genius. However, ours is at least partially an "age-graded society" where age, position, and prestige are correlated.

Arguments against. Excessive emphasis on seniority, however, may violate employee attitudes about the "right" way of getting ahead: Indeed, the promotion of incompetents solely on the basis of length of service clearly violates another strongly entrenched cultural attitude that rewards should be somehow commensurate with accomplishment.

The top-skilled members of glass- and steel-making crews are typically men who have worked their way up through a lengthy, informal apprenticeship system. In the old days they worked long hours, often without pay, under the far-from-tolerant tutelage of a craftsman who would put up with his younger assistants only in return for numerous services. It was a long, hard, grueling road to the top, and those who have made it frequently resent the rather automatic manner in which men can now work themselves into similar positions primarily by accumulating seniority.

Contribution to ability. Up to some point, it seems likely that the longer an employee works at one job, the more qualified he becomes for promotion to the next-higher job. Research among production workers suggests that the employee with the longest service often is better prepared for promotion than management is initially willing to admit. [16] For many jobs, particularly those at the lower levels, differences in ability from one employee to another may be less important than management tends to think. Consequently, the gain in morale derived from promoting the most senior employee may more than offset any slight loss of efficiency.

But the correspondence between seniority and ability undoubtedly diminishes as length of service increases, and beyond a certain level, continued service brings very little gain. Indeed, after a point, increased length of service on a given job actually *reduces* an employee's ability to change jobs, producing in him what is often referred to as "a trained incapacity to learn"; that is, he becomes so imbued with the problems and procedures of his present job that he is unable to adjust to new circumstances and situations. The expert becomes simply too expert in what he is doing.

[16] James J. Healy, "The Ability Factor in Labor Relations," *Arbitration Journal*, Vol. 10 (New Series), No. 1 (1955), pp. 3-11.

Reward for loyalty. In a sense, to grant promotions on the basis of seniority is to reward employees for loyalty. In an organization that wants to keep its employees and avoid costly turnover, a type of guaranteed promotion plan may be an effective personnel policy. Traditional Japanese industry believed this.

No one would deny that loyal service deserves reward. But the question is, how many loyal employees become discouraged about their future with the organization when they realize that they can be promoted only as fast as length of service permits? Also, the emphasis on longevity induces a "ritualistic devotion to duty" in which perfection in the small things, the job routines, and the avoidance of mistakes take precedence over imaginative and energetic pursuit of more challenging goals. Further, those characteristics that were most associated with job success at lower skill levels may not be as useful in higher level jobs. Balancing this, however, is the reduction in destructive interpersonal competition that can occur when there is too much uncertainty about who will be promoted.

Striking a Balance

Every organization must decide on the relative weights it will give to merit, ability, and seniority in making promotion decisions. Even when company policy or the union contract sets up merit and ability as the prime determinants, many an organization succumbs in time to the presumably more objective criterion of seniority. Supervisors in general believe that relations with their subordinates will be easier if they promote the most senior employee. Almost all companies give some weight to seniority in practice, although firms that are unionized give it greater weight than those that are not. See diagram.

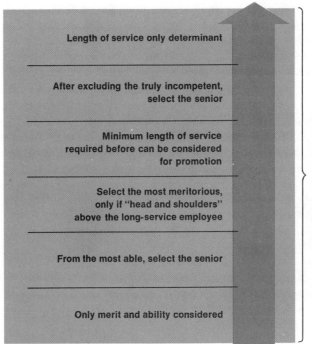

Length of service only determinant

After excluding the truly incompetent, select the senior

Minimum length of service required before can be considered for promotion

Select the most meritorious, only if "head and shoulders" above the long-service employee

From the most able, select the senior

Only merit and ability considered

INCREASING WEIGHT ON SENIORITY

SPECTRUM OF MERIT-SENIORITY CRITERIA FOR MAKING PROMOTIONAL DECISIONS

ADMINISTERING THE PROMOTIONAL PROGRAM

Dealing with the Individual

Handling employees who are unlikely to be promoted. A boss must be able to predict what members of his group will be the most likely candidates for promotion when openings occur. And he must try to keep those who are unlikely to be promoted from taking it for granted that they will soon be moving up the ladder. For example, a long service employee may assume he is promotable even if he is not. If his boss allows that misapprehension to continue, the employee will be sadly disappointed when someone else gets the job. And if his buddies encourage him to think that he is wronged, he is likely to create a serious problem.

Problems of this sort can be avoided if the boss makes a point of discussing with the hopeful candidate the exact nature of the new responsibilities long before the opening actually occurs. Then, if the employee is clearly not qualified for the promotion, he may be brought around to accept his unsuitability. The supervisor may be able to suggest a way in which the employee can supplement his background or improve his performance so that he will eventually become eligible for a promotional opportunity. If he shows himself unwilling to make the extra effort required, the job of winning his assent to being "passed over" becomes much easier.

Dealing with the employee who doesn't want to be promoted. In our culture, anyone who does not want to advance is regarded as somehow queer or lazy. Many individuals take on higher-level jobs even when they are not suited for additional responsibility; but the cost is high to themselves and to the organization. In fact, people who really should not be promoted may come to feel that a failure to show interest in advancement is a black mark against their record. Actually, a clear recognition of each employee's psychological and intellectual limits is valuable both to the organization and to the individual.

The employee who has reached the limit of his ambitions or abilities still has a vital role to play. The armed services have discovered the value of long service "old-line" master sergeants who stay with a particular unit, providing stability and continuity, while its commissioned officers come and go. So, too, employees who have been in one department for a long time may help to break in newcomers, particularly new supervisors.

But nonmobile people must not be permitted to monopolize the training jobs in which more suitable candidates can be prepared for higher positions.

Helping the successful candidate. Serious problems are experienced by the man who does move up into a new position, particularly if it involves supervision. Unless he has been with the group for a long time, and unless the group has concurred in his promotion, he is bound to encounter some measure of fear and resistance. His new subordinates will be uncertain at first about what his new leadership will mean to their future. (This is sometimes called a "succession crisis." See Chapter 12.)

The employee who is promoted to a nonsupervisory position has his problems, too, for he may be facing new responsibilities for which he is not wholly prepared. Nothing is "automatic" in a strange job, and the new man is under great strain. In worrying about what he should do and how to avoid mistakes, he may become so tense that he performs clumsily or forgetfully. If his supervisor is aware of these strains, he can provide the understanding that will help the new man over the hump of the first days on the job.

Craft Consciousness

Where promotion ladders are short and narrow, employees are more likely to perceive the job as being a part of their personal property or territorial preserve. Any threat to an element of the job situation becomes a threat to the employee.

This is one of the primary sources of resistance to technological change; the employee is reluctant to see his work modified for fear of his job status. His income, his security derived from knowing everything there is to know about the job—any or all may be threatened.

Craft-consciousness—the feeling that no one should work outside his narrowly defined job duties—has traditionally been strong in the construction and maintenance trades. A carpenter will refuse to do any work but carpentry, and he will refuse to let other employees do carpentry work—even if this means that other employees must stand idle or be laid off. [17]

Other groups that lack the traditional craft status of the building trades try to erect barriers around their particular skills. The primary motivation seems to be job security, for workers feel that if they can prevent other men from doing their work, they will be able to make their own jobs more secure. Unions in general encourage craft-consciousness, because they look upon it as a means of restricting management's power to make transfers. And every time management gives in to a union demand to make craft boundaries more sacred, a past practice is established, which is in a sense frozen into the union contract.

In one company, machinists were prohibited from picking up any material that had fallen on the floor. This was the janitors' work! Even valuable parts were sometimes swept away by the clean-up crews because the machinists refused to pick them up.

Management itself, by carrying specialization and division of labor to extremes, may be responsible for proliferating an unwieldy number of narrowly defined jobs. Where jobs are defined narrowly, each with a limited number of highly specific duties, the problem of shifting employees is accentuated. Employees, taking their cue from management, then proceed to erect artificial barriers that inhibit flexible transfers designed to expedite the flow of work and to even out work-load inequalities.

[17] An unresolved problem, of course, is always this: What is the jurisdiction of the carpenter? He may want to include things that others claim as their rightful work or exclude tasks that management believes he ought to do.

"I am the only girl in the office who can run this mimeograph machine. It's not easy, let me tell you; it's old and has got lots of tricks to it and it takes years to learn. I don't want other girls using it; this way I know they really need me around here. When we occasionally run out of work on the machine, I don't think its fair for me to have to do other odd jobs. After all, this is what I am getting paid for."

Reducing craft-consciousness. How can management deal with excessive craft-consciousness? First, by accepting as natural the work group's efforts to protect its members. Very little is accomplished by accusing employees of "feather-bedding," for employees are anxious to strengthen their "property right" in their jobs.

A second way of meeting this problem is to develop job descriptions that define jobs in terms of the work that needs to be done rather than in terms of abstract craft skills. In short, determine job duties by the requirements of the work process, not by traditional concepts of what a craftsman is.

In inducting new employees, the supervisor should try to instill in them the broadest possible definition of their jobs. A good recruitment and training policy helps, for employees with diversified skills and good training are more easily transferred.

TRANSFERS

Not all movement is upward. Particularly where career ladders have substantial "breadth," employees may shift sideways. To be sure, the transfer that is a lateral move may involve greater salary and responsibility, but there may also be times in which the individual accepts an assignment at a comparable level in order to broaden his experience or in order to get around a "blockage" in his career ladder. Transfers are also used by management to cope with incompatibilities between the job and the person holding the job. When an employee has trouble doing his work or develops personal friction with his boss or fellow employees, the answer may be to transfer him to another job. Remedial transfers, however, are often used as a means of glossing over serious problems. Where the manager is arbitrary, where newly hired people receive inadequate training, or where employees discriminate against members of minority groups, it is far better to resolve the problem directly, rather than postpone it through a transfer. After all, the replacement for the man who is transferred may face the same problems again.

Nevertheless, when technological change is introduced or customer demands change, then the manpower needs of some departments may decline while the needs of other departments expand. To safeguard the jobs of long-service employees and to avoid losing the skills of trained personnel, most companies try to transfer employees to other jobs. Moreover, a company that follows a liberal transfer policy and provides retraining for employees who are transferred to new jobs has less difficulty in introducing changes.

Good evidence of intelligent manpower planning is stability of employment. Erratic "ups" and "downs" in employment levels, expedient hiring, substantial overtime during some periods and layoffs and short workweeks in others, are prima facie evidence of poor planning. Well-managed companies seek to avoid hiring surges and plan for cutbacks far enough in advance so that *attrition* (normal quits and retirements) will bring employment levels down to efficient levels.

Many companies take great pride in their policy of resisting layoffs and providing stable employment. They claim it pays off in a more secure work force, more loyal to the organization, and less fearful of management changes costing jobs. Obviously a utility or a company fortunate enough or skilled enough to create a stable (or better, expanding) market for its goods or services finds such a commitment easier to make and keep than a company facing cyclical markets.

There are many incentives to encourage management to provide stable employment. (However, the difficulty of doing so varies from industry to industry. Compare a public utility to a manufacturer of machine tools!)

Many state unemployment insurance plans, as well as company-sponsored supplementary benefit plans, are designed to penalize the employer with a record of unstable employment. (This is called *experience rating.*) In addition, the process of laying off and rehiring is expensive to administer, and valuable employees may eventually be lost to other employers. Changes in employment levels involve expensive shifts of workers within and between departments. Just the fear of layoff may encourage employees to consider "stretching out the work" as they mark time, waiting to see "who will be the next to go." Disagreements over seniority criteria result in costly, time-consuming grievances, as do intergroup arguments over short workweeks.

All these possibilities provide a stimulus for the firm to seek means of regularizing employment by using techniques such as the following:

1. Trying to develop a more flexible work force through careful selection and training, supplemented by contractual provisions that permit relatively free transfers between departments—though craft consciousness makes this more difficult.

2. Using temporary employees or overtime in peak volume periods.

3. Taking on additional products or service lines whose variable demand will complement the demand for existing products—for example, if peak demand occurs in the summer, seeking products that are used primarily during the winter.

4. Exploring the possibility of warehousing goods during periods of slack demand, and offering new incentives for customers to stockpile during normally slow periods or order longer in advance.

5. Contracting-out work that would require the employment of new people who might not be needed when the job is completed—for example, maintenance or construction work. [18]

Merely listing alternatives, of course, is an oversimplification of the problem. Temporary personnel agencies typically have higher hourly rates than employees can be hired for directly. Overtime, when continuous, can lead to employee expectations concerning future earnings levels that may be unrealistic and cause resentment when the overtime is reduced. Also excessive overtime reduces efficiency. Inside employees can also resent "losing" work to outside contractors. Among the problems encountered in transfers are the resentments associated with being wrenched out of one's normal work and routines and familiar social group. Also the employee may complain, and often legitimately, that the temporary work is more difficult and is beneath his accustomed status (and dignity). At the very least the supervisor has to be sure that his earnings are maintained and that if the temporary work is distasteful, such transfers are shared equally.

Whatever its policies or intentions, most organizations at some time do have to face up to the painful decisions surrounding a reduction in the size of the work force.

REDUCED EMPLOYMENT

Management must provide orderly pathways downward as well as upward and seek to minimize the personal and organizational disruption associated with cutbacks in employment. If the cutback is a small one, the least painful method is *attrition*, allowing normal turnover, retirement, and cessation of hiring to bring employment levels down.

Reduced Hours or Layoffs

When instabilities in work load persist and attrition is not adequate, then the next choice is usually between shorter work weeks for everyone or laying off the least senior employees, keeping the remainder fully employed. Sharing work—which is what reduced working hours implies—means in effect that unemployment is distributed equally. Depending on circumstances, this may or may not be an advantage to the firm. Sometimes the exact procedure is specified in the union-management agreement, thus making discretion impossible.

What criteria does management use in deciding which procedure to favor? The nature of the industry itself is a critical factor in this decision. A department store could not arbitrarily reduce the hours it is open to the public without seriously damaging its business. Other firms have more flexibility in resorting to a reduced schedule when business warrants.

[18] For a survey of the problems involved in using this method, see Margaret K. Chandler, *Management Rights and Union Interests* (New York: McGraw-Hill, 1964).

Naturally enough, longer-service employees are likely to press for the laying off of short-service personnel, in an effort to secure higher income for themselves. The availability and the magnitude of *unemployment insurance* benefits may also influence the choice between laying off employees and reducing work hours. At some point it becomes more desirable, from the employee point of view, to accept these insurance benefits and avoid the travel expenses, taxes, and effort associated with reporting to work for relatively brief periods.

Seniority vs. Merit in Layoffs

When business is poor and costs are relatively high, management becomes more sensitive to productivity issues. It is regrettable that such slack periods alert management to problems that have probably existed for some period of time. Layoffs are usually more painful to employees in such a period when other companies may also be experiencing cutbacks because alternate jobs are scarce.

The first temptation is to dismiss marginal performers, say the bottom 10 per cent in terms of existing appraisals. In fact, this is done in many organizations. However, where there is a union or where very long service employees are involved, there are a number of impediments to this policy.

Most employees and their supervisors will assert:

"Look, James was here almost 20 years before they discovered his work was unsatisfactory. Sure, we know he wasn't the best by any means, but don't you think the company could have noticed this and have done something about it a lot earlier? Now he's got family responsibilities and debts, and a man in his late 40's can't just step into another job that easy if these layoffs should last for long."

Of course, almost every industrial union (craft unions are often an exception) makes sure that its contract with management includes a clause requiring that employees be laid off in reverse order of their hiring: last hired, first to be dropped. [19]

Ambiguities in counting years of service. But even with the acceptance of this principle of length of service governing such manpower decisions, the question remains as to how seniority is "counted." Here are some alternatives:

1. Company-wide seniority: the length of time an employee has worked for the company.
2. Department seniority: the length of time an employee has worked in a particular department of the company.
3. Job seniority: the length of time an employee has held a specific job in a particular department of the company.

[19] As unemployment benefits (both state unemployment insurance and supplementary benefits paid by the employer) become more generous, approximating take-home pay in some industries, the strong feelings surrounding seniority for layoffs subside and in some cases even reverse: The senior workers sometimes prefer to collect benefits rather than work. This can provide problems for both management and the union.

Many union contracts allow an exception to the seniority rule for a small number of key employees whose work is indispensable to operations or who would be difficult to replace.

The method used obviously has a significant effect on the choice of which employee is laid off when, for example, there is a surplus of clerical help in the Accounts Receivable Department.

The "youngest" employee (with least seniority) under formula 1 might be a recently hired stenographer in the Engineering Department. Then a girl from the Accounts Receivable Department would be transferred into the Engineering Department to take the job of the laid-off stenographer.

The employee with least service under formula 2 might be a secretary who has been with the company for several years, but who recently transferred into the department when an opening occurred. (She will probably regret having shifted jobs!)

Under formula 3, the company would be required to lay off the youngest employee doing the specific clerical job in the Accounts Receivable Department where the surplus existed.

Bumping. Let us introduce another complication: *bumping.* The application of seniority may mean that a whole series of moves is generated when a single employee is laid off.

Let us look again at our earlier example. Under formula 2, the following would be a more typical sequence of events: The Accounts Receivable Department has too many stenographers. The stenographer with the least service in that position would lose her job. However, she would have the privilege of taking another job she could perform in the department, which is currently held by an employee with less department service than her own. Thus, the girl first displaced might "bump" a tabulating clerk with less service. In turn, the tabulating clerk may bump a file clerk with even less seniority than hers. And the process repeats itself as long as displaced employees can find other workers with less seniority than themselves occupying jobs that they are able to perform. Larger companies find that cutbacks in manpower may generate thousands of job shifts, which in turn create massive record-keeping and personnel problems. Shifts of this sort are bound to provoke countless grievances and complaints about alleged inequities in the demotions.

Selecting from among Alternative Seniority Systems

Which seniority system is best from the point of view of the firm? Though there is no simple answer, the following criteria may help management in arriving at a solution.

Reducing frequency of movement. One criterion to apply in evaluating a seniority system is whether it reduces the frequency of job-shifting. Shifts create grievances, and they also give rise to training and efficiency problems. Although management may require that an employee be able to perform the job for which he exercises his "bumping" privileges, it is hard to measure performance. Under the pressure of events, employee job shifts inevitably result in workers being displaced from jobs which they do efficiently and being placed on jobs for which their performance is marginal. "Bumping" works best when the movement takes place down a promotional ladder and where everyone in the department has worked his way up from the bottom jobs. In summary, to satisfy this criterion, management often favors a relatively "narrow" seniority unit, such as job or departmental.

Retaining valuable employees.   The use of "narrow" seniority units may be costly to the company, however. Assume that the need for machinists has declined temporarily. Under a system of job seniority, the company would be required to lay off machinists with long training and experience. Then, if these machinists accepted jobs elsewhere, expensive recruiting and training would be required to acquire new machinists when business picked up. Obviously, management would like to shift these employees to other jobs, and allow less valuable employees to be laid off. Many times some form of department seniority is a good compromise solution to a problem of this sort.

Encouraging requisite mobility.   "Narrow" seniority units discourage employees from accepting transfers, for they lose their seniority when they transfer from one unit to another. Thus, "wider" seniority units make it easier for the company to provide a flexible work force.

Swift return to normal production.   After the need for layoffs has passed, management seeks to return to normal production as quickly as possible. Naturally, key employees must be the first to be recalled. The seniority system usually specifies that those who were laid off last will be called back first. [20] Presumably the more senior workers will have held the more important positions. This correlation is not always a perfect one, however, and management may seek to recall junior employees whose skills are essential to the resumption of production.

Employees' desires.   Management also wants to be fair. But what is fair is not easy to determine.

In theory, employees and unions favor "wider" or more inclusive seniority units than does management. They argue that it is unfair to lay off employees with 15 years of seniority in one department, when there are employees with only one year of service in another department. Unions have sometimes sought corporation-wide seniority agreements to enable an employee whose job is terminated in one company location to shift to another; on occasion, they have even demanded that moving expenses be provided.

In actual practice, employees very often favor narrow units much as management does, only for quite different reasons. Because the employee tends to consider his job as a piece of "property," even though management has a very different interpretation, he seeks out the help of his fellow workers who share the same or nearby jobs to help him protect this valued possession.

The importance of seniority and the careful calculations of self-interest that go into employee decisions impinging on this area are revealed by the following case:

In the ABC Chemical Company, John Jones was seriously injured in an explosion. After his recovery, the company sought to transfer him to a department where his resulting physical impairments would not be much of a handicap. The workers in the new department, even though they were aware of the reason for the transfer, protested strongly. Since plant-wide, not departmental, seniority determined eligibility for layoffs, and this injured worker had very long service, each junior employee felt that his security would be worsened by this move.

[20] This last-out-first-back method means that newer employees are most directly exposed to the threat of unemployment—another reason why employees seek to build up seniority.

Either management or the union may seek modification in existing seniority regulations when changes in technology or in the company's business threaten widespread loss of their jobs.

The Furst Corporation is eliminating its consumer product lines. Under the terms of the existing union-management agreement, even employees with 30 years of service expecting to retire in six months or a year will have to be laid off since the seniority clauses forbid interdepartment "bumping." Recently hired young men in adjacent departments will retain their jobs while these senior employees are separated.

These are very delicate problems of equity and contract. The union finds it difficult to decide what to ask the company, because inevitably some of its members will be injured and others will benefit.

Termination or Layoff?

Management has a responsibility to inform the employee when a layoff is assumed to be permanent. Many union-management agreements and company policies specify that an employee's right to be recalled, with a priority determined by his length of service, will not continue beyond one or two years. Thus, if the layoff persists for this length of time, the employee also loses his claim to other employment benefits associated with accrued service. If he is rehired, he will come back as a new employee. Many companies pay a *severance* or *termination* allowance when an employee loses his job through no fault of his own (see Chapter 26).

An alternative to dismissal for older employees is early retirement, an option which is being used with increasing frequency particularly by relatively profitable companies. Realistically they compare the cost of maintaining the employee through to normal retirement at full salary (and perhaps doing make-work jobs or jobs which could be better filled by others) with the additional cost of a more generous early pension.

A SYSTEMS APPROACH TO MANPOWER PLANNING

During recent years the terms *human resources management, systems* and *manpower planning* have come to the fore. Their usage reflects a growing concern for personnel systems as distinct from compartmentalized personnel policies. Another way of saying this is that there is growing awareness by managers and personnel specialists that the organization is an *organic* entity. All of its parts are so interdependent that a change cannot be introduced in one place without affecting the total.

One of the unfortunate legacies of the scientific management tradition was the encouragement given to managers to compartmentalize their problems. Just as the job of the managers was divided up by the fathers of scientific management into separate components (planning, controlling, directing, etc.), there is still a tendency to classify personnel problems into watertight categories.

We have a shortage of people qualified to be sales managers: This is a *recruitment* problem.

Too many engineers are requesting a transfer out of the power division: This a *transfer* problem policy.

We are losing many of our best craftsmen that have been hired in the last several years: This is a *turnover* problem.

In fact, every one of the above designations may be incorrect. What appears to be a changed recruitment requirement may, in fact, be a training problem. Excessive transfers may reflect inadequate pay or promotion procedures, and turnover can be symptomatic of the same or other defects in internal personnel policies.

In the effort to identify the underlying manpower system that shapes the flows of personnel through the organization, personnel research analysts examine critical comparisons. For example, comparisons like the following may be useful in examining the backgrounds and career patterns of those who quit, those who are asked to leave, and those who are promoted.

Do engineers who quit during their first three years of employment graduate near the top or middle or bottom of their class?

Do we lose more young managers who begin their careers with us in our trainee program or more who go directly to a first non-training assignment?

How do the internal company careers of staff people who go "up" rapidly differ from those who promote more slowly?

Traditional management thinking often involved a search for simple cause-and-effect relationships. Poor performance must mean poor selection procedures. Absence of qualified candidates for a middle-level position must mean poor promotional policies. In practice, it is rare to find such simple causality operating. More often they result from a complex interaction among a number of company processes, including supervision, remuneration, career paths, performance appraisal, and others. The managerial challenge is to identify the *interrelationships* among these various organizational processes. Such analyses do *not* automatically tell the organization what it has been doing right and wrong, but simply what has been happening. However, such new understanding can play a highly useful role in decisions concerning promotion, management development, and selection policy.

Another example of the significance of interrelationships is provided by the manpower implications of various job-security provisions, such as guaranteed annual wages or SUB plans. On the surface these appear very costly since they penalize management heavily for layoffs and job insecurities. But these costs have to be balanced against potential benefits to be derived from a work force that feels more secure and, therefore, may be more willing to accept new technology and job changes. [21]

[21] Japanese companies tend to hire employees for their entire work careers and appear to experience less resistance to change since employees know they do not risk discharge.

Manpower planning requires management to assess the total impact of existing company procedures on the utilization of manpower. It is not unusual to find organizations failing to recognize that the impact of a given personnel policy depends upon its interaction with other company policies; there is no such thing as separate compartments for remuneration, selection, promotion, etc. Decisions made by individual department managers ramify throughout the total organization.

Companies may have a non-discrimination policy in employment, but unless it is backed up both by suitable training of supervisors and effective monitoring, such policies may be ineffectual. Similarly a great deal of effort may be devoted to selecting high potential graduates of technical schools, but if placement and promotion policies do not reward their abilities, it is likely that the effort placed on selection will be vitiated.

A manager may be reluctant to promote anyone to a middle-level position in his department who does not have a unique and narrowly defined experience; yet this job is a critical stepping stone to broader, general management positions in the company. His immediate needs for fully qualified personnel may have to be modified in the light of the larger organization's needs.

We cite examples like these to emphasize the need for synthesis and integration in viewing management decisions and policies. Too often their values or "correctness" are assessed independently one from the other.

Long-run vs. Short-run Costs and Benefits

A manpower planning approach to personnel problems should also counter the tendency of all managers to neglect long-run considerations. An investment in training may not pay off for many years and not until the employee has moved up to other jobs. His present manager can be disinclined to "invest" in the future when his incentives motivate him to look only at the present. The organization requires some process by which these longer run considerations can be factored into today's decisions. As in all planning, that is the contribution of manpower planning—to make sure that choices are made today which will assist the organization in moving to the objectives it has set for tomorrow.

A Definition of Manpower Planning

Manpower planning then is an integrated view of the personnel systems of the organization, which allows individual managers to make improved day-to-day decisions that will be consistent with the total organization longer run needs. Its successful operation requires:

1. An understanding of the existing interdependencies among personnel systems and personnel flows.
2. The establishment of guidelines and policies based on this understanding within which managers will make their personnel decisions.
3. Some mechanism to detect when these policies either need changing or are being violated.

If this is done successfully, the organization will be in a better position to decide such questions as:

1. Where should we begin hiring people?
2. Where should we reduce hiring and allow attrition (i.e., quits, retirements, etc.) to decrease the size of the group?
3. Where should promotion rates be accelerated, slowed down; similarly where is more training required, less?

CONCLUSION

The prime objective of any manpower-planning system is the provision of adequately trained and qualified personnel to meet the future staffing needs of the organization. Accomplishing this requires a *quantitative* understanding of the past and predictions of the future.

Over time, any organization develops fairly well-worn routes by which human resources flow from hiring jobs through various promotional or transfer steps up through the organization through retirement or resignation or discharge. Since these flows are not accidental or random, but are determined by how the organization is put together and the kinds of incentives and punishments that are meted out to people, identifying the flows and their constraints facilitates the effective utilization of manpower.

Our discussion has emphasized the system comprising manpower flows and career paths from a total organizational point of view. Our next chapter deals with the critical point of entry and with the problems associated with recruitment and selection.

problem 1 • SENIORITY

When Bill Jones, with six years' seniority, was promoted to the position of straw boss, Al Smith complained. Smith, with fourteen years in the department, argued that he could do the job himself, and furthermore the company in the past has promoted the senior man to such jobs.

As divisional superintendent, you are notified by the Industrial Relations Department that a union grievance is pending. Here are the two sides of the case:

Supervisor's argument: The job of straw boss requires good judgment in making work assignments. Jones has held the job temporarily several times and has demonstrated this competence. Smith, on the other hand, some years ago in another department, failed when he was promoted to a foreman's position. His records were always "mixed up"; he used poor judgment in requesting repair help, assignment of men, and so forth. Furthermore, Smith is not a good "leader" from the point of view of his own colleagues. He was appointed to fill a vacancy as a union steward, but was not elected when he ran at the next regular election.

Smith's argument: He has never been given a chance to try out as a leader—Jones always was given these chances. His "failure" took place ten years ago when he was young and less mature. The supervisor has never criticized his work; the company and the supervisor are discriminating against him because of his union record. While he was steward, he fought through many difficult grievances that embarrassed management. He lost the election because he was Polish and a majority of the department are of Italian descent. In general, it is company practice to promote by seniority unless there are overwhelming reasons favoring the less senior man, although the contract states that management will give substantial weight to merit and ability and will use seniority as a criterion only when there are no significant differences in ability.

1. How would you investigate this case?

2. What further information would you need? How would you assess the facts you now have?

3. What responsibilities does the supervisor have in this case?

4. What criteria would you use in making your decision?

While you are evaluating this situation, the Industrial Relations Department reports the following comments to you—from another company supervisor in a different department:

"Sure, our union contract says that management can promote the employee with the most ability, and only when there are no substantial differences do we have to take the most senior. But try and do it! I have tried it. The men get together and almost force the oldest guy to file a grievance, and then the union opens up on you. As a supervisor, you are put into the position of having to come up with solid-gold proof that the senior man isn't as good as the man you selected, and believe me, it is hard to get such proof. Sure there are no problems when the older man has been constantly absent, drunk, or a troublemaker. But if he has 'kept his nose clean,' the union can put up an awfully good case that you are discriminating against him for something he did 15 years ago. Then during the grievance procedure your relations with the rest of the men in the department are strained; it's like a cold war. In the end, the Industrial Relations Department may reverse your decision anyhow because they feel that they can't win the case in arbitration or for some other reason. Then you swallow your pride and take the man off the better job whom you promoted (and is he upset!), and put the other guy on the job whom you first turned down—and his feelings toward you are nothing to write home about either. Your reward for following the contract out to the letter of the law is poor morale and a lot of lost time for yourself in grievance meetings, and in the Industrial Relations Department. Do you blame me for taking the easy way out?"

1. Does this statement alter your evaluation of the case?

2. As the divisional superintendent in this company, how concerned would you be if these sentiments were prevalent in the organization?

3. If you wanted to change the situation, what steps would you take?

4. Does the prevailing situation mean that the union-management contract is not really a contract?

problem 2 • INFORMAL PROMOTION

Myers was a mechanical engineer himself before being promoted to supervise a department of engineers. The new job provided a great deal of challenge. Time, however, was always a problem. While Myers believed in delegation, he couldn't resist getting involved in the technical problems of the work in his department, and this took time away from the daily round of administrative questions that came to him, largely on personnel and scheduling problems. Therefore, when Myers found that one of his subordinates, a young engineer by the name of

Thompson, was eager to take on new responsibilities and handled them well, he began assigning certain administrative detail work to him. Thompson filled the job of assistant supervisor, which appeared nowhere on the department's organization chart, and he handled many of the work-assignment decisions and relationships with other departments.

After four months, in which this informal arrangement had worked well in relieving the pressures on Myers, the supervisor requested a formal promotion for Thompson to a managerial job classification. While Myers' superiors were willing to add an additional manager to the division, they turned down Thompson as being too inexperienced and lacking in adequate formal education (Thompson did not have a college degree).

Myers was left with a difficult problem. He could not get a salary increase or change in status for Thompson, although he had pressured for this. Should he take away the additional duties from Thompson, although his subordinate did not request him to do so, or should he encourage him to seek a job in another division of the company that would recognize his managerial capacities and not discriminate against him for his lack of a college degree?

1. What should Myers' decision be?

2. Did Myers handle the informal upgrading of Thompson appropriately? (Remember that Thompson liked his administrative work, wanted additional responsibility, and was, in fact, receiving good training.)

3. Are there circumstances that justify a "promotion" without a commensurate increase in income and status?

problem 3 • THE SKILLED AND THE UNSKILLED

The Frank Home Oil Service has had a long-standing tradition of promotion from within, largely on the basis of length of service. Men were hired as laborers and moved up through several promotional ladders to higher-paying positions, including maintenance work. Older workers typically "bid" on the mechanics' jobs when there were openings, because this work was easier than delivery and pumping jobs. Recently the company became concerned that its maintenance mechanics were less skilled than those of its competitors. As new and more complicated equipment was purchased, the company found itself without adequate maintenance personnel.

The company was finally able to negotiate an agreement with the union permitting it to use aptitude tests in selecting new mechanics. The steady stream of older workers bidding on these jobs was now halted. To fill openings as they occurred, the company for the first time was able to go outside the organization and hire young trade-school graduates who quickly learned the requisite skills. Over time the older mechanics who had come into their jobs "unscreened" were shifted to the less-skilled work in the department—largely building-maintenance work.

The immediate problem is that declining business is forcing a cutback in the size of the maintenance department. Normally, department seniority is used to determine who will be laid off. The result in this case will be that nearly all of the relatively new and more able younger mechanics will be laid off, except those who have enough seniority to "bump" the few unskilled laborers in the department. The company fears that its maintenance work will be crippled, and that a good share of the mechanics will leave the company permanently to take jobs elsewhere.

1. How would you analyze the company's problem? What mistakes have been made that other organizations can profit from?

2. What are the alternative solutions, and how would you go about trying to put any of them into effect?

problem 4 • THE WRONG JOB

Bill Allen accepted a new promotion with mixed feelings. He was proud of having his work recognized, but he had some doubts about how he would like the new work. His former job had involved regular contacts with salesmen—trouble-shooting, helping them with special customer problems, and so on. His new job in market research was essentially a research job, working with population data, industry marketing reports, and the like.

Bill missed the routine of his old office and the men he had worked with. He had a private office now, but he felt he really did not have the educational background for the job. When he submitted his first report, the division head was nice enough—suggesting some changes that in fact meant that Bill had really used the wrong approach. His boss said not to worry, "We all have to learn a new job." The more Bill thought about it, the more he wanted to go back to the old job. But he hesitated for fear that he would be considered a failure by management and thus disqualified for any further promotion.

1. If you were Bill's boss, what could you do to correct this situation?

2. What would your objectives be?

3. Could this situation have been avoided altogether? How?

problem 5 • NEW ENGINEERS

The Firstway Aircraft Company has just received a government contract to develop a new military transport plane. At least 175 additional engineers will be needed to initiate this program, although it is uncertain how long the contract will remain in effect. The funds will be cut off unless Congress increases the military budget at the end of the year.

Management is faced with several problems in recruiting the personnel required by this program:

1. Because of the recent cancellation of other projects by government cutbacks, the company has been left with a surplus of engineers. Unfortunately, however, they will not have completed their present assignment until one or two months after the new program is scheduled to get underway. Further, most of them are not experienced in designing transport planes. What criteria should management use in deciding whether or not to select engineers from the anticipated surplus to staff the new activity?

2. The new program may be short-lived. But if the company publicizes this fact, it will hamper its recruiting activities in a tight labor market. Is the company under any obligation to disclose that the work may be short-term? If so, how can it discharge that obligation?

RECRUITMENT AND SELECTION

19

Logically, the first step in the development of an organization's personnel activity is to acquire the people to operate the organization. Not only is this first in theory, it is one of the most critical steps in the establishment and growth of a business. The supply of qualified people limits organizational success just as sharply as does the supply of money, materials, or markets. Obviously the recruitment and selection process is intimately connected with the over-all manpower system.

The process we are to discuss begins of course with recruitment—and the decision as to where and how to look for job applicants. Next these applicants must be evaluated in terms of how their individual patterns of personality and ability fit organizational needs. A number of evaluation instruments are available, among them testing, interviews, application blanks, and the like. All of these can serve—some better than others—as means of predicting behavior on the job. The ability of these instruments to predict (technically known as *validity*) can be increased by careful research and design. But this is expensive. And so the personnel decision-maker is forced to choose the degree of sophistication of his selection process, always taking into account the fact that selection techniques are costly and have an impact on the manpower system generally.

RECRUITMENT

The Nature of the Labor Market

In recruiting new employees, management must consider the nature of the labor market: what sorts of potential employees are available and how do they look for work? These are questions that economists have studied for years; their findings are relevant to the understanding of the recruitment process.

Labor market boundaries. Knowing the boundaries of the labor market helps management estimate the available supply of qualified personnel from which it might recruit. A labor market consists of a geographical area in which the forces of supply (people looking for work) and demand (employers looking for people to hire) interact and thus affect the price of labor (wages and salaries). The actual boundaries of the market depend on the type and number of job candidates being sought. The labor market for certain unusual skills may be half or all of the United States. Top-quality hotel chefs may move from resorts in Maine to Florida when appropriate openings occur. At the other extreme, married women seeking clerical positions may be unwilling to take jobs that are not within a few miles of their homes.

Available skills. Few companies hire "labor"; rather, they hire specific kinds of worker. Many large offices that move out of cities to suburban areas find that although there is a readily available blue-collar labor supply, there may be a severe shortage of young girls with clerical skills. Companies that want to hire large numbers of highly skilled tool and die makers must locate in areas where these tradesmen have established homes. Where fully trained workers are required, a new firm may have no choice but to locate near the plants of competitors. Auto stylists are most likely to be found in Detroit, and photographic engineers in Rochester, New York.

Companies that require relatively large numbers of a particular type of employee often have a severe recruitment problem. If a firm needs only a single bookkeeper, it usually has little trouble finding one—even though it pays less than competitors and has a poor reputation in the community. But in an insurance company, for example, which must hire hundreds of stenographers every year, relative wages and working conditions are critical.

Economic conditions. Economic conditions in the labor market itself affect recruitment. A new plant located in a depressed labor market may be swamped by unemployed workers. On the other hand, a firm trying to establish itself or to expand in an area where few qualified workers are out of work has quite a different recruiting problem.

Attractiveness of company. Potential employees find some organizations far more attractive than others. Company A is engaged in an expanding, profitable industry and can afford to pay high wages. It guarantees steady employment, high wages, rapid promotions, clean work, and attractive fringe benefits. This company may never really have to recruit, for a steady stream of prospective employees will come seeking work. Company B is in a highly competitive industry in which profit levels and wages are relatively low. The company has a reputation for unsteady work, and many of the jobs it offers involve dirty, dangerous work. This company has a difficult time recruiting employees, particularly in times of relatively full employment.

Manpower Sources

The next question is this: what sorts of employees are available and how do they seek employment? [1]

The new employee taking his first job. An inexperienced employee has only a sketchy idea about job possibilities. He is likely to take several jobs during his first five or six years of employment (the "trial period," as it is called). His final settling down is likely to be as much a result of growing family responsibilities and more realistic expectations as of his finding genuine job satisfaction. The job held by his father, the ambitions encouraged within his family, and his level of education all exert a major influence over what jobs he regards as acceptable.

The already employed, but dissatisfied employee. Firms that require special skills often recruit employed workers who are looking for a better job. Every job has its disadvantages; we all rebel to some extent against authority, and we are convinced that our talents are going unrecognized and uncompensated. Consequently, we might expect that most employees would constantly be on the lookout for a better job. The fact is, however, that at any given time only a small percentage of employees are actually seeking other jobs.

Family and friendship ties deter the worker from searching for opportunities outside his immediate neighborhood, and seniority and fringe benefits that are tied to length of service also reduce the motivation to look elsewhere. Furthermore, the early job-hunting experiences of a worker and his friends may have convinced him that good jobs are scarce, and that whatever its disadvantages a job in hand is worth innumerable possibilities in the bush. Even employees who quit voluntarily rarely have a specific alternative in mind.

There is one exception to this generalization, however. During periods of what has come to be called "over-full employment," when companies actively compete for labor and when jobs are remarkably easy to get, employees may begin to consider alternatives. Stories spread about how well Jim Jones did when he walked across the street to an employment office, and gradually other employees begin to follow the same route.

As a general rule, then, one can say that dissatisfaction with the present job does not make the worker search actively for a new job. It does make him more receptive to tips, rumors, and actual job offers which come to him. If none of these look promising enough and if his present job continues to be unsatisfactory, he will eventually (during a period of high employment) quit his job. *Active search for work usually does not begin until after he is unemployed.* [2]

A small percentage of the labor force consists of perpetual malcontents, who, for one psychological reason or another, are never satisfied with their work and cannot tolerate the normal restrictions imposed by life in an organization. They move endlessly from one job to another. In a sense, these workers fit the

---

[1] Chapter 21 will give special consideration to the problems of recruiting racial minorities.

[2] Lloyd Reynolds and Joseph Shister, *Job Horizons* (New York: Harper, 1949), p. 37. (Emphasis ours.) See also, Gladys Palmer and others, *The Reluctant Job Changer* (Philadelphia: University of Pennsylvania Press, 1963).

economist's model: They do indeed try to maximize the net advantages they receive in return for their labor, and they actively compare the benefits offered by various employers. Personnel directors find such employees poor bets and are unlikely to hire them.

Another group of potential dissidents is made up of new employees. Longer-service employees have usually adjusted to their job and typically expect to stay with it for some time to come; the newly hired employee has made no such adjustment. He is still trying to accommodate himself to his fellow workers, to supervision, to the pace and work requirements of a specific job, and to the organizational "climate" of a particular company. Voluntary quits are highest by far during the first year or two of employment on a new job. (It is for this reason, it might be added, that turnover is particularly costly. In order to replace one long-service employee who quits, the company may have to hire two or three or even four new employees.)

There is modest evidence that executives as well as staff and technical specialists are becoming more profession-oriented. Identifying with their field as much or more than their employer, they are likely to "job-hop" if their present post does not provide adequate psychological and financial returns. Although for an expanding firm with exciting promotional opportunities this situation may increase the supply of trained manpower available, for other employers it increases the costs of turnover. (Obviously, it should encourage greater efforts to diagnose the source of dissatisfaction and to provide countermeasures.)

Raiding.   The practice of hiring employees from other companies raises the question of "raiding." The term itself suggests that many employers consider this practice unethical. Some companies scrupulously refrain from recruiting employees from other firms in their community or industry. They may even require clearance from a potential recruit's present employer before they will accept his application. In actuality, however, so-called "no-raiding agreements" are honored more in theory than in practice. In order to avoid the stigma of raiding, employers sometimes use intermediaries, such as executive recruiting and consulting firms, to make contacts for them. Significant legal liabilities, however, can be incurred when a company lures a key employee from a competitor in order to learn trade secrets or technical "know how" from him.

The unemployed worker.   Ordinarily, the unemployed worker is a man who has been laid off because of slack times or because of an infraction of company rules or because of the permanent closing of his employer's business. If he has been laid off because of slack times, a company may hesitate to hire him for fear that he will return to his original employer as soon as possible in order to enjoy the seniority benefits he has accumulated there. Of course, firms are suspicious of those who have been discharged from another job—this can cause the employee who has been inequitably discharged a great deal of grief.

The unemployed worker is no more systematic in his search for a job than the potential recruit who is currently employed and is under less economic pressure:

Where the worker does not hear of a job through friends within a reasonable time [when seeking employment] he frequently resorts to direct application at a plant which is conspicuous because of its size, closeness to his home, or some other reason. In most cases, however, he knows little about conditions in the plant before applying for work.[3]

Methods of Recruitment

The mere availability of jobs will not bring applicants into the employment office. True, a firm with an outstanding reputation in the community (for providing "good" jobs) may have a steady stream of applicants. But most companies must engage in active recruitment.

Paper

1 *Word of mouth.* Recommendations from satisfied friends and relatives are among the best sources of recruitment that a firm can have. Many companies conduct regular programs to encourage their employees to speak to friends about job openings in the company; some even give bonuses to employees who introduce applicants who are actually accepted for employment.

Word-of-mouth recruiting has a real disadvantage, however, for it may lead to nepotism, particularly in management positions. Such an emphasis may arouse resentment in the present staff and may impair morale and long-run efficiency. Further, as we shall discuss in Chapter 21, word-of-mouth recruitment may be inconsistent with a policy of reducing racial minorities since minority members are less likely to have friends or relatives among present employees.

2 *Government employment agencies.* State employment agencies are located in almost every major city. They charge neither the employer nor the prospective employee for their services, for they have a public responsibility to service both. Further, they have access to a nationwide network of job opportunity information sources and can provide their clients with a wide variety of testing and counseling services. Unfortunately, many employers, believing that well-qualified employees look for work through other channels, have learned to look upon the government employment service as a source of unskilled labor only. State employment services are closely connected with the administration of unemployment insurance benefits. At times, people getting benefits pretend to be interested in a job in order to continue their insurance payments; such applicants too often disappoint the personnel departments to which they are sent.

3 *Private employment agencies.* These tend to specialize in specific occupations and skills—clerical, manual, craft, or technical, for example. Sometimes the employer pays the fee, sometimes the employee; in either case, the fee may be quite substantial. Specialized executive recruiting companies are utilized to find new managerial talent. They may scour the country looking for a man with highly specialized experience (such as directing a marketing program in household detergents) and prescribed personality attributes. Most of the men they

3 Reynolds and Shister, *op. cit.,* p. 37.

look at will already be employed but will have indicated confidentially a willingness "to be considered." Indeed, an unemployed executive may have difficulty getting himself considered seriously by these search firms.[4] He may be considered a failure.

4 *Advertisements.* Advertisements in daily newspapers, over local radio stations, in trade journals, and in the magazines of professional associations usually attract applicants in great numbers but of highly variable quality. A more homogeneous group will respond to an advertisement in the *Journal of the American Chemical Society,* for example, than to one in the community's local newspaper. Similarly, papers catering to a black readership will be useful in recruiting members of this minority group.

5 *School recruiting.* Many companies send representatives to interview seniors in high schools and colleges. This technique enables the company to paint an attractive picture of its employment opportunities and to do advanced screening of candidates. The better candidates are then invited to visit the company for further consideration. In addition, good contacts with school placement officials help in channeling suitable candidates to the company.

6 *The union as recruiter.* Particularly in the building trades and in the maritime industry, the worker feels a stronger attachment to the industry as a whole than he does to an individual firm. In these occupations, the union is the traditional clearinghouse for jobs, and both employer and employee have come to accept the union hiring hall as a combination employment agency and recruiting office. To a lesser extent the union provides this service in the printing and entertainment industries, restaurants, and hotels (when union-organized), and sometimes in the manufacture of men's and women's clothing. (The Taft-Hartley Act, in part, regulates these hiring halls.) Note that in all these industries employment is unstable. Thus the worker feels a stronger attachment to the industry as a whole than he does to an individual firm.

Clearly it is to management's advantage to be able to tap a ready supply of skilled, experienced workers merely by lifting the phone and calling the union. This saves management the expense of recruiting and screening, and also means that management will be less hesitant to lay off an unneeded or incompetent worker. The union's stock-in-trade becomes its ability to maintain a full complement of readily available skilled employees.

7 *Professional contacts.* As a work force becomes more professionalized, recruitment takes place through networks of personal relationship and small specialized labor markets. Even in a country as large as the United States, many individuals sharing similar training and work experience get to know one another. Through trade association meetings, professional-society conventions, execu-

---

[4] For a good summary of the labor market techniques open to an executive seeking employment see Aurens Uris, *The Executive Job Market* (New York: McGraw-Hill, 1965). Ordinarily private employment agencies are subject to government regulations with regard to fees, the nature of their operations, etc. Some of the more expensive "headhunting" firms pose as management consultants and thus escape regulation (even though their operations may be perfectly ethical).

tive-development sessions sponsored by universities and management groups, and day-to-day business dealings—managers and technical specialists develop wide circles of friends. For example, although the stated purpose of professional societies for economists and electrical engineers is to exchange learned papers, much time is devoted to exchanging job information. When an opening occurs, a manager can telephone an acquaintance who might be interested in the job or who can recommend another personal friend. Thus, personal circles of acquaintanceship overlap and intersect to such an extent that a well-placed executive might locate the "two dozen people who know the most about solid state circuitry" in a matter of a few days.

ALTERNATIVE SELECTION PHILOSOPHIES

Attracting qualified job applicants is only the first step in the process of acquiring new employees. Next, the firm must develop techniques for selecting, among these applicants, those to be accepted for employment. Management wishes to avoid hiring the employee who will either quit or turn out to be unqualified. Hiring and training costs are usually substantial. Several hundred dollars can be expended in placing a relatively unskilled employee on the payroll; several thousand dollars or more in the case of a professional or manager. Further, union standards and the expectations of employees and the community can serve to limit management's ability to discharge those who fall below performance standards. In many foreign countries, government regulations restrict such decisions more severely.

Such pressures sometimes encourage management to avoid permanent commitments. A firm can do so by using temporary workers supplied by agencies specialized in "lending" manpower. (The hiring company usually pays a daily fee for each employee based on the skill required, but the employee remains on the payroll of the agency.) Also, the company thus gets to hire employees who know from the outset that they are temporary and cannot qualify for the security of the regular work force.

It should be noted, further, that most organizations use a probationary period as a check on their selection system. The newly hired worker does not become a regular employee until he has successfully completed a one- to three-month or even a one-year trial.

Alternative Selection Policies

Organizations tend to develop hiring methods that are consistent with their over-all philosophy of selection. These methods differ significantly from company to company.

Screening out applicants who don't fit. The primary objective of the selection procedure may be to obtain applicants who fit the company's image of a "good, reliable" employee. Such a program aims to screen out those who "don't belong."

Some employers look for the "right type," right in terms of physical appearance, background, age, degree of drive, and similar characteristics. Banks, at one time, tried to maintain a homogeneous group of employees, who place security above advancement, lack aggressiveness, and prefer to be left alone.[5] Brokerage houses may favor applicants with an "Ivy League" college background. Some companies restrict their top jobs to handsome, white Protestants.

There is evidence that even when the company sets up no formal restrictions, an informal self-selection process will operate. Certain types of people gravitate to and find working in certain kinds of organizations compatible with their own personalities. This pattern has been observed among operators in clothing manufacturing plants, retail store personnel, and government employees. Thus, there may be some justification for attempting to avoid mismatching by weeding out those who will be uncomfortable in their new work environment. On the whole, however, most of these "right type" criteria, which usually represent irrational discrimination, are ethically indefensible and now legally wrong.

There are other, more concrete, general selection criteria that may appropriately be utilized as screening variables. Where most jobs in the firm require technical ability, some minimal education requirement may be imposed on all entrants—for instance, completing of high school or college. (Of course, there is the real possibility that a good candidate may have achieved equal proficiency through less orthodox channels or the standard may be unrealistically high.)

Fitting jobs to people. Alternatively, management can go in the opposite direction and seek to adjust the jobs themselves to the people who are available to fill them. For example, during World War II, many male jobs were, with slight modifications, made suitable for women. Great progress has been made in recent years in modifying or redesigning jobs for those who are blind, infirm, or otherwise incapacitated. Experiments in adjusting working hours to permit housewives to be employed for split shifts have proved successful. Skilled craftsmen's jobs have been broken into components that could be learned by relatively untrained novices. Jobs have also been redesigned to suit them to members of minority groups.

Psychologists in particular have been active in "human engineering." While industrial engineering has stressed fitting people to satisfy the time and motion requirements of machinery and production schedules, these psychologists have sought principles and methods to make equipment design better adapted to typical human characteristics.

Fitting people to jobs. The typical selection program tries to fit applicants to particular jobs—to match jobs and people. This selection philosophy assumes that the requirements of a given job, and the characteristics of a given applicant, are sufficiently unique and explicit to make possible an intelligent match between them. Most of the rest of this chapter will be devoted to discussing the problems involved in implementing this philosophy of finding the best man for the job, not just screening out the worst.

[5] Robert McMurry, "Recruitment, Dependency and Morale in the Banking Industry," *Administrative Science Quarterly*, Vol. 3, No. 1 (June 1958), pp. 87–117.

Essentially, the selection process is one of prediction—making an informed estimate as to which of the various applicants is most suited for the job being filled (or, more strictly, since prediction is never perfect, which applicants have the highest odds for job success). But to make such decisions, one needs information about the jobs being filled and the applicants themselves. Our last chapter dealt with jobs and career ladders. Let us now look at alternate techniques or instruments for gathering information about job applicants.

There are at least five major selection instruments, four of which will be discussed here: application blanks (or, in their more carefully designed form called biographical inventories), interviews, physical examinations, and formal tests. (A fifth, assessment centers, will be discussed later.) Each of these instruments has its advantages and disadvantages. Each can be utilized with various degrees of scientific precision. For example, an organization may use standard tests without much concern as to their relevance to the needs of the job being filled, using the test results only as a means of weeding out the "undesirables"— or it may go through the expensive process of developing tests that are specifically validated in terms of the jobs in question and then base its decisions almost entirely on these results. Similarly, physical examination can be cursory or extremely thorough. Application blanks may ask for only the most essential data (name, address, social security number) or they may be multipage biographical inventories, with each question bearing a carefully researched relationship to job success. Interviews too can be highly informal, or they can be minutely structured and graded, almost as if they were oral examinations.

As we shall see, even the best measures are poor. The main reason for using them is that hopefully (though this is not always the case), they add useful information to the decision process, and that decisions made on the basis of them are at least slightly better than chance.

Application Blanks (Biographical Inventories)

The application blank is the traditional device for recording biographical information, such as age, marital status, and number of dependents; previous education (subjects, degrees, and grades) and training; previous work experience, including nature of duties, salary, length of time on the job, and reasons for leaving; and such personal items as association memberships, police records (if any), outstanding debts, home ownership, leisure time activities, and health histories.[6] Although applicants may lie in giving this information, most of it can be checked by independent means. In addition to purely objective items, questions may also be asked about applicants' goals and interests, thus converting the application blank into something like a personality or interest test (to be discussed below).

---

[6] The Fair Employment Practice laws adopted by many states make it illegal to ask questions about the applicant's religious affiliation, wife's maiden name, parents' names, race, and similar points, on the grounds that such questions constitute either direct or indirect attempts to ascertain race, religion, or nationality, and provide a basis for discrimination.

Application blanks may be used for a number of purposes. They test the candidates' abilities to write, to organize their thoughts, and to present facts clearly and succinctly. (Thus they serve as a simple literacy or intelligence test.) They help the interviewer with leads and a point of departure for the formal job interview, and they provide the company with data for its permanent employee record. The application indicates, further, whether the applicant has consistently progressed to better jobs, and whether his education and occupational experience have been logically patterned.

Recent years have seen increasing use of the biographical material on the application blank as if they were items on a test. A statistical analysis can be made of the relationship between each item and the actual job success. For example, a study in a given situation might find that the following characteristics correlate with success on certain management jobs: being a college graduate with good grades, participation in at least one competitive sport, election to at least three collegiate offices, and being the eldest (or only) child in a family. On the other hand, the study might find that for certain sales jobs high grades are merely a predictor of high turnover, and that the most successful men (measured in terms of turnover and annual sales per salesman) may be those with relatively average grades. Once studies such as these are completed, scores ("weights") can be assigned to various items on what is now often called a biographical inventory; these scores can then be used to predict success on the job. [7]

Often references are to be listed in the application, though these may be of limited value because most people named will provide very favorable references, being loath to handicap the applicant in finding employment. There is a very low correlation between ratings given by references and observed job performance. Furthermore, when former employers are interviewed about candidates, there is almost no relationship between their full report and what they put on a short reference form.

Interviews

The interview is used almost universally as a selection device. The interview enables the person responsible for hiring to view the total individual and to appraise the person and his behavior directly. The effective interview involves two-way communication. It permits the interviewer to learn more about the job applicant's background, interests, and values, and it also provides an opportunity for the applicant to ask questions about the organization and the job.

Ideally, the interview provides a valid sample of the applicant's behavior. Even though the applicant is "on guard," careful to present the best picture possible, the skilled interviewer can draw him out far more successfully than can an application blank. Using the information recorded on the application blank as a springboard, the interviewer can guide the applicant into explaining why certain jobs appeal to him and others do not, and into speaking freely about the influence of family and educational experiences. Furthermore, the interviewer can uncover clues to the applicant's motivation, to his attitudes toward himself

[7] A critical review of this type of testing procedure is provided by Harrison Trice, "The Weighted Application Blank—A Caution," *The Personnel Administrator* (May-June 1964), pp. 17-19.

and to the kinds of situation he finds either troublesome or satisfying to his level of aspiration, to his ability to deal with interpersonal situations, and to his readiness to take the initiative in conversation and in dealing with strangers.

Although interviewing is the most widespread selection device, a high percentage of interviewers have had no training in the art and few have given much conscious thought to what information they seek to obtain from the interview, or how they will go about obtaining it. Good interviewing requires great skill. Many supervisors discover this when they are required to interview an applicant, only to find that the conversation lags, embarrassment grows, and the procedure is stressful for both themselves and the other person.

Even trained interviewers differ in their approach. In one sense the interview is a battle of wits. The applicant who wants to put his best foot forward engages in "impression management," seeking both to cover up his deficiencies and to provide answers that will please the interviewer. The latter tries to penetrate these defenses and catch a glimpse of the "real person" underneath. Opinions differ about how best to do this. Some favor putting the applicant at ease as much as possible and using nondirective methods (see Chapter 11). Others favor more structured or patterned interviewing in which the questions are asked in a predetermined manner and the answers score almost as in an examination. [8]

Particularly in the military and civil service, it is common for the interview to be conducted by a panel of interviewers who pool their final judgments. In any case, it is always possible to introduce stressful elements into the interview to assess the interviewee's reaction to frustration and pressure.

Thus the interview is a flexible tool; it can be used for many different types of jobs and people. It can emphasize the applicant's formal qualifications or seek to plumb the depths of his personality. Because of this flexibility, there is sometimes a division of labor in interviewing—personnel seeks to assess personality, and the line manager interviews for technical ability and experience.

Even at its best, the interview is not a precise technique, and skillful interviewing is difficult to conduct. Candidates react very differently depending on who is interviewing them and how the interview is handled. Since there are no fixed criteria for success or failure, the prejudiced interviewer can easily evaluate the interviewee's performance in accordance with his own stereotypes. (If the applicant is interviewed by several people, it may be possible to cross-check observations.) Unfortunately, there are still people who believe that they can assess other people on the basis of the type of necktie they select, their tone of voice, or whether they "look you straight in the eye."

Each interviewer brings his own special frame of reference or "personal construct" to the interview setting and this colors the way he perceives others. Each interviewer also possesses a stereotype of what he expects in the ideal job candidate, depending on his own characteristics. ... Once the interview is under way, the interviewer forms a quick first impression (within the first four or five minutes) of the interviewee. ... Many interviewers will then tend to gather subsequent information selectively in order to confirm the first impression. [9]

[8] The military has also experimented with efforts to standardize the interviewing procedure by means of a fixed format and the use of a panel of interviewers. The applicant is evaluated, not only in terms of the content of his answers, but also in terms of his reactions to the stress introduced by the situation.

[9] John Campbell and others, *Managerial Behavior, Performance, and Effectiveness* (New York: McGraw-Hill, 1970), p. 143.

Too many interviewers look primarily for "negative information" (slip-ups which show that the applicant is not the "right type") rather than for positive evidence of job potential. They also tend to rate interviewees who are like themselves higher than those who are different. One study suggests that the more the interviewer talks during the interview, the higher he rates the interviewee.[10] Obviously, some interviewers use the interview as a chance to talk with a captive audience.

Given these limitations, how well do interviews shape up against tests as a means of accurately predicting employee behavior? The evidence suggests that decisions made on the basis of interviews "are generally no more (and frequently less) accurate than those based on tests alone"[11]—and, as we shall see, the predictive value of tests is also fairly low. By and large the validity of interviews is higher when interviews are structured rather than unstructured, and when the interviewer is looking for specific elements from the applicant's past history rather than seeking to assess the interviewee's psychodynamics.

Physical Examinations

Many jobs require unusual stamina, strength, or tolerance of unpleasant working conditions. Physical examinations reveal whether or not a candidate possesses these qualities. Furthermore, the company's responsibility (both legal and ethical) for employee health and safety encourages widespread use of physical checkups. Health insurance costs are increased when employees in poor health are hired. Thorough physical examinations also provide valuable records in the event of accidents.

FORMAL TESTS

To many people, tests are synonymous with selection methods, although many companies do not use tests at all. Tests have been developed in an effort to find more objective means of measuring the qualifications of job applicants, as well as for use with employees who are candidates for transfer or promotion. One of their major advantages is that they may uncover qualifications and talent that would not be detected by interviews or by listings of education and job experience. Tests seek to eliminate the possibility that the prejudice of interviewer or supervisor, instead of potential ability, will govern selection decisions. Because of their importance, we shall look closely at their design and their

[10] D. Sydiaha, "Bales's Interaction Process Analysis of Personnel Selection Interviews," *Journal of Applied Psychology*, Vol. 45 (1961), pp. 399-401. See also Robert E. Carlson and Eugene Mayfield, "Evaluating Interview and Employment Application Data," *Personnel Psychology*, Vol. 20, No. 4 (Winter 1967), pp. 441-460; D. Keith Baker, "Correlates of Effective Interviewing," *Personnel Journal*, Vol. 48, No. 11 (November 1969), pp. 902-906.

[11] Eugene Mayfield, "The Selection Interview—a Re-evaluation of Published Research," *Personnel Psychology*, Vol. 17, No. 3 (Autumn 1964), pp. 239-260. In this careful study, Mayfield is cautiously optimistic about structured interviewing.

limitations, as well as at some of the policy problems involved in applying them to personnel selection and placement. [12]

Types of Tests

First we shall examine some of the more commonly used types of tests and the purposes for which they are designed. With this as background we shall consider the limitations of formal testing, stressing the extreme care that must be used in evaluating test results.

Performance tests. The simplest and perhaps most obvious type of testing procedure is the work-sample or performance test in which the applicant is asked to demonstrate his ability to do the job. For example, prospective typists may be asked to type several pages and their speed and accuracy are then calculated. Or a prospective machinist is asked to interpret a blueprint and to make certain adjustments on the equipment he will be expected to operate.

But how about jobs like sales representative or plant manager? Here the characteristics that make for success are less obvious, the requisite skills not so easy to test. Nor are performance tests useful in selecting inexperienced workers.

Intelligence tests. On the assumption that quick-learning, alert, bright people can learn almost any job more quickly than those who are less well endowed, many companies use general intelligence tests, sometimes called IQ tests. On the other hand, for some simple, repetitious jobs management wishes to assure itself that intelligence is not *over* a certain level, to reduce employee dissatisfaction.

Psychologists are not unanimous in recommending the use of intelligence tests, nor is there general agreement on the concept of "intelligence" itself—that is, on what is being measured by the test. Some argue that intelligence tests measure not just a single factor, but a combination of factors such as verbal comprehension, mathematical aptitude, inductive reasoning, and straight memory, and that the relative importance of these various factors varies from job to job. The typical test gives greater emphasis to "convergent thinking—organizing content in such a way as to produce a single correct solution to a problem" than to "divergent thinking—utilizing content to produce a wide range or variety of possible solutions to a problem." [13] Theoretically, intelligence tests measure raw, native ability and not extent of education. However, there is reason to believe that many intelligence tests are "culturally biased" in favor of those who have had extensive education and have come from middle-class backgrounds (for further discussion, see Chapter 21).

Aptitude tests. In a sense, an intelligence test is a kind of aptitude test that measures the candidates' overall learning ability. However, psychologists have

[12] Two valuable testing texts are Marvin Dunnette, *Personnel Selection and Testing* (Belmont, California: Wadsworth, 1966) and Robert Guion, *Personnel Testing* (New York: McGraw-Hill, 1965).
[13] Dunnette, *op. cit.*, p. 50.

also developed a large number of much more specialized aptitude tests which seek to predict the likelihood that an applicant can learn specific jobs. Individuals differ markedly, for example, in their ability to learn work involving precise eye-muscle coordination, such as the work done by the skilled shop craftsman or mechanic. It is difficult for some people to learn to do jobs that involve quantitative computations or that require the ability to visualize solid objects in space. There are tests of a person's potential to become a programmer, just as there are examinations to predict the likely success a student will have in law, medical, or business schools.

Aptitude tests obviously do not test motivation and, on the job, motivation may be more important than aptitude. For this reason many companies supplement aptitude tests with interest and personality tests.

Interest tests. These measure the applicant's interests; for example, whether he prefers to work outdoors or indoors, or with people or things. Though frequently used for vocational testing (for example, to help students choose among careers), interest tests are also used by companies to determine suitability for specific jobs. The Strong Vocational Interest Inventory, for example, helps predict adjustment to dozens of occupations. Research suggests that male college students scoring high on specific scales are four times as likely to be in these occupations twenty years after college than those who score low on them. Similarly, these tests help predict whether men will be happy in these occupations. [14]

Personality tests. Personality tests are much like interest tests. For example, neither one has a specific set of "right" answers. Interest tests, however, are concerned chiefly with a person's liking for various types of work. Personality tests seek to determine how people will relate to interpersonal and situational stress.

Many observers feel that more employees fail on the job because of personality defects than because of lack of aptitude or physical ability. A psychologically well-adjusted employee who is highly motivated to do a good job may be worth more to the company than a man with great potential who is emotionally upset or lazy. At times, personality affects job performance in the most unexpected ways.

During World War II, when great numbers of trained technicians were in demand, it was assumed that those who had mechanical aptitude would make good airplane mechanics. A careful analysis of this assumption proved otherwise. It turned out that a good shoe clerk in civilian life would become a better mechanic for military purposes than someone who had fixed cars most of his life and learned on a Model-T Ford. The critical trait was not mechanical aptitude but the ability of the trainee to follow instructions. The Army then worked out its instruction manuals so meticulously that the best recruit turned out to be a mildly obsessional person who could read and follow directions. The last thing they wanted was someone with his own ideas on how to fix equipment. [15]

In fact, for management jobs, personality tests may well be the equivalent of work-sample tests, since the most important component of many managerial

[14] Dunnette, *op. cit.*, p. 63.

[15] Edward T. Hall, *The Silent Language* (Garden City, N.Y.: Doubleday, 1959). p. 94.

jobs is the ability to deal effectively with people. As a result, many large companies now use personality tests, particularly at the executive level. There are hundreds of consulting firms that specialize in providing testing services as well as large numbers of full-time staff psychologists within personnel departments who conduct elaborate testing programs.

Personality tests seek to assess an individual's motivation, adjustment to the stresses of everyday life, capacity for interpersonal and self-image. These are expressed in terms of the relative significance of such traits within the person as self-confidence, ambition, decisiveness, optimism, patience, fear, and distrust.

The most popular personality tests are also of the pencil-and-paper variety; the applicant is given a test booklet in which he writes his answers. A typical question might be "Do you ever feel that people are staring at you and laughing at your appearance? Yes ____ No ____." A standard key is provided with these tests to enable employment department technicians to process them easily with limited training and expense.

Most of these paper-and-pencil tests claim to give a well-rounded picture of the applicant's personality, but many observers argue that they are superficial, easily faked, and misleading. Clinical psychologists favor depth interviews and projective tests (such as the Rorschach "Ink Blot Test" or the TAT) that require many hours to administer and that must be interpreted individually by trained experts. Originally, these tests were developed to analyze the abnormal or deviant personality. Only recently have they been used to assess the more "normal" personality.

DEVELOPMENT OF TESTING PROCEDURES

In order to understand the use and limitation of tests, it is important to get at least some slight understanding of the problems involved in their development. The main steps are outlined in the box on p. 424. Each step involves difficulties. First, let us look at the major assumptions behind testing procedures and then consider the main problems in greater detail.

Underlying Assumptions of Testing Procedures

1. Testing procedures assume that there are significant differences in the extent to which individuals possess certain characteristics—such as intelligence, finger dexterity, knowledge of blueprint reading, and motivation.

2. Testing procedures also assume that there is a direct and important relationship between the possession of one or more of these characteristics and the individual's ability to do certain jobs. This relationship should enable the manager to predict the candidate's eventual job performance.

3. Finally, testing procedures assume that the organization can measure selected characteristics practically and evaluate the relationship between test results and job performance.

At first glance, all these assumptions seem perfectly reasonable. Actually, however, they often lead an unsuspecting management into trouble. For example, in some instances the degree of individual differences does not justify a testing program. As one psychologist points out, it would be wasteful to try to test differences in color discrimination among female applicants for inspection jobs, because "Color blindness in women is about as rare . . . as appearances of Halley's Comet." [16] Similarly, a self-selection process, by which people themselves decide whether or not to apply for a specific job in a particular company, may minimize differences among applicants to the point where they are hardly worth the expense of testing.

The fact that some jobs can be handled successfully by more than one type of person throws doubt on the assumption that there is a close relationship between certain employee characteristics and job performance. For example, the older worker, who is slower and less agile, may compensate for his liabilities by displaying greater attention, persistence, and energy.

The validity of these assumptions generally can be evaluated only after we have additional knowledge about the problems in developing tests.

IDEAL TEST DEVELOPMENT PROCEDURE

1. Personnel specialist interviews current managers on characteristics that distinguish good from bad employees on particular job, or "what it takes to do well on this job."

2. Interview results are analyzed and consensus summarized in list form. These listed characteristics are sent back to managers to rank order.

3. Psychologist prepares test items that he believes will measure highly ranked characteristics in job applicants.

4. These questions are tried out on a random sample of potential applicants to see which do the best job of differentiating (that is, items which roughly half the test takers will get "right," half "wrong"). Also, intercorrelations are sought, often by factor analysis.

5. On the basis of these results, a tentative test is prepared from questions which differentiate among people.

6. A decision is made as to how to distinguish between "good" and "bad" employees (the *criterion*). This may be in terms of over-all performance as subjectively rated by the supervisor, or in terms of objective measures such as average daily sales, percentage of production passing inspection, or absentee rates. If several criteria are used, some formula must be developed to weigh them so that a single over-all dimension can be determined.

7. Test is then given to all new applicants, but not used for selection.

8. After some time (say 18 months), the scores of those hired are compared with their performance as measured by the criterion (see figure on next page). Test items (such as Question 1) that seem to correlate with the criteria are used in the test battery, which is now introduced into the employment procedure. Other items (such as Question 2) are discarded. If too few questions remain, start again at step 3.

9. Several years later, revalidate the test (as in steps 7 and 8) to insure that the test is still adequately predicting performance.

[16] Mason Haire, "Use of Tests in Employee Selection," *Harvard Business Review*, Vol. 28, No. 1 (January-February 1950), p. 44.

PERFORMANCE

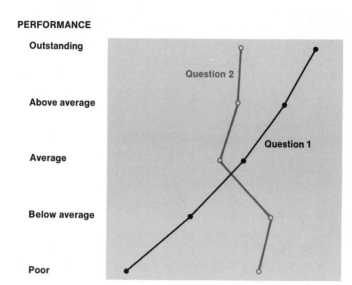

Question 1 is a good predictor
Question 2 is not

SELECTION

Criterion Measures

The use of any predictive method assumes that the organization can identify who is successful and who is not, distinguishing "good" from "bad." The dimension used in the measuring is called the *criterion*. One method of measuring is simply to ask each supervisor to rate his subordinates on a scale from outstanding to poor. At times, such subjective judgments are the best that can be obtained, but it is generally believed that more objective standards should be used, where possible. Among these may be production (units of output), quality (perhaps measured in terms of per cent of output passing inspection), absentee rate, turnover rate, promotion rate, and the like.

In many cases, one measure is not enough. In selecting typists, for example, one may look for speed, accuracy, sound judgment (a subjective measure), and a good attendance record. Unfortunately these various criteria may not be closely correlated. Fast typists are not necessarily accurate. Thus one must give arbitrary weights to each factor.

To complicate matters further, employee ability may change over time. Tests that are designed in terms of predicting success over an employee's first six months of employment may do a poor job of predicting success over the long run. No wonder the criterion problem has been called the "Achilles' heel" of testing.

Trait Stability

The next question we must ask is a fairly technical one, but also one of considerable practical significance. Can we be sure that the test result "is not due to luck, error or chance, but that it selects a stable individual quality that has been measured with some precision?" [17] (At times this question was called "reliability.")

Measurement "errors" may be introduced by a variety of means. To take a very few examples: The test may be too short and so give an inadequate sampling of the attribute being measured. It may be so long that the test-taker becomes bored and begins to answer at random. Or it may ask such personal questions that the test-taker refuses to give an honest answer.

Among the techniques used to insure test stability is checking to see if slightly different versions of a test given to the same person at different times, or the same test given to matched samples of people, give approximately the same results. Frequently, the test results obtained by scoring only the odd-numbered questions are checked against the scores derived from only the even-numbered questions. In addition, items may be introduced which word the same question differently; if different answers are given to these questions, one has good reason to doubt the test results as a whole.

Despite increasing attention to eliminating error through elaborate statistical techniques, it is obvious that some forms of contamination will remain in even the best-designed test.

Test Validity

The truly critical question is *validity:* Does the test actually predict what it purports to predict? Does it distinguish effectively between those who will be successful from those who will fail on a job? The best technique for validating a test (called *predictive validation*) is to administer a series (battery) of tests of different types to potential employees or candidates for a given position. The results of the tests are *not* used at this point to make hiring or placement decisions. Rather, the scores are filed, and then, after some extensive period of time has elapsed, the job-performance records of those who took the tests are examined. The test scores are then compared with the performance records to determine which, if any, of the tests helped predict who would be successful on the particular job (see figure above). [18] After this comparison has been made, and assuming that one or more of the test items have a significant correlation with performance on the job, a new battery is developed using those tests or parts of tests that were shown to be useful predictors.

This appears to be a straightforward and reasonably simple procedure. Unfortunately, it is not. Most companies have neither the facilities nor the

[17] Dunnette, *op. cit.*, p. 28.

[18] Note that on some jobs the relationship between test scores and performance may be negative, i.e., those with high intelligence may do less well than those with low intelligence. Or the relationship may be curvilinear—those in the middle range do best.

patience to undertake this type of program (after all, it requires that the company hire men whom the tentative test says should not be hired). As a result, they begin giving a test and use the results immediately to make selection decisions. This means that the evaluation data are "contaminated," for there is no way of knowing how those who were not hired, because of poor test scores, would have performed.

When the results of the testing program become generally available to supervisors before the test is validated, the test scores themselves may influence managerial decisions. Employees with relatively high scores may be given more personal encouragement and opportunities for promotion. Understandably, these high-scoring candidates are evaluated as being "superior" to those who came through with lower scores.

Concurrent validity. For many companies that find predictive validation too costly and time consuming, *concurrent validation* seems a likely short cut. Present employees are tested rather than job applicants. However, this procedure may not accurately reflect the population from which selections in fact have to be made (for example, current employees may be entirely white, while a large number of applicants are black). Further, some of the qualities being tested may have been acquired through a man's experience on the job. His test score today may be very different from what it might have been had he taken the same test when applying for the job. Finally, a validation study using only employees presently on the job provides no means of predicting the test answers of those who are fired or perhaps promoted to higher positions.

Low validities. Even with the most careful techniques, tests predict inaccurately. Back in 1928, the famous psychologist, Clark Hull, noted that the best tests of the day had a maximum validity of .50. In technical terms this meant that at the most these tests could predict only 25 per cent of the differences among peoples' performance. [19] Over 40 years later this ceiling still stands. Indeed a comprehensive 1966 review of testing studies showed that the average validity of tests for most occupations was below .40, with tests doing a better job of predicting performance in training than performance on the job. [20] Indeed, these "statistics are far from gratifying and offer little support for *anyone* claiming to do much better than chance." [21]

These disappointing results have led many psychologists to become disillusioned with testing generally. Some urge that greater emphasis be given to training. However, the major effort of those doing original research in this field has not been to raise the traditional over-all validity measure, but to get around it by improving the prediction of specific aspects of job performance for specific subgroups of people, in particular by seeking practical (as opposed to statistical) validity, the use of moderator variables, and the development of synthetic validities.

[19] After all, individual performance is a function not just of innate ability but also of his supervisor's ability, peer group work standards (Chapter 4), and so forth—all of which improve or harm his performance.

[20] Edwin E. Ghiselli, *The Validity of Occupational Aptitude Tests* (New York: Wiley, 1966).

[21] Marvin Dunnette, "A Modified Model for Test Validation and Selection Research," *Journal of Applied Psychology,* Vol. 47, No. 5 (October 1963), p. 317.

Practical vs. statistical validity.   Statistical validity is a summary measure of the relationship between test results and job performance of *all* those who take a test. Practical validity may be something else again, as the following illustrates:

Recent research has emphasized that, in practice, many tests are not equally effective with high scorers and low scorers (jaw-breaking name for this phenomenon: nonhomoscedastic). Thus a test which may be useful in discriminating between "outstanding" candidates and those who are merely "very good" may be totally useless in discriminating between "average" and "poor." Consequently test batteries that are useful when there is an abundance of highly qualified applicants may have little value when the labor market becomes tight.

Moderator variables.   Tests do not predict equally well with all classes of applicants. Research on *moderator variables* has been concerned with the classes of jobs and job applicants for which tests have strongest predictive power (sometimes reffered to as the "prediction of predictability"). For example, certain tests have been shown to be more useful in predicting the college success of women than of men, and of anxious students than of those who are not anxious. Within industry, aptitude tests seem to be more highly correlated with job performance for those who are highly motivated than for those who are not.

The object of this research, then, is to determine which tests work best with which class of applicants. For example (see figure below), the test results on one test may correlate better with performance on the criterion for whites than for blacks, and on another the results may be the opposite. Or the performance of one group may be predicted fairly well by tests, but that of another better by interviews or biographical inventories.

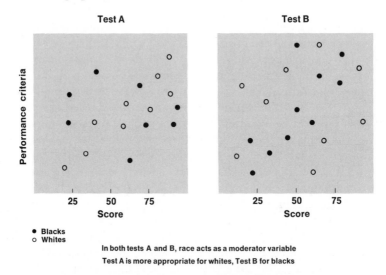

In both tests A and B, race acts as a moderator variable

Test A is more appropriate for whites, Test B for blacks

TEST RESULTS WHERE RACE IS A MODERATOR VARIABLE

Synthetic validation.   A test can do a better job of predicting performance in accordance with a single criterion, such as work quality, than it can on a "composite" criterion, such as "over-all performance," which is itself only a summation of a number of specific criteria. Thus validities tend to be higher when tests are used to predict performance with regard to specific elements on the job, rather than total results. If one were concerned with hiring parcel deliverymen, different tests or parts of tests might be used to predict their safe driving, flexibility, work output, relations with customers, and record-keeping ability. For this reason a psychologist might feel much more confidence in saying "Our tests predict that Jones will be a hard worker, but he may have trouble getting along with customers," than in making a summary judgment—"Jones is the best man in the batch."

But in selection, management must often make a decision as to who is the best man. Test experts who have worked with *synthetic validation* have sought to determine the essential qualities required to perform specific jobs, and then to test applicants for each of these qualities. Thus, for a given job, a test of speed may be given a 75 per cent weight while a test for accuracy is given only 25 per cent.

Among the advantages of the synthetic validity approach is that it permits test batteries to be designed for jobs on which only a few employees work. The orthodox form of validation is statistically meaningful only if at least a fair number (30–50) of workers are employed on the job. Synthetic validity is also useful in vocational guidance, determining the best job for the man, as it is in selection, determining the best man for the job.

Other Limitations of Tests

Statistical rather than individual predictions. Test scores can never make firm predictions on what will happen if a specific individual, Mr. Jones, is hired. They can't say absolutely that one man is better than another; all they can do is give the odds. At best, test scores simply tell management that a greater proportion of the people who score above a certain point will be more successful than those who score below that point. However, test results can never predict precisely that Jones himself will succeed or fail. The testers tell management that, in general, people whose test results look like Jones' are successful or are not successful. The degree of accuracy of their prediction depends on how closely the test scores are correlated with job-performance evaluations, and these correlations are never perfect. Thus, some people who do poorly on the test might do well on the job, and some people who score well might fail on the job.

Correlations not causes. One must remember that a test does not tell you why someone succeeds or fails. Even if a testing program discloses that job success is associated with a particular personality characteristic, the trait does not necessarily contribute to performance. Individuals with that trait may simply have some other unmeasured and unknown characteristic that helps them on the job, or supervisors may respond favorably to it (even though it may have nothing to do with the work). Of course, this is the limitation of all correlations; they are not meant to indicate causality.

Labor market limitations. The use of tests assumes that the supply of recruits is so large that management can afford to reject those who don't pass, even though some of them might have proved satisfactory employees. Often, however, the number of job applicants is limited, and recruitment costs are high. The introduction of a new selection requirement—for example, all applicants must pass an employment test—may mean that the company will have to double or even treble the number of applicants recruited in order to find enough who can meet the new requirement. But conditions in the labor market may make this impossible. Unfortunately, the amount of improvement that tests can generate is a function of the number of applicants that can be *rejected!*

Actual Practice

Despite new developments, such as the use of moderator variables and synthetic validities, which have helped raise testing's batting average, only a few organizations (mostly the armed services and large companies) follow proper scientific procedures in test development. Many companies buy standard tests developed by professional testing services (at times merely at the say-so of salesmen) without any attempt to measure the appropriateness of the test for the situation in which it is to be used. Or they develop "homemade" tests on their own, again without proper validation.

The reason for this apparently slipshod approach is very simple. The careful validation of tests is costly and time consuming (predictive validation normally takes at least a year). Many a personnel man has decided that it is better to use a poorly validated test than none at all. Recently, however, as we shall discuss in Chapter 21, the Civil Rights Act of 1964 has been interpreted as prohibiting the use of improperly developed tests if such tests in fact discriminate against minority job applicants. These decisions have done much to increase company interest in psychologically correct test development procedures. Tests may be less common in the future, but they will be more carefully designed.

DECISION-MAKING

Our discussion so far has dealt with the process by which personnel decision-makers gather bits of evidence on which to make their hiring decisions. But how is this evidence pulled together? And how much evidence is required? These questions must be answered in terms of the over-all manpower system.

Clinical vs. mechanical decision-making. How is the final decision made? Typically the line manager or the personnel man (or the two together) look over the application blanks, test results, and interview summaries, and make their decision on the basis of their subjective weighting of these imperfect indices and any other facts (or prejudices) they have at hand. Though this process can be called a *clinical approach*, often it is pure hunch. But most experienced personnel men feel that only in this way can the various important but unmeasurable intangibles be given proper consideration.

In recent years there has been an attempt to reduce this subjectivity through what has been called the *mechanical approach*. The data gathered through interviews and application blanks is quantified and, along with test scores, subjected to elaborate computer analysis in order to determine the highest possible correlations between predictors and the criterion measure of performance. At the end, weights are given to each of the predictor items. In other words, all of the selection measures (tests, interviews, and the like) are treated as if they were part of a single test. The studies to date suggest that the mechanical approach may have greater validity than the clinical, or, in other words, that computers can make better decisions than personnel men. [22]

Given these findings, why do personnel men persist in using the clinical approach? Part of the reason may be inertia. More important, most personnel men insist that computer-developed mechanical decision-making rules cannot be trusted to do the job alone—selection requires human judgment. [23] In addition, the mechanical approach is expensive to develop (though once developed it permits decisions to be made by clerks rather than by better-paid personnel men). It can easily get out of date as job requirements change. Further, the approach is feasible only for jobs for which a substantial number of men are hired. [24]

Costs. As the foregoing suggests, cost enters the picture. The selection process is expensive. As of 1966, according to one study, the cost of hiring a single executive, professional, or technical employee averaged over $1,000. [25] Since almost endless sums can be expended in increasingly high-powered selection techniques, the organization must at some point ask whether the added expense is worth the results in terms of better-qualified employees.

Some researchers have treated the selection process as an exercise in decision-making. The better the information the decision-maker has, the better his decision. But information costs money. If the organization intends to develop, validate, the administer its own testing program, it must hire well-trained, high salaried professionals. Moreover, most of the commercially available test batteries contain copyrighted elements, for which a fee must be paid each time they are used. Even companies that use outside consultants to administer and score tests incur substantial expenses. Interviewing is expensive, too, in terms of executive time. Recruiting costs mount up also (in 1966, for an average of $350 per executive or professional hired). [26]

[22] Campbell and others, *op. cit.*, Chapter 7; J. Sawyer, "Measurement and Prediction, Clinical and Statistical," *Psychological Bulletin*, Vol. 66 (1966), pp. 178-200.

[23] An extreme example would be the case of the applicant for a salesman's job who has a horrible case of body odor. If, as likely, (a) the quantified interview summary has no place for an evaluation of body smell, or (b) no study has been done in this company as to the relationship between body smell and efficiency, this perhaps crucial characteristic will not be properly noted or considered.

[24] Supporters of the mechanical approach argue that these limitations can be overcome through synthetic validation.

[25] John G. Myers, *Job Vacancies in the Firm and the Labor Market*, Studies in Business Economics, No. 109 (New York: National Industrial Conference Board, 1970), pp. 86-87.

[26] *Ibid.*

The higher the company's standards, the more costly the program becomes. If the company sets its "cutting scores" so that it hired only the top 20 per cent of those who apply, five applicants must be recruited, tested, and interviewed for every man employed. If almost all qualified men are already employed (as was the case for engineers through much of the 1960's), the company is forced either to increase its recruiting efforts vastly or to lower its standards.

The company's degree of selectivity, in turn, depends on the costs of making a wrong decision. Obviously more care will be given to the selection of an executive than of an unskilled worker, or to the hiring of a permanent employee as opposed to a temporary worker. Standards will be looser if it is easy to discharge an employee once it becomes obvious that he was a poor choice, and tighter if he is protected against discharge by a union contract, especially if (as occurs in some industries) the man hired can progress almost automatically, through seniority, to a highly responsible position.

Selection is often viewed as an alternative to training. If a man can be easily trained, less effort need be spent to find those who are already qualified. On the other hand, the need for an expensive training program may make management especially careful in whom it hires.

In short, selection decisions cannot be considered alone, but only in terms of their impact on other aspects of the manpower system.

SELECTION OF EXECUTIVES

Executive selection involves some special problems of its own:

1. Most blue-collar or white-collar workers are selected for specific jobs (though there are exceptions). Executives, for the most part, are selected not for specific jobs but for a career. This means that the job requirements and the criteria for success are much more nebulous than for other jobs.

2. Blue-collar and white-collar workers generally require manual skills, or at least skills that are rather easily tested. Executive skills, to the extent they can be defined, are generally in the areas of decision-making and human relations.

In part because of this greater vagueness as to what it requires to be an executive, there is also less agreement as to how to pick one. Some companies rely almost entirely on interviews. Others also make use of personality tests, while still others have experimented with what have come to be known as assessment centers.

Interviews

Interviews vary greatly in their sophistication. Too often, however, decisions are based on first impressions, "I like the cut of his jib," rather than on careful evaluation. Indeed one study of a business school graduating class concluded that handsomeness correlated with job-hunting success better than other factors such as college major, previous work experience, or holding of leadership positions in college organizations. [27]

Personality Tests

Though personality tests can be used for the positive purpose of identifying leaders or innovators, they are used most commonly to weed out misfits. Since executive positions require people who can work closely with other people, personnel selectors look for adaptable, conformist personalities who fit the overall organizational "climate." But by trying to make everybody alike, management runs the risk of excluding creative, imaginative talent, including the type of people who can become strong managers.

Personality tests . . . are loaded with debatable assumptions and questions of value. The result . . . is a set of yardsticks that reward the conformist, the pedestrian, the unimaginative—at the expense of the exceptional individual whom management most needs to attract. [28]

Ethics. Personality tests sometimes probe highly personal areas: unconscious sexual tendencies, family life, hidden fears and urges. These responses are highly confidential and are subject to serious misinterpretation except in the hands of a trained clinician. There can be serious ethical questions concerning the desirability of putting such information in the hands of supervisors and employers. In fact, the U.S. Civil Service Commission has restricted their use in the government on the grounds of invasion of privacy and potential misuse. [29]

Low validities. Personality tests generally show discouragingly low predictive powers. One reason for this defect may be that many of the tests utilized (such as the Minnesota Multi-Phasic Personality Inventory) have been designed to assist in the diagnosis of mentally ill people. They were not intended to predict on-the-job behavior. They may indicate only the presence of certain traits, not whether these traits are indicative of success within a given company. In any case, given the wide variety of situations within which executives work it is reasonable to assume that no two jobs require the same mixture of traits.

There seems to be general agreement among the experts that unless personality tests are carefully validated in the particular situation in which they are to be used, their predictive validity is little better than chance (and frequently they are less valuable than weighted application blanks or interest tests). On the other hand,

. . . in *some* situations, for *some* purposes, *some* personality measures can offer useful predictions. . . . [However,] a homemade personality or interest measure, carefully and competently developed for a specific situation, is a better bet for prediction than is a standard personality measure with a standard system of scoring. [30]

[27] Stephen J. Carroll, "Relationship of Various College Graduate Characteristics to Recruiting Decisions," *Journal of Applied Psychology*, Vol. 50 (October 1966), pp. 421–423.

[28] William H. Whyte, Jr., "The Fallacies of Personality Testing," *Fortune* (September 1954), p. 118.

[29] In a somewhat similar vein trade unions have objected to the use of lie-detector tests designed to uncover deception in the pre-employment background information supplied by applicants.

[30] Robert M. Guion and Richard F. Gottier, "Validity of Personality Measures in Personnel Selection," *Personnel Psychology*, Vol. 18 (Summer 1965), p. 159.

On balance, if personality tests are used at all they should be considered as only one of a number of factors entering into the final selection decision.[31]

Assessment Centers

In part because of the limitations of interviews and personality tests, some companies are experimenting with *assessment centers*. Here potential executives are submitted to a variety of assessment techniques. Those participating may be graduating seniors or MBA's being considered for employment (as at Sears), blue- or white-collar workers being considered for promotion into management (as in the Bell system), or young managers in the 25–30 age bracket being considered for promotion to higher levels (as at General Electric).

Assessment centers typically process candidates in groups of ten to fifteen, putting them through up to four days of exercises. These may include standard instruments, such as depth interviews, personality, interest, and intelligence tests, and biographical inventories. But the unique aspects of the assessment center approach is that candidates are given a series of typical management problems to work on as a group.[32] For example, a group of five may be set up as a "company" to make toys, a problem that involves aspects of purchasing, sales, design, manufacturing, finance, and inventory control (real toys are made with real parts). No formal leaders are appointed.

While the five wrestle with their problem they are observed by experienced managers who note the behavior of each candidate and the patterns of interpersonal relations that develop.[33] At the end of each period the observers gather together to make an over-all evaluation of each candidate's performance in the light of all available evidence. These judgments are passed on to management. However, each candidate if he desires it, is given a frank appraisal of his strengths and weaknesses, along with some counseling as to how to overcome the latter.

Assessment centers bring greater realism to the selection process. They measure behavior rather than just personality or aptitude. Over-all, both candidates and observers have greater confidence in the results. Early findings indicate a strong correlation between assessment center predictions and later performance on the job (even when the predictions are kept confidential).

Our discussion so far has dealt with the mechanics of selection. But what are the roles of management and staff in this process?

[31] Standard Oil of New Jersey, for example, has found high correlations (as high as .70) between managerial success and a battery of job-potential measures, including a biographical inventory, two measures of intelligence, a specially scored personality test, and a test of "managerial judgment." No one of the instruments alone proved as effective in predicting performance as the battery as a whole.

[32] These problems may include cases, in-basket exercises, and management games, all of which are also useful in training (see Chapter 24).

[33] The experience of observing is itself a valuable form of training for these managers. To spread this opportunity and to avoid anyone's becoming stale, observers normally are rotated.

We have spoken before about the relative authority of staff and line executives. Since selection procedures contribute significantly to a manager's effectiveness, ultimate responsibility for decision-making must reside with the line. Personnel specialists can help the manager select his subordinates by recruiting and screening appropriately qualified candidates. But the final decision on whom to hire for a specific job must rest with the manager.

The danger is that managers tend to ascribe more validity to test scores than test specialists do. When a test claims to measure the "impulsiveness" or "self-sufficiency" of an applicant, the manager may ignore the fact that these are just *labels* attached to test results, and that a given applicant who scores high in these categories may or may not demonstrate these characteristics on the job. The specialists readily admit that test results do not guarantee success or failure; they know that test scores are simply another set of data to be added to information about the applicant's previous experience, training, work evaluations, interview information, and the impressions of those who know him.

Tests for Present Employees

So far, we have been talking about the selection of new employees. Tests are also used by many companies as one means of determining promotions and transfers.

The use of tests for such purposes may threaten the leadership position of the immediate supervisor. If good test performance is required for promotion in the organization, what happens to successful job performance as an incentive? As Whyte observes:

The weight now being given test reports makes it clear that for those who aspire to be an executive the most critical day they may spend in their lives will be the one they spend taking tests. [34]

Employees often resent the great weight given to the results of tests that they do not understand. The problem is further aggravated by the statistical nature of test results. It is difficult to use test results to explain to an employee why he did not get a given promotion. At best, one can say that, "In general, those with scores like yours are less successful than those with higher scores." Many times the material covered by a personality or aptitude test bears little logical relationship to the job to which the employee aspires. And those who develop the tests are not much help here; as one expert remarked candidly:

"All we look for are correlations between test items and our criterion of job success. We don't care whether it is the height of the applicant's grandfather or how much he likes to fish. As long as it correlates, we will use it in the battery."

A company that bases its promotion decisions primarily on such test results must be prepared to inform employees how and why the tests are used. Other-

[34] *Op. cit.*, p. 174.

wise employees will feel that they are subject to mystical forces and that hard work counts less than test-writing and interviewing skills. "The headshrinkers decide which way you go in this company."

If the testing program has been carefully chosen and well administered, management can justify it to employees. Personality tests, for example, uncover talent that would otherwise go to waste. An immediate supervisor may overlook or be prejudiced against the abilities of a given subordinate, but an impersonal test may bring these abilities to the attention of higher management. Moreover, management can make it clear that test results are not the *sine qua non* for advancement, but only one type of evidence that is used. And the employee can be made to realize that tests are valuable for his own purposes, for they identify attributes that suggest types of jobs and training that he will find satisfying and rewarding. (Many of these problems, of course, are diminished when assessment centers are used.)

THE ROLE OF THE PERSONNEL DEPARTMENT

Recruitment and selection are probably the Personnel Department's two single most important functions. But Personnel is a staff department. It can perform advisory, service, and even research functions, but the final responsibility for deciding who will be employed (except, perhaps, for some very routine jobs) belongs to line.

Chapter 17 has discussed the delicate diplomatic problems arising out of staff-line relations and p. 368 suggests one possible division of activities in this area. At this point we should stress the fact that while line managers may be thinking of the interests of their own particular departments or groups, Personnel must keep in mind the needs of the manpower system as a whole and the possible impact of recruitment and selection decisions on that system.

Personnel should advise managers on hiring standards. For example, many managers may set standards too high, thus increasing recruiting costs and leading to serious morale problems, particularly when employees are overqualified by education for their jobs. By setting more realistic hiring standards many companies could enlarge their pool of potential recruits and provide opportunities for the underprivileged.

On the other hand, some automation decreases the number of menial jobs and raises hiring standards. Even shipping room personnel often have to read complicated instructions printed out by a computer, and many simple, repetitive jobs are now done by machine. Also, as we saw in Chapter 3, in automated plants, managers want to hire people who can be promoted through the ranks. All of these developments make it unlikely that anyone without a high school education can be hired.

Actually, Personnel's work in this area can destroy stereotypes. The assumptions that all salesmen have to be highly sociable or all managers have to be highly intelligent may not stand up under the scrutiny of a selection-research program. In one department store, Personnel's research on job requirements showed that very different personal characteristics were required to sell "big ticket" items from those needed for housewares and clothing.

In order to survive, every organization must attract an adequate supply of employees and must then assign them to the jobs for which they are best suited. In administering its recruitment program, the company must devise specific programs tailored to the numbers and skills to be recruited and to prevailing conditions in the labor market. Moreover, it must make a systematic evaluation of alternative selection techniques in light of their relative advantages and costs.

When psychologists first began to explore individual differences, the application of their research to selection promised to introduce a new era in employee relations. Theretofore, employee failures had been attributed to laziness or recalcitrance; now it could be argued that the real fault lay in trying to force square pegs into round holes. Testing enthusiasts claimed that careful appraisal of individual capabilities would solve most personnel problems. Placing the employee in the right job would assure a high level of performance and eliminate employee discontent.

These predictions have proved somewhat extravagant. The individual human being has shown himself to be more difficult to appraise and categorize than was anticipated. Frequently an employee with the requisite skills and learning potential has failed for lack of motivation. Personality attributes like motivation, although difficult to measure by simple tests, are often more important in explaining job success or failure than more tangible characteristics.

There is a vast difference between selecting people for jobs that have very predictable and controlled behavior (a draftsman or machinist) and selecting people who will be creative or innovative. For many of these more complex jobs we are not even sure what abilities or behavior patterns will lead to success. Nor are jobs themselves easy to classify, particularly the more complex managerial positions. Different people will handle the same job in strikingly different ways. The requirements of a job may change radically when a new supervisor takes over, and there is no way of predicting organizational changes of this sort. Jones, who was selected to work in a department headed by Brown, finds himself unable to work effectively under the new head, Smith.

In recent years greater emphasis has been given to biographical inventories and assessment centers as supplements to or even substitutes for testing. But research also suggests that the effectiveness of the various selection instruments can be substantially increased through detailed validation studies (both predictive and synthetic) and the use of moderator variables where these are appropriate.

These new developments have combined with federal anti-discrimination regulations to make management increasingly aware of the potentialities of carefully devised selection programs, along with the difficulties of achieving them.

One of the main questions today is the extent to which selection decisions should be made "mechanically," primarily on the basis of elaborate statistical studies, or "clinically," on the basis of sound judgment and common sense. Either way, selection's batting average will be well under 1.000.

As suggested earlier, selection and training can be viewed as alternate means of obtaining qualified employees; the more thorough the selection process, the less the need for training. With this in mind, let us now consider how training fits into the over-all manpower system.

problem 1 • HOW DO YOU SPOT A GOOD COPYWRITER?

Springfield, Zoar and Gowanda is a large, successful advertising agency. One of the reasons for its success has been its ability to produce fresh, creative, eye-catching copy. The company employs about 60 copywriters working in 15 different departments.

The department heads, who are responsible for hiring, have different ideas on what makes a good copywriter. Their predilections are based pretty much on chance experience and ingrained stereotypes. One supervisor will tell you: "I can tell a good copywriter right away—all you have to do is to give him two minutes to come up with an original advertisement for something like condensed milk and see what he does." Others use this criterion: "I have him bring in all the ads he has ever written and ask him for his 10 favorites and 10 worst. Then I spend the next evening reading them all over and comparing my judgments to his."

The results of this haphazard approach to selection have not been good. At present the company needs five new copywriters, and one-third of the present staff have not worked out well. The agency's personnel department would like to use a more systematic procedure for evaluating applicants, including some technique for testing writing skill. The new program would be costly, however, and there would be little point in setting it up if the department heads ignored its findings.

1. If you were head of the agency, how would you set up an improved selection procedure that would not detract from the department heads' responsibility for turning out high-quality copy?

2. What information would you need before deciding on such a new policy?

3. How would you introduce and gain acceptance for the new approach?

problem 2 • APPLICANT

The Ripley Paint Company trains the salesmen it hires to sell its product line to retail stores. The company seeks personable young men who have the energy and initiative to make the requisite calls on customers and the ability to speak enthusiastically and intelligently about the company's products. Flexibility and patience in meeting a wide variety of people, and accuracy in transferring orders to order forms, are also important requirements.

James Henry has applied for a sales job. The interviewer who is going to talk with him has noted the following entries on his application blank:

Henry is 25 years old.
He has completed one year of college, at a small teachers' college in the Midwest.
He was divorced after three years of marriage, no children.
He has held two jobs since leaving school; he had had no work experience prior to that time. The jobs were: laboratory assistant, Memorial Hospital (2 years), New York, and credit manager for collection agency (2 years), Buffalo.

No job is listed for one year. James notes on his application that he was recovering from an illness during that period.

1. If you were the interviewer, what objectives would you set for your interview with James?

2. How would you phrase your questions?

problem 3 • WANTED: CUSTOM TAILORS

You are the executive vice president of a large "high-style" women's dress manufacturing organization. Your firm finds it increasingly difficult to find candidates for custom-tailoring positions. These craftsmen, in the past, at least, have been apprentice-trained in Europe, and most of the better American tailors have been immigrants.

1. What proposals would you make to your company concerning means of increasing the supply of custom-tailors available to your organization? (You employ about a hundred of them, many of whom are nearing retirement.)

2. In your proposal, consider the sources of information and the channels of communication you would explore in developing a proposal with reasonable chances of success. Remember that costs are a significant factor.

problem 4 • A PERSONNEL POINT OF VIEW

"Personnel should provide advice and service; line should make the final hiring decisions." That's a lot of nonsense. In my company line doesn't want to be bothered. They hire us to be the experts. If the wrong hiring decisions are made, we are held responsible in any case. So we have to use the techniques which our professional experience tells us are best. Research tells us that the so-called "mechanical" approach to decision-making in this area is superior to the "clinical" approach and so we have completely automated our selection process. Our tests are scored by IBM machines, interviews and application blanks are coded, and the whole shooting match fed into the computer. It makes the final decisions, certainly not line.

Comment on this point of view.

20 TECHNICAL TRAINING

The efficiency of any organization depends directly on how well its members are trained. Newly hired employees usually need some training before they can take up their work, while older employees require training both to keep them alert to the demands of their present job and to fit them for transfers and promotions.

Training also motivates employees to work harder. Employees who understand their jobs are likely to have higher morale. And the very fact that management is confident enough of their abilities to invest in training provides an assurance that they are valued members of the organization. This is particularly important in dynamic companies undergoing changes in technology. Such changes as automation are resisted when workers fear that they will be incapable of handling newly-created jobs.

Effective managers recognize that training is an ongoing, continuous process, not a "one shot" activity. New problems, new procedures and equipment, new knowledge and new jobs are constantly creating the need for employee instruction. This explains why next to public schools and the military, industry is the third largest educational institution in the U.S. Many companies spend millions annually and the total budget of all firms probably runs into the billions of dollars annually.

The chapter begins with the role and objectives of training in any organization, then considers what psychologists have discovered about learning patterns, and concludes with more specific examples of types of training programs and technologies. (The special problems of training minorities are discussed in Chapter 21 and training programs for managers are assessed in Chapter 24.)

At one extreme, training consists of a few hours (or only a few minutes) of induction by the supervisor, who gives the new employee a skeleton outline of company policies, the location of the locker room, and a summary of work rules. At the other extreme, training consists of formal courses designed to develop qualified specialists over a period of years. In between these extremes are countless programs tailored to fit the needs of particular organizations: short courses on local safety hazards (one of the most common training areas and often handled by a safety specialist), or on customer uses of company products or services; instruction in writing sales slips; and courses in sales techniques or internal auditing.

But it is misleading to think of job training purely in terms of formal courses and programs. Almost everything that happens to an employee after he joins a company serves as a training experience. Those elements in an employee's repertoire of behavior that are rewarded and thus provide him with satisfaction tend to be repeated; those that are punished tend to be abandoned.

There are many people within the organization who provide these rewards and punishments in addition to those who are formally assigned to train employees. The informal work group, with its clearly defined codes of behavior, has a potent influence on its members; formal groups like the union also exert a strong effect. Many times the supervisor may be training his subordinates without even being aware of it. The acts that provoke discipline or that fail to provoke discipline tell an employee what is expected of him and what he can do with impunity. Good housekeeping practices that are praised and slovenly workmanship that goes uncriticized both are learning experiences. Similarly, the methods, short cuts, and routines practiced by fellow employees all carry important meanings that are assimilated by the novice as he learns his way in a new job situation.

The training derived from all of these varied sources may be in sharp conflict with the prescribed ways of doing things. So management must be careful to see that the impact of casual, day-to-day experiences does not nullify the practices stressed in the more formal training sessions.

WHO SHOULD TRAIN?

In many companies training is very informal. It consists of assigning new employees as helpers to old employees, or telling an old employee to "show this fellow what he should do." At times the results are excellent, but often the old-timer fails to train adequately. Sometimes the failure reflects the old-timer's indifference or even hostility to "breaking in a new employee," a job he feels he isn't being paid to do or that may create a competitor for his own job. More often, the old-timer fails because he is unable to communicate and lacks systematic knowledge of learning principles. The "generation gap" accentuates this problem, as can differences in background, say between white and black workers. In some companies, where supervisors can't speak the same language used by employees, training may be nonexistent.

Most managements today make formal provision for training, either through holding line management directly responsible or by hiring training specialists, and sometimes both. Sometimes these training specialists report directly to line management; more frequently, a special training section is established in the personnel department.

As a staff expert, of course, the training specialist faces the problems of staff men everywhere: Line management may resent his efforts as interference; he may try to teach employees methods that conflict with those their boss wants them to use (either because standard company procedures are not being followed, or because the trainer has not kept pace with developments "out on the floor"). Conflicts often arise when the training specialist insists on telling employees who are under the direction of line supervisors how they should do their job. Equally unfortunate, once a training specialist has been appointed, the line supervisor may decide to pass the buck and give up all responsibility for training. Some companies have tried to create an amicable division of responsibilities by having the staff trainer conduct classes off the work floor and advising the line supervisor on how to do better training on the floor (in a sense the staff trains the trainers), and by holding the line supervisor responsible for all training in production areas.

OBJECTIVES IN TRAINING

Induction Training for New Employees

Sometimes, the busy, hard-pressed supervisor tends to neglect what he considers the mere formalities of induction training and concentrates exclusively on the immediate job assignment. Haste and lack of sensitivity at this early stage, however, will spawn unnecessary personnel problems later on—for example, an employee refusing to do a task claiming it's not part of his job, having never received a complete explanation of his duties.

Progressive companies have long recognized the need for properly introducing a new employee to his job. Not only do they familiarize him with the tasks he will be expected to perform, but they also provide him with information about company rules and personnel policies, introduce him to his fellow workers, and give him an idea of where his job fits into the total operation. A carefully planned orientation-induction program helps the new employee to identify with the organization and its procedures and gives him some feeling for the significance of the work he will be doing and thus helps him overcome the fears and anxieties that are bound to arise on a new job. It also makes him feel a part of his new group.

A study conducted by General Electric suggests that employees on machine-paced jobs who are shown how their jobs fit in with others, the uses of the product, and who are given tours of adjacent work stations and the larger plant exhibit more positive work attitudes and produce higher quality work. [1]

[1] Marvin Sorcer and Herbert Meyer, "Motivation and Job Performance," *Personnel Administration*, Vol. 31, No. 4 (July 1968), pp. 8-21.

More profound uncertainties and anxieties relate to the problem of adjusting to a new culture, a new way of life. Just as travel to a new country or changing residences can mean "culture shock," so the student fresh from school discovers many of his preconceptions about industry and the theories he has learned don't fit. The shock resulting from disorganization can be ameliorated by understanding supervision utilizing patience and tact. [2]

Proper induction training also makes it unnecessary for the employee to unlearn methods and procedures that prove unacceptable. Unlearning is both difficult and time-consuming. However, no supervisor can expect to communicate everything about a new job at the outset. And some of the information he presents is bound to seem meaningless and confusing to the inexperienced subordinate, who simply has not had enough experience to appreciate the significance of what is being told him.

Cashier trainees in department stores report that they found much of their induction training meaningless because, never having been on the job, they knew nothing of the situations to which the information would apply. Once they had gone out on the job, however, and started receiving mutilated, faulty sales slips, they felt a need for the training they had considered worthless.

Learning New Techniques

Even with excellent induction training, most organizations can anticipate that jobs will change. Even highly trained professionals such as doctors and physicists find that they must periodically take new courses that reflect changes in the "state of the art" that have occurred since their formal graduation. New equipment and new products require employees and salesmen alike to learn new skills. Many times both managers and employees alike are lulled into a false sense of security by the gradualness of change which, in time, makes many skills obsolete.

A shift to centralized buying and higher level management participation in buying decisions has created the need for a very different set of selling techniques than were used when salesmen contacted lower level executives or purchasing agents. Many companies have found that they have large sales staffs who do not have the requisite abilities. [3]

Thus continuous monitoring of the actual jobs being performed, the skills required, and equipment utilized is necessary to identify evolutionary changes that periodically ought to call forth new training efforts. A major policy question is, how much should the organization do to keep employee knowledge and skills updated, and how much should the individual do for himself? Here is a typical problem; ask yourself if management was right.

Carters was the chief engineer on the Pluto project. For more than 3 years he worked 50-plus hours a week to deal with a never-ending series of technical and managerial problems. It was an exhausting pace. Two years later Carters was bypassed for promotion because he did not have up-to-date knowledge in the laser field which was the current major thrust of the division. In conjunction with a nearby university the company regularly sponsored a variety of math and physics courses, but Carters never enrolled.

[2] Cf. Edgar Schein, "How to Break in the College Graduate," Harvard Business Review, Vol. 42 (November 1964), pp. 68–76.

[3] E. B. Weiss, The Vanishing Salesman (New York: McGraw-Hill, 1962).

Handling such problems involves management in weighing very subjective factors: motivation and responsibility. A study committee made up of engineers, educators, and administrators in a major corporation made the following recommendation:

The professional must have the means to keep up with his field: the time and the facilities. If the company will establish a carefully planned program of continuing voluntary education, the conscientious professional will supply his own motivation, which will be the most fruitful. Management, however, must recognize the ensuing basic conflicts between immediate job demands and continuing professional growth.

Among other things this policy can require tuition rebates and time off at company expense to attend courses, some of which the company itself must staff and finance; generous leaves of absence (for instance, to acquire advanced degrees); and the inclusion of course attendance as a part of performance evaluation. It may even require the company to help in the establishment of a branch of a college or university where the community lacks adequate educational resources.

Remedial Training

A narrow line separates remedial training from learning new techniques, particularly for professionals. Where skills and knowledge have been unused (or poorly learned in the first place) they need to be "refreshed" by additional training. Such training tends to be tailored to individuals rather than to occupational groups. The usefulness of a constructive management response to on-the-job difficulties or poor performance is attested to by the rather substantial numbers of employees who exhibit such problems. [4]

Such training can impede this typical vicious cycle: Employee demonstrates below average performance → manager grows increasingly discouraged about employee's prospects → employee detects this as hostility and lack of encouragement → performance declines further, confirming supervisor's judgment that employee will not succeed. Thus when an employee fails to measure up to established standards, his performance may signal the need for additional training. Over time, an employee may forget procedures he learned during induction, or he may develop slipshod short cuts that require less energy and thought. Or management itself may introduce new procedures and equipment that alter the employee's job. Thus training is not a one-step process; it is a continuing managerial responsibility.

Training employees with some experience on the job may be a more difficult task than giving them induction training, however. Oldtimers may resent being told that they can't do their job, or may suspect that the training is an attempt to "show them up," perhaps for disciplinary reasons, or to step up output—all at their expense. Telling an employee that he needs remedial training may embarrass him before his colleagues, for it is a threat to his status as an intelligent, competent workman.

[4] Cf. John B. Miner, *The Management of Ineffective Performance* (New York: McGraw-Hill, 1963).

As an alternative to remedial training for individuals, some companies use regular refresher courses in such areas as safety, job methods, and housekeeping. This practice avoids spotlighting the poor performers and may head off the tendency to slip into short cuts. Periodic training also permits the regular introduction of new methods and techniques. New accounting practices, new company products or engineering standards, new equipment—all require explanation. If these explanations are presented regularly, the possibility that important changes will be overlooked is substantially reduced.

Aiding Displaced Employees

Increasingly, farsighted management takes the view that if an employee is displaced by new technology, management has a responsibility to endeavor to retrain him so that he will be able to maintain comparable earnings and status. Guarantees also serve to decrease worker and union resistance to change. Federal legislation also provides funds to subsidize training for unemployed displaced workers who are taking retraining programs sponsored by companies and schools. [5]

Among the special problems faced in such programs are the age and previous education of the displaced employees. Particularly in companies where automated equipment is replacing unskilled and semiskilled labor, the employee may be handicapped by inadequate basic training in arithmetic, English, and so on. He may not even be literate. Thus pretraining preparation may be necessary.

Further, the older employee is likely to lack confidence in his own flexibility and to be upset by the threatened elimination of long-established work customs, social groups, and job skills. Matching this may be supervisory bias against the older worker and doubts concerning his ability to develop new skills. However, there is increasing evidence that, properly handled, the over-40 employee is capable of very substantial retraining. [6]

Here are two examples of such retraining programs: [7]

INDEPENDENT TELEPHONE CO.

Telephone messages are now transmitted by microwave and the cable splicer has been partially replaced by the expert in microwave transmission. The company coped with this largely by retraining existing personnel and training new people as they are hired. The company arranged with a state industrial education agency to give courses in electricity and related mathematics, telephone equipment and circuits, plant construction principles, and basic technical writing.

Classes were held four hours a night for 10 weeks. Employees paid a $2 registration fee and the company furnished textbooks and materials. Employees with practical experience were used as instructors.

The company makes use of suppliers' educational offerings as well. For intensive training in the use of new telephone equipment it sends selected employees to a supplier's school in Chicago.

[5] Current developments in the field of manpower training and development grants and activities are featured in the *Journal of Human Resources* and also in a new monthly publication, *Career Development* (Washington D.C.: University Research Corporation). See also Chapter 21.

[6] *Cf.* A. T. Welford, *Aging and Human Skill* (London: Oxford University Press, 1963).

[7] *Personnel Management Bulletin,* Report No. 147, December 15, 1961, pp. 2-3.

Installation of automatic reservation machinery made retraining of clerical employees a must. The new machinery, specially developed electronic data-processing devices, did the posting work of 75 pairs of reservation clerks. However, a large number of clerks were still required to answer telephones and to operate the "Reservisor," as it is called.

The airline set up a special classroom program during working hours for both reservation clerks and supervisors. The first step was training instructors and preparing an instructor's manual. Classes were begun while the new equipment was being installed. About 40 supervisors and lead agents received a week's intensive instruction from the company's research engineer.

Training for Advancement

Effective training may help individuals to climb promotional ladders to more responsible and better jobs. (Of course, this is the function of all education in a free society: to permit individuals to advance on the basis of merit and ability.) Careful ordering of jobs in promotional ladders also permits individuals to learn, primarily through observation, some of the skills of higher-ranked positions while doing their present job. Filling-in for higher-ranked colleagues during vacations or absences also provides a type of informal on-the-job training.

Many companies have developed their own internal schools, which offer a range of courses relevant to self-development (from speed reading to calculus), and others make use of nearby educational facilities to sponsor special or existing course programs. Thus secretaries can learn to be administrative assistants, and technicians may become full-fledged engineers.

The key element in such programs is the opportunity provided for highly motivated individuals to attain more responsible and more highly paid positions. While the company may provide facilities or even tuition moneys, the employee must provide the energy, the dedication, and the willingness to assume additional burdens beyond his immediate job. Such self-selection procedures are sensible components of a good personnel program because they reward the well motivated and are not simply an additional company benefit bestowed on everyone.

Apprenticeship

Organizations that employ skilled tradesmen like machinists, construction workers, or printers, may conduct formal apprenticeship programs. Here, on-the-job training, directed by skilled journeymen, is supplemented by classroom instruction. Smaller companies that cannot afford programs of their own often join together to sponsor community-wide training programs, usually in collaboration with unions and the public-school system.

Trade unions that represent skilled craftsmen have a strong interest in these. At times, they want to keep down the number of men trained, so that excessive competition for job opportunities can be avoided. In fact, many agreements specify a definite ratio between the number of journeymen and apprentices, thus limiting the number of trainees. [8]

[8] Cf. U. S. Department of Labor, *Admission and Apprenticeship in the Building Trades Unions* (Washington, D.C.: Government Printing Office, 1971).

The typical apprenticeship takes two to five years to produce a journeyman. The school portion of a typical program for an electrician might include among other subjects shop math, blue-print reading, basic physical science, and local building codes. This material is "sandwiched" into more practical on-the-job training. The best programs provide for rotation among jobs and even among employers so that the apprentice learns all aspects of his trade.

Such programs are more common in Europe, where a much wider variety of jobs (such as hotel and office work) have formal apprenticeships, and one boy out of five participates. Apprentice-like programs extend to other jobs in this country as well. For example, the distributive trades (retailing) are often taught in cooperative training programs involving technical institutes and department stores.

Traditionally, would-be accountants and lawyers apprenticed themselves to fully qualified professionals who taught them the "trade." After a given number of years of supervised practice they were allowed to take the examination to qualify for *certification*. It is possible that as more occupational groups seek to professionalize (see Chapter 3) and establish experience and examination requirements for their members, the apprenticeship or internship type of training program will become more widespread.

USING LEARNING THEORY

Whatever type of training management decides to provide, some attention to the principles of learning is worthwhile. Most of these have been formulated by psychologists.

Motivation

The indifferent, reluctant student will learn little, even from a brilliant instructor. For an employee to benefit from training, he must be anxious to improve his abilities and job performance and thus enhance his opportunities for advancement. Clearly, the return the company receives from its investment in training will depend upon the over-all level of morale in the organization.

On the other hand, overly intense motivation may actually inhibit learning. If an individual becomes too tense (too fearful) or if he sets goals for himself that are greater than his ability to attain them, the results may be acute disappointment and loss of motivation.

Reinforcement

Related to motivation is the need for *reinforcement*—that is, for learning to take place, the individual must receive some encouragement or reward. The reward need not be tangible. Usually there is a balance between intrinsic rewards (sense of personal progress and accomplishment) and extrinsic rewards (encouragement and praise provided by an outsider such as teacher or supervisor).

Reinforcement is also provided by the learner's own sense of progress, of growing competence (the ability to master more difficult parts of the job).

Student nurses in medical wards occupied chiefly by chronically ill patients complain that they are always doing unimportant jobs that teach them nothing: custodial duties like bed-making and water-carrying. On the surgical floors, however, where each patient requires one or more of the "nursing arts," every student and assistant gets assignments commensurate with her growing ability. [9]

Psychologists distinguish between one-to-one and random reinforcement in what they call *conditioning*. Learning is much quicker when, each time a task is done correctly, the trainee is provided with some positive reward or encouragement. Regrettably, forgetting (or extinction) is also rapid with this method. On the other hand, random reinforcement (rewards received irregularly), while providing slower learning, also provide much slower forgetting.

We have referred consistently to rewards, not punishments, because of their more desirable effect on the learning situation. Punishment can breed resentment or even *fixation* in which the same unsuccessful response is repeated over and over again. The *law of effect* is a powerful tool for the manager in teaching: behavior that is rewarding tends to be repeated.

Feedback

For reinforcement to be effective in improving performance, there must be feedback, or *knowledge of results*. Imagine how difficult it would be to improve one's marksmanship without being able to see the target. If self-correction is to take place, the trainee must know the relationship between his behavior and the impact, or result, of his behavior. Unless he knows how close his achievement is to the desired standard of good performance, he will not be able to improve his performance, no matter how hard and how frequently he tries. This means that the supervisor should resist the temptation to contact the subordinate *only* when he has made a mistake. The learner also needs to know when he has made the right decision. And when he has made a mistake, he needs to recognize *why* and *how* he went wrong and how close he came to doing the work properly. Feedback of results should be provided as quickly as possible after the trainee's performance.

Here are two examples of the effective use of feedback in improving job performance:

Previously, furnace crews had no measure of the effectiveness of their work. When gauges were installed to indicate the efficiency of individual boilers graphically, it was estimated that $333,000 was saved in fuel costs.

A recording device was invented to show employees their cutting patterns on a foot-operated abrasive wheel used to cut tungsten discs. The device revealed learner errors so dramatically that training time was cut almost in half. [10]

---

[9] T. Burling, E. Lentz and R. Wilson, *The Give and Take in Hospitals* (New York: Putnam, 1956), pp. 252–253.

[10] Both examples are adapted from James N. Mosel, "How to Feed Back Performance Results to Trainees," *Journal of American Society of Training Directors* (February 1958).

Finally, feedback should be presented in a nonthreatening environment; the learner should be made to realize that mistakes will not cost him too dearly and that difficulties in learning are natural and expected. It is the supervisor's responsibility to provide this feedback, not just during the so-called training period, but on a continuing basis.

Learning by Doing

Learning is most efficient when the learner is actively involved in the learning process, rather than merely listening to a description of it. Motor activity (muscular movement) directly stimulates the higher mental processes, such as learning.[11] In fact, the greater the number of senses involved, the more effective the learning. To learn a poem quickly and accurately, it is much more efficient to recite it aloud than to read and reread it silently. Doing rather than just seeing or hearing also means that the individual is more likely to devote more of himself to the task; he becomes more *involved* in the learning process.

This principle has obvious implications for the supervisor's role in training. Instead of relying exclusively on lectures, or on training films and manuals, he should encourage the employee to try out new jobs, to ask questions, and to go through all the requisite motions. Of course, he watches for mistakes and insures that they are corrected, but he reinforces the correction by having the trainee repeat the activity properly. Active repetition is useful only when the training situation permits the trainee to try out alternative approaches in the full assurance that he can make mistakes and learn from them. Newly-acquired techniques that are not utilized are quickly forgotten.

Spaced Repetition

Training need not be continuous, however. Many experiments have shown that *spaced repetition*—that is, learning periods distributed through time—are more efficient than attempts to learn "all at once." Apprenticeship programs, in which the trainee learns by repeated doing, are an excellent example of this approach. Another obvious value of repetition is that it serves to inhibit forgetting.

Appropriate Size or Scope of the Lesson

Learning is expedited when the total process or skill to be mastered is broken down into small, "digestible" segments. Thus, the trainee can obtain satisfaction from reaching each one of the subgoals, and these, in turn, help him to reach his objective of learning the whole job. Whether or not this type of training is possible depends in part on what is to be learned. For example, the electrician can learn simple wiring and the associated arithmetic and then gradually move in logical steps to more complex circuitry.

[11] See Gordon Allport, "The Psychology of Participation," *Psychological Review,* Vol. 53 (May 1945).

On other jobs, this progression is hampered by the indivisibility of some work and learning is inhibited if the segments to be mastered are too small. Anyone who has learned to swim knows how difficult it is to combine leg movements with arm movements. If a job is broken into fragments, each of which must be mastered by itself, the problem of learning to integrate them into a whole activity, as a smooth, continuous process, becomes extremely difficult.

But how "small" a part of the job is "too small"? Wherever possible, the learner should try to master as a single unit all those activities that must be performed in a smooth, continuous sequence. In this way, each subpart becomes an internalized "cue" that stimulates the next part of the sequence. The trainer may have to encourage the learner to try out what seems at the outset to be an impossibly large segment. But it is more efficient in the long run for him to make many mistakes in trying to master a logically constituted unit, to fumble badly because of the number of coordinations required, than to concentrate on learning the parts as if each were to be performed in a compartmentalized fashion.

In addition, emphasis on these larger segments of the job may de-emphasize the trainer's tendency to assume there is only "one best way." When arm, hand, finger, and body motions are taught individually, in violation of what is easiest and most natural for the trainee, the training degenerates into an artificial, stilted ritual. Further, when these theoretically correct motions are combined, the resulting behavior pattern may be unsuited to the idiosyncrasies of the individual worker's nervous and muscular system (see Chapter 27).

Providing Theory

One of the more controversial training questions concerns the amount of *theory* or *background* the trainee needs to learn most effectively. Obviously the electrician has no need to go back to quantum mechanics. However, the effectiveness with which he learns repair or maintenance methods will be materially enhanced if he has some knowledge of electrical theory. The theory itself may not be essential to the specific tasks he will be performing, but it will help him to *transfer* his knowledge to new jobs, equipment, and processes. If the employee is to develop insight into new problems that arise during the course of his work, he must achieve more basic understanding of his activities than that provided by the "this-is-how-you-do-it" type of training. "Logical" training is always more effective than "rote" training—at least for jobs that call for any degree of sophisticated performance. As we noted in our discussions of management, the manager explains *why* when he gives directions, to insure that the employee will be able to handle unusual, unanticipated situations that may occur.

Typical Learning Patterns

Managers need some understanding of the pattern in which new skills are learned—of what are called "learning curves" (see figure p. 451). When the employee first begins to learn a new skill, he is likely to find himself unusually clumsy or inept—"all thumbs." This can be very discouraging, particularly to a

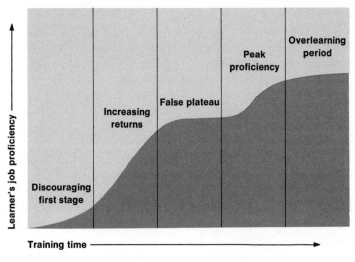

HYPOTHETICAL LEARNING CURVE

man who prides himself on his agility and ability; and so, during this early stage, the learner needs the supervisor's encouragement. (This, of course, is one justification for conducting certain kinds of training off-the-job.) The duration of this first stage is a function of the complexity and newness of the skill being learned—it may be only a few minutes or a few weeks.

After this period, the typical learning rate is rapid. This is the stage of increasing returns, in which small additional amounts of practice by the trainee produce substantial increases in job-proficiency. During this second period, the employee's confidence and satisfaction rise.

After more training time has elapsed, a "plateau" develops. Now additional training time does not result in very significant increases in proficiency, and both the supervisor and the learner may be deceived into thinking that the maximum proficiency has been attained.

These plateaus seem to be the result of two factors: (1) a loss of motivation as early surges of progress are dissipated and as further progress becomes more difficult, and (2) the trainee's need for substantial blocks of time to develop new and improved skills. Initially the employee may be forced to learn a new job in segments, thinking consciously about each part of the job. A great deal of practice is required before a real "break-through" takes place that permits these separate parts to become merged and the motions to be joined into a single, coordinated sequence of actions. Ghiselli and Brown describe this stage as follows:

Through practice, certain phases of the action patterns are automatized, superfluous activities are dropped out, precision of movement and smoothness of coordination are effected, excess tension is eliminated, the energy requirements of the total performance are greatly reduced, and the trainee develops self-assurance and confidence in his performance. [12]

[12] E. E. Ghiselli and C. W. Brown, *Personnel and Industrial Psychology*, 2nd ed. (New York: McGraw-Hill, 1955), p. 384.

The supervisor must also be wary of assuming that the employee's training has been completed once he has achieved a peak skill. Continued repetition needs to be encouraged so that *overlearning* will take place. An experienced automobile driver can refrain from driving for six months or even six years, and still be able to drive when the occasion demands. This is largely the result of overlearning, which diminishes the likelihood that forgetting will take place. Apparently, the reflex sequences that relate muscular responses and sensory stimuli become more deeply ingrained when the individual continues to practice even after he has reached top performance.

One note of caution: The learning curve of all employees is not the same. On the contrary, there are profound differences in native ability to synchronize muscular movements, to effect eye-hand coordinations, and to sense subtle differences in tactile and muscular responses. When these individual differences are added to differences in motivation and morale, they result in wide disparities in learning rates.

These differences pose serious problems for the supervisor. Should the same or greater rewards go to the highly motivated employee with lesser ability who achieves the same level of performance as the less highly motivated employee with greater ability? Would your answer be the same if you knew that the more gifted employee was working less hard and performing at a lower level of accomplishment than he would if he were to exert himself? (Professors face such questions every day!)

TYPES OF TRAINING

Classroom Training

Copying traditional education, the most obvious type of training places the trainee in a classroom. Larger companies can afford to provide their own classes. Sometimes they meet just before or just after regularly scheduled work shifts (and therefore represent uncompensated time). Where management deems the material sufficiently important, employees may be excused for one or two hours to attend class.

Off-the-job classroom training may be provided by correspondence courses, in nearby schools (which may be persuaded to offer a special course tailored to company needs), or by professional societies or training institutes. In recent years, more private companies have gone into the business of providing courses for industry, but organizations like the American Management Association are still among the largest in their field.

Where company trainees enter programs sponsored by external organizations, there may be a side benefit obtained in being able to compare experiences and ideas with outsiders drawn from diverse environments. This can reduce "provincialism."

Employees may be encouraged as individuals to enroll in various courses or conference programs that may last for one day or an entire college year. Tuition is often paid by the company, assuming that the course relates to the employee's job and he completes it with a satisfactory record. [13]

On-the-Job Training

"OJT," as it is known, may simply involve the supervisor paying some extra attention to the trainee, occasionally giving him criticism and suggestions. Or an experienced employee may be assigned to help break in the new worker (with the limitations that we have described).

During such informal training, the supervisor may be told to rotate the employee through a number of assignments in order to provide breadth of experience. Production requires that the man work at the job he is best at; training requires that he work at the job he is least good at, for this is the job he needs most to learn. This poses a dilemma for the supervisor who may find that his production objectives conflict with his training objectives. Unless upper management utilizes controls that measure the supervisor's training accomplishments, he is likely to keep the trainee on the job he does best. [14]

Recognizing the time pressures on supervisors and their lack of preparation for extended training activities, personnel specialists evolved a quick, easily-mastered training format for managers during World War II (called Job Instruction Training). As described below, it embodies sound learning principles.

1. A job description is worked out that breaks the job down into a series of motion sequences that can be described. The trainer identifies the special techniques required, the special precautions that need to be taken, the criteria that indicate whether the job is being performed correctly, the quality and safety levels required, and so forth. These are the *key points* of the job.
2. At the beginning of the training session, the equipment and supplies are arranged in the way in which the worker is expected to keep them.
3. The trainer puts the learner at ease, finds out what he already knows, explains the relationship of his job to other jobs in the organization, and shows him the correct working position.
4. The trainer describes the job completely, stresses the key points, and then performs the job, describing "what" and "why" at each step. The learner is encouraged to ask questions.
5. The learner then tells the trainer how the job is to be done and the trainer follows his instructions.
6. The learner does the job, explaining to the trainer at each step "what" he is doing and "why."
7. The trainer follows up with periodic checks and tells the trainee where he can go for help if he runs into difficulty.

[13] Obviously this can become a delicate subject. Who gets sent to the conferences meeting in Hawaii or on shipboard? Can a secretary be reimbursed for an accounting course (assuming she hopes to qualify for a staff job in the company)? Does your answer change if the company hires only accountants with university degrees and the secretary will require 8 or 10 years to complete such a course of study?

[14] *Cf.* Earl Gomersall and M. Scott Myers, "Breakthrough in On-the-Job Training," *Harvard Business Review*, Vol. 44 (July 1966), pp. 62–72.

Combinations

Management often tries to obtain the realism of OJT and the reduction in pressures for immediate production provided by off-the-job courses. One such compromise is called *vestibule training*. This kind of training is desirable where the job is difficult, where mistakes or slowness will materially impair production schedules or methods, and where very special coaching is required. On certain jobs, placing the new employee in the work situation immediately would endanger his own safety and the welfare of others, and would risk damage to costly equipment.

"Simulation devices" are an invaluable form of vestibule training. For instance, computers make it possible to simulate the operations of an entire refinery, enabling employees to learn to cope with emergencies and to make the proper responses at minimal cost. In this way, the learner is shielded from the pressure of the actual job situation and the demands of supervisors who are primarily interested in getting out production.

Off-the-job training does have certain disadvantages. Many skills simply cannot be learned in "slow motion." In effect, doing a task slowly may transform it into an entirely different kind of task; this is particularly true of certain difficult muscular-sensory coordination jobs. Also, the noise and other distractions of the real work-place may be factors that the trainee must learn to accommodate, just as he must also master specific body motions and intellectual responses. Finally, vestibule training is expensive, and the employee is being taught by instructors who will not work with him and evaluate his performance when he moves on to the actual job.

We have already referred to another combination: apprentice training. This is similar to college work-study programs in which classroom efforts are supplemented with actual work experience. Apprenticeships, like internships, however, involve more carefully-designed work experiences which are sequenced and graded so that an individual moves from simple tasks to the more complex, and in pace with the "theory" he is receiving in the classroom. Ideally, such training, by providing almost immediate opportunities to try out theory, should be highly conducive to motivation and learning.

Newer Training Technologies

In-company training, along with education in general, is being changed by the growing use of technical aides. Computers, projectors, and even closed circuit TV are often utilized. For example, in learning a complicated new assembly operation, each employee is placed in a booth where visual and auditory stimuli are presented in a carefully designed step fashion. Questions or challenges are posed which enable the trainee to assess whether or not progress is being made (and to receive regular reinforcement). Mistakes cause material to be repeated or remedial "branches" of the program to be displayed. Each learns at his own pace with very little need of external instruction and since the student is actively participating and having to make constant responses, learning is facilitated.

Supplementing these teaching laboratories are programmed text materials. Unlike a traditional textbook, a programmed text utilizes the principles of reinforcement, feedback, involvement, and repetition we have discussed above. After each element of new information, the reader is queried to test his comprehension. If he has the correct answer, the program is designed to carry him forward one small additional step and to require another response on his part. Each new step both helps cement the previous learning and assesses his capacity to absorb new knowledge. When a mistake is made, the trainee is made aware of this immediately (negative reinforcement) and is referred to a branch program which either repeats earlier information or provides another approach. While the steps may at first appear very elementary and some of the answers almost self-evident, the process builds confidence and increases motivation.

While there is no question that programmed learning facilitates self-study, some of the more unrestrained enthusiasm and claims for its efficacy have been dimmed because of more sober evaluation during the past several years. One of its motivational appeals—its novelty—pales after extended use, and boredom can develop given the monotony of the "frames" (embodying short statements and short questions to be answered). It is useful primarily for factual material; it is not very applicable to skill training or to changing attitudes. The programs themselves are relatively expensive to develop and practical only when large numbers will use each program.

There are also changes in classroom technology. Increasing use is being made of closed circuit TV and playback equipment so groups can experiment with a variety of supervisory, sales, and negotiating techniques and observe themselves "in action." Such methods have been used for years by football teams who, while viewing a tape of the previous game, criticize their performance. Such equipment also allows organizations to tie together geographically dispersed units.

Video-cassettes are just becoming available and they combine some of the flexibility of TV with the operator control available with motion pictures.

HOW MUCH TRAINING?

As we noted in Chapter 18, management cannot answer the question of how much to spend on training without considering a whole range of manpower questions, particularly hiring and remuneration policies. How much can a company afford to spend on developing employees who may leave at any time, permitting another firm to harvest the fruits of the effort? Some companies have no choice in this matter: Their needs are so acute and the supply of trained personnel so meager that training programs are an absolute necessity. These firms must insure that their wage and salary levels, the quality of their supervision, and promotional opportunities are sufficiently attractive to hold trained personnel. They cannot assume that their employees' gratitude for the training received will outbalance genuine disadvantages or a gap between newly-created expectations and reality. In fact, those employees who are most ambitious and most eager to grasp educational opportunities are the very ones who will be most alert to other job offers.

How much "credit" should the company assign an employee who has successfully completed a training program, particularly if the training has been taken during uncompensated time? Should those who undertake extra training be guaranteed advancement in preference to those who do not elect to do so? If so, all employees should be made aware of the policy and its implications. In one organization, we observed that certain technical courses were designated as "voluntary" and "optional," although attendance was a prerequisite to promotion.

Resolving questions like these require that Personnel be able to measure the contribution of any training effort. On some routine jobs this may be simple; productivity before and after can be calculated. On many more jobs it is difficult to measure the performance or contribution of the employee since many people jointly contribute and other factors are changing at the same time training is proceeding. As we shall see in Chapter 23, performance evaluation is an imperfect technique. Thus, it is difficult to show that helping an engineer obtain a master's degree improves his work; but management in this, as in other personnel programs, wants the evidence that dollar expenditures are providing comparable gains in operations; in other words, cost-effectiveness measures.

The organization faces agonizing problems when existing skills and hard-earned knowledge have become obsolete, and its new activities cannot make use of current employees without massive retraining. Responsible firms make this investment although the short run costs of hiring new people might appear less. In the longer run they believe that the increased commitment of employees who recognize the investment being made in their development will more than make up for the added costs.

CONCLUSION

Training means changing behavior patterns, and this is always a difficult task. An individual's method of doing a job, the skills he employs, the energy and thought he applies, the checking and coordinating with other people he undertakes—all partly reflect his own personality structure. The manager must assume that the employee's old pattern of behavior brought certain satisfactions—else he would have abandoned it. Since a change in work methods will be a threat to these satisfactions, the employee will resist new learning (see Chapter 12). This resistance may be bolstered by his desire for the approbation of his work group and by his psychological needs for security and a sense of accomplishment. Efforts to increase productivity through teaching better work habits may run counter to group-enforced production "bogeys" or behavior norms.

The trainer, in developing even an informal course of study, ought to know something about human learning, including the role of motivation and reinforcement. He must also consider the structuring of the material to be learned, seeking to balance theory with practice, identifying natural sequences which facilitate learning by providing internal cues, and moving from the simpler to the more complex.

The success of any training program is a direct function of the success of other aspects of the personnel program. Where employees are already highly motivated and closely identified with the goals of the organization, well-conceived training programs will lead to better performance. On the contrary, where morale is low and employees are suspicious and resentful of management, training will be ineffective. For example, in one company a course in work-simplification was seriously handicapped because it was associated in the workers' minds with the widely disliked time-study department. If the trainees fail to see how they will benefit by adopting the techniques being taught, no amount of good teaching will change their behavior.

Nevertheless, the satisfactions an employee derives from his work experience depend on his knowing what to do and how to do it. The employee who lacks confidence in his ability to perform successfully can never do his job well, no matter how vigorously management pursues the other aspects of its personnel program. And training can influence attitudes toward the personnel program. Employees develop more favorable sentiments for an employer who invests in their development. Education and training have become central values in American life. There is wide recognition that one cannot "cantilever" an entire career from the base of pre-employment, formal school education. Periodic infusions of new knowledge are essential.

problem 1 • WHAT REWARD FOR DILIGENCE?

John Adams with 10 years of service was eager to take courses to improve himself and to get an advanced degree. He was a purchasing invoice clerk with the Draper Equipment Company and was never considered outstanding as an employee. Starting with a night school degree in business, he began taking graduate courses when the company adopted a tuition-rebate plan. He also participated in several of the company's voluntary, after-hours training programs and computer courses taught by faculty members from a nearby college. After 7 years he qualified for a master's degree in accounting at the City University. However, when recently he discussed promotional opportunities with his supervisor, he was told that his work record was just average and there were no openings coming up for which he would qualify.

1. Does the company owe Adams something for his diligent pursuit of an advanced degree?
2. How should this kind of problem be dealt with to avoid the disappointment and frustration associated with being overqualified for a job?

problem 2 • HANDLING UNSATISFACTORY PERFORMANCE

Wilma Granger works in the accounts receivable section of a large department-store billing department. Her supervisor has found a large number of mistakes in a random check of the accounts she is responsible for, and her over-all output of work is lower than the department standard.

1. What "checks" should the supervisor make in evaluating whether this poor work is due to inadequate training or other causes?
2. If this investigation discloses inadequate training, how should he introduce remedial training?
3. How should the training be carried out?

problem 3 • WHEN TRAINING FAILS

The packaging department was the most troublesome department in the U.S. Auto Parts Company. The employees' job in this department was to watch high-speed, semi-automatic packaging machines and make adjustments and compensations for unexpected operating difficulties. Though the work was simple and easily learned, productivity was low. Employees frequently neglected obvious danger signals and failed to make the proper adjustments.

Management tried all sorts of solutions to this problem: employees were disciplined for making mistakes (they objected violently); supervisors were sent through a training program; a new incentive system was introduced. When all these efforts failed, management decided to experiment with a retraining program. Some of the employees may have forgotten their initial training, or perhaps it had been inadequate. In any event, many employees were using clearly inefficient, fatiguing motions on the job, and improved job performance would actually make the work easier.

Management had another reason for introducing training: It was contemplating discharging some of the worst offenders, but felt that it should give these men every opportunity to improve before it took such drastic action. Systematic training would head off union charges that the men had not been properly instructed.

The department head, in collaboration with the Industrial Engineering Department, prepared a training manual that outlined all the steps required in doing this particular job. One of the first-line supervisors was chosen to administer the training during the regular work routine of the department. He spent several hours with each employee, going over the procedures step by step in good J.I.T. fashion. (See p. 453.)

The results were discouraging. No improvements in productivity were forthcoming. The operators claimed that the trainer was a spy seeking evidence that they were malingering rather than trying to train them. Furthermore, "He knows less about the job than we do—we should be training him."

1. What mistakes, if any, were made in this training situation?

2. Describe completely how you would handle these problems, including the selection of the trainer.

MINORITY EMPLOYMENT

21

Minority employment is perhaps the most urgent and perplexing personnel problem faced by management in the second half of the twentieth century. Persistent poverty in the midst of plenty, demands for civil rights, and riots in major cities have forced our society to face up to racial injustice. Faced with this challenge, companies have made modest progress, though not as much as anyone except the defenders of status quo would like. Even with the best will in the world (and this frequently is not present) the elimination of the impact of past discrimination has been difficult.

Inequality is not confined to Negroes. Mexican-Americans and Puerto Ricans, particularly those who speak English poorly, are little better off. And Indians are clearly the most disadvantaged group of all in our society, their unemployment rates ranging around 40 per cent and average life expectancy two-thirds that of whites. Discrimination against women has somewhat different effects than does discrimination against minority groups, but it also results in maldistribution of income and in talents being inadequately utilized.

For the most part this chapter will deal with discrimination against Negroes, though much of what we have to say has relevance for other minority groups. We will look first at the abuses and then at governmental policies designed to reduce inequality in employment. After this background, the bulk of the chapter will be concerned with organizational personnel policies. The last part of the chapter is concerned with discrimination against women.

THE NATURE OF THE PROBLEM

During the 1950's and 1960's, the unemployment rate of nonwhites was twice that of whites. In 1969, unemployment was lower than it had been in 15 years; nevertheless, as the following table indicates, nonwhite teenage unemployment was 24 per cent—and considerably higher in central ghetto areas. (Militant, unemployed black youths provided the explosive core of riots.)

Unemployment Rates, 1969

	White	Nonwhite
	(per cent)	
Men, 20 and over	1.9	3.7
Women, 20 and over	3.4	5.8
Teenagers, 16–19	10.7	24.0

Stark as they may be, the figures in the table may understate the problem, because nonwhites are more likely than whites to be working on casual, short-term or part-time jobs, such as maids, loaders, sweepers, or delivery boys. Further, these figures exclude a substantial number of "discouraged" minority workers who would like work but have given up seeking it.

Not only do nonwhites suffer from a higher rate of unemployment than that of the population as a whole, but those who are working are concentrated in relatively low-status, low-paying occupations whose numbers are growing relatively less fast than the labor force as a whole. When they have found employment in the better paying industries, they have been hired for the heaviest, least desirable jobs. For example, despite breakthroughs in recent years, blast furnaces in the steel industry have traditionally been black departments, while rolling mills (much cleaner work) have been almost "lily white." In many industries, nonwhites are customarily "last hired, first fired." In 1968, these various forms of inequality were apparent in the median income of black families, which was but 60 per cent of that of whites. [1]

Inequality in employment hurts individuals and society, generally, and is an enormous waste of potentially useful manpower.

CAUSES OF INEQUALITY

Inequality in employment can be explained by two sets of reasons: (1) employers tend to hire proportionally fewer blacks than whites, especially for the better paid jobs, and (2) for a variety of reasons, blacks, on the average, tend to be less qualified than whites. Particularly in the past, even if blacks were as well qualified as whites, they found it harder to get equivalent work. But the very fact that blacks were convinced that they would suffer discrimination reduced their motivation to become qualified. Let us examine these two explanations.

---

[1] This represents considerable progress, however. Median income of nonwhite (not just black) families rose from 50 per cent of that of white families in 1958 to 63 per cent in 1968.

Inequality in Hiring

Outright discrimination.   There is a long history of racial bias in this country, some of which was once enshrined by law. Even companies which have believed themselves socially responsible have engaged in discrimination. Managers want to be considered good citizens, but for many, being a good citizen may mean adjusting to community values rather than trying to change them. In engaging in discrimination, management merely followed what it felt the community wanted (and in many cases this corresponded with the managers' own prejudices). Nor were managers the only ones to discriminate. As we shall see, some unions discriminated too.

Nonperception of discrimination.   Despite their willingness to follow community patterns, few managers today consider themselves discriminatory or nonobjective in their selection policies. Certainly few northern businessmen have justified a refusal to hire *qualified* Negroes. The problem was that of defining qualification. At least unconsciously, many managers felt that certain jobs were not suited for Negroes, just as some jobs were not suited for women or old men. Management often just did not see the black applicant as a potential skilled tradesman, salesman, or executive. Stereotypes (see Chapter 10) such as these were easy to maintain because there were in fact few qualified blacks and those who were qualified realized there would be very little point in applying for jobs not available to them.

Poor communications.   In some cases, discrimination has occurred by default: a sincerely felt, top-management policy not to discriminate has not been implemented at operating levels. In a hierarchy, as we saw in Chapter 14, such policies are not self-enforcing. In most cases they represent sharp contrasts with past practice, and many employees tend to resist them. Since there is such a sharp conflict between creed and deed in this area and pious platitudes are so frequently uttered, it is understandable that many employees are uncertain whether new nondiscriminatory policies are to be taken seriously.

"Others may object."   Managers at times have justified discriminatory policies along these lines: "Personally, I would like to increase the number of Negroes we hire, but my employees might object (remember I hire a lot of women) and so would a lot of my customers." Of course, there is some validity to this point of view: many employees and many customers are, in fact, prejudiced. But once management takes a firm position that it is going to integrate a department, most employees go along. Customers, too, adjust eventually. (Black waiters are well accepted in the South; only in the North do they find it hard to get jobs.)

Hiring practices.   Hiring practices are often stacked against Negro job applicants. Many companies do their hiring chiefly on the basis of word of mouth (see Chapter 19) or give preference to those recommended by friends. Their recruiters most frequently visit predominantly white high schools or colleges, while their want ads are rarely placed in black papers.

Hiring standards are often unnecessarily rigid: high school graduation may be required for unskilled jobs, thus eliminating the black dropout, and tests may be "culturally biased"—but all of this will be discussed later.

Technological change and plant location. Recent developments have tended to reduce further the number of jobs traditionally open to blacks. Black employment opportunities were best in hard, dirty jobs that no one else wanted, jobs that are being eliminated by technological change.[2] The few skilled trades that have employed significant numbers of blacks—carpentry, bricklaying, plastering, and painting—all offer declining or unstable employment. Blacks are largely unrepresented in the expanding trades related to electricity, plumbing, and sheetmetal work.

To make matters worse, older manufacturing plants in central cities have shut down, while new plants have been built in locations difficult to reach by public transportation from black ghettos. The kinds of jobs which are growing in the central city—managerial, professional, and clerical—require at least a high school diploma and conformity to white middle-class standards of clothing, speech, and behavior.

Inadequate Background

Discrimination and the decline in the number of traditional minority jobs are not the only causes of employment inequality. Poor education and the culture of poverty have contributed to the problem.

Since the 1960's, governmental and civil rights pressures have had their effect, and many major companies have made extensive efforts to increase the number of their minority employees. In some cases, they have in effect discriminated in favor of minority members and yet have found disappointingly few qualified applicants, especially for the better paying jobs. Applicants have been easier to find for relatively unskilled jobs such as those on automobile assembly lines; but here (for reasons we shall discuss) rates of tardiness, absenteeism, and turnover have been quite high, and attitudes toward work somewhat negative.

Until very recently there were substantial numbers of qualified blacks working at skills well below their competence (college graduates, for example, working as postmen), and blacks found it harder to get work than did equally qualified whites. This situation has been far from eliminated; nevertheless, for many jobs and in many communities, the reverse is true: the demand for black engineers or well-trained secretaries, for example, is far greater than the supply. In some cities, a high percentage of those who are easily trainable have already been hired. The hardest group to employ consists of "hard core" minority members who lack not just job skills, but also the attitudes necessary to hold steady jobs. These deficiencies in skill and attitude derive in large part from inadequate education and from growing up in what has been called "the culture of poverty."

---

[2] Technological changes may also make some jobs more desirable, thus encouraging the redefinition of former "colored" jobs into "white" jobs. At the time when locomotive firemen had to shovel coal, there were large numbers of black firemen in the South. Once automatic stokers were introduced, the job became less unpleasant and black firemen were displaced by whites. Today, diesels have eliminated even white firemen.

Inadequate Education

As the table indicates, fewer Negroes than whites have graduated from high school and far fewer have gone on to college.[3] Since predominantly black schools tend to be inferior to those predominantly white, the average black high school senior in 1967 was performing at only an eighth grade level.

Key Indices of Inequality

	White	Nonwhite
Finished high school: Males, 18 years or older (1969)	63.3%	40.2%
Finished college: Males, 18 years or older (1969)	14.7%	6.5%
Median years of education (1969)		
Males	12.4	10.8
Females	12.4	11.9
Median income, males, 25–54 years old (1968)		
Some college training	$10,149	$7,481
Did not enter high school	5,944	3,900
Families headed by a female	8.9%	26.4%

Though a much higher percentage of blacks are finishing high school today than in the past,[4] just going to school isn't enough. College trained blacks earn substantially less than do their white counterparts.

The Culture of Poverty

A significant minority of blacks belong to what has been called the hard core; that is, they have grown up in a culture of poverty, which has conditioned their attitudes toward work, given them a sense of defeatism, and failed to equip them with the skills necessary to find and hold a steady job. (Lest this discussion itself help propagate some very unrealistic stereotypes, two important points should be stressed: (1) the culture of poverty is far from a minority group monopoly; there are far more poor whites living in a culture of poverty than there are poor blacks; and (2) since most black men hold steady jobs, those in the culture of poverty constitute a minority of a minority.)

[3] Statistics in this section come from Herbert R. Northrup and others, *Negro Employment in Basic Industry* (Philadelphia: University of Pennsylvania Press, 1970), or from the *Manpower Report of the President, 1970.*

[4] In 1952, the median years of education for black males was 7.2, for whites 10.8. From 1952 to 1969, blacks gained 3.6 years; whites, only 1.6.

White middle-class children have learned from their parents that getting ahead means hard work and that having a job means getting up every morning, working fixed hours, and taking vacations and holidays only as scheduled. But if one grows up in the ghetto, one learns not the Protestant ethic but some very different lessons indeed.

Young people living in ghetto communities of New York, Chicago, Los Angeles, and other large cities grow up amidst a bewildering set of economic, social, and psychological barriers to adequate preparation for work. Poverty, disorganized family life, and the effects of past and present discrimination permeate their lives. [5]

Physical isolation in the ghetto plus black youth's needs for self-expression, racial pride, and uniqueness create a distinctive style of dress, manner, and speech. These, in turn, make job finding more difficult. Furthermore, there are relatively few role models in the youth's circle of friends and families who provide examples of success through education and mastery of nonmenial occupations. Although Willie Mays, Ralph Bunche, Sammy Davis, Jr., and Muhammed Ali are sources of racial pride, they are no substitute for knowing what it means to be a successful draftsman, electrician, or car salesman. Also, black parents are often unable to provide vocational counseling because of the restricted nature of their own working lives. Nor do black kids have the advantages of many white kids whose parents and friends can help them find jobs.

The role family weakness plays is clearly revealed in a story told by X [a black social worker] who was trying to convince an eighteen-year-old Negro youth that it *is* possible for a Negro to rise out of the slum and acquire the perquisites of American crime without resorting to crime. By way of illustration, he pointed to the fact that the boy's new boss, a Negro, drives a Cadillac. "Yeah man," the youth replied, "but that cat was born with a silver spoon in his mouth. . . . I mean for one thing, that cat had a father; for another, his father taught him a trade." [6]

Although an affluent society surrounds Negroes and appears daily on TV to demonstrate what "whitey" has accomplished through education, blacks have little proof that education and hard work pay off. This is especially true for the large number of black families who come from agricultural regions in the South where the economic value of education to the Negro is low and the quality of education is inferior. [7]

Experience has taught hard-core members that they have little chance to get ahead, that there is no point in even trying. Just to hold on to what they have is hard enough. Thus they have what psychologists call a short-term time perspective. From their point of view luck is a more important determinant of success than hard work.

---

[5] "The probability is strong that only one Negro child in two grows up in what could be defined as a normal family—one in which he lives with parents throughout his childhood." Eli Ginzberg and Dale L. Hiestand, "The Guidance of Negro Youth," in Arthur M. Ross and Herbert Hill, eds., *Employment, Race, and Poverty* (New York: Harcourt, 1967), p. 441.

[6] Charles E. Silberman, *Crisis in Black and White* (New York: Random House, 1964), p. 226.

[7] A high percentage of the hard core comes from families that have recently migrated from the South. Black agricultural workers fell from 1,447,000 in 1940 to 356,000 in 1969—a decline of more than a million people, most of whom migrated to northern and western cities and many of whom have found it difficult to adjust to the discipline of industrial work or even to living in big cities.

Only when one knows where his next week's or next month's shelter will come from can he and his children afford to go in for long-term education and training, the endless search for opportunities, and the tedious apple-polishing that attainment of higher skills and occupational status requires. [8]

In terms of Maslow's need hierarchy, since their physical needs are inadequately satisfied, they are little motivated by higher level needs.

Their generally defeatist attitude affects their job hunting approach. Having learned that certain companies and certain jobs are closed to minorities, they confine their job seeking efforts to the low status occupations in which blacks were traditionally employed. They tend to be apprehensive in entering employment offices where they feel they are not wanted. They have been discriminated against so long, they don't trust or believe advertisements that say "Equal Opportunity Employer."

Even their limited job experiences sometimes teach them the wrong lessons. Having short-term jobs, they have learned that the slower they work, the longer the job lasts. Prejudiced employers, justifying low wages on the ground that minorities are "lazy and dishonest," sometimes tolerate slipshod workmanship, petty thievery, and casual attendance practices. [9] Above all, members of the hard core learn not to trust the "Man" (the white boss), to be suspicious of his motives, and to expect little from the job.

Each man comes to the job with a long job history characterized by his not being able to support himself and his family. Each man carries this knowledge, born of experience, with him. He comes to the job flat and stale, wearied by the sameness of it all, convinced of his own incompetence, terrified of responsibility—of being tested still again and found wanting. [10]

As a result of this experience, many members of the hard core begin to value independence above all. "Many of them are similar to the old frontiersmen, the mountain people," one observer commented. "They value freedom. They don't like to be forced to report to work every day, to show up on time." [11]

This attitudinal barrier helps explain why turnover has been so high among members of the hard core who have obtained regular jobs. For this group, provision of a well-paid job is not enough. They need assistance in adjusting to a new life-style and culture. Among other things, they need a new sense of self-worth.

Black Militancy

Black pride ("black is beautiful"), has emerged along with black militancy, which itself may be essential to self-pride; but from the point of view of the

[8] Allison Davis, "The Motivation of Underprivileged Workers," in William F. Whyte, ed., *Industry and Society* (New York: McGraw-Hill, 1946), p. 89.

[9] Furthermore, many of these jobs pay little more than one can get on relief or from "hustling" (illegal activity). Hustling, in fact, may be less demeaning than many of the jobs blacks can obtain.

[10] Elliott Liebow, *Tally's Corner* (Boston: Little, Brown, 1966), pp. 53-54.

[11] Cited in Ralph Campbell, "Employing the Disadvantaged: Inland Steel's Experience," *Issues in Industrial Society*, Vol. 1, No. 1 (1969), p. 38. It should be emphasized that high hard-core absentee rates are not entirely due to attitudinal factors. Health problems, difficulties in arranging baby sitters, and even tangles with the law are more common in the ghetto.

company seeking to integrate its work force, black pride can create additional difficulties. For many young blacks, the Afro haircut is a symbol of pride and manliness, but for the company that insists on its employees being neatly groomed, the Afro is a symbol of nonconformity. The belief that everything that the "Man" does is motivated by discrimination sometimes leads to the rejection of rules that other employees accept as normal. And the combination of new pride and old insecurity may possibly lead to a "chip on the shoulder" attitude toward supervision. Finally, the black militant's demands for good jobs *now*, coupled with the belief that lack of preparation for such jobs is not the black man's fault, occasionally leads to a certain impatience with training and to the rejection of "crummy, second-rate" entry level jobs.

A Vicious Cycle

Black militancy, a middle-class as well as a hard-core attitude, complicates (yet also helps solve) the problem, but essentially the hard-core member is involved in a vicious cycle. His limited education and experience and his failure to adopt middle-class attitudes toward work all make it harder for him to find or hold a steady job. At the same time, the fact that he is unable (or believes he is unable) to hold a steady job is a major cause of his attitudes and failures.

GOVERNMENT PROGRAMS

Government efforts are designed to help break the cycle: to eliminate discriminatory barriers, increase job opportunities, and raise minority qualifications. (We will not discuss governmental programs designed to foster minority-owned business or to reduce discrimination in areas other than employment.)

Eliminating Discrimination

The federal government and many states have passed laws against discrimination in employment. These laws have been less effective than civil rights advocates would like. In the first place, enforcement proceedings are often cumbersome. Second, at least until recently, the absence of minority employees was not proof of discrimination. It had to be shown that a qualified minority job applicant did in fact seek a job and that a less qualified white was hired in his stead. Proof of this sort is difficult to obtain.

Nevertheless, these laws have had some impact. They have set a moral standard, which most socially responsible employers have sought to meet. As a consequence a vast majority of cases brought to the attention of governmental regulatory agencies have been settled informally; most employers seek to avoid the stigma of being involved in formal proceedings. More importantly, agencies have begun to look at results, rather than the methods by which they are achieved. If a company located in a community with a substantial minority population has only a token number of minority employees, the agency may inquire into the company's recruitment and selection techniques and may order it to change these so that they no longer have the effect of screening out minorities.

Also significant in reducing discrimination, the so-called *contract compliance* procedure takes advantage of the government's role as a purchaser. Each year the federal government spends billions of dollars on supplies, equipment, and roads, and ever since World War II major government contracts have included provisions requiring contractors to provide equal employment opportunity. Over the years, the enforcement of these rules has become tougher and tougher. No longer is it enough not to discriminate. The contractor must take *affirmative action* to ensure equal employment. Each company is required periodically to report the racial composition of its work force on a job-by-job basis. If there are an insufficient number of minority members in any job category, the company is required to specify steps it will take to eliminate the imbalance. The Philadelphia Plan, applying to governmental building contractors in that city, goes even further, providing specific employment goals *(ranges)* which indicate the minimum percentage of minority employees to be hired in each craft by specified dates.

Employers often complain that contract compliance rules are unreasonably enforced, that they induce a form of reverse discrimination, which requires that people be hired and promoted on the basis of race rather than ability, that duplicate inspections by various government contracting agencies consume much time, set up conflicting requirements, and harass the employer who refuses to go beyond the strict requirements of the regulations. [12]

Training Programs

Over the last decade the federal government has instituted a wide variety of training programs designed to improve the skills and job-holding capabilities of the disadvantaged. These programs are essentially of two types: *institutional*, conducted in the classroom, and *on-the-job* (OJT) conducted at the work place. (A third type—of which the Neighborhood Youth Corps is an example—provides work experience in governmental and nonprofit agencies.)

The first institutional programs were designed to provide retraining for experienced workers who had lost their jobs because of technological change. But these programs were accused of "creaming," taking the best prospects, who would have found work anyway without training. By the late 1960's, the emphasis switched to the hard core. With this group, training for specific jobs is normally preceded by remedial training in basic skills such as reading and writing. Often it is accompanied by counseling, testing, and job placement services. For many high school dropouts, institutional training is another form of school with all its negative connotations. They object to book work and have doubts whether training will even lead to a serious job. (In fact, the ability of program graduates to obtain and hold steady jobs seems to vary considerably from one situation to another.)

[12] The attitude of some governmental inspectors seems to be, "Don't tell us your excuses. We don't care how you do it, but we are going to keep pushing you until your work force is completely integrated."

On-the-job training avoids some of these problems. Trainees work on real jobs, which, in most instances, they keep upon graduation. The training is obviously practical, even though some auxiliary instruction may be provided each week.

In 1967, the National Alliance of Businessmen (NAB) was established under the leadership of Henry Ford II, for the purpose of placing 500,000 hard core members in permanent jobs by June 1971, as well as hundreds of thousands in summer jobs. Men are hired who cannot meet normal company standards (for example, those with prison records). Training—including, where required, classroom training in reading, writing, and arithmetic—is provided by the company. To reduce redtape, the program is administered by businessmen, many of whom are volunteers. For companies willing to sign a specific contract, the government grants a subsidy of up to $3,000 per trainee to offset additional costs.

The NAB program has been reasonably successful. Thousands of jobs have been provided, though somewhat fewer than originally planned. Numerous imaginative approaches to training the hard core have been developed. On the other hand, there is some question as to whether many people were hired who might not have been hired without the program. During the recession of 1970-1971, the number of job openings dropped precipitously and many of those employed were laid off. Only about one-quarter of the jobs were obtained through programs involving training contracts and subsidies. Most companies seem to prefer not to be tied down to the rigidities and possible governmental interference that a contract entails.

Thus the government has used a stick (fair employment practice laws and government contract compliance procedures) and a carrot (training programs, including that of the NAB) to increase the qualifications of those who might be hired. Now let us see how business has reacted.

ALTERNATE MANAGEMENT POLICIES

What are management's choices in this area? It can

- Discriminate against minorities, even though such a policy now violates the law.
- Be neutral and "color blind," not changing its recruitment or selection policies but insisting that decisions be made strictly on ability without regard to color.
- Change its recruitment policies to attract a larger number of minority applicants and modify its tests and other selection techniques to ensure that they fairly measure minority members' *real* abilities. In other words, it can maintain its personnel standards intact but make an effort to hire blacks who meet these standards, and it can develop better methods of determining ability.
- Pick minority members for job vacancies, even though they are not the *best* qualified candidates, just as long as they meet minimum standards. And it can reduce excessively strict standards, such as a high school diploma or a prison-free record for assembly-line work.
- Provide special training for those who do not meet minimum standards but eventually might be qualified, the *qualifiable*. (This is the principle behind the NAB program.)
- Try to adjust the job to the man and rearrange job responsibilities to create jobs within the capabilities of hard core members.

Generally speaking, management's choice focuses on two alternatives. Some believe that it is enough to be color blind and scrupulously impartial. Others feel that their company should take affirmative steps to recruit and develop Negroes.

Color blindness. Many who believe in color blindness, or neutrality, feel that reverse discrimination in favor of Negroes is just as unfair as discrimination against them. Further, they often doubt whether management has a moral responsibility to solve social problems, and they object to demands that they lower their standards. Two psychologists stated this position well:

It is clearly the obligation of the employer not to discriminate among persons on the grounds of race, religion, or national origin, but it is clearly not the obligation of an employer to hire or to promote the less qualified in an attempt to compensate for some injustice of society in general. [13]

Affirmative action. Affirmative action is demanded because color blindness rarely results in integration. "You can post an equal-employment sign for a hundred years," the director of an employers' association remarked, "and a hundred years from now there will be no change in the work force."

Does affirmative action mean reverse discrimination? This is largely a semantic question. Those who are committed to the principle of integration normally use the euphemism affirmative action in public but in private admit that this involves reverse discrimination, at least in the sense that opportunities that are not available to whites are granted to blacks and that where there are two candidates equally qualified, the black will get the job.

The rest of this chapter will consider the kinds of adjustments required if companies intend to engage in affirmative action to obtain truly equal employment opportunities. Perhaps in no other personnel area is it as important to view the organization as an integrated system and to consider the interrelationship, for instance, among recruitment, job requirements, training, and discipline.

RECRUITMENT

Effective affirmative action frequently requires radical redesign of the organization's recruitment efforts. Traditional recruitment has too often been directed toward whites only. Many blacks have never learned how to look for jobs. Further, they are convinced that they are unlikely to be hired for previously "white" jobs, regardless of equal opportunity laws.

As a consequence, special recruitment efforts must be directed toward blacks, to convince them that jobs *actually* are open to them. As a first step employers should advertise job openings in minority newspapers and over minority radio stations. In addition, they should send recruiters to minority high schools and colleges and cooperate closely with agencies such as the Urban

[13] J. E. Doppelt and G. K. Bennett, "Testing Job Applicants from Disadvantaged Groups," *Test Service Bulletin No. 57,* The Psychological Corporation, May 1967.

League, which specializes in working in the ghetto, and with natural leaders of the minority community. Greater use can be made of the public employment service.

Working in the minority community requires special skills, and a number of companies have hired minority group specialists, many of them minority members themselves. As the pool of qualified blacks diminishes, imaginative methods of recruitment have become necessary. In the months after the Detroit riot of 1967, GM and Ford set up recruiting offices in the black ghetto. A number of companies have arranged plant tours for students of largely black high schools, so that these students may come to think of the plants as possible places to work. Companies have been required to use the same imagination in recruiting blacks that they used to recruit all applicants during World War II.

SELECTION

The selection process is, of course, critical to successful integration. Even apparently trivial incidentals make a difference. Black applicants can be easily scared off by unsympathetic receptionists. Long waits, complicated application blanks, or an official-looking employment office make applicants ill at ease.

Interviewing involves subjective judgments. The prejudiced interviewer finds it easy to give a negative rating to almost every black applicant. Even the middle-class interviewer who tries conscientiously to be unprejudiced finds it hard to establish communications with the hard-core applicant. The words they use and the values they hold may be so different that each finds it difficult to understand the other. Interviewers must understand "street talk" (and yet, for a black interviewer, being black may not be enough—hard-core youths are often suspicious of middle-class Uncle Toms).

For these reasons it was once argued that selection should be made on the basis of objective criteria, such as years of experience or test results. Unfortunately, the use of presumably objective criteria has not helped advance the cause of racial equality. The heart of the black problem is insufficient opportunity to acquire experience on the most desirable jobs. And very significantly, there is evidence that blacks tend to do better in interviews than they do on tests. Indeed, tests constitute a major barrier to black employment. They are the object of attack from black militants and the source of a great deal of concern among psychologists and personnel experts.

TESTING

It is argued that all tests are unfair because they fail to make allowances for the inadequacies of black education. But if tests do relate to the job, and if blacks do not score highly because of the inadequacy of black schools, then the schools are at fault, not the tests. On the other hand, if tests do not measure some abilities related to the job, then their exclusive use could lead to bias.

Even if we can dismiss the argument that *all* tests are unfair, still there is considerable evidence that tests are frequently used in a discriminatory fashion.

Unfair administration.   Recent studies show that frequently tests are administered in a slipshod manner with confusing instructions and little privacy. In most instances, blacks and whites are equally subjected to this treatment, but blacks are harmed by it more. By and large, hard-core blacks have had relatively little experience taking tests, and this limited experience has often been associated with failure. As a consequence, they tend to feel more tense in a test situation. Equally important, studies show that blacks do better in tests administered by black examiners or when the applicants feel a sense of approval on the part of the examiner. [14]

Improper validation.   As we have seen (p. 430) only a small minority of companies follow standard psychological procedures to validate tests for *specific* jobs. Most companies either buy standard tests or develop tests of their own. The homemade test may seem to do the job; but unless it is properly validated, it is difficult to say with any certainty that it is not discriminatory.

Cultural bias.   Both kinds of tests, standard tests and those developed for use in a particular company, normally are validated, if at all, in terms of white norms only. Thus, there is reason to doubt whether they can adequately predict the abilities of hard-core blacks. Many so-called intelligence tests measure information that is more common in a white community than in a black one. The vocabulary section of a typical intelligence test may ask for the meaning of words such as *jumble, obstinate,* or *ameliorate* rather than words used in the ghetto.

A vocabulary test may reveal only cultural background, but culturally biased tests may be useful for certain purposes. A "ghetto vocabulary test" may be useful for selecting supervisors (both black and white) who will be expected to work with ghetto workers. On the other hand, secretaries of all races should be able to pass a "middle-class" vocabulary test if they are to work for white, middle-class bosses.

The real question is the relationship between test results and job performance. If blacks do less well than whites on a test, but equally well on the job, obviously the test is biased. How extensively such bias exists is hard to tell. Until recent years, tests were almost never separately validated for blacks and whites. Since blacks were excluded from many jobs, most validation has been in terms of an exclusively white population.

Only in the last few years has there been much research on the extent of cultural bias in testing. The results so far suggest that testing practice in general is quite unsatisfactory. Some tests are nondiscriminatory only in the sense that their predictive power is equally low with both blacks and whites. Other tests predict white success but not black—or vice versa. Obviously, race serves as a moderator variable (see p. 428). [15]

[14] See Irwin Katz, Thomas Henchy, and Harvey Allen, "Effects of Race of Tester, Approval-Disapproval, and Need on Negro Children's Learning," *Journal of Personality and Social Psychology*, Vol. 8, Part I (1968), pp. 38–43.

[15] Race may make a difference not only in tests, but also in the interpretation of job application blanks. An arrest record or failure to complete high school may have different meaning in terms of predicting job success in the case of whites than blacks.

Testing and the Law

The Civil Rights Act of 1964, which prohibits discrimination in employment on the basis of race, creed, or sex, also contains the Tower Amendment, which provides that

It shall not be an unlawful employment practice for an employer ... to give and act upon the results of any professionally developed ability test provided that such test, its administration, or action upon the results is not designed, intended, or used to discriminate because of race, color, religion, sex, or national origin.

What does "professionally developed" mean? Is any test developed by a professional psychologist a professionally developed test? Is it enough that it be validated for some general use, or must it be validated in terms of a particular job? *Griggs* v. *Duke Power Company,* one of the first cases to deal with such problems, considered the legality of requiring black laborers to pass the Wonderlic intelligence and the Bennett aptitude tests before they could be promoted. Both tests have been developed by professionals and are widely used in industry; neither had been validated in terms of the jobs in the Duke Power Company.

Among the questions asked in the Wonderlic are the following: [16]

Two of the following proverbs have similar meanings. Which ones are they?
1. Perfect valor is to do without witnesses what one would do before the world.
2. Valor and boastfulness never buckle on the same sword.
3. The better part of valor is discretion.
4. True valor lies in the middle between cowardice and rashness.
5. There is a time to wink as well as to see.

The District Court ruled in favor of the company, finding that "Nowhere does the Act require that employers may utilize only those tests which accurately measure the ability and skills required of a particular job or jobs. . . ." Obviously this was a controversial ruling. The opposite position was expressed in one of the briefs filed on appeal on behalf of the black employees which argued that the questions presented in the Wonderlic "*perhaps* have utility in a law school aptitude exam. As a measure of ability to fill jobs in an industrial plant they are ludicrous. And as a barrier to Negro advancement they are vicious—the more so because employers are growing increasingly enamoured of these kinds of tests and Wonderlic is one of the most popular."

In a strong opinion, the Supreme Court ruled for the black employees, saying in effect that a test could not be used where (a) in fact it operated to exclude Negroes from jobs, and (b) it did not "bear a demonstrable relationship to successful performance of the jobs for which it was used."

"Nothing in the Act precludes the use of testing or measuring procedures; obviously they are useful. What Congress has forbidden is giving these devices and mechanisms controlling force unless they are demonstrably a reasonable measure of job performance. ... What Congress has commanded is that any tests used must measure the person for the job and not the person in the abstract."

[16] *Daily Labor Report,* June 29, 1970, p. A–13.

Recent Developments

What has been the reaction to these growing government pressures and the accumulating evidence that tests are both generally misused and often subject to cultural bias?

Some psychologists have attempted to develop "culture free" or "culture relative" tests, but with little success. There is reason to believe that performance or nonverbal tests generally tend to be less culturally biased than intelligence or personality tests. Most psychologists seem to agree that the most useful approach is to analyze moderator variables (see p. 424) and develop separate scoring procedures for each major cultural group.[17] Sound as this may be in theory, it is not really practical except for jobs on which many people are employed.

The considerable cost of validating every test for every job plus the fear of government inspections and litigation have caused companies to de-emphasize their use of tests. Ford, in 1967, abandoned tests for hourly workers. Other companies seem to be giving greater weight to factors other than tests or ignoring test results altogether when evaluating members of the hard-core—especially when an organization is seeking people who are trainable rather than those who are already qualified. A few organizations informally give all blacks a few bonus points to counteract possible bias.

Over-all Philosophy

The above discussion touched technical questions of psychology and law. More important is company philosophy. If organizations look upon the selection procedure as a means of *selecting out* candidates who either are not the best they can possibly find or who fail to meet their preconceived notion of a good employee, then they adopt statistically more and more high-powered testing procedures, thus living by the letter of the law.

Being truly color blind is difficult with all the unconscious factors influencing choice. But if a company wholeheartedly wants to be more than "color blind" and seeks to increase the number of its minority employees, it will be concerned less with the niceties of validation. Its approach will be to *select in*, and it will abandon its normal selection standards where these bar the employment of seemingly attractive minority candidates. This is a risky approach, since a number of those hired may not turn out well. It may not yield the best qualified of all candidates, and it raises some serious moral questions about the rejection of qualified whites just because of their color. But it does lead to increased black employment.

How far any organization goes in this policy of *selecting in* may well depend on its sense of social responsibility and the degree to which it is subject to governmental pressure. Some companies now seek to hire not the best man,

[17] There are a number of problems here. Perhaps tests should be scored differently for hard-core blacks than for middle-class whites. But how about a middle-class black or a hard-core white straight from the hills of Appalachia?

regardless of race, but as many minority candidates as they can, provided these candidates can be trained to meet the minimum standards required by the job.

CHANGING JOB SPECIFICATIONS

Sometimes these "minimum standards required by the job" can be lowered without serious harm.

Job entry standards tend to rise during times of unemployment and to fall when manpower is scarce. Thus, during the recession of the late 1950's, when numerous high school graduates were looking for work, companies began to require a high school diploma for even the simplest jobs. Other requirements—age, weight, sex, and the like—have been adopted because qualified candidates were available. When companies carefully re-examine qualifications, they find that many can be lowered. Some companies that refused to hire anyone who had ever been arrested (though perhaps acquitted), even for laborers' jobs, now hire released convicts.

On occasion, it is enough to relax job requirements slightly while the new worker develops qualifications.

A large company sought to introduce at least one black into its accounting department. Not finding anyone who met the normal requirement—a bachelor's degree in accounting—they hired a junior college graduate who had majored in bookkeeping. He was fully trained for most aspects of the work normally handled by new hires, and while he learned the job he worked for his accounting degree at night.

Job standards may be set high with promotions in mind (see p. 384). Particularly when the collective bargaining contract includes a strict seniority clause, companies set their hiring standards in terms of the top jobs that employees are likely to reach. Government agencies may place pressure on companies to lower these standards to the requirements of the job being filled. Arguably, skills necessary for promotion can be developed on the job—but companies are worried about the people who fail to develop.

There may be charges of discrimination if those who do not develop are not promoted, particularly if promotions have always been almost automatic. The only solution—expensive and not always successful—is to give underqualified employees continual training, perhaps far more than had previously been given "majority" workers.

Jobs have even been redesigned to fit the abilities of those available to fill them—a fairly common procedure during World War II—but this fosters specialization and routine, the opposite of job enrichment. Understandably, blacks often resent being placed on the "Mickey Mouse," "second-class" jobs thus devised. Like most humans, they may aspire to more than they are ready to handle.

TRAINING

Training is a critical part of an equal employment program. Intensification of the regular skills training program is often enough, but instruction in reading, writing, and what might be called industrial survival skills has been added by companies that hired the hard core and found "the difficulties and frustrations turned out to be greater than expected. To turn the recruits into useful workers, corporations had to assume the role not only of employers but of parents and schoolteachers as well." [18]

The better programs include considerable individual counseling and informal group discussion (at times almost a form of sensitivity training, see p. 536). The subjects may include family problems, money management, and handling debt. Program length varies. In some, after a week or so of orientation, men are placed on regular jobs. Alternatively, trainees may spend several hours each day in class and the remainder at work, often in vestibule training (p. 454), which shelters them from the social and physical pressures of full-scale production as well as from the layoffs that normally hit low-seniority minority workers the hardest.

Training for Advancement

The training we have been discussing is designed to help minority members hold jobs. Equally important is training for advancement, since blacks have traditionally been concentrated in unskilled, bottom-level jobs. A number of companies offer remedial education—including reading and writing—to prepare their older minority employees for promotion.

In the building trades, blacks have been excluded from apprenticeship, a major "port of entry," by the requirement of a high school diploma and fairly rigid examinations. Under great government pressure, efforts have been made to increase the size of minority representation through eliminating discrimination, lowering entry standards, and preparing minority youths through special preapprenticeship classes to pass the admissions examinations. Equivalent programs exist in some manufacturing plants; however, some companies have reported difficulty in persuading their minority employees to accept the short-run cut in pay that apprenticeship involves, even though when they become skilled craftsmen their pay would be considerably increased. Once again there seems to be lack of faith that the long-run results will be as favorable as pictured.

SENIORITY

Promotion is blocked not only by lack of training but also by collectively bargained seniority rules. It was common in the South, for instance, to have two seniority rosters, one black, one white. A black man could not bid for a white man's job, and vice versa; however, the white jobs were always the better ones.

Such blatant discrimination is clearly illegal today, but equivalent results can be obtained through departmental seniority, which is the rule in many industries. In the steel industry, for example, Negroes were hired primarily in

[18] Allan T. Demaree, "Business Picks Up the Urban Challenge," *Fortune*, Vol. 74, No. 4 (April 1969).

blast furnaces, coke ovens, and labor gangs, while rolling mills were almost entirely white. A high seniority man may exercise his seniority to obtain a promotion in his own department, but he may not bump into another department except under very restrictive conditions. Since primarily white departments tend to have long career ladders, culminating in top paying jobs, while career ladders in black departments are short, the effect is to reserve the best jobs for whites. (On the other hand, if future hiring in all departments is not discriminatory, eventually the white departments will include a fair quota of blacks in top positions.) Discriminatory as departmental seniority may seem, there are some legitimate arguments in its favor (see p. 399), and neither union nor management seems likely to change the rules.

UNIONS

The racial issue presents problems to unions, just as it does to management. The union movement has traditionally been the champion of the underdog, and its gains have helped blacks perhaps more than any other group. Unions have consistently fought hard for civil rights legislation. Most international unions have insisted that strong anti-discrimination clauses be included in collective bargaining contracts.

On the whole, however, international unions have been more active in fighting discrimination than have unions at the local level. Local unions in manufacturing, on occasion, have stubbornly supported discriminatory seniority systems, even against the combined pressure of their international union, the government, and the company. Local 189 of the Papermakers threatened a strike against Crown-Zellerbach when the company began to introduce a government-ordered program of desegregation in its Bogalusa, Louisiana plant. Some local union leaders were in the forefront of the "hard-hat" anti-Negro backlash of the early 1970's.

Such prejudiced attitudes are understandable. White workers who are only slightly higher than blacks in the socio-economic pecking order are afraid that black advances threaten their hard-won security and that society is appeasing black demands at their expense.

Blacks, for their part, have sought to protect their interests through organizing black "unions" (for example, the Dodge Revolutionary Union Movement, DRUM) or black caucuses within established unions.

MANAGEMENT

Despite strenuous recruitment efforts, relatively few blacks today are in the ranks of management in large companies, and most of these are concentrated in two categories: either they are supervisors of largely black departments or they are in departments such as personnel, public relations, or urban affairs, handling relations with blacks.

Why are there so few black managers? One reason is that until recently blacks were not considered management material at all. Even today, many managers have serious reservations about the appropriateness of blacks in responsible line positions. Relatively few black college graduates are available, and few of these have engineering or business administration degrees commonly expected for such jobs.

Even when blacks do move into management, turnover is often high. Black managers frequently complain that they have been given token, meaningless jobs and that they are treated like little more than errand boys. Many feel not only rejected by their fellow managers but isolated from their black brothers and the mainstream of the black movement.[19] Indeed, black militants often look upon them as little more than bootlicking Uncle Toms. In order to regain their "souls," a number of black managers have quit big business altogether, to accept less well paid jobs in black-owned companies or civil rights organizations.

Obviously, this problem is likely to continue until companies give their black managers meaningful, responsible jobs and until the number of these managers is sufficient to overcome their feeling of isolation.

INTRODUCING MINORITY EMPLOYEES

Equal employment requires that the policy be accepted by line supervisors and the men on the job. Subordinate line managers may resist change in the composition of their workforce, not just because of prejudice but because they fear that integration will reduce production and disrupt interpersonal relations on the job. All reports indicate that the first step toward eliminating opposition of this sort is for top management to communicate a firm no-nonsense position that it intends to enforce its equal employment policy. But sometimes actions as well as words are required to get the message across.[20] Variants of the following are told in a number of companies which have successfully introduced integration:

During a meeting that a company called to announce a new equal employment policy, one supervisor stated that he would submit his resignation as soon as the first black was placed in his department. The top executive countered quickly, "If your resignation is submitted on that ground, it will be accepted immediately." This stilled all opposition.

But more than a firm policy is required. Steps can be taken to reduce as well as overcome resistance to change (see Chapter 12). Some of the more successful company programs include discussion sessions in which supervisors, their bosses, and outside consultants deal frankly with problems that the intro-

---

[19] See, for example, "More Negroes Enter Management, but Some Find Role Frustrating," *The Wall Street Journal*, May 22, 1969.

[20] Equal employment policies have required some companies to centralize some personnel decisions. Subordinate managers have less freedom to select new hires, and often top officials are appointed to monitor the program. "A historic problem at General Motors was the reluctance of some decentralized managers to give effect of equal employment opportunity. The corporation then adopted a strong policy that reduced local managerial discretion in this regard and then brought it under even stricter central office control." Northrup, *op. cit.*, p. 98.

duction of black workers might create. [21] Attempts have been made to equip supervisors with insights and skills necessary to understand and deal with the background and motivation of workers whose cultural values are very different from those of middle-class whites. These programs may include role-playing, in which individual supervisors take on the role of a confused minority worker dealing with an unsympathetic supervisor (see p. 535).

Programs of this sort help supervisors understand company policy and prepare them for the problems they may face on the job. In addition, they help them avoid inadvertent mistakes. All too often weeks of supervisory effort to win the confidence of hard-core employees can be destroyed in minutes by a simple mistake, such as calling a grown man "boy."

Changes in the managerial reward and control systems may be necessary to make equal employment work. The foreman who agrees to train a group of minority workers may have less time for his other duties; in the short run, too, his costs may rise and his departmental productivity fall. If promotions and bonuses are based entirely on meeting production and budget goals, he will hardly be sympathetic to accepting added responsibilities for which he will not be rewarded.

Problems on the Job

Tardiness, absence, turnover, wearing unconventional clothing and hairdos, poor quality and low quantity of work, resistance to rules—these are some of the complaints heard from supervisors of minority employees. Some complaints may be exaggerated. Others represent a generation gap; what might be considered weird and unconventional in an office or plant may be quite normal on campus.

In any case, hard-core employees who have never before held regular jobs often find it difficult to adjust to the stern demands of industrial discipline. As a means of bridging the gap between white workers and blacks some companies have assigned each new minority worker an older "big brother" to give him advice and assistance. Other companies have hired special minority counselors who presumably are conversant with the mores of both ghetto and business (just as counselors were used during World War II with great success to help women adjust to factory jobs).

But how tough should the supervisor be in dealing with his minority employees? If he enforces the rules on attendance, production standards, and the like, hard-core employees may quit (thus making it more difficult for his company to reach its equal employment goals); or they may even file charges of discrimination with appropriate government agencies. But if he permits minority employees to "get away with murder," other employees will demand equal rights. One possible solution to this problem is to allow minority trainees considerable leeway during their first few weeks of work, but to tighten up gradually, so that by the time they gain the status of regular employees they are subject to generally the same standards as other employees are.

---

[21] On the other hand, there is the danger that excessive emphasis on racial differences may merely perpetuate stereotypes. It is just as dangerous for supervisors to treat minority-culture workers as being very different from the majority whites as it is to treat them as being exactly alike.

Discrimination against women in employment opportunities has been even more pervasive than discrimination against racial minorities. Certain jobs in our society are viewed as appropriate for women; others are not. Women tend to become domestic servants, typists, sales clerks, or nurses. If they go to college, the major jobs open to them are those of grade school teachers, librarians, social workers—and if all else fails, secretaries. Other occupations, such as being a truckdriver, shipyard worker, engineer, architect, or business executive are largely closed to women, even though many of these jobs were filled by women during World War II and are performed by women today in Russia.

In factories, women typically are paid less than men even when they do the same work (or at least this was the case until the passage of the Equal Pay Act of 1963). Traditionally, too, there were separate seniority ladders, with the male list naturally leading to higher, better paid jobs. In the office, men and women with similar education may be doing equivalent work, but the man gets the job title with the higher status, pay, and opportunity for promotion.

As with racial minorities, a high percentage of women are engaged in casual, part-time, temporary work. As a consequence, female unemployment is much higher than male, with nonwhite female unemployment highest of all (see table, p. 460). Even women with full-time jobs, however, earn much less than men: in 1969, only 58 per cent as much. This tremendous disparity is sometimes justified on the grounds that most women workers are either single (and therefore have limited needs) or are working merely to supplement the earnings of their husbands, who are assumed to be the breadwinner. This logic fails when women are heads of families. Understandably, fatherless families constitute the single most poverty stricken group in the country.

Why the Recent Interest?

Discrimination against women has existed for years, and few women objected, at least openly. Why has the subject recently been a major subject of interest to those dealing with personnel?

More women working.   More and more women are working each year and for longer periods of their lives. In 1969, 43 per cent of all women aged 16 and older were in the labor force (either working or looking for work)—up from 28 per cent in 1940. Over half of all women aged 26 to 60 work at least part of the year, as do two-thirds of those aged 18 to 25. Women now constitute about 38 per cent of the labor force.

At one time it was the custom for women to work only until they got married. Later on the practice developed of having a "second career" after children had grown up. But today an increasing number of women are combining child raising with careers, and this combination is not confined to mothers of fatherless families. The labor force participation rate for women living with their husbands with children under 18 years of age rose from 9 per cent in 1940 to 39 per cent in 1969. Women no longer have to choose between marriage and a career; it is increasingly possible to combine bringing up a family with a single job career which will extend with little interruption from the time a girl leaves school to the day she retires. As work becomes more important in a woman's life, so does her insistence that she be treated fairly.

Women's Liberation Movement. The Women's Liberation Movement constitutes an additional reason for the growing interest in equal employment. Encouraged by the success of other minority groups, more and more women have shaken off their "slave mentalities" and have taken militant positions against "sexist exploitation." And "those who maintained that a woman's place was in the home, or that they were happy in their role as wives and mothers, were scorned and branded as 'Aunt Toms'." [22]

Legal developments. Sometime before Women's Liberation hit the front page, there were important developments on the legal front. The Equal Pay Act of 1963 prohibited differences in pay based on sex. And in 1964 an attempt was made to kill the Civil Rights Bill, then before Congress, by tacking on a rider adding a prohibition of discrimination because of sex to the bill's original prohibition of racial discrimination. Though the initial debate treated the rider as a joke, the joke backfired and the law passed, outlawing both forms of discrimination.

Discrimination against women has also been outlawed by the federal contract compliance procedures that were developed to reduce racial discrimination by federal contractors. Continual lobbying by Women's Liberation groups has prodded often unwilling male officials to enforce these rules with increasing rigor.

Legal Questions

The impact of these new regulations has already been considerable. Most major companies have revised their personnel rules. Women have moved into jobs reserved for men. Female pay scales have been realigned upwards. Job vacancy ads rarely specify sex. Seniority ladders have been merged. And in 1971, in its first ruling on sexual discrimination, the U.S. Supreme Court held that the Martin Marietta Company could not refuse to hire women with preschool children as long as it hired men with such children.

As might be expected, the new laws have raised a number of difficult legal questions, two of which are discussed below.

BFOQ. The Civil Rights Act makes it illegal to discriminate on the basis of sex except where sex is "a bona fide occupational qualification" (BFOQ). But what is BFOQ? It is not enough that the job might be too hard for some women to do or that men can do it slightly better (this can be decided on a case-by-case basis). Nor is it a BFOQ that customers expect to be served by salespeople of a particular sex or even that to hire women would require building a whole new set of restrooms. Freighter crews have traditionally been all male, but recently

[22] Doris Hardesty, "The Continuing Fight for Women's Rights," *AFL-CIO American Federationist*, (January 1971), p. 12.

women have won the right to ship out as members of the galley crew, despite company claims that there was insufficient space to provide separate sleeping and washing quarters for both sexes. Still to be decided is whether Bunny Club Hostesses must be exclusively female.

State protective legislation. Since the turn of the century laws have given women special protection regarding night work, rest periods, weight to be lifted, and the number of hours they could work. Some laws even restrict women from entering certain occupations (for example, being a bartender in Michigan). One of the effects of these laws has been to limit the jobs available for women.

An unsettled question is whether these state laws have been superseded by the federal Civil Rights Act. Can a company refuse to hire a woman for a job that requires lifting 25-pound packages if the state law says that no woman may be required to lift more than 20? If a company lets men work six hours overtime, can it rely on a state law and not refuse women the opportunity for equal earnings? As this was written, the issue was not finally resolved, but it seems likely that the Supreme Court will rule that the state laws will have to give way. If so, a number of important protections for women will be eliminated.

Problems Created by Female Employment

As the years go by, most job distinctions between the sexes will be blurred, yet the change will not be easy and we should examine some of the problems, real or imaginary, which women's employment may create.

There is a widespread belief that female turnover is higher than that of males, that women have higher absentee and tardiness rates, and that they are more prone to illness and accident. Statistics on these points vary, but there is no strong evidence that female employees are less reliable than men.

Another reason for not hiring women for responsible jobs that require long training is the belief that they are likely to get married and quit as soon as they become pregnant. This fear has some validity; but as more and more women combine careers with motherhood, companies may adjust to the special needs of mothers: long leaves may be granted at childbirth; provisions can be made for part-time work; and day care facilities can be provided for children (as they are in many European countries).

There is still a considerable prejudice against putting women in management. Typical male views include the following:

"Management is hard enough without introducing the sex element."

"How can I work with an employee if she breaks into tears every time she makes a mistake?"

"Women don't want to work for female supervisors, and you certainly can't ask men to do so."

"Every time I want Jane to do something, she rolls her eyes and smiles. She's too cute to get mad at, but it's a stupid way to have a business relationship." (Female counterthrust: "That's what he expects—and like it or not, that's what you have to give. ... If you do too good a job, you threaten the male's ego. The smart gal knows better ways to get what she wants.")

As radical feminists point out, our culture has established fairly rigid role requirements governing the behavior of men and women when they meet together. Obviously, these roles will have to change if there is to be true equality on the job, and they are changing rapidly.

CONCLUSION

The searching questions asked by racial minority and women's groups have revealed that few personnel policies are unbiased. Recruitment, selection, training, promotion, and compensation policies all have been found to discriminate. Stereotypes as to the capabilities of women and minority groups preserve irrational personnel policies.

But it is no longer enough to eliminate overt discrimination. Social and governmental pressures are forcing companies beyond "color blindedness" to "affirmative action." For the most part, management has accepted the responsibility of making a positive contribution to reducing racial discrimination, even at the cost of reducing profits and productivity.

problem 1 • ARCADE CHEMICAL COMPANY

The Arcade Chemical Company is located in Franklinville, a small town of about 10,000 with about 500 blacks. Most of the adult blacks grew up in the South and have come to Franklinville to work on the surrounding farms. Few of the older generation have gone to high school at all and even among the younger generation the dropout rate is high.

At present the company has only two black employees (both janitors) and there is strong government pressure to expand this number.

The plant is highly automated and most jobs, except for janitor and laborer, require considerable technical skill. Most new employees are hired as laborers and from this job they normally are promoted, on the basis of seniority, to successively more responsible jobs till finally they become chief operators, in charge of $5 million worth of equipment. The union contract provides that promotions will be on the basis of seniority, where merit and ability are equal, but in practice this has been interpreted as meaning that the senior man is to get the job unless the company can prove that he is not qualified to handle it. The company has an intensive training program for all its employees.

Because of these technical demands, the company has, since 1952, required all new employees to be high school graduates and in recent years a majority of those hired have been graduates of the local community college.

In addition to requiring a high school diploma the company insists that all new hires pass a technical aptitude test which has been validated (concurrent validation) in terms of the present chief operators.

Last year the company had ten black applicants, none of whom were hired. Six were rejected because they lacked a high school diploma while the other four scored quite low on the entrance test (and two had arrest records).

1. What steps can the company take to reduce its racial imbalance?

2. What problems are involved in each and how can these problems be resolved?

problem 2 • ELIMINATING THE EFFECTS OF PAST DISCRIMINATION

The Swormsville Company has a job career ladder which starts at job class 1, the lowest paid, and ends at job class 24, the highest. Normally one moves up the ladder, from job class to job class, with the man who has had the job longest in any one job class being given preference whenever there is a vacancy in the next higher job class. In the past, however, there was one major exception: no black could be promoted above job class 5.

Assuming this discriminatory provision is eliminated, what should the rights be of Mr. X, a black with 24 years departmental seniority, who is still in job class 5 while whites with equal seniority are now in job class 15? Three possibilities have been suggested:

1. Mr. X moves immediately to job 15, even though this means displacing someone currently on the job and even though he does not have the training and experience to handle the job.

2. Mr. X will be given special training and he will be moved upward from job to job as fast as his abilities permit him, in each case having first priority for any vacancy, but not displacing anyone from a job.

3. As the longest-service man in job class 5, Mr. X can move to job class 6 when there is a vacancy, but he can't move to job class 7 until all those presently in job class 6 are promoted.

Which of these alternatives seem fairest? Can you devise a fairer one? Would the nature of the jobs make any difference to your answer?

problem 3 • POLICE APPOINTMENTS

For selecting policemen, the city uses the following techniques: (1) the Strong Vocational Interest Inventory (see p. 422); (2) a paper-and-pencil personality inventory, which, among other things, probes into sexual interests; (3) a verbal comprehension test; (4) a physical examination; and (5) interviews by the city's personnel director and the chief of police.

A rejected black applicant appeals to the city council and alleges that these techniques are biased and unfair. He argues: (1) None of the tests have been validated in terms of applicants (especially black applicants) for jobs with this city's police department. (2) The verbal comprehension test reveals knowledge of middle-class words, not the language of the ghetto. Anyway, policemen don't have to be scholars. (3) Personality and sex interests are personal matters that the government has no right to probe. (4) The personnel director and the chief of police are both white and prejudiced, as shown by the fact that though the city's population is 10 percent black, only 3 percent of the police force is black.

The personnel director answers: (1) Verbal comprehension is important for a policeman, who must understand laws and instructions couched in middle-class language. (2) The verbal comprehension test has been validated (concurrent validation) in terms of performance of present policemen (as rated by their superiors). Correlation between test scores and rated performance is low (.10), but this is expected, since verbal comprehension is obviously only one of a number of factors relevant to police performance. The test does contribute useful additional information to the selection decision. (3) The personality test is used solely to weed out psychopaths and sexual deviants. Surely, these are not wanted on the force. (4) The Strong Inventory has been validated in terms of the population as a whole: it does predict who will be happy as policemen. Obviously, unhappy policemen are not likely to be good policemen. (5) The city has been making a determined effort to find qualified black applicants. Of the fifteen new policemen appointed in the last two years, three have been blacks (two of whom, unfortunately, have recently resigned to accept much better-paying jobs in private industry).

Evaluate these arguments. What do you propose?

6

Management and Organization Development

Managerial effectiveness is the most critical element in organizational effectiveness. As we have stressed throughout the text, managers have substantial opportunity in the modern organization either to contribute substantially to employee performance or to act as a brake on motivation and results. Thus, identifying and evaluating differences in managerial effectiveness as well as methods of improving these skills are critical responsibilities. They are also more difficult and challenging tasks than comparable appraisal and development activities for non-managerial personnel.

The overall setting and the major issues are discussed in Chapter 22, "Management Development." Preparing managers for advancement and properly motivating them to accept additional responsibilities fall within the province of several key personnel programs: training, appraisal, job rotation, and promotion systems. As we saw in Chapter 18, "Manpower Planning," the interrelationship and harmony among these programs is critical to their successful operation; therefore, these "system" issues have to be resolved if the total development program is going to be successful. Chapter 23, "Performance Appraisal" concentrates on methods of evaluating individual performance; but managerial work is not easy to assess, and the problems are analyzed with some of what we believe to be the more useful solutions.

The final chapter in this section, Chapter 24, "Management Training and Organization Development," reviews and compares the programs and techniques that have been devised to improve managers' behavioral skills. Such training, which concentrates on achieving on-the-job attitude and behavioral changes, is one of the most ambitious and controversial types of training. Company experience and the pros and cons of various types of behavioral training are reviewed.

MANAGEMENT DEVELOPMENT

22

Management development is the subject of our next three chapters. An effective management team may be as important to the survival of an organization as any tangible item on the balance sheet. Good managers don't just turn up when needed; a great deal of development effort is required. But neither can managers be produced on an assembly-line basis. After all, people are involved: people are unpredictable, have interests of their own, and so cannot be molded like plastic soldiers. Thus, a meaningful development program must consider both organizational and human needs. This chapter will be concerned with the general problems of providing experience that will enable managers to develop their fullest potentialities. The next two chapters will handle specific areas: performance evaluation (Chapter 23) and management training and organization development (Chapter 24).

Interest in management development is high partly because of the shortage of well-trained managers. The number of managerial jobs is rising much faster than the size of the work force generally. This growth in the number of "chiefs" may foreshadow a completely automated world where all "Indians" have been eliminated. The shortage in managers is rendered more acute by competition for high-talent manpower among business, the professions, and government. And yet the size of the male labor force between 40 and 50 years of age (the age range from which most top executives are selected) is likely to decline over the next ten years.

In addition, there is a growing feeling that management is a *profession* for which special training is required. Over the last fifty years, "getting ahead" in business has come to mean rising within the "management profession," rather than going into business for one's self. In the near future, almost every middle- and top-ranking manager will have a college degree, and an increasing proportion will have gone to graduate school (very frequently in business administration). According to the 1965 survey, 76 percent of one sample of managers had college diplomas and 31 percent had advanced degrees. [1]

Ever since World War II, the average age of top executives has dropped. The typical newly appointed vice-president or general manager today is in his middle forties. On the other hand, higher educational standards have deferred the age of entry into employment. Thus, the period between first entry into employment and attainment of a top management position has been reduced to not much more than twenty years, a critical period in the aspiring manager's life.

The object of a good management development program is to make each of these twenty years count and to provide each manager with as rich a learning experience as possible, but also (as we will discuss in Chapter 23) to permit his performance to be carefully observed, so that in this highly competitive race the truly best men get to the top.

Management development, however, has other objectives. Only a few executives are "fast track" men with a real potential for getting to the top. The management development program must also provide opportunity for personal growth for the vast majority of those who are destined to go no further than the middle and lower levels of the management hierarchy.

Finally, the opportunity for advancement has an important motivational value. Managers will work harder if they feel that their effort is likely to be rewarded by promotion. If they feel that promotional decisions are made on inequitable grounds, morale and motivation will be reduced. Thus (to use the terms introduced in Chapter 6), management development can be both a hygienic factor and a motivator.

SOME BASIC ISSUES

Before we look at the details of management development, it may be useful to introduce some basic controversial questions that will underlie our discussion in the next three chapters.

Special Programs or Good Environment?

The first controversy relates to the effectiveness of special developmental programs, such as planned rotation, performance evaluation, and training classes. On one side are those who argue that such programs develop proper attitudes

[1] Stanley C. Vance, "Higher Education for the Executive Elite," *California Management Review*, Vol. 8, No. 4 (Summer 1966).

Another possible sign of professionalism is increasing managerial mobility, the willingness of managers to move from company to company, thus suggesting identification with profession rather than company. Managers are showing, also, a greater sense of professional and social responsibility—toward minority groups, for example, or the environment.

and skills. But those on the other side claim that attitudes and skills (at least in the management area) can't be changed directly; the most that can be done is to create a challenging and permissive environment in which people can develop themselves. In a sense this is a question of strategy: Should our first emphasis be on changing people or on changing the organization? If we change people first, then hopefully they will make the organization work better. But if we change the organization first (through changing elements such as organization structure, work-flow, and methods of reward), then hopefully this changed environment may produce, if not better people, at least a situation to which people can adapt more successfully.

To take a specific example (to which we shall return more fully in Chapter 24), training programs accomplish little if the new behavior learned is disapproved by the trainee's boss; after all, a man is more likely to be concerned with what his boss thinks than what he learns in class. This may suggest that it is best to have each manager train his own subordinates. But the boss's behavior itself may be far from ideal. Even if it were exemplary, he may not have the ability to engage in training, and organizational pressures may not give him the time to do so. So special development programs may be needed, if only to provide the manager with some "ideals" which he may aspire to practice on the job.

Conformity or Diversity?

Should the purpose of development be to instill certain common values in managers, or should it be to encourage each individual to develop his own style of behavior, one which seems best to fit his own personality and the requirements of his special job?

Many development programs are, in effect, forms of indoctrination. As we have seen, indoctrination, through providing a uniform way of thinking and a standardized approach to problems, permits a substantial amount of innovative behavior within a common frame of reference, without the need for close supervision.

Yet some observers are concerned lest developmental procedures, as used in many companies, create too many "organization men," conformists who are mainly concerned with pleasing the boss, and fail to produce enough of the nonconformists who are needed at the top. [2] Indoctrination has been attacked on practical grounds as stultifying individual growth and on moral grounds as a form of brain-washing inconsistent with individual dignity.

Generalists or Specialists?

Should companies develop all-purpose *generalists* with broad points of view or more narrow *specialists* who think in terms of their own particular functions? With the development of specialists, organization-man conformity is reduced, but perhaps a new conformity to the specific viewpoint of the given specialty is

[2] William H. Whyte, Jr., *The Organization Man* (New York: Simon and Schuster, 1956).

encouraged. A man trained as a computer programer, for instance, is likely to think in terms of problems which can be expressed in computer language. There is a dilemma here. Each boss wants to hire specialists and reward specialization at the lower level, yet each company wants generalists at higher levels. Where are the generalists to come from?

Open Systems or Closed Systems?

Related to the conformity issue is the question of the degree to which an individual should be free to choose his own career path.[3] In many companies the individual has little choice in the kind of job he does or the kinds of training or developmental opportunities he receives. For example, when caught in an unrewarding, seemingly dead-end job, he is not allowed to apply to fill a job opening elsewhere in the company which seems more promising. In effect, this is a "closed system" in which the individual's freedom is greatly restricted.

Other companies have more "open" systems. They publicize job openings or training opportunities and let managers "bid" on them. They let individuals who wish take risky assignments, even though there is a good possibility they may fail. Rather than train personnel for specific jobs, they allow subordinates to pick their own training programs. Both the boss who has a job to fill and the subordinate who bids for the job have a wider range of options than under the closed system. And the individual is less dependent on his own particular boss.

Decision-Making or Human Relations?

What is the main job of the manager: to make decisions or to deal with people? As we shall see, two frequently used forms of training today, the T-group and the business game, involve these two radically different concepts of the nature of the manager's job.

The T-group technique (see pp. 536-40) assumes that the manager's main function is to deal with people. The T-group is designed to help executives develop greater sensitivity to their own behavior and in their perceptions of others. By contrast, business games, particularly those which involve a computer, generally require analytical ability and little or no human-relations skills. They assume that all relevant problems of decision-making can be quantified. Once a decision has been reached there is little problem of implementation;[4] all the participant need do is write his answer and the computer obeys without question.

Naturally the arguments can be overstated. We need better decisions and better means of implementing them. As we shall see, training programs have

---

[3] Theodore M. Alford, "Checkers or Choice in Manpower Management," *Harvard Business Review*, Vol. 45, No. 1 (January 1967), pp. 157-167.

[4] True, if teams are involved in the game, then there is a human-relations problem of getting team members to agree to a decision. Interestingly, advocates of T-groups and business games both claim that their techniques improve decision-making abilities, but they use the term decision-making in different ways. One group is concerned with the social process by which the group makes a decision, the other with the intellectual process by which the individual makes one. For an example of the first view, see Robert R. Blake and Jane S. Moulton, *Group Dynamics—Key to Decision-Making* (Houston, Texas: Gulf Publishing Company, 1961).

been developed which provide experience with both aspects of decision-making. And yet the question is related to those we have already discussed. What kinds of executives should we develop? Executives who make risk-taking decisions and set the general tone and direction of the firm in ways that are difficult to program? High-level executives who work toward goals in a rational fashion, evaluating alternative goals, appraising and re-appraising results? Organization men, skilled in carrying out orders and reducing human frictions? Or technicians with specialized interests in narrow areas?

Crown Princes or All Employees?

Who should be developed—just those with special promise or everyone? Because of the critical shortage of manpower after World War II, the early emphasis was on crash programs to discover individuals (both inside and outside the company) who would be capable of moving to top-management jobs. In the effort to ferret out such exceptional men, there arose a widespread use of tests (see pp. 433–34) and evaluation forms designed to identify traits that might point to *future* ability rather than to *present* performance. The men thus singled out (the "crown princes") were given special training away from the job (often at universities) and were marked for rapid promotion.

As might be expected, this program led to a wave of resentment among those who had not been selected and to a feeling that it was unfair to base promotions on vague character traits instead of on proven performance. Also, since the selection process tended to emphasize the safe, conformist, all-round man, there seemed to be a prejudice against the unusual individual who was able to get things done in spite of "character deficiencies." In other words, observers began to suspect that, by weeding out deviationists, management might also be weeding out the very men who would produce the original ideas of the future. Further, by emphasizing those who began their careers with a quick burst of speed, the "crown prince" program places late bloomers at a disadvantage. (Recent research indicates that there is a relatively low correlation between early increases in salary and salary later in one's career and that many apparently late bloomers do make it to the top.)

Recent Trends

The emphasis in recent years has been on providing a diversity of programs designed to help *all* managers (not just crown princes) perform more adequately on their present jobs, as well as to provide special training for those who show promise of moving higher up. Companies are not trying so hard to mold managers into a single form. Increasingly, managers are being helped to design their own custom-made developmental programs, thus creating a more "open system." (In some companies these custom-made programs are designed after managers have gone through assessment centers.)

Evaluation forms are being used as a tool to enable the manager to discuss with his subordinates how they can improve their performance, rather than as a means of selection. There have been other changes as well: personality traits (which cannot be changed easily) are receiving less emphasis than performance (which can); training is coming to be regarded as an essential management function rather than a peripheral frill; hence the primary responsibility for training is being shifted from staff to line management.

CHARACTERISTICS OF TOP MANAGERS

It may help us to understand the management development process if we look briefly at the findings of recent research dealing with successful, rapidly promoted managers.[5] According to this research, the successful manager in the large firms has the following characteristics:

1. He moves rapidly from job to job. "It now takes 20 years on the average to go from first-level manager to president, during which time there are seven geographical moves, 11 positional ones, and countless numbers of special and project assignments."[6] More than before the successful manager's career may include moving from one company to another.

2. He is flexible, realistic, and sensitive to the complexities of his work environment. Compared with less successful managers, he is both challenged by, and comfortable in, situations filled with high risk and ambiguity.

3. He earns his spurs handling critical assignments; these seem to be more important than doing well on routine work.

4. Very often he has a "sponsor," someone from higher management who is impressed with his abilities, finds him useful to have around, and who looks after his interests. It helps if the sponsor is moving up rapidly himself.

5. He engages in "anticipatory socialization": at each step he copies the values of those a step above him.

6. He is not necessarily an "organization man" conformist. High-level managers tend to be more "inner directed" and less "other directed" and less concerned with pleasing others than are those at lower levels.

To summarize, it is necessary for the rising young executive to persuade those above him that he has the human relations abilities to be a good member of their "team." But getting along with people is a less significant criterion for advancement than having the analytical ability to diagnose problems, evaluate information, and make sound recommendations.

[5] See William R. Dill, Thomas L. Hilton, and Walter R. Reitman, *The New Managers* (Englewood Cliffs, N.J.: Prentice-Hall, 1962); Lyman W. Porter, *Organizational Patterns of Managerial Job Attitudes* (New York: American Foundation for Management Research, 1964); Fred H. Goldner, "Success vs. Failure: Prior Managerial Perspectives," *Industrial Relations,* Vol. 9, No. 4 (September 1970), pp. 453–467; George Strauss, "Organization Man: Pattern for the Future?" *California Management Review,* Vol. 6, No. 3 (Spring 1964).

[6] Eugene Jennings, "Mobicentric Man," *Psychology Today,* Vol. 4, No. 4 (July 1970), p. 36.

To put it another way, the successful rising young executive may be the man who can be either conformist or nonconformist as the situation demands. In terms of social behavior and attitudes, he conforms; but in his own area of job competence he takes the initiative *at the proper time*. Perhaps the sense of timing—knowing when is the proper time—is among the necessary requirements of a good executive.

With this background, let us look at management development programs in practice. The first step involves planning.

PLANNING FOR DEVELOPMENT

In planning for management development the organization must predict its long-range managerial manpower needs and decide how to meet them. But, as we saw in Chapter 18, long-range planning must be highly tentative. In the shorter-range development of individual managers, far more precise planning is possible.

Scheduling of Promotions and Transfers

Many large companies keep careful track of the progress of each of their managers and tentatively schedule their future movements from job to job in order to insure that they will get optimum training and experience. An attempt is made to mesh individual careers with company growth and development. Normally, policy in this area is the responsibility of a top-level management committee, while the administrative work is handled by the personnel director or a special coordinator of management development who reports directly to the president.

The key tools in scheduling programs of this sort are *executive inventories* and *replacement charts*. An executive inventory consists of a file card for each executive with such information as: age, length of service, education, positions held within the company and with other companies, results on psychological tests, hobbies, membership in outside organizations, and so forth. More important are evaluations by superiors of his work since he first came with the company, a statement by his present boss about the type of experience he still needs, and an estimate of how far he might go in the future.

Frequently these data are computerized. When a new job opens up, all management need do is to set the standards as to the type of man best qualified. The machine does the rest. There are those who claim that once the standards are properly set, only a minimum of human judgment is required.

Many companies like to look several jumps ahead. They are interested in more than just finding who is most qualified at the moment. Some try to schedule moments five or ten years in advance. Here's where replacement charts are useful. The accompanying chart is typical, though it somewhat exaggerates the range of possibilities among six men.

REPLACEMENT CHART

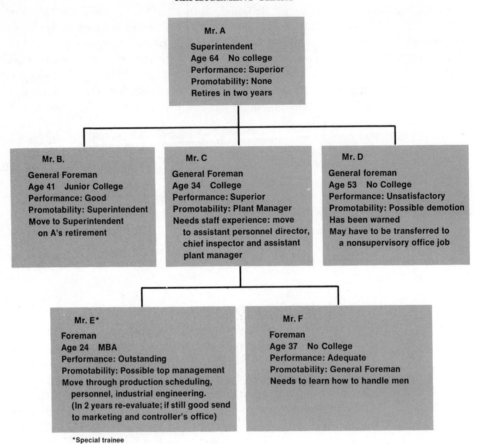

Mr. A

Superintendent
Age 64   No college
Performance: Superior
Promotability: None
Retires in two years

Mr. B.

General Foreman
Age 41   Junior College
Performance: Good
Promotability: Superintendent
Move to Superintendent
   on A's retirement

Mr. C

General Foreman
Age 34   College
Performance: Superior
Promotability: Plant Manager
Needs staff experience: move
   to assistant personnel director,
   chief inspector and assistant
   plant manager

Mr. D

General foreman
Age 53   No College
Performance: Unsatisfactory
Promotability: Possible demotion
Has been warned
May have to be transferred to
   a nonsupervisory office job

Mr. E*

Foreman
Age 24   MBA
Performance: Outstanding
Promotability: Possible top management
Move through production scheduling,
   personnel, industrial engineering.
   (In 2 years re-evaluate; if still good send
   to marketing and controller's office)

Mr. F

Foreman
Age 37   No College
Performance: Adequate
Promotability: General Foreman
Needs to learn how to handle men

*Special trainee

From individual file cards and replacement charts it is possible to plan many years in advance. For instance:

Mr. A
Jan.   1972 Superintendent
Jan.   1974 Retires (to be replaced by Mr. B)

Mr. B
Jan.   1972 General Foreman
Summer 1973 Executive Development Program at X University
Jan.   1974 Superintendent

Mr. C
Jan.   1972 General Foreman
June   1972 Assistant Personnel Director
Jan.   1973 Chief Inspector
June   1973 Assistant Plant Manager (position to be created)
Jan.   1974 Plant Manager

Mr. E
Jan.   1972 Foreman
June   1972 Assistant Chief, Production Scheduling
Jan.   1973 Assistant Personnel Director
Jan.   1974 Assistant Director, Industrial Engineering
Jan.   1975 Marketing Department, Corporate Headquarters
Jan.   1976 Controller's Department, Corporate Headquarters

Note that Mr. B is to receive special training to prepare him for Mr. A's job. Mr. C is to move three different jobs to gain breadth of experience. Mr. C, whose performance is superior, will jump the Superintendent's post altogether and eventually become Plant Manager, though not until he has served in inspection and personnel and then gained six months experience as an understudy to the man he will succeed. Mr. E, with an MBA degree, may have a still more brilliant future ahead. After short tours in three staff departments, he will move on to broader horizons in corporate headquarters. (He is lucky to stay in this one plant so long; in many companies, promising young executives move more frequently than once in three years.)

Note, too, that all these plans must be extremely tentative. If Mr. E fails to develop as anticipated, the schedule must be changed. Yet the very existence of such forecasts may lead to what some observers call a "self-fulfilling prophecy." The very fact that Mr. E is tagged as a "comer" means that he receives special opportunities and so is likely to become a good manager because everyone expects him to. Those who are less favored get less attention and so tend to lose hope. Furthermore, the system we are illustrating is "closed": Managers are rarely consulted about their future moves; indeed, not uncommonly they are kept completely in the dark.

The purpose of all this planning is to insure that the right man is available with the right experience at the right time. Naturally there is no absolute agreement on the best way of providing men with the experience they need. For instance, how long should a man stay on a given job before he moves on? How much variety of experience should he get? How much special attention should be given to the unusual "comer"? How should men be handled who have ceased to "grow"?

MANAGERIAL CAREER PATTERNS

The career of most managers goes through three stages: an initiation period, a period of upward movement, and a period of peaking out. Each of these periods presents problems for the individual manager and the organization as a whole. In the sections that follow we shall look at these problems and at developmental programs designed to deal with them.

The Initiation Period

Most large companies make major efforts to recruit and hire new college graduates, believing—in our opinion correctly—that a continual inflow of highly talented manpower is essential for organizational success. Yet the typical experience of many companies is that 50 per cent of their college graduates leave their jobs in their first five years, and those who leave are, on the average, every bit as good as those who stay.

Reasons for discontent and turnover. In part, high turnover results from a clash between what new graduates expect and what the jobs actually offer them. The typical graduate expects his first job to be challenging and meaningful.

Especially if he graduates from a business school, he wants to be able to use the skills he has developed in class. (Often these unrealistic expectations are encouraged by lavish promises made by corporate recruiters.)

The company, however, "may assign tasks to a new employee that are so trivial as to carry the clear message that a new man is not worthy of doing anything important. Or, in contrast, assignments can be made which require such specific and technical knowledge that failure is inevitable, thereby proving to the new man that 'he really isn't so smart after all.' Obviously, both strategies seem purposely designed to threaten the self-esteem of the newly hired college graduate."[7]

Considering the effort that many companies make to hire new graduates, why are the new people put through such a disillusioning experience? In part, this is the normal clash between generations. Older men at lower levels of management understandably feel threatened by brash youngsters whose education is better than theirs was. Particularly since the middle 1960's, younger men have different life styles, modes of dress, and scales of values. Thus younger men are likely to reject traditional concepts, for example, that a newcomer should show subservience, and instead they may ask that the company subscribe to their own enlarged sense of social responsibility.

Misuse of recent graduates is in part a result of poor planning. The number of challenging jobs that neophyte managers can handle is quite limited, and few companies have given sufficient thought to how these new men are to be used. Many companies hire more young managers than they have meaningful jobs for, because they expect (quite rightly under the circumstances) that a high percentage of these men will quit. In some cases, stockpiling of managers, especially of young MBAs, is a matter of prestige—the belief that hiring a lot of MBAs is itself a sign of progressive management.

But more than the generation clash and poor planning is involved. In many organizations the beginning of a new manager's career serves much the same purposes as a fraternity initiation or boot camp. Remembering our analysis in Chapter 12, we see that the initiation period serves to "unfreeze" the manager. Those who survive this painful process of "organizational socialization" become better indoctrinated with organizational values, just as those who survive Marine boot training often identify more closely with the Marines.

But the trouble is that a high percentage of young managers fail to "survive." When the turnover rate passes 50 per cent, it is obvious that the initiation is not working effectively, especially since at times the net result of the process, even for those who stay, is the creation of conformist "organization men," while the more innovative independents move on.

Executive training programs. Most companies know that newly hired graduates need a smooth introduction into management, and a number of compa-

---

[7] Marvin Dunnette, Richard Avery, and Paul Banas, "Why Do They Leave?" mimeographed, 1970, pp. 10-11. This article suggests that first jobs of college graduates tend to offer considerably less sense of status, accomplishment, use of ideas, and interesting work than they had expected to obtain upon being hired. Those who in a reasonably short length of time were moved on to jobs that offered more of these satisfactions tended to stay with the company. Those whose jobs remained unchallenging tended to leave for other companies.

nies have established special training programs. The programs—which typically last from six weeks to more than a year—are a general orientation to the company and its policies and a means of observing and evaluating the trainee.

Typically, trainees are rotated from department to department every few months, working perhaps as salesmen or assistant foremen. Often, on-the-job training is interspersed with formal classes, seminars, and discussion groups. Every month or two the trainees are carefully evaluated by their supervisor of the moment and by the over-all program coordinator. Trainees who completely fail to measure up to expectations are dropped; others are counseled on how to do a better job. At the end of the formal training period, each trainee is assigned to the department to which he seems best suited.

Such programs are designed to provide the recent college graduate with an easy transition from the campus to the very different atmosphere of business. Further, they give him a breadth of experience and insight that he never would obtain were he to stay in a single department. Indeed, the whole process is designed to help trainee and company pick the job for which the trainee is best qualified.

In practice, however, these programs have serious limitations. The "experience" of the trainee in any one department often consists of little more than superficial observation. And the trainees are never evaluated under natural conditions; everyone knows that they are special individuals and treats them accordingly. Also, the noncollege men in an organization sometimes display intense antagonism toward these so-called "crown princes." The fact that the company is hiring college men and training them specifically for management positions means that promotional opportunities for noncollege men are reduced. As one foreman commented:

"Look at that kid there. His dad had money enough to send him to college and so he is a big shot. Right now he's assistant foreman and he don't know one per cent of what the men he bosses know. Five years from now he'll be my boss and he still won't know anything. So I got to watch how I treat him. Look how he struts around. The men hate him."

Finally, trainees are often given trivial assignments that make little use of their college training: either routine, nonmanagerial work or the most insignificant form of managerial duties. Of course, many higher level managers feel that everyone who is to act as a supervisor of rank-and-file workers should have some experience doing the work. On the other hand, as we have seen, young college graduates find this kind of "Mickey Mouse work" quite frustrating.

Recognizing this problem, some companies such as A.T. & T., Procter and Gamble, and Ford have developed programs in which prospective managers are given relatively challenging assignments at the very outset—problems which will test their ingenuity but presumably not be beyond their capacity to solve. Typically, such assignments initially concern responsible operating activities and, after a year or so, require leading an ongoing work team. These assignments are difficult enough that a significant proportion of trainees fail. (At A.T. & T., one in every five trainees is separated from the company after the first year.) Early evidence suggests that for those who succeed, however, the experience is extremely worthwhile.

On the other hand, challenging assignments suitable for an inexperienced man may be hard to develop. In addition, much depends on the manager to whom the trainee is assigned, particularly on whether he is aware of the problems discussed above and sympathetic to the trainee's life style and aspirations (rather than looking upon him as a potential rival). In A.T. & T., managers who work with such trainees are specially selected and trained themselves, with no manager allowed to supervise more than one trainee.

To summarize this section: the evidence suggests that the new manager's experience in an organization during his first months and years after graduating from college may be critical for his career.[8] When the organization sets a high level of expectations for its new managers, these managers tend to meet it. Similarly, when the organization sets low levels of expectations, these expectations are also met.

Upward Movement

Once past the initiation period, how is the lower-level manager trained for higher positions? A number of programs offer "guided" experience that will help prepare the maturing manager for promotion, three of which we shall consider here: understudies, rotation, and special broadening assignments.

Understudies. In some organizations before an executive can be moved to a higher position, he is required to train a replacement. The understudy program is the least ambitious form of development program and requires the least centralized control and use of replacement tables. Yet, modest as it is, it raises many problems. Should there be a single understudy or several? If there is only one, those who have not been chosen may give up all hope of getting ahead. If there are several, rivalry may spring up among them.

When should understudies be selected? Some companies require a new manager to select a successor almost as soon as he moves to his desk,[9] early selection giving maximum opportunity for the understudy to gain experience, while insuring that someone is immediately prepared to take over in case of emergency. If the appointment is made too early, however, it may impair the morale of other men who feel qualified for the job.

Systematic rotation. As suggested earlier, one striking characteristic of the successful manager in most companies is his rapid mobility. He moves frequently from job to job and city to city. Some of these movements involve promotions; others, lateral transfers at the same level. In any case, "zigzag mobility," not straight upward progression, seems to be the typical path to success.

In many companies rotation is unplanned, but movement is regarded as a

---

[8] John P. Campbell and others, *Managerial Behavior, Performance, and Effectiveness* (New York: McGraw-Hill, 1970), pp. 407–408. According to one study there is a close correlation between the organization's expectations of a manager on his first job and his over-all success in the organization five years later. David E. Berlew and Douglas T. Hall, "The Socialization of Managers: Effects of Expectations on Performance," *Administrative Science Quarterly*, Vol. 11, No. 2 (September 1966), pp. 207–224.

[9] Often the selection is made by a management-development committee, and the manager has relatively little to say about the choice.

sign of progress: to stay frozen on one job for too long often signifies failure. Rarely is a man *forced* to move; but if he declines an opportunity to transfer, he knows his chances for advancement will be severely limited. Other companies have a planned rotation program which makes extensive use of replacement charts and schedules. The decision on who is to be moved, where and when, is made on a coordinated, company-wide basis.

Rotation, whether planned or unplanned, is expensive. Besides the company's out-of-pocket expenses for administering the program and defraying the costs when managers move their residence from one location to another, there is a substantial loss in executive time when a man gives up an old job and sets about learning a new one. Why, then, are so many companies willing to undergo this expense?

1. A systematic rotation program develops not specialists, but generalists—men who can take a broad, company-wide point of view, men whose chief ability is handling people and making decisions.

2. Rotation provides challenge. The man who is transferred is faced with a whole new set of problems and is less likely to get stale.

3. The outsider who comes into a department often brings with him new ideas and fresh points of view. Having no vested interest in the old ways of doing things, he can make changes quickly. In contrast, a man who has been in the department for many years has many personal ties and must always be careful not to step on his friends' toes.

4. Rotation makes it possible to compare one man against another, and so it tends to give everyone an equal chance. With a program of understudies, by contrast, no man can advance till his boss dies, retires, quits, or moves up, and, in departments where there are lots of good men, some talent is bound to be wasted. Rotation also protects a man from being frozen in a job merely because his department is expanding less rapidly than the rest. And it gives him a chance to make a good showing in the line of work for which he is best suited. Further, it reduces the chance that his advancement will be stymied just because of personality differences with his boss.

5. Rotation fosters organizational flexibility. In case of sudden expansion of one line of work, there will always be a number of people around who have had some experience in it.

6. Rotation also avoids the problems which arise when a newly promoted manager is required to supervise his former peers.

But in spite of the obvious advantages of systematic rotation as a program of management development, it does give rise to certain problems.

1. Rotation often means that the manager must pull up stakes and move to another location. This is particularly hard on children who must constantly readapt to new schools and new friends; after a while they learn not to make close friendships and to withdraw into themselves.

Beyond the time and emotional strain involved in packing, unpacking, and finding a new house, constant movement makes it difficult for managers to sink their roots into the community, and it disrupts their ties with relatives and friends. Particularly to the adult who has poured love and energy into creating a garden or fixing up a house, giving up one's home is a painful experience.

Sooner or later most people who are obliged to move around a good bit learn to adjust. They learn not to make close friends, not to become closely involved in community affairs, not to develop long-term ties of any sort. By ruthlessly rooting out all other ties, rotation may develop the Organization Man who identifies only with the company for whom he works. Of course this company-centered manager may not be the all-around well-adjusted individual some companies purport to desire. Dedicated individuals are rarely "well rounded." But the question arises whether men who are so largely dependent on their job for satisfaction are really mature.

Many outstanding managers have simply refused to continue in the "rat race" (these are the heroes of many contemporary novels). Fully aware that to refuse a transfer may kill all chance of further advancement, they still insist on staying put. Clearly, men are not being used to the best advantage when top managers are picked on the basis of their willingness to be rotated rather than just innate capability.

Rotation may, in fact, cause good men to leave the organization. If they have to change jobs and homes anyway, many feel they might as well look around for the best offer and change companies, too.

2. Just as moving around discourages the executive from undertaking long-range projects at home, so it makes him reluctant to take a long-range approach to his job. If a man knows he will be transferred in two years' time, he will concentrate on short-range projects with a quick pay-off—immediate cost reduction, for instance, rather than personnel development. He knows that he will have none of the satisfaction of completing long-range projects and, when they are completed, the credit will go to his successor. Understandably, he is tempted to make changes that *look* good, since there rarely is time to test how they will work out in practice. Thus rotation programs tend to inhibit basic innovation and change.

Rotation penalizes the slow starter who never has enough time on a given job to prove his ability. Yet the man who takes a long time to adjust to the people he works with and to learn his way around may at times be the best man.

3. The rotation system is like a highly competitive game of musical chairs. Every time there is another round of promotions and transfers, some people are left behind. And the system, as practiced by most companies, puts a high premium on conformity. As long as you perform *adequately* you are retained. An *outstanding* job may help you somewhat, but a *mistake* may result in being "selected out." As a consequence, the smart

rising young executive plays it safe; he avoids taking risks. Knowing that he may be judged more by whether he sticks to the rules than by long-term accomplishments, he learns not to raise a fuss or rock the boat.

4. Rotation means that a man spends a large part of his time learning the job.[10] Since the purpose of rotation is training, the new manager is assigned to the job not because he is the best man for it (that person might be an underling with years of experience in the department), but because the job is the best for him (that is, it provides him with the most training).

It may take a new manager months or years to learn both the technology and social geography of his department. At first, all he knows are the formal rules, so he enforces these even when they are inappropriate.

If he is wise, he lets his subordinates train him for the job. In the early months, in most instances, it is the subordinates who help the manager, rather than the manager who helps the subordinates. Often, just after the department and the manager become accustomed to each other's idiosyncrasies the manager is transferred, a new man comes in, and the process begins all over again.

If carried too far, the policy of regular rotation may throw the affected departments into almost constant turmoil. The employees, knowing that their boss won't be with them for long, never develop respect for him. They learn to resist the supervisor's attempts to introduce change (which are often inept due to his lack of knowledge) and to develop strong group standards, which the supervisor of the moment finds almost impossible to modify. As a long-service clerk in one office put it:

"Bosses come and go. Each one has his pet peeves. We pretend to go along; but to tell you the truth we run things our own way."

Thus, changing managers rapidly may in fact inhibit change.

5. Rotation sometimes leads to subtle class distinctions. The men who are not rotated tend to develop defensive reactions and identify with their own department against the "carpetbaggers" from without. This cleavage leads to misunderstanding and poor communications, with top management exerting pressure to get the local "stick-in-the-muds" to accept change and with local management strongly resisting every effort.

In an earlier chapter we pointed out that the manager is a man in the middle. His job is to represent his subordinates to his superiors and his superiors to his subordinates. He must try to maintain a balance, and if he favors anybody it should be the subordinates. The rotation system swings the balance sharply the other way. The man who is being rotated cannot afford to take the time and energy to develop relations downward; he must always look ahead to that next promotional shift.

[10] In an organization that practices rotation extensively, there is a need to standardize jobs so that each man performs as the man before him. But even standardized jobs take considerable time to learn.

6. The rotation system may easily become overcentralized, inflexible, and "closed." The plant manager, for instance, may have little to say about who is moved into his plant and may be forced to accept as an assistant someone whom he has never seen before. A manager who is promoted under these circumstances is less likely to show loyalty to his boss than he would if the boss had been personally responsible for the promotion.

Long-run replacement schedules often look better on paper than in practice. People quit or die; business recessions dictate cut-backs in operations; products fail to develop as expected; men turn "sour." In short, there are too many variables to make planning for very far in the future much more reliable than crystal-gazing.

In conclusion, rotation has both advantages and disadvantages. Some managers find it challenging and exciting. Others find it frustrating, for both themselves and their families. Some departments would benefit from being shaken up by outsiders, but others would suffer in morale and efficiency in the hands of an outside manager unfamiliar with the special human and technical problems of the situation.

Special broadening assignments. Although rotation gives trainees a broad experience, this experience is all at a relatively low level. Yet different kinds of skills are required at various levels of the organization. At the lower levels perhaps technical ability, a willingness to obey orders, and skill in dealing with people are the chief requirements. At higher levels the ability to innovate and to make bold, long-range decisions becomes more important. The men who do outstanding jobs at lower and middle levels of management may be totally ineffective at the top; on the other hand, the brilliant innovator might seem very inadequate in a subordinate post.

Since, at the lower levels, getting ahead depends on the recommendations of one's immediate boss, some men get no chance to advance because the boss is too unimaginative to appreciate their abilities (or even feels threatened by them). Thus, the "organization man" conformist will be favored rather than the kind of daring innovator needed at the top. In addition outstanding men sometimes lose their spark as they work their way slowly upward.

As a means of distinguishing the men who are outstandingly qualified for high positions, some companies are giving their promising junior executives special assignments which permit them to sample top-level responsibilities. The nature of these assignments varies greatly. Normally they are devised on a temporary or part-time basis—in addition to the executive's regular job. Some organizations have "junior boards of directors" or "management cabinets" to which the senior board of directors may refer special problems (or the junior board may consider substantially the same agenda as the senior board). More frequently, trainees are assigned to capital budgeting, product development, or long-range planning committees where they work in the company of more senior executives. At times a trainee may be assigned to study a problem area, prepare recommendations, and present and defend them in person before a top-management committee. Or he may be assigned as an "assistant to" a member of top management and work as his personal aide.

If such special assignments are to be successful as development tools, three requirements must be met:

1. The problems assigned must be genuinely "broadening"—that is, they must cut across departmental lines and involve long-range planning.

2. The trainees must operate under the direct observation of top executives who are personally responsible for evaluating the trainees' performance.

3. The problems must be *tough*, challenging ones—tough enough so that the merely adequate answer appears unsatisfactory and so that the truly outstanding man can show his real merits.

Special assignments should be designed to give the rising junior executive top-level experience both in operating on his own and in serving as a committee member.

There must be evaluation of the results not only by the senior committee members but also by the juniors themselves. The juniors' evaluations must be evaluated. There must be a chance for juniors (anonymously?) to indicate those of their colleagues whom they judge to show superior intelligence, ability to accomplish, leadership, etc. [11]

In general, programs of this sort permit the junior to be observed and evaluated by a group of top executives, and they reduce his dependence on a single boss. The junior is judged on his ability to handle a top-level job, not just on his ability to cope with lower-level jobs. The "crown-prince" problem is minimized since the trainee performs his special assignments in the presence of higher management rather than in the presence of subordinates. The program may bring a wealth of useful suggestions to the attention of top management, as well as provide the junior men with invaluable experience.

Of the three forms of planned career development discussed, each has its own special merits. An understudy program is well designed to provide a successor for a particular manager. Rotation, despite its costs, does develop well-rounded managers. Special broadening assignments seem best adapted to fast-track executives on their way to the top executive suite.

Peaking Out

Eventually everyone reaches his peak, even the president of the company. For a high proportion of managers, this occurs by age 45. For a high proportion, too, the peak occurs at relatively low levels of management.

In some circumstances, peaking out means merely that a man stays on his present job indefinitely. In others, he moves laterally from positions typically reserved for those who are still upward bound, or he is demoted or fired. But discharge at the managerial level poses such a threat to security that it is rather rare (early retirement is much more common).

[11] Thomas L. Whisler, "Performance Appraisal and the Organization Man," *The Journal of Business*, Vol. 31, No. 1 (January 1958), p. 26.

Frequent movement is so accepted in many companies that a man may be transferred from one job to another without his knowing that he has reached his peak or even that he is actually being demoted. [12] The fact that a man has peaked is often cloaked with an ambiguity which helps the employee cushion the shock and save face.

Organizational survival depends as directly on strong middle and lower management as it does on strong top management. The manager whose career has peaked out at a relatively low level has little opportunity to make major innovations or long-range decisions and is likely to function primarily as a specialist in one aspect of the organization rather than as a generalist. Still, broadening assignments and training programs will be quite useful for him too, both to prevent obsolescence and to keep him from slowing down.

Even the man who will never be promoted can improve his performance on his present job. Often it is necessary to move such men laterally so as not to block promotional opportunities for younger, promising men. For managers whose ability is actually declining, it may be useful to "kick them upstairs" in a way which is not obviously a demotion, or to cut down discreetly on the responsibilities of their present jobs.

Particular attention must be given to men who are likely to feel passed over when promotions are made. As soon as it becomes known that there is a vacancy in higher management, great hopes are kindled at lower levels. Unless management handles the situation with great care, many people will be so disappointed when the final decision is announced that they will lose their desire to cooperate.

A boss should be able to predict which members of his group will be the most likely candidates for promotion when openings occur. And he must try to keep those unlikely to be promoted from assuming that they will soon move up the ladder. For example, a poorly qualified long-service manager may mistakenly feel that he is promotable. If his boss allows the misapprehension to continue, the employee may be sadly disappointed when someone else gets the job. And if his peers encourage him to think that he is wronged, he may create a serious problem.

Problems of this sort can be avoided if the boss makes a point of discussing with the hopeful candidate the exact nature of the responsibilities, long before the opening actually occurs. Then, if the employee is clearly not qualified for the promotion, he can be brought around to accept his unsuitability. Possibly the boss may be able to suggest a way in which the manager can supplement his background or improve his performance. If he shows himself unwilling to make the extra effort required, it becomes easier to win his acceptance of being passed over. The grounds for making promotions should be made clear, particularly to those who are apparently passed over. In the long run, an explanation of a promotion makes it easier for subordinates to accept the legitimacy of the man who is moved up.

A regular program of appraisal interviews (see Chapter 23) may help each

---

[12] Fred H. Goldner, "Demotion in Industrial Management," *American Sociological Review*, Vol. 30, No. 5 (October 1965), pp. 714-725.

employee achieve a realistic attitude toward his prospects and give him a clear indication of how he stands. Such interviews tend to counteract overoptimism and provide

ladders of escape which will insure [subordinates'] being able to accept adverse decisions and still maintain a normal self-respect . . . Also-rans are happier in their organization when they feel the race has been fairly run; when they have positive evidence of thought being given to them; and when they know that some recognizable procedure—not favoritism—has been used. [13]

There is much that a company can do to reduce the feeling that a manager is a failure merely because he has stopped advancing. If salary schedules make allowance for years of service on the job, for example, the manager who has been bypassed can still look forward to increased earnings. As mentioned, he can be given broadening assignments and training courses to help him improve his performance on his present job. And his boss can show that he values the man's opinion by asking for his suggestions on matters of importance. Indeed, the more intimately a man participates in the organization, the less importance he attaches to the formal status of his job.

DEVELOPMENT AS AN ORGANIZATIONAL RESPONSIBILITY

The emphasis in this chapter has been on formal programs that provide managers with exposure to a variety of problems. These programs differ in the level at which the exposure occurs and the degree of challenge each exposure provides. But mere exposure does not guarantee learning.

The growth of any individual in the organization depends to a large extent on the attitudes of his superiors. True, superiors can't develop subordinates; they must develop themselves. Nevertheless, superiors can provide the atmosphere in which subordinates can experiment and grow, or they can stifle any attempt at self-development. For a development program to be effective, every manager must assume personal responsibility (1) for helping his immediate subordinates develop, and (2) for insisting that these subordinates in turn contribute to the development of those under him.

Thus we ask: What importance does management place on development? Are managers ever rewarded for doing an outstanding job of training subordinates? Or do the chief rewards always go to the manager who keeps immediate costs low and gets production out?[14] Does the reward system encourage the manager to think that developing subordinates is a waste of time?

One unpublished study made within a gigantic corporation indicated that those who had reached the highest positions were not remembered by anyone in the company as having done anything significant in developing men, while those who had achieved the reputation of being wise and effective counselors invariably reached only modest levels. [15]

[13] Virgil K. Rowland, "They Also Ran . . . ," *Executive Selection, Development and Inventory,* Personnel Series, No. 171 (New York: American Management Association, 1957), pp. 55 and 58.

[14] "Managerial compensation plans that reward managers for converting valuable human resources for a fraction of their actual value represent poor financial management." Rensis Likert, *The Human Organization* (New York: McGraw-Hill, 1967), p. 114.

[15] Whisler, *op. cit.,* p. 22.

Often managers learn that their only reward for training a subordinate is to have him leave and be replaced by someone with less experience. Knowing that a good subordinate is hard to find, the manager is tempted to recommend his poorer subordinates for special training programs in order to get rid of them. Too often, units that do a good job of training find themselves raided by other units.

The most effective development occurs in an atmosphere where management permits self-development. "Is management willing to take a chance on its men, greeting an occasional failure as the price of taking risks?" [16] Does the manager feel free to make suggestions? Is he encouraged to contribute his ideas? How much responsibility does he have? Does he take part in making management decisions? Does the manager feel that he has to cover up when he makes mistakes, or can he talk his problems over with his boss without fear of being blamed?

CONCLUSION

The strength of any organization depends largely on its management. If the organization is to remain strong, it must give to the development of human assets the same priority it gives to the development of physical assets.

Development is a matter of demand and supply. It is important to predict future needs for management manpower and to establish programs designed to supply competent men to fill vacancies as they occur. However, since it is impossible to look to the future with certainty, any development program must be flexible. Clearly it is desirable to have an orderly system that gives everyone an equal opportunity (dependent on real ability) for training, experience, and consideration for promotion. But an over-rigid rotation or promotional system can put the company into a straitjacket.

Organizations are learning that human resources are wasted if everyone is treated the same way, but promotional opportunities must be available to all, including rank-and-file workers and supervisors who have not graduated from college. However, the twenty-year period—between the time a potential top manager leaves college and the time the decision is made on whether he will be a top manager—is just too short to permit every manager to start at the very bottom and work his way, step by step, to the top. Talented men demand tough challenges, and they prosper best when they have it. All of which emphasizes the importance of a custom-made program of development for each manager, preferably one that is designed with his help.

Management development requires more than formal programs and individual effort. Top management support of such programs and an exciting, challenging organizational climate are both necessary to foster self-development. As we shall discuss in the next two chapters, performance appraisal, management training, and organizational development programs all can contribute to individual development.

[16] Robert K. Stolz, "Getting Back to Fundamentals in Executive Development," *Personnel*, Vol. 30, No. 6 (May 1954), p. 456.

The Bemus Company was founded in the basement of its president, Andrew Bemus, about ten years ago. Mr. Bemus had developed a highly sensitive instrument which immediately found use both in defense and civilian production fields. As a consequence, the firm grew very rapidly. It had seven employees nine years ago, 200 employees five years ago, and over a thousand today.

As of today, most of the company's top management consists of Mr. Bemus' earliest associates, many of whom are under the age of 45. They are a highly self-confident group who have worked together closely over the years.

And yet trouble seems to lie ahead. Sharp competition from other companies has developed for the first time and profit margins have fallen. Labor costs are obviously too high and there is much confusion and divided responsibility in management. Most decisions are made by the top-management group and there is little delegation of authority. Many of the more recently hired engineers complain that their ideas are given very little consideration by the inner clique—and that there is little or no chance for promotion since all the top jobs are handled by younger men. As a consequence, three of the more brilliant recent hirees have resigned after spending only a short time with the company.

1. What sort of management development program does this company need?
2. Assuming that you were recently hired from the outside as personnel director, what steps would you take to win acceptance for this program?

23 PERFORMANCE APPRAISAL

In the typical large company every manager is subject to a periodic appraisal of his performance. As with other aspects of management development, the primary purpose of these appraisals has shifted in recent years. Originally a device to provide guidance to management in selecting managers for promotions or salary increases, they are now also used as a coaching device to help men on all levels of management to improve their performance.

An effective performance-appraisal program provides management with a rational basis for determining who should be promoted or receive salary increases. It permits each man to be considered on the same basis as everyone else. Thus, hopefully, fewer charges of favoritism are made and better men are selected for promotion. Long-range personnel planning is also facilitated, since it becomes easier to determine who should be promoted now, who should be ready after further experience and training, and who, while satisfactory on his present job, is not a likely prospect for a more difficult one. Further, transfers can be more easily custom-tailored to meet the needs of individuals, while managers who need special training can be identified. Finally, appraisals are useful in helping a company to make an evaluation of the over-all effectiveness of its program for management development and selection.

Performance-appraisal techniques can be used for more than just pinpointing those who should be promoted, receive pay increases, or obtain special attention. They can also be used as a springboard for coaching and for helping individuals set goals for their own development. Unfortunately, the procedures which are most useful for selection purposes are less useful for self-development. As a consequence, many companies have abandoned their *traditional* proce-dures, which often emphasized the rating of an employee's personality traits by his boss, for newer, hopefully less biased methods. And some companies have abandoned ratings as such for *results-oriented* evaluation procedures, which frequently involve the setting of goals by superiors and subordinates working together.

We shall look first at traditional procedures and then at various newer ones. Before doing this, let us point out that performance appraisal is often conducted at the hourly-paid level as well as at the management level; in the former case it is often called "merit rating" (see pp. 575–78). Although we shall emphasize management appraisals in our discussion, most of what we say applies to merit rating as well.

TRADITIONAL PERFORMANCE RATING

Stripped to its essentials, traditional performance rating is a matter of thoughtfully filling out a rating form (see illustration on p. 510). Normally the form is completed by the immediate supervisor of the man being rated, then checked by the supervisor's boss. Sometimes the rating is made by a committee consisting of the direct supervisor, the supervisor's boss, and one or two others who are in a position to judge the man who is being rated. Committee ratings have one great advantage: By bringing several viewpoints to bear on the rating, they offset the immediate supervisor's special bias.

Rating Scales

A conventional rating form of the check-the-box type is sometimes called a "graphic rating" or a "rating scale." The important part here is the over-all summary rating or score, which makes it possible to compare large numbers of managers. The ratings on specific factors do serve a purpose, however, in helping to pin-point areas in which a subordinate needs further development.

In one variety of rating scale, the over-all score is determined by adding up the scores given to specific factors (as in the upper portion of the form illus-trated). In spite of its deceptive simplicity, this approach has severe limitations. Note, for example, some of the basic assumptions lying behind it: One is that each of the factors (cost control, judgment, and so forth) is of *equal* importance and that this holds true on all jobs. Yet clearly, on some jobs creativity is more important than effectiveness in dealing with people, and on others just the reverse is true. Another assumption is that these qualities are "additive"—for instance, strength in job knowledge will offset lack of leadership.

Unwilling to accept these assumptions, some companies permit their manag-ers to give their subordinates an over-all rating directly, without the necessity of adding up separate factor scores. This summary rating of over-all ability may be given either in numerical terms, from one to one hundred, or in descriptive terms, from "unsatisfactory" to "outstanding."

Name _Wilson Olcott_   Position _Asst. Director Marketing Research_   Date rated _6/25/71_

Date hired _Apr. 12, 1960_   On position since _Aug 8, 1967_

	Unsatisfactory	Fair	Good	Very Good	Exceptional	
Job knowledge: Extent of theoretical knowledge and practical know-how as related to present job.	1	2	3	4	(5)	5
Judgment: Ability to obtain and analyze facts and apply sound judgment.	1	2	3	(4)	5	4
Organizing ability: Effectiveness in planning own work and that of subordinates.	1	2	(3)	4	5	3
Attitude: Enthusiasm shown for job; loyalty to company and superiors; ability to accept criticism and changes in company policy.	1	2	(3)	4	5	3
Dependability: Reliability in carrying out assignments conscientiously and with effectiveness.	1	2	3	(4)	5	4
Creativity: Ability to apply imagination to job, to develop new plans, cut costs, etc.	1	2	3	4	(5)	5
Dealing with people: Ability to get along with others; tact, diplomacy; ability to command and influence people.	1	(2)	3	4	5	2
Delegation: Ability to assign work to others and coordinate others through distribution of workload and responsibility.	1	2	(3)	4	5	3
Leadership: Ability to stimulate subordinates to perform their jobs effectively.	1	(2)	3	4	5	2
Personal efficiency: Speed and effectiveness in carrying out duties not assigned to subordinates.	1	2	3	(4)	5	4

Total points _35_

In order of importance, state three performance characteristics which need improvement with respect to his present condition.

1. _Emotional stability_
2. _Dealings with subordinates_
3. _Cost control_

What might he do to improve his job performance? _Try harder to get along with other people. Don't blow his stack all the time. Be more practical._

Are there any factors in the health, personal life or other outside influences which may have affected his performance during this appraisal period? _Divorced wife last month_

Comments _A very able researcher who finds it hard to get out of the clouds. His subordinates respect his ability though many are irritated by his moodiness. Possibly he may settle down when he solves his family problems._

Evaluated by: _Burt Renfare_
Title: _Director Marketing Research_
Approved by: _Gerry Falconer_
Title: _Marketing Manager_

Unsatisfactory: 10-16 points
Fair: 16-25 points
Good: 26-35 points
Very good: 35-44 points
Excellent: 45-50 points

**CONVENTIONAL
RATING FORM**

Both forms of rating are often supplemented by open-ended, essay-type questions. At times the essay portion of the evaluation form takes considerably more space than does the quantitative portion. These subjective, qualitative evaluations tend to give a fuller picture than is presented by numerical ratings alone.[1] They are also more useful for coaching, but they are of little help in comparing large numbers of people for purposes of pay increases or promotion.

Human Errors in Rating

Both forms of numerical rating are subject to certain human evaluative errors. (Incidentally, these same errors distort merit rating and job evaluation, to which we will return in Chapter 25.)

Clarity in standards. Unless all raters agree on what terms such as "good" or "excellent" mean, their final ratings simply cannot be compared. To cite an extreme example, the rating scale in one hospital included Excellent, Very Good, Fair, Satisfactory, and Unsatisfactory. Several head nurses objected to using the term "satisfactory" on the grounds that "no nurse is ever really satisfactory." To them "satisfactory" meant "better than excellent."

Insufficient evidence. The boss frequently gets but a limited and often distorted view of his subordinate's performance. Particularly where actual results are difficult to measure, the subordinate's ability to get along with his boss may have a greater impact on his rating than does his performance on the job. "The manager who communicates his own ideas clearly and forcefully, whose analytical skills impress the boss is likely to be highly recommended even though he may create a very poor climate within his own work group."[2]

Differing perceptions. People differ in their standards of judgment. Even where there is no conscious prejudice, unconscious factors may bias a superior's evaluation of his subordinates. Even the fairest of people find it difficult to be impartial when judging the actions of individuals who differ greatly from themselves in terms of background, values, and style of behavior. More than obvious factors, such as racial discrimination, are involved here. The man who is accustomed to making quick decisions may be antagonized by the man who moves ponderously and deliberately—and vice versa. And "appraisal also requires that we ask people who are perhaps not themselves good managers to rate the managerial competence of others who may have more managerial competence than their bosses."[3]

[1] But a real problem arises because bosses with writing skills are able to get bigger promotions and salary increases for their subordinates than are bosses who write less persuasively.

[2] Herbert Meyer, in Renato Taguiri and George H. Litwin, eds., *Organizational Climate* (Boston: Harvard School of Business Administration, 1969), p. 164.

[3] George S. Odiorne, *Personnel Policy: Issues and Practices* (Columbus, Ohio: Merrill, 1963), p. 310. A number of recent studies indicate that a boss's attitude toward performance appraisal procedures and his ability to make effective use of them are closely related to his over-all competence as a manager.

Excessive leniency or strictness. As every student knows, there is a big difference between hard and easy graders. Supervisors in industry often hesitate to give low ratings for fear of antagonizing their subordinates and making them less cooperative.[4] Furthermore, the supervisor may be afraid that low ratings will reflect on his own ability. There is always a chance that his boss will say, "If your subordinate is as bad as all this, why don't you do something about it?" Some executives regularly rate new employees very low, then gradually raise them—thus making the employee feel good and displaying to their superiors their excellence as trainers.

In many organizations there is a tendency for average ratings to rise over time. Thus, during World War II practically every enlisted man got the highest rating. To get the next-to-highest rating was evidence of downright incompetence.

The halo effect. There is a natural tendency (sometimes called the "blending tendency") for the rater to be influenced in rating one factor by the kind of rating he gives on another. In fact, the individual rater tends to give each man approximately the same rating on all factors. If a supervisor has a general feeling that a man is good, he will rate him high on all factors—and vice versa.[5] Or his rating on the first factor listed or on the factor he thinks most important may "contaminate" his ratings on all others.

Influence of a man's job. Performance rating is designed to evaluate how well a man does on a particular job. Although in theory it is vastly different from job evaluation (which rates the job, not the man), in practice there is a common tendency to give a man on a higher-paid job a higher rating just because of his position.

All these human errors in rating can be at least partially counteracted by insuring that the managers who do the rating are properly trained.

Traits or Performance?

A more fundamental criticism of the traditional rating scale is that excessive emphasis is placed on personality traits as opposed to measurable objective performance. Management development was originally introduced into many companies as a crash program designed to reveal executives who were promotable to top positions. Actual performance on the job was often considered secondary, in part because the emphasis was all on *potential* for development.

In any event, many organizations ask raters to evaluate subordinates on

[4] One study showed that supervisors in a government department gave much higher ratings if they expected to have to show them to the men they had rated than if they expected the ratings to remain confidential. Fred Massarik, Irving R. Weschler, and Robert Tannenbaum, "Evaluating Efficiency Rating Systems through Experiment," *Personnel Administration,* Vol. 14, No. 1 (January 1951), pp. 42-47.

[5] The supervisor can reduce this halo effect by rating all his men on a single item before going on to the next, rather than rating one man at a time.

factors such as optimism, drive, and ability to learn. Among the armed forces, for instance, ratings are required of qualities such as "initiative," "force," "moral courage," and "loyalty." [6]

What has proved wrong with this emphasis on traits? In the first place, the ratings secured are of little use in helping an employee do a better job. For instance, it is hard for a man to make a real change in his "personality," though he might put up a false front and pretend to be, in the words of one typical form, "radiant, confident, cheerful, courteous."

In trait-rating, standards are often unclear. Although there may be considerable agreement among managers about what constitutes acceptable standards of output in a given department, degrees of "loyalty" and "moral courage" are particularly subject to personal bias.

Trait-rating shares with some forms of personality testing the assumption that there is one psychological configuration that makes the best executive. Yet jobs do differ in their psychological requirements: Sales managers, for example, may require more aggressiveness than do laboratory managers. And even where jobs are alike, people with vastly different personalities may perform equally well.

More important, an emphasis on traits gives the advantage to the conformist, "the individual who has nothing wrong with him. More particularly, [the] emphasis on human relations favors the individual who always gets along with other people and never rubs anybody the wrong way." [7] A large chemical company, for example, offers the following choices for the single trait "cooperation": [8]

1. Concedes nothing. Obstructive, antagonistic.
2. Poor mixer. Tries to run with the ball. Occasionally indulges in obstructive argument.
3. Generally adapts self to person and situations. Responsive to leadership and reasonably tactful.
4. Willing and eager to please. Works in complete harmony with group. Adaptable and courteous.
5. Adapts self very well without sacrificing standards. Goes out of his way to promote common end.

Note that by favoring the man who is "willing and eager to please" over the one who "tries to run with the ball," this company is in effect molding its own character. It is giving first priority to good human relations as opposed to decisive decision-making. [9] Yet those at the very top often are 100 per cent rugged individualists. How many of the great tycoons of industry have been "radiant, confident, poised, courteous"? "Henry Ford, Sr., got along pretty well

---

[6] Harold L. Jones, James L. Keating, and George Postich, "Officer Appraisal in the Armed Forces," *United States Naval Institute Proceedings*, Vol. 91, No. 4 (April 1965), p. 80.

[7] Robert K. Stoltz, "Is Executive Development Coming of Age?" *The Journal of Business*, Vol. 28, No. 1 (January 1955), p. 50.

[8] Ernest Dale and Alice Smith, "Now Report Cards for Bosses," *New York Times Magazine* (March 31, 1958), p. 56.

[9] This is not so much the fault of rating traits as of the frequent emphasis on the wrong traits. A company could just as easily use trait-rating to pick nonconformists. See Stanley Stark, "Executive Personality and Psychological Testing," *Current Economic Comment*, Vol. 20, No. 2 (May 1958), pp. 15–32.

without too much sense of humor. And Abraham Lincoln would never have been given a passing mark if his contemporaries had thought to grade him." [10] As Stoltz puts it, "realistically speaking, most executives are curious combinations of strengths and weaknesses." [11]

NEWER RATING METHODS

As a consequence of these criticisms of traditional rating scales, personnel researchers have tried to develop new rating procedures that are less affected by raters' personal biases and less concerned with imponderables such as traits. Among the best known of these new forms of rating are *forced distribution, forced choice,* and the *critical incident* technique.

Forced distribution. This method is familiar to many students as the old principle of "grading on the curve." The manager who uses this system of rating is expected to rank subordinates by class, instead of ascribing a set of rating points to each individual. In a typical system the top 10 per cent of the men are placed in the highest class, 20 per cent in the next, 40 per cent in the middle bracket, 20 per cent in the next-to-lowest, and 10 per cent in the very bottom class. Ordinarily, only one over-all rating of ability is given, rather than a series of ratings on separate factors.

This system obviously eliminates any danger that the manager will be over-lenient or the possibility that the standards will be interpreted in different ways by different managers. Moreover, the system is easy to explain and administer. Yet this scheme has distinct drawbacks: In effect, it assumes that all groups have the same proportion of average, poor, and outstanding men. But this is not likely to be true, particularly where there are only a few men on a given job.

Forced choice. This radically different approach was developed at the end of World War II for use in rating army officers. Its purpose is to reduce human bias by setting up a system in which the rater is presented with four possible statements about a person, such as:

	MOST	LEAST
Doesn't try to pull rank	_____	_____
Knows his men, their capabilities and limitations	_____	_____
Low efficiency	_____	_____
Uses a steady monotone in his voice	_____	_____

The rater is expected to check two items, one of which is the *most* and the other the *least* characteristic of the person being rated. Two of these are apparently favorable and two apparently unfavorable. However, only one of the favorable items gives a plus credit; the other, if checked, gives no credit at all. Similarly, only one of the two negative items affects the final result. The zero-credit items (in this case, possibly, "Doesn't try to pull rank" and "Uses a steady monotone") are ones that have been shown by tests to have significantly less

[10] Dale and Smith, *op. cit.*, p. 58.
[11] Stoltz, *op. cit.*, p. 51.

correlation with efficiency than the two that give a score. The important thing is that the rater doesn't know which items are the ones that count. His own prejudices and biases are minimized, since his only function is to give an objective description of the subordinate's performance by checking the blanks.

Following the war, the forced-choice technique was adopted by many industrial firms. It has the advantage of reducing such forms of bias as leniency and the halo effect; no training is required to prepare a supervisor to use it; and there is some evidence that it does a better job of pin-pointing the best men than do simpler forms of rating—that is, it correlates more highly with ratings by fellow employees and with objective factors such as productivity.

Though from many points of view forced choice seems clearly the best system of rating, its use has not spread widely. In the first place the system is expensive to install, for the items must be custom-tailored to the demands of the particular job and company. (Suppose a set of four items contained these two favorable items: "Has a constant flow of new ideas" and "Shows careful judgment." The first choice might represent a good mark for an advertising executive and the second one for a banker.)

Forced choice is often resented by both raters and ratees. The implicit assumption behind the system is that supervisors cannot be trusted to rate fairly, an assumption that naturally prejudices them against its use. A department manager summarized the common attitude: "I try to reward my good men by giving them good ratings—but you just have to guess what those psychology boys [who set up the items] want. No one understands how it works. Some of the men call it promotion by Ouija Board." (Actually there is some evidence that raters can figure out which items count, and so give the kinds of ratings they want.) A final objection is that forced choice makes it difficult or impossible to use ratings for the purpose of counseling employees.

Critical incidents. The critical-incident technique of rating is also known as the "critical requirement system" and the "performance-record program."

The first step is to draw up for each job a list of *critical job requirements.* For a foreman, for instance, these requirements might include "improving equipment," "getting along with staff," "meeting schedules," and so forth. Typical job requirements for a sales manager might be "developing new customers" and "avoiding losses."

Once the critical job requirements have been determined, the next step is to train managers to be on the lookout for *critical incidents* or outstanding examples of success or failure on the part of the subordinate in meeting the requirements. The manager lists the incidents as he observes them and gradually builds up a record for each subordinate, with the "debits" on one side and the "credits" on the other:

Dealing with Unions

9/21 Failed to consult with steward before making transfer.	8/6 Persuaded steward to withdraw grievance in regard to employee discharged for excessive absenteeism.
11/7 Made transfer in violation of sect. 39 (c) of contract.	12/3 Gave excellent answer to union grievance.

Normally, no attempt is made to balance the "debits" and the "credits." And yet the critical-incident method does provide the raw materials for other forms of appraisal.

The great advantage of this approach is that all ratings are based on objective evidence rather than on a subjective evaluation of traits. It is no longer enough for the boss to say, "Joe has trouble in dealing with people." The boss must cite specific incidents to prove his contention. To insure objectivity, the manager is requested to record each incident immediately instead of trying to think back over, say, the last six months before making a rating.

On the other hand, care must be taken to insure that the manager's record-keeping does not degenerate into supervision in detail. He should emphasize *what* is accomplished, not *how* it is accomplished. Further, keeping a "little black book" in which all mistakes are recorded conflicts with the philosophy that management should not overemphasize blame-finding.

THE EVALUATION INTERVIEW

Many companies now require each manager to sit down periodically with each of his subordinates to discuss his performance with him. The evaluation report is ordinarily used as a springboard for the discussion. Evaluation interviews serve two purposes: (1) They enable the evaluation to serve as a form of feedback, which helps the individual know his progress and where he stands in the eyes of his boss, and (2) they provide an opportunity for the manager to counsel the subordinate on how to improve his performance.

In some companies the subordinates are never told how they have been rated; they don't know where they stand, which may be bad for morale. In other organizations, however, management feels that it is only fair to inform men of the results of ratings. As one junior executive commented, "Before this evaluation system was installed, the only time the boss would tell you how you were doing was when you were really in trouble. If he'd say 'I'd like to talk to you about your future' that meant you were really going to get chewed out."

Yet too often managers recoil at the thought of having to tell another man how he stands or what he needs to do to improve himself. "They fool themselves into believing that the subordinate knows all this from day-to-day contacts on the job, and they are often shocked to hear that 'the boss never told me how I was doing.'" [12] Actually, the evaluation interview may reduce misunderstanding between manager and subordinate.

Evaluation interviews are not easy. Poorly handled they may lead to hostility and greater misunderstanding. Consequently, many companies have spent a great deal of time and effort on training their managers to handle evaluation interviews, giving particular emphasis to skill in the use of nondirective techniques. To ensure that no essential part of the interview is left out, managers are often encouraged to follow a standardized outline. For example:

[12] Paul Pigors and Charles A. Myers, *Personnel Administration,* 3rd ed. (New York: McGraw-Hill, 1956), p. 124.

1. The superior tells the subordinate the purpose of the interview, and that it is designed to help him do a better job.

2. The superior then presents the evaluation, giving the strong points first and then the weak points. (There is no reason why the superior has to show the entire evaluation to the subordinate, nor, as we shall mention later, does he have to be 100 per cent frank about the subordinate's prospects.)

3. Next the superior asks for general comments on the evaluation. He anticipates that the subordinate may show some hostility to negative evaluations and allows him to blow off steam.

4. The superior then tries to encourage the subordinate to give his own picture of his progress, the problems he is meeting, and how these can be solved.

5. The interview ends with a discussion of what the subordinate can do by himself to overcome his weak points and what the superior can do to help. The superior tries to accept any criticism or aggression on the part of the subordinate without argument or contradiction. He helps the subordinate save face and does not expose his unjustified alibis.

Some managers start the interview by asking the subordinate, "Tell me, how do *you* think you are doing?" Then they show the subordinate the evaluation. This approach has the advantage of letting the subordinate tell his side of the story first; it is often easier for a man to criticize himself than to accept criticism from others. Were it not for the fact that the subordinate knows that he is about to receive an evaluation from his boss, this would be an excellent form of training. Under the circumstances, however, the subordinate may look upon this as a cat-and-mouse affair and wonder what the boss wants him to say and how much it is safe to reveal.

Difficulties in Conducting Evaluation Interviews

In recent years many companies have become discouraged with the type of evaluation program just described. The rating period often turns out to be a time of apprehension and discomfort for managers and subordinates alike. True, most managers endorse performance appraisal as a matter of principle: They believe that people should know where they stand.

In actual practice, however, it is the extremely rare operating manager who will employ such a program on his own initiative. Personnel specialists report that most managers carry out performance appraisal interviews only when strong control procedures are established to ensure that they do. [13]

[13] Herbert H. Meyer, Emanuel Kay, and John R. P. French, Jr., "Split Roles in Performance Appraisal," *Harvard Business Review*, Vol. 23, No. 1 (January 1965), p. 123. For a somewhat different view, see Harold Mayfield, "In Defense of Performance Appraisal," *Harvard Business Review*, Vol. 38, No. 2 (March 1960), pp. 81–87.

Many managers just go through the motions of conducting interviews and some "forget" about them altogether. It is not uncommon for managers to hand subordinates their rating without comment, or to explain the rating in a rather embarrassed fashion without giving the subordinate a chance to comment or reply.

Why are managers generally so unenthusiastic about the evaluation program? Many have little skill in interviewing procedure; others, feeling that their primary function is "to get production out," have very little interest in taking time from their "main job" to develop subordinates. As one executive put it, "This is personnel's idea, personnel ought to carry the ball. I think it's a bunch of nonsense."

Yet even managers who are sympathetic to the principles of management development feel uncomfortable when they have to criticize subordinates. As one manager said, "I dread the time when I have to give ratings. Nobody appreciates them and I get into an endless series of arguments which make it just that much tougher to get the work out." This reluctance is particularly evident when the rating plan requires the manager to discuss the subordinate's personality traits. It is reflected by the tendency to avoid, if possible, giving anyone a low rating. Douglas McGregor concludes: [14]

The conventional approach, unless handled with consummate skill and delicacy, constitutes something dangerously close to a violation of the integrity of the personality. Managers are uncomfortable when they are placed in the position of "playing God." The respect we hold for the inherent value of the individual leaves us distressed when we must take responsibility for judging the personal worth of a fellow man. Yet the conventional approach to appraisal forces us, not only to make such judgments and to see them acted upon, but also to communicate them to those we have judged. No wonder we resist.

Subordinates also tend to react to performance evaluation with defensiveness, suspicion, and hostility. They hope that the boss will recognize their merits, but fear that he will criticize them unfairly. Since many are primarily concerned with defending themselves, they resist the boss's criticisms and suggestions. Subordinates in this state of mind are hardly in a mood to "learn" from the interview. In fact, evidence suggests that subordinates tend to rate their own performance higher than do their bosses; as a consequence the interview turns out to be a deflating experience. [15] Criticism may result in lower performance not higher, particularly in the areas most criticized. [16]

Thus, the interview may seriously impair the supervisor-subordinate relationship by creating animosity and misunderstanding. To prevent ill-feeling many managers avoid unpleasant truths. And "evaluation often becomes a ritual devoid of real meaning. Executives report that they never know what their bosses want

[14] "An Uneasy Look at Performance Appraisal," *Harvard Business Review*, Vol. 35, No. 3 (May 1957), p. 90.

[15] Meyer, Kay, and French, *op. cit.*, p. 126; James W. Parker and others, "Rating Scale Content: III. Relationship Between Supervisory and Self-Ratings," *Personnel Psychology*, Vol. 12, No. 1 (Spring 1959), pp. 49-63.

[16] Meyer, Kay, and French, *op. cit.*, p. 126.

them to do,"[17] where they really stand or what is required of them to get a promotion or salary increase.

Another explanation for the widespread resistance to conventional forms of evaluation interviews lies in certain assumptions that lie behind them: (1) People want to be told where they stand, and (2) if they are told, they can change for the better. Neither assumption is universally valid. Let us look at two examples:

A liberal-arts college decided to rate all faculty members on a scale from 1 (drop from faculty) to 5 (deserves immediate promotion) and to reveal the results to each faculty member. The rating program was conducted by a joint faculty-student committee. A 65-year-old professor was given a 2 grade on the grounds that his teaching lacked luster and he was hard to understand. Thus, the professor's grade for a lifetime of devoted service to his college was a D! He was too old to change his ways, and in any event the college had no intention of dropping him a few years before his retirement. Some people don't really want to know where they stand, nor will the knowledge help them.

The second case involves a laboratory division head who was brilliant technically, but suffered from shyness and insecurity in dealing with people. Would telling him of his failing improve his dealings with people? Of course not. Certainly it would not help him gain self-confidence. The only thing that might help him would be a form of psychotherapy much deeper than his superior could offer.

Obviously there is no simple answer to the question of whether an evaluation interview will be useful or what sort of interview should be used in a given situation. The choice depends directly on the personality of both the superior and the subordinate. Moreover, the manager should use the form of interview that he finds most comfortable. For instance, the supervisor who tries to use the nondirective interview with no understanding of the approach will simply give the subordinate the impression that he is two-faced, particularly if the nondirective approach is totally inconsistent with his normal pattern of supervision. In any event, the manager should recognize that the objectives of the interview vary from one person to another. For example:

1. Where the fault is difficult or impossible to correct, as in the two cases described above, there is no point in discussing it at all (unless the subordinate demands to know why he hasn't been promoted).

2. If a man has faults that are correctable, it may be better to let him bring them up himself when he sees fit. Since evaluation interviews are held periodically, there is no need for the supervisor to be disappointed if the subordinate doesn't give a perfect self-analysis during the first session. The important thing is that the subordinate make gradual progress in correcting his limitations where he can, and in accepting his limitations where he cannot overcome them.

[17] William R. Dill, Thomas L. Hilton, and Walter R. Reitman, "How Aspiring Executives Promote Their Careers," *California Management Review*, Vol. 2, No. 4 (Summer 1960), p. 12. This point can be exaggerated, however. The evidence suggests that some appraisal is better than no appraisal. Where managers engage in regular appraisal interviews with their subordinates, the subordinates report they know better where they stand and superior-subordinate relations are significantly better. Walter R. Mahler, "Improving Coaching Skills," *Personnel Administration*, Vol. 27, No. 1 (January 1964), p. 28; and Kenneth E. Richards, "Performance Rating as a Supervisory Tool," *The Personnel Administrator* (January 1965), p. 7.

3. In some cases an individual's performance may be so poor as to raise the possibility of his being discharged. Under such circumstances it is only fair that he be given warning, even though there is little chance of changing his behavior.

The appraisal interview is actually a form of coaching. So why formalize the process? After all the good manager recognizes that coaching should occur more frequently than once every six months; he holds the equivalent of an evaluation interview whenever he thinks a subordinate will profit from it. On the other hand, the poor manager will probably only go through the motions of a proper evaluation interview (which may do more harm than good) or perhaps ignore it altogether.

Thus, a company-wide policy requiring periodic evaluation interviews is most useful for the *average* supervisor, for it forces him to take time off from his duties, to think through how each of his subordinates has been progressing, and then to sit down with each man to talk over their long-range relationships.

Still, one fundamental objection remains: The conventional appraisal interview demands that the supervisor be a part-time psychiatrist. As the management development chief at Standard Oil of Ohio once asked: "Are we in the business of changing people or are we running a business? Are we interested in personalities or are we interested in on-the-job results?"[18]

MANAGEMENT BY OBJECTIVES

Designed to overcome the limitations of more traditional systems, results-oriented appraisals (also known as Management by Objectives or MBO) have been widely adopted by a number of companies. This new approach to appraisal is based on quantitative, measurable (or at least concrete) performance goals that are often set jointly by superior and subordinates. Instead of requiring the superior to rate his subordinates, under this approach each subordinate is requested to establish, for himself, short-term performance goals or targets, ways in which he can improve his own efficiency and that of his department;[19] for example, cut idle machine time by 5 per cent, reduce scrap by 3 per cent, or install a new production line by January 30. Together the superior and the subordinate talk over what is required to meet these goals and to adjust them to make them consistent with goals of other subordinates and of the organization as a whole. At the end of a set period (say six months) they meet again to evaluate how well these goals have been met, to discuss what could be done better, and to set goals for the next period. Instead of having the superior write a detailed

---

[18] O. A. Ohmann, "Executive Appraisal and Counseling," *Michigan Business Review*, Vol. 9, No. 6 (November 1957), p. 21.

[19] In addition to performance objectives, the subordinate may set personal development objectives, which will help him meet his performance objectives (and perhaps prepare him for promotion). Such a personal development objective for a design engineer might be to spend more time with the marketing staff, so that his product design might better anticipate changes in customer preferences—or to attend a leadership program to improve his relations with subordinates.

evaluation of the subordinate, the subordinate writes his own "accomplishment" report.

This procedure gives the subordinate an opportunity to make his own evaluation of the operation results. When he is discussing results he is actually appraising himself and probably gaining some insight on how he might improve his own attitudes, methods, or behavior. [20]

Of course, there is always the possibility that the subordinate may set his targets too low or rate himself too highly. However, "most subordinates normally have an understandable wish to please their bosses and quite willingly adjust their targets or appraisals if the superior thinks they are unrealistic." [21]

In effect, with MBO, the subordinate evaluates himself against standards that he has set himself. If handled correctly, the atmosphere becomes less punitive and anxiety-provoking than it is with conventional appraisals. At its best, the MBO process is a two-way street. Not only the subordinate's performance is reviewed, but also the relationship between the subordinate and the superior. For example, the superior can ask the subordinate what he, as the superior, can do, refrain from doing, or do differently to help the subordinate do an even better job. This approach gives a better balance to the interview, since each party is evaluating the other and there is clear recognition that the subordinate's efficiency is greatly affected by what the superior does. Also, it gives the subordinate a chance to bring up problems that he might otherwise have kept to himself.

Successful MBO requires more than setting individual goals. Individual goals should be consistent with each other and with the over-all goals of the work group and the organization as a whole. It would make little sense for the sales department to try to raise sales by 10 per cent by introducing a new product in June, when the goals of the product development and manufacturing departments didn't call for this product to be available before October. To help resolve these problems of coordination, the practice in some companies is for managers who have overlapping and conflicting responsibilities to set joint goals. Joint goal-setting is still not enough, however. An effective MBO program requires that managers anticipate snags and barriers and that they work out an "action plan" which shows in detail how mutual problems can be solved. Goals set by MBO must be made consistent with organizational budgets and long-range plans. Properly used, an MBO program helps to set the direction for individual managers and the organization as a whole; but to do this requires intensive participation on the part of managers at all organizational levels, from top to bottom.

Advantages

The advantages of MBO over conventional appraisal are many. MBO creates for each man a standard of evaluation based on the special characteris-

---

[20] Ohmann, *op. cit.*, p. 24.
[21] McGregor, *op. cit.*, p. 91.

tics of his particular job. He knows the standards on which he will be judged. MBO emphasizes the *future*, which can be changed, rather than the *past*, which cannot. The emphasis on forward planning helps clarify responsibilities, organize the job, and iron out problems in advance. The job of the superior shifts from that of criticizing the subordinate to that of helping improve his record. He becomes less a judge and more a coach.

MBO is consistent with the psychological principle that people work better when they have definite goals to meet in specified periods. By providing feedback, it helps subordinates discover where they stand and thus enhances learning. By allowing subordinates to set their own goals, it facilitates internalized motivation.

The emphasis on specific performance, rather than character traits, permits recognition for the nonconformist who obtains results by nonconventional means. In contrast to the "closed system" implied by traditional ratings according to which the subordinate is rated in terms of the supervisor's value system, MBO permits the subordinate to participate in setting his own goals. It gives him a more active role, increases his sense of control over his environment, and reduces his dependence on his boss. Applied throughout the organization, MBO becomes more than a method of appraisal: it becomes a style of management, emphasizing forward planning rather than the aimless fighting of fires. It facilitates interdepartmental communications and coordination. It promotes delegation and decentralization. Anticipating our next chapter, we may say that since MBO forces managers to think about improving interpersonal effectiveness, it is a program of organizational development.

Limitations

Despite the initial enthusiasm with which this new approach was greeted by a number of companies, experience suggests that MBO has a number of limitations and drawbacks.

In the first place the theory that the subordinate sets goals by himself (or jointly with his boss) may in practice turn out to be illusory. It all depends on whether the nondirective approach, which is required for goal-setting by the subordinate, is consistent with the boss's ordinary management style. The boss who regularly consults with his subordinates finds this new approach to appraisal quite easy. Not so the boss who is decisive and directive and never takes the time to listen. Under such circumstances MBO may be merely another form of "be strong"; even so, the subordinate may feel more secure because he knows what is required of him.

In any case, knowing that his boss is the one who hands out rewards, the typical subordinate may look anxiously for some indication of what the boss thinks are proper goals. Once these become clear, he will quickly adopt them with "enthusiasm." Indeed, some subordinates might prefer that their boss indicate his wishes frankly from the start, instead of make them go through guessing games. Further, with organization-wide goal-setting, the individual's freedom to set his goal is sharply reduced. If top management sets a goal to increase production by 15 per cent, a foreman can only suggest means of reaching that goal.

MBO places heavy stress on performance, and this may lead to all the problems that we previously discussed under "statistical controls" (see pp. 300–306). It leads subordinates to emphasize the *measurable*, such as production, at the expense of the unmeasurable, such as morale. For example, creative work, such as in engineering, personnel, or advertising, is often difficult to quantify, as is indeed most staff work. Because of this difficulty, quality may be sacrificed for sheer quantity; trivial items may assume undue importance just because they can be counted.

An engineering director set as a goal the enhancement of his laboratory's professional prestige, but since prestige is difficult to measure, he set as a performance target a certain number of papers to be read at professional meetings. And to fill this quota he "encouraged" individual subordinates to accept the writing of papers as goals for themselves. The result, as might be expected, was that the required number of papers were read, but they were of such poor quality as to lower rather than raise the laboratory's prestige. (The story might have been less unfortunate, however, if the director's subordinates had felt really free to reject their assignments.)

Overemphasis on measurable factors may also encourage the covering up of poor performance, actual falsification of data, or the setting of low goals. Since each person is anxious to make himself look good, cooperation is discouraged. When joint goal-setting is practiced, it is hard to fix individual responsibility, and if a manager's over-all performance is evaluated on the basis of a relatively few measures, there is always the risk that accidental factors may distort the picture. A good manager with bad luck may well look worse than a bad manager with good luck. Furthermore, in a period of rapid change, goals may become outmoded long before the next review period comes around.

In any case, a manager's apparent "performance" is a function of his initial goals. If his goals are set low it is easy to look good. And so the trick (where results appraisal is working poorly) is to set a low initial goal and sell one's boss that this goal is really very hard.

We can conclude, then, that MBO is a useful management tool, but if too much emphasis is placed on measurable results, the technique may boomerang. Used with discretion, goal-setting provides a framework within which subordinates are better motivated and receive more specific cues about how they stand and what they should do to improve themselves. Goal-setting by subordinates is more effective than goal-setting by the boss, but only if the boss uses participative techniques on a day-to-day basis. Goal-setting by the boss may be useful even in the absence of participation. [22]

[22] A number of studies suggest that various forms of results-oriented appraisals or MBO may give better results than do conventional appraisals. Setting specific goals is the important procedure, not whether it is the boss or the subordinate who sets them. The impact of subordinates' participation in setting goals depends on (1) the superior's everyday supervisory style and (2) the subordinate's self-esteem and need for independence. See, for example, John R. P. French, Emanuel Kay, and Herbert H. Meyer, "Participation and the Appraisal System," *Human Relations*, Vol. 19, No. 1 (1966), pp. 3–20; and Stephen J. Carroll and Henry Tosi, "Goal Characteristics and Personality Factors in a Management-by-Objectives Program," *Administrative Science Quarterly*, Vol. 15, No. 3 (September 1970), pp. 295–305.

For Promotions and Salary Increases?

Should results-oriented appraisals techniques, such as MBO, be used as a means for determining who should get promotions or salary increases? Here the experts disagree. It can be argued that, even at best, MBO measures only how a man has done a specific job. It provides little indication of how he might do on other jobs. For example, a man who does well under close supervision may do poorly under general supervision. In addition, managers should not be promoted to higher-level jobs purely on the basis of performance at lower levels. As a consequence, some companies isolate any evaluation of a man's potential almost completely from an evaluation of performance on his present job. They use different forms for each purpose, with the form used to measure potential putting greater emphasis on traits. Often the evaluation of potential is not even shown the subordinate. Hopefully, this separation of the two forms of evaluation reduces the unsatisfactory compromise that results when evaluation is used for a variety of purposes. And it avoids "undue emphasis . . . on 'upward-and-onward' possibilities to the neglect of improvement in present responsibilities." [23]

MBO may not be appropriate for determining who should get a salary increase either, since it provides little basis by which to compare one man against another. Yet any salary program that seeks to pay higher salaries to men who do better work must make such comparisons. And so a separate procedure may have to be established for salary purposes. Thus, a company may have as many as three appraisal programs, each for a different purpose: for coaching, for promotions, and for salary increases.

But having three different procedures may lead to chaos, particularly if the ratings are inconsistent with each other.

"Often men find themselves appraised for development by one method and for rewards by a second. The most meaningful appraisal, the one that will prove most effective in inducing developmental action, is the one that 'pays off.' " [24]

The dilemma is not an easy one to escape. Certainly salary increases should be consistent with appraisals, whether or not the latter are based on subordinate-set goals. How well these goals are met should be a major consideration in determining whether a subordinate should get a salary increase, though other factors such as seniority, the company's financial position, and salaries paid by competitors might also be taken into account. Further, as we shall emphasize in Chapter 25, salary is unlikely to act as a motivator to high performance unless salary and performance are closely tied together.

[23] Earl Brooks, "An Experimental Program for Executive Development," *ILR Research*, Vol. 1, No. 2 (March 1955), p. 12; see also Richards, *op. cit.*, p. 529.

[24] Walter Mahler and Guyot Frazier, "Appraisal of Executive Performance: The 'Achilles Heel' of Managerial Development," *Personnel*, Vol. 31, No. 5 (March 1955), p. 432. See also Paul H. Thompson and Gene Dalton, "Performance Appraisal: Managers Beware," *Harvard Business Review*, Vol. 48, No. 1, (January 1970), pp. 149-157.

Promotions

Promotion to a different position involves another matter. A man's past performance on his present job may be only an imperfect indicator of his potential for a new job. Other factors must be taken into account, such as his success on special assignments (see Chapter 22). Even personality traits, as disclosed by good selection tests and in assessment centers, may be relevant (certainly more relevant than trait-rating by the manager's immediate boss).

CONCLUSION

Performance evaluation serves two important purposes in the management-development program: (1) It provides a systematic, objective means for selecting those who should be promoted, and (2) it provides a tool to help managers train subordinates (as well as to help subordinates to improve themselves). In addition, it can play an important role in a salary-administration program. Yet, as we have seen, objectives often conflict. It is largely because of this conflict that the whole field of performance appraisal has become so controversial and has given rise to so many clashing schools of thought.

In theory, selection, salary administration, and training can be combined into one attractive management-development package. Ratings can be used by higher management for selection purposes and also as a form of feedback, through the evaluation interview, to inform subordinates on where they stand and to suggest ways in which they can do better. Unfortunately, the information management receives from an evaluation program designed primarily to permit an objective comparison of a large group of employees is seldom useful in the coaching of individuals. Many observers feel it wise to separate the selection and training aspects of evaluation altogether.

Both superior and subordinate, in many organizations, have come to dread the day when evaluation interviews must be held: The subordinate is afraid of being criticized unjustly and the superior is apprehensive about provoking the subordinate's antagonism. Because of the general inadequacy of traditional appraisals many companies have switched to MBO. MBO is hardly the perfect solution to the problem, yet its emphasis on specific goals makes evaluation more objective, and subordinate involvement in goal-setting tends to make "goals more realistic and more palatable to the individual. . . . No small accomplishment." [25]

But other objectives besides development must be considered. The organization also needs some information which will help in determining promotions. "The vital test of appraisal is whether or not it allows the right men to rise and prevents others from doing so." [26] Certainly no one approach can answer all the

---

[25] William G. Rothstein, "Executive Appraisal Programs," *ILR Research*, Vol. 8, No. 2 (1962), p. 17.
[26] Odiorne, *op. cit.*, p. 307.

problems, and the wise organization will proceed flexibly, without becoming wed too closely to any one method.

As far as development itself is concerned, appraisals are only part of the picture. We now turn to management training and organizational development.

problem • ROBERT JACKSON

Robert Jackson, 25, has been an advertising copywriter in your department for three years. He designs advertisements to be placed in newspapers and magazines. He must work closely with girls in the art department, with the sales department, and with the vice-president in charge of the whole division.

Bob is an extremely enthusiastic worker with good ideas. When you, the manager of the department, hired him, you hoped that he would advance rapidly. He still can, but he has considerable trouble in dealing with people. He is too impatient with the girls in the art department, seems to fidget whenever he notices one of them taking a break, and is constantly pushing them to finish his work. In dealing with the people in the sales department, he makes it perfectly clear that his ideas are always best. During a recent conference, when the Vice President was thinking out loud, Bob shouted out his own answer, and cut the VP off. It was a good answer, and the VP didn't mind, but some of the other people thought Bob had behaved badly. You are quite concerned about the animosity he is creating in your department.

A new company policy requires that each employee have an evaluation interview every six months. There are no performance-rating forms. This is Jackson's first evaluation under the new policy.

1. What should your strategy be in handling the evaluation interview with Jackson?

2. Role-play this interview. Jackson is quite sure that his ideas are good and will press for a substantial pay increase.

MANAGEMENT TRAINING AND ORGANIZATION DEVELOPMENT

24

Although management training is concerned primarily with individual managers, whereas organization development perceives the organization as a whole, the two subjects overlap, as we shall see, and they can conveniently be considered together.

Management training takes many forms and deals with many subjects. Coaching by one's boss, planned job rotation, and performance evaluation are all in a sense forms of management training. The manager also learns important lessons every time he is praised or reprimanded by his boss or achieves or is denied a promotion. The subjects dealt with by management training may range from public speaking to the impact of new tax legislation. This chapter, however, will be focused on just one kind of management training: formal programs designed to improve managerial skills, chiefly in the human relations areas—how to get along with one's boss, subordinates, and peers.

Historical development. Management training became significant first in World War II, when crash programs were instituted to train new foremen. After the war, the spread of human relations and foremen's unions led companies to engage more extensively in foreman training as a means both of persuading foremen that they were indeed part of management, and of reducing the petty tyrannies that earlier had contributed to the growth of blue-collar unions. At about the same time, selected groups of managers began to attend university-run executive programs, typically from two to six weeks full time. From these humble beginnings management training spread until it now covers all levels of management.

Over the years, a number of ingenious training techniques have been developed by training staff personnel and by outside consultants. For the most part, these techniques suffer various limitations as means of inducing behavioral change (even though they may be quite useful in disseminating facts). During the 1960's a number of major companies experimented with a new and seemingly more powerful technique, T-group training (to be discussed later). Powerful as this technique is, when applied to management it, too, has shortcomings, among which are the problems of transferring abilities learned in the T-group to the job. Most recently a more eclectic approach—organizational development, often called OD—has developed out of T-groups, a development which gives hope of overcoming many of the T-group's limitations.

We will consider all these developments in turn.

REQUIREMENTS FOR EFFECTIVE TRAINING

Through trial and error, those concerned with training programs have begun to learn some of the conditions that are required for successful interpersonal training. These conditions relate both to the nature of the training program and to the organizational environment in which it occurs.

Nature of the Program

Problems as the trainees see them. The training program should start with the felt needs of the trainees themselves, and they should see it as a means of solving their *own* problems. Training in some companies is on the level of the charm school or the booster talk. Or it may be presented in theoretical, abstract terms that participants are unable to translate into practice. One way to ensure that a training program is built around problems as the trainees see them is to invite them to participate in setting up the program (or at least to survey their felt needs before launching the program).

Unfreezing. The people who take part in the program must be dissatisfied with their old ways and willing to unfreeze their attitudes (see p. 254). A wise personnel director once told us that he never starts a training program until the people to be trained (as well as their superiors) are anxious for the program. If the men are forced into a training program against their will, they may well resent and sabotage it.

Evidence suggests that training is more valuable for managers who have just been promoted or are about to be promoted, since these are the ones most in need of an expanded viewpoint; confronted by a new job, they are anxious to develop new skills and willing to discard old points of view. This enthusiasm for learning is especially strong among staff specialists, such as accountants or engineers, who are being promoted into line positions where they will be faced with an entirely new set of problems.

Moratorium. A training program should provide a moratorium from the pressures of immediate problems. It should get participants away from their regular environment and give them time to reassess their present behavior and to examine alternatives. For this reason full-time training away from the job is often more effective than training an hour or two at a time. (On the other hand, too much isolation may lead trainees to ignore their back-home problems.)

Involvement. Trainees must be encouraged to work through to their own conclusions. The only way they can understand a problem is to think it out for themselves. They suspect the fast talker who tries to trick them into accepting ready-made solutions. As Robert Burns warns, "He who is convinced against his will, remains of the same opinion still."

A trainee can memorize what the instructor thinks is right, but this does not make it his own. Particularly in the area of emotional (as distinct from conceptual) learning, people learn primarily through experience, not through passive listening. Real learning is "gut" learning. If there is to be a carry-over from the classroom to the office or shop, it is essential that the trainee *feel* through the problem, experiencing and overcoming its difficulties as he works toward a solution. We emphasize the word *feel* because many of the problems in this area are emotional, involving the ways managers see, and feel about, the people and events that affect them deeply.

Without emotional involvement trainees are likely to develop intellectually satisfying answers which they fail to implement in practice:

Executives have been observed to analyze beautifully and verbally solve a case that focuses on "understanding the other person" and five minutes later show little or no ability to use this knowledge in a hot argument with the man across the table. [1]

Group influence. Human-relations training is often more effective when it is conducted in groups, for most attitudes in this area are group-conditioned. For instance, a foreman will be less likely to consult with his steward if his fellow foremen feel that to do so is being soft.

We have already discovered that group discussion at times provides an effective means of changing attitudes. When group norms are involved, it is easier to change members as a group than it is to change individuals. When a group of managers with common problems decides to change together, no individual has the unsettling feeling of being a pioneer, of being different. The group provides its members with emotional support and they learn from each other.

Typically, attitudes and behaviors begin to change only when the trainees recognize that they all have problems in common which they have not been able to handle satisfactorily (for instance, handling an unreasonable steward and living under a tight budget). It helps if they can work off their resentment—let off steam—a bit before moving on to the next step. The opportunity to share one another's burdens reduces frustration and makes them more willing to consider new approaches.

[1] Chris Argyris, *Personality and Organization* (New York: Harper, 1957), p. 221.

Experiments with change.   A training program is more effective if it makes allowances for the difficulties of giving up old ways of doing things. Understandably, people feel more secure with old patterns of behavior that have proven reasonably satisfactory in the past. And they resent suggestions that their performance is unsatisfactory. Similarly, they object to outsiders telling them what to do; they feel that their long experience makes them more qualified than any trainer.

One approach to handling this problem is to encourage trainees to consider new practices without attacking the old ways directly—that is, to ask them to consider a range of alternatives without committing themselves to any particular one. They should be encouraged to try new ways tentatively. Only after they have tested the new procedures on an experimental basis can they be expected to change their behavior permanently.

Even after the training program has been completed it is often useful to reconvene the training group to permit participants to discuss the problems they have faced in trying to implement new ideas on the job. Otherwise trainees may try these new ideas out for a while but abandon them just as soon as the going gets difficult. The reconvened training group provides the trainee support in carrying change into practice.

Carry-over.   For training to mean anything it must move from the intellectual to the practical level. It must provide skills that are useful to the manager in solving problems on his job—and skills that higher management will permit him to practice.

To summarize much of the above: Effective training that changes attitudes should run through three stages. In the *unfreezing* stage trainees learn to be dissatisfied with their old patterns of behavior. In the *change* stage they experiment with new patterns in a safe environment away from everyday pressures. And in the *refreezing* stage they adopt these forms for practical use and carry them to the job. Indeed, the problems connected with human relations training have much in common with those involved in introducing change generally (see Chapter 12).

Of the various points listed above, the last one, carry-over, may be the most critical. Training rarely results in lasting behavioral change unless there is a supportive organizational atmosphere.

Organizational Atmosphere

Training is difficult to evaluate, for reasons we shall discover. By and large, the results of conventional training programs and even T-groups have been somewhat disappointing. Managers may report enthusiastically about the course, and their behavior may change a bit in the first few days after leaving class; but long-range improvements resulting from training—at least from conventional training—are rarely observed.

How can we explain these negative results? Except for boredom, some programs have little impact on trainees, even while they are in class. More important, what is learned in class is too often not useful on the job, especially when it conflicts with the behavior expected of the trainees by their bosses and even by their subordinates. If training is to be worthwhile, trainees must feel free to apply what they learn and to change their behavior if they wish. When the organizational climate denies this freedom, subordinates are more likely to imitate their boss than to follow what they have learned in class.

The influence of the organization—in particular, the attitude of top management—is crucial to the success of a training program. In many companies management regards training as of only marginal importance and consequently gives it only token support. Many managers feel that training is purely a staff function for which line has no responsibility, or they institute training programs merely because it is the fashionable thing to do. Yet attitudes of this sort are quickly discerned by the trainees themselves, who may begin to feel that training is a waste of time and resent being held as a captive audience in a training class. As long as management thinks of the training process as something apart from everyday activities on the job, the chances that training will affect behavior are slim indeed.

Where higher management does not *in practice* support the objectives of training, managers feel uncertain about whether to follow the theory of the course or the example of their boss. As a result, they appear vacillating and inconsistent. For instance, subordinates might well become confused if their hard-as-nails supervisor started to listen to them before bawling them out. Naturally, subordinates, uncertain of whether their boss is going to be "tough" or practice "human relations," find this unpredictability highly frustrating. Under the circumstances, it may be a blessing that so many supervisors leave their training in the classroom and never let it interfere with their daily behavior.

In the establishment of a training course, there is often little effort to find out why managers behave as they do or to consider whether company policy or top management behavior may be the cause of whatever seems wrong; instead training is viewed as a magic cure for all ills.[2] Managers often talk as if only their subordinates' behavior needed changing, not their own. Trainees often say, "I wish my boss would take this course. He's the one who needs it."

Too often, training programs stress dealing with only subordinates, yet the trainee's biggest problem may be dealing with his boss. Foreman training may "increase the foreman's internal tension, his feelings of hostility toward management, and his sense of separateness in the organization, because it never comes to grips with his true predicament—the fact of his being a man in the middle."[3]

---

[2] One of the authors was once asked by a personnel director to set up a training program because:

> "We know that front-line supervision isn't giving us the loyalty and enthusiasm it should. We want them to feel part of the organization. We know that lots of times they get policy from our level which they only go through the motions of carrying out, or they tell their men, 'That's what top management wants.' We want them to understand that they are part of the team."

Note that the trainer was expected to build up enthusiasm and loyalty. There was no suggestion that top management had any responsibility for the existing situation or that perhaps top management itself should change. (Later it developed that the real reason for the foremen's lack of loyalty was fear of a substantial cutback in production which would lead to many of them being laid off.)

[3] Chris Argyris, "Employee Apathy and Non-Involvement—the House that Management Built," *Personnel*, Vol. 38, No. 2 (July 1961), p. 11. For a good example, see A. J. M. Sykes, "The Effects of a Supervisory Training Course in Changing Supervisors' Perceptions and Expectations of the Role of Management," *Human Relations*, Vol. 15, No. 3 (August 1962), pp. 227-243.

Only limited results can be obtained by training lower management alone, particularly if the training is of the typical classroom variety. Possibly the best way to train a foreman is to train his general foreman first; but it is difficult to train the general foreman until the superintendent has been trained, or at least induced, to behave in a manner that permits those on lower levels to try out new techniques.

Does this mean that the only way to start is with the Board of Directors? Perhaps. The Board of Directors of one of the nation's largest companies established a Human Relations Committee, whose job, in effect, is to train top management. Top management then trained the next lower level of management and so on down the line in a carefully planned program until finally the general foreman trained the foremen.

As we shall see, there are very definite advantages in having every boss train the people he supervises. Yet there are managers, otherwise competent, who are just poor trainers. Further, if all training is done by the boss there is a real danger that the organization will perpetuate its past mistakes and allow little room for new ideas. Training conducted by line personnel is not the complete solution to the problem.

More important than the person who conducts the training is the organizational atmosphere in which it occurs. For training to be effective this atmosphere must permit the manager to experiment with new patterns of behavior and to learn through making mistakes. But even changes in atmosphere must come from the top (or at least be approved by the top). Organizations are social systems, and it is difficult to change one part without changing the rest. It is the growing recognition of this interdependency which in recent years has led many companies to introduce integrated programs of organization development and to place less stress on individualized management training.

CONVENTIONAL TRAINING TECHNIQUES

Now let us examine some of the more common conventional training techniques. These techniques are designed for many purposes, and few, if any, completely satisfy the criteria listed above. Yet all of them have some value either as part of a comprehensive program or in organizations which for one reason or another are unable to mount such a comprehensive program.

Lectures

Lecturing, the traditional form of teaching, gives the trainer the greatest degree of control over the training situation. It enables him to present the material exactly as he wants to, with little danger that anyone will talk back.

But lecturing has obvious limitations as a training technique. As every student realizes, many lecturers are boring and some are entertaining without being instructive. Communications are but one way and lead to little involvement.

The instructor who can keep his class constantly stimulated through the sheer force of his ideas—and who is powerful enough to effect a change in the behavior of those who listen to him—is rare indeed. A lecture is unlikely to change fixed attitudes and certainly is of little help in developing skills. It is useful chiefly in presenting background facts—for example, the meaning of a new union contract.

Guided Conferences

In order to escape the limitations of straight lecturing, many companies have turned to the "guided discussion" type of conference. In a guided conference the instructor typically knows in advance what information or procedures he wants to bring out. The training sessions are similar to small discussion classes in a university.

These conferences have certain pitfalls, however. Unless the discussion is directed to the felt needs of the participants, they may well decide that the whole session is useless. Or the session may be little more than obvious manipulation of the participants' thinking, steering it toward the discussion leader's predetermined solutions. Such conferences deserve certain criticisms:

They do not accomplish what they are supposed to do, that is, to help supervisors with the human aspects of their jobs. Many of them raise "loaded" questions, give facile answers that cannot be applied to concrete situations, and discuss unreal situations, situations that have never existed except in someone's imagination. In many of these the conference leader is armed with points the trainees are supposed to make. He is allowed so much time to draw these points out, and should the trainees fail to respond, he is instructed to draw them out himself. . . . What so often astonishes me is how docilely supervisors go through these verbal hoops and how readily they learn the proper verbal response to please the instructor. [4]

There is a constant danger in a guided conference that the group will become overdependent on the leader. Expecting him to give *the* answer to their problems, the trainees are reluctant to go through the hard work of puzzling out their own answers.

The Case Method

This technique, which has been popularized by the Harvard Business School, is a common form of training. (Many of the cases that we present at the ends of chapters are typical of those used in this method.)

The success of the case method depends directly on the ability of the instructor. Under an unskilled instructor, the trainees tend to look upon the case as a puzzle that can be solved by finding the right answer. They make value judgments about each character and try to identify the "villain." Often, too, a poorly conducted discussion will degenerate into a rambling session from which the participants derive no learning. A skillful instructor, on the other hand,

---

[4] Fritz Roethlisberger, "Training Supervisors in Human Relations," *Harvard Business Review*, Vol. 29, No. 5 (October 1951), p. 51.

emphasizes useful ways of thinking about human relations rather than ways of reaching specific conclusions. He puts his stress on:

1. Increasing the trainee's power of observation, helping him to ask better questions and to look for a broader range of problems (for instance, not "Who is to blame?" but "Why did it happen?").

2. Encouraging the group to look for more and more implications in each solution, keeping them away from pat analyses and oversimplified solutions.

3. Helping the student to discard vague principles, such as "Be tactful" or "Apply the golden rule," and urging him to consider not only *what* to do but *how* to do it.

4. Encouraging the trainees to test their solutions against reality.

In the university classroom the case method introduces a note of realism that is absent from abstract, theoretical discussions. For management trainees in industry, however, cases are always less realistic than the actual problems that arise on the job. Even though practicing managers may discuss cases with enthusiasm, they tend to look upon the discussion as a game in which they solve the *other* company's problems, not their own. This lack of *emotional* involvement may make it difficult to effect any basic change in the behavior and attitudes of the trainees.

Simulation

By *simulation* is meant a broad range of techniques in which trainees act out samples of real business behavior in order to get practice in making decisions or in working together as a group, or both. It involves learning through doing rather than through memorizing principles. In effect, it is a form of vestibule training. Since it is more realistic than the case method it may lead to greater involvement.

The *management game* is one form of simulation that involves several teams, each of which is given a "firm" to operate for a number of "periods." In each period each team must decide what prices to set, how much to produce, how much to spend on advertising and on research, how much of an inventory to maintain, and so forth. Since the teams are competing with each other, each firm's decisions will affect the results of all the other firms. Typically, these decisions are fed into a computer which is programed to behave somewhat like a real market. At the end of each period the computer reports back how well each firm has done. This report provides the data needed for the next period of play. The winner, of course, is the firm which has accumulated the largest profit by the end of the game. Often the game ends in a postmortem in which the participants analyze their mistakes and attempt to generalize from their experience.

What do participants learn from such games? Primarily how to make better decisions, to select and analyze relevant data, and to choose from among alternatives. Most management games are concerned with the external environment of business, particularly marketing, and the aspects of it which can be quantified. Though participants gain some experience in working together, their chief concern is with making decisions, not implementing them. They provide little insight into the problems connected with organizational structure or personnel management. Only rarely is the game enlarged to afford each team an opportunity to analyze its own interpersonal problems. (In some OD programs the teams are large enough so that they can be divided into departments— finance, marketing, and the like—each with its own department head.) Evaluation periods permit each team to examine the stresses that developed in its communications and decision-making patterns during the last period of play— and also to experiment with alternate means of making these more effective.

Management games often generate much enthusiasm among players. There is still a good deal of doubt, however, about the extent of carry-over from game to job.

The *in-basket* technique is a form of simulation which permits emphasis on internal as well as external problems. A typical in-basket exercise might be as follows:

An "executive" (the trainee) is catapulted into a new job on the sudden death of predecessor. His secretary presents him with an in-basket containing a number of letters, memos, and notes of phone conversations—all accumulated over the last few days. A host of urgent problems face him, such as a union grievance (as well as a poorly written proposed reply drafted by a subordinate line manager), a complaint from an important customer, and a sudden supervisory vacancy for which there are three obvious candidates.

The trainee is given a short period of time to deal with these problems, either by drafting a reply at once or getting further information. Once each trainee has handled his own in-basket, he meets with other trainees who have handled identical in-baskets to discuss the logic behind how they handled them.

This technique provides experience both in making decisions and in implementing them. It differs from the business game in that there is no feedback on how well the decision "worked."

Role-playing is a form of simulation emphasizing human-relations problems. Parts are assigned to students to act out as they would in real life. It differs from ordinary drama in that the actors are given no lines to memorize; rather, they must improvise as they go along. (For examples of cases susceptible to role-playing, see pp. 279, 327, 526.) Role-playing is far more fruitful when it is followed by class discussion. Before the session starts, the trainer may suggest crucial areas for the students to observe and then use these areas as a framework for the subsequent discussion.

Among the advantages of role-playing are these:

1. It helps participants to appreciate other points of view, as, for example, when a foreman plays the role of a union steward.

2. It helps trainees to experience a situation emotionally.

3. It makes trainees more self-conscious and analytical of their behavior than they would be in real life.

4. It permits trainees to show imagination and daring in devising solutions, since they are not playing for "keeps." No harm is done if they make a mistake.

Even the trainees who merely observe a role-playing session profit from observing the mistakes of others. Certainly this is a highly dramatic technique for arousing interest and stimulating class participation.

Nevertheless role-playing has some disadvantages. It deals with problems formulated by the instructor, not with those which are bothering the trainee. Thus many are viewed as unrealistic. Further, the cases must of necessity be oversimplified, since they focus on the players' interactions and tend to ignore the environment in which the problem arises.[5]

Other forms of simulation may also be utilized. Individuals may be given roles, such as plant manager, sales manager, purchasing agent, and comptroller—and information about their jobs which these individuals might normally have. Then several emergencies are assumed to occur—for instance, a large rush order and a major equipment breakdown—and the trainees are required to solve the problems. Such simulation provides training in both decision-making and human relations, and after each "period" the participants can profitably hold a post-mortem about how they handled their problems.[6]

The main techniques discussed share one common characteristic: the problems they consider are presented by the trainer rather than the group, and are therefore looked upon as somewhat artificial or not pertinent. Thus, participants tend not to become emotionally involved or to develop insights relating to their own values or behavior. In order to obtain greater participation, a number of companies turned to T-groups.

T-GROUP TRAINING

T-group training (the "T" stands for training) is also known as *sensitivity training* and *laboratory training*.[7] Regardless of the name, the technique has strong supporters and strong detractors. For some, it is almost a religion; others see it as a quack nostrum.

Though T-group training dates back to the 1940's, only around 1960 did interest spill out into private industry. Yet by the mid-1960's, the list of firms

---

[5] "Spontaneous role playing," a technique little used in industry, makes use of problems generated by the participants themselves. Wallace Wohlking and Hannah Wiener, "Structured and Spontaneous Role Playing," *Training and Development Journal*, Vol. 25, No. 1 (January 1971), pp. 8-14.

[6] See for example, P. Hesseling, "Using a Communication Exercise for Training Managers," *British Journal of Industrial Relations*, Vol. 3, No. 1 (March 1965), p. 76. For programs of this sort, used to train prospective top management of a new plant, see John H. Wakeley and Malcolm E. Shaw, "Management Training—an Integrated Approach," *Training Directors Journal*, Vol. 19, No. 7 (July 1965), pp. 2-14.

[7] See Leland P. Bradford, Jack R. Gibb, and Kenneth Benne, *T-Group Theory and Laboratory Method: Innovation in Re-education* (New York: Wiley, 1964); Warren G. Bennis and Edgar Schein, eds., *Human Relations Laboratory Training: Theory and Practice* (New York: Wiley, 1965); and Warren G. Bennis and Edgar Schein, *Personnel and Organizational Change through Group Methods: The Laboratory Approach* (New York: Wiley, 1965). For an excellent overview both of T-group theory and how it can be abused, see Chris Argyris, "On the Future of Laboratory Education," *The Journal of Applied Behavioral Science*, Vol. 3, No. 2 (April 1967), pp. 153-183.

which had at least experimented with this radically new form of training read like a blue book of American industry (and in government it spread even through the State Department and the Internal Revenue Service).

T-group training differs from the kinds of training previously discussed in that it is concerned with real, not simulated, problems existing within the training group itself—not in the organization outside or in some hypothetical case. Rather than just teach skills and intellectual understanding, it seeks to change underlying attitudes and thus behavior on the job.

Although individual trainers may differ in emphasis, T-group training can be used to help participants:

1. Learn more about themselves, especially their own weaknesses and emotions.

2. Develop insights into how they react to others and also how others react to them.

3. Discover how groups work and how to diagnose human-relations problems.

4. Find out how to behave more effectively in interpersonal relations, and in particular, how to manage people through means other than power.

5. Develop more "competent," "authentic" relations in which feelings are expressed openly.

6. Confront interpersonal problems directly, so that they can be solved, rather than trying to avoid them, smooth them over, or seek a compromise that is not really a solution.

T-group training is often called *laboratory training* because T-groups are, in effect, laboratories in which people experiment on themselves and generate data for their own discussions. T-groups are really small discussion groups with no set leader. (The trainer merely raises questions and provides occasional comments.) Usually the groups are totally unstructured; they have no set task or agenda except for a strong focus on the feelings and mutual impact of the participants.[8] Learning takes place through analyzing one's emotions rather than intellectually through logic. The group talks about what seems important at the moment. It is felt that the lack of structure will motivate people to bring their feelings out in the open where they can be analyzed and dealt with in a more rational fashion. An example may illustrate how such groups operate.

At one early meeting, in a recent workshop, one executive got up from his chair and remarked to the stunned group: "I don't think this discussion is getting anywhere! I move that we appoint a committee to set up an agenda and report back their recommendations. Maybe this way we'll get something done. Are there any *serious* objections?" No one said anything. "All right, then, who would like to be part of this committee?" Four men raised their hands. The five left for an adjacent room.

[8] Most forms of T-group training are supplemented by lectures, which provide participants with suggestions for what to look for in their own groups, as well as, often, by simulated problems to provide further material for discussion.

During their absence, those remaining seemed infuriated. Their displeasure toward the five who had left was obvious. When someone asked why no one had objected, he was told there was no point "in getting killed by a steam roller."

The "secessionists" returned after a few minutes. When asked how they thought the group would respond to their recommendations, they felt sure there would be great interest in what they had to say. The trainer asked for a show of hands. The overwhelming majority was interested in neither the report nor its recommendations.

The rest of the session was spent in helping the five see what had happened. Much was said about authoritarian attitudes, "talking down," lack of respect for the integrity of the group, and aggressive, irritating mannerisms. A rude shock was followed by a slow awakening. [9]

In a well-conducted T-group, the trainees in effect train one another, though the trainer helps by asking a few skillful questions that the group may purposely (but perhaps unconsciously) have been ignoring. [10] Or he may provide feedback as to the interpersonal processes developing within the group.

T-groups go through periods of shock, frustration, and hostility, but hopefully all these stages lead to understanding. Indeed, T-groups make much use of feedback techniques, such as evaluation forms filled out by participants, process observers, and playbacks of tape recordings of critical sessions. All this is to help the participants learn more about their own behavior and to test out new forms of behavior.

Effective T-groups go through the three stages discussed in the early part of this chapter: unfreezing, in which the participant develops, often through shock, a sense of dissatisfaction with his present behavior; change, in which he experiments with new behavior; and refreezing, in which he develops an internalized commitment to a new approach.

Though all T-group training generally takes the same over-all form, T-group trainers differ somewhat in their emphasis. One school focuses upon *individual* emotions (and the training this school offers is often called *sensitivity* training); the other is more concerned with relations *among* members of the group. Sensitivity training is in a sense the deeper form of training, and the line between it and psychotherapy sometimes becomes vague. Sensitivity training is also akin to such movements as encounter groups, Synanon and Esalen groups, and Alcoholics Anonymous. In recent years, some sensitivity trainers have "experimented with the use of body movements, rhythm, form, color, and similar interpersonally expressive and receptive modalities." [11] Physical contact, games (in which a rejected person breaks his way into a circle of clasped hands), and even just plain screaming are among the methods used to permit fuller expression of feelings on a nonverbal, nonintellectual level. As might be expected, the more experimental techniques have been looked upon with little favor by adherents of the more orthodox, group-oriented school.

[9] Robert Tannenbaum, Verne Kallejian, and Irving R. Weschler, "Training Managers for Leadership," *Personnel*, Vol. 30, No. 4 (January 1954), pp. 257-258. Reprinted by permission of the American Management Association.

[10] Some T-groups function without the presence of a trainer. Self-rating scales, which the participants use to evaluate their group effectiveness, take the place of the trainer in providing feedback.

[11] Robert Tannenbaum, "Reaction to Chris Argyris," *Journal of Applied Behavioral Science*, Vol. 3, No. 2 (April 1967), pp. 205-206.

Debate

Both forms of T-groups have been subject to much debate. Three main arguments have been made against their use as a form of management training.

Excessive stress. Critics argue, first, that T-group trainers create stress situations for their own sake. At times, the groups are "converted into psychological nudist camps which end up mainly as self-flagellation societies."[12] There is a danger that training of this sort may do a better job of tearing people apart than of bringing them together. At worst, T-groups may trigger hidden psychological instabilities, leading to mental breakdown or, at best, to a frustrating experience which interferes with real learning. (In addition, it is argued that such training interferes with personal privacy, particularly in firms where attendance at such programs is almost compulsory.)

Defenders counter that one of the hallmarks of a skilled trainer is that he keeps tensions within bounds and that he makes sure that critical comments are "caring" rather than destructive. Further, the tensions generated in T-groups are no greater than those endemic to any large organization. To these arguments critics reply that many companies send to T-group training only those who "need" it most—frequently the most unstable. And too often groups are started by unqualified trainers who lack the skill to keep pressures at tolerable levels.

The impartial observer must note that there have been cases in which T-group training has led to personal damage. But this may be an argument chiefly for better care in selecting trainers and trainees, particularly when the deeper, more individual-centered type of training is used.

Carry-over difficult. It is charged that whatever changes occur in the T-group tend to fade out once the trainee returns to an unsympathetic environment where company policy and his boss's attitude may inhibit the exercise of his newly learned skills. T-group members learn chiefly to get along with other T-group members. The manager who has learned to express his emotions openly may find his honesty misunderstood by those who have not shared his experience. "Laboratory values are so different from the values of most organizations that if individuals learned well at the laboratory they would probably tend to conclude that they should not use their new learning back home except where they have power and influence."[13]

Because of this problem, acknowledged by all, there has been a trend toward "family" T-groups consisting of all those who work together. Thus, all the top men in a given department are trained at once. But such grouping raises serious ethical questions since attendance is scarcely voluntary. Further, as long as only part of the total organization has been trained, difficulties in communications may arise between those who have adopted the new values and those who adhere to the old ones. The answer may be to provide T-group training for

---

[12] George Odiorne, "Managerial Narcissism—The Great Self-Development Binge," *Management of Personnel Quarterly*, Vol. 1 (Spring 1962), p. 8.

[13] Argyris, *op. cit.*, p. 63.

everyone, but this may be prohibitively expensive. And even if it were possible to send everyone through T-groups, the kinds of "dirt" aired in such sessions and the intense feelings often engendered by them may in fact make it harder for some managers to work together after the session is over. T-group training may improve the interpersonal relations of some managers, but may be harmful for others.

Loss of managerial decisiveness. Another charge against T-groups is that they make managers so sensitive to the feelings of others that they are unwilling to make hard decisions—and so "open" and honest in the expression of their own feelings that their behavior approaches downright rudeness.

Obviously, there is a danger that this might occur, particularly where the T-group has been poorly led. Maslow suggests that since T-group training teaches people to behave more openly, with less defensiveness, it also teaches them not to fear to act in a forceful manner if the situation requires.[14] For example if a staff meeting seems unproductive and lengthy, a T-group trained manager will say so on the spot, rather than covering up his feelings and taking out his aggressions on his subordinates or his family. In any case, the fact that managers take feelings into account means not that they avoid making decisions, but that they make better ones. Only when problems are faced squarely can organizational tensions be resolved in a productive fashion.

ORGANIZATION DEVELOPMENT

Since 1965, in part because of the problems discussed above, a number of companies have switched away from T-groups toward broader, more eclectic forms of management training, now generally known as *organization development.* OD trainers (now more often called *consultants* or *change agents*) use a variety of techniques,[15] depending on what the situation requires. As the name implies, all forms of OD share the common objective of seeking to change not just individuals but also the values of the organization within which they work. Compared to T-groups, OD is characterized by less deep intervention (therefore less danger of engendering excessive psychological stress) and greater emphasis on carry-over and on organizational (as opposed to group or individual) factors.

Like T-groups, OD encourages managers to recognize and express feelings and to improve relations *within* groups. In addition, it seeks to reduce friction *between* groups and to improve communications generally. Some approaches to OD make use of T-groups, at least in modified form; but they do this only as one step in an integrated program that seeks eventually to involve all members of the organization in a coordinated effort to identify and resolve causes of interpersonal conflict.

Confrontation. Most approaches to OD assume that change will not occur unless the participants feel dissatisfied with their current performance (what

[14] Abraham Maslow, *Eupsychian Management* (Homewood, Ill.: Dorsey, 1965), p. 186.
[15] Including what we have called conventional techniques, role-playing, lectures, and the like.

some observers call "a conviction of sin"), and this requires some sort of feedback or "confrontation" that makes participants more sensitive to their own behavior and its impact on others.

Forms of confrontation vary greatly. T-groups, of course, provide a great deal of feedback to their members, but even as simple a device as closed-circuit TV playbacks of ordinary management meetings can be extremely effective in illustrating weaknesses. Simulations, such as the management game, can generate data as to how a group performs. After the simulation is over, the group evaluates the effectiveness of its internal processes.

The best-known OD technique, the *management grid*, uses a series of questionnaires (as well as simulations) to force managers to confront the gap between their idealized and their present behavior. "You have to build a model," says Robert Blake, the grid's originator, "as if you had no past tradition, no past practices, cult, or ritual. Then you see how lousy you really are in comparison with where you should be. So the ideal is a searchlight for seeing the actual. You have to close the gaps once you see them. You can't live with contradictions." [16]

Other OD programs begin with an employee attitude survey (see p. 356) or with a series of interviews with subordinates and peers. The findings of these studies are then reported to the management group with identification of source removed. If the studies are well conducted, they identify problems that require management's attention; often, these problems are ones that management had been unaware of or had ignored.

A fairly typical OD effort involved a hotel chain. Here the president was concerned with the relations between headquarters staff (such as accounting and sales) and their counterparts in individual hotels.

The consultant intensively interviewed a sample of people from all levels and then reported back to a meeting consisting of the president, the heads of the headquarters' staff groups, and the general managers of the various hotels. Sample items from his report:

Headquarters staff people: The president expects us to introduce change and upgrade quality, but the general managers won't let us into the hotels to do it.

General managers: The corporation talks decentralization but we have little voice in setting our own advertising policy.

Hotel staff people: Our rewards come entirely from the hotel managers. We have no chance of being promoted into headquarters and no one in headquarters is interested in our future. [17]

The range of problems presented indicated that efforts were required of not only those present but also of the hotel staff people if these problems were to be solved.

Another approach may involve two groups that have had difficulty working together in the past. Each group is instructed to meet by itself and to write down answers to questions like the following:

How do you view the other group?

How do you think the other group views you?

What's your best guess as to how the other group thinks you view it?

[16] *Business Week*, October 18, 1969, p. 159. In 1969, Blake's organization numbered among its clients 45 out of the country's top 100 industrial corporations. Blake seeks to create what he calls the "9,9" style of management, a style akin to maximum concern for interpersonal relations and production.

[17] Adapted, with slight modification, from Richard Beckhard, "An Organization Improvement Program in a Decentralized Company," *Journal of Applied Behavioral Science*, Vol. 2, No. 1 (January 1966).

The two groups meet together, and each divulges its list. Each group is permitted to ask the other to enlarge upon its answers, but argument is not permitted. Exercises such as this often reveal misunderstanding, which sometimes can be easily cleared up. In any case, the parties have obtained considerably greater insight into the sources of their difficulties.

Introducing change. Confrontation techniques help identify problems and create a desire for change ("unfreezing"). Using the data disclosed by feedback as a springboard for discussion, the OD consultant next seeks to induce managers to examine the cause of these problems and then to suggest means of solution. The group is challenged to develop new ways of relating to each other and to test out their choices in terms of their impact on the larger social systems. In the hotel case (discussed above) a list of recommendations was developed, many of which were implemented. For example, one of the hotel staff people was appointed to provide needed liaison between headquarters and the hotels.

Involving the entire organization. As mentioned earlier, the OD effort is not confined to a single group of managers but seeks to involve more and more people in the organization. As a result, OD proceeds on a step-by-step basis. T-groups are commonly followed by "team building" (to improve on-the-job relations of a work team) and then by activities devised to improve relations among teams. The managerial grid, for example, is a six-step program, starting with grid training itself, running through teamwork and intergroup development, the development and implementation of a "Strategic Model" that sets up company goals and how they are to be reached, and ending with a systematic evaluation of progress to date. The entire program may take three to six years.

Evaluation

Despite the claims of some of its adherents, OD is not a cure-all for organizational ills. It is more a philosophy than a rigid formula for success, and its effectiveness depends on the extent to which this philosophy is applied in everyday work relations and not just in training class.

Though OD may start out as a formal program, when it really gets under way obtaining feedback—checking on how others are reacting to you—comes automatically. Nevertheless, outside consultants and inside staff people may still, on a daily basis, give fresh insights into the particular interpersonal hangups that are hindering organizational effectiveness.

OD has been criticized for overemphasizing personal sensitivity and interpersonal relations—factors deeply rooted in the human personality—whereas changes in structure, workflows, and reward systems—the organizational constraints under which people work—can achieve results more economically and with less pain. Critics argue that job enrichment (Chapter 2), reorganization of work assignments to reduce communications blockages (Chapter 15), or improved compensation systems (Chapter 25) all have more direct effects on attitudes and behavior than any OD program is likely to have. OD supporters disagree. They insist that reforms of this sort are likely to be resisted as long as individual attitudes remain unchanged. The basic question is whether one should start from within or from without. The two approaches have been called by their critics "conversionalist" and "engineering."

Actually both approaches have merit. Structural changes lead to attitude changes. Favorable attitudes help make structural change a success. OD may be at fault in neglecting many of the personnel questions discussed in this book but, by emphasizing the importance of human feelings, OD offers a valuable counterweight to a mechanistic emphasis on purely structural changes.

OTHER FORMS OF MANAGEMENT TRAINING

The main emphasis in this chapter has been on formal training to improve interpersonal relations. But a complete management training program will include other forms of training.

Special Classes

On many campuses in the 1950's it was common to see middle-aged, balding businessmen back at school, sent there by their companies for advanced training. Now, college courses have been replaced by OD programs to some extent, but promising executives are still sent to universities for periods ranging from two weeks to a year.[18] They learn new subjects, such as operations research, and gain fresh points of view from their counterparts in other companies and from college professors.[19]

University-run programs are not the only opportunities available to executives to develop a broader, fresher point of view through exchange of ideas with executives from other institutions, or to acquire special training away from the job. The American Management Association offers a number of seminars similar to the university development programs, but they are shorter. Various professional associations and conventions also give executives a chance to make intercompany contacts and compare experiences. In addition, many concerns pay part of the expenses of managers who take night-school courses. In few of these instances, however, is there the feeling of retreat that marks the longer, on-campus course in which the executive is isolated from his daily routine.

A few large companies have set up their own management-training programs. Those chosen are sent to some isolated, attractive location for a training

[18] Since only a limited number of executives can be sent to university programs, management must exercise great care in making selections. The man who is picked may feel that he is slated for rapid advancement and may alter his expectations and behavior accordingly. If he is not promoted soon after he returns, he is likely to feel cheated and demoralized. On the other hand, those who are not selected may consider their being passed over almost a demotion. Sending a man to the university often makes him a "crown prince."

[19] Special programs of this sort are threatened by new media, such as closed-circuit-TV classes or video cassettes (video tapes available to the manager in his own plant), which make it possible for the manager to receive training on his home ground and frequently at the time most convenient to him.

program of a week or more. These firms feel that company training provides the same benefits as university programs, and, in addition, may increase company loyalty and inculcate a common company point of view. The function of company schools in indoctrinating managers has been described by IBM President Thomas J. Watson as follows:

> These schools were not only to teach general management but—most important—they were to give our managers a feeling for IBM's outlooks and beliefs. After a time we found that the schools tended to place too much emphasis on management, not enough on beliefs. This, we felt, was putting the cart before the horse. We felt it vital that our managers be well grounded in beliefs. Otherwise, we might get management views at odds with the company's outlook. [20]

The danger of such an approach, as of all forms of indoctrination, is that it may lead to excessive uniformity of thinking and behavior.

Coaching

Perhaps the most important form of training is provided by one's boss. Every manager trains by example, and individual coaching is an important form of training. Similarly, every time a manager talks to a group, he is in effect conducting an informal class. There is little point in making a sharp distinction between training and management, for each partakes of the other. Perhaps the best training program of all is the supervisory conference called to discuss current production problems.

Like other forms of teaching, coaching is most effective when it encourages the trainee to learn by himself. What does this mean in terms of day-to-day activities?

1. The coach should provide for enough delegation of authority to enable the trainee to learn from his own mistakes.

2. The coach should set goals and standards of performance toward which the trainee can work—or these standards should be set jointly.

3. The coach should adopt a relatively nonpunitive approach to the trainee's mistakes—and remember that the functions of judge and coach don't mix well. (But the coach, as boss, can't sit idly by while mistakes are repeated too often.)

4. The coach should require the trainee to be very explicit about the steps he takes in handling a problem. He should ask such questions as, "How much authority did you delegate to subordinates? What standards did you set up? How did you communicate to those below?"

5. The trainee should be given special assignments that require him to develop new experiences outside his normal routine.

6. The supervisor should give constructive criticism, encourage the trainee to talk through his problems, and help him discover for himself how and why he has made mistakes.

[20] *A Business and Its Beliefs* (New York: McGraw-Hill, 1963), p. 91.

Above all, the supervisor must practice good human relations himself. Since his subordinates copy him, they learn his bad traits as well as his good.

Training through coaching is successful on a company-wide basis only if each level of management holds the next level responsible for training results— in other words, only if the supervisor's boss starts asking questions when the manager's subordinates are inadequately trained. Unfortunately, many otherwise good executives are very poor at developing those under them. In some instances a manager's training ability can be improved through classroom instruction in training techniques or through coaching by his own boss. However, since there are many "hard-core" managers who do not respond to this sort of training, there will always be a place for the other forms of training we have discussed.

There is a further danger that coaching will turn the subordinate into a carbon copy of his boss. Slavish copying of the boss's behavior is desirable only when (1) boss and subordinate have identical personalities, so that what is good for one is good for the other; (2) the boss is already an ideal manager; and (3) there is no need to experiment with new approaches. Since these three conditions are never met in practice, coaching should be supplemented with other forms of training.

Choice of Program

Traditionally, a manager was "sent" to a training program either because everyone in his particular group was expected to go or because it was felt that he needed some special help. In neither case was the manager's own preference asked. Understandably, many managers resented being treated as schoolboys, and this fact hardly increased their willingness to change their behavior as a result of training.

In recent years, however, a number of companies have begun to permit managers considerable choice in choosing their own developmental programs. If they wish to attend a special university class, a regular night school, a T-group, a meeting of a professional society, or even to take a lengthy leave for an advanced degree, many companies encourage them to do so and even pay part of the cost. Training thus becomes the manager's own responsibility and is consistent with what has been called the "open system" of career development (see p. 490).

EVALUATING TRAINING EFFECTIVENESS

Management training and OD are still in their infancy, and much of the activity in this area is done on faith, with very little hard evidence of its effectiveness. Organizations seem to be following a "policy that is best characterized as spending millions for training, but not a penny for training evaluation."[21]

[21] John R. Campbell *et al.*, *Managerial Behavior, Performance, and Effectiveness* (New York: McGraw-Hill, 1970), p. 49.

Yet evaluation of any form of training is difficult. Students may judge the program and suggest improvements, but the value of such "customer reactions" is doubtful since participants try to be tactful. Moreover, real learning is often frustrating, and the inspiration peddler may win the popularity contest over the trainer who poses difficult questions.

It is possible, perhaps with before-and-after tests, to measure changes in student attitudes during training; but as we have just seen, attitudes developed in class may fade away rapidly in an unsympathetic back-home environment. A more important consideration is whether training changes on-the-job behavior. The trainee's performance can be evaluated by his boss, subordinates, and fellow workers, and this evaluation may be made just before training, immediately after training, and well after training (the last series to see whether change has persisted). Unfortunately the fact that the evaluators know that the trainee has gone through training may influence their judgments.

To many members of management the crucial test is whether training increases efficiency and profits. Yet in practice it is extremely difficult to isolate the impact of training on organizational effectiveness, because so many other factors may be responsible, such as changes in technology or market conditions. Ideally, one should take a number of identical groups doing the same work under identical conditions and then train the managers of some of these groups and leave the others as controls. Yet in real organizations (as opposed to those created in the research lab) it is difficult to find groups that will remain identical (except for the characteristics being studied) throughout the research.

Persistent current research into the lasting impact of training, particularly T-group training, is demonstrating that T-groups do change attitudes and even (according to a few studies) behavior.[22] Whether trainees benefit seems to be related to (1) how well they react during training and their willingness to accept feedback reports (and these, in turn, seem to be related to basic personality variables such as ego, strength, and flexibility) and (2) the trainee's security, power, and autonomy on the job.

But there is still some argument over whether such research is valid. On one side it is argued that most of this research fails to adhere to standard scientific procedures, such as the use of controls. The studies are defended on the grounds that the standard measures are inappropriate and may indeed contribute more error than they eliminate. The argument itself is somewhat technical; regardless, meaningful evaluation techniques are necessary if management is to make intelligent decisions in this area.

CONCLUSION

Management training, an essential part of management development, supplements other developmental techniques such as job rotation and performance evaluation. Such training is necessary to help promotable managers prepare for

[22] For a summary of the main research and discussion of the issues see the debate between Chris Argyris and Marvin Dunnette and John R. Campbell in "A Symposium: Laboratory Training," *Industrial Relations,* Vol. 8, No. 1 (October 1968).

advancement, to assist managers in keeping up with technological developments, to build morale in lower-level managers by demonstrating top management's interest in them, and, above all, to help improve interpersonal relations.

Technical training is fairly straightforward. But if training in interpersonal relations is to result in behavioral change on the job, two difficult conditions must be met. First, it must lead to attitudinal change and this means that the training must be focused on feeling as well as on intellectual principles; usually this also requires some kind of confrontation and unfreezing. Second, the organizational environment must permit the trainee to practice on the job the skills he has learned in class.

Conventional training techniques, such as lectures, case discussion, and even role-playing meet these two conditions only to a very small degree. For a while, a number of companies looked to T-groups as the sure-fire answer. But in the hands of some trainers, T-groups were excessively stressful and there was the problem of fade-out in an unsympathetic home environment.

Faced with either restricting training to a rather superficial level or seeking to change the organizational environment, a number of companies have selected the second course. OD is still experimental, but it represents our most ambitious effort to make training realistic and sustaining, and to eliminate the barrier between the classroom and the job.

problem • TRAINING PROGRAM

The Stockton Company had 15 plants scattered through the country. As a professor and training consultant, I was involved in only one plant, where I worked with Otto Fitch, the plant training director. After I had known him for a while, Otto told me that the training program had started at a meeting of the 15 plant managers. Allen Higgins had just been put in as company-wide training director.

"He sold the president on the idea there ought to be a development program in every plant; it was the modern, progressive thing. Higgins is a great salesman. So the president brought him to the meeting and said, 'We've been thinking about a supervisory development program and Higgins will tell you about it.' I doubt if any of the plant managers knew the slightest bit about training before Higgins spoke and I doubt if they knew much more after. One man spoke against it. He said, 'My foremen are pretty good as they are. I don't want anyone changing them.' The rest were quiet."

So the program was initiated. Each plant manager was asked to pick a training director from among his men. Otto's manager asked Otto, his safety director, to take on the job. The program got off to a flying start; all the new training directors spent three weeks learning their job at a resort hotel.

"We really got the works; how to run movies, buzz sessions, role-playing, conference leadership, just about everything except how to handle management back home. There were outside speakers, a big banquet every week. We figured the company put out $2,000 on each of us— companies don't spend money like that unless they are serious. I went home in a blaze of enthusiasm.

"Only there were no brass bands to meet me. Now I was safety *and* training director. That was a blow. I figured someone else would take over safety. But I was going to get a training program somehow. The plant manager said he would back me up on anything. However, when I tried to get the foremen released for classes, the production superintendent said he needed them on the job. I took that to the plant manager; he felt maybe we ought to hold the classes after work on their own time. I asked for suggestions on what to cover. He said anything I said went; I was 100 per cent in charge.

"I waited till Higgins came in town. He sized things up quickly and soon it was settled that foremen would get overtime for coming to class. So I started my classes. We had sessions on first aid, safety, job evaluation, and conference leadership. But this wasn't going so well—not enough interest—so that's why we went to the University for help."

Of course, I didn't know all this background when Otto and Humphrey Cadiz, the personnel director, called on me to ask if I would conduct an eight-week course for their foremen. I asked, "What do you want? What do your foremen need?" Cadiz replied, "Well, we came to you because you are an expert. I understand you have done a good deal of this before. We'd like our foremen to get all the latest information on human relations. We've got a pretty old group, most of them have been with the company for 25 or 30 years and all they know is production."

We talked a while. I suggested that it might be desirable for me to work with the superintendents and general foremen to get their ideas on what should be done with the foremen. Even some of the general foremen might be trained as instructors so they could teach the foremen themselves.

"No," said Cadiz, "our top management is just too busy and frankly I don't think one of them has the temperament to be a teacher. We want the best. That's why we picked you."

The job was going to be a tough one, but I agreed to take it on. The first class was not too bad. I lectured on what workers want from their jobs. Cadiz was there and so was the plant superintendent. Next session the superintendent was absent (he never returned). I switched the subject and tried to get discussion on day-to-day problems of supervision. Cadiz took part and it seemed that when the other men talked, they were looking to him for approval. After the session was over, Cadiz told me he thought it would be better if I lectured, since the men were really interested in hearing my ideas, not their own.

For the next few weeks I plunged into interview techniques, starting out with a lecture on why it pays to listen. Soon I had the class broken down into pairs, each pair enacting an interview. The group seemed to do reasonably well, but I sensed a certain hostility toward me—and each session it got worse. Getting discussion was like pulling teeth. When I got what I thought were good answers, I had the feeling that the people didn't believe what they said.

On the sixth session Cadiz was out of town. I decided to take advantage of his absence by bringing the problem out in the open. I said, "I have the feeling that a lot of you think this kind of approach, listening and all, might be fine for a professor, but just doesn't have any practical value, that it is a waste of time." I stopped and paused for a reply. Over a minute rolled by until somebody was brave enough to say, "You tell us we should listen to our employees' problems. But how are we going to get them to talk to us in the first place? They take their problems to their stewards."

I wrote his objection on the blackboard and waited for some more.

"Also, you say we should consult with the steward before we make any changes. I agree. But if we do that the personnel department will be on our neck for instigating grievances. Anyway the stewards get information from management before we do."

"Why do we have to listen politely to worker grievances when management won't listen to ours?"

Now it was my turn. "All right," I said. "Why do workers go to see the stewards instead of you? What can you do to get them to see you?"

Everyone had an answer to that. I've rarely seen so enthusiastic a group. "They see the steward because management listens to them and not us. In fact the only way we foremen can get a needed improvement in the department or get a man a raise is to see the steward. . . ." And so on.

Things died down for a second. Then a hand popped up. "I have a question for you, Professor. The men in my department all stop work about fifteen minutes before quitting time and gather around the time clock. How can you get them to stay on the job?"

(A wonderful question for discussion, I thought, but I suspected it was loaded.) "What have you tried so far?" I asked.

"Well I tried asking them not to congregate, but they laughed at me. I gave one a warning slip, but management tore it up. Unless I get some backing, I can't do a thing. What do *you* think?" I ducked the question, and tried to explore some more positive approaches without much luck. The group was too interested in telling me their troubles. And I was worried what management would think when they found I was running a session like that.

It was probably fortunate that Cadiz attended the rest of the sessions. I suggested it might be useful for him to spend a little time explaining the company's interpretation of the union contract. He felt not: The foremen were too close to the union as it was, and if he were to discuss company strategy it would soon leak back to the union.

A year later, Otto, the training director, and I were reminiscing. Otto had been sounding out the foremen on their reactions to the program, asking questions like, "How did you like it? Did you get anything from it?" His conclusions:

Well, they enjoyed it. It was something very new. And they would like another course like it. But, if by "get anything from it" you mean a change in behavior—no, I'm afraid there is no change. They still think the only thing the company wants is production and that is what they try to get. I doubt if the course changed anyone at all. There was one fellow who was rather disappointed. He told me, "When the program started I thought there would be great changes. At last the company has found the foremen and we will be in on things. But I guess it doesn't mean anything at all."

1. What was wrong with this training program?
2. If you were Otto Fitch, the training director, and had to work under the conditions described here, what kind of program would you set up? How would you go about winning acceptance for it?

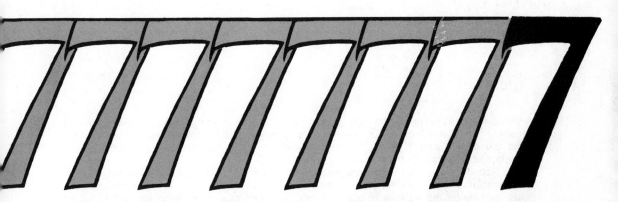

Reward
Systems

Having the right people in the right jobs at the right time is only one part of management's responsibility to develop and maintain effective personnel policies. Employees and managers—and the organization in which they work—are also vitally interested in the conditions of employment. These affect every working hour.

Nobody is surprised to find that employees expect payment for the services they render. The problem arises when the organization has to determine how much money each employee is to receive for the work he or she performs. Each firm must make a number of interrelated decisions concerning the relative magnitude of its wages and salaries (as compared with those in other organizations) and the relative rates for different jobs within the firm. Chapter 25, "Wage and Salary Administration," presents criteria for both kinds of management decisions.

The cost of employee compensation is not limited exclusively to wages and salaries. Another source of employee remuneration—and one that is continuously increasing in importance—is discussed in Chapter 26, "Benefit Programs: Rewards for Loyalty." Popularly known as "fringe benefits," these programs are now an established component of nearly every organization's personnel program. Their administration involves much more than mere agreement to pay for vacations and insurance. In fact, some of the most perplexing questions in personnel arise in this area. How successfully management answers these questions determines whether or not the benefit programs serve as an incentive for increasing productivity.

Employees receive income from the firm in exchange for work performed, but how much work constitutes a "fair day's work" or the effort that management can reasonably expect? Work measurement techniques can be employed, but these do not provide precise, incontrovertible results. If equitable standards can be set, however, incentive plans can be designed to provide financial rewards commensurate with employee performance. Setting work loads and administering individual incentive plans are dealt with in Chapter 27, "Incentives and Performance Standards."

The incentive programs discussed in Chapter 27 have been developed for individual employees. The shortcomings of these programs have motivated a search for other means of rewarding employee productivity, ingenuity, and group effort. A variety of techniques have been tried, and their relative advantages are summarized in Chapter 28, "Organization-wide Incentives and Participation."

WAGE AND SALARY ADMINISTRATION

25

Ask a man why he works and chances are he will say to make money. True, men and women want more from their jobs than just a wage or salary—yet this is a basic need. Even teachers and ministers, who may willingly accept less take-home pay for more on-the-job satisfaction, regard *relative* pay as highly important. A professor may be unconcerned about the fact that he earns less than a bricklayer, but still he may become enraged if Professor X across the hall, with six publications less than his, gets a salary increase while he does not. Pay provides more than a means of satisfying physical needs—it provides recognition and a sense of accomplishment. Obviously, people object to being underpaid, but experimental evidence suggests that they also feel upset when they are overpaid.[1] Alleged wage and salary inequities are among the most dangerous sources of friction and low morale in an organization.

Without a sound policy of *wage administration*, wages are often determined on the basis of "personalized," arbitrary decisions without regard for the over-all wage structure. (For the sake of brevity, we will talk of "wage administration" rather than "wage and salary administration," since roughly the same problems are involved.) Wage administration is a *systematic procedure* for establishing a sound compensation structure. By reducing inequities between employees' earnings, a good wage-administration program raises individual morale and reduces

---

[1] For a review of some of this research, see Karl E. Weick, "The Concept of Equity in the Perception of Pay," *Administrative Science Quarterly*, Vol. 11, No. 3 (December 1966), pp. 414-439.

intergroup friction. It also sets wages high enough to permit the company to recruit satisfactory employees (but not so high as to cause unnecessary expense), motivates people to work for pay increases and promotions, reduces union and employee grievances, and enables management to exercise centralized control over the largest single item of cost: wages and salaries. But, as we shall see, some of these objectives are in conflict.

ASPECTS OF WAGE AND SALARY ADMINISTRATION

There are four closely related aspects of wage administration: wage and salary surveys, job evaluation, merit rating, and incentives. *Wage and salary surveys* are designed to determine the general pay level in the community and industry, thus giving a company a base for setting its own rates. *Job evaluation* establishes the relationships between wages on various jobs within the company. Together, wage surveys and job evaluation set the "base" or minimum rates for each job.

Instead of setting one rate for each job, many companies establish a series of rates or *steps*. A new employee normally starts at the *base rate* for the job; then, as he gains proficiency and seniority, he advances through *merit rating* to higher steps. (Merit rating on one job should not be confused with *promotion* from one job to another.)

Companies with *incentive* plans pay the base rate only for a "normal" amount of production, as determined by time study. If a worker produces more than normal, he receives an extra incentive bonus. Similarly, salaried personnel may qualify for bonus earnings of one kind or another.

The personnel department is normally responsible for the administration of the wage and salary program and often has a special division that concentrates on this function. Top management, however, has a continuing responsibility to review wage and salary policies, and every level of management may become involved in merit rating and in introducing a new job-evaluation program.

In this chapter we shall review the factors that must be taken into account in setting the over-all wage level through wage and salary surveys, then we shall look at job evaluation and merit rating, and finally we shall consider some of the special problems involved in salary administration for executives and engineers. (Incentives will be considered in Chapter 27.)

DETERMINING THE OVER-ALL WAGE AND SALARY LEVEL

Determining the over-all wage and salary policy—whether to pay wages and salaries that are high, average, or below-average as compared with standards elsewhere—is one of management's most difficult decisions. What factors must management take into account in making this decision?

1. The company wage policy is related to its recruitment and selection policy, for high wages attract more job applicants and permit management to choose employees from a wider reservoir of talents. Moreover, they help maintain morale and make employees more reluctant to quit their jobs. And yet, as we saw in Chapter 6, high wages in themselves do not guarantee motivation for high productivity unless the employee somehow perceives that harder work will in fact be rewarded by higher pay. (But a sound merit-rating and promotional policy may provide such motivation.)

2. Employment conditions in the area naturally affect wage policy. When there is a great deal of unemployment, a nonunionized company may be able to hire all the men it needs at little more than the legal minimum wage ($1.60 an hour, in interstate commerce, as of 1971). When the labor market is tight, an employer may have to pay more than the going rate if he is to recruit qualified new employees.

3. If a company is anxious to gain a reputation in the community as a good employer and a good citizen—as are many public utilities—it may decide to pay high wages to insure good public relations. Small companies not in the public spotlight are not under compulsion to follow suit.

4. Unionized companies may be forced to pay high wages as a result of union pressure. Nonunionized companies may pay equally high wages to keep the union out. Yet if wages are too high, other employers may object that the company is "unstabilizing the market" and may exert subtle pressures to bring the company into line.

5. A company's profitability sets limits on its wage policy. The company that is losing money cannot afford to pay more than the minimum; the company that is known to be profitable is expected by the community and its employees to pay liberally.

6. Wage policies may be influenced by other factors too. Companies known for their stability of employment need not pay wages as high as those in which layoffs are frequent. Substantial fringe benefits may also reduce the need for high wages. And pay levels in unionized companies are inevitably affected by collective bargaining agreements providing for wage increases based on changes in productivity or the cost of living.

Once the company has decided on its over-all wage policy, the next question it must answer is this: What are other companies paying on *comparable* jobs? This information is useful in determining whether the company is meeting community standards and also in bargaining with the union. The U.S. Bureau of Labor Statistics collects data for many jobs in large cities, and local chambers of commerce and employers' and trade associations often make available more detailed data. There are times, however, when a company is obliged to conduct a *wage survey* itself.

This is not an easy task. What are "comparable" jobs in other companies? It is simple enough to call another company and ask, "What are you paying your machine operators?" The other company answers $4.10 an hour; that makes you feel good, since you pay $4.20. But the other company failed to mention that their operators also earn incentive bonuses and do easier work than yours. To insure getting data that are really comparable, the survey should be made in person by means of oral interviews.

Rarely are two jobs performed in exactly the same way in different firms. Consideration must also be given to fringe benefits and continuity of employment. It is traditional, for instance, for maintenance men in factories to get lower pay than maintenance men who work for construction firms, because the latter are less assured of steady employment.

What companies should you use as the basis of your comparison—companies in the same community regardless of industry, or companies throughout the country in your industry? The management of nation-wide firms faces the problem of whether to pay uniform wages throughout all their plants or to adjust to the local wage patterns in each community. At times it is far from clear in what industry a firm should be classified. For instance, is a firm that makes rubber soles in the shoe industry or the rubber industry? Unionized firms are under pressure to pay the wages equivalent to those paid by other firms that have contracts with the same unions, even though these firms may be in other industries.

After the wage-survey figures have been gathered, great caution must be exercised in interpreting them, particularly if, as often happens, there is no central tendency or clear "going rate." The survey itself, however, does provide a series of bench-marks against which the company can compare its present wage and salary rates and decide whether adjustments are necessary to make them consistent with its over-all wage policy. Surveys are meaningful chiefly in regard to "key" jobs which are common to many firms. Wages for jobs which are unique to a given firm cannot be set by wage surveys alone.

The company should keep its rates under constant review—if the workers are unionized, of course, management will have little chance to forget this need. New wage surveys should be made periodically to determine whether the company's rates are getting out of line. Wage rates undergo constant change—in recent years, in an almost steadily upward direction. Adjustments may also be dictated by changes in the cost of living or in company profitability or productivity.

Once the over-all wage level has been set, the company can turn to a consideration of individual rates. Here job evaluation is widely used.

JOB EVALUATION

Strictly speaking, job evaluation is a method of determining the *relationship between* wage rates, not the rates themselves. In practice it is hard to consider these two questions separately. In theory, for instance, the completion of a job-evaluation program need not lead to any increase in the total wage bill: Some people will get increases, others decreases. In practice, however, some increase in the wage bill is necessary if the program is to be accepted by the employees; normally no one gets his wage cut. Furthermore, if the rates that are finally set for any job are out of line with prevailing rates for that job in the community, the job-evaluation program may have to be adjusted.

Job evaluation is a systematic way of applying judgment, but it does not eliminate the need for exercising judgment. It is not an automatic process, for it is administered by people and is subject to all the human frailties.

In this section we will first present a very general picture of how a job-evaluation program is conducted. This background will make it easier for you to understand the problems involved in applying job evaluation to a particular situation. Our purpose is not to transform you into a job-evaluation expert, but simply to present some of the policy questions that job evaluation raises.

There are many methods of job evaluation, some of which are quite simple, but many of which are extremely complicated. In essence, however, all forms of job evaluation are designed to enable management to determine how much one job should pay relative to others. Most companies use one variation or another of the *point system* of job evaluation, though the *factor-comparison, ranking,* and *job-classification methods* are also quite common. [2]

THE POINT SYSTEM

The point system involves four steps, which we will first describe briefly and then discuss at some length:

Step 1: A manual or yardstick is drawn up (for an example, look at pp. 587–88), which provides a set of standards against which each job can be compared. Notice that the manual lists a number of *factors* on which each job is to be rated and then breaks each factor down into a number of *degrees.* Each degree is worth a certain number of *points.*

Step 2: The requirements of each job are described and listed in a standardized fashion in what is called a *job specification* (see p. 589 for an example).

Step 3: Each job—as described in the job specification—is rated, one factor at a time, in accordance with the manual. A point value is assigned to each factor. Then the points are added up.

Step 4: Each job is slotted into a *job classification* in accordance with its evaluated point total. A wage rate is then assigned to the job.

[2] The standard method of factor comparison is described in Eugene J. Benge, Samuel L. Burk, and Edward N. Hay, *Manual for Job Evaluation* (New York: Harper, 1941). For variations, see Edward N. Hay, "Four Methods of Establishing Factor Scales in Factor Comparison Job Evaluation," *The AMA Handbook of Wage and Salary Administration* (New York: American Management Association, 1950).

Two somewhat simplified job evaluation techniques are *ranking* and *job classification.* Ranking, as its name implies, involves listing a given set of jobs in order of importance, from highest to lowest, taking into account the characteristics of each job as a whole (though sometimes specific factors, such as job difficulty, are given special attention). The job classification system, used by many government agencies, is also somewhat self-descriptive. First, a set of job classifications or grades are established (say from Grade 1 to Grade 12); then the level of difficulty of each classification is carefully described; and finally individual jobs are fitted into what seems their most appropriate classification. All this is done without the elaborate analysis which occurs in the factor comparison or point systems.

Step 1: Setting up the Manual

It is very difficult to draw up a job-evaluation manual that is consistent and free from ambiguity, and that will give a fair evaluation of the relative worth of each job. Because of this difficulty many companies adopt standardized, ready-to-use plans prepared by such organizations as the National Metal Trades Association or the National Office Management Association. Yet other companies, particularly those that have jobs with unique characteristics, prefer to draft their own custom-made manual. In either case, management should be aware of some of the problems involved in preparing job-evaluation manuals.

Selecting factors. What are the factors or dimensions on which the jobs are to be evaluated? Each factor represents a certain characteristic of the job that management feels is worth compensating. Two of the best-known plans, those of the National Metal Trades Association and the National Electrical Manufacturers Association, use the following factors, with the weights indicated:

Skill (total 50%)	*Responsibility (total 20%)*
Education 14%	Equipment, process 5%
Experience 22%	Material or product 5%
Initiative and ingenuity 14%	Safety of others 5%
	Work of others 5%

Effort (total 15%)	*Job Conditions (total 15%)*
Physical demand 10%	Working conditions 10%
Mental or visual 5%	Hazards 5%

Naturally, different factors are used in evaluating supervisory jobs than in evaluating, say, production or clerical jobs. A job-evaluation manual for supervisory jobs might list such factors as public contacts, staff contacts, complexity of duties, responsibility for money, and number of employees supervised—factors that would be largely irrelevant on hourly-paid jobs.

Some plans have used as many as 40 factors, but the trend has been to use considerably fewer. A plan with fewer factors is simpler and easier to understand, and statistical studies have shown that almost the same results are obtained when only two or three factors are used.[3] There are two reasons:

The first is the *halo effect* (see p. 512), the tendency of evaluators who rate a job high on one factor to rate it high on others, particularly if the factors are closely related.

The second is that in practice some factors are more *effective* than others. An example may help clarify this concept of effectiveness: Suppose an examination has only two questions, each worth 50 points. The instructor grades each paper exactly 30 points for Question I, but disperses his grades on Question II from zero to 50. Since all students receive exactly the same grade on Question I, obviously Question II has the crucial "effectiveness" in determining differences between a high and low total grade on the over-all examination. Similarly in industry, the majority of jobs in a given situation may be pretty much alike, with differences concentrated on a few effective factors.

Thus, increasing the number of factors may not result in a more "accurate" job evaluation. Still, it may be desirable to have a reasonably large number of factors to help "sell" the program to employees and to reduce complaints that important factors are not being considered.

[3] For a list of such studies, see David Belcher, "Employee and Executive Compensation," in Herbert G. Heneman and others, eds., *Employee Relations Research* (New York: Harper, 1960), pp. 118-119.

"Time span of discretion." A novel and highly controversial approach to job evaluation takes into account only one factor, "the time span of discretion"; that is, the longest period of time in which an employee is permitted to exercise discretion, judgment, or initiative without having his actions reviewed by his superior.[4] (Thus, an unskilled worker might have his work checked once an hour; a skilled craftsman, once very three days; an executive might go for six months before his work is reviewed.) Presumably, the time-span of discretion measures the weight of responsibility, a factor common to all jobs, since the activities at higher levels of responsibility take longer to complete and are therefore more difficult to review. Supporters of this approach claim that employees who enjoy equal time-spans feel that they should, in fact, be paid equally. Indeed, it has been argued that the widespread adoption of this single standard might permit a nationwide system of job evaluation that would eliminate much of the cause for industrial strife.

Selecting degrees. Just as inches are a basic unit in determining length, so degrees are the basic unit in measuring the importance of any one factor in a given job. There is no set rule governing the number of degrees into which a factor should be broken down. If the scope of the jobs to be evaluated covers a wide range, from unskilled through highly skilled, there will be a large number of degrees. However, if there are too many degrees it may be hard to distinguish one from another.

It is helpful to define the degrees as closely as possible (for example, see manual, pp. 587–88). "Lifts weights in excess of 50 lbs." is more specific than "Lifts heavy weights." But there is a danger in being *too* specific. For instance, physical effort is more than a matter of pure weight-lifting; constantly carrying a number of small bulky objects may be more tiring than infrequently lifting an easily grasped heavy object.

Assigning weights to factors and degrees. Next, point values must be assigned to each degree of each factor. The table below summarizes the point values that have been assigned by the manual on pp. 587–88.

POINTS ASSIGNED TO FACTORS

Factors	Degrees						
	1	2	3	4	5	6	7
Education	20	40	60	80	100	120	140
Training	20	40	60	80	100	120	140
Physical effort	25	50	75	100			
Dexterity	60	120	180	240			
Mental effort	20	40	60	80			
Responsibility	25	50	75	100			
Working conditions	20	40	60	80	100		
Safety	20	40	60	80	100		

[4] See Elliot Jaques, *Equitable Payment: A General Theory of Work, Differential Payment and Industrial Progress* (New York: Wiley, 1961). Controversy centers over (1) whether the concept is at all meaningful; (2) whether time-span can be measured; (3) whether it is in fact seen by employees as a fair method of setting earnings; and (4) whether it can be introduced in the face of market pressures. For a critical view see Alan Fox, *The Time-Span of Discretion Theory* (London: Institute of Personnel Management, 1966).

At best, this process must be completely arbitrary. One must, for example, decide whether a requirement of "two years of college or equivalent" is worth more or less points than "hard work with constant physical strain."

The number of points may total 500 or 1000 or even more. The reason is purely psychological: It is easier to justify not putting a man into a higher rate range if he is 10 points off out of 1000 than if he is 1 point off of 100. Similarly, the lowest degree is never fixed at zero. Presumably to give a man a zero on any factor would be insulting. Note that since the relative standing of the jobs is the thing that counts, it makes no difference if point values are added or multiplied, provided each factor is treated in the same way.

Step 2: Drawing up Job Specifications

Although many knotty problems of judgment are involved in drawing up the job-evaluation manual, in practice the really difficult disputes start when job evaluation moves from the general to the specific—that is, with the drawing up of job specifications when specific individuals become first involved.

Job titles. The first question is one that we discussed in an earlier context (pp. 379-80): What does a particular job consist of? How should one draw the boundaries around a specific job title?

The common union insistence that a man should not work outside his classification has important ramifications here (see p. 395). Questions of status are also involved. A highly skilled maintenance man might object to the same job title as someone with no skill at all. A man who is proud of being "in charge of incoming vouchers" may be very unhappy to have his title changed to "Clerk II."

Job description. Next, each job must be described—that is, a list must be compiled of its duties and responsibilities (see figure on p. 561 for an example).[5] Particularly in unionized plants the job description must be prepared with great care, since many union members refuse to work outside their job description.

Management faces a dilemma here. If it includes only a few of a man's duties in a job description, he may well refuse to perform others. Yet every additional requirement in the description tends to inflate the number of points given to the job and therefore improves the union's case for getting more pay. Further, a job's real nature is misrepresented when the job description gives equal weight to main functions and to those performed rarely.

---

[5] Especially in evaluating management posts, some companies use "functional job descriptions" which avoid ambiguous terms such as "have general responsibility for sales" and instead specifies the employees' functions in great detail, such as, "...2. (a) Receives daily machine-load charts from each of his departments. Analyzes to see what machines were down and for how long. (b) If he was not notified by foreman as to the reason on the preceding day, goes to him to find out the cause. (c) If he and the foreman agree that faulty material caused the down-time, gets a sample and takes it to the superintendent of the responsible department to request corrective action. (d) If the cause is mechanical, goes to the chief mechanic to determine whether the cause is routine maintenance, operating or machine construction..." Eliot D. Chapple and Leonard Sayles, *The Measurement of Management* (New York: Macmillan, 1961), p. 49.

	Factor	Rating	Basis of Rating
	Code No.		X 100
	Total Points		281

Job Title _____ Grinder – Rough (Castings) _____

Department _____ 49 – Grinding _____ **Section** Foundry _____

	Factor	Rating	Basis of Rating
S K I L L	**1** General Knowledge	1 (5)	Requires the ability to understand English, understand and carry out specific oral instructions and recognize signs.
	2 Experience	4 (48)	Requires 6 to 9 months experience to perform routine semi-skilled work of grinding fins, burrs, gates, etc., from a wide variety of Blanko attachments and castings using various sizes and types of grinding wheels on stand grinder and hand air grinder.
	3 Judgment	3 (21)	Some judgment required on standardized rough grinding operations where there are variations in location of burrs, fins, gates, etc., on a wide variety of Blanko attachments and castings. Involves making decisions such as correct grinding wheel to use, distance between wheel and rest and type of rest best suited for job and maximum production.
	4 Initiative & Ingenuity	2 (14)	Performs work of grinding gates, fins, burrs, etc., off castings, according to limited detailed instructions in following standard grinding methods but makes occasional changes in grinding rests and set-ups to grind castings in more efficient manner.
	5 Manual Dexterity	4 (24)	Considerable manual skill and speed in the use of fingers, hands, and arms on repetitive operations of holding castings between rest and grinding wheel and manipulating part in most efficient manner and against wheel without use of grinding rest and burring of Blanko attachment where burrs are ground off by rapid touching of head and open end on side of wheel.
	6 Accuracy	2 (16)	Moderate accuracy required in performance of rough grinding duties involving removal of fins, burrs, gates, etc., from a wide variety of castings where care must be taken to insure removal of the proper amount of metal.
	7 Physical Activity	4 (28)	Sustained repetitive physical activity in manipulating Blanko attachments and castings between rest and wheel and burring of Blanko attachments and castings on wheel when rest is not used. Requires manual pressure for all types of grinding.
	8 Strength	5 (25)	Requires the strength and physical activity to constantly handle castings weighing up to 5 lb and lift 30 to 50 lb.

Total Points 281

Date 1/20/71

Source: L. C. Pigage and J. L. Tucker, *Job Evaluation* (Urbana: Illinois Institute of Labor and Industrial Relations, University of Illinois, 1955), pp. 28–29. Reprinted by permission.

JOB SPECIFICATION WITH POINTS ASSIGNED

Job description cannot be performed in a vacuum, for it impinges on many areas of status and informal organization. An impressive job description builds up one's prestige. Purely as a matter of pride, everyone wants his job description to sound difficult. Companies that have tried to base their job descriptions on questionnaires filled out by the employees themselves have discovered that there is a strong tendency to puff up one's job beyond recognition.

Job specification. The next procedure is to formulate the job specification itself, which involves breaking the general job description down into specific categories, one for each factor. Here, for each job, one must decide such questions as how many years of schooling are required, how much noise is involved, and so forth. (An example of a job specification is illustrated on p. 561.) A careful job specification is useful in selection and training as well as in actual job evaluation.

Step 3: Assigning Points

Now we come to the critical point: rating each job by assigning a certain number of degrees to each factor. The points are then computed and added together. The total is the *evaluated point score* for the given job (in the example on p. 561, 281 total points).

Though job specifications and the job-evaluation manual may make rating easier and more systematic, rating is still entirely a matter of judgment. As such, it is subject to all sorts of human bias, including:

The halo effect. (See our discussion, p. 512.)

Leniency. Raters tend to be overly generous in handing out points. There is no harm in this provided they are equally generous with all jobs, since job evaluation is a matter of *relative* standing.

Consistency. Regardless of how carefully the manual has been written, there will be countless questions of interpretation. The problem is to achieve consistency in interpretation. Seemingly irrational decisions that are consistent with each other may be better than more rational decisions that are inconsistent.

One plan assigned 100 points for constant noise and 80 points for intermittent noise. A machine on which many of the employees worked made a great deal of noise 300 times a minute, but this job was classified as having intermittent noise. When a new job was established in this shop, the union insisted that it should be evaluated as being subject to "constant noise." Management objected on the ground that this noise had been rated as intermittent for years, that if 20 points were added to this new job for constant noise, then 20 points should be added to all other jobs in the shop and that doing this would amount to giving a general wage increase to 30 per cent of the employees. The company argued that the union should wait until the contract expired to demand a change.

Eventually the matter went to arbitration. Though the arbitrator agreed that the noise sounded pretty constant to him, he still ruled for the company. He pointed out that the purpose of job evaluation was to establish *relative* wage rates, and that to give this one job an additional 20 points would disturb the traditional relationship between jobs.

Step 4: Determining the Wage Rate

From this point on, evaluation schemes vary a great deal. We will describe one common variety.

Once the point scores for each job have been calculated, they are plotted on a graph with point scores on one axis and present wage rates on the other. Notice that in the graph below, the utility assembler is evaluated at 300 points and now makes $3.65 an hour.

Next a trend line is drawn through the data, either freehand or in accordance with some mathematical formula. Jobs that lie above the trend line

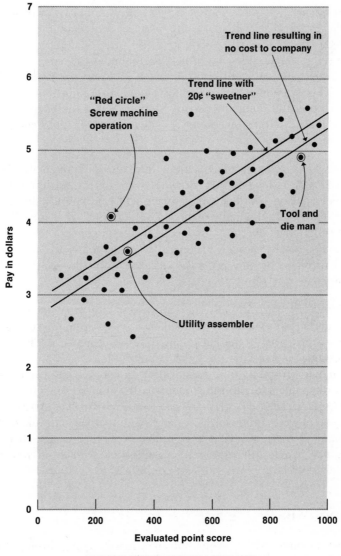

DETERMINING THE WAGE RATE

presumably are overpaid; those that lie below are underpaid. In the example given, the assembler is overpaid by 10 cents an hour, the tool and die man is underpaid by 20 cents.

If the trend line has been properly drawn, the cost of bringing the underpaid jobs *up* to the trend line is just balanced by the savings achieved by bringing those that are overpaid *down* to the line. If the rates are adjusted in this way, roughly half the employees will get wage increases and half will get wage cuts. However, such widespread wage cuts will make it extremely difficult to win acceptance of the plan (since the man who is about to get a cut will normally react much more violently than the man who is about to get a raise). Management can adopt two approaches to make the change more palatable:

1. *"Sweeteners."* Management may decide to offer a "sweetener"—that is, a wage adjustment that will make the plan more acceptable. For example, it may draw the trend line 20 cents above the present mid-point, causing fewer workers to suffer wage cuts. The utility assembler, for instance, would get a 10-cent raise instead of a 10-cent cut, while the tool and die man would get a 30-cent raise. This sweetener is sometimes called an "adjustment for inequities." Note that it costs the company as much as an across-the-board wage increase. (Normally the size of the "sweetener" is determined by reference to collective bargaining or wage surveys.)

2. *"Red-circle rates."* Management may also guarantee the men who are now overpaid that as long as they *personally* are on this job the rate will not be cut. However, anyone who takes their place will receive only the rate set by job evaluation. This is traditionally called "red-circling" the job. (Note that on p. 563, the screw-machine operator has been red-circled.)

Often, too, where there is a general wage increase, the men on red-circle jobs get no increase, or only a partial increase, until the evaluated rate catches up with the red-circle rate.

Job classifications. Actually, instead of separate wage rates for each job, it is common under job evaluation to bracket jobs with roughly similar point totals into *job classifications* (sometimes called labor grades), each of which will receive the same rate of pay (see chart on p. 565).

Since moving from one job classification to another constitutes a promotion, management should give careful thought to the number of job classifications it establishes (see pp. 389–90). If there are too few classifications, it will be hard to promote employees and give them the feeling that they are moving ahead. On the other hand, if there are too many grades, every time a man changes his work slightly, he may move into a different classification with a different rate of pay. Too many changes create expense and confusion.

POLICY PROBLEMS

There is far more to job evaluation than merely going through the mechanical procedures that we have just described. True, by following these procedures management can tentatively slot each job into a classification and for each

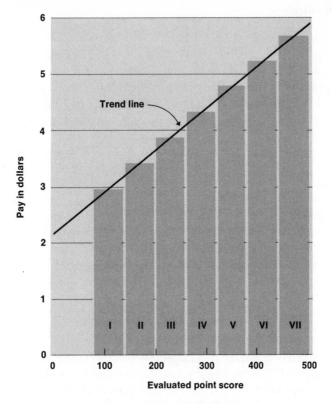

JOB CLASSIFICATION CHART

classification it can set a wage or salary rate. However, job evaluation cannot provide scientifically determined or objectively fair rates. As we have seen, it is a highly subjective process and there is much room for judgment and human error.

But it is not enough to strive for complete, laboratory-like objectivity. [6] The crucial question is not whether management has followed the job-evaluation procedures with scrupulous care, but whether the resulting wage and salary structure meets the objectives of sound wage administration that we discussed on pp. 553-54. In particular, does the structure provide rates that (1) seem fair to those concerned and (2) will attract and retain enough competent employees to do the job?

In short, an effective program of job evaluation should be concerned with employee values on the one hand and with going market rates on the other. These criteria are sometimes called "internal" and "external" standards. A technically sound job-evaluation plan that ignores either of these standards is bound to lead to tremendous friction and to fail in achieving its objectives. To complicate matters even further, these standards themselves are often in conflict.

[6] For a discussion of some of the efforts to improve the statistical reliability and validity of the system, see Belcher, *op. cit.*, p. 91.

Internal Standards

Who gets compared. Usually there are separate job-evaluation programs for production, technical, supervisory, and clerical personnel. Perhaps from a theoretical point of view it would be fairer to compare jobs in all these categories against each other, but the practical difficulties would be enormous. The less jobs have in common, the more difficult it is to compare them.

The job requirements of nurse, sales engineer, and riveter, for example, have so little in common that it would be almost impossible to get agreement on which factors are the relevant ones to compare. How is one to compare the skill or responsibility required by these very different jobs? Fortunately, there is little need to do so. People tend to compare their jobs only with those "close by" them. A clerical worker is unlikely to compare her wage with that paid for any specific production job (though she may feel that all production workers earn too much). Consequently, it is possible to establish separate programs for each group and to exercise a separate set of criteria for each program.

It has even been suggested that there should be separate job-evaluation programs for automated and nonautomated jobs. On automated jobs, responsibility is the most important factor; on nonautomated jobs, skills are most important. A program that gives equal weight to both factors might not be fair to either kind of job.

Rates should seem fair. In Chapter 4 we discussed the determinants of status and suggested that a major cause of employee discontent is the *status inconsistency* that develops when various measures of status, such as job title and size of office, get out of line. Two of the major determinants of status are the nature of a man's work and the size of his paycheck. Great dissatisfaction arises when the *people concerned* decide that these determinants are out of line. One purpose of job evaluation, therefore, is to realign the status ladder so as to reduce the perceived inconsistencies between pay and job requirements. Here, it is the view of the people affected that is important, not the so-called objective measurements of some staff man or outsider.

Employees in most situations have a pretty good idea of what various jobs are worth. In part this is a matter of tradition. Job A has always paid more than Job B. Yet the "accepted" wage structure varies widely from one situation to another.

A number of specific examples come to mind: (1) In one company all the major maintenance crafts are in the same labor grade and rate range. The evaluated result follows the previous custom of equal payment. In a neighboring plant these same craft skills carry historical differentials. In each instance they are accepted as correct. (2) Within one industry several different skilled jobs are at the top of the pay ladder in different companies. Where Job A is at the top it appears to be regarded as the most skilled by management and employees alike. The same holds true where Job B is most highly paid. [7]

For this reason job evaluation may be most readily accepted—and most acutely needed—in new plants where there are no traditional rates and in old

[7] E. Robert Livernash, "Wage Administration and Production Standards," Arthur Kornhauser, Robert Dubin, and Arthur Ross, eds., *Industrial Conflict* (New York: McGraw-Hill, 1954), p. 336.

plants where technological change has thrown all the old job responsibilities and wage relationships into a state of flux.

In any case, care must be taken not to disturb established status hierarchies. If employees are generally satisfied with current pay relationships, why upset the applecart to achieve the theoretical equity afforded by job evaluation? If Job A has always paid more than Job B, in the eyes of the employees Job A is a better job. An "A" man has always had a tendency to look down on a "B" man. Now suppose job evaluation leads to higher pay for Job B than for Job A. The pay on Job A has not been cut, but status is a relative thing and Job A now has lower status than Job B. The "A" men consider themselves demoted; they are frustrated, lose interest in their work, and may even quit or take a militant antimanagement position in the union.

Job evaluation can also unwittingly upset promotional sequences. Let us assume that Jobs A and B are in the same "seniority district"—that is, when there is a vacancy in either job, men from the entire "district" may bid for it. Naturally if Job A originally paid more than Job B, the senior men would tend to move to Job A and turn down Job B. Moving to Job A would be considered a promotion. Now job evaluation reverses this relationship: Job B becomes the better job. The men who had previously chosen Job A over Job B are understandably bitter. Then senior men on Job A will be getting less than the junior men on Job B. Of course, management may permit the senior men on Job A to "bump" the junior men from Job B, but the bumping period will be one of confusion and expense to management and of great ill-feeling on the part of employees.

Another problem arises in evaluating hard, dirty jobs. According to worker logic, clean jobs are better than dirty ones. A new man should start at the bottom, at the hardest, dirtiest, least desirable job. Then, as he acquires seniority, he should move up to better, easier, higher-paying jobs. But this is contradictory to the logic of job evaluation, which says that more points should be given for hard work and dirty conditions. Yet people will resist being "promoted" into a higher-paying job that has lower status. In practice, this problem is solved by giving very low point values to the factors of physical effort and job conditions—or by socially separating the two kinds of job so that there will be little invidious comparison. At times management disregards the logic of job evaluation almost completely; dirty jobs are paid less than clean jobs. But the dirty job is a starting job through which all employees must move. As a man gets promoted, he moves by the ordinary process of seniority from a dirty, low-paid, low-status job to a cleaner, higher-paid, higher-status job.

Similar problems arise when job evaluation fails to take into account such job characteristics as opportunities for overtime or promotion. For instance, Job X pays 5 cents more an hour than Job Y, but Job Y is generally considered a better job because it presents greater opportunities for overtime. If evaluation raises Job X's differential to, say, 30 cents an hour, the men who had previously picked Y over X will feel cheated. On the other hand, if Y's hourly pay is increased still further, others may say that this is unfair, since Y's weekly pay may now exceed that of Z, a job that everyone agrees is more demanding than either X or Y.

Similarly, a man who has a so-called dead-end job, on which there is little opportunity for promotion, feels that he should be somehow recompensed for this disadvantage. So does the man whose job has been automatized. Perhaps his work requires less skill and effort than before, but his output has vastly increased and he feels that some of the benefits should go to him. Yet strict job evaluation would say that since less skill and effort are required, the wage for the job should be cut.

Under strict job evaluation, too, it makes no difference whether the work is performed by a man, a woman, or a member of a minority group, and this is also the requirement of the law. Yet, as we have seen in Chapter 21, strong traditions lower the pay for women or members of minority groups, even though they hold jobs comparable to those of white males.

Another question concerns the differentials between skilled and unskilled workers (in effect, the slope of the trend line mentioned on p. 563). All through the 1940's and early 1950's wage increases were given generally on an "across the board" basis (so much per hour for all employees), thus reducing the differential. Since then pressures by skilled employees have tended to restore the previous balance by increasing differentials.

Thus, there are many factors that wage administration must take into account other than the abstract requirements of the job as determined by job evaluation. It should be emphasized again that the objective is to obtain wage standards which *seem fair* to the people involved. The outsider should not substitute his frame of reference for that of the people involved (except on moral and legal grounds to prevent sex or ethnic discrimination).

External Factors

It is not enough for wage administration to achieve internal consistency, however, for employees and their unions compare their wages with those paid on comparable jobs in other companies. If wages lag behind those paid for similar work elsewhere, some employees may quit, the rest may grow dissatisfied, and it will be harder to hire new men. External comparisons are more likely to be made in some situations than in others.

1. Skilled maintenance men and unskilled common laborers are more likely to make such comparisons than are workers who hold jobs in the middle range of the spectrum. Maintenance jobs are pretty much alike throughout the community; the carpenter, for instance, knows what he can earn elsewhere. To a lesser extent the same is true of unskilled laborers' jobs, the starting jobs at which new employees are hired.

    Since 1965, wages in the unionized building trades have risen much faster than they have in manufacturing. As a consequence, manufacturing firms have been placed under pressure to give special increases to their skilled maintenance men (such as plumbers or electricians)—increases not justified by job evaluation (and of course, when one group receives a special increase, other groups insist on them too).

There is less market pressure on semiskilled jobs. These are not hiring jobs; instead, one must have considerable seniority to earn them. A semiskilled employee may become dissatisfied with low pay but he is less willing to quit because he will lose his seniority, pension rights, and so forth. In any case, most semiskilled jobs are relatively specialized; there are fewer comparable jobs, so fewer comparisons are made.

2. Comparisons are more likely to be made in times of full employment when a new worker can choose among employers and when older employees can transfer to jobs elsewhere.

3. Workers are less likely to make comparisons if the plant is geographically isolated or if the type of work is so highly specialized that there are few comparable jobs.

4. Research suggests that there are considerable differences among employees in terms of the "reference groups" with which they make wage and salary comparisons and that these differences relate to background, personality, and occupation.[8] For example, blue-collar workers, generally, and lower-level managers tend to compare their earnings with co-workers and relatives; upward-mobile employees and those with higher education tend to make comparisons outside their own company. Among staff personnel (such as personnel men or engineers) the higher their professional orientation, the more likely that their comparisons will be with jobs in other companies.

Thus, the pressure to meet comparable rates is higher in times of full employment and in certain job ranges. Many companies use wage surveys in order to keep their wages from getting inadvertently out of line, either in terms of over-all wage levels or of specific jobs which are common to many enterprises.

Reconciling Internal and External Standards

What should a company do when internal and external standards conflict, when the rates set by job evaluation are lower than those set by the market? High-wage companies need not worry too much about this problem, since most of their evaluated rates are well above those of the market. However, the lower the company's average pay, the more likely there is to be "conflict between the disorderly operation of the labor market and the orderly operation of the internal wage system."[9]

Job evaluation frequently favors groups different from those favored by the market.

[8] See Martin Patchen, *The Choice of Wage Comparisons* (Englewood Cliffs, N.J.: Prentice-Hall, 1961); I. R. Andrews and Mildred W. Henry, "Management Attitudes Toward Pay," *Industrial Relations*, Vol. 3, No. 1 (October 1963).

[9] Frank H. Cassell, "Corporate Manpower Planning," *Stanford Graduate School of Business Bulletin*, Vol. 34, No. 1 (Summer 1965), p. 31.

The jobs which tend to rate high as compared with the market are those of janitor, nurse, and typist, while craft rates are comparatively low. Weaker groups are better served by an evaluation plan than by the market; the former places the emphasis not on force but on equity. Ideally, for a system of factors to accurately reflect the market, it should give heavy weight to those considerations to which the market most responds: skill, job conditions and bargaining power. [10]

Some sort of adjustment is required when the market rate on a specific job is higher than the evaluated rate. Many companies pay an "out-of-line" rate. Other companies engage in trial-and-error adjustments to make their job-evaluation scheme conform more closely to market forces. For instance, if some rates are well above the market and others below, the job-evaluation manual may be giving the wrong weights to the various factors, and these weights should be corrected. "If working conditions were given the major weight and skill a minor weight, there would be no correlation with the realities of the market place." [11]

The greater the difference between evaluated rates and market rates, and the lower the company's average pay, the more point-juggling and factor-balancing will be required to devise an acceptable wage structure. Finally, there comes a point where job evaluation simply isn't worth the trouble. A really low-wage employer in a highly competitive industry, for instance, will have little use for job evaluation. He will just pay the lowest rate he can to recruit or retain employees for each job.

Many companies follow market rates exclusively for skilled jobs and use job evaluation only for semiskilled jobs on which it is difficult to make comparisons with other companies. Or a company may pay prevailing rates on jobs where such rates exist, and then use job evaluation to interpolate other job rates between those set by the market.

Thus, if job evaluation is flexible enough, there need be little conflict between the rates it establishes and the external standards set by the market. But this very flexibility may lead to conflict with internal standards. According to job evaluation, Jobs Q and R are equally difficult, and for years they have been paid the same rate. Then a tremendous demand arises in the community for workers to do Job R. So on the principle of adjusting to market rates, R's pay is raised while Q's remains the same. The man on Q protests, "My job is as hard as his. Why shouldn't I get an increase too?" Wage administration must constantly face dilemmas of this sort. Whether satisfactory adjustments can be made, however, depends at least as much on how the plan is administered as on the rates that are set.

Automation

Automation reduces physical effort and often dilutes job skills. Thus, by some standards the worth of the job declines. But workers (and their unions)

[10] Clark Kerr and Lloyd H. Fisher, "Effect of Environment and Administration on Job Evaluation," in Paul Pigors and Charles A. Myers, eds., *Readings in Personnel Administration* (New York: McGraw-Hill, 1952), p. 392.

[11] Livernash, *op. cit.*, p. 336.

insist vehemently that pay should be increased, since readjustment to new work is difficult and the new equipment involves vastly greater responsibility and mental fatigue (a factor often not measured by job-evaluation plans).[12] In addition, since the new systems are more productive, workers whose jobs have changed argue that they should share the "fruits of progress." And, understandably, workers on adjacent jobs claim that productivity gains should not be hoarded by one group but divided among all those in the bargaining units. To alleviate problems such as these, some companies, such as Kaiser Steel, have introduced group incentive plans (see pp. 637–38).

ADMINISTRATION

Any system of job evaluation is doomed to failure unless it is accepted as fair by all parties concerned. Introducing a job-evaluation plan involves all the problems of introducing change discussed in Chapter 12. Employees fear that job evaluation will upset the old structure of social relations; supervisors fear that it will deprive them of their traditional prerogative to set the wages of those who work for them; the union fears that it will reduce the scope of collective bargaining. All may well look on job evaluation as an impersonal, impossible-to-understand system which threatens their old established ways of doing things.

One way of reducing these fears is to make the plan easier to understand; indeed, there is a trend toward greater simplicity. Another is to involve the maximum number of people in administering the plan. In general, the larger the number of people who take part, the more likely the plan is to be accepted— though there is always danger that if too many people are involved in the early stages, so much time will be spent in discussion that the plan will never be put into effect at all.

In a nonunionized organization the job-evaluation program is at times administered by a committee representing a broad range of departments and levels of management. The line supervisors involved are consulted and their approval is required before a job specification is made final. Moreover, the individual workers are consulted when the job specifications are drawn up. Usually the personnel department acts as general coordinator for the program, though a few companies assign this task to the industrial engineering department or even to an outside consultant. (It can be argued that job evaluation is more properly the personnel department's function, since above all the program demands flexibility and skill in dealing with people.)

One of the problems of administration is deciding on the proper degree of centralization: Should job evaluation be conducted on an office-wide, a plant-wide, or a company-wide basis? To what extent should the individual supervisor be permitted to make exceptions in special cases (*e.g.*, to grant a salary increase to avoid losing an exceptionally good man)? Too much centralization severely

---

[12] After the workers have adjusted to automated work, they may find it easier than their old work; but at the time of the change, they find it harder and demand an immediate increase as a *quid pro quo* for their cooperation during the transition period.

limits the freedom of the individual manager; too little makes it possible for a manager to be exceptionally liberal, thus adding unnecessary expense and raising the danger that others will feel discriminated against. The trend is toward allowing supervisors to make exceptions, but only with the approval of the personnel department.

Once a plan has been set up, constant "maintenance" is needed to keep inequities from arising. Changes may occur either in wage rates elsewhere or in the job requirements of particular jobs. New jobs are created and must be evaluated. Suppose, after a plan has been put into effect, that one group is still very much upset over the wage rate it has received. Neither wage rates elsewhere nor job requirements within the company have changed. Should the job-evaluation administrator give this group another hearing and perhaps yield to its pressure? Many authorities suggest that the administrator should be quite willing to make adjustments *before* the plan is finally adopted, but that it should strongly resist pressure for change *after* the plan has been adopted. If the administrator does not stand fast, every discontented group in the organization will continue to make trouble and unrest will persist indefinitely.

Wage Drift

Regardless of the care shown by job evaluators, average ratings tend to drift upward. Jobs are constantly changing over time. The man whose job has become harder will almost certainly ask that his job be evaluated upward, and his boss will be hard pressed not to recommend that this request be granted. But the man whose job has become easier and less challenging is likely to keep very quiet about this fact (psychologically he may not even accept that it has occurred). If his boss is aware of the change, he will doubtless feel that to initiate a pay cut will be a sure way to lose popularity and to break the "psychological contract" with his employees.

If a job is filled by an exceptionally competent person, there will be pressure to rate the job higher, and it will be difficult to downgrade the job when the person leaves. Finally, even on jobs on which there have been no changes at all, as the job holders get older and see their colleagues on other jobs get raises, they begin to lobby both union and management to get their own jobs upgraded too (often calling for a "long overdue increase" if there is no recent change to justify it).

Thus job rates are flexible only one way—upward—and the drift may be substantial. If it leads to a great feeling of inequity among employees or if the resultant wage rates are unrealistic in terms of the labor market, then a totally new job evaluation may be required.

The Role of the Union

Union attitudes toward job evaluation vary greatly, more in response to the over-all quality of union-management relations than to union policy toward job evaluation as such. Union objections center around the charge that job evaluation is a management tool used to restrict or eliminate collective bargaining. By its very nature, some union leaders argue, job evaluation prevents a realistic consideration of market forces or bargaining strength, and makes it impossible to work out adjustments suited to individual needs. It is "just hocus-pocus which prevents workers from understanding the pay system under which they work . . . a cumbersome calculus in which nothing seems to add up." [13]

Nevertheless job evaluation is often introduced in the first place in response to the union's insistence that something be done to eliminate wage inequities. Union proponents of job evaluation argue that "the basic concepts of job evaluation were used by trade unionists long before these ideas were formalized into a systematic body of thought. . . . As soon as negotiators recognized that a tool and die worker warranted a different scale than a broom sweeper, then job evaluation had been introduced into collective bargaining. Like Molière's famous character, many trade unionists may be surprised to find that they have been talking prose all their life." [14] Job evaluation, they would argue, is merely a systematic framework for negotiation.

In practice, the role of the union varies from outright opposition to complete participation. The UAW, for instance, is firmly opposed to evaluation. As a consequence, some automobile manufacturers engage in informal evaluation for their own purposes, but make no use of it in negotiations.

In contrast, some of the unions that believe in complete participation appoint specially trained international representatives to assist in the process. Local unions often select members, who are then trained by management, to sit on joint union-management evaluation committees. These committee members participate equally with management in writing job descriptions, rating jobs, and setting rates. A different approach is for the company to conduct the entire evaluation, but to secure union approval at every stage, or to guarantee the union the right to object only to the end-product.

One reason for the union's reluctance to take an active part in the evaluation procedure is its realization that job evaluation is a dirty job. Many of the questions that arise concern disputes between union members over who should have higher status. Regardless of how impartial the union officers try to be, some members will accuse them of favoritism. Rather than make themselves the butt of complaints, many officers would prefer to let management take the responsibility and reserve for themselves the freedom to criticize from the sideline. For this same reason, management is often glad to pass the buck to the union, if it will accept it.

Job evaluation is more difficult to administer if the company is obliged to deal with several unions, for each will be concerned with how it makes out relative to the others, and each will be reluctant to make concessions in its relative position. For that matter, job evaluation is also difficult to administer if there are internal disputes within one union.

13 Boris Shiskin, "Job Evaluation: What It Is and How It Works," *American Federationist* (July, August, September, 1947), as cited in Edward N. Hay, "The Attitude of the American Federation of Labor on Job Evaluation," *Personnel Journal*, Vol. 26, No. 5 (November 1947), pp. 168-169.

14 William Gomberg, "A Collective Bargaining Approach to Job Evaluation," *Labor and Nation* (November 1946).

Management has good reason to encourage the union to take an active role in job evaluation and not just to force it to accept partial responsibility for the final result. To repeat the theme of this chapter, one of the primary objectives of job evaluation is to devise a wage structure that workers regard as fair. And the union is in an ideal position to sample and present worker opinions.

Whether job evaluation is desirable depends directly on the state of union-management relations. Certainly a joint committee will turn into a battleground if a cold war is in progress between the parties. On the other hand, if management is flexible in its attitude toward job evaluation and if the union is favorable to it, there may be very little distinction between bargained and evaluated rates.

WHEN SHOULD MANAGEMENT ENGAGE IN JOB EVALUATION?

Job evaluation has been adopted in many companies just because it is the "proper" thing to do. Those responsible for its administration are often more concerned with developing a technically perfect product than in measuring its impact on people or in finding out whether it is accomplishing what it is designed to do.

Job evaluation is always expensive to administer and to keep up to date. It almost invariably leads to headaches for management and to friction with workers and unions. By altering relative wage rates, job evaluation disrupts established social and psychological relationships and opens a Pandora's box of troubles. Even though management institutes evaluation in response to the union's demands for fairer wage rates, friction with the union over the administration of the program is almost inevitable. As a consequence, many personnel directors feel that job evaluation should be avoided as long as problems are not too serious. The real question is whether evaluation will improve matters enough to be worth the trouble—or whether it will actually make matters worse.

We shall conclude this section with a list of some of the circumstances under which job evaluation has the best chance of success:

1. When it does not cause undue disruption of either traditional wage patterns or established promotional ladders.

2. When the company's over-all wage level is relatively high, so that not too many adjustments or exceptions must be made to meet market pressures, *or* when the company is so isolated from other firms (either in terms of geography or job requirements) that comparisons with wages elsewhere are difficult to make.

3. When relations with the union are generally good, when the union accepts an active role in administering the program, and when there is little internal conflict within the union.

4. When there is broad participation in administering the program throughout all levels of management.

5. When the company is willing to pay a "sweetener" to encourage acceptance.

Merit rating is used by many companies to determine which employees should receive *merit increases* that will lift their wages or salaries above the minimum rate set by job evaluation. These companies hope to reward outstanding performance and provide motivation for all employees to work harder.[15] Indeed, even a smoothly functioning job-evaluation system will operate primarily as a "hygienic" factor preventing employee *dissatisfaction*. A merit-rating system should provide positive motivation for hard work.

Instead of a single wage or salary rate for each job, companies that practice merit rating normally have a *rate range*. For instance, the rate range of Job Class III might be from $3.90 to $4.70 (see chart below). Typically, each range is divided into a series of intervals or *steps* (the steps are $.20 apart in the chart). A new employee starts at the bottom step and is subject to periodic *merit reviews*, usually conducted by his supervisor. These reviews determine whether the employee should receive a raise that will carry him up one or more steps. They are made at regular intervals, possibly every four, six, or twelve months. In

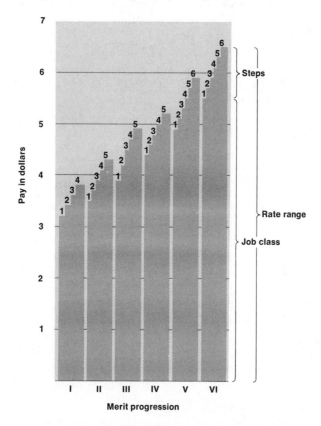

JOB CLASSIFICATION AND MERIT PROGRESSION CHART

---

[15] Merit rating is useful in deciding who will be promoted from one job to another as well as in deciding who will get raises.

conducting the review, the supervisor often makes use of a *merit-rating form* (see p. 577), which provides a convenient means of summarizing the employee's weaknesses and strong points. After the review has been completed, the supervisor at times sits down with the employee to communicate the results in a *merit-rating interview*, which is analogous to the appraisal interview at the management level.

Merit rating gives rise to several special problems, each of which we will discuss in turn.

Rate Ranges

Rate ranges normally overlap—that is, the highest step in one job classification may pay more than the lowest step in the next job classification. In the chart on p. 575, for example, the top step of Job Class III pays $.30 more than the lowest step of Job Class IV. What happens if an employee is at the top step of one job classification—must he take a cut in pay in order to move into a higher job classification? Normally he does not; he carries his old rate of pay with him and starts from the equivalent step in his new classification.

Not uncommonly, the rate ranges for higher job classifications are wider than those for lower job classifications. In our example, Job Class I has a range of only $.60 while Job Class VI has a range of $1.00. Wider ranges are customary on higher-paid jobs to provide employees with more opportunity to display unusual skills on more difficult work. Also, as jobs become more difficult and important, it is more worthwhile to give employees a substantial financial incentive to contribute outstanding work.

Merit Reviews and Merit Interviews

Merit rating of hourly-paid and lower-ranking salaried employees involves many of the problems of performance rating that we discussed in Chapter 23. There are numerous types of rating forms, though the check-the-box type illustrated on the opposite page is the most typical. As in performance rating, numerous sources of bias such as the halo effect and over-leniency serve to reduce the effectiveness of the rating process.

In theory, the merit-rating interview gives the supervisor a chance to discuss each subordinate's problems with him and to coach him to do a better job. In practice, supervisors show little sympathy for the interview process and tend to conduct their interviews in a mechanical and insensitive manner; it is possible, of course, to improve their proficiency through careful training.

Union Attitudes Toward Merit Reviews

Unions in general oppose merit rating, insisting that it opens the door to rivalry and bad feeling between employees and to favoritism on the part of supervisors. They would prefer that all employees receive the same rate, and feel that if there is to be a rate range, employees should move up from step to step purely by seniority.

When merit-rating systems are established in unionized plants, the union tends to pressure management into giving each employee an increase every time a rating period comes around. If an employee is skipped over, the union files a grievance and requires management to explain why he did not receive an increase. Understandably, grievances of this sort often lead to recriminations and bad feelings. Yet where management yields to such pressures, wage increases from one step to another become completely automatic and depend exclusively on seniority rather than performance. Sometimes a compromise is worked out whereby employees automatically move up one step each review period until they reach the "mid-step" halfway between the top and bottom of the range. Pay increases above the mid-step are given purely at the discretion of management. (In government service, however, it is quite common for increases to be based entirely on seniority.)

NAME *Howard Bowman* JOB *Pool crib attendant*
DATE *7/16/72* FOREMAN *David Thatcher*
If on job less than six months, state time _____

Supervision required	4	Attendance	4
Job knowledge	2	Adaptability	2
Attitude, conduct, cooperation	4	Judgment	1
Safety	3	Quantity	4
Housekeeping	2	Quality	2
		Rating	22

Remarks *An able employee who shows a tendency to be lazy. He knows his job well but is frequently late to work and uncooperative with other employees.*

Reviewed by Board ☑
Total ③

Rating Code
1. Top
2. Above average
3. Average
4. Below average
5. Unsatisfactory

MERIT RATING FORM

When Should Merit Rating Be Used?

In theory, merit rating should relax the rigidity of job evaluation (which emphasizes the job, not the man who performs it) and should provide recognition for performance. It should also raise both productivity and morale, since employees who do a good job are rewarded. In practice, however, employees often come to expect that raises will be given automatically, instead of as a reward for good work. Indeed, for an employee to be denied an increase is sometimes regarded as a form of discipline and is sharply resented unless it is clearly justified. Moreover, a poorly administered merit-rating program may lead to constant tension and ill feeling between supervisors and subordinates (and between management and union). Employees may become demoralized when they reach the top of their range, particularly if there is little realistic chance of their being promoted to a higher ranking job. Understandably, they become upset when they see younger (and presumably less competent) employees getting raises, which are denied to them. Under these circumstances there is often great pressure to raise the top of the range.

In general, merit rating should not be introduced unless the employees themselves accept the principle that there may be a legitimate difference in compensation among employees who hold the same job title. If employees think such distinctions are unfair, they are bound to resist any attempt to create them. Such distinctions are most likely to be accepted by highly skilled workers and by white-collar workers. On highly skilled production jobs there is a significant difference between outstanding performance and merely adequate performance, while white-collar workers are particularly anxious to advance in their work. For this reason, and because of blue-collar union opposition, rate ranges are considerably more common among white-collar than among blue-collar employees.

Finally, merit rating should not be attempted unless subordinates have confidence that the rating will be fair. Ratings do more harm than good if employees assume that there is any arbitrariness or favoritism in the way they are made. Thus, a company would be wise to forego merit rating unless its supervisory practices are generally sound and it enjoys good union-management relations.

SALARY ADMINISTRATION FOR EXECUTIVES

Salary administration for executives involves most of the problems that apply to clerical and production employees, but it also involves certain peculiar problems of its own. Indeed, some argue that principles of wage administration, developed at the factory level, are completely inappropriate for management.

Generalized vs. Individualized Increases

In this inflationary period, employees generally—both blue-collar and managerial—have come to expect regular pay increases. For blue-collar workers these increases normally take the form of across-the-board pay hikes given simultaneously to all employees (supplemented at times by promotions and merit raises). In unionized companies, the size of the increases is naturally determined by collective bargaining.

Some companies give their white-collar and managerial employees increases identical to those given blue-collar employees, the logic being that to treat one group differently would result in great antagonism. But other unionized companies feel such uniformity is unwise because it makes nonunion employees dependent on the union for the size of their increase and perhaps leads these employees to identify with the union. Furthermore, if increases are given across the board, individual differences are not taken into account, differences that are especially important at the managerial level. For these reasons, across-the-board increases, given all employees at the same time, are less frequent at the white-collar than at the blue-collar level, and are utilized less frequently still for managers. The typical practice is a periodic review of each manager's salary, perhaps every six months or year, often on the anniversary date of his entrance into the company. This is the equivalent of merit rating at lower levels. In such a salary review, the size of an increase is largely determined on the basis of an evaluation by his direct superior (see Chapter 24). Under such circumstances most executives will receive an increase at least approximating the change in cost of living since the previous review (zero increases are rarely given except to the downright incompetent), but really large increases go only to those whose performance has been truly outstanding.

A modification of this approach is to require the salaries of all managers to be reviewed at fixed, fairly infrequent intervals (say, every two years). But the boss of an outstanding manager may initiate an earlier review of the manager's salary. Thus the up-and-coming managers tend not only to receive increases more frequently than do run-of-the-mill men, but also to get larger increases each time around.

Managerial Job Evaluation

To determine managerial salaries, many companies use a modified version of the standard job-evaluation procedure—that is, they go through the normal steps of job description, point rating, and establishing salary grades and salary ranges. And yet executive jobs are particularly hard to describe. They are more complex than lower-level jobs, and, particularly at higher levels, no two jobs are alike. The manager of Plant A, which concentrates on experimental work, has a different set of responsibilities from those of the manager of Plant B, which specializes in routine, mass-production work. Yet both executives have the same title: "Plant Manager."

Obviously most of the factors used to evaluate subordinates' jobs (such as skill or working conditions) are not appropriate to an evaluation of executive responsibility. Executive jobs, after all, require a great deal of decision-making, planning, and supervision of others. Yet these special executive skills are often difficult to define, measure, or reduce to the "degrees" that are required by most forms of job evaluation.

Moreover, since there is usually a great difference between the efficiency with which two men perform the same job at the executive level, executive jobs are usually assigned salary ranges (for instance, $18,000 to $25,000) rather than a specific salary ($20,135).

The width of salary grades—the within-grade progression or percentage by which the salary of the man classified at the top of the grade exceeds that of the men at the bottom of the grade—should depend theoretically on the extent to which the performance of the individual job holder can determine the value of the job. In other words, how much can man-worth affect job worth? [16]

[16] Robert E. Sibson, "Plan for Management Salary Administration," *Harvard Business Review*, Vol. 34, No. 3 (November 1956), p. 112. Since the individual is so much more important than the job at these levels, it has been suggested that job evaluation should never be applied to top management.

Keeping Costs in Line

Since individual differences are so significant at the executive level, performance evaluation may be more important than job evaluation. The two programs must be closely coordinated, however, to prevent inequities from arising (for instance, to prevent executives of equal merit from being paid more in Division A, which has a generous division manager, than they are in Division B, whose manager is more cost-conscious). Many companies permit a certain amount of flexibility in their evaluation system to provide for individual bargaining—that is, to make it possible to grant a special raise to keep a good man who has had a better offer from another company.

Excessive flexibility can cause trouble. In being overgenerous in granting salary increases to his subordinates, the executive can both jeopardize his company's profit position and create inequities between departments. Expectations arise in some departments that all employees will receive merit increases annually. When this happens the "merit" increase becomes the equivalent of an across-the-board increase and those who fail to get increases feel very much discriminated against. To keep costs down, prevent inequities, and preserve merit rating as a means of rewarding good performance, some guidelines are necessary. Departments can be given quotas which they cannot exceed without special authorization. For example, the average increase may not exceed 5 per cent, or not more than half the employees may receive increases in any one year.

Regardless of how the quota is set, problems are likely to occur. [17] Often each department is given an equal merit-increase budget (say 5 per cent of present salaries), which can be allocated among deserving managers as the department head feels appropriate. But an equal budget for each department is equitable only if, on the average, the managers in each department are equally deserving of salary increases. Suppose we have two adjoining departments. Department A has many long-service managers, most of whom are already at the top of their salary ranges. Department B has a number of younger managers, many of whom are growing quite rapidly on the job. Clearly, it would be inequitable to give the same quota to each department.

Obviously no one guideline is sufficient. Nevertheless, even in companies which do not follow rigid programs, higher management, the personnel department, and the accounting department all police the salary structure. An executive whose structure gets out of proportion may well have to give some careful explanations to his boss.

Communicating Salary Positions

The details of the executive salary program are often kept secret—either by design or because of poor communications. Top management fears that all sorts of rivalry and bad feeling will develop if each executive knows what his

---

[17] See Thomas H. Patten, Jr., "Finding Merit Increases for Salaried Employees," *MSU Business Topics* (Summer 1968), pp. 7–18.

colleagues are getting. But there is little justification for keeping an executive from knowing how he himself stands. At times, for example, in companies with managerial rate ranges, an executive who receives $25,000 a year has no idea whether he is already at the top of his salary grade, or whether he can reasonably expect to receive several thousand dollars more in salary increases without having to go to a higher-ranking job. Typically, executives are in the dark about the basis upon which their work is judged, or what they are required to do to increase their earnings. Uncertainty of this sort leads to the suspicion that raises are distributed in an arbitrary manner or purely on the basis of favoritism. Nothing is more harmful to morale motivation than the fear that one is being cheated on his salary.

According to one study, company managers have generally inaccurate pictures of how their pay stacks up against others. [18] They tend to *over*estimate the pay received by their subordinates and peers and to *under*estimate the pay received by their superiors. Thus they undervalue both their own present position and the worth of a possible promotion. Doing better than the other person serves as an effective form of motivation for many, but how can such motivation operate if the employee doesn't know what the other person is getting?

A final argument in favor of eliminating secrecy relates to pay's function as a form of feedback concerning performance. We have considerable evidence that feedback on performance tends to raise productivity, but secrecy about relative pay eliminates one important form of feedback. Thus a strong case can be made for letting each man know where he stands relative to the average earned by his colleagues (even if he is not told precisely what everyone makes). Once secrecy is reduced, however, it becomes extremely important that the method by which compensation is determined seem fair and defensible. Indeed it has been argued that the main reasons for keeping compensation confidential are managerial laziness and unwillingness to devise rational, equitable compensation schemes. [19]

Extra Compensation

As one goes higher in the management hierarchy, one finds that base salaries are supplemented more and more heavily with extra compensation in the form of bonuses (often based on the profitability or effectiveness of the executive's own department or of the company as a whole) and fringe benefits, ranging from free life insurance and liberal retirement benefits to company-paid membership in the country club. [20]

---

[18] Edward E. Lawler III, "The Mythology of Management Compensation," *California Management Review*, Vol. 9, No. 1 (Fall 1966).

[19] Lawler, *op. cit.*

[20] There are some interesting differences in the forms of compensation stressed as means of motivating top management. Banks emphasize pensions; manufacturing firms, stock options; and retail stores, bonuses. John P. Campbell and others, *Managerial Behavior, Performance, and Effectiveness* (New York: McGraw-Hill, 1970), pp. 55–57.

It is estimated that the value of all forms of "extra compensation typically averages from 10 per cent to 15 per cent of the base compensation for middle management, and as much as 100 per cent at the top."[21] Indeed, in recent years extra compensation seems to have grown much more rapidly than base compensation, again particularly at the highest management levels. The income tax laws have been largely responsible for this development. Deferred income, such as retirement benefits, is subject to tax only when it is received (when presumably the recipient will be in a lower tax bracket), while benefits such as country-club memberships and liberal expense accounts do not count as income at all (provided some showing can be made that these have a relationship to company business). Recent laws have reduced tax advantages of extra-salary forms of compensation. Nevertheless these are still quite substantial.

Tax advantages are an attraction chiefly for the older, higher-paid executives, and this same group places greatest importance on pensions. Junior executives with growing families and large mortgages seem to be interested primarily in take-home income. Indeed, one psychological study indicates that executives as a whole want only a small proportion of their income in the form of benefits.[22] By in effect imposing a ceiling on their own income, top executives have squeezed salary levels below them and have imposed their own scale of compensation preferences upon those who have different needs and interests. Recently some companies have begun to experiment by permitting each executive to decide for himself how he will divide his compensation among take-home pay and various fringe benefits.

Stock options. Stock options have become an important form of compensation, particularly for top management. Stock options permit a participating executive to purchase a specified number of shares of company stock at some future period, but at a price close to that prevailing when the options are issued. Thus, if the price of the stock goes up in the future, the executive can buy below market and so stand to make a profit (taxed at the low rate for capital gains), whereas if the price falls he does not have to pick up his option. (Some companies even lend money to their executives at low interest rates to permit them to exercise their options.)

The advantages of stock options are twofold: they are a means of increasing the manager's after tax income, and they are designed to increase his motivation by giving him a stake in the financial success of the enterprise. In this way, large companies compete with small, aggressive, competitive companies that offer their managers a sense of direct ownership and the possibility of winning a big jackpot if the company is successful.

Despite these advantages, the use of options has fallen off in recent years. To qualify for favored tax treatment, options must conform to increasingly stringent regulations that prescribe the issue price (market price at the time of

[21] Sibson, *op. cit.*, p. 103. For more recent information as to the impact of supplemental forms of compensation, see Harland Fox, "Top Executive Compensation," *Studies in Personnel Policy*, No. 213 (New York: National Industrial Conference Board, 1969).

[22] Thomas A. Mahoney, "Compensation Preferences of Managers," *Industrial Relations*, Vol. 3, No. 3 (May 1964), pp. 135–144.

the grant), the duration of the option (five years maximum), and the period that the acquired stock must be held (three years). Because of these restrictions, companies are increasingly turning to so-called non-qualified stock-option plans, which do not require approval of the Internal Revenue Service. Non-qualified plans allow the company greater flexibility, but are less tax-advantageous than qualified options. [23]

Stock options involve other problems as well. They may lead the executive to concentrate his attention on day-to-day fluctuations in the stock market and thus neglect long-term reforms that might have an immediate adverse effect on the market but a beneficial effect over the long run. Major market declines, such as that which took place from 1969 to 1970, can demoralize executives who observe the value of their stake dwindling, despite their years of effort. If very large grants of options are taken, substantially increasing the number of shares on the market, earnings per share will be reduced and the price of the stock will go down. Finally, plans must be constantly changed to adapt to revisions in the tax laws, and their complexities provide a field day for lawyers and accountants.

Salaries and Bonuses as Motivators

Some critics argue that the whole concept of salary administration, which has grown up in the factory, is inappropriate at the managerial level. They argue that money can be an effective motivator for higher productivity only if managers perceive that increased effort will in fact lead to increased monetary rewards. [24] The trouble with most compensation plans, the critics suggest, is that managers do not see such a relationship existing and instead believe that compensation is primarily a function of seniority, education, performance in years past, and even more irrelevant criteria such as favoritism or sheer luck. [25] To put it another way: pay is important to managers, not just for the material goods it buys, but because it is concrete feedback as to how well they are doing. When pay is not seen as a measurement of performance, it does not motivate performance. Thus, the sooner and more directly increased effort is followed by increased compensation, the greater will be the motivational value of such compensation.

Supporters of fringe benefits argue that fringes are incentives to harder work and that they tend to reduce turnover. Key managers are hard to replace

[23] To complicate matters further, companies have devised other modifications; for example, so-called phantom stock plans. The company simply credits the executive's account with a block of imaginary stock and at some future payoff date he receives the stock at its current value. Of course, this payoff is taxable as earned income, but recent tax-law changes make this less disadvantageous than it once was.

[24] See Frank H. Cassell, "Management Incentive Compensation," *California Management Review*, Vol. 8, No. 4 (Summer 1966), pp. 11–20; Edward E. Lawler III, "The Mythology of Management Compensation," *California Management Review*, Vol. 9, No. 1 (Fall 1966), pp. 11–22.

[25] For most managers, "getting ahead" means promotion to a higher-ranking job, rather than salary increases in a particular job. Promotions, however, are based upon factors other than performance in the recent past—factors such as apparent qualifications for the job to which the man is being promoted, special training, and being in the right place at the right time. None of these is necessarily or directly related to the manager's recent performance; and to the extent that these factors determine who is promoted, the motivating impact of promotion is reduced.

and can represent a high investment for the company.[26] But critics have warned that fringes can be carried too far. They claim first that deferred benefits such as life insurance and retirement are not incentives, because the period between performance and reward is too long; and second, that such benefits serve primarily to keep the barely competent from leaving, rather than to motivate the really dynamic.

The practical implications of these arguments are that greater emphasis should be placed on bonuses for individual productivity and less emphasis on straight salaries, standardized fringe benefits (which are received regardless of individual effort), deferred compensation, and group incentives generally. The amount of the bonus should be permitted to fluctuate substantially from period to period and should be tied in closely with measures of individual performance.

Logical as this approach may seem, a number of problems have inhibited its widespread implementation. Research suggests that though managers feel that compensation should reflect performance,[27] they also feel that factors such as past service should be taken into account. Managers want stable, reasonably predictable income. Thus considerations of motivation and equity may conflict. Further, as we have seen in Chapter 23, appraisal of individual performance was never easy; but with technological change requiring more teamwork, it is becoming increasingly difficult to isolate individual performance. The need for teamwork makes it inadvisable to foster competition among managers. In addition, for ease of administration, it is often desirable to treat managers similarly if their work is similar. Trying to measure exactly the contributions of each manager takes too much time and may be too threatening to the boss's relationships with his subordinates. The gains in increased motivation may be more than offset by various costs involved.

As a consequence, bonuses in some companies are computed as a percentage of over-all profits, thus making them into a form of profit-sharing (a subject to be discussed in Chapter 28). Other companies make a real effort to measure individual contributions despite the difficulties involved.

SALARY ADMINISTRATION FOR ENGINEERS AND SCIENTISTS

The application of standard job-evaluation techniques is even more difficult with engineers and scientists than it is with executives. In professional work there is even ambiguity about when an employee has moved from one job to another, for job definitions here are quite elastic. An engineer, for example, may be required to work on a more difficult assignment for several months before the change in his job status is officially recognized by a formal promotion. And the distinction between an engineer doing "more responsible" work and an engineer doing "less responsible" work is often vague. The jobs of both may change over time as new projects come in and old ones are completed.

[26] In addition, top level managers learn a good deal of proprietary information about the firm that would be damaging if they joined a competitor.

[27] David C. McClelland, "Money as a Motivator: Some Research Insights," *The McKinsey Quarterly* (Fall 1967), pp. 10–21.

In any case, it should be clear from the above that job classification means relatively little in engineering and scientific work. An engineer's salary may increase year by year, through merit rating. In many companies, when he reaches the top step of one job classification, he is almost automatically advanced to the next higher classification. But this promotion may mean relatively little change in work.

As a consequence, the emphasis in salary administration for engineers is usually on the individual worth of the particular engineer rather than on the job he is doing at the present. Yet engineering supervisors often claim that it is hard to measure individual professional ability. Since engineers normally work on projects that have never been attempted before, it is difficult to predict in advance how long a given project should take. Two engineers may be assigned to what seem to be equally time-consuming projects. Yet Engineer A finishes long before Engineer B. Is this because Engineer A is better? Or because his solution is slipshod? Or because the two projects were not really of equal difficulty?

Engineering supervisors may tend to exaggerate the difficulty of making judgments on the quality and quantity of professional output: the evaluation of professionals may be no more difficult than the evaluation of managers, with intangibles playing a major role in both cases. In any case the trend is toward setting engineering and scientific salary rates largely on the basis of a man's education and seniority. Thus, two engineers, both with a master's degree and ten years' experience, will get roughly the same salary unless one is clearly outstanding. Many national scientific and engineering societies publish statistics on the salaries received by men with various degrees and various years of experience following graduation. Depending on the company's over-all wage policy (pp. 554–55), it can decide to base its salaries on the median, above the median, or below the median shown by these "maturity curves."

Unfortunately, the rigid use of career curves as the sole basis of setting salaries leaves little opportunity to reward individual excellence. Most companies use such curves merely as guidelines. They permit larger-than-average salary increases for those who have done exceptionally well and withholding of increases for those whose work has been poor. Even so, the following criticism is relevant: [28]

The maturity curve approach is wrong because it emphasizes personal characteristics [education and seniority] and ignores work. And, while it does consider performance, it does so in a manner that does not enable pay to motivate performance. In fact, it has been suggested that maturity curves can be viewed as similar to a union wage scale.

During the 1950's the starting salary for newly graduated engineers tended to rise faster than the salary paid to more experienced men. In some firms engineers with five or ten years' experience were paid little more than recent graduates. Consequently, many engineers felt that the only way to get a salary increase was to take a job with another company. The discontent provoked by inept salary administration even led some engineers to form their own unions.

[28] D. W. Belcher, "The Changing Nature of Compensation Administration," *California Management Review*, Vol. 11, No. 4 (Summer 1969), p. 90.

But by the early 1960's the traditional differentials were gradually being restored.

A salary increase is one way of rewarding good work, but public recognition of competence is usually given through change of title or promotion. During the early stages of an engineer's or scientist's career, it is possible to reward merit by promoting him through several nonsupervisory ranks—junior engineer, engineer, senior engineer—but in most companies the only way to reward continued excellence is by promotion into management. But many outstanding engineers and scientists are poor administrators. Promoting such an individual may merely make the company lose a good engineer and gain a poor administrator.

Some companies try to get around this dilemma through the use of "dual ladders of promotion." In addition to the first, purely administrative ladder, there is a second ladder which is used to reward technically competent individuals with titles such as engineering consultant and senior engineering consultant. Engineers and scientists on the technical ladder receive salaries equivalent to those of their administrative counterparts. (Thus, a senior engineering consultant may receive as much as a laboratory manager.) Also, they are given greater freedom to choose their own research topics and receive status privileges such as private offices or labs and admission to the executive parking lots and dining rooms. But dual ladders are rarely perceived as an ideal solution to the problem, if for no other reason than the fact that positions on the technical ladder are seen as "booby prizes" for those who fail to make the more prestigious administrative ladder. The dual ladder seems to work better with research scientists than with engineers. For most engineers, success seems to consist of winning a place in management.

NONFINANCIAL COMPENSATION

Those who argue that salaries and fringe benefits are overemphasized as a means of attracting, holding, and motivating high-level executives and professional personnel urge instead that companies should move away from grimy industrial centers to areas that offer a "university environment, good schools for children, and pleasant living conditions."[29] Even if this is impractical, buildings can be made more attractive, working conditions can be improved, and organizational policies changed to make executive and professional work less frustrating. Though this approach may seem hygienic rather than motivating, it is undoubtedly true that most people prefer to live in a pleasant environment.

As self-realization becomes a more sought-after goal, employees want their jobs to be fulfilling.[30] Since few jobs provide an exact match between company needs and employee desires, employees want released time (at their regular salaries) to pursue personal professional interests, not leisure. Thus law firms get requests from their younger, community-conscious attorneys to have some time

[29] Cassell, *op. cit.*

[30] For managers, "money is seldom enough. Rewards and incentives must also be supplied in terms of organizational factors and variables. Autonomy, for example, becomes more than an organizational concept useful for accomplishing goals—it is a form of payoff. Funding for programs, powers of decision-making, and permissible experimentation are all used as compensation. . . . Organizational policies become a medium of exchange." Fred H. Goldner, unpublished manuscript.

to take civil rights cases that provide no fees. Research scientists want time to pursue their own experiments, apart from their normal assignments. Many employees expect the organization to allow them to go to professional meetings (on company time and expense account) and even to take company-paid college courses or other self-development programs.

CONCLUSION

Monetary reward is the primary motivation for most employees since it helps satisfy lower-level physical needs and also higher-level needs for recognition and accomplishment. Yet many employees are more concerned about how their earnings compare *relatively* to the earnings of other employees than they are about their absolute take-home pay. Without a sound wage and salary administration program, it is difficult for management to recruit or maintain a motivated work force.

Wage administration is a particularly delicate activity, since it deals with one of our most sensitive areas, our pocketbook. And, since it results in the comparison of one man with another, it cannot help but lead to emotionally fraught rivalries and resentments. The struggle for a salary increase often shows human behavior at its very worst.

There are some managers who feel that the way to avoid all these problems is to retreat to the Olympian heights of "scientific objectivity." But, as we have seen, such aloofness requires that they ignore many of the most troublesome economic and human relationships in our society.

At best, wage and salary administration can only channel conflict and provide for a systematic review of difficult problems.

problem 1 • JOB EVALUATION MANUAL

The following is a simplified example of a *poorly designed* job-evaluation manual. Read it carefully and try to find the bugs, the areas of inconsistency, and the areas of ambiguity.

DEGREES	POINTS
Education	
1. None required.	20
2. Ability to speak English.	40
3. Four years school or equivalent.	60
4. Grade school or equivalent.	80
5. Graduate of high school or equivalent.	100
6. Two years college or equivalent.	120
7. College degree or equivalent.	140
Training required	
1. Less than one week.	20
2. One week to four weeks.	40
3. Four weeks to six months.	60
4. Six months to a year.	80
5. A year to two years.	100
6. Two years to four years.	120
7. More than four years.	140

Physical effort

1. No significant amount required.   25
2. Frequent handling of lightweight material. Must lift or handle objects of less than
   five pounds.   50
3. Repetitive or sustained physical effort. Usually handling light or average weight
   material or occasionally working with heavyweight material. Lifting not over 30
   pounds.   75
4. Hard work with constant physical strain or immediate severe strain. Lifting over 75
   pounds required.   100

Dexterity

1. None required.   60
2. Low degree of dexterity required.   120
3. Considerable skill and craftsmanship required.   180
4. Very high order of skill.   240

Mental effort

1. Flow of work is intermittent. No pressure of work. Attention required only at
   intervals.   20
2. Operation requires frequent but not continuous attention. Inspection work where
   flaw is easily detected.   40
3. Close attention is required at all times. Eye-hand coordination needed.   60
4. High degree of concentration. Very close, exacting use of eyes.   80

Responsibility

1. Little possibility for mistakes.   25
2. Small losses might occur but mistakes are easily caught. Errors might go up to $15
   a week.   50
3. Substantial loss possible before errors are discovered. Worker must exert care.
   Losses might be very great but normally shall not exceed $50 a week.   75
4. Responsible for an important operation. Errors oould cause substantial damage to
   equipment or material.   100

Working conditions

1. Works regularly under desirable working conditions.   20
2. Works regularly under poorer than average working conditions; illumination and
   ventilation are considered only adequate (as in enclosed vault or work-room
   space).   40
3. Works under conditions which entail some sacrifice of personal comfort. Subject
   to heat, noise, dirt, and cold.   60
4. Works under difficult conditions such as high, though not continuous noise, heat,
   cold (such as work in refrigerator), and so forth.   80
5. Works under highly hazardous or difficult conditions, such as continual high noise,
   constant movement from refrigerator or hot room, constant dust.   100

Safety

1. Almost no hazards.   20
2. Some chance of personal injury such as scratches and bruises.   40
3. May be subject to moderately serious injury if proper precautions are not taken.   60
4. Exposure to health hazard which might result in incapacitation if proper precautions are not observed. Minor accidents are common.   80
5. Must be constantly on guard against serious accidents which often occur in spite
   of precautions.   100

Using the preceding job-evaluation manual and the following job description, evaluate the job of a press and liner operator. Notice that this job description is also inadequate. Observe the areas of ambiguity that develop as you try to apply the manual.

Job Description of Press and Liner Operator

This girl works in a can-making factory. She stamps out ends for the cans on a machine which makes 200 ends a minute.

The girl works in front of the machine. Sheets of metal are put into the rear by men. Circular ends are punched out by a metal punch which resembles a cookie-cutter. These ends pass through several complicated operations and drop onto a rack.

The girls take piles of ends and put them in crates. Each pile includes about 40 ends and weighs about 3 lbs. A good deal of dexterity is required, otherwise the ends will slither all over the floor. Lift-truck operators take filled crates to storage until needed.

The girls also watch the machine closely, stop it when something goes wrong and make minor repairs. Major repairs are made by mechanics.

Usually the girls can tell if something is wrong by changes in the noise. The punch makes a very loud staccato sound.

When ends are coming through poorly, each one can be inspected separately. Otherwise a girl can talk to the girl next to her. Girls must stand all day except for short rest periods.

Girls can and do cut their fingers on ends, although they are encouraged to wear gloves. Also, if they don't shut the machine down when making repairs (they are instructed to do so), they can seriously injure their fingers.

If they fail to pay attention to their work, a lot of bad ends can go past them. These must be re-inspected by inspectors and discarded. Such inattention rarely lasts more than 20 minutes. Ends are worth perhaps ½ cent.

About three weeks are required to train a girl. There are no education requirements other than the ability to speak English. However, the company believes that girls with low intelligence are not aware when the machine is operating improperly.

problem 3 • FOUNDRY WAGES

The foundry has always been regarded as one of the worst places to work in the Pushem Manufacturing Co. The work is hot, dirty, and heavy. Brawn rather than brains is considered the chief requirement to get the job done.

Yet according to the job evaluation plan, "physical ability" and "working conditions" are weighted relatively lower than "responsibility," "training," and "skill." As a consequence, most of the foundry jobs are rated at the bottom of the wage scale.

In recent years it has been increasingly difficult to get foundry help. Management has had to take men who could not get jobs elsewhere—thus further lowering the already low social status of the foundry in the eyes of the other men in the plant. The whole matter has now reached a crisis. There are now 17 vacancies in the foundry and it is impossible to hire new men at the evaluated rate.

1. How should this problem be handled? Should management completely revise its job-evaluation program? Should it make foundry jobs an exception to job evaluation?

2. How should management deal with the reactions of other workers if it decides to increase foundry wages but not other wages?

problem 4 • BANK WAGES AT BEMUS BAY

The Busti National Bank has just decided to open a branch in Bemus Bay, an exclusive resort located about 20 miles from Arkwright, a large city. There is no bank there at present.

Busti is anxious to determine the appropriate wage for the clerical staff it expects to hire. Clerks in the bank's offices in Arkwright receive a starting wage of $125 a week, but through promotions they can work up to $160. As a matter of company policy, these wage rates have been set at the midpoint of the range for other banks in Arkwright.

A survey of the local businesses at Bemus Bay, primarily realty and insurance offices and offices for local stores, indicates that the "going rate" for qualified clerical personnel is $150–$175 a week. The higher rates in Bemus Bay may be attributed in part to the substantially higher cost of living in this resort town, the limited number of young women seeking employment, and the fact that there are no other banks in Bemus Bay. Banks in Arkwright have traditionally paid lower wages than other businesses, on the grounds that banks offer better working conditions and higher prestige.

1. What should the Busti Bank establish as its hiring rate for clerical personnel? What factors should be considered in making the decision?

2. Could the bank justify to its Arkwright employees the fact that it was paying higher wages in Bemus Bay?

BENEFIT PROGRAMS: REWARDS FOR LOYALTY

26

Fringe benefits—compensation other than wages or salaries—today comprise about one-quarter of the compensation of the typical U.S. employee,[1] and this proportion is ever increasing. In recent years, fringes have grown twice as fast as wages and salaries; since 1959 they have expanded an average of 10 per cent annually (even after cost-of-living adjustments).[2]

Certainly today the term *fringe* is a misnomer. Fringes are no longer "extras"; a vast majority of Americans rely on them as their first line of defense against illness, unemployment, and old age, as well as the source of their vacations and holidays. Today fringes provide protection from the contingencies of life from day of employment to retirement and beyond (and many programs provide protection for the employee's widow as well).[3]

[1] The one-quarter figure is reached if overtime and shift-differentials are included. Fringes play an even more important role in many foreign countries. They are higher in Western Europe than in the U.S. and reach 150 per cent of direct labor costs in some Latin-American countries.

[2] T. J. Gordon and R. E. LeBleu, "Employee Benefits, 1970-1985," *Harvard Business Review*, Vol. 48, No. 1) (January 1970), p. 93. Benefit levels, in part related to profitability and tradition, vary by industry. One survey suggests that banks are likely to pay 50 per cent more of their payroll into employee benefits than are textile manufacturers. (*U.S. Employee Benefits 1967*, Chamber of Commerce of the United States, Washington, D.C., 1968, p. 5.)

[3] This chapter emphasizes the more generous programs often associated with larger and more profitable firms. It is worth remembering that many employees do not share in these. A 1970 survey by the U.S. Department of Labor disclosed that 41 per cent of all American workers do not receive paid sick leave, 39 per cent have no retirement program, 28 per cent have no medical insurance, and 27 per cent do not get paid vacations.

Why this growing emphasis on fringes? Why should fringes be preferred to their dollar value in actual pay, which the employee presumably can spend as he wishes? Several factors seem to be involved.

Employee Demands

Paradoxically, as our country has become richer and more self-assured, the desire to eliminate risk and increase personal security has grown stronger. The prevalence of fringe benefits reflects a strong urge to eliminate insecurity of every conceivable kind. It also represents a demand for more leisure—paid holidays and vacations—with money to enjoy it.

Of course, employees might buy these benefits out of their own pocket. But in general they find it more convenient to have their contributions for benefits deducted from their paychecks. If the money never appears in their paychecks and is never available for them to spend, the whole process becomes less painful. In most instances, too, fringes provide important income tax savings. Since they are paid for by the company, the employee does not have to pay tax on them. As one study concluded:

> For many workers, compulsory purchase of benefit protections had advantages apart from tax savings through group purchase. The automatic character, convenience, and security of a company program are attractive features to persons on hourly pay. Under a company program, the individual is spared the problems of choosing an insurance company, a proper program, and the extent of his coverage and also the problems of accumulating funds to meet periodic premiums on due dates and of processing his own papers to establish his eligibility. [4]

Unions

Collective bargaining has also contributed to the growth of fringes. Unions compete with each other, and there is a considerable amount of prestige attached to being the first union to win a "new model" fringe, such as dental insurance. Union members may give their leaders more credit for a new benefit than for an equally costly increase in pay. And if one union wins such a benefit other unions feel pressured to follow suit. Non-union firms feel compelled to join the parade if they are to maintain their status and continue attracting good, new employees.

Employers

Among an employer's reasons for providing fringes are his desire to raise employee morale, to meet his social responsibility, and to make more effective

[4] Richard Lester, "Benefits as a Preferred Form of Compensation," *Southern Economic Journal*, Vol. 33, No. 4 (April 1967), p. 490. These arguments apply equally well to salaried employees.

use of his work force. Here is an example of these three factors working simultaneously.

Joe, who is 64, has worked for a small company for more than forty years. During this time he has won a host of friends and has earned a reputation as a hard worker. In recent years he and his wife have suffered several spells of illness that have almost wiped out his savings. Now his eyesight is failing, and the quality of his work is falling.

Without a pension plan, Joe's company has two choices. It can leave Joe's personal problems to Joe and discharge him, hoping that he can survive on his social security benefits. [5] But discharging Joe would undoubtedly result in deep resentment among his fellow employees, who would feel that the company's action was unjust. Many would wonder if the company will treat them as callously when they get old. Management itself might feel uncertain about whether it has met its social responsibilities.

Alternatively, management might keep Joe on indefinitely and provide him with whatever work he could do. But this would mean that Joe's department would be burdened with a largely unproductive employee, and it would make everyone's work much more difficult. Eventually, the day might come when Joe would be able to do no work at all, and the company would still be faced with the necessity of terminating his employment.

Obviously, in such a case, the provision of a pension reduces the employee's sense of inequity, satisfies management's need to feel socially responsible, and also permits it to make more effective and flexible use of its work force.

But management is interested in fringes for other reasons as well. Fringes are often tied in with length of service: vacations get longer, the more years one works for a company; at the managerial level, benefits such as bonuses and stock options accrue. Thus fringes serve as "golden handcuffs," in that they reduce turnover. (But fringes also make it more difficult to pry loose an incompetent or dissatisfied employee, either voluntarily or at his company's request.)

Some fringes, such as profit sharing or bowling teams, are designed to promote teamwork and a sense of identification with the company.

Over-all, fringes are a prime example of the "be good" approach to motivation. At one time the typical company's approach to fringes was essentially paternalistic. Fringes, it was believed, would make employees grateful, and gratitude would motivate them to work harder. In addition, some fringes helped satisfy what might be called the "lady bountiful" approach to social responsibility. Today, paternalism is somewhat out of date, but many managers are convinced (with considerable justification) that fringes raise morale and make it easier to hire competent personnel. [6]

What is the impact of fringes on productivity? With the possible exception of profit-sharing plans, there is little evidence that fringes provide any direct motivation for higher productivity. On the other hand, fringes help meet employees' need for security. The frustrations caused by insecurity may lead to lower output, and fear of unemployment may result in workers' slowing down to make the available work last longer. By and large, however, fringes are hygienic rather than motivating factors.

[5] The dilemma discussed here would have been even more difficult in the days prior to social security.

[6] Do fringes or an equivalent increase in salaries do the better job of attracting personnel? The answer is far from clear. Indeed there is some evidence that younger employees prefer their income almost entirely in the form of straight salaries.

MAJOR BENEFIT PROGRAMS

Cost-wise, the fringe package [7] (see following table) is made up of three main components:

- *Supplementary pay:* vacations, holidays, and other forms of paid leave.
- *Insurance:* health and life insurance programs, sick leave, and workmen's compensation.
- *Retirement:* private pension plans and the federal old-age, disability, and retirement program.

AVERAGE WEEKLY FRINGE BENEFIT COSTS PER EMPLOYEE

	1969	1959	Increase (per cent)
Paid time off			
Vacations	$ 6.17	$ 3.83	61
Holidays	3.85	2.19	76
Paid sick leave	1.25	.67	87
Insurance			
Health, life, accident, hospitalization, etc.	5.00	2.19	128
Workmen's compensation	1.29	.67	93
Retirement			
Taxes for Federal Old-Age, Survivors, and Disability Insurance (Social Security) and for other government-sponsored health insurance	6.44	2.15	200
Private pensions	5.88	4.12	43
Other programs			
Paid rest periods, lunch periods, wash-up time, etc.	4.12	2.29	80
Profit-sharing payments	1.63	.87	87
Unemployment compensation taxes	1.10	1.02	8
Free meals for employees	.29	N.A.*	N.A.*
Discounts on goods and services purchased from company by employees	.17	.10	70
Other employee benefits	2.27	1.67	36
TOTAL EMPLOYEE BENEFITS	39.46	21.77	81
AVERAGE WEEKLY EARNINGS	141.44	95.48	48
Benefits as per cent of employee earnings	27.9	22.8	

*Data not available

Source: Based on a study of 1115 manufacturing and nonmanufacturing firms. *Nation's Business,* Vol. 58, No. 9 (September 1970), p. 84.

[7] The term *package* is often used in labor relations to refer to the total economic settlement agreed to by management. Since the costs of many insurance and other employee benefits cannot be precisely determined in advance of actual company experience, such "package" settlements (e.g., "And the company agreed to 25¢ in fringe benefits") allow both parties to exaggerate, if they wish, the magnitude of the costs or benefits involved in the contract. They are stated in "per hour" terms.

Other fringe benefits include retraining, severance pay, and a variety of company-financed or subsidized savings, recreational or special benefit programs. Some authorities add to the list overtime pay, shift differentials (extra pay for night shift), and various forms of profit sharing and deferred compensation.

Now let us open the package and examine its components: how do they meet critical needs of employees and what administrative problems do they create?

SUPPLEMENTARY PAY

Pay for Leisure

The demand for leisure is being met with more holidays, longer vacations, and shorter workweeks. Employees have received more and more paid holidays in recent years, with the typical organization now providing eight to twelve per year. Often, if the holiday falls on Sunday, Monday is the day off. Less frequently, Friday is the day off if the holiday falls on Saturday. Some companies treat an employee's birthday as a holiday, and half-days off before Christmas and New Year's Day are becoming increasingly common (after all, management feels, little is done then, right before Christmas or New Year's Day, and the extra time off is a small holiday gift).

Paid vacations are getting longer. Normally, the length of an employee's vacation depends on his length of service. In a few industries (steel and the California canning industries, for example) sabbatical leave programs permit long-service employees to take extended paid vacations at lengthy intervals (for example, thirteen weeks' vacation every five years, but only for employees with eight or more years of service). When these plans were first established, it was hoped that employees would use this time to go back to school or to take extensive trips, thus widening their horizons, but there is little evidence that much of this has occurred.

At one time, the six-day, 48-hour (or even 54- or 60-hour) workweek was the rule in this country. The 40-hour workweek (usually 5 days) became standard only during the New Deal days of the 1930's. Ever since that time, unions have passed resolutions asking a further reduction to 30 hours.[8] For the most part, such demands have relatively low priority, for the average worker seems to prefer increased pay to shorter hours. Indeed, most workers want to work overtime (at time-and-a-half or double-time pay), and companies that have scheduled such overtime for a lengthy period of time often find it difficult to eliminate. A considerable number of workers use their free time to "moonlight" on other jobs, thus demonstrating that leisure is not universally preferred to income.

Four-day workweeks. A number of smaller companies have been experimenting with four-day workweeks, each day being 9 or 10 hours long. The extended weekend privilege attracts some employees who want more leisure (or more moonlighting time). It is difficult to summarize briefly its relative attractive-

[8] A few unions, especially in the building trades, have won workweeks considerably shorter than 40 hours. A notable example is the New York City construction electricians who have negotiated a 25-hour week plus 5 hours guaranteed overtime.

ness since so much depends on the nature of the business, its staffing needs, and equipment utilization efficiencies. Some companies report significant morale boosts. [9] While unions object, the trend appears upward.

Many of these leisure fringes involve administrative problems. Scheduling vacations is complicated. Do senior workers get choice vacation times, even though they have three weeks, leaving junior employees to take their one week at undesirable times? Petty jealousies and coercive comparisons flourish. Similarly, there can be many ambiguities surrounding pay for holidays. If an employee entitled to sick leave is ill on a holiday, should he be given another day off? There are also questions surrounding how the employee must spend his vacation time. Can he accumulate leave time? Over how long a period—years, for example?

Overtime and Similar Penalty Provisions

Overtime pay penalizes the employer who violates the normal workweek. It also compensates employees for working extra hours.

The federal Wages and Hours Act (which applies to firms affecting interstate commerce) requires that hours worked in excess of 40 per week be paid at the rate of one-and-a-half times the regular hourly rate, [10] but company policies and union-management contracts often go beyond this requirement. Overtime may be paid for hours in excess of eight in a single day. In some industries, especially the building trades, overtime is paid at twice the regular pay (double-time) rather than just one-and-a-half times it.

Numerous other provisions penalize the company for disturbing the normal workweek. Shift differentials, perhaps 15¢ an hour, are often paid to men working the evening (4 P.M. to midnight), night (midnight to 8 A.M.) or split shifts (bus drivers, for example, working 7 A.M. to 10 A.M., 3 P.M. to 6 P.M.). In some companies there is week-end pay for working Saturday and Sunday. "Call in" pay is often given to those who are "called in" but not given work. Similar provisions apply when workers are called in on short notice.

All these provisions are designed to protect the employee's leisure time. They also help to spread work and reduce unemployment.

Unemployment and Job Protection

The imposed leisure of layoffs can have catastrophic effects on an employee's living standards. To reduce the impact of unemployment, the government has established an unemployment insurance program, largely financed by employer contributions. Benefits paid by such programs vary greatly from state to state but generally amount to less than 50 per cent of prior earnings. (The net loss of income is reduced by the facts that unemployment benefits are not taxable and unemployed workers save the cost of going to work.)

---

[9] As of this writing, the only extended survey of experience in companies endeavoring to adopt this procedure is contained in Riva Poor, ed., *4 Days, 40 Hours* (Cambridge, Mass.: Bursk & Poor, 1970).

[10] There are a few, notably managers, who are exempt from this provision. Many are also subject to the Walsh Healy Act, which requires overtime pay after eight hours in any one day.

Because of the relative inadequacy of these benefits, a number of unions (especially those in industries with cyclical employment patterns, such as steel, autos, rubber, and cement) have obtained contract provisions for *supplementary unemployment benefits*. These SUBs, when combined with ordinary unemployment insurance, can bring the employee's income much closer to his pre-layoff earnings. (Indeed, some older, senior employees feel discriminated against in having to work while their unemployed junior workmates receive substantial weekly checks.)

Governmental and SUB plans both contain provisions relating to *eligibility* (the length of time an employee must be employed in order to qualify for benefits) and *duration* (the length of time in which these benefits can be received). Together these provisions considerably restrict benefits. For example, "In steel, with two-year eligibility and 52-week protection typically available for employees with a few years seniority, the proportion of those on layoffs receiving SUB in seven large companies for the period 1961 through 1965 was almost always less than fifty per cent and quite commonly less than 25 per cent." [11]

To receive governmental unemployment insurance, the employee must be willing to take another suitable job. But this requires an administrative determination of what jobs are suitable. For example, may a machinist turn down a job offer as tool crib attendant and still retain his benefits?

Since the cost of SUB and (in most states) unemployment insurance is closely related to the company's unemployment record, the existence of these benefits provides an incentive for companies to keep their employment stable. Indeed, the programs were designed with this objective in mind. SUB is a direct outgrowth of union demands for a guaranteed annual wage. In a few instances, *guaranteed employment plans* are in effect. For example, management may guarantee all employees with at least two years seniority that they will receive at least 2,000 hours of work per year, and management must pay a worker his regular wages even if there is no work available. In return for these guarantees, management often obtains greater flexibility in transferring employees to different jobs or—as in the case of longshoremen—the right to introduce labor-saving techniques.

Work guarantees reduce fluctuations in employment; unemployment insurance and SUB benefits lessen the impact of short-term unemployment; but what happens when plants are shut down forever or technological change forces a permanent reduction in the size of the workforce? To meet these problems, a number of plans have been developed, again largely as a result of union pressure. Perhaps the simplest of these plans provides *severance pay*, usually a lump-sum payment related to length of service, which helps tide the worker over until he finds another job. Such payments can be as high as two year's income.

More complicated plans involve the establishment of special funds under which displaced workers can receive a variety of benefits including weekly payments, job training (to make them qualified for new careers), and vocational guidance. Sometimes union-management administered, these plans represent an imaginative effort to recognize management's responsibilities to employees

11 E. Robert Livernash, "Wages and Benefits" in Woodrow L. Ginsburg and others, *A Review of Industrial Relations Research* (Madison: Industrial Relations Research Association, 1970), p. 125.

whose skills and experience have been devalued through no fault of their own. Perhaps the best-known plan is Armour's "automation fund," which has helped to pay for relocation, early retirement benefits, severance pay, and retraining allowances.

Another form of job protection has been written into union-management agreements, guaranteeing the same pay for an employee who is transferred from a discontinued job to a lower-rated one in the same company. [12]

Layoff benefits vs. new job. There is a conflict between layoff benefits and finding a new job. On extended layoffs, both the law (governing the payment of unemployment insurance benefits from state funds) and an employee's self-interest may dictate finding a new job. However, employers are likely to be dubious about offering employment to an employee who has seniority benefits accrued at the company from which he has been laid off. They say

"Why should we invest in hiring and training costs if there is any chance that his old job will open up again and he will go flying back?"

Although severance pay avoids this conflict, there are obviously times in which the employer may not know for how long a period the decline in work will last. In the interim the employee is caught in the middle.

HEALTH PROTECTION AND LIFE INSURANCE

Most organizations now provide several forms of protection against the loss of income and extra expense caused by sickness.

Workmen's Compensation

This, perhaps the longest-established form of protection, provides benefits for workers injured on the job. Prior to the passage of workmen's compensation laws, a man injured at work could sue his company for damages, but this was not an easy recourse. He had to hire a lawyer and sue through the courts, an expensive, time-consuming, and perhaps unsuccessful process, because the company had a number of ways to avoid liability. Through the *fellow-servant doctrine*, it could prove that another worker was responsible; through the *contributory-negligence doctrine*, it could prove that the worker himself was at least partly to blame; and through the *assumed-risk doctrine*, it could show that the work was inherently dangerous and the worker knew this when he took the job.

Now, instead of going to the courts, all a worker need do is file a claim with the compensation board. Although the board's proceedings are often time-consuming, too, and technical, they are far less so than the usual legal proceed-

---

[12] Some idea of the magnitude of costs involved here can be gleaned from the experience of the New York Central and Pennsylvania railroads, whose wage protection and severance pay costs totaled nearly $65 million in the first two years after their merger. (*Wall Street Journal*, Aug. 25, 1970, p. 30.)

ings. A lawyer is not necessary, although sometimes desirable. More important, management is directly responsible for all accidents *arising out of and in the course* of a worker's employment. A few examples may indicate what this phrase means. Management may be responsible if: [13]

Two workers engage in rough-house in the company cafeteria at lunch hour and one knocks out another's tooth.

After work is over, an employee stubs his toe in the company parking lot.

A painter with a heart condition gets a heart attack and falls off a ladder.

A salesman away from home is injured in an auto accident while driving to a movie at 10 P.M., after his sales calls.

A man gets a slight bruise. Six months later cancer develops on the site and evidence indicates it was caused by the bruise.

In most states, if an employee is injured under circumstances such as the above, he receives free medical expenses plus a proportion of the income he loses for all the weeks he cannot work. In New York (in 1970), for instance, he would get two-thirds of his previous weekly pay—but no more than $85. There are many who consider this compensation inadequate, particularly if a man and his family must live on it for the rest of his life.

Most employers take out insurance to meet these risks, either through a state insurance fund or private companies, though some large firms are self-insured. In any case, the company's insurance costs depend on its "experience." By keeping its accidents infrequent, a company can reduce its costs substantially. A poor safety record can be enormously expensive.

Added to the cost of insurance are other expenses that make safety a goal: the cost of lost production, as a result of an accident; the cost of training a new man to take the injured one's place; the cost of dislocations created by the sudden loss of a skilled man.

Furthermore, it often becomes difficult to find people to work in dangerous departments. Some authorities estimate that for every dollar of direct compensation cost there are four dollars of indirect costs plus, in the case of a serious accident, intangible costs in loss of morale and community reputation.

Hospital and Medical Bills

Workmen's compensation covers only injuries arising out of employment. Most medical bills arise from other causes. To help meet these expenses, many organizations pay all or a major share of the cost of health insurance programs, such as Blue Cross (chiefly hospital bills), Blue Shield (chiefly doctors' bills), or the equivalent sold by private insurance companies.

An insurance program rarely, if ever, covers all medical costs, although there has been some tendency to increase the comprehensiveness of such programs.

[13] The laws vary considerably from state to state. Under the circumstances listed, however, the company would be liable in many states.

To understand the nature of the restrictions on medical protection, two sets of distinctions must be made. The first relates to the differences between *indemnity* and *service* plans. Indemnity plans are usually cheaper because they provide an upper limit to the costs per unit of service, such as $35 per day for a semi-private hospital room or $15 to have a cyst removed. Because of inflationary increases in medical costs, indemnity plans often do not cover a substantial proportion of the bill. Service plans, such as Blue Cross (in most states) provide full coverage regardless of cost, but even Blue Cross plans normally place a limit on the number of days of hospital care (say 60 days) which they provide.

The other distinction relates to *first-dollar* and *last-dollar* protection. First-dollar protection sets an upper limit to the amount of benefits; for example, it may pay the first $500 of doctors' costs or for the first 60 days in the hospital. Last-dollar protection is a form of deductible insurance. Usually the last-dollar benefits involve coinsurance. That is, the employee must pay a certain percentage (for example 20 per cent) of the costs. Major medical insurance is a good example of the last-dollar benefits combined with coinsurance. Typically such a program might pay 80 per cent of the medical costs in excess of $250 in any one year. Thus, major medical insurance helps reduce the cost of catastrophic, extended illness, which may involve expenditures of $10,000 to $15,000.

Insurance experts often argue that last-dollar protection is socially more desirable than first-dollar, since most families can afford to pay first dollars. What really destroys a family's financial independence is the last-dollar expense of a major illness. Yet, if forced to make a choice, unions frequently prefer first-dollar insurance because a higher percentage of their members will receive benefits from it (even if catastrophic illness is uncovered).

The best and most expensive plans combine first- and last-dollar insurance. An example of this might include Blue Cross, Blue Shield, and major medical. But even a program such as this may provide limited, if any, protection against mental illness or tuberculosis.

Companies and unions both are worried that the increasing availability of health insurance will: (1) further inflate the costs of scarce medical resources and (2) encourage physicians to hospitalize patients and too frequently prescribe complex procedures. As examples of increased costs, General Motors estimated that its medical-hospital costs jumped from $29.96 per employee per month in 1967 to $37.38 in 1969, while Ford claims that sickness and accident payments went up to 64 per cent in the three-year period 1967 through 1969.

On the other side, unions and employees fear that the rise in medical costs will make the benefits too low. Further, there are continuous pressures to extend medical coverage to the entire family. (But what happens when the wife and husband work for different employers?) There is also pressure to include such heretofore excluded items as prescription drugs, eyeglasses, dental bills, and psychiatric services. (The last two are particularly expensive, and they raise management control problems such as when is psychotherapy a matter of employee preference and when is it a critical medical need?)

Employees and their unions may still be dissatisfied with the sum total of medical insurance provided by employers, as suggested by this statement:

[For those Americans covered by private insurance plans often provided by employers] only 36 per cent of costs are paid. The average insurance plans pay a high percentage of hospital costs, 76 per cent, but only 38 per cent of doctors' charges. And the virtual noncoverage of such items as prescription drugs and nursing care hauls the over-all average down.... [14]

Because of skyrocketing medical costs, there is increasing interest in more effective health care "delivery systems." A few companies and unions (such as Kaiser and the Clothing Workers) have pioneered in family health plans, including diagnostic clinics for preventive medicine and group medical practice.

In-plant medical programs also help maintain employee health. Company medical departments, clinics, and nurses can reduce time lost because of illness. They can also identify dangerous or unhealthy work areas and procedures. Pre-employment physical examinations can reveal health problems that may make an applicant unsuited to a particular job. Some companies provide all their employees (or at least their executives) with an annual examination. [15]

Sick Leave

Medical plans provide for the costs of doctors and hospital services, but what about the loss of income when an employee is unable to work? To meet this need organizations often allow a certain number of days as paid *sick leave*, particularly for salaried employees. [16] Sick leave can be easily abused. Employees who are not sick may take advantage of it; those who do not use it sometimes feel cheated. Comments like this are common. "I've still got 11 days of unused sick leave this year. I don't see why I haven't got that time coming to me." To deter the use of sick leave as an extra holiday, thus vastly increasing its cost, companies may require a doctor's certificate to prove illness; they may refuse to pay sick leave for the first day or two of illness; and in some cases they pay a bonus to employees who don't use their entire leave (for example, an extra day's pay for every three day's of unused leave).

Life Insurance

Fairly frequently, companies make available low-cost or no-cost life insurance, its face value often related to the employee's annual income. Especially liberal life insurance benefits have been provided for executives.

[14] AFL-CIO *American Federationist* (February 1971), p. 24, quoting Daniel Schorr's *Don't Get Sick in America.*

[15] The use of company physicians raises an ethical question related to privacy and patient–doctor relationship. How much should the doctor tell the company or place in company records about the personal life of the employee-patient? Obviously, many such matters can affect the employee's reputation and his chances for promotion or even retention, and yet the professional also has responsibilities to the organization that has hired him. What are the criteria to determine what is confidential and what can be told the company? (The problem is more difficult when the physician is also a psychiatrist.)

[16] Mention must also be made of disability benefits paid under the federal social security program to employees who are totally disabled from doing work and various state programs (notably in California and New York) which provide short-term benefits for employees who cannot work because of illness or accident.

RETIREMENT

Since no employee expects to work his entire life, pension demands tend to be strong, although younger employees, particularly when they are unmarried, may not have the same degree of interest as older employees. Traditionally, management gave little thought to retirement plans. When employees were too old to work, they were either unceremoniously dropped from the payroll or given a small lump sum payment as a "reward" for their years of service. People were expected to save for their old age, or their children were expected to take care of them—and then there was always the county old folks' home.

By the 1920's a few responsible companies pioneered with formal retirement programs, which typically included fixed retirement age (often 65) coupled with a guarantee of a regular (but often very modest) monthly income thereafter. The Social Security Act of 1935 established a federal program of retirement benefits that now provides a base level of protection for a majority of American families. But the federal program provides little more than the bare minimum necessary for survival, and today most large organizations supplement this with private programs of their own.

Like any form of insurance or annuity, pension programs can be legally and financially complicated. Here are some of the major issues.

Size of benefits. Most pension plans relate benefits to past earnings, but there is a trend to weight more heavily later or higher income. Also unions press for higher and higher minima, which tends to reduce the relationship to actual earnings. Today, in the more liberal companies, pensions and federal social security benefits together may total as much as three-quarters of an employee's pre-retirement income (after tax), while one-quarter was much more common a decade ago. [17]

Who pays? Early pension plans typically provided for a significant employee contribution, perhaps half. The trend, however, is clearly toward having the employer pay the full cost. Nevertheless, many managers believe that it is desirable for the employee to pay at least part of the cost in order to help keep demands for greater benefits in reasonable perspective.

Age of retirement. There has been a modest trend toward reducing the age of *mandatory* retirement from 68 or 65 to 62 or even younger. More common has been the tendency to provide for *voluntary* retirement at lower ages. If the retirement age is early enough, employees can seek a second career. This is one of the attractive features of a military career, since the military permits retirement at half pay after twenty years of service. The 1970 General Motors-UAW contract (as of 1972) allows employees with thirty years service to retire at age 56 at $500 a month.

---

[17] In many cities, policemen, firemen, and even garbage men and subway workers are permitted to retire at half pay after 20 years of service, and in New York City, in some cases, with almost full pay after 40 years. These extremely liberal pension provisions—far more liberal than in the private sector—have been a contributor to the financial crises affecting many cities.

The GM retirement benefits are received by all blue-collar employees, regardless of the age of retirement. Other organizations permit retirement as early as 50 (particularly for reasons of health), but only at reduced benefits.

An organization may use early retirement to solve a problem of obsolete skills or an overage work force. During a period of diminishing employment the average age of the work force tends to increase, and it becomes more difficult to hire young employees with critical technical skills. Encouraging early retirement may open up additional opportunities for promotion and hiring. Early retirement may also be used as an alternative to severance pay when layoffs are necessary, owing to a plant being shut down permanently or its workforce cut back severely.

Mandatory retirement creates problems. People age at different rates: some are physiologically and mentally ready to retire at 60, others at 75 or 80. With a fixed retirement age, some are retired too soon, some too late; but making a ruling for each person involves all sorts of difficulties. Without a fixed date, it is hard to make a man retire against his will. To resolve this problem, many universities permit early retirement at the professor's option, set a "mandatory" retirement age of perhaps 68, and then permit a limited number of people to continue employment on a year-to-year basis by mutual agreement. Some companies have similar rules.

Vesting. Most pension plans assume continuous employment with a single employer. What happens to an employee's accrued benefits if he is laid off, changes employers, or his company ceases operation prior to retirement? Unless there is some sort of *vesting*, these benefits are lost.

Private pension plans hold well over $100 billion in assets. About 17,000 such plans covering about 21 million workers are on file with the Labor Department. . . . Pension plan coverage has become increasingly generous over the years—yet Congressional committees and others looking into pensions are discovering that because of high industry turnover even in good times, stringent eligibility requirements and today's widespread layoffs, many workers "covered" by such plans will never be eligible to collect a penny.

Just how many workers lose out is a hotly debated question and no exact figures are available. "My very rough estimate is that it is quite possible that over one-third of all workers in pension plans will never get anything from them," says Michael S. Gordon, special minority counsel for pensions for a Senate subcommittee. [18]

With vesting, the employee carries the accumulated-to-date pension account with him even if he changes jobs. (A typical vesting plan may provide that pensions become vested only after ten years of service.)

Vesting considerably increases the costs of pensions. Further, it makes them less effective as a "golden handcuff," which reduces turnover. For these reasons, most employers seek to minimize the extent to which pensions are vested, while employees and unions seek to expand it.

Where there is substantial movement of employees among a number of employers in the same industry, union pressures have sometimes resulted in the formation of multi-employer pension plans that allow a worker to move within this industry without sacrificing any of his accrued pension rights. In 1970 it was

---

[18] *The Wall Street Journal* (November 4, 1970), p. 1.

estimated that such plans cover 30 per cent of the employees covered by private pension plans.

Funding. If pensions are not funded, the company pays for pensions only after the employee has retired. If pensions are funded, money is set aside in advance, year by year, in a pension trust that is usually administered by a bank or insurance carrier. The amount set aside must be enough to pay for all benefits that have accrued to date. [19] With a funded plan, employees are assured that their pension benefits will be paid, regardless of whether their company goes bankrupt or out of business. [20]

Parenthetically, the savings created by funded pension and other fringe benefit plans represent an enormous aggregation of capital. Some unions are beginning to propose that the company direct the trustees of such funds (usually, but not always a major bank or insurance company) to invest them in projects, such as low-cost housing, that will directly or indirectly benefit employees. Also, there have been some serious scandals in which unscrupulous union and management officials have used such funds for risky projects that endangered the payment of future benefits.

Pensions for executives. Pensions can be combined with other forms of deferred compensation to be paid after retirement. When these expanded pension benefits are not available to the entire work force, the Internal Revenue Service considers them "nonqualified" pension plans and does not allow the same tax advantages that "qualified" plans are given. To receive these extra-pension, postretirement benefits, an executive sometimes makes himself available as a consultant to the firm and promises not to work for a competitor.

THRIFT PLANS, STOCK PURCHASE PLANS, AND BONUSES

In Chapter 25, we discussed how bonuses and stock option plans are used as a means of motivating top managers and increasing their sense of identification with the organization. Programs with somewhat similar objectives have been developed to cover employees at *all* levels. [21] In Chapter 28 we shall deal with formal profit-sharing plans. Here let us consider thrift and stock purchase plans as well as bonuses.

Thrift plans are designed to encourage employees to save for emergencies and retirement. The typical plan permits an employee to set aside some percentage of his total earnings (usually up to 10 per cent), and this amount is then supplemented by a matching company contribution. The proceeds for each

[19] The precise amount is determined by actuarial considerations, such as the probable longevity of the employees and the probable interest and dividends the fund will earn.

[20] The problem with funded plans is that when pension rates are increased, the company must pay into the fund at once the full cost of all increased benefits accrued from past service, even though employees themselves may not receive these benefits for years to come.

[21] The tax laws require that certain benefit plans be made available to all employees, regardless of level, if the company is to receive a tax deduction for its costs in operating the plan.

employee are then invested in company stock or in some combination of stock and government bonds. The bonds may be preferable if there is concern that volatility in stock prices may depress morale in a falling market.[22]

Other plans provide that some share of the pension funds be kept in company stock. In a company that has grown rapidly and consistently, even relatively modestly paid employees can retire with sizable nest eggs. Often there is a combination of pension and deferred compensation. After some years of service (or in specified emergencies) an employee may begin to withdraw some percentage of the fund kept in his name. Assuming again that the stock has increased in value and the employee is limited in the timing and amount of his withdrawals, we can easily see how this benefit will defer voluntary turnover. As one employee told us, "I want to quit, but how can you leave $50,000 sitting there in a kitty with your name on it?"

A few corporations, such as IBM, also subsidize the purchase of their own stock as a means of allowing employees to share in the capital growth enjoyed by shareholders. Some years ago the United Auto Workers turned down Ford's offer to contribute to employee stock ownership, but recently the union has had some second thoughts on the matter, another indication, perhaps, of the long-run trend toward obliterating class differences in the United States. Just as an increasing number of employees receive salaries instead of hourly wages, more of them are interested in stock ownership.

Stock purchase plans, of course, are designed to give employees a stake in the company's ownership. Hopefully, that stake will help employees identify with the company's welfare, and they will come to understand the need for efficiency and profitability in a free enterprise system. As a result, corporate profits will appear not as unearned windfalls to stockholders, but as necessary compensation for investors' risks.

Paying year-end bonuses is perhaps more typical of Japanese and British firms than it is of those in the United States. Except insofar as they are directly related to production (see Chapter 27) or are a form of profit sharing (see Chapter 28), such bonuses are largely a vestige of paternalism. They are designed to demonstrate management's gratitude for the loyalty of its employees over the past year and to show that management is concerned with their welfare. In unionized firms it has been held that the amount of such bonuses is subject to collective bargaining.

PERQUISITES AND JOB AMENITIES

Companies provide a wide variety of goods and services for employees. Some—liberal expense accounts, trips to exotic resorts, the free use of automobiles, club memberships—are designed to give a status boost to managers and

---

[22] The magnitude of such plans can be inferred from General Electric Company's contribution to its "Savings and Security" plan in 1970, to which the company contributed $45.9 million in GE stock, $64 million in U.S. Savings Bonds, $14.7 million in units of their plan's own mutual fund, and $1.4 million in cash.

help them enjoy tax-free luxuries.[23] Executive dining rooms and employee cafeterias frequently offer subsidized meals. Some companies sell their own products at a substantial discount to employees. Where work is arduous, clothing may be provided. In remote locations, employees can receive free transportation, generous travel allowances, and even free or subsidized housing. It is common to pay moving expenses when an employee is required to move from one location to another. At times, moving expenses are construed broadly to include trips back and forth from the old location to the new one until a new house is found, a realtor's fee, and mortgage financing.

The list grows: For example, companies now face demands for day-care centers, so that working mothers can have reasonably priced baby-sitting, and requests for on-the-job personal counseling. Companies provide recreation centers (camps, country clubs, lakes, athletic fields) and sports equipment, to allow employees and their families to enjoy modestly priced week-end or holiday vacations. The companies hope to develop *esprit de corps* and loyalty, as employees from various departments and levels interact.

For the most part these perquisites, whether recreational facilities, paid travel, educational opportunities or day-care centers, represent a growing demand for a more well-rounded, fuller life style, on the job and off. They also represent an important element in the status system of the organization. Higher status employees want their status to show in larger expense allowances (even in the use of company planes).

Amenities

Attractive working conditions can also be conceived as an employee benefit: air conditioning, modern furnishings, comfortable and spacious lounges, auto parking, even gardens and art displays. Obviously, the facility's age and location are critical factors here. New office buildings in the suburbs can provide more of these benefits than older factories can, especially those in the inner city. What is interesting, however, is the increasing attention to aesthetics, often manifested in construction that is both a one-time cost, and a continuing maintenance expense. Although few industrial psychologists now attribute greater productivity to working conditions, employees *are* attracted by pleasant surroundings, particularly in a more affluent world with little desire to work eight hours a day in a grin-and-bear-it mood. Thus, in Herzberg's terms these amenities are not motivators; they are a form of hygienic management.

Companies having large white-collar staffs find it particularly expensive to provide private offices, but prospective employees turn away from huge, unbroken desk-strewn spaces in which dozens or even hundreds work in close proximity. A number of innovative efforts are being made to use growing plants and new types of partitioning to break up such areas and give employees some sense

[23] Overseas, such managerial perquisites are even more common. Managerial salaries are lower, taxes are higher, and only through such perquisites can managers afford an upper-class standard of living. For example, Japanese and British executives may enjoy expense-account luxuries that contrast sharply with their modest home lives. Tax authorities here and abroad have taken conflicting stands on the degree to which such perquisites are taxable.

of "territory" and privacy. The energy drain of high noise-levels also encourages such developments.

Although these amenities never appear in fringe benefit budgets, they can represent significant outlays and require careful planning to make sure that the benefits are worth the expenditure.

BENEFIT PROGRAM ADMINISTRATION

In providing benefits, sooner or later each company must decide how much is "enough." It must decide where the line should be drawn between services that ought to be provided by the employer and services that ought to be offered by the family, the community, and church and social organizations. The simple criterion "satisfying employee needs" is not adequate. Human needs are multitudinous, and dissatisfaction that will affect job performance may come from many sources beyond the reach of management.

Services designed to build employee morale may backfire with disastrous results, as some companies that operate plants overseas or in company towns have discovered. Service programs that provide housing, food, schools, and the like often develop into rich sources of employee grievances. Who gets the company cars or club memberships? When is it fair for the company to raise house rentals or the price of food in the company restaurant? How often should hash be served?

Most companies seek to get out of the housing business, even in so-called company towns, and out of the food business by bringing in food-service concessionaires. (But even when concessionaires are brought in, the average employee will blame the company for poor food or high prices.)

Obtaining Employee Preferences

Relatively few organizations ever ask their employees' preferences among benefit programs. Normally, employers institute programs because they think they are good for their employees or, more commonly, because other organizations have done so. Even unions are more likely to follow the leader than to engage in extensive consultation with their membership as to its wishes.

A modest number of studies have measured employee preferences among alternative forms of compensation; for example, between straight pay and various forms of fringe benefits. Much of this research has confirmed the obvious, such as older managers being more interested in pensions than are younger managers. But some of these studies have had unexpected findings. For example, in a 1963 study, workers in one company indicated preference for a dental insurance program over a four times more costly life insurance program.[24]

Even within a company, employees differ considerably in their compensation preferences. With such variety in mind, some conclude that companies

[24] Stanley Nealey, "Pay and Benefit Preferences," *Industrial Relations*, Vol. 3, No. 1 (October 1963), pp. 17–28.

would be wise to poll their employees before giving them benefits that may not be greatly appreciated. A few companies have gone further and have established "cafeteria" plans of benefits, which allow each employee to pick his own combination of benefits within a set cost limit. Thus, a young bachelor may decide to spend most of his "allowance" on a long vacation, while employee B, with a large family, may spend it on health and life insurance. Attractive as "cafeteria" programs may seem—especially since they give employees greater control over their own destinies—they raise many administrative problems.

Eligibility

The sheer administration of benefit programs can be expensive and time-consuming. A vast number of records must be kept. Health and retirement programs can be administered by insurance companies, but the company bares the cost in the end.

Benefit programs also require constant decisions about seemingly petty details that are of considerable importance to employees (and may set precedents for expensive action by the company).

Suppose the plant closes down for a national day of mourning on the death of an ex-President. Should employees be paid for the days' work lost? Including or excluding lost opportunities for piecework? Should those (such as watchmen) who are required to work anyway receive double pay? (Or even double-time-and-a-half, on the assumption this is the equivalent of overtime?) Should an employee who is on vacation at the time get an extra day of vacation? How about the employee who regularly works Saturday and Sunday and observes the day in question as part of his "weekend"?

Or suppose the company's medical coverage excludes routine medical examinations. Where does one draw the line between these and genuine medical emergencies? How does one deal with a doctor's bill that seems to be completely out of line (and is submitted by the employee's cousin)?

Inept handling of service programs injures employee morale as easily as inept supervision does. Thus, what started out as *fringe* benefits, a marginal aspect of the personnel program, has become a sensitive area requiring considerable managerial planning and skill.

CONCLUSION

Although many benefit programs began as aspects of paternalism, employees now take them very seriously and consider them one of the most important elements of their compensation for working. Indeed, many employees believe that they have the equivalent of a property right in their perpetuation.

Today, benefits typically comprise more than one-quarter of total compensation costs, and their rate of growth may accelerate in the years to come, as new ones become popular and old ones continue to increase in size. Employee counseling programs (for example, preretirement, personal finances, and career interests) are on the increase, as are demands for group rates on auto insurance. There is greater interest in postretirement benefits (medical insurance and improved pensions to reflect continued increases in the cost of living). Further, as the work force becomes increasingly salaried, more white-collared, and service-industry oriented, it is reasonable to assume that income-protection plans, longer paid vacations, and educational opportunities will all become more expensive for companies.

In the face of these pressures, management must constantly decide on (1) the *total* expenditure on benefits—would the money be better spent on increasing wages and salaries, or must it be spent at all? and (2) the *division* of funds among alternative programs—an extra ten cents an hour for holidays will have an impact on morale and motivation that is different from the impact of the same money spent on retirement benefits. But it should be emphasized that management is not completely free to give employees only the benefits it thinks desirable. Employees (and their union) expect that their employer will keep up with his neighbors. As new programs are introduced in other organizations, management comes under pressure to go along. And as changes are made in tax laws and in the social security program, management must undertake compensating adjustments.

In addition, management needs to keep costs under control. Fringes may be more difficult to budget than salary items, and often they turn out to be much more expensive than predicted. [25]

There will continue to be controversy over the dividing line that separates public and private concerns. Insofar as a greater share of pension benefits and accident and health insurance is provided by government administered programs (even though the costs may be borne directly by the firm or shared with employees) the individual's tie to a single organization is reduced. Also there is more uniformity in benefits, regardless of where one works, and concern about management *paternalism* is reduced. However, employees and their employers may not want to lessen this tie, since there are some satisfactions to both in the sense of loyalty and identification that may be a by-product of well-administered, generous fringe benefits.

Recently a personnel executive observed tartly that in the 1950's employees resisted and resented any intrusion on their lives by the company, but now they want extensive services: [26]

Then, it was "stay out of my life." Now, with the sad state of society, with family, churches, and the schools often disqualified, the job and the employer becomes central. . . .

Above all, management must consider the motivational aspects of fringes. What sorts of behavior do fringes motivate, and are these reactions and attitudes desirable? Does the employee take fringes for granted, since he does not know the cost of what he is getting? Or does he mentally add the cost to his paycheck? Some managers are disappointed because they are not compensated by at least a recognition of the expense involved, but those who are looking for "credit" are often accused of taking a paternalistic attitude.

[25] Changes in interest rates (affecting funded plans), in tax laws, in employee turnover, in the average age of employees, in the incidence of illness and accidents, and many other difficult-to-predict items all affect costs.

[26] Robert Feagles, Senior Vice-President for Personnel, First National City Bank (New York), quoted in *Fortune* (December 1970), p. 80.

Other managers look not for credit or gratitude from their employees, but for a sense of loyalty and attachment to the organization. Lavish recreational, health, and educational benefits, however, may foster a sense of overdependence among some employees and among others a destructive resentment against paternalism.

Fringe benefits, then, are often on the border between benefits and detriments. Pensions, stock-purchase plans, and vacation benefits may be instituted to reduce employee turnover, but many dynamic organizations question the value of having employees place strong emphasis on seniority. Fringe benefits make it difficult for an employee to leave his job and for an employer to discharge him. As the employee has more to lose with his job, arbitrators in grievance cases require more conclusive evidence of wrongdoing before they will sustain a discharge. Similarly, early retirement programs make opportunities for promotion and for new talent and energy, but they may also remove valued, experienced people who are still needed.

In general, fringes benefit all employees equally, or they reward tenure rather than performance. As a consequence, they are hygienic factors, not motivators. If management is primarily concerned with motivation, it might be better advised to consider incentive plans, which seek to relate earnings directly to performance, and we turn to these in our next chapter. [27]

problem 1 • HOW MUCH PRIVACY FOR EMPLOYEES?

The Platform Drilling Company provides all of its managers with an annual physical check-up. The primary purpose of this examination is to encourage good preventive medicine, alerting key employees to the need for giving attention to problems that could become more serious.

These examinations are provided by an internist, Dr. Amos Rawley who gives about one-fifth of his professional time to the company and has an office in the company's dispensary. Occasionally, top management consults Dr. Rawley when they are contemplating giving an executive very great additional responsibilities.

Recently, the company decided to transfer Harvey Lobsenz to South America to direct its growing off-shore drilling program there. Since sending a man and his family overseas involves a minimum expenditure of $15,000 and a good deal of psychological adjustment for all concerned, Dr. Rawley was consulted.

At the time of Harvey's last examination, Dr. Rawley had noticed some evidence of hypertension. In discussing this with his patient, Dr. Rawley learned a good deal about Harvey's home and personal life. Reticently at first and then with an emotional outpouring, Harvey revealed that he was having both marital and financial problems. At the conclusion of the examination, Harvey became quite embarrassed because of what he had said and asked the doctor to forget it because of the potential effect on his career and because he was sure that both problems could be resolved satisfactorily. Dr. Rawley was less optimistic, viewing the severity of the situation—at least as it had been described to him—the emotionality of the patient, and some of the physical strain that was beginning to show. His prognosis was that here was a man whose physical condition should be watched closely.

About a month later, when the executive vice-president of the company approached Dr. Rawley in a rather routine way about making sure that Harvey was in "reasonably" good health to take on this new assignment and change of location to a very different culture, he empha-

---

[27] For a good overview of the fringe benefit field see Donna Allen, *Fringe Benefits* (Ithaca, N.Y.: New York State School of Industrial and Labor Relations, 1969).

sized that Harvey was most anxious to assume this new challenge, which involved a substantial salary increment.

1. Describe the conflict in the doctor's mind concerning his responsibilities: what is appropriate to discuss with the company's management and what should remain confidential.
2. Would it make any difference if the doctor was full-time on a company salary? If he examined company officials in his own office, off the premises?
3. What criterion should govern what remains confidential and what can be discussed with company management?
4. What if any, medical records should the company have access to, and who, if anyone, should have access?
5. What role should Harvey play in this disclosure question?
6. Do any of your answers depend upon:
   a) How critical is the new assignment to the company.
   b) How critical is Harvey's condition.

problem 2 • EMPLOYEE DISCRETION IN ASSIGNMENTS

Among the amenities sought by employees are job assignments consistent with their social and political convictions. This is a small but significant aspect of the employee's search for fulfillment on the job as well as off the job.

Newspapers recently have carried stories describing three such demands:

A pilot for a major airline was disciplined when he refused to dump excess jet fuel over the ocean, according to long established company procedures. He refused to do this because he considered the resulting pollution undesirable, although there were good company reasons why the request would be made.

Certain TV announcers have been insisting that they be allowed to pick and choose among the products they will advertise, since some products offend their personal tastes.

Young lawyers in several large metropolitan firms have been requesting time off from regular assignments to take on volunteer work with local poverty agencies and for destitute clients who are members of minority groups.

Assuming you are advising the managements of these companies, what are the various factors you would consider (and their relative weight) in providing them with personnel counsel?

problem 3 • RELIGIOUS VALUES AND THE COMPANY

Your plant is located in a medium-size midwestern city. It employs 800 workers. You have recently received a petition signed by 200 employees requesting that an annual Catholic holiday be observed as a company-wide paid holiday. At the present time you have six paid holidays. You have only a modest allowance for fringe benefits. Two smaller companies in the area observe this day as a paid holiday, but other large firms in the community do not recognize it as such. About 50 per cent of your employees are Catholics, and half of them have children in parochial schools that give the day off.

1. Should the company grant this request?
2. What additional information would you want before making a decision?
3. What criteria would you use in making the decision?

4. If you granted the day as a holiday, would you be willing to give compensating time off for workers who do not celebrate it? (Christmas is a paid holiday, although 10 per cent of the employees are of Jewish origin.)

5. If the union had made a formal request on this issue during negotiations, would your decision be any different?

6. What difference would it make if this were a branch of a multi-unit company, with other plants in communities in which there were few Catholics?

problem 4 • CREEPING COSTS

The Faraday Insurance Company undertook a blood-bank program in response to what seemed to be an important employee need. When a company employee or a member of his family was ill and required a transfusion, one or more other employees who had voluntarily signed up would be called by the company personnel office to report to one of the local hospitals. Recently, the personnel department has noted that the costs of this program are greater than originally anticipated. Often a great many telephone calls have to be made before a donor can be located. This task requires almost full-time services of one clerk. Moreover, some donors do not return to work until the next day, even though the transfusion has been given in the morning, and overtime replacements have to be brought in.

1. How would you weigh the cost of this program against the benefits it provides?

2. Is there any way of cutting costs without nullifying the advantages of the program and without damaging the company's reputation?

problem 5 • CARE FOR WORKING MOTHERS

Crittenden Electronics in Los Angeles has received a petition signed by three-quarters of its women employees, requesting that the company sponsor a day-care center for children of working mothers. The union has not been enthusiastic, although it has not taken a stand against the proposal. The workforce of 2,800 has 1,500 women, of whom 500 have children below school age. Such programs are expensive (estimates vary widely, but $500 per child per year would probably be conservative). The issue has attracted a great deal of attention in the plant, and it has become a focal issue for women's rights groups, blacks, and other cause-oriented younger employees. Management expects to keep increasing its proportion of women workers, but the union and the company are concerned about the possibility that heavy expenditures in this area may limit wage increases.

1. Consider the criteria you would use in evaluating the proposal for this new benefit.

2. What studies would you undertake in the evaluation process?

3. How would you handle the problem of this benefit that has special appeal to what is now only 15 percent of the workforce?

INCENTIVES AND PERFORMANCE STANDARDS

27

Management often supplements wages and salaries with increments related to employee performance. These are variously called incentives, commissions, bonuses, and piecework plans, all designed to motivate employees to improve their performance.

Such incentive compensation plans must have a "base line," or normal work standard, so that performance over and above this standard can be rewarded. The base must be high enough so that employees are not given extra rewards for what is merely an average day's work, but it should not be so high that additional amounts are almost impossible to earn. And the level of difficulty should be the same for all. Management may also set work-load standards (often called measured day work) to use as a relatively objective definition of the job—an important supervisory tool even when no financial incentives are provided.

In this chapter we shall want to look first at the contribution of such standards of measurement, then at the use of work-load standards and incentives in white-collar jobs, and at their use in blue-collar, production jobs.

WHY MEASURED PERFORMANCE IS IMPORTANT

Productivity is increased when an employee has as an objective a specific, easily viewed target, rather than a vague job description or a supervisor's exhortations. Compare the motivational impact of telling a salesman to "work harder" and telling him, "Your quota is 100 gross per month." The growing emphasis on "management by objectives" (see Chap. 23) reflects the need for these targets at managerial levels, as well. Such objectives are sources of feedback *(How close am I getting? How "good" am I?)*, and they can provide the ego satisfactions associated with a sense of accomplishment *(THIS is how much I've done!).*

Work-load standards make it easier to set work assignments equitably. Can Bill Jones operate two machines? Can a receptionist announce visitors, answer the telephone, and also type correspondence? Management must be able to measure the quantity of work that can reasonably be expected of each employee. In turn, such measurements should result in a fairer distribution of work and fewer disagreements over who is or is not doing more than his share.

A manager may need an operational definition of a job to be able to judge whether an employee is performing adequately. Merely looking at whether the subordinate is busy or idle is often a poor measure of his effectiveness. The bustling employee may be doing many unnecessary things; or he may spend too much time on some tasks, to the detriment of others. Also if an equitable work load can be specified, an employee can be provided with a means of earning more than the base salary for the job. Such *incentive plans* have many problems, as we shall describe later, but their appeal is great, even among diverse cultures.[1] Let us examine this appeal.

Built-in Economic Motivation

Incentive systems allow an employee to earn more by working more—without the need for any outsider to award him a merit increase or recommend a promotion. As we have seen, salaries and fringe benefits are usually the same for mediocre or outstanding performers; but with financial incentives the superior employee can receive substantially more, and he knows that there is a direct relationship between effort and reward. A pay plan that provides immediate, as distinct from delayed, rewards for performance can be a powerful stimulus. (Of course, employees will be responsive to such a system only if management can convince them that there is equity in the determination of the basic work load and the measurement of performance, problems that we shall deal with in this chapter.)

Greater Autonomy and Job Interest

Clear, unambiguous targets can add job interest. They provide a catalyst, a focal point and an inner direction which helps organize the working day.

"It gives you a good feeling to know that you can knock off 30 per cent of your quota right away; you have to be good to do that. And then there's that nice feeling of knowing you can coast anytime you want, because that big chunk is under your belt already."

---

[1] *Cf.* Clark Kerr, John Dunlop, Frederick Harbison, and Charles Myers, *Industrialism and Industrial Man* (Cambridge, Mass.: Harvard University Press, 1960), p. 252.

Thus the employee can periodically change the "trade off" he makes between an easier pace and more income. The supervisor is less likely to be pushing for higher output, and employees feel they can vary their pace to suit their moods and needs. Moreover, the opportunity to set goals, improve one's "score," and race the clock may add interest to tedious jobs.

Increased Control over Labor Costs

Incentive plans also help the firm to control its labor costs. By ensuring that employees will be paid on the basis of production, rather than on the number of hours they work, incentive systems enable the firm to predict its labor costs. Particularly in highly competitive industries like textiles and clothing, this ability to look ahead is highly important. Incentives also make it possible for management to develop more accurate cost-accounting estimates in establishing budgets and in preparing bids on new contracts.

Performance standards have been established for both white- and blue-collar jobs, but the approaches to these two areas involve elements of commonality and difference. We will look at performance standards in both white- and blue-collar settings in turn, and then compare the two.

WHITE-COLLAR AND MANAGERIAL WORK-LOAD STANDARDS

How hard is an executive working, and what will motivate him to work harder? Upper management jobs are not easy to define explicitly, and how they are performed depends a great deal on the style and personality of the manager. "Output" may not be seen for some period of time: a manager may spend months, even years consummating a merger or assessing the worthwhileness of a large capital appropriation. Most companies, therefore, devote little effort to calculating work loads. Instead, top managers receive broad over-all targets that, it is hoped, will both motivate high performance and provide a yardstick for measuring the executive's worth. The measurements may be

> Growth in earnings per share of the company's stock
>
> Penetration of new markets or number of new, successful products
>
> Success of diversification or integration programs

Many companies (as described in Chapter 25) build executive bonus plans and deferred compensation schemes around these kinds of broad targets or goals.

As one moves down the organization hierarchy, jobs can be defined more clearly, and shorter-run goals and targets can be established. Well-managed companies give middle managers specific objectives in sales, costs, and profits. Managers are not told *how* to achieve these objectives, but their progress is monitored monthly or quarterly. Accomplishment is reinforced by bonuses, merit increases, and promotions.

Still further down the line, employees may be paid largely in terms of how well they meet or exceed their standards. Stockbrokers, department store clerks, most field salesmen, and other service workers receive commissions based on the business they generate. Since the standard or quota that is established for each job will be critical in determining employee income, it becomes important to ask how these standards are established.

Historical Records

For many jobs, historical records provide the basis for setting performance standards. Looking back over the past several years, Company X sees that in Ohio it has sold an average of $162,000 worth of tools per year. A new salesman is hired, and that becomes his quota. Of course, if economic conditions change in Ohio or new competition comes in, the quota may appear unfair. In fact, such standards tend to overreward employees when business conditions are good and penalize them in bad years.

There are other obvious defects here. An employee following an enormously energetic predecessor may receive a more difficult standard or quota than one coming after a poor performer. In some instances salesmen actually hold back on their performance for fear that "too good" a month or a year will saddle them with an unbeatable standard for the upcoming accounting period.

It is obviously helpful in setting quotas to have a substantial number of similar records to examine. A department store chain with many similar stores and many similar people selling women's stockings can establish more credible performance standards than can an organization in which each employee has a different job. Even in the chain, however, there can be doubts concerning the equity of standards. A salesperson in a store in a growing city located at a busy crossroads will have more opportunities for sales than will her counterpart in a town with declining population or one suffering economic dislocations or bitter competition among stores or where the store has an undesirable location. Adjustment is usually a highly subjective process.

Diversified Jobs

Quota systems are based on an assumption that an employee will be more highly motivated to do his job if he is compensated in proportion to how hard he works. Many jobs, however, are really more complex than they first appear, and a single standard or quota may not be a fair measure of how well the *total* job is performed. Two examples:

A. A salesman markets small pumps to machinery manufacturers. A naive view of his job is that it simply involves selling. But observing the salesmen in action, one quickly learns that an effective salesman spends considerable time
   1. analyzing and reporting back to his company on changing customer requirements and the impact of competition;
   2. helping customers with their service problems in using the company's merchandise and with delivery and quality problems;
   3. investigating potential new customers and new applications of the company's product (so-called missionary work).

B. Mr. Egbert uses his secretary to make his full travel plans and itinerary, to arrange conferences, and to compose his more routine correspondence. Grimshaw, in contrast, uses his secretary for only routine tasks: filing, typing, and making phone calls. At the end of the day, Egbert's secretary may have her more *observable* work load—typing and filing—back up, and she may appear less productive than Grimshaw's secretary, who has completed all her work.

Under a simple quota system a salesman might be receiving high earnings and encouragement for ignoring all but the easiest-to-sell customers, high-pressuring people to buy the wrong equipment, failing to ensure proper installation and service, and ignoring new trends in competitor equipment and marketing tactics. To avoid this, many sophisticated companies seek ways of measuring more than gross sales.

In our example above, the salesman might be asked to keep track of the number of visits he made to prospective as well as established customers, to write field reports on what he learned about customers' needs and intentions, to detail his service work and handling of complaints. Conceivably he might receive bonus credits for winning a new customer from a competitor or selling a product that the company was most anxious to move.

Even with such elaborations, management must recognize that its standards (and the financial incentives that bolster them) are at best subjective and perhaps not totally equitable.

To provide real equity in earnings opportunities, management would have to first study each job and determine how much work could be accomplished by a typical employee working at an average pace. This would then become the baseline for some bonus system to reward above-average performance. But even if management does not make incentive payments, it has good reason to measure the time required by various elements of a job.

Carol was always running around the department, talking on the telephone, or poring over the seemingly endless pile-up of papers that were in large measure the result of her own inefficiency. Her day was full of stops and starts and never finishing a job.

On the other hand, the highly efficient employee who distributes his time properly and in relation to the importance of the tasks he has to do may appear relaxed and even leisurely at times!

Most nonproduction jobs have an important unmeasurable quality; they cannot be precisely programed. The best employees will use discretion and will add or subtract tasks to meet job problems. A good file clerk, for example, will assign priorities, decide when to ask for help on a problem, and develop new files if they are needed. Such discretionary components, while not quantifiable, may make the difference between a good and a mediocre employee.

Although there have been efforts to make complete studies of white-collar jobs, particularly clerical positions, in order to establish unambiguous time standards for each job component, for the most part these have not been very successful. We shall have to turn to blue-collar production jobs in order to understand how difficult this is.

WORK-LOAD STANDARDS AND INCENTIVES
FOR PRODUCTION WORK

Factory production jobs seem to be ideally adaptable to objective work-load standards and opportunities for incentive earnings. Typically, they are highly repetitive, have a short job cycle, and produce a clear, measurable output.[2]

Before explicit work-load standards can be set, however, management must:

1. Describe the job (see discussion in Chapter 18).
2. Decide how the job is to be performed by the employee (motion study).
3. Decide how fast the job can be performed (time study).

Motion Study

The purpose of making the job absolutely explicit and invariable is to allow the various elements of the job to be timed and appropriate quantitative standards to be established. Unless management knows these components of the job precisely, it is obviously impossible to set any such standards.

At first glance, describing a job so that it can be timed may seem simple. Let's take our classic assembly-line worker who is helping to make washing machines. The one we shall follow is using a power screwdriver to tighten fourteen bolts that hold the frame together. How many such bolts can be tightened in an hour? The answer to that question will depend upon factors such as these:

1. Is the condition of the power screwdriver and its location constant?
2. Are some bolts more difficult to tighten than others (perhaps because they are faulty or have been improperly inserted)?
3. Does the supervisor ever ask the worker to do other things such as clean up his area, move supplies, fill-in for others?
4. Does the employee use his hands and arms in an efficient manner, or does he waste motion and effort at times?

Essentially, motion study involves: (1) analyzing how the job is currently being done, (2) questioning whether steps can be eliminated or combined, and (3) setting up a quicker, easier way of doing the job. To do this the engineer looks at the flow of work to and from the employee, the actual motions and movements the employee uses (even including his walking and finger motions). The main purpose of such a job study is to question existing procedures and to suggest both job simplifications and easier ways of working to save time and employee effort. What motions can be eliminated? Can gross, simple movements be substituted for fine, more complicated movements, which require greater

---

[2] Of course, this output is not always proportionate to the amount of effort that the employee is willing to expend. For example, an assembly-line worker cannot produce more than the number of units that pass before him, and many machine operators control equipment with pre-set speed limits.

dexterity? Can the sequence of operations be rearranged so that both hands will be kept busy where before one was idle? Can symmetrical, rhythmic, or circular motions be substituted for straight-line, jerky, or uncoordinated motions?

Limitations of "one best way." The industrial engineer uses all these motion-study techniques in an effort to determine the *"one best way"* for a worker to do a particular job. Behind this effort, of course, lies the assumption that there actually is one best way. What are the limitations of this assumption?

First, it tends to force everybody to work in the same way; it seems to ignore the fact that people are different. The best method for a right-hander, for instance, might be different from that for a "leftie." Moreover, it disregards the fact that, over a long period of time, varying one's work method may be less fatiguing than constantly doing the same thing.

Motion study often pays little attention to the sequence in which motions are taken or to the value of pauses. Carried to its logical extreme, this insistence on the "one best way" would eliminate the windup from the baseball pitch. The tendency in motion study is to consider each motion separately, rather than to determine whether it contributes to *over-all* efficiency. Considered by itself, the windup is clearly an unnecessary motion.

More important, behind this assumption lurks an implication that the seasoned worker's years of experience on the job are useless and that an engineer with a few hours' observation can find the one best method. To be sure, the engineer with his trained and questioning mind can spot mistakes that the worker on the job has always overlooked. Yet it is not safe to ignore the worker's experience altogether.

Further, even if the method that the engineer finally devises is clearly better than the existing method, there may be trouble in getting workers to accept it. Certainly if they are skeptical of the engineer's method and enthusiastic about their own, chances are they will turn out higher production by sticking with the less efficient method.

Time Study

Once the proper way of doing a job has been determined by motion study, it is possible to begin time study. Time study is a procedure for determining the *standard time* required to do a job. Usually it consists of four steps:

1. Selecting the employee and describing the job.
2. Determining the *observed* time.
3. Applying a correction factor.
4. Introducing *allowances* for fatigue, personal time, and contingencies.

Selecting the employee and describing the job. A typical union contract includes the following provision:

The time standards shall be based on the time required by a qualified normal employee working at a normal pace under normal conditions, using the proper method with normal material at normal machine speeds.

Notice how often the word "normal" is used: What are the normal machine speed, normal material, and normal conditions? Usually these are prescribed by the industrial engineer and all the details are listed on the time-study form. It is essential that these details be listed accurately, for if, some months later, a worker feels that, say, the sheet of metal on which he is now working is thicker than that which was used when the original time study was made, he can always claim higher piece-rate earnings than originally allowed.

What is the "proper method"? That is the one best way, of course, which we have already mentioned.

What is meant by "normal" worker, "normal" work pace? Behind these questions lies a major area of contention between management and union. In most cases the industrial engineer makes no effort to find a "normal" employee. Instead, he times a more or less typical employee, and, then, if the man seems to be working at a pace which is slower or faster than the engineer's preconception of "normal," he applies certain corrections (as we shall discuss) to bring the employee's observed speed in line with that conception of "normal."

Timing the job. Once the worker has been selected and the job conditions thoroughly described, the engineer is almost ready to start timing. But first he must break the job down into *elements*, each of which will usually be timed separately. An element is a clearly distinguishable motion, such as "place piece in jig." It should have a definite starting and stopping point, and it should last long enough to make accurate timing possible. The engineer is interested not only in the total time for the entire *cycle*, but also in the time for each element. Close examination of "elemental" times enables him to determine exactly in what parts of the job there are needless operator, machine, or materials delays.

How long a time should the study cover? Practice varies, but it is usual to time enough job cycles to insure that an adequate sample is obtained. Unless the whole operation is unusually long, at least 10 or 20 cycles are observed.

The engineer usually works with a stopwatch and a form on which to record the time measured for each element. Once the timing has been completed and the necessary calculations made, the observer is left with a number of readings for each element. If he has observed 20 cycles, he will have 20 readings for each element. Doubtless these readings will vary. The usual practice is to throw out all abnormal values—those that are too high or too low—before taking an average. (Of course, deciding which readings are *too* high or *too* low can be highly subjective.)

Applying a correction factor. The next step is to apply a correction factor to adjust for the fact that the worker observed may be working at a pace slower or faster than "normal." Correction factors are applied frequently through effort-rating.

Effort-rating means merely that the time-study man estimates at what percentage of normal the operator is working. (He can make an effort-rating for the job as a whole or a separate rating for each element.) If he estimates that the operator is working at only 90 per cent of normal pace, then the observed time is obviously too long. The normal time can be obtained by multiplying the observed time by .90.

Effort-rating assumes that the observer has in the back of his head some standard of what constitutes normal pace. Time-study engineers once felt that normal pace could be determined objectively and *scientifically*, but today it is pretty generally conceded to be purely a matter of judgment. What one man considers normal performance, another may consider "goofing off."

How is the standard to be determined? Basically this is the age-old question of what constitutes a "fair day's work," the subject of frequent union-management negotiation. According to one union contract, "A normal pace is equivalent to a man walking without load on smooth, level ground at a rate of three miles per hour."

Nonunion plants (and many unionized plants as well) normally follow bench-mark standards set by leading industrial engineers. One such standard calls for typing 50 words a minute or dealing a deck of cards in 30 seconds (but one engineer insists that only 27 seconds are required).

Often, movies are taken of employees working at standard pace. When run at the speed that has been negotiated as "normal," they provide criteria by which to judge the pace of men on new jobs. Such films are also used in training time-study men to judge "normal" pace.

In spite of its seeming simplicity, effort-rating, with some justification, has been attacked as being arbitrary and imprecise.

Predetermined time systems.   Because of the obvious disadvantages of traditional forms of time study, industrial engineers are turning increasingly to predetermined time systems (sometimes known as synthetic data). The use of standard data completely eliminates the need for timing each job. How?

First, the one best method for each job is determined, as discussed above, and waste motions are eliminated. Then the basic motions for each hand are carefully listed. Once this is done, reference is made to the "standard times" developed by engineering firms for each basic motion. The standard times allowed for each motion are merely added together to get the equivalent of "corrected time."

The advantages of this technique are many. By sidestepping time study and the rating problem, it eliminates endless union-management wrangles (if the union accepts the standard data and, what is more unlikely, if its members accept the results). A worker can no longer fool the time-study man by pretending to work fast, nor does the time-study man (now better called an industrial engineer) have to worry about being outsmarted. Nor is there any problem of consistency. Predetermined data make the whole rate-setting process quicker, cheaper, more mechanical, and less subject to personal discretion. Indeed, computers can be used to calculate piecerates.

But if the predetermined time method is so advantageous, why isn't it used universally? There are many objections to it.

The method assumes that the time for each motion can be determined without considering its place in the complete sequence. But this would be true only if each movement started at rest and ended at rest. An efficient worker develops a rhythm in his work, and his speed in any one part of the job depends in part on what he has just done and what he intends to do next.[3] (Some predetermined time systems distinguish between the time required to lift an object when the hand starts from rest and when it is already in motion. Few go further than this and most do not go this far.)

In spite of these criticisms, standard-data systems do provide a rough check on the times obtained through direct observation. And when such a system is applied to a number of roughly similar jobs, such as using a drill press in a standardized fashion, it may result in considerably greater consistency between standards than does time study. Indeed, one union, the International Ladies Garment Workers', has developed its own standard data for use in setting piecerates for dresses.

Allowances

Once the time for a particular job has been determined, either by corrected time study or on the basis of standard data, the time-study man adds a certain percentage *allowance* to this time to account for what the worker may lose in personal time (going to the washroom, getting a drink of water) or because of fatigue or unexpected contingencies.

The *fatigue* allowance is designed to compensate for the worker's increasing tiredness as he does the job. Fatigue allowances are often set uniformly for all jobs, although larger allowances are sometimes made for heavier jobs. As we have seen, fatigue is partly a psychological factor that is influenced by the worker's home life, his relations with his fellow workers and his foreman, and his attitudes toward his job. Theoretically, it might be possible for a worker to claim a higher fatigue allowance because he has a poor foreman. In practice, no such nonsense is allowed.

Allowance for contingency is a general catch-all category that may include setup time, delay for materials, delay for minor breakdowns, time for oiling, and other stoppages beyond the operator's control. Sometimes an arbitrary allowance is made to cover all such contingencies. More often, a contingency allowance is computed on the basis of a rough time study made over a period of several days.

Establishing Standards

After these time and motion study procedures are completed, management is in a position to establish work-load standards specifying the quantity of work that reasonably can be anticipated from an average employee in a particular job. To be sure, as we have already noted, numerous subjective calculations embodied in these standards make it pretentious to call them "scientifically determined rates," as did the early "scientific management" advocates. Applied with good judgment and good faith, however, the procedures do narrow the difference between what employees feel they ought to do and what management

---

[3] The speed at which a baseball player can run from home plate to first base depends on (a) whether he has just bunted or driven a line drive, and (b) whether he intends to stop at first or go on to second. It might also depend on whether he is first man up and still slightly tired from running in from center field at the end of the previous inning.

wishes they would do. The process of measurement can stop here, and it will provide what is typically called *measured day work*. Now the supervisor has quantitative performance standards to give the employee and to judge him by.

Many companies, however, prefer to go one step farther and develop an incentive payment plan by which workers who *exceed* these standards receive extra pay (usually proportionate to the amount by which they exceed the standards). Such incentive or piecework systems are designed to allow most employees to earn 20 per cent to 25 per cent more than they would under daywork conditions. This increment assumes that employees under incentive conditions will be working harder than their counterparts without this opportunity for additional income.

Surely it seems that incentive systems should eliminate many of the sources of industrial conflict and employee-relations problems—after all, they encourage delegation of responsibility, increase worker motivation, and strengthen management's control. Unfortunately, the results have often proved disappointing, for incentive plans have been the source of serious friction between labor and management. Why should a program that is theoretically sound prove so deficient in practice?

EMPLOYEE RESPONSES THAT CHALLENGE INCENTIVE SYSTEMS

To understand why incentive plans tend to generate conflict, we must first assess employees' reactions to incentives.

The Work Group Imposes a Ceiling

Employees rarely produce as much as they can in response to an opportunity for additional earnings. The members of certain inexperienced work groups may react that way, but most employees are quick to learn that such behavior is *dangerous*. Employees fear that if they begin to pull down earnings that are too high under a particular piecerate, management, particularly the time-study department, will decide that the rate is too generous.

Management usually promises it will not cut rates except when changes are made in working conditions or in the methods by which the job is done. Employees, however, believe that management will always be able to find an excuse to restudy a job on which incentive earnings are obviously very high.

Further, many workers fear that if they increase their production markedly they will work themselves out of a job—that is, that management won't be able to sell the increased output, and some workers will be redundant.

Moreover, incentive plans may threaten the status hierarchy within the group, since older workers—who customarily have the highest status—may be unable to match the pace of their younger colleagues and thus find that their relative earnings have declined. Naturally, to protect their social position the older workers put pressure on the younger ones to take things easy.[4]

[4] *Cf.* D. J. Hickson, "Motives of People Who Restrict Their Output," *Occupational Psychology*, Vol. 61 (1961), pp. 110-121.

In response to all these factors, the work group begins to establish ceilings ("bogies") of what is the proper or safe level of output; the employee who overproduces is belittled as a "rate-buster." New employees are indoctrinated into the group's standard almost as soon as they enter the department:

This was my first job. The foreman told me I was on piecework and to make just as much as I could. I was scared and anxious to make a good impression so I tried pretty hard.

About an hour had passed when several guys told me "Take it easy, guy—don't knock yourself out." I thought they were showing kindness, so I thanked them and kept plugging ahead.

Then an older man came to me and said, "Let me give you a piece of advice. The most we ever make on that piece is sixty an hour, and a new man doesn't make that much. If you want to make any friends here, I'd watch your count pretty closely."

"How come?" I asked.

"Because if we put out more than that, they'll cut our rates. We will have to work that much harder for the same amount of money."

Those men, who do not rely on group acceptance as a source of job satisfaction, ignore the group's norms and produce at a level substantially above the agreed-on ceiling. They trade their social acceptability in return for higher income. The friction that develops between rate-busters and the other group members may explode into severe supervisory problems. Efforts of the group to get the rate-buster to conform may show themselves in the sabotage of equipment as well as in ostracism—neither of which is conducive to harmonious working relationships.

As a result of pressures, most workers will try to maintain and report approximately the same safe output. If the group inadvertently overproduces, this excess is concealed and reported on a day when the group falls short of its normal output.

Struggling for "Better" Rates

Employees under an incentive plan often struggle with management and the time-study department to obtain more desirable or "looser" rates. They believe that the time-study engineer cannot evaluate precisely how many pieces per day or per hour each worker should be able to complete; they know that he must resort to certain subjective judgments. Consequently, they suspect that management will try to make them work harder than they should to obtain a reasonable bonus.

This distrust shows itself most dramatically when the time-study engineer appears in the shop, for example:

(Starkey is advising Tennessee, a relatively inexperienced worker, in the ways of dealing with time-study men.)

"If you expect to get any kind of a price, you got to outwit that——You got to use your noodle while you're working, and think your work out ahead as you go along! You got to add in movements you know you ain't going to make when you're running the job! Remember, if you don't——them, they're going to——you! . . . Every movement counts!

". . . You were running that job too damn fast before they timed you on it! I was watching you yesterday. If you don't run a job slow before you get timed, you won't get a good price. They'll look at the record of what you do before they come around and compare it with the timing speed. Those time-study men are sharp! . . ."

(Later Starkey describes Ray Ward, one of the "heroes" of the department.)

"Ray knew his drills," said Starkey. "He'd burn up a drill every four or five pieces when they were timing him, and say the speed was too high for the tough stuff he was running. Tough stuff, nuts! They'd lower the speed and feed to where he wasn't burning up the drills, then afterwards he'd speed up and cut through that tough stuff like cheese."

"What I want to know," said Tennessee, "is how in hell could Ward burn up the drills like that? You can't just burn up a drill when you feel like it."

"It's in the way you grind the drill," said Starkey. "Ray used to grind his own drills, and he'd touch them up before they timed him. The wrong kind of a grind will burn up a drill at a lower speed than the drill can take if it's ground right for the job."[5]

Both sides may legitimately disagree over the frequency and importance of equipment failures, material shortages, or imperfections that delay and hamper the employee in his production. Obviously the employees want to insure that the allowances are ample; management wants to insure that they are kept within reasonable limits.

Time-study engineers come to see the employees as tricksters who feign difficulties when jobs are being timed, are dishonest about their ability to do the job within the time allotted, and are always pressuring for looser standards, whether legitimate or not. Time-study engineers may even overcompensate for the expected bluffs and shenanigans of employees. They fear being tricked into setting too "loose" a rate, and consequent embarrassment. Expecting the worst, they take extra pains when first setting a rate to make sure it is reasonably tight. Employees recognize this tendency and try to make sure that they don't have to accept the rate the company first establishes for a new job.

The Negotiation Process

Thus, the introduction of new jobs often marks the outbreak of an extended cold war between employees and management. Employees may have learned by experience that if they object vigorously to the rates and fail repeatedly to meet the standard output, eventually they may be able to win a slight loosening of the rates. Management recognizes that by giving in to such pressures it may only encourage further slowdowns, grievances, and similar protests. The war rages until the employees are convinced that they can do no better and management is satisfied that it has won something approximating a reasonable standard. The ultimate result is a "negotiated" rate that may depart significantly from the time-study data. Particularly when a situation involves only a small group of workers who control a potential bottleneck in the work flow, management is tempted to concede rather than suffer a prolonged loss of output.

Here is a colorful description of this cold war.

The setting of rates and the reaction by the operators is a routine you have to go over again and again, forever and ever apparently, as long as there shall be garment rates, and broken needles. You study carefully and set the rate, say $49\frac{1}{2}$ cents a dozen for hemming. You post the rate and then the operator has a fit. She says she "can't make nothing on that rate." She says she's been here on the line for 23 years and no young squirt time-study man is going to push her around. You tell her there's a lot of factors involved (what would we do without those involved factors?), and that management wants to meet the operators half way and continue to enjoy mutual confidence for the highest production, Sleep Tite quality, and high earnings based on output and ability. The operator says she "can't buy no groceries on mutual confi-

5 William F. Whyte, *et al.*, *Money and Motivation* (New York: Harper, 1955), p. 32.

dence" and is going to go to work at the Packing Plant unless something is done about the rate. The other girls in the unit glare at management and exchange significant looks and talk so much about it all day that production goes off 12 dozen. You promise to analyze the situation and make a "eight-hour study" to check for any factors that might have been overlooked (or involved). . . .

You agree to raise the rate from $49\frac{1}{2}$ cents per dozen to $50\frac{1}{4}$ cents. Two weeks later the operator is running away with the rate and making $1.33 an hour, within 17 cents of the machinist, who is the best machinist in the area and knows more about a Singer machine than the Singer people. [6]

Living with the Rate: Rising Costs

While they are being observed by the time-study man, employees try to prove that they have to work very slowly indeed. Then, after the rate has been set, they do just the opposite. They try to find short cuts: devising ways of running the machine faster, using special jigs or fixtures, leaving out some of the required operations. To avoid punishment for using unapproved short cuts, and to avoid retiming of the job, all these tricks must be kept secret.

Thus employees may earn large incentive bonuses but productivity may not increase proportionately. Or sometimes management is deceived into thinking its rates are "in line" because the incentive earnings do not appear abnormally high. Of course, as we have seen, this in part merely reflects the adroitness of the work group in establishing output ceilings. "Loose rates" are hidden by carefully controlled output restriction, and the benefits from these rates are taken in the form of increased leisure on the job rather than increased earnings.

In their efforts to earn high bonuses, employees may pressure management for higher-quality materials and better maintenance. They are also likely to neglect work that does not help them increase their earnings—for example, keeping their work area clean, oiling equipment, and caring for tools. As a result, management is confronted with higher overhead costs.

Frequently, too, these plans provide that employees will receive "average earnings" during delays that are beyond their control. This provision, in turn, motivates employees on occasion to seek delays and to fail to take adequate care of their own equipment. By pressuring job-setters, maintenance men, tool-room personnel, and even supervisors to "adjust" the time records and to report incorrectly the time when an employee began a particular job or the time when a breakdown occurs, employees can inflate the amount of time their machines were idle due to factors "beyond" their control, and can understate the time they were actually able to devote to their job. Thus employees can earn more money without working harder. The emphasis on quantity may induce employees to pay only perfunctory attention to quality. As a result inspection costs rise significantly.

In administering incentive plans it is assumed that job changes which make the employee's work easier or faster will be reflected in changes in the incentive rate for the job—that is, as improvements are made in the process, new rates will be established calling for lower rates. In practice, however, management is often reluctant to begin the long tedious struggle over rate-setting, and therefore

[6] Richard Bissell, $7\frac{1}{2}$ Cents (Boston: Little, Brown, 1953), pp. 132-134.

does not insist that a new rate be set every time a minor change is made on the job.

Thus, these minor job changes have a cumulative effect. Just as job evaluation rates tend to drift upward, so incentive rates tend to become "demoralized" and looser. The result is unjustifiably high earnings in relation to employee effort, and failure of the company to benefit from the investments it makes in improved technology, scheduling, and supervision.

Coercive Intergroup Comparisons

Because incentive plans may affect relative earnings, potentially they can upset long-established status relationships between groups. Certain groups do work that has traditionally been considered as relatively low-paying and undesirable. Under a loose incentive rate, these groups may begin to earn substantially more than do workers on higher-status jobs. Almost invariably, intergroup bickering and dissatisfaction will arise, leading eventually to pressures on management to re-establish the traditional relationship between rates. A slight concession made by management in order to avoid serious disagreement on one job may mushroom over time into substantially higher labor costs throughout the organization.

When, for whatever reason, one group of workers begins to earn bonuses so large that their relative position in the earnings hierarchy is altered, the unstabilizing affect on other groups may force management to take action—sometimes a contrived engineering change that will justify retiming. Thus, management cannot really live by the maxim, "We never cut a rate." But reducing a rate is a painful process for all concerned. The lesson it teaches employees with high earnings is to exercise greater restraint—that is, greater control over output—next time.

Union Attitudes

Because incentives can create unfavorable intergroup comparisons (between those with incentive pay, or loose rates, and those without incentives, or tight rates), because they can pit worker against worker (more energetic against lazy), and because incentives can affect employment, many unions have policies discouraging their use. To craft unions, they are an anathema, since they encourage "rushing the work."

Once installed, however, they are tenaciously kept because of the extra earnings. In the late 1960's, the Steelworkers' Union insisted that steel company management extend incentives to nearly all workers, including maintenance employees and technicians, whose work was in any way related to production. [7] Many unions find themselves in the position of being against incentive systems in principal but fighting for them in practice!

[7] When Western Electric and General Electric sought to abolish incentives, the Electrical Workers' Union fought to keep them. *Cf.* William Gomberg, "Collective Bargaining and the New Industrial Engineering," *Essays in Collective Bargaining Theory*, Gerald Somers, ed. (Ames, Iowa: Iowa State Univ. Press, 1969), pp. 69-78.

THE SUPERVISOR'S CONTRIBUTION

One of the most rewarding starting points in meeting incentive problems is the supervisor-employee relationship. The effective supervisor must be willing and able to *represent* his subordinates, to respond to suggestions from them, and to bring their problems to the attention of higher management. Where the supervisor has no voice in the incentive system and no specialized knowledge of how it works, or where he feels that the whole process is out of his hands, it is highly unlikely that the system will function successfully.

The rate-setting process is in the hands of industrial engineers. Fearing that concessions in one department will cause a mushrooming effect, management frequently discounts supervisory criticisms, fearing that they are the result of employee pressure. Thus, the supervisor is tempted to respond to an employee question about his standard by saying, "Look, I don't understand it either; those engineers in time-study work these things out, not me. If you're dissatisfied, they're the ones to argue with."

But this attitude undermines the whole system. Once the employees realize that their supervisor is isolated from the rate-setting process, they fear that they will be taken advantage of. The supervisor must be trained in the administration of the incentive plan and made to feel that it is part of his job. When employees find that he is informed, willing to go to bat for them when they are right, and unwilling to collude with them when they are wrong, the whole tenor of the system is likely to improve.

Improving the Supervisor / Time-Study Relationship

Before this improvement can be achieved, however, the relationship between time-study personnel and the supervisor must be put on a sound basis. This is one of the stabilization relationships that we described in Chapter 15, and as such it is well stocked with problems. There is also the natural antipathy between the production man, who is likely to have been promoted through the ranks, toward the smart specialist who may be a relative newcomer to the organization.

Actually, the foreman has a strong incentive to support his work group in its struggle with management. Loose rates leave employees happy and eliminate the "cold war" type of grievances, slowdowns, and the like. Employees working under loose rates have energy left over to pitch in during an emergency when the supervisor needs their help. In addition, his own production record is likely to look better when employees have easy rates and always make a 20 to 30 per cent bonus.

To the time-study man, such supervisory attitudes are an anathema, for he knows that even slight concessions quickly grow to major proportions as other groups demand rates that are equally loose. Intraplant pay distortions spring up when easy rates make it possible for some employees to make disproportionately high earnings, and the time-study men are embarrassed. As a result they feel that the supervisor is too weak, too willing to concede to employee and union pressure.

The following hypothetical dialogue between a supervisor and a time-study man illustrates their different points of view.

Supervisor: "It looks to me as if that rate is pretty tight and we are going to get a lot of gripes from the operators."

Time-study Man: (To himself) "How does he know; he hasn't even looked over the study—in fact, he probably doesn't even understand time study; he just wants to avoid any personal troubles with the men."

(To Supervisor) "Well, I've done a careful job, and I think it is a good standard."

Supervisor: (To himself) "Here is another one of those know-it-all kids who thinks he has learned in a couple of days what it took me 15 years to learn. There's no use trying to reason with them."

(To Time-study Man) "I've already heard a number of complaints from the men that they can never make out under this new standard. I wonder whether there might not be some factor that was overlooked in the study."

Time-study Man: (To himself) "Just as I thought, he doesn't have the ability to get his people to accept the new standard; they are so used to only doing half a job that tightening up seems unfair."

(To Supervisor) "If they would only give it a chance and really try it out, I know they could make it, but they prefer to gripe rather than work."

Supervisor: (To himself) "There is not much use even talking to him; he doesn't care about what happens *after* he sets the rate. In fact, he probably gets a pat on the back from his boss for the amount he increases the standard on the job; the greater the increase the more likely he is to get a raise himself. I'm left holding the bag as far as dealing with the men is concerned and with the new quality problems that are going to come up when they try to beat it and with more tooling breakdowns and costs which those guys never figure on."

(To Time-study Man) "O.K. We'll see what happens but I can tell you right now we are in for trouble on this."

Time-study Man: (To himself) "Sure, if that's the way the supervisor feels about the standard already, what can you expect from the men? We'll have trouble from them."

(To Supervisor) "If they'll only give it a fair trial I know it's going to work out."

The solution of such conflicts of interest demands both organizational change and training. William F. Whyte, generalizing from a study of the Inland Steel Container Company, has described the type of reorganization that will eliminate many of the problems we have described:

No longer was he [the time-study man] to be a free-wheeling, apparently autonomous agent who carried the threat of change with him wherever he went in the plant. Instead, management decided that he should not enter a department for purposes of making a study unless he had written approval by one of two production management officials. Furthermore, he had to present this clearance to the foreman in whose department he was to work, and the foreman then took the initiative in bringing in the union steward so that the three of them could discuss the work that was to be done. Then, before the work was started, the foreman and steward would accompany the time-study man to the worker or workers whose jobs were to be studied so that the next steps could be explained to them. [8]

Notice that this approach shifts the time-study man in the direction of an advisory relationship. The next step is for management to train the supervisor in industrial engineering techniques, so that he can deal intelligently with the problems and grievances raised by time and motion study.

Effective handling of incentive problems at lower levels also assumes the use of simple formulas for converting production into earnings. Many companies develop unnecessarily complex formulas that supervisors and employees cannot understand nor can they calculate their own earnings.

[8] Whyte, *op. cit.*, p. 229.

INCENTIVES FOR AUXILIARY EMPLOYEES

In addition to the immediate supervisors themselves, employees who transport materials, maintain equipment, distribute tools, and do inspection are in a position to influence the pace and efficiency with which incentive employees work. These service workers resent not getting extra compensation although their efforts are essential to the incentive employees' earnings, and whenever the incentive employees work harder, they must work harder, too.

In many companies, auxiliary employees receive extra compensation in proportion to the piecework earnings of the incentive workers, the assumption being that auxiliary work increases roughly in the same ratio as the size of the bonus earnings. For a toolroom worker, the formula might be based on total plant production; for material-handlers, the bonus might be based on the production of the department or departments they service.

The manager must be careful, however, not to let auxiliary bonuses encourage undesirable practices. An inspector who is paid a bonus in proportion to the incentive earnings of the group as a whole may decide to be less diligent in looking for rejects. Extra precautions need to be taken to check his work (and this means extra costs). A supervisor who is rewarded in proportion to the incentive earnings of his subordinates may be similarly motivated to agitate for looser rates for his men.

There are sensible industrial engineering techniques for developing incentive formulas for continuous or semicontinuous processing equipment. Here the employee's real job is to keep the equipment going. As we noted in Chapter 3, his job becomes easier if he can spot minor troubles early enough to make the proper adjustments. His bonus is calculated on the basis of the percentage of the eight-hour day that the equipment is operating at or near full capacity.

THE CHALLENGE OF INCENTIVES FOR MANAGEMENT

Incentive payment plans are most popular where individual effort appears to have a major influence on the rate of production (clothing and steel production, e.g.) and lowest where assembly lines or continuous process production (chemicals, e.g.) make it more difficult for the individual to affect the work pace. Although one might assume that increased automation would decrease their use, the evidence is not convincing. The percentage of manufacturing employees covered by such plans has been relatively stable over a number of years (about one-quarter of manufacturing employees in the U.S.).[9] Of course, the growing importance of service occupations relative to manufacturing will decrease the relative importance of incentives.

[9] Cf. George Stelluto, "Report on Incentive Pay in Manufacturing," *Monthly Labor Review*, Vol. 92, No. 7 (July 1969), pp. 49–53. Also, for critical reviews of the status of the incentives field see Garth Mangum, "Are Piecerate Incentives Becoming Obsolete?" *Industrial Relations*, Vol. 2, No. 1 (October 1962), pp. 73–96; R. Marriott, *Incentive Payment Systems: A Review of Research and Opinion*, 2nd ed. (London: Staples Press, 1961); and Robert McKersie, "Wage Payment Plans for the Future," *British Journal of Industrial Relations*, Vol. 1 (June 1963), pp. 191–212.

Automation highlights a flaw in most traditional incentive systems. With automated equipment continuity and regularity become more important to high productivity than bursts of speed or effort.

Incentives typically reward employees for extra effort, not for productivity as such. Management therefore puts itself in the position of bargaining over how much effort should be expended. Although industrial engineers assume that there is a direct connection between the two, this is not always the case. (For instance, employees may be rewarded for complicating their job and causing more breakdowns, and they may be penalized for finding shortcuts.) In fact, technological changes that increase productivity are often accompanied by retiming and rate cuts! (In the next chapter, we shall look at some other incentive plans, which encourage employees to increase productivity and give them financial rewards even when their effort expenditure has not increased.)

Incentive plans may generate healthy pressures within the work group: employees becoming concerned about raw material shortages, equipment problems, and scheduling can urge management to expedite the flow of work. After all, they now have a stake in conditions which foster high productivity.

On the other hand, some naive managements regard financial incentive plans as a cure-all. Faced with weak and ineffective supervision, difficulties and delays in work flow, low morale, and unsatisfactory output levels, management decides that all these problems can be solved by incentives. Also, shortsighted managements may neglect nonmonetary incentives, which can be powerful motivators, in favor of too exclusive reliance on monetary rewards.

Where companies have been oversold by enthusiastic consulting firms to expect enormous labor cost savings from installing incentive plans, they have often become disillusioned. Workers can restrict output, and there are heavy costs associated with the special engineering, accounting, work inspection, and grievance negotiations.

Actually, an incentive plan neither eliminates nor reduces the need for good supervision; it requires alert, skilled supervisors who can facilitate the rate-setting process and handle the difficulties inherent in any plan. Worker confidence and good relationships with employees and union are essential if the plan is not to become bogged down in constant bickering.

Incentives can also discourage some management from making technological changes, because employees will resist retiming and new rates. But if the jobs are not retimed, management may not be able to recoup the capital costs of what was designed to be labor-saving equipment.

Management, in instituting an incentive plan, must be willing to pay the price of administering it. It must be willing to struggle with grievances and to correct inequities and imbalances in the wage structure resulting from differences in the relative "tightness" or "looseness" of incentive rates in various parts of the organization. It must also avoid the temptation to establish a looser rate when critical production is at stake or to offer incentive pay as "extra remuneration" to gain acceptance of technological changes. Concessions made during good times will cause trouble when profit levels decline. Otherwise there is the strong tendency for rates to become looser and looser, for more money to be paid for less productivity. Incentives are wasteful when they are used to bring production levels *up* to reasonable standards; they should be used only to compensate employees for performance *above* such standards.

BLUE-COLLAR VS. WHITE-COLLAR INCENTIVES

Some of the problems management faces in deriving adequate returns from the *potential* of incentive payment plans may be summarized when we contrast salesmen's commissions with production workers' piecework plans.

Group restrictions. Salesmen typically work alone or at least are less bound by group norms of what is suitable output. Inclined to be more individualistic, perhaps in McClelland's terms, more achievement oriented, they are more responsive to the opportunity to earn more, and less concerned with protecting the rate (from being cut) or with their fellow group members. [10]

Flexibility. When management wants to push a particular item, it is easier to offer an especially high temporary commission rate than it is to change a piecerate. The latter involves meticulous, invidious comparisons among large numbers of employees. Their surveillance typically is aided by the union who insists that no one be given the opportunity for greater earnings unless all receive it, and that such changes cannot be rescinded, once established, without additional study and negotiation. Thus factory piecerates and work study may make the introduction of change more difficult because of the implications these changes have for employee take-home pay and work load. But commission structures can be changed and can provide for quick responsiveness of employees to management's changed priorities.

Validity. Given the larger group and its demands for equity and comparability, management has had to develop relatively (although by no means perfectly) scientific methods for measuring work load and thus relative performance in blue-collar work. Such methods have not been widely applied to white-collar work, largely because of greater variability among jobs and the possibility of variability within jobs. So most commission plans assume comparable territories, etc., but the measurements are subjective at best. Salesmen (who are generally nonunion) accept the likelihood that inequities will be ironed out when eventually they move to better (more lucrative) territories. The factory worker demands equal opportunity now!

Unmeasured work. Most white-collar jobs, being more complex, are likely to contain unmeasured aspects; and management can find that salesmen, for example, neglect "missionary work" or other sales services in being too responsive to those target activities from which they derive extra income. The factory worker is more constrained, more tightly supervised, and more likely to be performing a job in which the incentive can take into account almost the total task. (Poor quality, for example, work will not receive payment.) All incentives, however, run the risk of biasing job performance.

[10] *Cf.* David McClelland, *The Achieving Society* (Princeton: Van Nostrand, 1961).

Cost of administration. Being more informal and less precise, and involving fewer coercive comparisons, sales incentive plans are relatively inexpensive to administer. There is real danger, however, that the cost of production worker piecework plans can begin to approximate the benefits received. A great deal of managerial effort must be devoted to handling grievances, retiming jobs, calculating earnings, and the impact of changed jobs, downtime, changes in quality of materials, and so on.

CONCLUSION

There is little question that objective measures of work performance can motivate increased productivity. They provide employees and their supervisors with comparable data as to how well jobs are being performed and where rewards are due (or the opposite). Management should seek to develop these measures for a wide range of jobs, not just production and service employees but staff and managerial jobs as well. Where these measures are combined with immediate financial returns, the motivational effects may be even stronger.

Unfortunately, these advantages cannot be secured without costs. The most serious of these costs involves the possible redirection of effort away from work responsibilities that may be more difficult to measure (such as quality, investment in activities that have longer-run payoffs, improved cooperation with fellow employees) to those job elements that are easiest to measure. Also the rate-setting process itself can become a source of controversy and injury to on-the-job relationships. Particularly with incentive plans, when earnings are directly affected, employees become very sensitive about even slight inequities in standards. A production worker becomes enraged when he feels he is getting a heavier proportion of tight-rated jobs compared to his neighbor who gets more loose-rated jobs. Management must be willing to invest heavily in continued administrative vigilance because job content and surrounding working conditions, which affect the work load, are constantly changing. Introducing changes also becomes more difficult where the impacts on work load and earnings must be calculated precisely and explained to employees. These problems are reduced somewhat by organization-wide incentives, a subject to which we now turn.

problem 1 • LEISURE AS AN INCENTIVE

Berea is a supervisor in a parts clean-up department. When the laboratory finds that some piece of equipment has failed or has a serious quality problem, and repair is too costly, the equipment is sent to Berea's group. They, in turn, dismantle the equipment, clean up the components, and place them in stock, to be available as spare parts.

Berea has noticed that his men will work very hard for several hours if they know they can "win" an extended work break. Last week when they finished an especially large group of motors, he told them they could leave early. It was about an hour before quitting time. They returned the next day with enormous vitality, worked at a similar pace, and finished what Berea considered a good day's work in about five hours. He told them it was all right to leave early again, and for about two weeks the same pattern was followed with unflagging effort and great esprit. When Berea's manager heard about the practice, however, he said it had to stop, since the working hours for all employees had been established by the laboratory, and discrimination should not be practiced.

1. What do you think of "free time" compared to money as an incentive? (It has been used, of course, by numerous organizations.)

2. Assuming that these employees worked in an isolated location, would this affect your judgment of Berea's action?

3. How relevant is the fact that the employees responded very favorably to this type of incentive and appeared likely to continue to do so? What other savings were being made? Are there other hidden costs?

problem 2 • WHEN CAN INCENTIVES BE IGNORED?

A group of production employees is refusing to work any faster than "base rate" in protest against the elimination of a soft-drink machine near their work area. Top management is pressuring supervision "to do something" quickly, for scheduling throughout the plant is being affected by the decreased output here. The foreman is reluctant to succumb to employee pressure, both because of the bad precedent that would be set and because the machine itself was a nuisance—cups, bottle caps, and bottles were strewn about the area, and the dispenser encouraged loitering. Disciplinary measures are being considered against the ringleaders for organizing a "slowdown." Some members of management are urging caution, claiming, as the men themselves do, that the employees do not have to work at an *incentive pace*. The company provides the opportunity for workers to earn a bonus if they wish to work more intensively than a *daywork pace,* but this decision is up to the employees. Other members of management take the opposite point of view: in accepting work on a job with an incentive rate attached, the worker obligates himself to try for such additional earnings, and this is a concerted effort to hold back production.

1. Comment on the merits of the divergent opinions within management on the employees' obligation to seek incentive earnings.

2. Discuss what management's approach should be to the workers' protest action. (There is no union in the organization.)

problem 3 • WHO GETS THE "TIGHT" AND "LOOSE" JOBS?

Machine-shop employees are constantly wrangling among themselves and with their supervisor over work assignments. Several senior employees have filed grievances claiming that their foreman is discriminating against them. Here is a typical case:

Waljack claims that his incentive earnings were cut 40 per cent the previous week because the supervisor assigned him several jobs that had very "tight" rates. During the same period most of the other employees, nearly all of whom had less seniority than Waljack, received highly desirable jobs with "looser" rates. Waljack further claims that the supervisor did all this on purpose, to punish him because the supervisor dislikes him.

When the superintendent reviewed this particular grievance he was told by the departmental foreman that it was not serious. "This is just another effort by the older men to get all the good jobs and leave the dregs for the younger employees. What they want me to do is to spend hours analyzing every job that comes into the department and figure out just how much bonus the operator is going to get on it. Then I am supposed to plan out the work so that the senior workers get only the high-paying jobs; and when they finish one good one, I will have another choice job to give them. This way I would spend my whole day working out earnings schedules rather than planning the most efficient way to schedule production in my department."

The superintendent also spoke to the union chief steward about the problem. The steward said that the union felt that the company's incentive system provided an easy means for the foreman to reward his friends and punish those whom he didn't like (and who might be vigorous union supporters). The union wanted management to come up with a proposal to take this power away from their foremen.

The superintendent learned that the department itself was divided on this issue. Some of the men were afraid that the union would set up a system whereby the good work was distributed according to length of service, which would mean that the newer employees might take a real wage cut. At the same time they were not happy about the supervisor holding these assignments over their heads "as a club."

The personnel department cautioned that any management decision here might have far-reaching implications. The supervisor's right to make work assignments was a crucial element in management's ability to run the plant efficiently. The union would be in a good position to limit this vital prerogative if it got a foot in the door in a case like this one.

1. As the superintendent, how would you evaluate the case? Assuming that Waljack had some grounds for making his complaint, how would you deal with it in a way that would avoid other problems?

2. Can the right to make work assignments be separated from other aspects of incentive-plan administration?

problem 4 • SALES QUOTAS

The Superior Floor Covering Company has an incentive program for its salesmen. Incentive earnings are based on the amount of sales in relation to an assigned quota. The quota is computed each year by management, taking into account the number and type of customers in each salesman's territory and the previous year's sales records for the company and for its competitors. In the administration of this incentive program, the following problems have arisen. Suggest the type of analysis you would undertake to provide data that might lead to a solution and the alternative plans you would consider in eliminating these difficulties. Note also the parallels between the problems here and those involving blue-collar, manufacturing incentive plans.

1. Some of the best salesmen now have too many accounts in the area assigned to them. From the company's point of view, it would be advantageous to reduce the size of the districts covered by each of these men and to add several new salesmen who could give more thorough coverage. The outstanding salesmen resent this proposal, however, claiming that it would penalize them for their success. Furthermore, they argue that although their sales records are high now, some of their good accounts may go to competitors, and then they will be worse off than other salesmen who have not had their districts "trimmed."

2. The top-earning salesmen also complain that their base quotas increase each year, reflecting their previous success. This, too, they feel is discrimination against success.

3. Management believes that the company is not acquiring as many new accounts as it should. So-called missionary work, trying to induce a store that has not previously purchased Superior products to become a customer, takes more time and energy than selling old customers. Also, the results of this missionary work may not show up for several years. The present incentive plan gives no credit for this type of work. Should extra allowances be given for new accounts? How will this affect the over-all sales effort of the company?

4. When business is booming within a salesman's territory, he may receive high bonus earnings even without great effort on his part. When there is a great deal of unemployment in his territory or when competition decides to lower prices to penetrate this new market, his bonus earnings may decline even though his sales efforts are at a maximum. How can these factors be taken into account so that the incentive plan will motivate and reward effort rather than reflect fortuitous circumstances?

28

ORGANIZATION-WIDE INCENTIVES AND PARTICIPATION

In this chapter we shall discuss some of the approaches that have been devised to provide broader employee motivation than is furnished by individual incentive plans. These approaches serve a dual purpose: (1) to increase productivity and (2) to improve morale by giving employees a feeling of participation in and identification with their company.

As we discussed in the last chapter, individual incentive plans often do not provide adequate motivation. Even when they are successful in inducing employees to work harder, their value as an incentive is reduced by output restriction, conflicts over rate-setting, and intergroup conflict. Nor are high wages, fringe benefits, and good working conditions in themselves a complete answer to the problem of motivation. These inducements may be effective aids in recruiting and retaining good employees, but they provide little help in motivating them to work harder.

We will make a critical examination of five techniques that are being used by management to provide greater motivation and a greater sense of identification with the company: (1) group incentives, (2) profit sharing, (3) suggestion systems, (4) employee-management and union-management consultative committees, and (5) the Scanlon Plan. Finally, we will compare these techniques with "workers' participation in management" schemes that exist in many countries in Europe and Asia.

With group incentives each member of the group receives a bonus based on the output of the group as a whole, unlike individual piecework, in which each employee receives a bonus based on his individual output. The "group" may include the entire plant or company. More frequently it consists of a single department of the men who work on a single process or product. In these smaller groups, output standards are usually set by time study, just as they are in individual piecework.

Group incentives are particularly useful when the job assignments of members of the group are so interrelated that it is difficult to measure the contribution of any single employee to total production. Group incentives make it possible to reward workers who provide essential services to production workers, yet who under individual piecework are usually paid only the regular day rates. Moreover, in theory at least, since everyone's earnings are dependent on everyone's efforts, the group may put pressure on the laggard individual to work harder. Certainly, as the spread of automation makes individual piecework less appropriate, companies that wish to retain some form of incentive may turn increasingly to group incentives.

Group incentives encourage cooperation among employees, whereas individual piecework militates against cooperation. Since all the members of the group share in the same bonus, conflict is reduced between workers on "tight" rates and workers on "loose" rates.

Rather than struggling with one another over choice work locations, materials, and job assignments—the sources of much friction under individual piecework—the employees work out their own allocation problems, knowing that everyone will share in the final result. For example, waitresses who pool tips are often eager to help each other out of jams.

On the other hand, group incentives share many of the disadvantages of individual-incentive plans. The workers still fear that if they produce too much management will cut the rates. Many of the intergroup differences that we discussed in the previous chapter remain. Also, since each individual may feel that his own efforts have very little effect on the over-all output of the group, he may experience less motivation to work harder than he would under individual piecework.

Group incentive systems that include an entire company or plant are less common than those that include only a single department. These broader systems are usually based not on time study but on some general measure of production, such as pounds produced or value of goods produced. For example, it was proposed in one union-management negotiation session in the automobile industry that the company put aside $10 for every car produced and that the whole fund be divided among all the employees. Company-wide systems often call for less than 100 per cent gain-sharing—that is, a 10 per cent increase in production results in a less than 10 per cent increase in earnings.

Company-wide plans naturally eliminate the intergroup incentive problems and fights over time study that we discussed in the previous chapter. Most important, they make employees less fearful of the introduction of new equipment, since all gains in productivity are usually shared by all employees (in contrast to individual piecework, where the gains can be taken away through a new time study).

Both of these factors contributed to Kaiser Steel's decision to introduce its group-incentive, or gain-sharing, plan. Rewards under this plan are based not only on gains in output but also on reductions in material costs. When set up, the plan also provided for substantial lump-sum payments to "buy out" workers who had been enjoying unusually high earnings from "loose" piece rates under the old individual-incentive plan. This plan, which now covers only part of the work force, has been at least moderately successful and has paid bonuses over the years averaging 15 to 20 per cent of employees' pay. The company credits it especially with reducing resistance to change.

In smaller plants, company-wide incentive systems may provide some incentive for the average employee to work harder. However, in larger plants where hundreds or even thousands of employees share in the bonus, the employee may feel there is little relationship between his own effort and the ultimate reward, and consequently may feel little motivation to increase production. Moreover, the union may oppose the scheme unless the amount of the bonus and the method of computing it are determined through collective bargaining.

PROFIT SHARING

In profit-sharing plans, employees receive a bonus that is normally based on some percentage (often 10 per cent to 30 per cent) of the company's profits beyond some fixed minimum.[1] For example, employees might receive 25 per cent of all profits in excess of 6 per cent of the company's net worth.

In a few profit-sharing plans, the bonus is paid directly to employees, usually at the end of the year. However, *deferred* plans, as they are called, are much more common. In deferred plans, the bonus is deposited in a fund to provide retirement or death benefits for employees (and perhaps made available for use in time of emergency). With such deferred plans, the company hopes to obtain the advantages of both profit-sharing and fringe benefit programs. (A third, fairly rare form of profit sharing allows the employee to choose between deferring his benefits or taking advantage of them at once.)

Profit sharing has a long history, but only in recent years has it gained widespread popularity. One of the best-known plans is that of the Lincoln Electric Company, which in some years has paid a bonus that doubles employees' pay. Sears Roebuck, Prentice-Hall, Procter and Gamble, and East-

---

[1] As we have discussed elsewhere, many companies have instituted a form of profit sharing through providing stock options for their top executives and encouraging their employees generally to buy the company's stock.

man Kodak also have profit-sharing plans of one type or another.[2] In 1966 such plans covered at least 2 million persons, coverage being more extensive in nonunion firms and in predominantly white-collar establishments (especially banks and retail stores) than it was in manufacturing or unionized firms generally. Eighty-one per cent of the plans involved deferred distribution.[3]

The advocates of profit sharing claim many advantages for it as a means of strengthening the sense of involvement that employees feel toward the company: It makes them feel like partners in the enterprise, it motivates them to work harder, cut waste, push sales, and so forth. And under the deferred plans, profit sharing makes it possible for the company to provide pensions and fringe benefits without increasing fixed costs, for the company makes contributions only in profitable years.[4]

Yet profit sharing has severe limitations, which may explain its failure to be more widely adopted. For one thing, it provides even less relationship between individual effort and ultimate reward than do group incentive plans. After all, profits depend on a great many factors other than individual performance: for example, the state of the market, sales efficiency, technological development, and so forth. Moreover, the fact that the payoff occurs years after it is earned means that there is a long delay between effort and reward, and this delay tends to impair the worker's feeling of working toward a goal. To complicate matters even further, many workers find it hard to understand how profits are computed, and particularly where labor-management relations are bad, they may suspect that a good deal of sleight of hand is involved in the calculations.[5]

What actually happens is that employees tend to regard profit sharing as just another fringe benefit ("added gravy"). Naturally they are happy to get a bonus once a year, but they recognize little concrete relationship between how hard they work and how much they get. Under deferred profit-sharing plans, pensions and welfare benefits are put on a rather insecure basis, for they depend not on how long an employee has been with the company but on whether the company has made a profit during that time. Still, in companies that can afford no other form of pension plan, even this is probably better than nothing.

Although profit sharing has been extremely successful in some companies, many have tried it for a few years and then abandoned it. Its success seems to depend to a large extent on the company's over-all personnel policy and on the state of union-management relations. Although it may provide motivation for employees to work harder, particularly in smaller companies, its chief merits would seem to lie in raising morale, in keeping the union out (if this is indeed a merit), and perhaps in reducing pressure for wage increases.

[2] Portions of Sears' savings have been reinvested in Sears stocks, thus multiplying employee returns. As of January 1970, Sears employees owned 33,600,000 shares of the company's stock through their profit-sharing account, and this stock was worth $2 billion. In 1970, Sears and Kodak each distributed close to $100 million in profit-sharing benefits.

[3] Gunnar Engen, "A New Direction and Growth in Profit-Sharing," *Monthly Labor Review*, Vol. 90, No. 7 (July 1967), pp. 1-8. One estimate placed the coverage of profit-sharing plans as high as 8 million employees, as of 1971, a fourfold increase over 1961. *The Wall Street Journal*, October 12, 1971.

[4] According to the 1966 survey, only "28 per cent of plant workers sharing profits had regular pension coverage, compared with 68 per cent of all plant workers." Engen, *op. cit.*, p. 7.

[5] The president of one company with a "profit-sharing" plan once told us, "I don't think my profit figures are any of my employees' business. I give them a bonus each year which is fair. They trust me." But do they? And do they really feel that they are *involved* in a profit-sharing plan?

SUGGESTION SYSTEMS

Suggestion systems are quite common in American industry. Their purpose is twofold:

1. To give management the benefit of employee suggestions on how to improve company efficiency. The average worker may have countless ideas on how to cut waste, eliminate unnecessary motions, prevent safety hazards, and so forth. Unless there is some systematic way of bringing these ideas to management's attention, a reservoir of ingenuity and experience may be overlooked.

2. To raise employee morale through giving them a chance to express their ideas on how the job should be done, to display their creative talents, and to take pride in seeing their ideas accepted—in other words, to reduce the employee's feeling that "as far as the company is concerned I'm just a machine. Nobody wants my ideas."

In the typical suggestion system a worker writes his idea out on a special form and drops the form into a special box. All suggestions go directly to the suggestion director or to a suggestion committee. The practicability of each suggestion is then explored and evaluated, usually in consultation with the supervisors who might be affected. If the suggestion is accepted, the employee receives a reward, often 10 to 25 per cent of the savings produced by the suggestion during the first year. For suggestions whose savings cannot be measured, token awards of from $3 to $25 are paid. If the suggestion is rejected, most companies insist that the employee be given a detailed explanation of why it was turned down, along with encouragement to make more suggestions in the future. It is customary to promote suggestion plans by means of active publicity programs, posters, articles in plant newspapers, award presentations, and so forth.

A reasonably successful plan may elicit 50 or more suggestions from every hundred employees each year, 25 to 35 per cent of which will be acceptable.[6] Frequently, however, results are a good bit less impressive than that. One explanation for poor employee response to a given suggestion plan may be that it is ineptly administered, with inadequate publicity or explanation of how the program is run. Moreover, delay in evaluating suggestions may give employees the impression that their ideas are not being given serious consideration. If the suggestion needs considerable time to be evaluated, progress reports should be issued to the employee to let him know that his idea has not been forgotten. If it is turned down, a careful explanation of why it has been rejected is important.

Even with good administration, suggestion plans often have only limited success. Employees may feel that the rewards are too meager, particularly when

---

[6] In 1968, of the 7 million employees of 233 firms belonging to the National Association of Suggestion Systems, 3 million (or 40 per cent) made suggestions. Of these, 725,000 received rewards, averaging $52 per suggestion. *Personnel Journal*, Vol. 69, No. 9 (November 1969), p. 861. General Motors in 1962 had 295 suggestions per 100 workers (in fact, 74 per cent of the work force made one or more suggestions); 25 per cent of these suggestions received awards. In 1966, G.M. paid out a total of $13 million in rewards.

they amount to only 10 per cent of the first year's savings. This means that management keeps the remaining 90 per cent the first year and 100 per cent of the savings in future years. Of course, even when awards are small on a percentage basis, it is not unusual for an employee to earn several thousand dollars for an especially good suggestion.

Employees may fear that their suggestions will backfire—that in effect they may be suggesting themselves out of a job. The man who makes a labor-saving suggestion is not likely to be very popular with his fellow employees, even though no one loses his job right away. The reward for the suggestion goes to the individual, but the suggestion may have disastrous effects on the entire group. Understandably, a group attitude may develop that discourages employees from making suggestions.

The very fact that suggestions are submitted and rewarded on an individual basis may generate serious resentment within the group. On the worker level especially, many of the best ideas grow out of long-term group discussions. If one man turns in an idea as his own suggestion, the rest may accuse him of larceny. In a sense, the suggestion system discourages teamwork in working out ideas and encourages individual workers to keep their ideas to themselves.

In addition, all suggestions must be submitted in writing, even though the average worker can do a much better job explaining himself orally, particularly if he can demonstrate his idea and answer questions directly.

In most instances the suggestion system bypasses the foreman. Yet many suggestions point up areas where the foreman has fallen down on the job or suggest ideas that the foreman should have thought of by himself. Understandably, employees fear that the foreman may retaliate if his failures are exposed, and as a consequence they hesitate to make suggestions at all. Some companies try to get around this problem by giving the foreman credit for all suggestions made in his department, by having his employees submit their suggestions directly to him instead of to the suggestion committee, and by involving the foreman in evaluating suggestions and handing out rewards. [7]

Suggestion systems sometimes arouse union opposition because, as a form of upward communication, they usurp what the union regards as one of its rightful functions. Consequently, many companies permit union representatives to sit in on the suggestion committee, in an effort to win union cooperation in implementing the plan and to alleviate workers' fears that their ideas are not being fairly evaluated. [8]

In general, the success of the suggestion system depends largely on the quality of the over-all personnel and labor-relations atmosphere. If the union

[7] In Russia foremen are given bonuses when their subordinates submit award-winning suggestions. David Granick, *The Red Executive* (Garden City: Doubleday, 1960), p. 16.

[8] Other problems with suggestions are: (1) administrative costs may run very high, sometimes as high as the value of the suggestions made; (2) managers may oppose the whole suggestion system because of the time and paperwork required to investigate them; (3) because of differences in jobs, workers who have relatively few opportunities to make suggestions may feel antagonistic to those who are better situated; and (4) over-all resentment on the part of those who don't get rewards may more than counterbalance the satisfaction of those who do. G. C. Gorfin, "The Suggestion System: Contribution to Morale or an Economic Transaction," *British Journal of Industrial Relations*, Vol. 7, No. 3 (November 1969), pp. 368–384.

suspects management's every move, and if supervisors discourage subordinates from doing things on their own—then employees will keep new ideas to themselves.

To sum up: a well-run suggestion system may yield a never-ending stream of ideas which cut costs and increase the employees' feeling of accomplishment and participation. Yet many plans are often poorly administered. And even when well administered, they often bypass both foreman and union, and place primary emphasis on the individual, though most problems involve the entire group.

CONSULTATIVE COMMITTEES

In an attempt to avoid the suggestion system's exclusive emphasis on individual workers, many companies have tried to elicit broader group participation by setting up consultative committees. The purpose of these committees is to improve two-way communication with lower levels of the organization. They give lower-ranking supervisors or employees a chance to express their points of view directly to top management, thus bypassing intermediate levels. For example, the first-line supervisors may elect representatives to meet weekly or monthly with the general manager to present and discuss current problems, ask about the rumors, pose questions, and ventilate gripes.

Management may institute similar committees for consultations with hourly-paid employees or their union. Joint worker-management or union-management consultative committees are involved in many activities such as solving production problems, cutting waste, reducing accidents, planning recreational programs, and soliciting for the Community Chest.

Union-management committees normally work in three areas:

1. *Collective bargaining.* Consultative committees have proved extremely useful in facilitating collective bargaining on such matters as job evaluation, incentive rates, and job transfers. These committees permit the orderly, systematic consideration of problems that would otherwise be handled piecemeal through the grievance procedure.

2. *Welfare activities.* Often joint committees assist in running athletic programs, handling welfare funds (perhaps derived from the profit from coffee machines), and so forth. These are areas in which the company has no special interest so long as workers are satisfied, and it is glad to let employees share responsibility.

3. *Production problems.* In some industries consultative committees have been established to explore persistent production problems, such as scrap, productivity, and safety. Committees of this sort are common only in companies that enjoy good labor-management relations, however, since production decisions are traditionally conceded to be management prerogatives.

In unionized companies, consultative committees give the union leadership an opportunity to make a positive contribution toward running the company rather than merely sitting on the sidelines or filing grievances. Often they provide management with a valuable source of information on worker and union problems, and provide union officials with a better understanding of management's problems. Thus, they have a potential ability to improve the general tenor of labor-management relations. Sometimes nonunionized companies set up consultative committees composed of representatives who are elected directly by the workers or appointed by the foremen.

When consultative committees, either union-management or worker-management, work effectively, they improve the quality of both upward and downward communication within the company. They give the workers a chance to bypass middle management and bring their suggestions, problems, and gripes directly to the men who actually make the decisions. Management may use these committees as a sounding board by releasing information on sales trends, safety problems, and so forth, in the hope that it will be passed along to workers at lower levels.

In short, consultative committees provide many of the same advantages that are derived from face-to-face conferences between subordinates and their immediate supervisor (see Chapter 9)—such advantages as lowered resistance to change, greater feeling of autonomy, better understanding of why orders are issued, and more effective implementation of instructions.

Nevertheless, joint committees labor under several disadvantages which sometimes limit their effectiveness:

1. Committee members may not communicate effectively with the workers back in the shop. Indeed, as they learn more and more about management's point of view, they may become more and more removed from the other workers. They may become extremely aware of production or safety problems, but they may fail to pass their enthusiasm on to the rest of the shop. Production committees, for example, are rarely successful unless the committee members energetically canvass their constituents for ideas.

The now-defunct Human Relations Committee in the basic steel industry suffered from the disadvantages of isolation from the rank-and-file membership. Consisting of top-level representatives of union and management, it operated largely without verbal fireworks and in secrecy—thus giving the average member little feeling of participation in collective bargaining and even leading some to suspect that their officers were in collusion with management against their best interests. This suspicion may have contributed to the defeat of union president David McDonald by I. W. Abel, a man committed to more conventional collective bargaining techniques.

2. Consultative committees run the risk of impairing the morale and status of the middle managers whom they bypass.

3. The success of these committees depends pretty much on the over-all quality of labor-management relations. If committee meetings are looked upon primarily as battlefields in a continuous war between union and management, then little will be accomplished.

4. Finally, consultation in itself does not provide a specific incentive for individual employees to work harder. True, employees do gain personal

satisfaction from influencing company policy and seeing their ideas adopted, but in our society we require a more specific goal toward which we can work, most often in the form of an economic reward. Thus the consultative committees that have proved most fruitful have been those with some highly specific incentive for cooperation: to win the war, to save the company from going out of business, to earn more pay, or to remove accident hazards.

If consultative committees are to be successful in solving production problems there must be participation throughout all levels of the organization as well as a definite incentive or goal to unite everyone's efforts. On the other hand, such complete participation is not required if the committee's efforts are restricted to handling collective-bargaining problems or fringe areas. Probably this explains why consultative committees have been most useful in solving specific, limited problems. They do not, in themselves, provide motivation for higher production or a general sense of participation.

THE SCANLON PLAN

The Scanlon Plan is one of the most interesting approaches to securing widespread employee participation and obtaining industrial peace and higher productivity as well. [9] Although the plan is not widely accepted, we shall discuss it in some detail because it seems to avoid many of the problems raised by other plans. The plan consists of two basic parts: (1) a wage formula or incentive, and (2) a new form of suggestion system.

The *wage formula* is designed to distribute the gains of increased productivity proportionally among all employees involved. Although each formula is tailor-made to the needs of the particular company, wages are typically tied to the sales value of goods produced, so that, for example, for every 1 per cent increase in productivity there is a 1 per cent increase in wages and salaries. In contrast to usual incentive plans, bonuses are paid to the clerical force, salesmen, supervisors, and sometimes even to top management.

Notice that this is really a form of group incentive covering the entire plant. As we have seen, a bonus of this sort is valuable not only as an incentive to productivity, but also as a form of feedback or yardstick by which the plant's success can be measured by the participants themselves.

---

[9] The late Joseph Scanlon, author of this plan, rose from an ordinary worker in a steel plant to be a top officer of the United Steelworkers of America and later a Lecturer at the Massachusetts Institute of Technology. For fuller discussion of the plan see William F. Whyte and others, "The Scanlon Plan," *Money and Motivation* (New York: Harper, 1955), Chapter 14; Frederick G. Lesieur, ed., *The Scanlon Plan: A Frontier in Labor-Management Cooperation* (New York and Cambridge: Wiley and The Technology Press, 1958); George Strauss and Leonard R. Sayles, "The Scanlon Plan: Some Organizational Problems," *Human Organization*, Vol. 16, No. 3 (Fall 1957), pp. 15–22; *Group Work Incentives: Experience with the Scanlon Plan* (New York: Industrial Relations Counselors, 1962); Frederick G. Lesieur and Elbridge Pluckett, "The Scanlon Plan Has Proved Itself," *Harvard Business Review*, Vol. 47, No. 5 (October 1969), pp. 100–118; and Herbert R. Northrup and Harvey A. Young, "The Causes of Industrial Peace Revisited," *Industrial and Labor Relations Review*, Vol. 22, No. 1 (October 1968), pp. 40–42.

The mechanics of the *suggestion system* are simple: In each department a union *production committeeman* is elected or appointed by union officers. The production committeeman and the foreman constitute a departmental *production committee*, which meets periodically to discuss suggestions from individual employees and to formulate general plans for the improvement of productivity. Rejected suggestions or suggestions that affect the plant as a whole are referred to a plant-wide *screening committee*, which includes top management as well as the union leadership.

Note how the Scanlon Plan differs from the typical suggestion system: Instead of individual rewards for accepted suggestions, the group gains as a whole through a higher bonus whenever productivity is increased. The union takes an active part instead of worrying whether suggestions will result in a speedup. Individuals cooperate with each other in developing suggestions instead of keeping their ideas to themselves. Further, under a suggestion system management normally waits passively for workers to submit suggestions; frequently under the Scanlon Plan management itself suggests problems for mutual discussion.

Before the Scanlon Plan was put into operation in a particular printing plant, management had tried to introduce a conveyor system. The plans had been developed exclusively by the engineers, without consulting the employees. The system immediately ran into trouble and the employees showed little interest in making it work.

After the Scanlon Plan was accepted management decided to try another conveyor system, but to introduce it in a different manner. Employees were shown a small scale model of the proposed layout and encouraged to make criticisms and suggestions for improvements. On the basis of these comments the joint production committee made modifications to eliminate "bugs" that the engineers had not foreseen. The new system was enthusiastically accepted by the employees. [10]

Both the quantity and quality of suggestions seem to be higher under the Scanlon Plan than under the typical suggestion system.

As a means of increasing productivity, the Scanlon Plan has met with varied success. For example, take the experience of the LaPointe Machine Tool Company over a period of 58 months. Here the monthly bonus ranged from 0 to 52.1 per cent, with no bonus at all during 16 months and bonuses in excess of 20 per cent during another 20 months. Gains of over 40 per cent are not uncommon, however. [11]

In summary, there are gains for everybody under a successful Scanlon Plan: (1) more and better suggestions, (2) higher productivity and profits, (3) decreased resistance to change, (4) better union-management relations, (5) greater cooperation among work groups and between individuals and their supervisors, and (6) increased motivation to work.

And yet the Scanlon Plan, promising though it seems, is not a cure-all for every industrial ill.

[10] Adopted from George Shultz, "Worker Participation in Production Problems," *Personnel*, Vol. 28, No. 3 (November 1951), pp. 201–211.

[11] George Shultz and Robert P. Crisera, "The LaPointe Machine Tool Company and the United Steelworkers of America," *Causes of Industrial Peace Under Collective Bargaining, Case Study No. 10* (Washington, D.C.: National Planning Association, 1952), p. 55.

1. If the plan is to be successful, management must be willing to make substantial changes in its attitudes. Traditional company prerogatives must be forgotten. Foremen, superintendents, and even the company president must learn to consult with subordinates and be willing to listen to sharp criticism. In companies that already practice general supervision and enjoy a good system of upward and downward communication, the transition to the Scanlon Plan may be relatively easy. Others may find that the plan requires adjustments that they are unwilling to make.

2. The Scanlon Plan presents the union with a real dilemma. In fact, the plan is bound to fail unless the union officers give up the militant view that the "member is always right." But there is also a danger that the officers may become too concerned with jacking up production. If they refuse to handle individual grievances and concentrate too much on pushing their members to work harder, the members may become resentful, give the plan only passive support, and even reject their officers at the next election. Indeed, as the officers become more and more closely identified with management's point of view, they tend to become alienated from the average member. This dilemma may be partly resolved if the officers are careful to explain new developments to the rank-and-file and to listen carefully to their reactions. Still, the plan blurs the union's primary function of providing representation for its members.

3. As we have seen, one of the disadvantages of traditional incentive plans is that they engender ill-feeling among groups—both where technology makes one group's earnings dependent on the production of another group, or where groups suspect each other of having "loose" rates. The Scanlon Plan presumably eliminates this problem by establishing plant-wide incentives. But a plant-wide incentive means that each individual's earnings are dependent on the effort of the entire plant. Harder work by any one individual will bring him only negligibly higher monetary return. Hopefully, self-satisfaction, the desire for praise from fellow workers, and interest in the group as a whole will be sufficient to elicit high productivity. But for this to happen there must be a high degree of cohesion and employee identification with the plant as a whole.

   How likely is this to occur? The answer depends on a number of factors, including the size, homogeneity, and history of the work group. One thing is certain: There are bound to be some rivalries among groups, and skill in human relations is constantly required of all parties to prevent these rivalries from reaching serious proportions. "Why should we work so hard when Department Y has fallen so far behind?" The larger the plant, the greater are the possibilities for dissension, and the more difficult it becomes to maintain support for plantwide production goals.

4. The Scanlon Plan has been successful both in very depressed companies, where, the employees have cooperated to save their jobs, and in prosperous companies, where the employees realized that there were big bonuses to be won. The plan may be less successful in industries where the

market conditions make it difficult to sell increased output and where greater productivity may in fact mean fewer jobs (in economic terms, where demand is inelastic). Nor do we know what happens when a successful plan goes through a long period of poor earnings (some have weathered short periods).

In short, the Scanlon Plan seems to be most successful where both union and management are able to make substantial changes in their patterns of behavior, where good internal communications exist within and between both groups, and probably only in smaller organizations.

WORKERS' PARTICIPATION IN OTHER COUNTRIES

The Scanlon Plan and other forms of workers' formal participation in management have received relatively little attention in the United States and Canada, where "participation" generally refers to the kinds of group decision-making and delegation discussed in Chapters 7 and 9. Elsewhere in the world, however, workers' participation has been the subject of much discussion and experimentation. Yugoslavian plants, in theory, are run by the workers themselves through elected work councils, which make general policy and have the right to hire and fire the plant manager. German coal and steel companies operate under "co-determination" in which seats on the "supervisory boards" (roughly equivalent to a board of directors in the United States) are filled half by employee representatives and the other half by management representatives. Joint consultation committees (often called work councils or production committees) have been established in companies in Sweden, Norway, Britain, France, Israel, and India.

Most of these participation schemes differ from the Scanlon Plan in three important ways: First, they provide no direct incentives. Second, the consultation committees operate at the plant or company level instead of at the work force level. Third, they deal chiefly with personnel rather than production problems.

Supporters of participation schemes argue that not only is participation morally sound, but that it reduces alienation, raises morale and productivity, and improves union-management relations. Generalization about these schemes in practice is difficult. By and large, their main impact seems to be in the area of labor-management relations. [12]

In most European countries collective bargaining has traditionally been restricted to establishing nationwide wage levels. Participation has, in effect, introduced plant-level collective bargaining of the United States variety, with its emphasis on subjects such as promotions, seniority, work conditions, and individual grievances. Yet consultative committees here and overseas seem to suffer from many of the same problems: their discussions are focused on company or

[12] For a discussion, see "A Symposium: Workers Participation in Management: An International Comparison," *Industrial Relations,* Vol. 9, No. 2 (February 1970), pp. 117–214.

plant-level problems rather than on those affecting the shop and the individual worker. Little effort is made to involve employees in solving work problems or providing positive internalized motivation for harder work.

CONCLUSION

We have looked at six plans designed to raise employee morale and promote a sense of identification with the entire organization. All six plans seem to reach these goals through changing human relationships. Group incentives and profit sharing aim for greater cooperation among individuals. Suggestion systems and consultative committees seek to improve communications between individual employees and higher management. Both objectives are sought by the Scanlon Plan and by the "workers participation" schemes that exist overseas.

Each of these plans has been adopted by management as a panacea for a whole range of industrial-relations ills. Yet none of them will work well except in an atmosphere of good labor-management relations and sound managerial, organizational, and personnel practices. Although all are designed in part to provide internalized motivation for production, they have been more successful as a form of hygienic management that tends to raise morale and reduce friction. Indeed, two of the techniques—group incentives and profit sharing—are often viewed as forms of fringe benefits.

problem • THE CONSULTANT'S STORY

It all started when Harry Beard phoned and asked me to "come out to the plant and give us a little advice on our suggestion system." I readily agreed, though I told him I was dubious about what I could do in a single visit. However, before hanging up I asked him how he was involved and what was the problem. He said, "My job is chiefly trouble-shooting, and right now I'm up to my ears on a new product line we're installing—almost completely automatic. But the Plant Manager wants me to do something about suggestions. We have a plan, but is isn't working. We get a fair number of piddling ideas on safety and housekeeping—but almost nothing which saves us any money. We have a new plant here and there must be lots of ideas around—lots of things need improvement and the workers must see them—but we have the worst record in the company—and you know how the Head Office watches these things."

I arrived at the plant at noon. Harry had invited me for lunch and I had visions of the nearby Country Club. Instead we went to the plant cafeteria with the Plant Manager, the Industrial Engineer, and the Personnel Man. Table talk was dull and the food worse. I decided to let them broach the subject at hand. I did notice that everyone deferred to the Manager's ideas—even on sports. Then to the conference room—attractive but noisy. Plant Manager opened up, "Harry brought you here because he said you had some ideas on suggestion systems."

"He wants his answer wrapped up 1-2-3 in cellophane," I thought, and countered. "Well, first I'd like to get a little idea of your problem."

The Plant Manager did most of the talking, though the others broke in at times to underscore his words. There was plenty of opportunity for suggestions, he felt, but no good ones were forthcoming. With a plant of 2,000 employees, last year they had 750 suggestions, but of these only 300 were acceptable—and on 230 of these the savings were unmeasurable, so only the minimum $3 reward was given. Total awards last year came to $1,940. The largest: $55.

I asked what determined the size of the award. "We pay 10 per cent of the first year's savings." He must have seen my inward shudder, for he asked, "Is that low?"

"Not very," I added tactfully. "Awards seem to vary from 10 to 25 per cent. Have you thought of raising it?"

"We can't. It's set by corporation policy. For a while we paid $5 as the minimum reward, but then we heard the company policy was $3. Of course it made us seem rather cheap to cut it down."

My questioning then turned to the mechanics of the program. "Suggestions are made on this form," he said as he handed it to me. "You see, the suggestor's name goes on a special tab which the Suggestion Director tears off, so that no one but he knows who made the suggestion. That way we eliminate favoritism."

"Are you the Suggestion Director?" I asked the industrial engineer.

"Oh, no," said the Plant Manager. "We have a full-time man. Possibly you might like to meet him—you might give him a few pointers." I nodded. He continued, "To get back to our system. The Suggestion Director refers each suggestion to the man in whose area of responsibility it lies—to the foreman, the maintenance department, and so forth. They investigate the suggestion. If they think it is good, they pass their recommendation back to the Suggestion Director, along with their estimate of likely savings. The suggestion committee takes up the accepted suggestions and decides how much the award should be."

"Has the union shown any interest?" I asked—hopeful that this question might lead to pay dirt.

"Oh, yes, the union president sits in on every meeting," he said.

Just then the Personnel Director interrupted: "I never got a chance to tell you that at the last meeting the International Representative showed up. The union wanted to have three men sit in on meetings in the future. I told the Representative that he could attend this meeting, but in the future we'd let only one man in. After all, it's purely a company committee."

"That's right," said the Manager. "We can't let the union run away with this."

"Do you have any idea how the union feels about this?" I asked. I knew the answer, but hoped to stimulate them to do a little thinking.

There was a slight pause, then the Industrial Engineer answered, "They take the position that these suggestions shoudn't force anybody out of a job. I think they're scared that just that will happen. Frankly, I think maybe the union is sabotaging it."

"Do you think there is any justification for their fears?" I asked, trying not to sound argumentative.

"I suppose there is," he replied. "Seventy per cent of our costs are in labor. You can't save anything in material. We're in a highly competitive industry and we're going to have to save on labor costs."

There was a pause. I said nothing, hoping for further discussion. There being none, I asked, perhaps a little gruffly, "Well, where do you think the weak points of the program are?"

They paused. Then the Plant Manager spoke up, "I've been wondering whether our form (on which the suggestions are made) is adequate. I wish you would look it over."

This set me back. I tried another tack. "How do the foremen feel about it? Is there any chance they think these suggestions threaten them—point out things they should have noticed themselves?"

"Not that I've heard," said the Industrial Engineer. "After all, good suggestions would improve the efficiency of their department—and they will do better on their EIP."

"What's that?" I asked.

"EIP—that's our Efficiency Improvement Plan. Every member of management is rated monthly on a number of factors such as cost control, production, scrap, and so forth."

"Are foremen rewarded under EIP for the number of suggestions made in their department?" I asked. The Industrial Engineer shook his head.

There was some more discussion, along the same vein. Finally, the Plant Manager said, "Well, I have another meeting. Harry will take you around the plant, answer any questions, and I will be anxious to get your recommendations."

After he left, Harry gave me the "Grand Tour." It was a beautiful plant—most of the operations involved assembling—almost all routine—a great deal of finger work.

Finally Harry pointed: "There's the Suggestion Director's office." He was in a glass cubicle, right off the main assembly line, with two other men, both industrial engineers.

Bill Dongle obviously had been waiting for us. He seemed a little nervous as he shook my hand. Harry was fairly tactful: "Bill, as you know, we've been talking a bit about suggestions among other things and we were sure he [me, the consultant] wanted to get the real picture from you."

"That's right, I do. I gather your program sounds pretty much like the normal—that is, you're having the normal number of headaches."

Bill looked a little relieved. I felt sorry for him as he started telling his problems. Among others they were:

"I don't get much cooperation from the foremen. They don't seem to talk it up among their men. When I do refer suggestions to them, they always seem to be negative. Lots of times they turn down ideas which I think are pretty good—in fact, sometimes they put them in later on—and do I catch hell from the men. Also they take so long to make a report. Sometimes it is six months till a man gets an acknowledgment that we have accepted his ideas—he may even see it being put into effect before he gets a report, but the procedure is, we don't tell a man his suggestion is accepted until the award committee figures out how much it is worth. Sometimes, of course, if the suggestion is not written up too well, I call the man in to talk about it—and that lets him know we're thinking about it. You know—maybe I should talk to every man who has a suggestion—that lets him know we're interested. It would be better than our usual short note saying that we have accepted it or rejected it."

"Harry, what do you think?" I asked.

Harry said, "It might be a good idea, but I don't know about taking all the men off their jobs."

"Maybe I could see them on the job," Bill volunteered. It was agreed he might do this—though Harry wondered whether Bill's presence might make the other workers think that the man who made the suggestion was a "company man."

I then asked, "I gather you feel that foremen turn down some good ideas. I wonder if anything can be done about this?"

(We discussed this for a while, but you can figure out for yourself what Harry and Bill decided.)

Near the end of the discussion Bill said, "What we've got to do is get the foremen to show more interest."

I asked, "To what extent does supervision indicate to the foremen that they are backing the suggestion plans?"

"Well," said Harry, "it's mentioned all the time in the company magazine and the plant newspaper."

To myself I asked, "Who writes these newspapers? Staff."

To them I asked, "Do you know of any situation where a foreman has been praised by his superior for getting good suggestions or questioned when he got none?"

Both shook their heads, but perhaps the import of my question slipped by them.

Later Bill returned to the original theme. "All the suggestions we get are trifles. Perhaps if we could get a few good ideas and give some really big awards, it would get the ball rolling. You know we have scrap and safety contests between departments. The record of all the departments are posted monthly as well as their improvements over previous months. Perhaps we could do this with suggestions."

We discussed this for a while. Then I had a bright idea. I asked to go over some typical suggestions. We took two from the file that seemed more complicated than most.

The first involved a change in the carrier that held the product as it passed through the assembly line. I noticed the company had spent $800 to make the change, but the suggestion was classed as "housekeeping—no measurable savings," and got the minimum $3.

"Why put it in," I asked, "if there are no savings?"

"Well," Bill said, "before we made the change there was always the chance that a piece might fall off. This would cause a great deal of damage—but you just can't estimate the chance of its falling off or how great would be the damage."

Another accepted suggestion involved a minor change in an operation. Harry said, "It did make the job easier to do and a little faster. But since the union wouldn't let us retime the job, there were no savings. So we paid just $3."

The phone rang and I had a short pause to collect my thoughts. I had a lot of questions to answer—and quick:

Why were so few suggestions made?

I hadn't talked to any workers, but what did they *probably* feel about the whole scheme?

How did the union officers feel?

How did the foremen feel?

Assuming I were plant manager (nice to daydream), what would I do to solve the problem?

Ah, I'm just a consultant and there are definite limits to the ideas they are willing to accept—no point in suggesting things they won't carry out. But what has my brief experience with this company taught me about the way they handle problems? How good is the union-management relationship, for instance? Why was the Suggestion Director so tense?

Are there any suggestions I could make that would be *likely to be accepted* and that would also change the attitude of the workers, of the union, of the foremen?

The Plant Manager wanted ideas on how to improve the application blank. What does this indicate?

Above all, what next? How should I go about putting my ideas across? Should I make a written report? Should I give my ideas to the Suggestion Director, to Harry, or to the Plant Manager? Or do I need to do further research? If so, what questions should I seek to answer?

More fundamentally, I wonder whether the whole situation might have some implications for staff-line relations.

How's my interview technique? What am I trying to accomplish? Should I have followed some of these points more deeply?

MANAGEMENT'S RESPONSIBILITIES IN DEALING WITH PEOPLE

Unlike such specialties as electrical engineering or finance, management involves *human beings*. The engineer, for instance, need never give a thought to the impact his maintenance program will have on the "personality" of his equipment. The accountant busies himself with tractable, obedient figures. But the manager must keep himself constantly alert to the impact of his personnel administration on the employee as an individual and as a citizen. And he must understand the subtle relationships that prevail between corporate efficiency and employee satisfaction.

HISTORICAL PERSPECTIVE

Private Charity

For hundreds of years, managers have been aware of their special obligations to employees. The early New England textile manufacturer, for example, often provided elaborate opportunities for his "charges" (typically young girls) to worship and to gain an education. Some owners, of course, were flagrantly paternalistic—eager to extend benefits in order to receive praise for their generosity. Rockefeller and Carnegie are today better known for their philanthropy than for their often ruthless business practices. Even the worst of the "robber barons" might provide housing facilities, grant Christmas gifts, and distribute other forms of largess to those who worked for him. Yet much of this philanthropy was personal (rather than corporate) charity, and benefits were given as gifts, not rights. By the 1920's many companies had institutionalized these obligations by establishing a special department—the personnel department—to deal with the legitimate needs of their employees. ("Legitimate" needs, as we have seen, can be defined in many different ways.)

The personnel department was sometimes regarded as a buffer between management and workers, as the workers' "representative" that could be counted on to intervene on their behalf. Although management often encouraged this attitude simply to keep the unions out, there was also a sincere feeling that every organization needed a "conscience," someone who could speak for employees and who would be responsible for their welfare. Many managers genuinely believed that their decisions should be guided by concern for human beings as well as by a desire for profit maximization. In making layoffs, companies often gave special consideration to men with families or with long service, even though they might be less efficient than the men actually dismissed.

Gestures of good will and efforts to be just were haphazard and erratic. John Jones, whose needs happened to come to the attention of top management, received excellent treatment; Gus Smith, who was not quite so lucky, lost his job, even though his claim for consideration was as valid as Jones's. Some personnel directors proved effective spokesmen for employees; others had neither the interest nor the ability to do so.

Cynics argued that these humanitarian policies were only a reflection of management's deep-seated opposition to unions, or evidence of a selfish desire to raise morale in order to boost productivity. Clearly, however, many managers went beyond dollars-and-cents considerations and were genuinely altruistic.

How Contemporary Managers View Their Role

Management attitudes have become more complex in recent years. Top managements of many corporations have become self-perpetuating groups who own relatively few shares of stock in the corporations they control. Since management's control can no longer be legitimatized purely on the basis of ownership, many managers are now seeking other bases on which to justify their powerful economic role. Increasingly managers look upon themselves as professionals, and as we saw in Chapter 3, professionals traditionally concern themselves with ethical bases for their actions.

Corporate objectives are less clear than they once were. Growth, share of the market, company (and managerial) prestige supplement the goal of maximizing profits. Some managers now claim that their function is to act as trustees for a number of interests (some of which admittedly conflict). It is not uncommon for managers to talk of being mediators among stockholders, employees, customers, and the community rather than solely representatives of the stockholders. [1]

[1] Committee for Economic Development, *Social Responsibilities of Business Corporations* (New York: CED, 1971)

Concern with corporate citizenship, aiding minorities, pollution abatement, and a healthy and livable community are becoming more central to the line as distinct from the staff's job description. (Of relevance to this subject, however, is the degree to which such new problem areas involve communications, negotiations, and leadership skills—the dealing with human beings—just as much as the more traditional production and selling functions.)

On the other hand, many sincere businessmen feel that business should not pose as the guardian of the general welfare. They, too, argue on practical and moral grounds. [2]

Many would claim that management cannot mediate among the competing claims of stockholders, employees, suppliers, and the community. The businessman owes his first responsibility to the owners of the business, which means that he must devote primary attention to profits and efficiency. When he takes other interests into account, he abdicates that responsibility. In fact, only by concentrating on profits and efficiency can he bestow the greatest benefits on the community as a whole. These observers argue that only then will he make economic use of the company's personnel and material resources, with maximum production and minimum costs.

Yet the close interrelationship between business and society seems more clearly recognized by businessmen today than it was before the Great Depression and World War II—and this is true even in industries not closely affected by government purchasing and government regulatory commissions. Many businessmen are beginning to develop a sense of having a special responsibility to behave in the interests of the national welfare, to function as good citizens.

There is also a more practical motivation. With improved and widespread public education and effective mass communication media, public opinion is a more potent pressure on business. The alert business leader recognizes that if he is to maintain reasonable autonomy in decision-making, he must maintain public good will. As the Celanese Corporation announced:

The company proudly cherishes its freedom to innovate and considers that corporate self-discipline, like personal self-discipline, is the chief condition of retaining that freedom. [3]

Ever since Taylor's scientific management, executives also have been endeavoring to increase their rationality. Objectivity is also another hallmark of professionalism. For example, it is felt that promotion and salary increases ought to be awarded on the basis of merit, not friendship, [4] since this policy is rational in

[2] In a letter to *The New York Times* (Western Edition, Nov. 8, 1963, p. 8), Roger Blough, Chairman of the Board of U.S. Steel, explained his attitude towards the suggestion that his company should play a positive role in solving racial problems in Birmingham, Alabama:

"As individuals we can exercise what influence we may have as citizens, but for a corporation to attempt to exert any kind of economic compulsion to achieve a particular end in the social area seems to me to be quite beyond what a corporation should do, and quite beyond what any corporation can do ... I believe that any attempt by a private corporation like U.S. Steel to impose its views, its beliefs and its will upon the community by resorting to economic compulsion or coercion would be repugnant to our American constitutional concepts, and that appropriate steps to correct this abuse of corporate power would be universally demanded by public opinion and by Government."

[3] As cited in Cheit, *op. cit.*, p. 188.

[4] The sociologists call this shift from personal to impersonal decision-making a move from *particularism* to *universalism*.

terms of the welfare of the business. The emphasis on behavioral sciences as a guide to solving human-relations problems is, in fact, an emphasis on what is presumed to be an orderly, scientific way of approaching problems in contrast to an emotional, personal-preference mode of solution.

Another aspect of this rationality is the greater use of rules and general policies. Both devices avoid the complexities of deciding each individual case by itself and the difficulty of justifying such decisions. In the broadest sense, it is a shift towards the rule of law. Leaves of absence and vacations tend to be granted in terms of general rules rather than managerial whim. Of course, union and government pressure for written contracts and better record-keeping have both been spurs in this direction.

Finally, professional managers tend to take a longer-run point of view. Although good human relations may not show up immediately in lower costs and higher profits, it is asserted that over the long run, investments in a more satisfied work force will show a return, just as do capital investments in any other area. Similarly, neglect of human resources produces obsolescence and diminished effectiveness.

Unfortunately, these various sources of increased managerial awareness of human-relations responsibilities may not always provide mutually consistent answers. For example, as we saw in Chapter 21, skewing of employment practices to aid minority group members can discriminate against others. This type of problem will be less abstract if we look at an actual case. In the Duffy Case, we shall see that decision-making in what first appears to be a small problem is made difficult by the large number of tough questions that have to be answered (questions on which data and behavioral principles are not easy to find).

SATISFACTION VS. PROFITABILITY

Rules, contract clauses, and even behavioral science findings often do not furnish a ready answer to two critically important questions: What are the legitimate needs of employees, and when is it justifiable to put those needs aside in favor of the profit needs of the company? Unfortunately, most personnel problems still cannot be resolved simply by reading the company manual or the union contract. And the most important problems of all have a dismaying tendency to crop up between the rules, in the uncharted territory where there are no clear precedents, no obvious "right" or "wrong" answers.

The Duffy Case

Bill Duffy is the head of a clerical department in a large brokerage office. Most of the work is relatively routine though of considerable importance to the company. Duffy's department has always been known for its high morale and for its ability to maintain work schedules.

Duffy started with the company right after finishing high school. Although he is just celebrating his 50th birthday, he has already accumulated about 30 years of seniority. In many ways, he seems much older than his years. He lacks stamina and his thinking processes are slower than those of many of his older colleagues.

Over the past year, the responsibilities of managing the department have been pretty much taken over by the assistant department head, Joe Jenkins. When a difficult problem comes up, the clerks now turn to Joe for an answer. Duffy continues to sign papers that need the signature of the department head, and he is consulted as a matter of form on all major policy questions. But Jenkins has become the real head of the department.

Top management considered Duffy's case at a recent meeting. A couple of the men present thought that the company should encourage him to accept early retirement, although they recognized that this would be a serious psychological and financial blow to him. His retirement benefits would be less than half of what they would be if he continued to work until 65. It might be possible to demote him to a less responsible position, but there were no jobs open that would fit his capacities. After reconsidering the matter, management decided to retain Duffy in his present position, feeling that too "harsh" an approach to the problem would prompt substantial dissatisfaction in the organization.

Nagging Questions

The Duffy Case presents us with a number of more explicit questions than did the question of employment policies in the racial area. These are questions involving all sorts of intangibles, conjectures, and risks.

Equity considerations and individual satisfaction

1. How much does the company "owe" an employee who has given 30 years of loyal service? What obligation does it have to him?

2. Can this obligation be met in financial terms? What is the relationship between Duffy's dissatisfaction, on the one hand, with being only a "figure head" and his satisfaction, on the other hand, with maintaining his salary and title?

3. Should management adopt a more liberal policy toward early retirement for long-service employees who become "disabled"?

4. Is it fair to Jenkins, whose salary is approximately 30 per cent lower than Duffy's, to let him assume the responsibilities of a managerial job without granting him both the prestige and the economic rewards that normally go with it?

Organization and profit considerations

1. What effect would Duffy's forced retirement have on the morale and performance of other long-service employees? Would it be more harmful than their realization that inefficiency and ineptness are protected by the fiction of having a formal department head and a real one? What impact

will management's decision have on employees' attitudes toward opportunities for promotion?

2. What would be the long-run costs of establishing more liberal early-retirement benefits? How would these costs compare with the apparent savings offered by the present policy?

3. What is the effect on department efficiency of having two managers? Can Duffy's salary be justified in terms of the contribution he is making?

4. Will management's decision have any effect on the company's ability to recruit highly motivated young men?

These are only a few of the highly complex short- and long-run questions raised by this case. There are two fundamental problems: (1) How much importance should management ascribe to efficiency as against human satisfaction, and where does one draw the line? And (2), assuming that management can resolve this first problem, what are the best ways of achieving optimal efficiency and human satisfaction?

What at first glance appears to be a single organization problem is normally intertwined with a whole host of other policy problems. This case, for example, is tied in with the company's promotion policy as well as with its policies on fringe benefits (pensions and severance pay). Also involved are job evaluation, recruitment, organizational structure, individual needs and motivations, and the attitudes of the work group.

The manager must constantly seek to resolve the diverse and conflicting claims of individuals and groups both in the short run and in the long run. And yet, since he cannot ascribe exact weights to each factor, or predict the future with any real accuracy, he must rely heavily on intuition, personal judgment, and probability.

Nor do employee needs and company needs fit into neat, separate compartments. There is no simple answer to what course of action is "equitable" or what decisions will improve "efficiency," for the two objectives are intimately associated. There are very few decisions that affect employee satisfaction which do not also have a direct bearing on work efficiency.

THE CONTEMPORARY SCENE:
HOW MUCH BEHAVIORAL SCIENCE?

Management in recent years undoubtedly has begun to show greater concern for the welfare of its employees. True, strong unions, government regulations, and labor shortages have contributed heavily to this shift in attitude, but enlightened executives are sincere in their acceptance of human relationships as a vital part of managerial responsibility. In fact, the human-relations movement has profoundly altered the qualities that have traditionally been associated with the successful business leader. No longer is he judged solely on his drive, ambition, decisiveness, or ability to make money. Now he is also expected to develop cooperative, satisfying relationships within the organization.

Both the economic position and the psychological position of subordinates have improved tremendously over the last generation. The emphasis on human relations has tended to take the bite out of authority and the harshness out of arbitrary rules; it has promoted compassion and dignity at the work place. There is less likelihood of arbitrary discharge, less discrimination in handing out rewards. Work loads are easier and supervision is fairer. At least in larger companies, employees have considerable opportunity to protest inequities through union or company grievance procedures. No one would pretend that we have achieved Utopia, but tremendous progress has been made.

In recent years, however, the behavioral science approach to management has been subjected to a sustained and unexpectedly strong attack from observers who stress efficiency and productivity above all other management objectives. These criticisms, which have come from many sources, reduce themselves to the following charges:

1. The behavioral science approach tends to complicate what are essentially very simple problems. All that is required in dealing with people is honest common sense and the application of the golden rule.

2. Computers will solve the problems, not managers.

3. Excessive concern with people leads management to interfere in the personal life of employees, to take over community functions, and to encroach on areas that are outside the province of the business organization. It manipulates people and dupes them into accepting changes that really are against their best interests.

4. Overemphasizing people at the expense of productivity may prove disastrous to the organization.

Let us look briefly at each of these charges. Since they are so commonly leveled, the student of management—whether in the university or the business firm—must expect to run across them in one form or another.

Do We Complicate Simple Problems?

Recently in a talk before a group of businessmen, one of the authors tried to explain how complicated human relations really are; he emphasized all the factors that the manager should take into account before making a decision involving people. He felt reasonably proud of the presentation, but complacency was shattered during the discussion period by the following comment from the floor: "Professor, doesn't everything you say boil down to the golden rule? I've had 40 years experience in industry and I've found that the important thing is to be honest and sincere with people. Show an interest in them and you'll never have any human-relations problems."

But are sincerity and good will and even common sense enough? We think not.

The findings of modern psychology suggests that applying the golden rule is just too simple an approach, mainly because it assumes that everyone has identical needs. In the Duffy case, for example, a great deal of insight into the total organizational situation would be required before management could make a truly ethical decision. Is it more ethical to transfer an older employee to a lower-paying job or to terminate his employment and give him early-retirement benefits? What does common sense tell you?

Unless management is aware of the impact of each decision on the individual and on the group, it cannot know whether it is acting to the advantage or to the detriment of the members of the organization. It is not enough to apply the golden rule or to ask, "How would I want to be treated in a similar situation?" This projection of oneself into the position of the other person may lead to unwise and highly unjust actions.

Many disastrous mistakes are made with the best of intentions. A kind-hearted supervisor decides not to penalize an employee who has family troubles even though he is persistently late and fails to meet production standards. The situation grows worse and worse until finally the employee is discharged. Were the supervisor's intentions good? Of course they were. But they led him to injure both the individual and the organization. No businessman really lets concern for others control everything he does. Were he completely motivated by charity and altruism, he would never try to take business away from a competitor and he would never discipline a subordinate. What the ethically motivated businessman *does* believe is that he should take into account the welfare of others *along with* other factors.

Won't Computers Solve These Problems?

With recent developments in the management sciences and computer technology, it is widely believed that many subjects which now take managerial resources and time will be handled in routine fashion by data-processing and operations-analysis techniques. It has even been argued that many human-relations problems are complicated needlessly by unthinking managers or those seeking to make work for themselves to justify larger staffs.

However, in reviewing this and similar cases, it does not appear that these problems lend themselves to the decision-making techniques that are useful in deciding what size batch of a variety of components to manufacture or where to locate a warehouse. There were such a multiplicity of considerations, each of which is laden with value judgments, and such heavy requirements for personal skill in the execution of any decision reached (or even in securing adequate data) that it is unlikely machines will ever do the job. In fact, in the future, because computers will handle effectively some other technical aspects of the managerial job, it is likely that an increasing proportion of the managerial work load will be in the human-relations area.

How Much Manipulation and Interference?

Managers are often charged with trying to manipulate their employees.

In many cases human relations has been used or is intended to be used, to manipulate, to adjust people to what the boss thinks is reality, to make them conform to a pattern that seems logical from the top down, to make them accept unquestioningly what we tell them. [5]

[5] Peter F. Drucker, "Human Relations: How Far Do We Have to Go?" *Management Record* (March 1959).

The ... evil of the "human relations" fad is its repeated violation of the dignity of the individual. It becomes a technique for manipulating people. There are certain areas that should be free of the boss's review and his standards of performance. Today, we stick our noses into other people's business, analyzing their motives and judging their lives. We should be able to take a man at face value and not always fret about what he really means. Too many of us are trying to be little tin Freuds ... consciously trying to be a gentleman. If it doesn't come from the heart, it is phony. [6]

It is claimed that such techniques as nondirective interviewing and group decision-making are designed to get employees to do things they don't want to do, or at least that they don't realize they are doing. A familiar example is the supervisor who pretends to be interested in his subordinates and to consult with them, but only in order to disguise his essentially authoritarian approach (see Chapter 8).

Also, these critics insist, excessive concern over the individual usually leads to paternalism, with all its attendant evils. Attempts to plumb the employee's personal feelings and attitudes thrust the company into areas that are properly the province of the individual, the family, and the community. (The union adds that only an organization which is directly responsible to workers—that is, the union itself—can protect the individual's welfare consistently and vigorously.)

Fortunately, most employees are quick to spot insincerity. Gimmicks and deceit are soon exposed, as some companies have learned to their sorrow. The only group that is duped is management itself, which has underestimated the intelligence of its employees.

We see little danger that brainwashing, mass persuasion, or subliminal suggestion will win much acceptance in organization administration. The power of suggestion may be quite effective in persuading a customer to buy one brand of cigarettes rather than another—but this is because cigarette brands are not very different and because most customers have no vested interest in which brand they smoke. Brainwashing may change basic attitudes in prisoner-of-war camps where the individual is isolated from alternative sources of information. In the typical work situation, however, personnel decisions are of immediate importance to the people involved; employees do have a vested interest in what happens to them on the job. Further, few companies can isolate their employees from other points of view. Whatever the company or the individual supervisor says and does is discussed and criticized by the employees on the job, by the union, and by other groups in the community. Management's pronouncements can always be checked against the viewpoints of others. Clearly, the employee is not likely to succumb to propaganda; indeed, his cynicism is often so great that it is hard for management to get the truth across to him (see Chapter 10), let alone falsehoods.

Some critics argue that the supervisor is resorting to manipulation whenever he tries to minimize conflict and gain acceptance for a point of view or for some change. But is there anything objectionable about efforts to weigh alternative courses of action and to select the one that avoids personnel problems? Is it not, rather, highly desirable for management to enlarge its perspective to include rational solutions to its human-relations problems? In short, are not human relations deserving of as much careful attention as engineering and finance?

[6] Malcolm P. McNair, "Too Much 'Human Relations'?" *Look* (October 28, 1958).

When Is Efficiency Impaired?

"Management has been sold a bill of goods by human relations. In the process of coddling people it has lost sight of its major objective—getting work accomplished profitably. Management's job is to get the work done and to let employees worry about themselves."

This is the considered view of many critics of the human-relations movement in management.

To assess the validity of this charge, we must place the problem in historical perspective. Only a short time ago business was being accused of neglecting personnel problems. Now it is being accused of ignoring business objectives in its attempts to "coddle" people. Why this remarkable shift?

Many companies discovered only quite recently that they had "people" problems. Years ago, when businesses were much smaller, most managers (who were also the owners) knew their employees personally and were able to handle problems informally. Turnover was not particularly worrisome, for good replacements were readily available. Unions were weak. Perhaps most important, there was no professional concern with the job of management—certainly not with personnel administration. Businessmen busied themselves with buying and selling in the marketplace and gave little thought to organizational problems. No manager considered himself inept or ineffective simply because he had high turnover or labor strife—this was the fault of weak foremen or troublemakers in the work force.

Today, businesses are large and impersonal. Trained employees are harder to replace, and alert unions are ready to transmute management's mistakes into costly grievances. It is generally accepted that all levels of management have a continuing responsibility for solving human-relations problems—that these are not just transitory phenomena or the result of bad luck.

In the course of this rapid transformation of the executive into a professional, and this rapid acceptance of personnel administration as a general management responsibility, it is not surprising that many mistakes have been made. Naive managers seeking quick and easy solutions have been victimized by charlatans. Companies have purchased expensive training programs, engaged enthusiastic speakers, prepared expensive give-away brochures, and have footed the bill for whole kits of supervisory gimmicks in the mistaken belief that there were simple, quasi-mechanical techniques for solving employee-relations problems. Rather than try to understand the functioning of organizations, the nature of groups, and the importance of individual differences, some companies have gone overboard in embracing such cure-alls as "participative management" or "public speaking for everyone." There has been a regrettable follow-the-leader fashion-conscious acceptance of anything called human relations or behavioral science.

Some managers have simplified human relations to the point of absurdity. They insist that good management is just a matter of liking people and inducing them to like you. "Getting to know your people" is the sure guarantee of success, perhaps tempered by this warning: "Don't get pushy about production; it annoys people."

The principle of two-way communication has been particularly abused. Some authorities seem to assume that all trouble within the organization is purely and simply the result of "misunderstanding." Jones misinterprets Brown's motives and Brown fails to realize that Jones is operating within a different frame of reference. The moment the communication dam is broken, understanding will flood through the organization.

Given this simple definition of the management problem, one might well ask why improvement has been so long in forthcoming. A ready answer is that the human being is recalcitrant, hard to change. Some ardent "human-relationists" throw the whole problem right onto the psychiatrist's couch. There has been a mushrooming of quasi-therapeutic cures for insensitive, uncommunicative people: role-playing, group therapy of one kind or another, sensitivity training, nondirective counseling. Apparently the hope is to change the manager's personality, to make him show more "consideration," to induce him to be less autocratic.

Many of these techniques have a useful role to play, but they may be overemphasized. What is wrong with this approach? At least four things, in our opinion:

1. True, some problems are created and others are magnified by poor communications. But many problems cannot be solved by better understanding alone. They can be solved only by carefully wrought changes in technology, work procedure, organizational structure, or personnel policies.

2. True, counseling and training may improve communications and may even help people develop skills—and that is all to the good. But changing personality itself is an expensive, arduous job, with a poor prognosis.

3. Human relations is not an end in itself. The purpose of business is not to make people happy (though some have argued otherwise) but to achieve its over-all goals of productivity and profitability. And the purpose of *human relations* is to help management elicit the cooperation of people in working toward those goals.

4. Many management development programs treat human beings as though they were motivated by a single need. Taylor thought it was money; thus the incentive systems produced by scientific management. Mayo insisted it was social needs; thus the emphasis on satisfying group relations. More recently, the emphasis has been on self-actualization through participation and job enlargement. To be sure, there are important partial truths here, but all men are not alike and the manager must deal with diversity if he is to be a successful leader.

Although we decry the uncritical acceptance of some organizational theories as magic cures, we feel that it is a mistake to go to the opposite extreme. The manager cannot be concerned about getting work done without also being concerned about people. Even in the fully automated factory or office, important jobs must still be done by human beings. Their willingness to coordinate their efforts with those of other people and with the system and equipment developed by engineers is an essential component of a successful organization.

In his efforts to conquer disease, man has resorted to charms, incantations, and witch doctors. But no one would suggest that just because he put his faith in gimmicks and myths in the past he would be better off today to ignore the problems of illness and concentrate on "living."

The manager cannot ignore the human-relations problems of his organization and concentrate exclusively on getting the work out. Getting the work out depends on getting cooperation out of people both inside and outside the formal boundaries of the organization. The future will see increasing, not decreasing, attention paid to the human-relations problems of the organization.

CONCLUSION

We hope you have not been discouraged by our survey of the human problems inherent in the organization. As most managers have learned, there are no perfect, final solutions to these problems. Every area we have explored is rich in challenges to the decision-making skill of the executive.

Only when we place these problems in the larger context of American life does their full significance become apparent. The individual human being, and his opportunities for development and satisfaction, have a high value in our culture. We expect our institutions to provide him with a chance to express and satisfy his needs and to fulfill his capabilities. The evolution of private organizations that are consistent with and complementary to our democratic political institutions is a high achievement in itself. Throughout the ages, man has struggled to achieve individual freedom without jeopardizing the safety and welfare of others, and to engage in productive work that will satisfy the economic and physical needs of himself and society. Not unexpectedly, severe conflicts arise between the needs of the individual and the needs of the groups and organizations that make up society. As the administrator makes choices between organizational efficiency and the satisfaction of individual needs, he is acting as a mediator in this inevitable, and, we believe, socially useful, divergence of interests.

We think the manpower policy statement of a major multinational company states this commitment very well and exemplifies the responsibilities of management for its human resources:

The role that Shell employees play in the conduct of the business is vital to success. We strive to create the conditions in which people can develop their full potential, and to do this we rely both upon our own knowledge and experience and on help from behavioural science studies and research. We believe that the human contribution can be dramatically increased and constantly seek greater insight into how this can be achieved.

Large and complex enterprises are often thought to be faceless and mechanistic, and inhibiting to the expression of individual personality. On the other hand a special pride is felt by many employees in belonging to one of the greatest industrial enterprises in the world. Moreover, they identify themselves with a particular Shell company for which they work. In most of these companies actual working units are comparatively small. There is, therefore, every opportunity to develop individual skills so that each man's capacity is fully used. Our annual staff reporting system is designed to foster this.

It is recognized that managerial leadership is a vital competitive asset. Participative management, in which the key is consultation and not command, brings out the best in people and assists us all to adapt rapidly to change. It demands, to a much greater extent than other styles of management, qualities of understanding and inspiration that must be developed alongside the more traditional managerial skills.

Many activities that Shell companies are apt to take for granted, because they have been part of our personnel policies for some time, are directed towards increasing knowledge and understanding so that individual effort can be more constructively applied. Among them are joint consultation; discussion of individual and company objectives and performance at regular intervals; employee information services; and a whole range of training and development programmes. [7]

problem 1 • MARY'S AILMENTS

The Ames Department Store prides itself on the excellence of its Medical Department. All new employees are required to take a rigid pre-employment physical. Because of an error, Mary Fillipi came to work as a salesgirl several days before completing her physical exam. She was a charming person and immediately made fast friends among everyone in her department including the buyer and assistant buyer.

Thus, everyone was disturbed when Mary received a notice from the Personnel Department that she could not be hired because the medical examination had disclosed two rather serious internal ailments.

The buyer represented the department in requesting that Personnel make an exception in this case because (1) the girl had already been working a week and (2) she promised to become, not only one of the most well-liked employees, but also an excellent salesgirl. Further, the employees, whose sympathies had been aroused, felt that Mary was being discriminated against because of a health problem when, in fact, Ames should help people with problems.

Personnel turned down the request on the grounds that the hiring requirement of passing the medical examination was a fixed, long-established company policy. Also, as the Director of Personnel put it,

"The employees should be told that the store's ability to pay unusually generous fringe benefits, including the best sickness plan in the city, is due to our selectivity in hiring. Should these standards be eroded, over time, the employees will receive less favorable fringe benefits."

Evaluate the decision of Personnel in this case and its implementation.

problem 2 • WOMEN'S LIB

Carol Marsio was transferred temporarily to the position of private secretary for Carl Marks, head of Sales for the World Watch Company. She was taking the place of Marks' regular secretary who was taking her annual three-week vacation. Carol knew Marks only as a face and a title, but she didn't object to the transfer out of the three-girl office that comprised the Advertising Department.

What did distress Carol, however, were the numerous requests Marks made for errands and the conduct of personal business. During the first week he asked her to go out and purchase a small gift for his wife, to stop by a camera shop to pick up his repaired movie camera, and to pick up a shirt at a nearby men's store when he received an unexpected dinner party invitation that did not allow him time to get home to change.

[7] From the Annual Report, Royal Dutch Petroleum Corportation, 1970; statement of the president, L. E. J. Brouwer.

The second week produced more of the same, and she began to think she was filling the job of a valet, not just a secretary. When she checked with other girls who had similar jobs she found that most had similar experiences, and a minority of the girls resented the imposition, but considered it part of the job.

Carol had been active in Women's Lib, and gradually came to the conclusion that women were being exploited at World Watch—treated as "vassals and handservants for dominant males," as she put it. During the lunch hour of her third week as private secretary she organized a meeting of all the private secretaries she could contact, and seven of the twelve in the company attended. Of those attending, five were willing to sign a letter addressed to the company president stating that personal errands and nonbusiness related service was both demeaning to women, wasteful, and a throwback to a male-dominated age.

When the president got the letter, he called in the personnel manager, Edgars, to discuss the problem. Edgars said that he had already heard about the letter and the meeting. "Carol is a real firebrand; she takes women's rights very seriously and has gotten people aroused. I really don't know what to say. If you talk to your executives they'll tell you as they have told me that *all* secretaries do these things, and after all it saves them time and energy which can be devoted to company matters. Further, how do you separate personal and business? Much of an executive's social life has some implications for business."

On further questioning the personnel manager admitted that some executives take advantage of their secretaries and request too much errand-running. But he also noted that Carol was only an average employee at best and frequently missed work. There were the extenuating circumstances that she had two young children, was divorced, and often had trouble getting baby sitters.

The conclusion of the meeting was to just ignore the letter and to leave things as they were, because any action would appear to recognize these girls as a pressure group and would get the company involved in a morass of trying to define rigidly a secretary's duties. However, the following week Edgars received a personal visit from Carol, who told him that she would guarantee that all secretaries would hold a two-hour work stoppage on company time unless the company issued a formal policy statement that secretaries were not required to do, nor should they be used for, any work not related directly to World Watch business.

After the meeting, through checking with employees he knew well, Edgars learned that Carol was spending a good deal of time agitating among the girls to undertake some formal demonstration that would accuse the company of violating women's rights. Also a crudely-drawn poster appeared on a bulletin board showing a secretary dressed as a household maid, curtsying to a fierce man behind a desk.

1. What should Edgars do at this point?
2. How relevant to the situation is Carol's personal situation, her small children and very obvious need for this job?
3. What is your opinion concerning the psychological impact of these personal errands on the secretary and her self-image?
4. Should the company's posture relative to this agitation be different if Carol was organizing a union rather than a "Women's Lib" movement?
5. What is your assessment of the arguments of executives that there is no possibility of drawing a clear line between the job and personal business?

problem 3 • SMALL-TOWN DISASTER

Changes in technology and sources of raw materials have made obsolete the Dunbar, Nebraska (fictitious name) plant of the American Fibers Company. Employing 800 people, this plant has been, for forty years, the sole industrial employer and the economic mainstay of Dunbar (pop. 8,500). American has no other nearby plants, but it does have a dozen other manufacturing facilities in various parts of the country. Except for the skilled mechanics, most employees are in the 40 to 50-year-old category and have little other industrial experience.

1. Making your own assumptions about manpower and economic variables, evaluate the company's responsibility to the community and to stockholders.

problem 4 • BUTTONS AND BANDS

Hemmings, Personnel Director of the City Diagnostic Labs, noted the increased popularity of various political and cause-oriented buttons worn by some of the technicians in the lab. Some referred to the Vietnam war; others to local housing issues, and they emphasized racial or ethnic pride. This week, several employees wore black arm bands, indicating sympathy for a prisoner killed in a riot in a nearby penitentiary.

This symbol, however, caused a pitched battle in the lunchroom. Apparently, the arm-band wearers were accosted by several other employees who said that the prisoner deserved to be shot. Other words were exchanged and led to a fist fight and some broken dishes.

1. Should the labs consider banning all such items from the premises, on the grounds that they are a needless irritant and source of disturbance and partisanship?

2. What about employees' rights and free speech? Would you, for example, forbid union buttons?

Indexes

NAME INDEX

Shaw, Malcolm E., 536
Shephard, Jon M., 160
Shils, E. A., 71
Shiskin, Boris, 573
Shister, Joseph, 17, 411, 413
Shultz, George, P., 17, 18, 645
Sibson, Robert E., 579, 582
Siegel, Abraham, 86
Silberman, Charles E., 464
Simon, Herbert A., 128, 134
Smith, Adam, 5
Smith, Alice, 513, 514
Snyderman, Barbara, 20, 126
Sorcer, Marvin, 442
Stark, Stanley, 513
Stelluto, George, 630
Stolz, Robert K., 506, 513, 514
Strauss, George, 20, 65, 91, 102, 103, 114, 492, 644
Strickler, M. D., 56
Sydiaha, D. 420
Sykes, A. J. M., 531

t

Tannenbaum, Robert, 512, 538
Taylor, Donald W., 191

Taylor, Frederick W., 14, 30, 310, 349, 654
Thayer, Clarence H., 341
Thompson, Paul H., 524
Tosi, Henry, 523
Triandis, Harry, 209
Trice, Harrison 370, 418
Trist, E. L., 337
Tucker, J. L., 561
Turner, Arthur, 36, 160, 171, 172, 288

u

Uris, Aurens, 414

v

Vance, Stanley C., 488
Vollmer, Howard, 156
Vroom, Victor, H., 126, 135, 158, 159

w

Wakeley, John H., 536
Walker, Charles R., 19, 23, 33, 36, 42, 172, 288

Watson, Thomas J., Jr., 149, 544
Weick, Karl, 389, 553
Weiss, E. B., 443
Weiss, Robert S., 20, 21
Welford, A. T., 445
Weschler, Irving R., 512, 538
Whisler, Thomas L., 503, 505
Whyte, William F., 81, 93, 144, 160, 173, 174, 181, 185, 192, 240, 254, 259, 385, 625, 629, 644
Whyte, William H., Jr., 15, 208, 433, 435, 489
Wiener, Hannah, 536
Wigdor, Lawrence A., 126
Wilensky, Harold, 57, 126
Williams, Whiting, 12
Wilson, Robert, 150, 152, 177, 293, 448
Wohlking, Wallace, 536
Woodward, Joan, 43, 286
Worthy, James C., 12, 331, 339, 341
Wright, Ormon, Jr., 380
Wyatt, S., 11

y-z

Young, Harvey A., 644
Zaleznik, A. 74, 86

SUBJECT INDEX

b

c

d

e

f

g

h

n

Need satisfaction (*See also* Job satisfaction):
   advancement, 9-10
   competition, 130-32
   egoistic, 11
     achievement, 11-14
     autonomy, 14-15
     knowledge, 15-16
   physical, 7-8
   role of money in, 19
   security, 8-9
   social, 10
Needs, hierarchy of, 16-20
   economic conditions, 17-18
   hypothesis criticized, 18
   personality differences in, 18-19
     McClelland-Atkinson theory, 18-19
Negotiation, 625-26
Neighborhood Youth Corps, 467
New professionals, 60-61

O

Occupational associations, 92
Occupational groups, differences among, 19-20
  blue-collar workers, 20
  craft workers, 20
  service workers, 20
  white-collar workers, 20
On-the-job training (OJT), 453
Orders, issuing of, 168-69
Organization, informal, 192-95
  leaders, 192-93
    managers working with, 193
  union steward, 194-95
  working supervisor, 194
Organizational development (OD), 528, 540-43
  defined, 540
  evaluation of, 542-43
Organizational structure, 331
  personality and, 343-44
Organization change:
  illustration of, 334-35
  research studies of, 337-38
Organization chart, 284, 352
Organization pyramid, 283-86

Organizations:
  "flat" vs. "tall," 331-33
  large, advantages of, 330-31
  lateral relations, 313
    audit, 320-21
    service, 313-16
    stabilization, 321-22
    work flow, 313-16
Overtime, 398

P

Parkinson's law, 311-12
Paternalism, 124-26, 349, 593, 609, 652-53
Paths-goals analysis, 135-37
Pay, and status, 80 (*See also* Wage administration)
Pension plans (*See* Fringe benefits)
Performance appraisal:
  evaluation interview, 516-20
  management by objectives (MBO), 520-25
    advantages, 521-22
    defined, 520
    limitations, 522-23
    for promotions and salary increases, 524, 525
    as useful management tool, 523
  newer methods of rating, 514-16
    critical incidents, 515-16
    forced choice, 514-15
    forced distribution, 514
  traditional rating, 509-14
    human errors, 511-12
    scales, 509-11
    traits or performance, 512-14
Performance standards:
  blue-collar vs. white-collar incentives, 632-33
  blue-collar work-load, 618-23
    allowances, 622
    establishing standards, 622-23
    motion study, 618-19
    time study, 619-22
  challenge of incentives for management, 630-32